THREE WHO
MADE A
REVOLUTION

THREE

WHO

MADE A REVOLUTION

A BIOGRAPHICAL HISTORY

BY

Bertram D. Wolfe

Foreword by Sol Stein

Cooper Square Press

FOR ELLA

First Cooper Square Press edition 2001

This Cooper Square Press paperback edition of *Three Who Made a Revolution* (originally published in 1948) is an unabridged republication of edition published in New York in 1984.

Published by Cooper Square Press, Inc.
A Imprint of the Rowman & Littlefield Publishing Group
150 Fifth Avenue, Suite 911
New York, NY 10011

Published by Cooper Square Press
An Imprint of the Rowman & Littlefield Publishing Group
150 Fifth Avenue, Suite 817
New York, New York 10011

Distributed by National Book Network

Library of Congress Cataloging-in-Publication Data

Wolfe, Bertram David, 1896–1977.
    Three who made a revolution : a biographical history / by Bertram D. Wolfe ; foreword by Sol Stein.
    p.   cm.
Includes index.
Originally published: New York : Stein & Day, 1948.
ISBN 0-8154-1177-4 (pbk. : alk. paper)
    1. Revolutionaries—Soviet Union—Biography. 2. Lenin, Vladmir Il§'ch, 1870–1924. 3. Trotsky, Leon, 1879–1940. 4. Stalin, Joseph, 1879–1953. 5. Soviet Union—Hitory—Revolution, 1917–1921—Causes. I. Title.

DK253 .W65 2001
947.084'092'2—dc21
[B]   2001042384

The Author

(above) Bertram D. Wolfe on his way to the Fifth Congress of the Communist International in 1924.

(left) Wolfe, when he was Chief of the Ideological Advisory Staff of the Voice of America, U.S. State Department; taken on Cape Cod in 1955.

(right) Wolfe was a Fellow and Writer-in-Residence at the Hoover Institution at Stanford University during the last twelve years of his life. This picture was taken in 1973.

BERTRAM D. WOLFE was born in Brooklyn in 1896, and educated in the local schools, the College of the City of New York, the University of Mexico, and Columbia University. His lifelong interest in Russia began in 1917, when after the First Revolution in March of that year he predicted a second revolution that would take Russia out of the war. He has visited Russia three times, lived in Moscow for a total of two years, made the personal acquaintance of Stalin, Trotsky, Bukharin, Molotov, Manuilsky, Kerensky, Tseretelli, Chernov, and many of the other personages that figure in his pages.

Mr. Wolfe lectured and gave courses on Russian history, politics, institutions and culture in many of our leading universities, as well as at Oxford and the University of Geneva. His last academic appointment was as Distinguished Visiting Professor of Russian History at the University of California. California gave him an honorary doctorate in 1962 for "his notable contributions to historical literature." He was awarded three Guggenheim Fellowships, and Senior Fellowships in Slavic Studies at the Hoover Institution (Stanford University) and the Russian Institute (Columbia University).

He contributed articles on Russian history and institutions, on Marxism, Communism, and the nature of totalitarianism to *Foreign Affairs*, *The Slavic Review*, *The Russian Review*, and other scholarly journals, as well as to *Harper's*, *United States News* and *World Report*, *Life*, *Readers' Digest*, and other general publications, and notable book reviews on works in his field to *The New York Times* and the New York *Herald-Tribune*.

Bertram Wolfe died in 1977 in the midst of writing his autobiography, *A Life in Two Centuries*, which was published in 1979.

Credo

"Time in its irresistible and ceaseless flow carries along on its flood all created things and drowns them in the depths of obscurity . . . But the tale of history forms a very strong bulwark against the stream of time, and checks in some measure its irresistible flow, so that, of all things done in it, as many as history has taken over it secures and binds together, and does not allow them to slip away into the abyss of oblivion."
—Anna Comnena

"The historian has a duty both to himself and to his readers. He has to a certain extent the cure of souls. He is accountable for the reputation of the mighty dead whom he conjures up and portrays. If he makes a mistake, if he repeats slanders on those who are blameless, or holds up profligates or schemers to admiration, he not only commits an evil action; he poisons and misleads the public mind."
—Albert Mathiez

"History does nothing, possesses no enormous wealth, fights no battles. It is rather man, the real, living man, who does everything, possesses, fights. It is not 'History,' as if she were a person apart, who uses men as means to work out her purposes, but history itself is nothing but the activity of men pursuing their purposes."
—Karl Marx

"Society can never think things out:
It has to see them acted out by actors,
Devoted actors at a sacrifice—
The ablest actors I can lay my hands on."
—God to Job, in Robert Frost's
"The Masque of Reason"

Contents

Full Circle
a foreword by
Sol Stein

In the early 50s, I came upon a publishing failure called *Three Who Made a Revolution*. Though Edmund Wilson, then the dean of American literary critics, had called it "the best book in its field in any language," its original publisher, the Dial Press, had sold fewer than 1,000 copies a year since its publication in 1948. It was ready for the scrap heap.

I was young, naive, inexperienced, and found it intolerable that a book that had influenced my perception of the century should be consigned to death. A book, unlike a magazine or newspaper, was supposed to be durable, an object of worth, permanent, to be passed on with lesser treasures to one's children. My heart cried out like a young lover's in despair. War, pestilence, traffic cut lives short, but should books, like people, be subject to premature death?

I was not then in publishing. So I ran about frantically seeking a reprieve, a cure. I spoke to my friend Nathan Glazer, then Jason Epstein's second-in-command at Anchor Books. He agreed with me about the worth of the book, but his prognosis was dire; *Three Who Made a Revolution* was far too long to fit into a pocketsized Anchor Book. It would take three volumes, and resetting it to fit the pocket format would cost too much: the patient was not immortal; it would die like an animal.

It is said that if you would stop a hunter from pulling the trigger, let him first see the eyes of a rabbit. Two years earlier, in 1951, I had met the author of *Three Who Made*. His eyes were not limpid like a rabbit's, but—one is tempted to play upon his name—like a wolf's, hunted (as he had been during his years of exile), cunning, and knowledgeable, cold to the advance of strangers. I was working then as an analyst in the Western European section of the U.S. State Department's Voice of

America; Wolfe, who had broken with Stalin in 1928, was now, in a country that elevated its Rubashovs instead of executing them, the chief of the Ideological Advisory Staff. The grapevine said he needed a writer. I asked for an interview. He let me remain standing. There was no point to an interview until he had sampled my writing. I carefully laid some short manuscripts on his desk.

A day later I was summoned to his presence. He offered me—it came across as an instruction—the post of senior editor and his second-in-command. He would arrange for a transfer. Yes or no?

My instinct cried *yes*, my inexperience waffled in trepidation of being exposed daily to Wolfe's scythe of a mind and his equally scythelike temper. Not without fear of his immediate wrath, I asked for a bit of time to think things over. It was a lie. I wanted to consult my various Dutch Uncles to get their views on my ability to survive the heat of Wolfe's demanding environment.

Everyone advised against. While acknowledging Wolfe's expertise (he knew more about the Soviet Union than anyone else in the State Department) and his methods of analysis (his record for predicting future Soviet actions was unmatched), he was hell to work for. As a stylist, Wolfe was unsurpassed by anyone in his field; as a department head, he wanted everyone to write as close to perfection as possible *daily*. He had a wide-ranging disrespect for the minds of the less knowledgeable. He defied protocol, rank, systems, procedures, conventions. He was not only intolerant of mediocrities, he was impolite to anyone, however good, who made a mistake. Among anti-Stalinists he was reputed to be a man of steel; if you were in his inner circle, your chances of survival decreased.

I am ashamed to say that it took me eleven months to plug my ears against the din and to accept his offer. Just as Wolfe was always patient with those who defected from their Communist allegiances much later than he, he was patient with me, a virgin who had never been a Communist. I could make any mistake *once*. Though I had taught a course on the Soviet Union at the City College during the late 40s, I learned more about the subject in the first few weeks with Wolfe than I would have in a lifetime of teaching. Being in the proximity of Bertram Wolfe meant you were constantly being bombarded by electrons. You learned fast or you were exploded.

When Joe McCarthy launched his attack against the Voice of America, I received Wolfe's approval for an act that some thought treasonable at the time. I wrote a broadcast denouncing McCarthy, and, with the official stamp of the Ideological Advisory Staff, it was broadcast to the world in forty-six languages. The Eastern Europeans who worked for the Voice were certain I would be taken out to the courtyard and shot. Wolfe and I had a resounding laugh together. Lesson: demagogues without a program retreated if you fought back without camouflage or cover.

It was about that time that Wolfe divided our ideological chores: he would deal with what we (meaning America as envisioned by Thomas Jefferson of Monticello and by Bertram Wolfe of Brooklyn) were against and I would deal with what we were for. He got the better end of the bargain. My position was cut out of the budget. I worked at other desks in other departments with room in their budgets, doing exactly the same work with Wolfe as always.

At least once each year Bertram Wolfe was denounced on the floor of Congress, and immediately protected by a cordon within the State Department that knew how desperately we continued to need him.

In addition to editing the writers on Wolfe's staff, I had a first startling experience of editing something of Wolfe's. An article promised to Norman Cousins at the *Saturday Review* by Wolfe was long overdue and a last, warning telegram arrived. Wolfe closeted himself in his office. When he came out, he threw the pages of his article on my desk and stood looking over my shoulder as I read. When I delivered my unhappy verdict, he grabbed the pages off my desk and stalked into his office, slamming the door so hard we all turned around in expectation that the top half of the door, made of glass and shimmering in its frame, would break.

At the appropriate hour, others left for home. I stayed amidst the cleaning ladies emptying the wastebaskets. Finally Wolfe came out of his office. He showed no surprise that I had remained behind. He put the fresh pages of a totally rewritten piece in front of me. It was perfect. As I handed it back to him, he didn't smile, he didn't shake my hand, he didn't say "thank you," but his quick nod of approbation was for me no less than the Pope's crown for Bonaparte.

A decade later, when I was editing Wolfe's *The Fabulous Life of Diego Rivera* (which was eventually nominated for a National Book Award), we would meet almost daily in my home because his afflicted back could not find comfort in office chairs. We would sit side by side as I flipped pages, revealing my presumptuous corrections, and Wolfe saying *No, no, no* to each. When we'd gone perhaps ten pages in this fashion, he'd ask to go back to the first page and query my reasoning behind the proposed changes, at which point, with thought, he would agree. And so page by page until he was too tired to go on. The next meeting would go exactly the same way, *No, no, no,* and then back to the beginning. Like all writers who command their ideas as well as their language, he was constantly on guard against disimprovement.

Along the way our relationship had changed. We were no longer just employer-employee, co-conspirators against barbarism, writer-editor. Wolfe had no son. I had no father. Though more than three decades apart in age, we became friends. One evening, as Bert and his wife, Ella (who remains as beautiful today as she was then), and I and my wife parted on a street corner after a social occasion, he took my hand in his and with embarrassment reddening his face, said, "Give my love to the parents of your children" and fled down the street, away from the terrors of expressing emotion.

And so it was in 1953 that acting not only as *amicus curiae* with regard to *Three Who Made a Revolution* but as a friend of the author as well, that I rushed around trying to save the book. After failing to involve Anchor Books, I sought to interest two other publishers in what seemed at first glance a harebrained idea: Why not put the book out in paper covers but the same size as the hardback, offsetting from the original to save composition costs. I suggested that Edmund Wilson's quote be put at the top of the cover, on the assumption that the right audience would know that Wilson meant it was even better than his own *To the Finland Station.* I was confronted by naysayers. Paperbacks, they said, were *pocket* books, and Wolfe's big book would never fit in the pocket. Costings were thrown back at me; the huge book would have to sell for $2.95, and the highest then projected price for a paperback was $1.25. Nobody would buy it, the naysayers choarused.

Men and women in love are unreasonable nuisances to the

sane world, and I was now in love not only with the idea of preserving the life of *Three Who Made a Revolution* but doing so in this new format, which was condemned, among other reasons, for "looking like a European book and not an American book."

To his everlasting credit, one of the publishers I'd approached proved as deaf to the naysayers as I was. Melvin Arnold, director of the Beacon Press and later president of Harper & Row, said he'd give the book and format a try.

Wolfe's "failure" sold over 500,000 copies in the Beacon edition until, many years later, Dell's Delta line, then commonly owned with Dial, wisely reverted the rights and reportedly sold another 300,000. A total of 800,000 copies of a serious book on the Russian Revolution became its own revolution. With each decade its relevance increased.

Wolfe, of course, went on writing and receiving ideological converts—some afraid for their lives—in his small, Brooklyn apartment. In time, he shifted his ground to the comforts of Palo Alto, California, where, with the resources of the Hoover Institution, he continued his work, taking his hydrochloric acid capsules and only the mildest of pain killers that would not numb his brain. I, by chance as it were, had become a publisher. We stayed in touch. Then in 1977, when Wolfe was midway in his autobiography, *A Life in Two Centuries*, came the terrible accident. At 82 he was cold in the Northern California mornings and would light the gas heater in his bathroom before his daily ablutions. He wore a long, flowing bathrobe that his wife, Ella, had warned him against. It caught fire, and when it was finally extinguished, the man who was perhaps the most astute perceiver of the central event of the twentieth century passed into legend.

Then one day in 1983 came a second terrible phone call from Palo Alto. It was Ella Wolfe with the news that her husband's greatest work had been put out of print.

Plus ça change, plus c'est la même chose. I made a few phone calls. I drew up a contract, and once more *Three Who Made a Revolution* lives. If after I die the book is allowed to go out of print, I leave a curse for whoever may be responsible, for this book is not merely a triple biography and a history, but an understanding our children and grandchildren need to grasp how, in this most horrific of all centuries, the impulse toward improving the lot of men resulted in the creation of man's greatest disease, the totalitarian state, for which this book is a vaccine and for which, at this writing, there is as yet no cure.

And to the Soviets, who have prohibited their people reading this book since it first saw life nearly half a century ago, I would say in my mother's tongue: Where is your Bertram Wolfe who understands us from his experience within as Bertram Wolfe understood you?

Scarborough
November 1983

THREE WHO
MADE A
REVOLUTION

Introduction

The work of one who writes a history of some large event of his own time is never done. Sealed archives are opened; colleagues publish books and monographs on various aspects of the same event; survivors grow old and write memoirs that reveal matters only a participant could have known. The very events that make up the large pattern keep revealing themselves in a new light as new consequences continue to flow from them; the ever-shifting kaleidoscope of time gives new shape to what seemed fixed and settled.

Internally as well, one's book begins to seem unfinished as soon as it is completed. Things said in closing chapters suggest changes in earlier ones. If it is a first volume in a contemplated larger study, later research keeps turning up fresh materials and inspiring new viewpoints concerning parts of what is already published. While the book is on press, the writer is already making changes in proof. When he looks at the first bound copy, his satisfaction diminishes as *"typos"* leap out of its pages, and fresh questions arise in his mind about things which yesterday seemed so certain.

Then come the reviews, the observations and corrections of colleagues. The meticulous reader—and every serious book merits one or more meticulous readers—finds an incredible number of minor errors. The author has barely seen the first copy off the press before he is longing for the entire printing to be sold out so that he can revise it.

In this regard I have been fortunate. The book's use as a university text over the past fifteen years has permitted three editions in cloth, eight printings in paper, and two printings for book clubs. Printing costs being what they are, corrections and alterations have had to be made by counting letters and spaces for each change so that the same pagination could be kept. Within this typographical straitjacket I have attempted to incorporate the suggestions of colleagues and critics (and the meticulous reader), and my own new insights and discoveries. But a number of methodological questions have been raised which do not permit of this skimped treatment, hence in this, the most sweeping revision, I have ventured to discuss some of these questions here, in a belated introduction.

Many readers have objected that the three protagonists, Lenin, Trotsky and Stalin, did not contribute in equal or comparable measure to the "making" of the Revolution. If to "make the Revolution" means to conceive and build the machine that seized power in 1917, then Lenin is without peer. If the strategy and tactics of the *coup d'etat* on November 7, 1917 is what is meant, then Trotsky as Chairman of the Petrograd Soviet and the Military Revolutionary Committee, made the chief contribution. Some critics have argued that Stalin merely inherited the power, having played a negligible role in the seizing of it. They are, of course, correct. Others have urged that Stalin "unmade" the Revolution, after Lenin and Trotsky "made" it. To resolve this matter is to go into metaphysical, ideological, quasi-theological definitions of what "the Revolution" was or was supposed to be; beyond the ambition pragmatically expressed by Lenin on its eve: "The point of the uprising is the seizure of power; afterwards we will see what we can do with it."

But the sense in which the title was originally conceived was quite different. The book was written during the years when Joseph Stalin was *Vozhd, Khozyain,* Leader. He was Boss and Dictator over the Party, the State and the People of Russia, setting his unmistakable imprint on the Revolution organized as Power, and on the new society it was shaping. In that sense, all three of these men "made" the Revolution for all three have set the imprint of their personalities, doctrines, passions and wills upon it. It is this impress of their personalities upon their time and land which explains the title, and also explains why it was sub-titled "A Biographical History."

Crane Brinton in a review of this work said of "biographical history":

It is a good kind of history, even if, indeed probably because, it is a kind men have been writing since the ancient Greeks and Hebrews. By his practice and by an occasional methodological aside, Mr. Wolfe indicates his belief that the character of the leaders has a great and abiding influence on the course of history.

To this I must add that in our present "time of troubles," when thrones tumble, empires break up, new nations come to life, regimes are transformed, "new orders" are introduced, and new men of power conduct ruthless experiments on their people, biographical history takes on an especially large importance.

Because in the century from 1815 to 1914, institutions and economic and political structures were, comparatively speaking, more stable, it was possible for the historian to believe that it did not matter too much which president, premier, sovereign, or political leader was in the key position. One of the weaknesses of much nineteenth-century historiography was the belief that one could write history largely in terms of institutions and impersonal social forces, though, of course, the great historians knew how to combine the man and the age.

Now, in an age when change is rapid and dizzying, when newly born nations have to construct their institutions *de novo,* when new men heading new movements come to power armed with the determination to remake human beings according to their blueprints, then the character, the passions, the theories, the spirit of the man who sets his stamp upon his movement and his land—in short his "biography" and his personal impress upon history—become vastly more important. He may never be as all-powerful as he fancies and the past may have sly and devious ways of reasserting itself, yet even from the past he selects kindred elements and neglects or combats those that he finds distasteful. Indeed, even the traditions that persist despite him, even the unintended consequences of his actions, and the very deeds and spirits of those who react against him, bear the marks of his impress.

How different India is today because Gandhi was murdered at the moment of independence and partition, leaving Nehru to set his quite different stamp upon India's spirit and institutions. How different was the Chinese Revolution under Sun Yat-sen than it is under Chiang and Mao, each of whom claims to be his heir.

If, in time of peace, the stability and efficacy of the Tsarist administration was so different under a Stolypin than under a Goremykin, how much deeper, in a time when everything was in chaotic flux, was the difference between a Russia with Kerensky at the helm and one ruled by Lenin. What a difference it has made in the history of the "new Russia" that a Stalin had the biological constitution to outlive a Lenin, and not the reverse.

It was considerations such as these which prompted me to combine with the study of social forces, institutions, traditions, a close study of the ideas and the persons of the men who were the prime historical actors in the Revolution of 1917, and who set their imprint upon the regime which emerged from it. That is why, too, the study of their opponents is usually a mere vignette, while that of the prime actors is something of a full-length close-up.

The protagonists of the revolutionary movement were ideologues, essentially men of a single idea, which motivated them and to which their lives were dedicated. If they invoked the name of the people, or a class, or the masses, it was not the people that they loved, but their idea. It is for that reason that the present volume might with equal justice have been titled not a "biographical history" but an intellectual, or more narrowly, an ideological history.

"Revolution," wrote Mussolini, "is an idea which possesses bayonets." Lenin did not misprize bayonets, but to *idea* and *bayonets,* he added something peculiarly his own: namely, *organization.* In the world of ideologues, Lenin's *idea* was an idea concerning the nature and role of organization. Not the organization of the entire people or an entire class, but a special type of organization of men who were to be specialists . . . specialists in revolution, and then specialists in the administration of power. As for the rest of the population, he was ready to content himself with the words of Lasalle to Marx: "*Hate* in the *multitude* is sufficient for everything, if there are five people in the country who also *understand*."*

For this reason it was impossible to write the history of the Russian revolutionary movement without trying to render comprehensible to the reader the obscure and unfamiliar world of inter-party and intra-party controversies, of fine-drawn doctrinal differences, of splits and splinterings, the world of the Russian underground.

Some have urged that in this work I have presented the Mensheviks as too doctrinaire, and Lenin as somewhat less despotic and totalitarian than in the end he proved to be. Perhaps this is so, if we examine Menshevism after it had assimilated the bitter lessons of defeat and gotten a clearer notion of the mischief in the ways of its adversary. And certainly it is so, if we contemplate what became of Lenin's doctrines and how they developed after they were implemented with the terrible instruments of absolute power. Bearing this in mind, I have introduced some corrections into the text in its latest revision. But because of the historical method I employed, these "ultimate" implications of character and doctrine had in the main to develop out of the events, and along with the story itself.

Those who read this work attentively will recognize that I have tried an extremely difficult historical design, but one necessary in my judgment to the living presentation of a historical sequence. The historian's most challenging task is to put himself, and his reader, back into the events he is treating as if they had not yet occurred and he did not yet know the "ultimate" outcome. Rejecting the deceptive omniscience of hindsight, he must look forward with his characters toward their future, which is to him already in the past. Only thus can he reopen what now appears to be closed, put himself in their places, see things as they looked to his protagonists before they made their choices among the possibilities of action. Only thus can he comprehend their dilemmas, appraise their achievements, misjudgments, errors, responsibilities, the consequences of their choosing to do one thing and not another, the results of their failure to foresee what might follow from what they do and leave undone. Only thus can he give to his story the breath of life, and extricate its human—that is to say, moral—significance.

Looking backward, the historian is seduced into regarding any large event as having been inevitable, is inclined to regard the consequences of the acts of willful and powerful men as having been all along intended. But looking forward, he cannot fail to see multiple possibilities all along the road ahead.

*From a letter dated September 11, 1860. It should be added that this thought was marginal in Lasalle, but central in Lenin.

Backward or forward, more than the tidy historian likes to admit, he finds at every turn the unexpected and the unpredictable: contingency, historical accident, biological accident intruding itself into history, as when the death of a history-making personage brings a change in direction; sudden changes of mood; emergence of totally new situations; leaps that seem to turn an accretion of ambiguous little events into a definitive big event; the complicated interaction of multiple and various determinants in every happening; the unintended consequences of intended actions, and the unexpected consequences which were not foreseen even when the event itself was foreseen and forewilled.

Huge events like wars and revolutions are so multiply determined and so fraught with striking consequences, that in restrospect decades may seem to have been preparing for this and no other outcome. The vacillations and uncertainties, the ebbs and flows, the countless actions and counteractions, the striving for quite other results than the event finally gives forth—all this tends to get lost from view. Choices of action and inaction have been made along the way, unnoticed or misapprehended, so that when the huge climax comes, it has the deceptive air of having been inevitable all along.

Afterwards, the historian can go back for decades, industriously picking and choosing among the welter of ambiguous and contradictory events just those actions, trends, forces, and proposals, which appear to have led up to just this denouement. He can ignore the ebbs for the now irreversible flood, overlook the turns not taken, the chances missed, that might have led better or more foresightful or luckier men to another outcome.

Be that as it may, the method I have used in *Three Who Made a Revolution* has been to put myself and the reader back into the time of the protagonists, looking forward and moving forward with them toward a future in essential respects still open. For this reason, the same problems pose themselves again and again in this history, each time on a later, more advanced and more explicit level of complication and meaning, as the "living dead" whose deeds and thoughts I treat face these issues under constantly developing and changing conditions, and add to their solution the ingredients of their own choices and perceptions.

Only in one respect, as I should here confess to the reader, have I consciously deviated from this method. When a man undertakes a large work, he does not know how much of it he will live to finish and publish. Therefore, after looking forward with my characters toward an issue or an event, every so often (or so seldom), I have permitted myself a side remark, or a leading question addressed to the reader to carry his thought beyond that of the protagonists and the action. Thus on page 510, for instance, the reader will find the story of the expulsion of Bogdanov, Lunacharsky and other Bolsheviks by Lenin:

By a small and safe majority [I wrote], Bogdanov and his associates were declared to have 'placed themselves outside the faction.'

'Not outside the Party,' Lenin explained precisely. 'A party can
include a wide range of opinions, the extremes of which may be
diametrically opposed to each other . . .'

This was as far as the method of "looking forward toward the
future" with my protagonists would have carried the story. But I
could not resist the temptation to add two "hindsight" sentences to
the episode:

But in 1912, Lenin's faction was to declare itself the Party! And
after 1917, he was to make even the State a mere instrument of
the Party. What then would happen to the 'wide range of opinions?'

Finally, this introduction would be incomplete without a word
on sources, annotation, and my indebtedness to various colleagues.
I have often been reproached for the lack of systematic footnotes.
The reproach is well taken. Certainly the sequels (beginning with
Marxism: Ambiguous Heritage—a work now on press which treats of
aspects of the intellectual history of Marxism and Marxism-Leninism),
will be annotated according to the prevailing rules. By way of ex-
tenuation if not disculpation, I should like to point out that many
"footnotes" are not at the foot of pages, but in parentheses and asides
in the text itself. If the text says, for example: "wrote Lenin in *Proletarii* of such-and-such date," any experienced researcher can find
the passage in a moment in the corresponding (dated) volume of
Lenin's *Sochineniya*. Especially where the reader might be inclined
to doubt or where the interpretation appeared most novel, I included
the sources in the text. And in my revisions for this edition I have
followed the usual practices of historical scholarship.

I am deeply indebted to those Russian men and women whom
fate has thrown on our shores, and whose spirits are irreplaceable
human archives of all they have lived through. Only now are we
beginning to get some of their memories in writing in such publishing
ventures as the Inter-University Project on the History of the
Menshevik Movement. When I did the first edition of this book, I
had to depend on their time and patience in the granting of repeated
personal interviews.

I owe a great debt to those who read the original manuscript in
whole or in part before publication, and to the much larger number
who read it in print, and kindly sent me their comments, suggestions
and encouragement from many lands:

To Solomon M. Schwarz, who read the manuscript twice over.

To Vera Alexandrova, my guide into the intricacies and glories of
the Russian tongue and Russian literature.

To Nikolai Vladoslavovich Valentinov, who read the work in

French and, despite his illness, sent me many long letters concerning various aspects of the work.

To Wladimir Woytinsky, who read it on the bed of his last illness, and communicated his suggestions orally.

To Michael Karpovich who read the difficult opening chapter and gave his encouragement to publish its generalizations concerning the historical heritage and the intelligentsia.

To Boris Nikolaevsky, himself a living archive, for reading the chapter on Roman Malinovsky.

To Rafael Abramovich, who read the sections concerned with his own personal experiences.

To Angelica Balabanoff, who answered all questions I had the wit to put to her.

To Leo Borochowicz, who offered many valuable suggestions.

To Sidney Hook, who read in manuscript the chapter on "Lenin as Philosopher."

To David Shub, who sent me evidence which left its traces on the revisions I have made in the chapter on Roman Malinovsky.

To Iraklii Tseretelli, who made many valuable suggestions and gave me the priceless encouragement of saying, "As I read it, I cannot believe that you did not live in our movement."

To Boris Dvinov, Boris Sapir, Raymond H. Fisher, Warren Walsh, Marc Szeftel, Max Nomad, Walter Goldwater, Mark Vishniak, all of whom made valuable suggestions and corrections.

To a number of Russians here and in the Soviet Union, who had best remain nameless, who answered questions put to them.

To the Slavonic Division of the New York Public Library, to the Hoover Library in Stanford, the Columbia and Harvard Libraries, the Library of Congress, and the British Museum, for the friendly cooperation of their staffs and for making materials available to me that were hard to come by.

To Leon Kramer, bookseller, who searched the Russian colonies of the world from Shanghai to Prague in an effort to secure for me obscure and out-of-print papers, pamphlets and books which might enable me to confront the "official truth" with the "truth of the defeated," so that out of the confrontation more of the historical truth might emerge.

To Edmund Wilson for lending me his valuable library of Leniniana which he had collected to write his own *To the Finland Station*.

It goes without saying that the defects in this book are my own and that none of those who so kindly helped, or sought to help, bears any responsibility for any of them.

The tentative large generalizations concerning Russia's history offered in the first chapter are my own, but I must acknowledge a debt to many Russian historians and thinkers, particularly to Klyuchevsky and his school, to Karpovich, Vernadsky, Berdyaev, and Milyukov, and to the sudden flashes of deep self-knowledge that abound in the nineteenth-century literature of the Westerner-Slavophile controversies and in the Russian novel. In order to "get back" into the vanished world I spent two years reading or rereading Russian novels and the literature of those great controversies.

The chapters on Lenin are based primarily on his writings and his letters, on the notes provided by the Third Russian Edition of his *Sochineniya*, on the memoirs of his wife and his sister Anna, and innumerable other memoirs friendly, hostile and hagiographical, concerning him. Special acknowledgment is due to Leon Trotsky for his brilliant fragment, "Vie de Lenine: Jeunesse."

The chapters on Stalin owe much to Boris Souvarine's groundbreaking biography, and to Trotsky's unfinished biography of Joseph Stalin. I am indebted to Charles Malamuth, editor and translator of Trotsky's *Stalin* for making available to me much unpublished documentation. Much more than for Lenin and Trotsky I have had to use for Stalin the "archaeological method" of uncovering successive layers of falsehood and juxtaposing them in the hope of extricating the truth. The reader can find a detailed account of these excavations in my article in *Foreign Affairs*, "Operation Rewrite: The Agony of the Soviet Historian." And I should record my thanks to Nikita Sergeevich Khrushchev for confirming much of my previously so hotly contested version of the truth concerning Stalin in his *Secret Speech* at the Twentieth Congress, and public speeches on the same theme at the Twenty-Second Congress of the Communist Party of the Soviet Union.

Bertram D. Wolfe
January 1, 1964

CHAPTER I

THE HERITAGE

Russia, whither flyest thou? Answer! She gives no answer.
The ringing of bells melts into music; the air, torn to shreds,
whirs and rushes like the wind, everything that is on earth
is flying by, and the other states and nations, with looks
askance, make way for her and draw aside.—*Nikolai Gogol*

The tradition of all the dead generations weighs like an
incubus upon the brain of the living.   —*Karl Marx*

The greatness of today is built on the efforts of past centuries.
A nation is not contained in a day nor in an epoch, but in
the succession of all days, all periods, all her twilights and
all her dawns.   —*Jean Jaurès*

THE GREAT Eurasian Plain opposes few obstacles to frost and
wind and drought, to migrant hordes and marching armies. In
earlier centuries the plain was dominated by vast Asiatic empires,
Iranian, Turkish, Mongolian. As the last of these melted away,
Muscovy expanded to take their place, expanded steadily through
several centuries until it became the largest continuous land empire
in the world. Like the tide over limitless flats, it spread with elemental force over an endless stretch of forest and steppe, sparsely
settled by backward and nomadic peoples. Wherever it met resistance, it would pause as the tide does to gather head, then resume
its inexorable advance. Only at the distant margins does the pla-
teau end in great mountain barriers: the snowy summits of the
Caucasus; the Pamirs, roof of the world—where two of our three
protagonists have peaks named in their honor, thrusting up over
four miles each into the sky; the Altai, Sayan and Stanovoi mountains forming China's natural wall. How could a people not be
great and not aspire to greatness, whose horizon was as unlimited
as this Eurasian Plain?

By the time our story begins, the empire of the Tsars sprawls
heavily across two continents, from the Gulf of Finland to the
distant Pacific shore. It includes most of the land area of the frozen
Arctic to within twelve degrees of the Pole, and stretches southward into hot desert sands and semi-tropical slopes bordering on
Turkey, Persia, Afghanistan.

History presents no parallel to this vastness. The Roman Empire at its height would have been lost in it. The other great continuous land areas, the United States, China and India, do not equal its extension, when all three of them are added together. Its European portion is equal to all the busy lands of Western Europe combined, yet two-thirds of its vast bulk lies outside that continent, on the Asiatic tundras and steppes. It embraces over 8,500,000 square miles of contiguous territory—approximately one-tenth of the human race and one-sixth the total land surface of the globe.

It gives us fresh perspective on the wars of our time to follow backward through the pages of history the ebb and flow of peoples over this limitless plain, recalling that the Elbe (Slavic *Laba*) was a Slav frontier in the time of Charlemagne, Hamburg a fortress erected to hold the Slavs in check, Prussia (anciently Borussia), once a Lithuanian land, and Breslau (formerly Breslavl, now Wroclaw), along with Dresden and Leipzig, once Slavic towns. Or to remember that Mongolia, now being torn from China, once ruled alike over China and what is now Russia and the whole Eurasian Plain.

Against every powerful invader, the chief defenders of this great open plain have ever been General Distance (with his aides, General Mud and General Winter) and his age-old strategy of the "scorched earth." No invention this, as recent "discoverers" of Russia have proclaimed, of socialism, or state property, or Stalin's military genius, but so venerable as to be known in Russian history as "Scythian tactics." For it has been used against every would-be conqueror from Hitler and Hindenburg in the twentieth century, Napoleon in the nineteenth and Charles XII in the eighteenth (Charles, be it remembered, got as far as Poltava in the Ukraine), to Darius the Great of Persia, who invaded the plain through the Pontic steppes in 512 B.C. Then the Scythians, as the inhabitants of what is now the Ukraine were called in those days, retreated inland, driving away their cattle, burning the grass and poisoning the wells. They drew the hosts of Darius inland until he was too deep within the scorched land, then counter-attacked, helping to save an Athens of which they had never heard, even as the Tsar's armies saved Paris in 1914 and the Soviet armies London in World War II.

At the beginning of the nineteenth century, one European in seven was a Russian; at the beginning of the twentieth, one in every four. As I write, the ratio is still changing in Russia's favor. If we include all the newly annexed lands, and all those being brought under the sway of occupying armies and puppet governments, approximately one European out of every two is today under Russian rule.

> The three holy capitals of the Russian Empire—wrote the Pan-Slavist Tyuchev—are Moscow, Saint Petersburg and Constantinople. Where are her boundaries in the North and East, in the South and West? Destiny will show that the path of the future will lead us to the seven inland seas and to the seven great rivers, from the Nile to the Neva, from the Elbe to the Yangtze, from the Volga to the Euphrates, from the Ganges to the Danube—this is the Russian Empire, and it will last through the ages. . . .

And fearfully Lord Palmerston, that same Lord Palmerston whom Marx denounced as a "hireling" of Russia, responded:

> The policy and practice of the Russian government have always been to push forward its encroachments as fast and as far as the apathy or want of firmness of other governments would allow it to go, but always to stop and retire when it met with decided resistance, and then to wait for the next favorable opportunity to make another spring on its intended victim.

The unity and expansive force of Muscovy have had about them something elemental, largely independent of differences in leadership and régime. The spread of the Russian people in earlier centuries was more the work of Cossack bands, fugitive serfs, outlaws, adventurers, freedom-seekers, than of the state itself. Sometimes the state sought to check or contain this process of overflow, yet, in the long run, it always reaped the harvest which swelled it into the super-state we know. Only at brief intervals, particularly in the later nineteenth century, has it been consciously expansionist. The Bolshevik leaders we are to meet will find in Russia's great distances the salvation of their revolution in its days of peril. Beginning with a sincere attempt at rupture with Russia's imperialist-expansionist past, in the end they will take over and develop further, under other forms, the same expansive force, the same far-flung centralism, ubiquitous bureaucracy, million-headed standing army, leviathan state, the whole imposing apparatus which binds this many-colored conglomerate of races into a single, ever-expanding domain.

An empire so huge and cumbersome is hard to tie together, inept at times in bringing its overwhelming force to bear at any given point. Yet four times in the eighteenth and early nineteenth centuries, victorious Russian armies stood upon the Rhine. They took

Paris from Napoleon and Berlin from Frederick the Great. Even under the palsied leadership of Nicholas II, they crushed the imposing forces of their Austro-Hungarian neighbor in 1914-16, compelling Germany to abandon its drive on Paris in order to contain them in East Prussia. Thus it is mere legend that Russia's armies were never great till now.

Behind the legend lies the fact that in the last two centuries the countries of Western Europe have made up for their inferior numbers by advancing technically faster than Russia. Therefore, five times did Muscovy meet checks in its slow expansion. Yet the expansion did not cease, while contact and conflict with the West gave rise to tremendous transformations, as if the law of Russia's being were to progress through defeats.

The first such encounter began in earnest Muscovy's modernization, when Peter the Great saw his armies melt away on the Narva, and answered with the forced "Westernization" and industrialization-for-war of his backward land. The second impulse came from the French Revolution, Napoleon's march on Moscow, and Russia's march on Paris. Out of these were born such diverse things as the moral unity of the nation, the early plans of Alexander I and Speransky for reform, the military-agricultural "communes" of Arakcheev, and the abortive revolt of the Decembrists, which opened a century of revolution. The third impulse came when the small forces of the Concert of European Powers defeated Russia's far-larger serf-formed armies in the Crimean War, leading to the emancipation of the serfs and an era of attendant reforms. The fourth was the defeat by Japan (this time, General Distance went over to the enemy), which precipitated the uprising of 1905 and gave rise to the beginnings of a constitutional regime. By none of these clashes, be it noted, was Russia's secular expansion more than given pause. At the end of each encounter, Muscovy was in possession of more territory, and mightier than before.

The fifth such event forms the central core of our story, when Russia's enormous military machine bogged down in East Prussia and Galicia because of demoralization in the rear and exhaustion of matériel, with no possibility of lend-lease to supply the defficiency —a defeat which helped to bring on, and was accelerated in turn by, the revolutions of 1917. This time the transformation was to be the most sweeping of all and would in the end provide the greatest dynamic power for expansion that Russia had known since Muscovy first swept through Siberia in the sixteen-hundreds. Such a record of mighty offensive force and stubborn staying power in the face of adversity makes it perennially impossible to "write off"

Russia in the hour of her reverses, or to contain her within her old limits in the hour of her victories.

In Russia, Europe and Asia meet. Throughout its history, East and West have striven for its soul. How often has it stood between Europe and Asia's migrant hordes? How many times saved Europe from conquest at the price of its own partial orientalization? Still today, as at the dawn of history, it stands at the boundary line, embracing half of the lesser peninsula called Europe and more than a third of the greater mainland called Asia, serving as the channel of the ebb and flow of Eastern and Western influence, partaking of both in its make-up. Though the center of gravity has long shifted from Asia to Europe, still Russia remains, in body and in spirit, a double nature, a Eurasian land.

Its window on Europe is narrow and small, and, even as its tiny casement *fortochkas,* likely to be nailed tight shut in winter. Behind that little vent upon the West (growing larger now), lies the overwhelming hinterland, stretching eastward a quarter way round the world. It is a hinterland localistic and passive enough to be held in control, but vast enough and sufficiently resistant to stifle or distort the most powerful movements for change. Again and again mighty impulses have come from the West only to weaken and lose themselves at last in the endless eastward-stretching plain, which again and again has reconquered its conquerors or transformed their dreams into something more in accord with its own patient and timeless image.

Though predominantly a European land it has long stood on the periphery of Europe. It formed a part neither of the Roman nor of the Holy Roman Empires. In its formative period, its culture came from the Near East, from the "Eastern Rome," Byzantium, and from the Caliphate of Baghdad. This did not then spell backwardness, for in the tenth century when these Eastern cultures rippled through the Balkans and the Caucasus into Russia, their centers were not behind but ahead of Western Europe. But, shortly thereafter, the life of Baghdad and Byzantium seemed to freeze into rigidity, and consequently their spiritual child, Russia, lagged behind too. The sudden shift of the currents of historical dynamism westward to the Mediterranean and then the Atlantic shore, left Russia outside the main stream. As the Arab Caliphate and the Byzantine Empire both fell to the Ottoman Turk, Russia retained for a while a precarious connection with the West through the Baltic and the Black Seas, then lost that to the Germans, Lithuanians, Swedes and Turks. But the decisive events which cut Russia off from Western Europe were the schisms between the Byzantine and the Roman Church, and the Tartar-Mongol invasion, followed by two centuries of Mongol domination.

The Mongol invasion was but one—the last before the formation of Muscovy—of a long series of such elemental floods of migrating peoples. Norsemen from Scandinavia, Poles and Livonians and Germans from the West, Greeks and Turks and Persians from the South, Ugro-Finns from Asia, Slavs from the Carpathians, Khazars, Kalmucks, Tartars and other nomadic hordes from the East, have rolled in endless succession over the great open Eurasian Plain, now as conquerors, now in flight, planting their successive deposits of race and custom, rooting up and scattering again and again the slow accumulations of settled civilization, retarding the progress of economy and laying on all the land the ineradicable imprint of pillage and enslavement and the sword.

Yet, when the age of the great migrations ceased in Europe, Russia, under the dominance of the Slavs, no less than the Western lands, developed its unifying language and culture and seemed ready, along with the rest, to make its first steps toward the economy and civilization that characterize the modern Western World.

The unifying impulses which radiated outward during the later Middle Ages from linguistic-cultural centers like Paris, London, Tuscany, Castille, and made French, English, Italian, Spanish dominant over neighbor dialects and languages within great regions of national cohesion, have been but obscurely studied. One thing, however, seems certain: that markets and trade routes and consequent cultural interchange have played an important role in begetting these centers. And yet another, that the experience of a common struggle for existence tended to give their leadership over "national" regions a permanent form.

The Little-Russians (Ukrainians) and the Great-Russians (Muscovites) were not behind the rest in developing the trading towns of Kiev and Novgorod, in exhibiting that potent expansive force of one tongue and people, in Russifying quite without compulsion the conquered Finnish peasants in the central plain and the conquering Viking boyars and princes who ruled the land. Russia-Ukrainia, no less than other countries, became an early highway of medieval commerce in men and things and ideas. At the very dawn of the Middle Ages, its network of broad, slow-running rivers, navigable by ships of trade through much of the year, connected by easy portages, and serving as smooth sledgeways for winter traffic, provided the main highway of the East European medieval world—the long continental route "from the Varangians to the Greeks," i.e. from Scandinavia to Byzantium. The river road ran through a land of forests and steppes. The nomads of the steppes provided the first trading-piratical bands. The forests supplied primitive forest products: honey and wax; pelts and furs; agricultural products crudely cultivated with wooden plough and hoe in the clearings around towns that raised the first armies to defend the highway; and the human animal, hunted in forest and steppe to be sold as a slave. Young Russian girls were famed in Arabia as concubines, while the very word slave is declared by most philologists to be related to Slav.

How far this early commerce might have carried ancient Russia toward urban culture and democratic or patrician town government we do not know; for in the thirteenth century the course of inner transcontinental trade was suddenly and permanently deflected to other routes. When the Crusaders took Byzantium in 1204, the Orient trade ceased to follow the route of the Black Sea, the Dnieper and the Baltic. It was diverted to the Mediterranean, going through Venice and Genoa to Syria, Palestine and Egypt, and through the passes of the Alps to the Rhine and northern Europe. Italian cities flourished while the great river highway from the Varangians to the Greeks became a turbulent backwater; the young Slav towns withered, the nascent burgher or aristocratic democracies died, the forest and steppe prevailed in Russia once more. The Renaissance flowed through other waterways, passing Russia by. It alone of the great nations never knew that spiritual stir, never felt the full force of the Reformation, never developed the widespread culture and individualism that those movements brought in their train. Indeed, it became a strangely silent land. In the centuries when Italy had its Dante and its Petrarch, when England had its Shakespeare, Spain its Cervantes, France its Corneille and Racine, Russia remained silent. The mighty land did not find its voice until the nineteenth century, when suddenly full throated, it astonished the world.

At the moment when the river highway was becoming a backwater and the dying towns had grown too feeble to offer successful resistance, came the last great Mongol-Tartar invasions from the Asiatic steppes. The moribund centers of trade were pillaged, burned, laid waste, their "principal men" exterminated or carried off as slaves, their primitive liberties and feeble shoots of lay culture destroyed. Urban and mercantile Russia, "bourgeois" Russia, received a blow from which it did not recover for several centuries.

And then it was another Russia, centering in Muscovy, and not the old Russia, or Ukrainia rather, centering in Kiev.

> One *Rus*—writes Tolstoy—has its roots in universal, or at least in European culture. In this *Rus* the ideas of goodness, honor and freedom are understood as in the West. But there is another *Rus*: the *Rus* of the dark forests, the *Rus* of the Taiga, the animal Russia, the fanatic Russia, the Mongol-Tartar Russia. This last Russia made despotism and fanaticism its ideal. . . . Kiev *Rus* was a part of Europe, Moscow long remained the negation of Europe.

Not that the Mongols contributed nothing positive. If, unlike the Arabs who invaded Spain, they brought with them "neither Algebra nor Aristotle," they did bring a technique of statecraft eminently suited to a great land empire. Guided by Chinese sages, these nomads of the Asiatic steppe had developed a considerable skill in bureaucratic administration of great areas, greater areas than had ever been held together by any people from a single center. They it was who contributed the loose and easy tolerance of local religions, local administrations and local customs, which enabled both Tsars and Soviets to hold together a diversity of peoples by varying combinations of centralism and autonomy. All they asked was submission from the indigenous, autonomous ruler, or, failing to get that, they set up a puppet from the same indigenous ruling layer. Provided they secured tribute and a military levy (the only centralist aspirations of that simpler day), they were content to let dukes and priests and elders remain in their posts. Finding that they could use the Russian Orthodox Church and the Grand Dukes of Muscovy as instruments of their rule, they favored them, while they destroyed the more advanced and democratic cities like Kiev, richer in booty and more zealous in their resistance. Moscow was aided by the Tartars against the West, and elevated into a collector of tribute, a center of religion, and a Tartar viceroydom. As the power of the Golden Horde began to disintegrate, the Grand Duchy of Moscow succeeded swiftly to the headship of the great vacant empire extending over the Eurasian Plain. Its sudden growth brought the other princes to the Muscovite Court, made Moscow into a holy city and a patriarchate, reinforcing the Byzantine principle of Caesaro-papism with the Mongol principle of unquestioning submission and universal obligation of service to the absolute military leader and the state.

But it is too frequently forgotten that this military autocracy had deep popular roots. Its successive struggles for Christian reconquest from the Tartar Khans, then with Roman Catholic Poland-

Lithuania, and much later with Sweden and Germany, made the Church into its banner and earned for tsardom as deep popularity among the masses of Muscovy as was won by the Spanish monarchy in its long struggle with the Moors. Thus a capital of popularity was accumulated that it would take until the twentieth century to disperse. In the year 1905, as we watch a gowned and bearded priest, Father Gapon, lead a procession of the most skilled and advanced workers of Russia, those of the famous Putilov machine and locomotive works, on a march to the Palace to petition the Dear Father Tsar, bearing on high the images of the beloved monarch, we will have cause to remember how deep were the roots of popular support of tsardom. It was the firing of the troops upon these unarmed and reverential workers that broke at last the Tsar's spell. But a feeling so deeply rooted is more likely to be displaced and transferred to other objects than utterly disintegrated. Still, today, as in the past, Russian workers march in all their processions bearing on high the images of their ruler and call him *Rodnoi Otets*, "Our Own Dear Father," or "Father in the Flesh."

After Muscovy shook off the Tartar yoke, all serious threats to Russia's existence were destined to come from the West—from the German knights, from Poland-Lithuania, from Sweden, from Napoleon, from the Concert of Powers, from Germany under Wilhelm II and under Hitler. Thus the bonds of loyalty that bound the people to the state and its military autocrat were continually being reinforced. And the barriers of Byzantine heritage and Tartar rule that had cut off Muscovy from the West were as constantly strengthened by the ever-present sense of Occidental threat and national danger.

Indeed, war, virtually unending war, was an all-powerful factor in shaping the Muscovite state structure and spirit. In the years from 1228 to 1462, the years conventionally given for Western Europe's Renaissance, Russian historians list 90 internal wars and 160 foreign invasions! During the seventeenth and eighteenth centuries, Western Europe's "Enlightenment," Russia fought three great wars with Sweden, ending with the annexation of Finland and the Baltic lands, and seven desperate struggles with Poland, ending with the Polish partitions.

Muscovy was slower to develop feudal bondage than the countries of the West, because, unlike those smaller realms, it possessed in the Eurasian Plain limitless reaches of free land. Whereas serfdom was reinforced in France and England and Germany by the

absence of unoccupied lands, in Russia, with its boundless steppe
and river bottom and Black Sea shore, fixity had to be created
by law. It was the drain and strain of unending war which caused
the Tsars to decree bondage (the Russian word for it, *Krepost*,
literally means "fixity"), fixity so that tax collector and recruiting
sergeant might always know where to find each individual and
might hold each village communally responsible for its share of
money and men. Bondage began to develop under Peter and
Catherine when, in Western Europe, the institution of serfdom
was already being abolished. In England and France, at the very
moment when medieval institutions began to develop into a juridi-
cal system, feudalism was already beginning to decay. The same
century which undertook to codify the variegated patchquilt of
Western medieval life saw the fabric wear thin and show great
rips and tears. But in Russia, several centuries later, the fabric
was sewn solid, reinforced, stiffened to outlast the storms of the
French Revolution. There were woven into it rich and unpliable
materials from the dying Byzantine East, bright metallic strands
contributed by the Tartar hordes, dark ones worked into the warp
and woof by never-ending war.

Still primitive and crude, the Muscovite state—cut to the pattern
of a mere dukedom—became the head of a great Eurasian empire
long before it possessed an apparatus or a technique equal to such
massive tasks. In the words of Russia's greatest historian, Klyuchevsky, "the state swelled up; the people shrank." Or, as Karpovich
has put it, "the body of Russia grew too fast for its soul." The military budget and the costs of the apparatus were always too big
for the productive economy (and are so still). Hence people had
to be fixed in their jobs and tied to their places, where tax-gatherer,
military levy, and army supply commissariat could find them. On
this military-feudal foundation Russia put into the field great standing armies while the Western powers were still contenting themselves with little companies of mercenaries or volunteers.

Thus, what today has come to be known as totalitarianism,
product of the gearing of modern life to modern total war, with
its perpetual sense of emergency and its omnipotent state, has deep
roots in the formative history of the Russian land. "All through
the state, nothing against the state, nothing outside the state"—
today the doctrine has a new technological base and completeness, but the spirit is not altogether new. Universal obligation
to service, universal fixity created by decree—*krepost* and *nevolya*
—have for centuries been characteristics of Russian life. Other
peoples, it has been said, consist of two parts, Body and Soul,

but the Russian of three: Body, Soul and Passport. Prior to World
War I, only two countries required passports for foreigners, Russia
and Turkey. Now, as all lands move towards leviathan statism,
documents and passports multiply. But today, as in the past, the
internal passport, occupational fixity, prohibition of the free movement of the individual from factory or farm, distinguish Russia
from other countries still. The countless reports on the "New
Russia" have not even posed the problem: how much of this is
socialism or Stalinism, and how much the heritage of Russia's past?

The greatest industrializer of Russia prior to Lenin-Stalin was
Peter the Great. His modernization, like that of his successors, was
intended primarily for the purposes of war and the state. Industrialization was an aspect of militarization. It came from the top
downward. It lifted, shoved, dragged, drove, booted the Russian
people toward Western technique by fiat of the state. Overnight,
Peter created alongside the cottage industry, a great textile and
clothing industry to produce uniforms in millions and a great iron
and steel industry to produce bayonets, cannon and the munitions
of war. The industries were created by state plan and *ukaz*. Sons
of the nobility were ordered to study science and technology; capital was invested by royal command; a laboring class was created
by assigning state serfs from the Crown estates. Thus, long before
Marxian socialism was so much as dreamed of, the Russian state
became the largest landowner, the largest factory owner, the largest employer of labor, the largest trader, the largest owner of capital, in Russia, or in the world. The needs of its huge armies made
it the largest customer for private industry as well.
    This brought into being the world's largest apparatus of bureauc-
racy. The destruction of the hereditary nobility, begun by Ivan the
Terrible in the sixteenth century with his substitution of a security-
and-service-to-the-state *Oprichnina* (curiously suggestive of the
GPU), was completed by Peter the Great in the eighteenth. The
bureaucracy was arranged in a fixed hierarchy, and the slow ascent
in the service from copying clerk to high dignitary was largely
dependent upon mere length of years spent at a rigidly determined
series of desks, each with its well-defined routines, duties, associates, grade and titles, salary and prerogatives. Nobility itself was
now so rooted in service to the state that it was automatically
attained by a plebeian who had put in a definite number of years
in possession of a government inkpot. The bureaucracy was graded
by Peter into a hierarchy of *chinovniki*, a ladder of precisely fourteen *chins*, or rungs, not as a rule to be ascended by impetuosity

or merit, but rather at an exact and monotonous pace, which could be varied only by the arbitrary decision of some higher being.

To this structure of state capitalism, Alexander I and Nicholas I added a system of military state farms, termed by Vernadsky an "experiment in military socialism." Its aim was to engage Russia's huge armies in productive labor and thus reduce the monstrous war budget. Whole regiments were settled in farming areas, whence the native peasants were deported. Whole villages had their male population put into uniform and drilled, while continuing to work the fields. New communities were constructed to plan, with farmhouses, barracks, communal buildings. They received cattle, horses, subsidies, tax exemptions, and were subject to discipline and continual drill. Though spiritually galling, physically they prospered, piling up a reserve of 32,000,000 rubles. Begun in 1810, by 1825 when Alexander I died, they embraced 138 infantry battalions and 240 cavalry squadrons: over 200,000 soldiers and their families, one-third of the standing army. The system continued for over 40 years, being abolished as part of the "loosening of the bonds" by Alexander II. It is suggestive of the militarized labor communes attempted by the Bolsheviks in 1920; many of its features can be found in today's state and collective farms and in Khrushchev's dream of the *agrogorod*.

After the emancipation in 1861, there was at last a rapid development of free labor and capital. But the state continued to expand economically, too, and to take on additional enterprises: notably, a vast construction of railroads and telegraph lines, with state operation; new trade monopolies; and large-scale state banking. Alexander III, according to Count Witte, declared in language befitting Lenin or Khrushchev: "The existence of Railroad Kingdoms ruled by little railroad sovereigns is incompatible with the dignity and security of the Russian autocratic empire." (Witte: *Vospominaniya*, p. 352.) In 1869, the state owned 23 percent of the railways; in 1890, 60 percent. Then it undertook the construction of the Trans-siberian, in ten years completing a greater mileage than any government before or since. In the twentieth century it was also the leading banker, the State Bank having a turnover of 234,009,000,000 gold rubles in 1913. During the War it continued to build railroads at a more rapid rate than the Bolsheviks have ever been able to achieve in a like period of time. About one-third of the pre-war tsarist budget was appropriated for government-operated industries and construction, another fourth for army and navy, the rest for the usual purposes of a vast state apparatus. The state's leading position in the economy (its possession of what Lenin would call "the commanding heights") was further strengthened by the conversion of industry to war after 1914. What the Bolsheviks really took over in 1917, even before they had nationalized a single industry on their own, was the largest state economic machine in the world.

"Europe is necessary to us for a few decades," Peter is supposed to have said, "and then we can turn our backs on her." But the new techniques, the new administrative forms, required new attitudes and were imported with an invisible aura of a new way of life and thought. Technologically one borrowed an end result without the organic cultural development which had engendered it. Or one borrowed the latest idea, wrenching it loose from the competing ideas which held it in check and the shadings which qualify it. From Peter's time to the present, Russia has often imported her ideas along with her machines, and often not known how to operate with one or the other. To import technicians along with techniques solved one problem only to raise another: offended national pride. The sudden injection of "Westernism" by "Eastern methods," by command from on high, did little to prepare the people spiritually for what was commanded, and much to offend them. The enforcement of the strange ways caused a deep split in the Russian psyche: a crisis in religion, culture, politics, feeling and thought, which has lasted three centuries and not ended yet. It deepened the schism between Old B. 'ievers and State Church, the cleavages between throne and people, nobility and peasant, bureaucracy and people, intelligentsia and people, and finally, inside the intelligentsia itself. In the nineteenth century the intelligentsia became conscious of this fissure in the Russian spirit, giving form to it in great battles of the Westernizer-Slavophile controversy.

In the present century, the same dualism expressed itself in the proliferation of splits among the opponents of the regime: between Miliukov and Maklakov in the Liberal camp; between Slavophile Social-Revolutionaries and Western Marxists; between Bolsheviks and Mensheviks—endless variations of the same psychic tug-of-war. The crowded years of the Revolution show a peculiar symbolic displacement: zealous Westernizers dominating the first three-fourths of the year 1917; then Lenin, whose complex blend of "Slavic" and "Western" we shall examine in this work. Next the Great-Russian from the Central Volga is succeeded by Stalin, a Georgian from the Caucasus, where Europe ends and Asia begins.

Yet even within the soul of Stalinism appeared the same schizoid inner war: between the Stalin of the twenties and early thirties who imported foreign technicians and machines and worshipped foreign techniques, who defined his "holy of holies," the very "style of Leninism" as "the harmonious union of Russian élan (*razmakh*) with American practicality in getting things done"—and the Stalin of the forties who feared and denigrated everything foreign and created the new thought-crime of contact with, admiration for, or "slavish kow-towing to the West." Now the more mercurial spirit of Khrushchev, his disciple, shuttles visibly back and forth between the same two poles of tension.

Suddenly, in the dawn of the nineteenth century, long-mute Russia found her voice and became aware of the rival spirits struggling for the possession of her soul. The first stirrings had come in the preceding century, but it was the contact with the West and the sense of national peril and national triumph in the Napoleonic Wars that gave new impulse to Russian industry and culture, brought young aristocrat-intellectuals of the officer caste into the camps and capitals of Western Europe, awakened the aristocratic intelligentsia to national self-consciousness. Not among the masses, but among these young noblemen of camp and court, stirred the first impulse to freedom.

> *We wait, our anxious hearts are beating,*
> *We yearn for sacred liberty,*
> *As a youthful lover yearns to see*
> *The lagging hour of sweetheart greeting*

sang the youthful Pushkin. Characteristically, it was from the Tsar that he expected the precious gift:

> *And shall I see, my friends, a people freed from burdens*
> *And serfdom's yoke struck off by royal hand,*
> *While at long last the sacred dawn of freedom*
> *Sheds its bright glow o'er our dear fatherland?*

For a time, the Autocrat on the throne seemed to share the bright dream. But then Alexander the liberal dreamer became Alexander the reactionary mystic. He who had written to Thomas Jefferson for advice on a constitution, commissioned Czartoryski to plan the charter of Polish freedom, and the commoner Speransky to draft a constitution for Russia itself—now fell under the influence of such reactionary figures as Arakcheev in domestic, and Metternich in foreign, affairs. Thereafter there was a displacement of the center of renovation from monarch to enlightened aristocrats, though these young radicals of the Court long continued to center their hopes on a revolution from above because they dared not think of a revolution from below. For a whole decade after Alexander withdrew his favor, they waited, dreaming, planning, plotting, in their secret societies and Masonic leagues, hoping for a change of heart, for death to bring a change of autocrats, for a palace revolution.

Most interesting of the officers' secret societies were those known as the Northen and the Southern. The program of the Northern Society, written by Colonel Muraviev, provided for a liberal constitutional monarchy on the English pattern, for federal decentralization, and individual civil rights. Muraviev would have preferred a republic; however, the people would have to be consulted, and their will could only be determined through a constituent assembly. The program of the Southern Society, on the other hand, was conceived in the spirit of French Jacobinism, curiously foreshadowing the ideas and methods of those twentieth-century Jacobins, the Bolsheviks. Pestel, its author, was determined to establish a republic by any and every means, in the interests, of course, of the people, but, if necessary, against the will of the people themselves. The members of his society were divided into a triple hierarchy of responsibility and initiation: a leading layer of conspirators that would alone know all secrets and make all important decisions; a middle layer that would participate in some degre in the knowledge and determination of these matters; and a lower layer whose duty it was merely to execute instructions. Below them was to be yet another group of "friends" or sympathizers, a species of fellow-travelers who were not to be initiated into any of the secrets of the society's existence. Pestel's plans involved a conspiracy which would overthrow the autocracy, execute the Tsar and all the members of the imperial family, then take power and set up a temporary military dictatorship as the lever for a sweeping program of social reform. The dictatorship was to be equipped with all the instruments of power, including police, spies, censorship. The serfs were to be freed, class distinctions abolished, the land was to be nationalized and divided into two equal portions, one of which was to be in the communal possession of the peasants, the other at the disposal of the state for fiscal purposes, or for sale or distribution as private holdings. In eight or ten years, Pestel thought, the dictatorship would have sufficiently transformed Russia and eliminated the danger of counter-revolution so that the land might become a firmly centralized republic with a popular council or *vieche* (the word is etymologically related to "soviet") as lower house, and a higher ruling body in the shape of a directory of five, a sort of Politbureau which would concentrate the administrative power in its hands.

When Alexander I died, the young radical officer nobility undertook a military coup, known to history by its date (December, 1825) as the Uprising of the Decembrists. It was the last of a long series of attempts at palace revolutions, and the first attempt at a socio-political revolution. It ushered in the period of Russian revolutionary history.

But the very sweep of its program made it less likely to succeed than previous palace revolutions since it involved the fate of the masses and they remained indifferent and unaware of what was planned for them. Nicholas I easily suppressed it, personally conducting the inquiry into the conspiracy. His temperament combined with the alarm attendant upon his accession to the throne to make his long reign (1825-55) a period of reaction. Seeing that a stay in foreign parts had proved so unsettling, he forbade Russians to go abroad except by special permission or on missions for the state. Regarding the discussion of ideas with suspicion, he set up rigid standards as to what must be taught and printed and discussed. As his chief instrument of rule he set up a secret "Third Section" or political police, with himself as chief judge and inquisitor, chief censor and policeman, and, in his own words, "first official" of his realm. Thus the autocracy set itself against the awakening nation, and entered upon the final and fatal stage of its existence.

With the Decembrist uprising of 1825, the frozen crust was broken. In vain did Nicholas, "The Cudgel," seek to stifle change under his iron rule. His own construction of the first railroad (characteristically, he drew two straight lines across a great map, ignoring towns and cities, and said, "Let it run so"), and his own policy of furthering industrialization and a modernized bureaucracy, were more disturbing in their effects than any plot that might have been conceived. When he died in 1855, literally of a broken heart because his rigid social setup had failed ignominiously in the test of the Crimean War, all the stout props he had put up against the work of time collapsed of their own weight. His son, Alexander II (1855-81), was to resume the work of transformation at a rate as rapid as that of Peter, going down in history as "the Tsar Emancipator." But he was to perish by a revolutionist's bomb. For the rest of the century, Russian life would be an unequal race between the waning force of reform from above and the waxing strength of unrest from below.

Inevitably, those who sought the way of revolution had to turn their attention to the still slumbering Russian folk. All possible attitudes mingled in their feeling concerning the people: self-abnegation, repentance, humility, mystic worship, blind hope, fascination, fear. Some appealed timidly and reluctantly, with incomprehensible hints and equivocal gestures; others with reckless abandon. But all appeals fell on deaf ears. The people neither stirred nor comprehended, or, worse still, indignantly turned in the would-be revolutionaries to the authorities, for the peasants' faith in the benevolence of the Autocrat was as deeply rooted as was their distrust of his officials, and of all refined, lettered, and city folk. Thus, the "way to the people" became the central problem of every movement for freedom. Many, even as they sought to approach the masses, felt an obscure foreboding that the entrance of this million-headed actor upon the stage of history might crowd the intelligentsia itself forever off that stage. This feeling is expressed again and again, from the Decembrists to Maxim Gorky, but even those who held it did not refrain from approaching the folk, and seeking to stir it to wrath. Five years after the crushing of the Decembrists, the sixteen-year-old Lermontov in his fearful "Prediction (1830)" gave voice to the darker side of the ambivalent hopes and fears involved in that way to the people:

> A year will come for Russia, a dark year
> When Royalty no more his crown will wear,
> The rabble who loved him once will love forget,
> For Blood and Death will richest feast be set;
> The fallen law no more will shield the weak,
> And maid and guiltless child in vain will seek
> For justice. Plague will ride
> Where stinking corpses fill the countryside,
> And flapping rags from cottages demand
> Help none can give, while Famine rules the land.
> Dawn on thy streams will shed a crimson light;
> That day will be revealed the Man of Might
> Whom thou wilt know. And thou wilt understand
> Wherefore a naked blade is in his hand.
> Bitter will be thy lot; tears flood thine eyes,
> And he will laugh at all thy tears and sighs.

Russian patriarchalism was rooted in the "undivided family" and the communal village *mir*. The village was dominated by its council of its elders, and each family by its patriarch. So long as he was in the years of his vigor, he was the autocrat of the family domain, where he ruled with absolute authority over grown sons and daughters, their spouses and children and their children's children. Both institutions, the undivided family and the communal village, survived into modern times. They set their unmistakable patriarchal, communal stamp on much of Russian life. To them is largely ascribable the peasant disposition to submit to authority and to give love, and faith and obedience to the patriarch of patriarchs, the "Dear Father Tsar." To them is attributable the corporateness of Russian rural life, the comparative speed with which the village could be collectivized into the *kolkhoz*, the readiness with which bolshevism was transformed from a program of rule from below into rule by a small élite and then into a personal dictatorship, once more of a "Father of the People." Perhaps, too, these forces help to explain such practices as the taking of hostages and the holding of an entire family legally responsible for the acts of any one of its members. The practices of taking hostages and of family responsibility were taken for granted by Russians, Red and White, during the Civil War, and became basic tenets of the new régime. Even such a "libertarian" as Leon Trotsky professed himself to be during his last years, still stubbornly defended to the end his use of hostages in the Civil War. To be sure, in Nazi Germany, too, and even in the unconscious thought of Western Europe and America, the doctrine of collective responsibility of entire families and peoples has been growing again, as a by-product of the modern total state and total war. Yet family and collective responsibility has not figured in our conscious thinking since we permitted to fall into desuetude the theological doctrine of the sins of the father, while our first statement of fundamental law specifically set it down that "no Attainder of treason shall work Corruption of the Blood." So alien has it been to our way of thinking that the average American does not even know what the words mean.

In a certain sense, all of olden Russian was one vast patriarchal family, with a single autocratic head. To the "Dear Father" of his people, every Russian owed obedience, material and spiritual. All partook in varying degrees of *nevolya*—absence of freedom or of self-determined will—excepting only the Tsar. He was at once self-willed and the sole source of will for all. In a world of universal hierarchical subordination, he alone knew no superior. He was

constrained neither by binding law theoretically superior to his
person, nor by theoretically unalterable institutions. For others
his will was law, until he might alter it, proclaiming the law and
cancelling it by simple decree or *ukaz*. Until 1905, all efforts of
the nobility, or the Senate, or of the earlier *Sobor*, to put definite
restrictions upon that power had ended in nullity. Even the constitutional *ukaz* extorted from Nicholas II by the Revolution of
1905 contains the revealing ritual expression, "it is our inflexible
will." *Samoderzhetz*, self-holder of power, was his untranslatable
Slavic title, itself a Russian version of *aùtokpátwp*, employed by
the Byzantine emperors of the late Roman empire of the East. In
the nineteenth century, the so-called "Fundamental Laws" still
designated the Tsar as "unlimited autocrat," the fourth article
thereof stipulating:

> To the Emperor of all the Russias belongs the supreme
> autocratic power. To obey his commands not merely from
> fear but according to the dictates of one's conscience is
> ordained by God himself.

The Tsar might, if strength and interest permitted, regulate all
matters throughout his vast domain, all details large and small,
make all appointments, dictate or overrule all verdicts, set aside
or impose all commands military or civil, take over a court of
inquiry, as Nicholas I did with the Decembrists, or command of
the armies in the field, as Nicholas II did in 1916. The only limits
on his power were those of tradition and wont, plus those dictated
by the possibility of rebellion or palace revolution, and those dictated by the need to delegate authority to officials and to rest his
power on some social support beyond the mere apparatus of police,
army, clergy and bureaucracy. "Russia is not ruled by me," said
Nicholas I modestly, "but by my forty thousand clerks." And his
Chief of Police wrote to him:

> The landowner is the most reliable bulwark of the sov-
> ereign. . . . No army can replace the vigilance and the
> influence which the landowner continuously exercises in
> his estates. . . . He is the most faithful, the unsleeping
> watchdog guarding the state; he is the natural police mag-
> istrate. . . . If his power is destroyed, the people will be-
> come a flood endangering, in time, even the Tsar him-
> self. . . .

And, of course, there were the inevitable limits imposed by
nature on the ubiquity, omnicompetence and powers of even the
mightiest of autocrats. "This is Her Majesty's will," Catherine II

had written in a characteristic *ukaz* intended to make Russia independent of imported silk. "Silk factories shall be established in
Astrakhan . . . to which shall be sent those who were found at
the previous census to be idlers, and those who do not remember
their origin." But the peasants did not take kindly to silk culture,
nor the worms to the Russian climate. "The works were founded
by *ukaz*," Prince Shcherbatov commented shrewdly, "and maintained by *ukaz*, but silkworms cannot very easily be multiplied by
ukaz."

Like the benevolent despotism, the cruelty that characterized
Russian life had in it a patriarchal element, too. In Western Europe
the last refuge of the flogging of adults was the navy, where the
captain is absolute autocrat on his vessel. But in Russia, flogging
continued as a dwindling device up to this century. Until 1904, it
was legal in rural penal law and in the armed forces. A strange
counterpart was to be found in the self-flagellation of the *khlysty*
as a mystical discipline of the spirit. Torture as an investigative
device disappeared after the judicial reform of 1864. The torture
introduced by the Cheka, and raised to a nightmarish system in the
purge trials and extraction of "confessions" which the accused could
not conceivably have committed, is in degree and principle somewhat new in the history of mankind. It is not to be derived from
earlier despotism but from totalitarianism, which holds that for its
apodictically noble ends "all things are permitted." The "scientific
experiment" to remake man totally according to an infallible blue-
print is modern. Only the cruelty has roots that are age-old.

An eighteenth-century "apostle of enlightenment," the landowner
Bolotov, author of a *Guide to Happiness*, relates, not without pride,
how he administered five successive floggings to a peasant suspected
of theft, to force him to confess and divulge the identity of his
accomplices. When at last he named names, their bearers were
flogged in turn to extort confessions, but in the end they proved
to be innocent. Fearing that a further flogging might kill the original
suspect, Bolotov records:

> I ordered that he should be tied hand and foot and
> thrown into a heated bathroom [a brick chamber such as
> is used for "Russian baths"], after he had been made to eat
> the saltiest kind of fish; and a strict watch placed over him
> to see that he had nothing to drink, and that he should
> suffer the torment of thirst until he spoke the truth. . . .

Nowhere in his memoirs does he suggest that there is anything
unusual or reprehensible in the flogging of suspects who later turn
out to be innocent.

The advanced Peter, creator of academies, hospitals, museums, industries, settled the revolt of the *streltsy* by the simple device of having twelve thousand of them decapitated on a single occasion. "The violence of his punishments for neglect of duty or for offenses against his policy," writes Klyuchevsky of Peter, "produced a neurasthenic condition in his subordinates."

Similarly, a century later, accounts of the reign of Catherine II, liberal blue-stocking and friend of the Encyclopedists, are full of floggings with rods and whips, and of tortures more refined and more abnormal. Wrote the visiting Frenchman, Passenans:

> I have taken precautions to avoid witnessing these cruel proceedings, but they occur so often, they are so habitual in the villages, that it is impossible to avoid hearing the cries of the unfortunate victims of inhuman caprice. Their cries followed me in dreams. Many times I wished that I had not understood the Russian language when I heard orders being given for punishments.

Not only revolution and counter-revolution have been accompanied by outbursts of violent cruelty. Terror and torture, physical violence, arbitrary, capricious and unrestrained, have been a regular feature of much of normal, peaceful, benevolently patriarchal life in old Russia, and part of the unconscious heritage of the new. The legendary-seeming acts of madmen related of so many Tsars were indeed not legend. "The trade of autocracy," as Mavor has written, "was an exhausting and dangerous business, imposing a severe strain upon the physical constitution and tending to the disturbance of mental equilibrium." And from that center of often well-intentioned and generous but as often brutal despotism, the same manners and methods filtered downward to manorial lords and overseers, army captains and factory foremen and provincial police chiefs.

During the latter half of the nineteenth century, the bonds that tied every serf to his land and lord, every man to his estate and occupation, began to dissolve. It was the hope of all democrats and lovers of the people that Russia, having "reached the limits of her natural expansion" and being comparatively secure from attack, might now turn from super-armies and military super-budgets to the "loosening of the bonds" and to the development of the cultural and physical well-being of its own people.

The last four decades of the nineteenth century, and the first two of the twentieth, were bright with this hope of the "loosening of the bonds." In 1861 serfdom was abolished by fiat of Alexander II. If that seems "late" in history, it is sobering for us to remember that the same year marked the outbreak of a great civil war in America, rooted in Negro slavery, and that Lincoln's Emancipation Proclamation of 1863 failed to endow the freed slaves with any of the land they had tilled, as Alexander did the freed serfs.

Followed the introduction of local zemstvo rule, trial by jury, irremovable judges, reduction in censorship, expansion of public education, town councils, factory inspection, social security legislation, shortening of the former "life-term" of military service, freedom of movement from the countryside into the cities, freedom to emigrate, freedom for foreigners to enter and move about the land. True, many of these reforms were incomplete, and were partially undermined by the reaction which followed the assassination of Alexander II. But, after 1905, they were further extended, a limited constitution was granted, a Duma or legislative parliament set up, a large measure of parliamentary immunity granted. In 1907 a new and sweeping land reform was initiated. In 1912, the revolutionary parties, not excluding the Bolsheviks, were permitted to establish legal daily papers. Finally, in the first revolution of 1917, literally all the bonds were loosened at once——save only the overweening bond of war. Why freedom did not come to flower and fruit in that swift growth is one of the tragic problems with which we shall have to deal.

Not stagnation, then, but the very rapidity and unevenness of change made increasingly intolerable all that was left of the old order. All through the latter half of the nineteenth century it continued to disintegrate, yet a new Russia seemed powerless to be born. Gradually, a sense of impending doom took possession of the ruling class and of the Court. The reform movement spread from the top downward, the history of the century presenting itself as a progressive widening of the circle of those who felt that change was necessary, and an increasing audacity in their conceptions of the nature of the change. Awakening from its millennial slumber, Russian public opinion took as its banner the words of a Dostoevsky: "In all things I go to the uttermost extreme; my life long I have never been acquainted with moderation." The reformer Tsars ended up in disillusionment. They were succeeded by lesser autocrats, unable to lead the nation boldly along the new uncharted ways, until at last the autocracy ceased to show signs of further adaptability, becoming the rallying center of opposition to change. Thereby it sealed its doom, handing over the initiative to the intelligentsia.

The Russian intelligentsia is a specific formation of nineteenth-century Russia, not to be identified with the "educated and professional classes" of the Western lands, or with the officials, technicians, and managers of present-day Russia. It was extruded out of a fixed society of medieval estates into which it no longer fitted, an ideological sign that that old world of status had been outgrown. It was recruited simultaneously from the more generous sons and daughters of the nobility, and from the plebeian youth: from above and from below. Its members were held together, neither by a common social origin and status, nor by a common role in the social process of production. The cement which bound them together was a common alienation from existing society, and a common belief in the sovereign efficacy of ideas as shapers of life. They lived precariously suspended as in a void, between an uncomprehending autocratic monarchy above and an uncomprehending, unenlightened mass below. Their mission as independent thinkers was to be critics of the world in which they had no place and prophets of a world that had not yet come into being, and might have no place for them either. They were lawyers without practice, teachers without schools, graduate clerics without benefices and often without religion, chemists without laboratories, technicians, engineers, statisticians for whom industry had as yet no need, journalists without a public, educators without schools, politicians without parties, sociologists and statesmen rejected by the state and ignored by the people. They anticipated and oversupplied in advance the requirements of a world that was too slow in coming into being, and sought to serve a folk that had no use for their services. In the decaying feudal order they found neither scope nor promise; in the gross, timid, and backward mercantile bourgeoisie neither economic support nor inspiration; in the slumbering people no echo to their ardent cries. Even while they sought to serve the unreceptive present, at heart they were the servants of the future. With all their being they longed for its coming, and all possible and impossible futures for Russia mingled together in their dreams.

Almost involuntarily they were forced into open enmity to the old order that had no use for them. Beginning as gentle dreamers, reformers, and humanitarians, they were constantly being punished for mere dreaming and forbidden to dream. In despite of themselves they were driven into open rebelliousness, a mood so general that the very word "student" would finally become synonymous with revolutionist. The better to regiment them and set them apart, the state devised a student uniform for them, and, sometimes, before their formal education was completed, exiled them to their native village, or to Siberia, for a "higher education." Many were lost and broken, many more forsook their generous vision as they grew older and adapted themselves to a career under the existing order. The noblest and the best sought to merge themselves with the people—who did not receive them; or hurled themselves single-handed, or in desperate little bands, against the still unshakable regime; or finished out their lives dreaming of home and freedom, in distant lands.

Their very culture was a source of torment to them. Their inherited or acquired privileges burdened them with a sense of guilt. How could they enjoy things of the spirit while around them the people remained in darkness and Russia decayed? Their deep love of their native land was transformed into a passionate hatred of all that was evil, backward, and degrading in it, and into a fierce belief in the nobility of its future destiny and mission in the world.

> *Thou are black with black injustice*
> *And slavery's yoke has branded thee. . . .*

wrote the Slavophile Khomyakov, welcoming the humiliation of his country in the Crimean War as a just punishment for its evils and a hope of its repentance and purification. In this he became the prototype of that apparent contradiction in terms, patriotic defeatism, which thenceforth was to characterize a good part of the intelligentsia.

When their efforts to rouse the people remained unanswered and their first attempts to shake the autocracy ended in deeper reaction, they came to be tortured by a sense of their own powerlessness, or they became more reckless in the scope of their dreams. Thought and feeling accumulated potential like a dammed-up stream. Over and over again they solved in agonizing theory the problems they were forbidden to touch in practice. They constructed grand systems, vast as Russia, embracing the whole of humanity. Their awareness of Russia's backwardness and lack of liberty mingled with their sense of Russia's grandeur, expansive force and imperial strength. That Slavic messianism which, after the fall of the Eternal City on the Tiber and the Eternal City on the Bosphorus, had seen in Moscow a "Third and Last Rome," now took on a new, a radical form. Even as they envied Western Europe they rejected it. The gospel that was destined to save and transform Russia would exalt that which made backward Russia different from and superior to the West; would make Russia capable of saving Europe from the evil which her own critics saw in her;

would give to Russia the leading role in the salvation and transformation of the world.

Each decade, each half-decade, saw a completely new version
of that evangel of universal salvation: through science, through
the negation of tradition and convention, through literature and
criticism, through nonresistance to evil, through a return to primitive Christianity, through the village commune, through love of the
people and adoption of their way of life, through anarchism, agrarian socialism, Marxism—whatever the gospel of the moment, its
disciples were ready to live by it and die for it and remake the
world utterly in its image.

Not having much else to live by, they acquired the power of
living by ideas alone. "The thoroughly true-to-type intolerance of
the Russian intelligentsia," observes Berdyaev, "was self-protective;
only so could it preserve itself in a hostile world; only thanks to
fanaticism could it weather persecution."

It was a fanaticism that served as a surrogate for the older religions. It idealized Russia, the peasant, the proletariat, science, the
machine. It made a true gospel of its particular brand of salvation.
It possessed singleness, exclusivism, dogma, orthodoxy, heresy, renegation, schism, excommunication, prophets, disciples, vocation,
asceticism, sacrifice, the ability to suffer all things for the sake of
the faith. Heresy or rival doctrine was worse than ignorance; it
was apostasy. To the disciple even of so rational a doctrine as that
of Marx, an *ipse dixit* was an irrefutable proof.

This energy of dammed-up thought, prevented from overflowing
into action, invested Russian literature with its peculiar intensity.
A charged atmosphere, a sense of coming storm and apocalyptic
revelation pervades the great works of nineteenth-century Russian
literature. They are full of forebodings and prophecies, bear de-
monic charges of inhibited energy, give glimpses of ecstatic heights
of hope, fearful depths of gloom. Their characters are driven by
obscure compulsions into the most violent gestures and grimaces;
their events take place against a background of preternatural darkness, illuminated by sudden flashes of blinding light; their sunlit
passages seem brighter than the light of day.

Even the humor of Russian literature, without losing its gaiety,
is yet grotesque and savage, full of violent and incomprehensible
actions, fantastical gesticulations, terrible caricatures that come
close to tragedy, laughter that verges on hysteria. What is *Dead
Souls*, a humorous masterpiece? a sanative satire meant to heal
Russia of deep maladies? the voice of a religious holy man, crying

of wickedness, salvation, and doom? Not only the critics, its very
author could not make up his mind or know what it was that he
had done, or ever finish the work.

The intensity of these works took the whole Western world by
storm; their love of humanity moved generous spirits everywhere;
their self-determined and almost unconscious technique became the
envy of every great novelist in a century of great novelists and in
lands with a far older literary tradition. As the grand century of
peace and progress came to a close, their forebodings began to
seem prophetic for a world that was moving toward universal war
and social upheaval. Now in retrospect we can see that not Dickens,
Thackeray, or Hardy, not Balzac, Zola, or Galdos, not even Turgeniev or Tolstoy, but Dostoevsky—whose voice sounded a trifle
mad—was the prophet who came nearest to foretelling whither
both Russia and the optimistic, self-confident, progressive West
were blindly driving. The sufferings of his demon-ridden spirit enabled him to see depths in human psychology that were covered
over, to discern the fearful outlines of the age in which at this
moment we live, to express the compulsive, uncontrollable furies
of our war-ridden, breakdown-tortured, totalitarian time—when an
old order, dying, seems powerless to die, and a new order, aborning,
seems powerless to be born.

Since direct political discussion was prohibited, all literature
tended to become a criticism of Russian life, and literary criticism
itself but another form of social criticism in the second degree. If
the censor forbade explicit statement, he was skilfully eluded by
indirection—by innocent-seeming tales of other lands or times, by
complicated parables, animal fables, double meanings, overtones,
by investing apparently trivial events with the pent-up energies
possessing the writer, so that the reader was compelled to dwell on
them until their hidden meanings became manifest. Men found
means of conveying a criticism of the régime through a statistical
monograph on German agriculture, through the study of a sovereign
four centuries dead, the review of a Norwegian play, the analysis
of some evil in the Prussian or some virtue in the British state.
There developed that peculiar "Aesop language" which would enable Lenin to fight Russian imperialism in wartime by a statistical,
theoretical analysis of the German variety. Still later Bukharin
was to employ the same device to circumvent a more vigilant and
ruthless censorship, when he wrote a pamphlet attacking the Vatican, in which his criticisms of Loyola and the "corpselike obedience"

and discipline of the Jesuits implied his criticism of the Stalinist régime.

Not only literature was charged with peculiar intensity and allegorical meaning. Often the most trivial acts became in some obscure fashion overpowering symbols. Whether to eat vegetable or animal food, whether to leave beard and hair uncut, whether to wear a peasant blouse or a flowing tie or a workman's shirt, might easily become, did become, matters of passion and banners of devotion.

The same energy charged the most abstract theoretical debates on philosophy or program and the most minute discussions of petty organizational detail. Conversation consumed the Russian intellectuals as a fever. They spent days and nights, weeks and months and years on end, discussing and rediscussing actions on which they were as yet powerless to embark.

If the peasant revolts of earlier centuries had been doomed for lack of urban leadership and thought-out program, now the situation was for several decades reversed. Russia was seething with programs and her cities crowded with would-be leaders; but the masses remained passive and indifferent, the countryside gave no sign. However, as the nineteenth century drew to a close, the atmosphere became charged with electricity. All signals presaged a coming storm. Theory and physical might, intellectual program and mass movement, city and countryside, began to approach each other.

The revolutionary intellectuals sensed that their day of isolation was drawing to a close; tomorrow they might find themselves captains of multitudes and determiners of Russia's destiny and perhaps the world's. With fiercer passion than ever, they fell to engaging in controversies of a minuteness, stubbornness, sweep, and fury unheard of in all the history of politics. At socialist congresses in 1903 and 1907, men who were hunted together and exiled together and shared a common basic program, yet wrangled endlessly with fanatical fury and subtlety—in the one case for three and in the other for five whole weeks of days and nights on end, reckless of financial cost, drain on health, buzzing of spies, and the fact that they were actually driven during the course of the exhausting debates from one land to another. Even on the boat going over the English Channel, they never stopped the argument for a moment.

The controversies of the period carried over into the underground movement inside Russia, into the prisons and places of penal exile in Siberia, into the cafés and hovels and lodging-houses of distant and alien cities. So great was the turmoil and the chatter, so unearthly the hours kept, so furious the quarrels, that it became a commonplace in hospitable Geneva and Zurich to see advertisements reading: "Roomers Wanted, No Russians."

The angry, intolerant battle went on under the very eyes of the tsarist police; government archives filled up with reports of positions and faction documents; police spies were as energetic as others in taking sides. Even as the revolutionists began the opening skirmishes with the common enemy, their war with each other continued to gain in fury.

The three with whom we are to deal grew up in the midst of it, and it absorbed their major energies for more than a quarter of a century. It was the touchstone by which they selected their followers and associated or quarreled with each other, the whetstone on which their minds were shaped and sharpened. With brief periods of truce or enforced silence, their whole lives were one long series of controversies. The aim they held in common was so easily realized, apparently, that the outlived institutions, drained of their content by a half century of intellectual mining and sapping, were to fall of their own weight. But not for that reason did the debate cease. The continued "discussion" was to make up the principal content of the two decades of Russian history from the Revolutions of 1917 to the purges of 1937, and its echoes were to shake the foundations not of Russia alone, but of all the world. The disinterested clash of theories was transformed into the interested clash of parties and factions, implemented by the terrible and categorical implements of power. Their lives were a duel to the death not merely with tsarism and capitalism, but equally with each other—with each other and with almost every one else whose name we shall meet in these pages. That struggle is an essential aspect of the revolution they made, and of the stuff their own lives were made of.

CHAPTER II

VLADIMIR ILYICH ULYANOV

Whoever wanted to learn to detest feudal barbarism should
be born in Simbirsk.   *—Leon Trotsky*

Let no one say that Lenin is an expression of some kind of
allegedly Asiatic 'elemental Russian forces.' I was born under the same sky, I breathed the same air, I heard the same
peasant songs and played in the same school playground, I
saw the same limitless horizons from the same high bank of
the Volga, and I know in my blood and bones that it is
only by losing all touch with our native land, only by stamp-
ing out all natural feeling for it, only so could one do what
Lenin did in deliberately and cruelly mutilating Russia.
                                        —Alexander Kerensky

Surely thou couldst only have been born among a spirited
people—in that land that does not care to do things by halves,
but has spread a vast plain over half the world, and one
may count its milestones until one's eyes are dizzy.
                                            —Nikolai Gogol

THE VOLGA is a slow, monotonous river that takes its rise at the
heart of Russia midway between Petersburg and Moscow, ma-
jestically winding its way eastward to Nizhni Novgorod and Kazan,
thence southward through the Tartar country, past Simbirsk, Samara
and Saratov down to Astrakhan, where it empties, still unhurried,
into the vast landlocked Caspian Sea. Around it cluster the songs
and legends of the Great-Russians. The land's few revolutionary
traditions—the fierce peasant and Cossack revolts of the seventeenth
and eighteenth centuries—are indissolubly linked with its name.
The true history of Russia, in contrast to the intrigue and turbulence surrounding the Muscovite court, is as slow and monotonous
and uneventful as is the course of this river. It, rather than the
Urals, forms the true boundary separating Europe from Asia. On
the "European" side, the shore rises into hills and bluffs as if nature
had constructed palisades to aid in repelling the Mongol invader.
On the other bank there are only the low plains and endless expanse
of the Asiatic steppe stretching out to the horizon.

On this river, as befits a leader and ruler of the Great-Russian
people, Lenin was born; on the hills of the "European" bank he

spent his childhood and youth; in his veins flowed its mixed bloods
of Tartar and Great-Russian and Volga German. From Astrakhan
his father came, and his mother from the province of Kazan. In
Simbirsk he was born, studied in Saratov and Kazan; near Samara
he lived through his brief experience as a landowner and exploiter
of peasants; in Samara, too, he began and ended his short career
as a law clerk or junior attorney and engaged in his first activities
as a revolutionist. When at last he left the banks of the Volga for
Saint Petersburg he was grown to man's estate, a fully formed
Marxist who had chosen revolution as his "profession."

Simbirsk, where the future Lenin was born, in 1870, was then
and still is a backward, desolate provincial capital. Its wooden
buildings are scattered in disorderly fashion up the sides and over
the summit of one of the more commanding hills of the "European"
bank, standing guard like a fortress against the endless steppes to
the East. On the "crown," as it elegantly called itself, were a few
unimpressive buildings of stone: the governor's palace, the cathedral,
the *gymnazia*,[1] the prison, and the little library dedicated to the
memory of the historian Karamzin. Its climbing roads were ruts
of sticky mud in the spring and repositories of light-flying dust in
mid-summer, yet it did not lack moments of physical beauty. No
town on the hills overlooking the Volga and the steppes can be
altogether devoid of beauty. "From the summit right down to the
waterside," writes Alexander Kerensky, who was born there ten years
later than Lenin, "stretched luxuriant apple and cherry orchards.
In the spring the whole mountainside was white with blossom,
fragrant, and at night breathless with the songs of the nightingales.
. . . With the melting of the snow, the river used to leave its banks
and flood the low-lying lands on the left, stretching like an endless
sea over the fields which, later, in the heat of the summer, would be
gay with the songs and games of peasants and townspeople come
to mow the rich fragrant grass. . . ."

Vladimir Ilyich Ulyanov—the boy whose underground name was
to ring round the world—was at birth one of a mere thirty thousand
souls who lived their quiet, undistinguished, routinary lives in this
most conservative and stagnant of the river capitals. No railroad
connected it with the rest of the country; one had to go many miles
by horse to Syzran to take the train. It was not even a significant
river port. Its peasants were more backward, its handicraft industries more local and insignificant, its nobility more impoverished

---

[1] The Russian *gymnazia* was a type of intermediate or university preparatory school roughly corresponding to our senior high school and junior
college.

and stubbornly reactionary, its life more stagnant than that of the other Volga capitals.

It was young, too, as river towns went, and poorer than the rest in history. It possessed no fabled past like Nizhni Novgorod, Kazan and Astrakhan; it was, indeed, scarce two centuries old when Vladimir was born. The revolutionary traditions of Pugachov, the Cossack pretender, and of Stenka Razin, the Russian Robin Hood—traditions which haunted all the rest of the length and breadth of the Volga valley—had no foothold here. Rather did Simbirsk find cause for boasting in the fact that its serfs had been too impoverished and apathetic to rebel, and that it alone had held out against Cossack and peasant risings as a bastion of reaction, while those two great movements swept by and around it to their short-lived triumphs and inevitable doom.

Its intellectual glories, too, were symbols of sloth and social backwardness. Its two great men before the time of Lenin were the historian Karamzin and the novelist Goncharov: that Karamzin who was the literary antagonist of the modest reform proposals of Speransky and who became the leading historian of reaction, creating in his works a vast and stately monument to despotism, written, Pushkin declared, to show the Russian people "the necessity of autocracy and the charms of the knout"; and that Goncharov whose one great fictional creation, Oblomov, had become a symbol of all that was torpid, apathetic, and impotent in the sprawling Russian spirit. It was here, in the shabby elegance of the nobles' quarter of Simbirsk, that Goncharov formed his melancholy impressions of the decaying gentry whose soul he embodied in the elephantine apathy of his anti-hero. Oblomov consumes over two hundred pages of the novel bearing his name in the mere effort to get out of bed and dress, and spends most of the rest of it in moving sluggishly from decrepit sofa to slovenly dressing gown, dreaming, amid intermittent snores, of the possibility of better things, of improving the lot of his peasants and the income of his broken-down estate, of wedding the girl he passionately adores, yet never rousing himself sufficiently to lift a finger toward the realization of his dreams.

But the boyhood years which Lenin spent in Simbirsk were far from unhappy. His father, Ilya Nikolaevich Ulyanov, was a solid and respectable figure in the bureaucratic and intellectual life of the provincial capital. Until the latter's death the family knew neither want nor rebellion. Their household was one breathing order, peace, conscientious devotion to duty, domestic simplicity and quiet affection. The boy, unsuspecting of the symbolism that might one day be read into his Christian name of Vladimir ("Lord of the World"), enjoyed the boyhood that goes with a healthy body, a lively brain, an ironical sense of fun, an ability to excel easily in studies and sports and childish tests of strength. He knew the peaceful and untroubled existence that springs from a modest and assured economic foundation, parents who respected themselves and each other and were respected by the community, and an atmosphere of family harmony in which brothers and sisters loved and cared for each other. There was fishing and swimming in the river, wandering over its hills, skating, sliding, sleighing on its frozen surface in winter, hunting as he grew older. There were long summer sojourns with mother and aunt and cousins of like age, at his mother's paternal estate in the village of Kukushkino in the Province of Kazan. There were games of sport and imagination and stories told or read aloud by the mother. She sang to her children and played for them on her pianoforte, and taught Volodya (affectionate for Vladimir) to play on it, as she did her other children. She and her husband were their first instructors in reading and writing. Volodya and his older sister, Anna, were each taught to read at the age of five, and his precocious older brother, Alexander, at the age of four. There were high marks at school and honors and prizes and the intellectual joys that come from the exercise of an able brain and entrance into possession of a goodly portion of the accumulated cultural heritage of the race. From his mother's example and teaching, the boy early learned to love books and learning, to find solace and absorption in the great Russian novels and poems that this remarkable century was creating, and to find deep joy in music.

In short, in all the reminiscences of brothers and sisters and family friends, as in Lenin's own occasional references to his childhood, there is nothing to accord with the fashionable "psychological" explanations of the careers of the world's great rebels, nothing to document the formula of mother or father fixation, no unhappy family life, maladjusted childhood, youthful rebellion against domestic tyranny, no traces of a sense of inferiority due to failure at school or in childish competitive sports, no sign of queerness or abnormality. True, the hanging of his older brother, Alexander, for an attempt on the life of the Tsar when Vladimir was only sixteen, was an event to put iron into his adolescent soul, but that only moves the question a little further back: what made brother Alexander into a plotter and a rebel? We shall have to look elsewhere than to the maladjustments of a miserable childhood for the motive forces that drove them to hate feudal barbarism and despotism and to choose revolution as a way of life.

Friends and enemies alike who knew the Ulyanov family have left testimony in their memoirs as to the bright and industrious harmony prevailing there. Its head, Ilya Nikolaevich [2] was somewhat given to the quiet exercise of patriarchal authority within the home (while he lived his wife looked up to him as her intellectual superior and the family's undisputed head). But the patriarchalism was no more, rather much less, than prevailed in other families of the same region, time and social class. Ilya Nikolaevich must have had a capacity for anger, since his eldest daughter, Anna, in a work of unmitigated piety, speaks of Lenin's having inherited his father's love of work, his gay, sociable nature and inclination to humor and jest "and also his quick temper." But there is ample evidence that his influence was exerted chiefly by the force of example rather than by coercion. The children did not remember ever having witnessed a quarrel between their parents or a disagreement in their presence.

All his life the head of the Ulyanov household bore on his spirit the sobering mark of a hard, orphaned childhood and a consciousness of how much an older brother had sacrificed and how he himself had labored to secure an education. From his pupils, his subordinates and his children, he expected the same devotion to duty, diligence and application, and the same respect for study that he had himself. Anna records that he feared for his young son, Vladimir, because learning seemed to come a little too easily to him, without arousing sufficient tension and effort. But if he had lived to see that son's bulldog intellectual tenacity and powers of sustained application and prolonged exertion in later days, he would have been satisfied that his fears had been vain.

Ilya Nikolaevich was universally reputed to be industrious, intelligent, respectful towards authority, and philanthropic in the older sense of that word. He was a deep believer in the meliorative value of education, unselfishly devoted to his profession, first as teacher of physics and mathematics, then as provincial inspector and superintendent of schools. He had come of a modest plebeian family

[2] The Russian custom is to give the Christian or given name and the patronymic or father's first name with an ending signifying "son of." Thus Lenin's father was Ilya Nikolaevich Ulyanov, signifying Ilya, son of Nikolai Ulyanov. Lenin's name, Vladimir Ilyich Ulyanov, means Vladimir, son of Ilya Ulyanov. "Lenin" is of course one of the pseudonyms he adopted in his prolonged duel with the police. His older sister Anna's married name is Anna Ilyinishna Ulyanova Elizarova, signifying Anna, daughter of Ilya Ulyanov and wife of Elizarov.

of Astrakhan (his father is believed to have been a tailor), which distinguished itself from its similars only by a certain devotion to learning and zeal for advancement. Astrakhan, at the mouth of the Volga, was an old Tartar town and the family, Great-Russians, had some Tartar blood in their veins. It showed in the high cheekbones, flat nose and deepset, small, slanting eyes of both Ilya Nikolaevich and of his son, Vladimir Ilyich (Lenin), who so closely resembled him.

The father of Ilya Nikolaevich (that is, Lenin's paternal grandfather) had died when Ilya was only seven. Grandfather, father and son were alike destined to die at a fairly early age. When Ilya became an orphan, an older brother, thirteen years his senior, dropped his own schooling to support the family and to see Ilya through school. Thus Lenin's father began, on behalf of the family, the upward climb that was to lead from the plebeian estate to that of nobility, by the only avenue of ascent open to it: service to the state.

The school career of Ilya Nikolaevich more than justified his elder brother's sacrifice. He graduated with honors from the *gymnazia* at Astrakhan, and then, also with honors, from the University of Kazan. Here Ilya attracted the favorable attention of a mathematics teacher, Lobashevsky (world-renowned today as the founder of non-Euclidian geometry), on whose recommendation he was given the post—unpaid—of director of the Meteorological Station of Penza. His living he earned as instructor in physics and mathematics at the secondary school of the Institute of the Nobility in Penza. The devoted filling of such unremunerated posts was typical of the fashion in which the old-time Russian intelligentsia built up Russian science and culture, and Russia's knowledge of her own resources.

When Ilya Nikolaevich left Penza at the age of thirty-three for a similar post as instructor in the *gymnazia* of Nizhni Novgorod, he took with him his newly acquired bride, Maria Alexandrovna Blank, twenty-nine-year-old younger sister of the wife of a colleague at whose home he had boarded in his bachelor days in Penza. In Nizhni, this secondary-school instructor founded a family, and there his first two children, Anna and the ill-starred Alexander, were born. In the sixth year of his marriage he was promoted once more, this time to the post of inspector of schools in the Province of Simbirsk. Simbirsk was a comedown from the great town of Nizhni Novgorod, but the new appointment meant advancement in grade and compensation and the abandonment of teaching and meteorological research for a bureaucratic career. It is not on record that

Ilya Nikolaevich hesitated to accept. His daughter Anna explains the change on the ground that the emancipation of the serfs by Alexander II (in 1861) and the subsequent reforms in local self-government and education had made possible the opening of new schools and the spread of instruction to new sections of the population. By the reform of 1864 the zemstvos were given the supervision of local schools, and, by the efforts of such enlightened and devoted officials as Ilya Ulyanov, public education spread—despite occasional setbacks—so that by 1914 there were fifty thousand zemstvo schools and a planned expansion of the educational budget envisaged universal education by 1922. The war of 1914 and the civil war of 1917 delayed but did not permanently hinder the realization of the dream of universal education and general literacy, the foundations of which were laid by the generation of zemstvo educators of which Lenin's father was one.

When the Ulyanov family moved to Simbirsk in 1869, the new school inspector was thirty-nine years of age, his wife thirty-five, and they took with them two children. A third was on the way. That third child, born on April 22, 1870, they were to name Vladimir, after the saint who was the first Christian ruler of Russia. One day the backward provincial town to which the Ulyanovs were moving was to have its name changed from Simbirsk to Ulyanovsk, in honor of the son who was born to them soon after they arrived in their new home.

Maria Alexandrovna Ulyanova, the mother of this little family, had more time than ever to devote to her children. She had few friends at first, and Simbirsk was much slower and duller than Nizhni Novgorod. The schools were scattered, the roads bad, the distances great; arduous trips by horse and sleigh or horse and carriage kept the new inspector away from wife and children for long stretches of time. His homecomings were remembered as festive occasions. The care, education and upbringing of the growing family—there were to be six children in due course, not counting one who died soon after birth—were largely left to the mother, and, as the family fortunes improved, to a hired tutor.

In the beginning the inspector met with little interest on the part of the local governmental régime in his efforts to improve the quantity and quality of the scattered schools of Simbirsk Province. He himself gave courses in pedagogy to prepare new teachers. In time, his self-denying zeal and devotion to duty attracted the attention of influential superiors so that he was promoted once more in the rapidly expanding school system to the new post of director of primary schools for the entire province, with several inspectors under him. His reliability and respectability made him acceptable to the authorities even as they were beginning to have misgivings about the spread of popular education, while his reputation among those really interested in education began to spread beyond the confines of Simbirsk. His ascent up the bureaucratic ladder now brought with it the honorific title of "Actual State Councillor" accompanied by hereditary nobility for him and his children.[3] Thus, in 1874, when Vladimir was three years old, the lad's status changed from that of plebeian to nobleman; so that all the ink that has been spilt in discussions as to whether the future Lenin was of one origin or the other has been spilt in vain, since he was each in turn. By the time he was old enough to fill out school or police questionnaires—and he filled out many of the latter in his lifetime— he was privileged, even obliged, to record himself as a member of Russia's state-created or bureaucratic hereditary nobility. Not from his father's title, but from his mother's modest estate, he was also for a time, a landowner.

Bolshevik prudery is reticent concerning the youthful Vladimir's slow mastery of the "political facts of life." Nowadays, he is habitually treated as if he were born a Bolshevik, and as if his father had been a revolutionist before him. The persistence of such a legend in his official biographies is illuminating. In a land where hereditary status is ingrained in the very texture of life, where one's right to schooling was denied under the old régime if one were "the son of a cook," and was later to be denied under the new régime if one were "the son of a kulak," such legends are more than an attempt to evade the problem of tracing the development of their subject's views. Moreover, the current cult of the infallibility of the leader and the apostolic succession requires him to have sprung, ideologically fully armed, from the womb, as the Greek goddess of wisdom from the forehead of Zeus.

Leon Trotsky in his brilliant study of The Youth of Lenin (the first volume of a life destined never to be completed) has examined all the evidence available in this matter. With patient and ironical persistence he reduces the official legends to foolishness. For the facts are, as he amply demonstrates, that Lenin's father was orthodox in religion—without that strain of mysticism which sometimes challenges the authority of the hierarchy and institutionalized church; a champion of domestic order and discipline—without that excess of tyranny and cruelty which, when it does not break the

[3] "Actual State Councillor" was one degree higher than "State Councillor" and carried with it the title of "Excellency" and the privilege of hereditary nobility. It corresponded to the rank of major general in the army.

spirit, is conducive to rebellion; a sincere servant of the state devoted to improving its foundations by the spread of religion and popular education—without ever dreaming for a moment of calling into question the established order, the authority of his immediate superiors, or the autocracy of the Tsar.

Ilya Nikolaevich was an earnest man of good will. Devotion to his duties in a land where popular education itself was frequently regarded with suspicion, represents the sum and substance of his "liberalism." Former students of his, who later attained sufficient importance to write their memoirs, mention with respect this hardworking instructor in mathematics and physics, who put his heart and soul into his teaching, and voluntarily gave up part of his Sundays to tutor the more impoverished and backward of his pupils without charge. Teachers who served under him as he advanced in official position speak favorably of his inspectorship and subsequent directorship. But there is no record—quite the contrary—of his having defended any of his subordinates from dismissal for radicalism. Indeed, his daughter relates how a niece came to him to complain of the unjust dismissal of a teacher by his superiors. Ilya Nikolaevich, she reports, listened without saying a word, "his head lowered, he kept his thoughts to himself."

Official documents reveal that in seventeen years of service as an education official he was credited with the construction of some 450 new tiny school houses in his backward province, and a doubling of the number of pupils enrolled. However, the period of his inspectorship coincided with a general period of growth of zemstvo or local educational facilities throughout the country, so that the achievement, while genuine, must not be writ too large, or ascribed too exclusively to his individual zeal and ability. Still, he was sufficiently above average to stand out among his peers so that a liberal zemstvo nobleman of his *gubernya* could write of him as a "rare, exceptional phenomenon," and, describing his tireless efforts in the face of difficulty and apathy, could say: "Such strength and vigor can come only from a devotion bordering on abnegation." (*Vestnik Evropy*, 1876.) Not every provincial official was sufficiently noticed to have himself written about in a metropolitan paper in Saint Petersburg! And even as late as 1906, in a history of public education in Russia published more than a quarter of a century after the inspector's death, and before his son's fame could give him retroactive importance, it was still recorded that among the educators of the Province of Simbirsk "the first place belongs, according to the unanimous opinion of his contemporaries, to Ilya Nikolaevich Ulyanov."

The very unanimity and continuity of official approval, however, is sufficient refutation of the theory that Alexander and Vladimir Ulyanov, and the other less celebrated children of Ilya Nikolaevich, "inherited" their revolutionary tendencies from their father. What they did derive from him were such things as a good head, an ability to move familiarly in the world of books, a tendency to application, hard work, unswerving devotion to duty as they might conceive it. But their conception of duty would likely have shocked their good father had he lived long enough to learn of it. That this is so, the available evidence leaves no doubt.

Thus we find that the zealous inspector of schools, Ilya Ulyanov, went beyond the obligations of his post to report to his superiors a lack of zeal on the part of the village priests in the teaching of the catechism. And the catechism of the Russian Orthodox Church goes beyond the simple rendering unto Caesar of that which is Caesar's, as the following passage will suffice to demonstrate:

> *Question.* What does religion teach us as to our duties to the Tsar?
> *Answer.* Worship, fidelity, the payment of taxes, service, love and prayer—the whole being comprised in the words, worship and fidelity.

It is interesting to pursue the legend of the revolutionary character of the elder Ulyanov a little further, since it provides a relatively innocent example of the retouching of the past to fit the dominant folklore, which makes so difficult the work of biographer or historian who must deal with Soviet sources. Trotsky quotes with angry irony from biographies of Lenin which portray his rather timid and moderate father as one who "regarded the revolutionary movement with great sympathy," and which make of his home on Moscow Street in Simbirsk a sort of revolutionists' club in which "the tone was given by Alexander (Lenin's elder brother)," while Vladimir also "participated frequently in the discussions and with great success." At that time, the youthful Vladimir must have been all of thirteen or fourteen years of age, since his father died before he turned fifteen! Even Lunacharsky, who was a more scrupulous writer than most and who wrote before a respect for historical truth had been completely purged from the printed page and from the heads of men, sets it down as fact that the father of the Ulyanov household "sympathized with the revolutionists and brought up his children in a revolutionary spirit."

Against this retroactive revision of ancestral traits, we have the testimony of Lenin's elder sister, Anna. "Our father, who was never a revolutionary, during those years—being more than forty years of age and head of a family—wanted to protect us, his children."

The state, too, as we have seen, gave ample testimony to its confidence in the reliability of Ilya Nikolaevich. From teacher to inspector of other teachers, from inspector to director of primary instruction for an entire province and superior of various inspectors —such watchdog posts were not knowingly given, in the reactionary Russia of the seventies and eighties, to men of doubtful loyalty. As early as 1859 the earnest teacher had received a bonus of 150 rubles "for his excellent services and his zeal." Though there were repeated investigations of the teaching staff for germs of sedition, Ilya Nikolaevich was never called in question. The creation of the posts of inspector and director of primary schools, which posts he filled from the moment of their respective creation, were steps in the calculated subjection of local educational institutions to the bureaucratic center at Saint Petersburg. All through the closing years of the reign of Alexander II, who was assassinated by revolutionists, and especially during the reign of his son, Alexander III, this process of curbing the autonomy of the institutions of local government, the zemstvos, continued as a part of the growing reaction. Years later, Lenin was to write of this reactionary process, and to pick out two symbolic dates, of both public and biographical interest, as mileposts in this backward march from the great reforms of Alexander II's earlier years. The dates he selected as markers on that road were the years 1869 and 1874. They were the dates when the posts of inspector and director of primary schools were created, and the very dates, as Lenin knew, when his father had been appointed to each of those posts in turn!

> In 1869—Lenin wrote in an article on zemstvo liberalism, published in 1901—the office of inspector of elementary schools was created for the purpose of taking the effective management of elementary education out of the hands of the zemstvo. . . . In 1871, instructions were issued to the inspectors of elementary schools empowering them to dismiss teachers who are deemed politically unreliable. . . . In 1874, a new regulation was passed which placed the management of the schools entirely in the hands of the school directors. . . . [*Zarya*, No. 2-3, Dec. 1901, signed T.P., Lenin's *Collected Works*, Vol. IV, pp. 133-4.]
>
> Who does not know—Lenin was to write eleven years after his father's death—how easily is accomplished in Holy Russia the transformation of a radical intellectual, of a socialist intellectual, into a functionary of the imperial government—a functionary who consoles himself by think-

ing that there is "a certain utility" within the limits of the routine of office—a functionary who justifies by that "utility" his own political apathy, his obsequiousness before the government of the *knout* and the *nagaika*.

Clearly there is more than an accidental touch of family biography in these two passages. "It would be unjust," comments Trotsky on the second passage, "to apply without reservation these severe words to Ilya Nikolaevich Ulyanov, but only because he had been neither socialist nor radical in his youth."

Thus, while educational reaction grew apace, Ilya Nikolaevich continued his unwavering devotion to his career, ascending with unbroken regularity the slow grades of civil promotion, until he received in good time the decoration of the Order of Saint Vladimir, the title of "Excellency" and the hereditary nobility of which we have already spoken. There is nothing to set in doubt the official epitaph written of him by the subsequent Deputy from Simbirsk to the Second Duma, Delarov:

"I. N. Ulyanov was a man of conservative views, but not reactionary or conservative in the ancient way—he had his personal aim in life . . . zeal in serving the good of the people." This zeal, and this alone, is the social heritage of Alexander and Vladimir Ulyanov from their father. The rest is legend, stupid, mendacious legend, serving no purpose the historian or the biographer can honor.

To this social heritage of zeal in the service of the people, respect for education, and ease in moving through the world of books, Vladimir added a physical and personal inheritance which he did not share with his older brother. Vladimir resembled his father in features and constitution; Alexander his mother. If Lenin in the prime of his maturity had let the fringe of reddish hair around the great bald forehead grow a little longer and his beard assume statelier flow and dimensions, if he had dressed himself in the respectable outfit of a late nineteenth-century functionary in the employ of the state in place of his own unvarying and no less respectable outfit of a bourgeois *bonhomme* of the early twentieth, old-timers in Simbirsk might well have thought that His Excellency, Ilya Nikolaevich Ulyanov, Director of Primary Schools and Actual Councillor of State, had returned once more. The same tiny, slanting, pale, chestnut-colored Mongolian eyes with the same little wrinkles of fun-loving laughter around the edges, the same plump cheeks and high cheekbones, the same strongly marked features, the same broad, flat and slightly curved nose, the same high forehead made yet higher by premature baldness in the days of young manhood, the same somewhat flattened back of the skull, the same short, pudgy, rotund, muscular body, the same hunch to the shoulders, the same solid, self-contained physique and spirit, suggestive of great physical and moral force, the same reddish hair—where there was any—and grayish complexion, the same hint of plethora of the blood, almost the identical winding up of the clock of life— a tense spring capable of running strong for some fifty years and then destined to snap suddenly—in both cases by a hemorrhage in the brain.

Much has been written of Lenin's wearing himself out in the hard exertions and cares of running one-sixth of the earth in the midst of universal ruin and chaos, and of the shortening of his life by the bullet from Dora Kaplan's gun. Trotsky has even hinted, in his last article in *Liberty* (August 10, 1940), that Stalin hastened the death of the bedridden man by administering poison. Certainly, any of these theories would greatly increase the drama and the conventional biographical suitability of Lenin's death. But the "evidence" which Trotsky adduces is too thin and insubstantial, too like the Moscow trials "evidence" against Trotsky himself. And while the ruthless pace of self-driving whereby this man, who died in his fifty-fourth year, seemed to crowd fivescore years of living into little more than half a century, may well have shortened his life, yet the biographer cannot help but note that his father, of whom he was the "spit and image," died in his fifty-fifth year and that the medical certificate offers cerebral hemorrhage as the cause, even as in the case of the son.

Lenin's mother remains a mystery in Soviet literature; and there are not presently available unofficial sources from which an inquiring biographer might safely learn anything to fill the great gaps in the otherwise prolix flood of memoirs and biographies. Her maiden name was Blank, Maria Alexandrovna Blank. The family name is obviously not Russian, but there is no hint in all the official literature as to the national origin of that Alexander Blank who was Lenin's maternal grandfather. The silence suggests deliberate reticence, for such matters are easily ascertained in a land where every man registered with the police, bore a passport for internal travel, and had all his goings and comings recorded from the day of his birth to the day of his death.

Alexander Blank was a medical doctor and landowner of the Province of Kazan. He married a girl from the German colony on the Volga, and their daughter, Lenin's mother, was brought up in the German tradition. This fact is more hinted at than stated in the existing literature. Decisive are the memoirs of Lenin's elder sister,

Anna—though even she is strangely vague on her mother's family origin. From Anna we learn that her mother did not manifest the same religious orthodoxy as the father, that the sum and substance of her religious tradition lay in the solemn-sweet observance of the Germanic tradition of the Christmas tree, and that "she visited the Russian church as little as the German temple." This implies that her family religion might have been Protestant. For the rest, Anna makes clear, her piety was an inward force which moved her to prayer only in moments of great trial. Twice, Anna records, her mother besought her to "pray for Sasha" (diminutive for Alexander, the oldest boy). The first time, he was desperately ill and the doctors had told his mother that he might not live. The second time, Anna was facing her mother through the double grille of bars through which prisoners are permitted to speak to their visitors. The girl hung onto the prison bars and inquired anxiously concerning the success of her mother's efforts to save Alexander from the hangman. Actually, he had already been hanged, but Maria Alexandrovna did not tell her daughter. Her only answer to the question was once more, "Pray for Sasha."

Lenin's mother came, it seems clear, from a higher social layer than the young secondary-school teacher whose bride she became, for she brought as dowry a modest landed estate in Kukushkino, presumably one-fifth of the estate of her father. Her education, like that of most women of her time, had been received entirely at home: a little desultory tutoring when tutors could be hired, instruction in languages and music and the domestic arts and the graces proper to her class. She knew German, French and English and taught the rudiments of these languages to her children. She early learned to read and love books, an affection which she communicated to her children, also. Reading aloud of an evening to her family circle was a common custom, so that the future Lenin acquired in childhood a wide acquaintance with the Russian novel and a love for the great classics of its sudden heyday, which he carried with him all his life. His plain, usually pedestrian writings display as almost their sole adornment an occasional illustration of some political trait by reference to a character known to the readers of Russian literature. These unostentatious literary allusions are to Gogol, Saltykov-Shchedrin, Griboyedov, Pushkin, Goncharov, Tolstoy, Krylov, and Turgeniev, whose newly written novels must have been coming into Lenin's home during his childhood, and whose work he loved best of all.

The one characteristic which stands out in the meager material on Lenin's mother is the steady, warm flame of her unquestioning devotion to her children. The family was—after the German rather than the Russian fashion—not a demonstrative one. There was little kissing or embracing, few tears at parting or in time of·misfortune. But Maria Alexandrovna Ulyanova was devoted to her children and tireless in bearing, rearing and training them and watching over them in illness and adversity. She sheltered them to the best of her ability from the difficulties of somewhat reduced circumstances after her husband died. She humiliated herself by pleading with the officials her husband had served under, when it was a question of getting her expelled son Vladimir reinstated in the university, shortening or moderating terms of prison or exile for one or another child, or shielding them from persecution as a result of their activities. All of her children were arrested at one time or another, sometimes several of them at once, and always if she could she moved near the prison, or into the town of administrative exile, of the one who seemed most in need of her ministrations. She never professed to understand the activities which brought her eldest son to the gallows and her two daughters and two other sons into the hands of the police on various occasions. But she sympathized in a general way, was even proud, as so many parents in those days were, of the abnegation, devotion to society and to freedom, which she understood to be the content of the activities that got them into trouble. She asked no questions, made no reproaches, wasted little time in lamentation and none in efforts to persuade them to abandon the paths onto which their consciences had led them. To her they were children who had grown up and were old enough to decide their own conduct. Her task was to follow their fate with anxiety or pride, to stand by them in their hour of need, to send them money, books, clothes, food, delicacies, to visit them when authorities and regulations permitted, never to waver in her loyalty however much official society branded them as criminals and monsters.

Maria Alexandrovna outlasted her husband by thirty years, all the years of her children's adversity. She went twice abroad to see her long-exiled son Vladimir Ilyich—the last time in 1913—and died in Russia at the age of eighty-one, a little more than a year before his return to become head of the new Russian state.

CHAPTER III

LIFE AND DEATH OF
ALEXANDER ILYICH

To you who desire to cross this threshold, do you know
what awaits you?
I know, replied the girl.
Cold, hunger, abhorrence, derision, contempt, abuse, prison,
disease, and death!
I know, I am ready, I shall endure all blows.
Not from enemies alone, but also from relatives, from
friends.
Yes, even from them . . .
Are you ready even to commit a crime?
I am ready for crime, too.
Do you know that you may be disillusioned in that which
you believe, that you may discover that you were mistaken,
that you ruined your young life in vain?
I know that, too.
Enter!
The girl crossed the threshold, and a heavy curtain fell
behind her.
Fool! said some one, gnashing his teeth.
Saint! some one uttered in reply.   —*Ivan Turgeniev*

Vladimir had been backward in learning to walk. He took his
first steps at the same time as his younger sister, Olga, some
eighteen months his junior, and then his efforts were not altogether
successful. For some time, each adventure in toddling was likely to
end in catastrophe, a fall on the nose and a howl that resounded
through the neighborhood. "Probably his head was heavier than
his body," is the explanation offered in the memoirs of his older
sister, Anna.

Despite his diminutive height he began to show great prowess in
trials of strength and speed. When those of like age did not offer
sufficient competition, he chose to emulate his brother Alexander,
four years his senior. Soon the effort to pattern himself after his
older brother was reduced to a formula.

"Volodya," his mother would ask him, "how do you want your
kasha?" (It is worth noting in passing that the family régime was
not so stern as to permit of no selection by the children.) Volodya

waited to see whether his older brother would take his cereal with milk or with butter, and then: "I want mine like Sasha." When Alexander came home from the *gymnazia* wearing his new student's uniform, his younger brother became fired with enthusiasm for learning: he too wanted to have a uniform like Sasha's.

Yet, in physique as in temperament they were as different as two brothers could possibly be. Alexander's face was long and brooding; his skin milky white; his hair, thick, turbulent, frizzy, deeply rooted, stood up in all directions from a line far down on the forehead. His eyes, set deep and on a strange angle in a nobby, overhanging brow, seemed to turn their gaze inward. It was the strongly chiseled face of a dreamer, a saint, a devotee, an ascetic. But Vladimir's head was shaped like an egg, and the thin fringe of reddish hair began to recede from the forehead before he was twenty, leaving him bald, like his father, in young manhood. His complexion was a blend of grayishness and full-bloodedness; his eyes tiny, twinkling, Mongoloid. His whole aspect, except in moments of intense thought or anger, was jovial, humorous, mischievous, self-confident, aggressive. Not knowing him, one might have taken him in later years for a hard-working kulak, a rising provincial official, a shrewd businessman. There was nothing in his build or appearance or temperament to suggest kinship with his brother Alexander.

The young boy was noisy and boisterous, a player of practical jokes, an inveterate tease, quick at repartee, sharp of tongue. He loved to exhibit the growing powers of his mind by raillery at the expense of his littler brothers and sisters, young cousins and playmates. The one bad mark in his high-school record came for playing pranks on a French teacher whose pomposity he disliked. Various people testify to the fits of ill-temper to which young Vladimir was subject on occasion, while his mockery and intellectual superiority created a certain wall between him and the other lads of his age. ("Vladimir Ilyich enjoyed the love of his schoolmates," writes the pious Anna, "although he had no very close friends.")

But the older boy was habitually silent and reserved. Throughout his school career there is not one bad report by any of his teachers recorded against him. He rarely spoke unless addressed, and then to the point, directly and briefly. No one, not even his mother or his sister Anna, the two that were closest to him, ever knew what was going on in his head. The great moments of his life came as a bewildering surprise to them. Even when they reviewed it all in retrospect, they could remember few signs that might have foreshadowed his destiny. He read much, meditated much, studied in

solitude, thought through his perplexities alone, then acted resolutely to carry out his conclusions.

The polarity of these two temperaments is symbolized in their
choice of favorite authors—a polarity which characterized the entire
nineteenth century Russian intelligentsia: Alexander's favorite was
Dostoevsky; Vladimir's was Turgeniev and the realistic, "precon-
version" Tolstoy. In Dostoevsky the older brother found the brooding introspection, the morbid saintliness, the terrible humility and
compassion, the compulsive urge to self-immolation that were to
reveal themselves as having been at the core of his character, in
the early hour when it was put to the test.

Each lad was invariably the best student in his class and they
received uniformly high marks in all subjects. Each won the gold
medal as the Simbirsk *gymnazia*'s "best student." But here too they
showed marked differences in intellectual character. Alexander's
predilection was for science, Vladimir's for Latin, history and literature. Both were thorough in their preparations, but the younger
boy was so swift that he seemed to finish his homework before he
was well settled down in the house, and then his noisy ebullience
disturbed his older brother. Sometimes his father put him through
his paces to ascertain whether he had mastered his lessons, and did
not know whether to be pleased at his speed or fearful that because
things came so easily, his son might never acquire the powers of
prolonged application.

Writing compositions was Alexander's most difficult exercise in
school. He labored long over them, then the ideas came out direct,
naked and stark. Vladimir went in for elaborate outlines, as a preliminary to vigorous and workmanlike expression of his thoughts.

Even when his feelings were hurt, Alexander was silent. Almost
in infancy he ceased to shed tears at anything. When he felt
wronged, or saw wrong done to others, the force of his unshed tears
accumulated within him.

Little Volodya was made of noisier stuff than his older brother.
His howls when learning to walk made enough noise to get themselves recorded in family memoirs. His boisterous shouts on the
Volga steamer when they were headed for the summer estate
brought a rebuke from the quiet mother: "One doesn't yell like that
on a steamer," she told him. "Well, the steamer is yelling loud
enough," cried little Volodya.

At least one childhood lie was recorded as having been told by
young Volodya—he had broken a decanter belonging to an aunt
while racing through her rooms, but at the solemn family inquest
denied all knowledge of how the bottle had met its fate. Three

months later, Anna records, he came to his mother in tears to make voluntary confession. Obviously, lying did not come easy to him, as his detractors were to insist when they discussed his later advice to use lies on occasion as a stratagem in the revolutionary struggle. But to the older boy, lying was an utter impossibility: it was absolute truth—or silence—for him from earliest childhood. Once some adult, probably a school inspector, asked him to name the two worst vices. "Lying and cowardice," was his answer. The response was not something drilled into him; it came from the depths of his own nature, to which untruth and cowardice were utterly alien.

"Very characteristic it was," writes his sister Anna in her memoirs, "that he was unable to lie. If he did not want to say something, he remained silent. That particular quality of his showed itself brilliantly before his judges."

> One feels like adding—comments Trotsky on the above— what a pity! In an implacable social struggle, such a mentality leaves you politically defenseless. Austere moralists, liars by vocation, have reasoned well, the lie is the reflection of social contradictions, but also, at times, a means of struggle against them. One cannot, by an individual moral effort, escape from the context of the social lie. In type, Alexander resembled a knight more than a politician. And that created a psychic separation between him and his younger brother, considerably stronger, considerably more opportunist in the questions of individual ethics, better armed for the struggle, but in any case no less intransigent in his attitude toward social injustice.

Trotsky's comment is interesting, not for what it adds to that of Anna concerning her two brothers, but for the indirect light it throws upon the attitude of Trotsky, and upon the ethics of Bolshevism—a subject to which we shall have to return.

Sometime during his early adolescence—the exact age is not recorded—Alexander suddenly ceased to be religious. The change, characteristically, was preceded by no discussion with parents, teachers or spiritual advisers. Whatever debate there was went on within him, until, one day, he stopped going to church. "Aren't you going to vespers tonight?" his father asked. The "no" was so firm and decisive that Ilya Ulyanov did not venture to pursue the subject further. "Devoted teachers," the school inspector had written, "do not need to have recourse to punishment." Whether it was his disbelief in coercion, or respect for the budding personality of his son, or hope that he "would get over it," Ilya Nikolaevich never raised the matter again, and from that day forward Alexander did

not set foot inside a church. Yet he made no demonstration when
the priest conducted services at the *gymnazia*, and his record for
outward conduct there continued to be perfect. There was, as we
have noted, not one complaint recorded against this quiet and
studious lad by any of his teachers during his entire life. Always
his marks were of the highest; always his lessons were prepared
with perfection; always he kept his doubts and disagreements to
himself. He graduated with highest honors, and was awarded the
gold medal. Though he was good in all subjects, his intellectual
predilections were already formed: he was determined to follow
in his father's earlier footsteps and become a scientist. He looked
with eagerness to Saint Petersburg, city of a great university, distinguished scientists, well-equipped laboratories. During his last
vacation before leaving for the metropolis he spent all his time in
a homemade laboratory on the maternal estate, performing chemical experiments, too absorbed for conversation, for meals, for sleep.
The only time which he took off from his scientific pursuits was for
hunting, and for shy courtship of a young cousin with whom he had
fallen in love.

When they succeeded in assassinating Tsar Alexander II in 1881,
the mysterious Executive Committee of the Narodnaya Volya ("The
People's Will" or "The People's Freedom"—the word *Volya* has both
significations) seemed to be all-powerful. The new Tsar, Alexander
III, a corpulent giant of a man, wept on the bosom of his confessor
as he implored guidance on how to answer the Executive Committee's ultimatum offering peace in exchange for a constitution. His
adviser strengthened his anger and pride. After a brief period of
vacillation, Alexander III answered by recalling the moderate constitutional rescript which the dead Tsar had been about to publish,
and by multiplying the police, enlisting spies, closing the feeble
liberal newspapers, purging the libraries, supervising professors and
curricula, reducing the local self-government of the zemstvos, prohibiting student organization, setting up the *Zemski Nachalnik*
(rural chief) as a permanent guardian over the peasantry, strengthening the restrictions on the Jews, and in general tightening all the
chains in the great prison house of peoples.

The Narodnaya Volya felt that it had no choice but to give out
the watchword: "One Alexander after the other!" But the new Tsar
had shed his frightened tears for nothing. The Executive Committee
was no longer anything but a signature on an ultimatum. Six prior
unsuccessful attempts on the life of Alexander II had cost them
twenty-one executions. "We are consuming our capital," Zhelyabov,

chief organizer of the successful assassination, had exclaimed in anguish. And now, two years after their great success (in 1883, the very year that young Alexander Ulyanov went to Saint Petersburg to enter the university), one Degaev, an informer in their ranks, betrayed to the police the last surviving member of the Executive Committee, Vera Figner. Next year she was condemned to die, but, being a woman, her sentence was commuted to life imprisonment in the Schluesselberg fortress prison. The dread Executive Committee no longer existed, nor any party to which it might serve as executive.

In a land of secrets and mysteries, there were many who did not know that. Here and there, for the next few years, little groups sought to act in its name, even though they had no contact with it. But they moved now in a nightmarish vacuum. The village had not responded to the deed, many peasants even believing that the nobles had killed the Tsar-Emancipator as an act of vengeance for his Emancipation Proclamation! And liberal public opinion, which at first had celebrated the assassination, later execrated it as the bringer of reaction. The police noose pulled ever tighter, the mighty body of Russia stiffened and grew still, its great voice choked on the gallows.

"The eighties cut across the history of Russian civilization like a belt of darkness," wrote the historian Pokrovski. But even in the darkness, here and there the heart of youth, being young, continued to glow. Everything about the next conspiracy, six years later, was naive and inexperienced. The continuity of the generations had been ruptured. The technique of conspiracy and the programs of freedom alike had died on the gallows, or been buried beneath tons of masonry in the dungeons of Peter-and-Paul and the Schluesselberg fortress. The young men of generous vision had to begin afresh spelling out the first letters of the revolutionary alphabet.

Not until 1886, five years after the assassination of Alexander II, was there any new activity amongst the students, and then—a measure of its modesty—it was but a decision to go to a cemetery (the Volkov Cemetery in Saint Petersburg) to lay wreaths upon the tombs of the thinkers and officials of the reign of Alexander II who had prepared and carried out the emancipation of the serfs. It is a measure of the change of mood that the older generation had declared war to the death on Alexander for what they considered the inadequacies of his reforms, and now the student youth was paying tribute to a time that seemed blessed in comparison. Of course, in their hearts some were perhaps paying tribute, too, to those martyrs and rebels who had gone before and whose deeds and dreams had helped to prepare the loosening of the bonds in the sixties. At any rate, the police made no move to prohibit or dissolve the demonstration. Some four hundred students, with no support from the older intelligentsia, marched to the cemetery, had a prayer said by a priest, chanted the requiem service and laid their wreaths on the tombs of the tsarist officials. Among the young men was Alexander Ulyanov. It was his first act of public participation in the student movement.

When Alexander Ulyanov went to Saint Petersburg in 1883 he had had no interest in student circles. They wasted his precious time, they violated his innate reserve, they were engaged in frivolities and dissipations which did not attract him, or in discussions of social questions on which he felt that he—and they—knew too little for profitable discussion. He was absorbed by science, and, unlike most Russian intellectuals, not given to the feverish pleasures of conversation.

At the university he had plunged into biological research, pored over the microscope, made observations on earthworms, made laboratory notes, read deep in the literature of science, accumulated knowledge enough to last a long lifetime.

His father had provided a comfortable monthly allowance of forty rubles. Alexander assured him that thirty would be sufficient, then ceased to insist, perhaps because he did not wish to embarrass his sister Anna, who received the same stipend. When he came back to Simbirsk at the end of his first school year he silently returned to his father the sum of eighty rubles, the excess saved from his pocket money. The episode was characteristic, and gives evidence both of his abnegation and the fact that he kept away from the rest of the students and their activities, else he would easily have found ways of spending the spare rubles. At the end of 1885, some of the students had approached him to join one of their clubs. His answer, as remembered by one of them: "One talks a lot there, and learns nothing."

In January, 1886—he had not even given up his research to return with his sister to Simbirsk for the Christmas vacations—the mails brought him the news that his father had died suddenly of a cerebral hemorrhage. "For various days," one of his schoolmates records, "he neglected everything. He walked up and down from one corner of his room to the other, deeply wounded." But he did not abandon his work, nor even then return to Simbirsk. A few weeks later he wrote to his mother: "For my zoological study on annelid worms, I have won the gold medal." The zealous school inspector would have approved his son's devotion to duty and rejoiced at his prospects for a brilliant future.

Freud has offered the theory that young men do not often undertake significant independent activity until after the deaths of their fathers. Be that as it may, the independence of spirit of Alexander had developed earlier. The first, almost the only, observable change was that during that next summer, for the first time in his life, he rebuked his younger brother, Vladimir, for rudeness to their mother, as if he felt himself now the responsible head of the Ulyanov household. There was one more change which might give support to Freud's theory: the year of his father's death, without slackening his scientific studies, Alexander decided to go with his fellow students to the Volkov Cemetery for the memorial services to the officials who had brought about the peasant emancipation. And that same year, when the students united into a single federation the only organizations not prohibited by the police: the regional clubs (they were mere groupings of the students by their province of origin)—the name of Alexander Ilyich Ulyanov figured as one of the leaders of the union of clubs!

A few months later they essayed again the sheltering device of a funeral demonstration. This time they chose the occasion of the twenty-fifth anniversary of the death of the radical critic, Dobrolyubov. Encouraged by success, they brought out greater numbers —estimates vary from six hundred to one thousand—but they found the cemetery barred by a cordon of police. They sought to break up and return to the city, but they were surrounded by mounted police and kept two hours in the rain. Forty of their number, alleged ringleaders, were expelled from the university and from Saint Petersburg!

Alexander was once more among the participants. He was not among the expelled, but he felt that if they were guilty of any crime, he too was guilty. If they should suffer, he would suffer also. Such was his nature. He brooded quietly and deeply upon the experience. He discussed it with several earnest young men who, like himself, could not forget the indignity or the unjust and arbitrary punishment.

What to do? The students drafted a "protest to society," but the police went from mailbox to mailbox, collecting the crude circulars. "Society," if it received any of them, gave no sign. Write? There was no liberty of press. Speak? It was not even permitted to hold a memorial meeting with priest and requiem in a cemetery! How make one's protest heard? There seemed to be only one possible answer. On a pitifully diminutive scale, only half realizing it, he and his young comrades were repeating in a few months the evolution of a great generation that had preceded them. "Peaceful methods had been forbidden me," the gentle Vera Figner had told her judges at her trial only two years previously, "we had of course no free press, so that it was impossible to think of propagating ideas by means of the printed word. If any organ of society had pointed out to me another course than violence, I would have chosen it. . . ."

Alexander Ulyanov, a young man of integral character, who could not accept the conveniences of a gulf between thought and action nor leave to others the dangers of things he thought needed doing, now added laboratory experiments with nitroglycerin and magnesium to his studies on annelids and sea spiders! Press and speech being choked off, dynamite, that democratic invention of the Swedish chemist Nobel, perfected twenty years earlier, would guarantee that their protest would at least be heard in the shameful silence. Once more they chose the anniversary of a death for their demonstration, but this time it was to link themselves onto the great tradition that had just perished on the gallows. They chose the date March 1, 1887, the dreadful anniversary of the day when, six years before, the Party of the People's Will had laid low the Tsar-Emancipator, Alexander II.

The plot was in all things pitiful. Scarce knowing the meaning of the words, they resoundingly called themselves "The Terrorist Section of the Narodnaya Volya." Before one has "sections" one must have a whole. There was no Party of the People's Freedom any longer. There were only seven earnest young men, the oldest twenty-six, the youngest twenty; four of them, including Alexander Ulyanov, just turning twenty-one. Alexander was not the leader or organizer of the attempt. That post was assumed by a sickly and intense young man, Shevreev by name, aged twenty-three. But Alexander became the official chemist of the little group, and his conscientiousness made him into the drafter of its vague, immature program. Still in love with life and his personal future, he could hardly tear himself away from a study he was even then completing, dealing with the habits and physiology of the sea spider, to pore uneasily through the pages of Marx's *Capital* and other forbidden and ill-comprehended books—it takes time to carve oneself out a revolutionary *Weltanschauung*, and time was pressing. On the very days that he felt might be the last of his young life, he still divided his time between sea spiders, chemical experiments with dynamite bombs, and Marx's *Capital*. The seven young men classified themselves, theoretically, into three "Social Democrats," three "Narodovoltsi" and one who took no part in the programmatic controversies. Young Ulyanov, despite his studies in Marxism, declared himself a member of the Narodnaya Volya or "People's Freedom" group. They pooled their meager resources to send one of their number to Vilna to purchase some nitric acid, which proved too weak to be usable. A pistol that one of the bomb-throwers possessed, intended to supplement the dynamite or aid his escape, likewise proved unserviceable when he tried to use it. Alexander's poor bombs were so inadequate that, when one of the students hurled one at a policeman who was placing him under arrest, it did not even explode! In order that one of the organizers of the plot might escape abroad, Alexander pawned the gold medal he had won in the *gymnazia* at Simbirsk. Such were the weapons and the resources, material and intellectual, with which seven young students set out to overthrow the mighty Alexander III, Tsar of All the Russias!

Even then the conspiracy was thwarted only by the merest accident. Its very obscurity escaped the vigilance of an overconfident police. On March 1, 1887, police agents followed a young man onto the Nevsky Prospekt, the broad boulevard to the banks of the Neva that runs past the Tsar's Winter Palace. He was carrying a thick "Dictionary of Medicine." The astonishment of the agents was boundless when they found that the "Dictionary" was hollow and contained a crude dynamite bomb. Two other students with him proved to have dynamite bombs in their possession and one an unserviceable pistol. The police had followed the young man almost as a mere matter of routine. Only the day before they had received a tip from the police in Kharkov that the youth they were shadowing had written a letter—six weeks earlier: there was little speed in the Tsarist bureauracy—to a friend in the latter city. The letter, being opened by secret agents, proved to be a confused hymn to terror. The student Andrushkin, the carrier of the "Dictionary of Medicine," was the author of the letter. "To enumerate the qualities and the advantages of the red terror, I shall not attempt," reads a typical sentence, "for I would have enough of them to take centuries, since it is my hobby, and it is from that, no doubt, that my aversion for the Social Democrats is derived." The police themselves did not dream that the young man who needed centuries had actually allowed himself only one more day for enumeration and exemplification together. The Tsar's thanks for "having watched well and acted efficiently" were not deserved by his loyal police.

Alexander Ilyich was not on the Nevsky Prospekt, for he had not been chosen among the three bombers. The police raided his lodgings and found his sister Anna there on a purely personal visit. They arrested her and posted a guard to waylay her brother, who was arrested the same day at the house of another student. To young Vladimir in Simbirsk, not yet seventeen but henceforth the acting male head of a fatherless household, a former teacher of the Ulyanov children wrote a letter telling of the danger to his older brother and sister and bidding him break the news as best he might to his mother. He didn't get far before she snatched the letter out of his hand. She made instant plans to join her two oldest children in their peril, leaving Vladimir in charge of the younger children in Simbirsk. All the friends who but a year ago had paid such eloquent tribute to the school inspector at his public funeral, those who had visited him, played chess with him, drunk his tea with him, shrank away from the accursed and perilous household.

> When we had become closely acquainted—Lenin's wife wrote in her memoirs—Vladimir Ilyich once told me about the attitude of the Liberals towards the arrest of his elder brother. All acquaintances shunned the Ulyanov family. . . . There was no railway at Simbirsk at that time, and Vladimir Ilyich's mother had to go by coach to Syzran in order to go on to Saint Petersburg, where her eldest son was imprisoned. Vladimir Ilyich was sent to seek a companion for the journey. But no one wanted to travel with the mother of an arrested man. Vladimir Ilyich told me that this widespread cowardice made a very profound impression upon him. This youthful experience undoubtedly did leave its imprint on Lenin's attitude towards the Liberals.

At the trial, each played the part that corresponded to his character. Some turned state's evidence. One, a young Pole who had lent his home to Alexander for the printing of their program, denied all sympathy for the movement. His name was Bronislaw Pilsudski. His brother Josef, future dictator of Poland, being brought in as a material witness, denied all knowledge of the affair, but was shown to have sent a coded telegram to Vilna for the conspirators. The organizer of the conspiracy, Chevreev, had disappeared from Saint Petersburg. Alexander Ulyanov took upon himself full responsibility. To a fellow-prisoner in the courtroom he whispered: "If you need to, you can put all the blame upon me!" "There is no finer death," he told his judges, "than death for one's country's sake; such a death holds no terror for sincere and honest men. I had but one aim: to help the unfortunate Russian people."

His power of speech in the prisoner's dock astonished his mother and sister. So this was their silent Alexander! "How well Alexander speaks!" his mother whispered. But she could not stand the new-found eloquence, and fled the courtroom before his address to his judges had come to an end. To his sister Anna, he confessed that he was torn between the desire to shield the others by taking all blame upon himself, and the fear of hurting their feelings by belit-tling their role and magnifying his own—a true character out of that Dostoyevsky who had been his favorite author!

Even the prosecutor was touched by his nobility. "I concede full confidence," he said, "to the declarations of the accused Ulyanov, whose admissions, if they are at fault, err only in taking upon himself what he has not done in reality."

A few weeks later, the mighty Tsar who was the target of this impotent conspiracy carefully read the entire record of the case, scribbling in the margin his loutish commentary. But when he came to the words of the accused Ulyanov, insisting that his was "the most complete moral and intellectual responsibility . . . all that my abilities and the strength of my knowledge and convictions permitted," alongside this sentence the Emperor wrote: "This frank-ness is even touching!!!" Whereupon the touched Emperor ap-proved the hanging by the neck until dead of young Alexander Ilyich Ulyanov and four of his comrades. Their lives ended before they had well begun.

And with them ended the "Terrorist Section" of their "Party of the People's Freedom"—the last, faint, childish echo of the heroic age of the populist terror, the pitiful *reductio ad absurdum* of its methods of seeking to revolutionize society behind its own back. Alongside the many mightier and more significant attempts and cele-brated trials that had preceded it, it scarcely deserves to be men-tioned at all. Its real importance to history lay in the deep impres-sion it made upon Josef Pilsudski, brother of defendant Bronislaw, and upon Vladimir Ilyich, sixteen-year-old brother of defendant Alexander Ilyich Ulyanov. It loaded young Vladimir with a man's responsibility; it put iron into his soul; it barred his path to respect-ability; it opened an unbridgeable gulf between him and the régime that had taken his brother's life. And it inoculated him with a profound contempt for the "liberal society" which had abandoned the Ulyanov family in its time of trouble. That con-tempt found far more frequent and eloquent expression in his writ-ings than did his opposition to the Tsar. It drew the line of dis-tinction between him and most of his associates in the socialist movement. Though, in the abstract, he would frequently preach the strategy of a common alliance of all "democratic and liberal and socialist oppositional elements," yet at every crucial point in his career when there was a serious proposal to implement that strategy, his fury knew no bounds. Greater than the anger of his denunciation of the régime would be his anger at the "unreliable and treacherous liberals," and greatest of all his anger at those of his comrades who proposed agreement with them. Again and again he did not hesitate to break with all and sundry on this issue, even his closest associates and the men he had most admired. Again and again he would split away from a movement he himself had helped to build, standing isolated and alone, as if he were repeating symbolically the tragic scene of the isolation of the Ulyanov family from all of Simbirsk "liberal society," at the hour of his bereaved mother's greatest need.

CHAPTER IV

AGAINST A STONE WALL

Repression is the only lasting philosophy. The dark deference of fear and slavery, my friend—observed the Marquis—will keep the dogs obedient to the whip, as long as this roof shuts out the sky.   —*Tale of Two Cities*

> *Their well-deserved hangman's fee*
> *My son and my sire received.*
> *But, a specter of ancient slavery,*
> *I ride through all eternity*
> *Derided by humanity.*

OTHER MONSTROSITIES were torn down by the cleansing wave of revolution, but on the pedestal of the equestrian statue of Alexander III—a huge-buttocked rider on a huge-buttocked horse that seems to sag under the rider's weight—the Bolshevik art commission merely carved these lines, and left it standing as a monument to the late autocracy's bad taste. The father of Alexander III died by a bomb. His son Nicholas would be shot to death with all his family in a cellar in the Urals. But he himself lived heavily and died heavily in his bed, and heavily weighed all his life upon the Russian people. With those powerful royal hands with which he could unbend a horseshoe (it was one of his proudest accomplishments), he personally horsewhipped his grown-up son, the future Nicholas II, so as to train him in obedience, and, no doubt, fit him for command.

His father had been "the Emancipator" and had even dreamed of issuing a moderate constitution. The reward had been Grinevitsky's bomb. For his part, therefore, Alexander III would "not grant Russia a constitution for anything on earth." He would maintain peace, as a graveyard is peaceful. He would freeze, for all eternity, the sluggish current of Russian public life. His Polish, and other non-Russian subjects would be made to talk Russian though it choked them.[1] Over the villages he would set his *Zemski Nachalniki*

[1] Contrary to general belief, Russification was intermittent and sporadic under the Tsars. For some time the Poles retained a wide measure of autonomy, and Finnish autonomy still sheltered Lenin from the Tsar's police in 1907. The conquered peoples of Central Asia were despoiled of their

67

(rural chiefs) to curb the zemstvos and to keep the peasants "eternally under age" even as he kept his son Nicholas up to the day when death took from him the crown and set it on the twenty-six-year-old boy's head. Alexander's Minister of Education, Delyanov, issued the celebrated *ukaz* directing that "the children of coachmen, servants, cooks, laundresses, small shopkeepers, and suchlike should not be encouraged to rise above the sphere in which they were born."

For spiritual advice, and for the education of his son, Alexander turned to the lay Supreme Procurator of the Holy Synod, the state's watchman over the Church, "a thorough despiser of human nature who had turned reaction into a system of philosophy." From this counsellor the Tsar learned that representative institutions are "the greatest falsehood of our time . . . serving only to satisfy the personal vanity, ambition and interests of the representatives"; that liberty, equality, freedom of thought, civil rights, trial by jury, are alien importations, elaborate deceptions and utter failures; that general education should be limited to reading, writing and arithmetic, beyond which "all else is not only superfluous but dangerous"; that fear was the sovereign principle of statecraft and that "fear of, not love of God, and fear of, and devotion to the Tsar, are to be cultivated as aids to government."

But the walls Alexander set up against change were so many dams behind which fresh pressure accumulated. The subsidies and tariffs he bestowed upon industry, the great network of railroads he constructed, called into being great concentrations of workingmen. At the very moment when his triumphant police were putting the finishing touches upon the Narodnaya Volya in 1883, an obscure "Union for the Liberation of Labor" was being founded by a few exiles in Geneva. In 1886, at the height of the period of stagnation and abject surrender of all liberal circles, the régime of granite and iron found it advisable to make its first social security concessions to the nascent working class. In 1891 a great famine, one of those periodic famines which had always been taken passively as incomprehensible acts of God, caused men to stir uneasily as if they were about to awaken from a nightmare. Three years later, when Nicholas II (1894-1917) succeeded to the throne, a sensitive ear might already catch sounds which told that the long sleep was coming to an end.

Thus Alexander III's "eternal" régime proved but to be a paren-

best lands but retained their local customs and leaders and were exempt from military service until 1916. Only the last two tsars were persistent and irreconcilable Russifiers.

thesis of sagging reaction between the rising movement of the People's Freedom that had laid low his father, and the rising movement of the Social Democrats and Social Revolutionaries that would lay low his son. It was during this parenthesis of reaction that Nicholas Romanov, born 1868, and Vladimir Ilyich Ulyanov, born 1870, received their respective educations and came to maturity. From its increasing industrial expansion, and from its rigid tyrannies, Lenin derived his political conceptions. Its very immobility sheltered him from premature exposure such as had cut short his brother's life, and taught him to estimate soberly the difficulties of the task to which he was to dedicate himself.

In the preceding chapter—following Lenin's own reminiscences to his wife—we portrayed the Ulyanov family as completely deserted by respectable Simbirsk society in the hour of its trial. But, among the colleagues of the deceased school inspector, Ilya Nikolaevich, there was at least one honorable exception who stood by the family. Feodor Kerensky (father of that Kerensky who will play a large role in our story) was the director of the *gymnazia* of Simbirsk, instructor in literature and Latin, and headmaster of the graduating class in which, at the moment Alexander was hung, his younger brother, Vladimir, was completing his high-school studies. Even while scandalized whispers still remarked the uses to which Alexander had put his gold medal (according to sister Anna, Kerensky received a reproof from his superiors for having given the medal to one so unworthy), the director had the decency and courage to award the gold medal once more to an Ulyanov for excellence in studies. He advised with Lenin's mother on the boy's future, suggesting that Vladimir apply to the University of Kazan rather than to that of one of the two capital cities, and that she accompany him to Kazan as a safeguard for his good conduct. Setting aside any fear of what might come of praising the brother of a would-be assassin of the Tsar, he wrote the following recommendation to help young Vladimir Ilyich get into the university:

> Very gifted, always neat and industrious, Ulyanov was first in all subjects and, upon completing his studies, received the gold medal as the most deserving pupil in ability, progress and conduct. Neither in the school nor outside of it, has a single instance been observed when he has given cause for dissatisfaction by word or deed to the school authorities and teachers. [A white lie, this, for Vladimir had gotten into trouble for ridiculing his French teacher!] His mental and moral instruction has always been well looked after, first by both his parents, and, after the death

of his father in 1886, by his mother alone, who devoted all
her attention to the upbringing of her children. Religion
and discipline were the basis of this upbringing, the fruits
of which are apparent in Ulyanov's behavior. Looking more
closely at Ulyanov's character and private life, I have had
occasion to note a somewhat excessive tendency towards
isolation and reserve, a tendency to avoid contact with
acquaintances, and even with the best of his schoolfellows
outside of school hours. Ulyanov's mother intends to be
with him throughout his university career.

Even the mild stricture on his excessive isolation and reserve
(which incidentally confirms what his sister Anna records about his
lack of close friends) was intended to convince the authorities
that the boy lacked the qualities which might make him into a ringleader and troublemaker.

At first glance, the above document does not seem to have anything remarkable about it. Why should an innocent youngster
suffer for the crimes of an elder brother? Why not be rated on his
own merits? Why deny him a gold medal merely because the previous winner in the same family had sold his to finance a conspiracy
against the Tsar? But it is well to remember that in Medieval England, and to some extent in pre-nineteenth century Russia, the
blood of whole families was regarded as "attainted" if one of their
members was guilty of treason. And in the Soviet Union today, far
from having declined, the doctrine of family responsibility has received unheard-of extension and legal codification.[2] In order to
see in its true perspective Director Kerensky's act on behalf of the
lad who was one day to become the leading antagonist of Kerensky's own son, we need only try to imagine an official of present-
day Russia writing such a letter concerning the younger brother of
one who had plotted to assassinate Stalin!

One hundred and fifty miles or so north of Simbirsk, Kazan was
the main capital of the middle Volga. Presiding over the Tartar
country, it had thirteen mosques scattered among its old streets.
Its university, not yet a century old, had been established to serve
as a fount of Slavic Orthodoxy and a place where the lesser provincial nobility and bureaucracy might send their sons.

But for the young Vladimir Ilyich, whose seventeen years had

---

[2] See, for instance, the decree of June 6, 1934, making all the adult members of a military deserter's family responsible, even though they did not
know of his intention to desert, and making them liable to a penalty of not
less than five years exile in a Siberian forced labor camp (*Izvestia*, June 9,
1934).

been passed within the confines of backward Simbirsk and rural Kukushkino, the journey up the Volga to his father's *alma mater* in Kazan was an entrance into an ampler, more modern world. On May 20 of that same year (1887), his beloved older brother died upon the scaffold. Just as Alexander had stayed in Saint Petersburg without interrupting his studies when he heard of the death of his father, so Vladimir had not ceased his scholastic work when his brother was tried and hanged. On June 22, a month after the execution, he graduated at the head of his class. Bearing the certificate, medal and recommendation of the headmaster, he applied for admission to Kazan. To the disappointment of Director Kerensky, his promising pupil did not heed his advice to choose letters or history, but entered the faculty of law and political economy. Was his interest in legal defense aroused by his brother's fate? Did he feel that some such profession as law would be more promising now that he was the male head of the twice-bereaved household? Or was it, as his sister Anna conjectured, the beginning of a newly awakened interest in public affairs?

Before we follow the Ulyanov family—all but Anna, who was rusticated by the police at Kukushkino as a dangerous person—to their new home in Kazan, we must examine the reminiscences collected from old-timers in Simbirsk, concerning Vladimir Ilyich's seventeen boyhood years, spent in that narrow provincial capital. We have little enough to go by for those crucial formative years, and from that little we must endeavor to squeeze the last drop of ascertainable truth. Our sources are the memoirs of the oldest Ulyanov girl, Anna, of two younger children, Dmitri and Maria, of a teacher or two, and some family acquaintances, none of whom suspected then that this stocky, homely, slant-eyed, mocking boy had greatness in him, or was one day to be the ruler of Russia. Thirty years and more would pass before they would rack their brains for memories of him.

Anna Ilyinishna, on whose memoirs we have to depend most, was six years Vladimir's senior. Moreover, it is significant that she had not even known of Alexander's revolutionary activities, although there was but two years' difference in their ages, until she was arrested in his lodgings. Clearly we will not learn much from her of what went on within the head of Vladimir. Dmitri, on the other hand, was four years younger than his famous brother; his memories yield nothing of interest beyond some superficial childish impressions. As for young Maria, born in 1878, when Vladimir Ilyich was eight years old, she records little more than that she was tutored by Lenin in various subjects and was impressed by the long, silent, solitary hours he spent in poring over books. For the rest, she remembers what is expected of her, or what might be "remembered" by one who has heard about things at second hand, years after they occurred.

If we go outside the family, we are no better off. Alexander Kerensky, son of the *gymnazia* director and one time Premier of Russia, has introduced a few sparse "memories" into his autobiographical writings, concerning the man whom he came to detest more than any other on earth. Though they were born in the same town and their parents moved in the same bureaucratic and pedagogical circles, there was eleven years' difference in their age. Kerensky's hostile reminiscences, like those of the adulators, are recalled *ad hoc* to fit a preconception, more than three decades after the events to which they refer.

> Lenin was cruel by nature—he writes.—As a boy he liked to shoot at stray cats, or to break a crow's wing with his airgun.

That Lenin went hunting as a boy, we already know. But a curious coincidence makes the above "memory" a bit suspect. In a novel written by Eugene Chirikov (schoolmate of Vladimir Ilyich in Kazan) we find the following passage:

> He—Ulyanov—always had moist hands! And yesterday he killed a little cat with a rifle shot. . . .

Kerensky's other memories do not stand textual criticism any better. He is at great pains to testify to the noble character of Alexander Ulyanov, the better to contrast him with Vladimir. But all he can actually recall of the martyred older brother is "a carriage with drawn green blinds; that carriage which mysteriously drove through the town at night and took people away into the unknown" when they were placed under arrest. Remarkable memory, since Alexander was not arrested in Simbirsk, but in Saint Petersburg!

> I have a strange, eerie feeling almost of mysticism—reads the longest of the passages concerning the boy Vladimir in Kerensky's memoirs—when I call to mind that scene: the school chapel—I picture it before my eyes on a festive occasion—a solemn service: the Holy Gates are opened, the headmaster's two little sons are led up to him: they are in white, with pink bows under their Eton collars; and behind them, from among the orderly rows of schoolboys, dressed in a tight-fitting blue uniform with silver buttons, looking at them, is the exemplary pupil—religiously educated and

first in his class—Vladimir Ulyanov. . . . Who would have thought by the looks of that precise, exemplary schoolboy living in the God-forsaken Simbirsk of fifty years ago and brought up in the best tradition of the humane and liberal Russian culture, that one day he would be the gravedigger of that culture?

"Who would have thought," we might as well ask the author of the memoir, "that the little, eight-year-old headmaster's son in white with a pink bow under his Eton collar in that God-forsaken Simbirsk of fifty years ago would one day become Premier and War Minister of Russia, flirt with the idea of taking full power into his hands, and then let it slip so easily into the hands of the "exemplary pupil"? Such memoirs throw more light on the rememberer than on the one remembered.

As against the Chirikov-Kerensky story of the cat and the crow, we have a statement of Anna's that Vladimir was always an indifferent hunter. ("At bottom, like my other two brothers, he was never a hunter.") Trotsky, a passionate devotee of hunting, disputes Anna on this score, while Krupskaya (Mrs. Lenin) in her memoirs of their stay in Siberia sets her husband down as "an ardent huntsman." Yet, in an immediately following passage she has this to say of his role in a foxhunt:

> We placed the hunters in such a way that the fox ran straight at Vladimir Ilyich. He grasped his gun and the fox, after standing and looking at him for a moment, turned and made off into the wood. "Why on earth didn't you fire?" came our perplexed inquiry. "Well, he was so beautiful, you know," said Vladimir Ilyich.

Finally, we have Vladimir Ilyich's own words in a letter to his mother from Siberia: "There is plenty of game but without a dog and I being such a bad shot, shooting is a difficult sport" (letter of May 18, 1897).

Whichever version we accept, the whole matter is not very illuminating and proves nothing about his real relations with ideas and men. But it will serve to give the reader a notion of the difficulty with sources, friendly and hostile, which are really an inflation of meager materials, recalled to order more than a quarter-century after they occurred, when Lenin was already leader of the Soviet Government, or still later, when his death called forth a steady stream of publications made up of the most insubstantial memories of his formative years.

Besides being trivial, they are often demonstrably false. Founders

and leaders of states and faiths are customarily surrounded by edifying or enhanced legend. It is the way of the folk in dealing with a
figure that has captured its imagination, and the lowliest adherent
thereby feels himself somehow enlarged. Moreover, in Lenin's case
such retouching has been a matter of plan and an affair of state.
Yet the very legends in his case are few and feeble. His personal
sobriety and modesty, his lack of fire and color—there was little
of the Promethean about him as there was about Trotsky, or of the
secretive and adventurous as in the case of Stalin—lend themselves
ill to legend. During his life he was sparing in personal reminiscence, and, unlike Stalin and Trotsky, not at all concerned with
the editing of his future obituary.

To make matters worse, as a lad Vladimir "never brought a
friend home with him" (Anna); had "a somewhat excessive tendency towards isolation and reserve, a tendency to avoid contact
with acquaintances and schoolfellows outside of school hours"
(Director Kerensky). When cousins, or his brothers' and sisters'
playmates called, he frequently climbed out of the window into the
yard, or, if escape were cut off, he could be heard to say with mock
courtesy, "Kindly oblige me by your absence"(Anna).

Indeed, all through his life there was a faint envelope of aloofness separating him from even close associates. In later years, as
Edmund Wilson has put it, there was always about him something
of "the respected headmaster who deals directly and frankly with
his charges yet who stands on a higher ground and always preserves a certain distance between him and them." None of the
intimates who shared his perils and his triumphs ever called him
"Volodya," except his wife. The others, however close, limited
themselves to the grave, formal intimacy of "Vladimir Ilyich" or the
more patriarchal "Ilyich." In many a village, there was a respected
elder thus addressed by patronymic alone, as a mark of intimacy,
respect and affection. In Lenin's case, the intimacy was lacking.
Both *Ilyich* and *Starik* were signs of his authoritative, charismatic
predominance over a group which was unconsciously saturated
with ways derived from the Orthodox folk. Even Krupskaya called
him *Ilyich*, more like a worshipful disciple than a wife.

The import of the few legends concerning Lenin's youth that have
received official sanction is invariably the same: they all tend to
increase the precocity of his intellectual development. It is deemed
unfitting to tell Komsomols and Pioneers (members of the Communist Youth Leagues and Boy and Girl Scouts) that their great
exemplar did not cease to be religious and a faithful attendant at

church until he was sixteen or over. Krzhizhanovsky, the old Bolshevik engineer who knew and worked with Lenin in Saint Petersburg when they were both young men in their twenties, has produced a more "suitable" memory, according to which Vladimir Ilyich told him how he had become irreligious when he was fourteen and "thrown his cross into the dungheap." But Anna records that during the autumn after their father's death she and the sixteen-year-old Vladimir were drawn more closely together, and took long walks in each other's company. Apparently due to first-hand experience with death, Vladimir showed a disposition to question religious teaching. Their father's closing years as an educator had been embittered by the tightening régime of reaction and he had suffered a premature pensioning off, without the customary five years of grace accorded to a faithful servitor. This, too, must have contributed to Vladimir's mood. At any rate, Anna notes that she found in him "for the first time an oppositional spirit on the direction and instruction of the *gymnazia*, as well as on religion." The words are fairly sober and specific. They do not speak of Marxism or revolution, merely of a mood of opposition concerning the things directly within the orbit of his youthful world. In any case, the question of the exact moment of his rejection of religion would seem to have been settled by Lenin himself, for on one of those party questionnaires which he himself invented and which he took very seriously, in response to the question: "When did you cease to believe in religion? he had written in his own careful hand: "At the age of sixteen." This would correspond with Anna's testimony, whatever its deficiencies as exemplary instruction to the Russian youth of the present day.

Anna's memoirs tend to destroy yet another favorite "cherrytree" legend of Soviet hagiography, which, in despite of historical materialism and suchlike trifles, would hold that great revolutionaries like Lenin are born, not made. Even the comparatively sober Lunacharsky portrays the boy Vladimir in earnest discourse with his father and elder brother on matters of revolutionary strategy and theory. Since Ilya Nikolaevich Ulyanov died at the beginning of the New Year, 1886, the discussions with his sons would have had to take place when the untalkative Sasha was eighteen or nineteen, and the bumptious Volodya (who "participated with considerable success") was fourteen or fifteen. But that should not surprise us too much since one of the recent official biographies of Stalin by Yaroslavsky) has the latter also, "while still a schoolboy"—in this case at the age of fourteen or fifteen—often conversing with workers and peasants and "explaining to them the causes of their poverty."

One anecdote, repeated by Lenin's wife Krupskaya, has the boy Vladimir shaking his wise young head over his elder brother's deep interest in natural science. "No," Krupskaya reports him as having said to himself, "my brother will never make a revolutionary —a revolutionary cannot devote so much time to studying annelid worms!" According to the old Bolshevik Shelgunov, when Vladimir read the telegram announcing the execution of his brother, "he rubbed his forehead and said: 'Very well then, we shall have to find a more efficacious path'." To whom did Vladimir address these sage words? his biographer, Trotsky, ironically inquires. Obviously not to Shelgunov, whom he did not meet until years later. Nor to his father, who had died the year before. Nor to Alexander, who had just perished on the scaffold. Nor to Anna, who was in prison. Nor to his mother, who had gone to Saint Petersburg to beg from ministerial door to door in an effort to save her boy. "Evidently," writes Trotsky, "Vladimir confided his revelations as tactician to Dmitri, who was thirteen, and Maria, who was nine!"

As against these portents of precocity we have the narrative of Anna, who has written, "Our father was never a revolutionary," and who places Vladimir's first oppositional questionings on the ways of school and Church in the autumn following the school inspector's death. To this we can add the report of another old Bolshevik, Lalayants, who got to know the future Lenin as a student in Kazan, while he was thus far more celebrated as the younger brother of a martyred would-be regicide than as a leader of men in his own right. Lalayants naturally questioned him on his memories of the affair. "For all of us," Vladimir Ilyich responded, "the participation of Alexander in a terrorist act was completely unexpected. Perhaps my sister knew something. As for me, I did not know a thing about it." Nor did Anna, as her later memoirs were to make clear.

According to Steklov, former editor of the Soviet organ *Izvestia*, Vladimir received a copy of the first volume of Marx's *Capital* "directly" from Alexander's hands. "Thus, Alexander Ulyanov installed not only his successor," observes Steklov, "but the inheritor and continuator of Marx as well." When we contemplate the role that the theory of apostolic succession was to play in the faction struggles of the Bolshevik Party, this anecdote takes on significance. Actually, however, Alexander did not begin to study Marx's *Capital* until the winter and spring that preceded his arrest. Copies of it were rare even in Saint Petersburg, and hard to lay hands on. He would have had to send the volume to his brother in Simbirsk by

mail or messenger, since young Vladimir never stopped his schooling during the trial and never saw Alexander again. It is not unreasonable to suppose, however, that he first heard the fateful name
of Marx in connection with his brother's trial.

In reality, Vladimir Ilyich was not one for sudden conversions.
He resembles but little those romantic revolutionaries who preceded
him: that generation of noble young men who brooded briefly on
the people's wrongs, rushed swiftly from brooding to conspiracy,
and died on the scaffold or by their own explosives within a few
months of their first impulse to action. Alexander was fashioned
thus, but not Vladimir. His was the kind of nature that grows
slowly and robustly, sending its roots deep into the ground, solid
and stout and destined to endure. He was not so much the man of
action as the shaper of the actions of men. There were four years
between Alexander and Vladimir which, in the discontinuity of the
experience of the seventies and the eighties was the equivalent of a
revolutionary generation. The depth of the reaction through which
Russia was going combined with Vladimir's temperament to favor
this slow, organic growth, this capacity to give material force to
his ideas not by enacting them into passionate drama but by making
them take possession of great masses of men. Strange to relate,
these official legends, which appear to exalt him, actually do injustice to his strongest qualities, his habit of many-sided examination of the matters he had in hand, his depth and solidity, his continued growth and flexibility to the end of his days, a certain
scientific experimentalism toward the problems he faced in applying
the certainties, which he in good time acquired, to the uncertain
world of day-to-day affairs.

Young Vladimir did not last long at the University of Kazan. The
year 1887, in which his brother was killed and in which he entered
into the law school was the very nadir of the prolonged reaction,
and the doctrine of family responsibility, though it had been relaxed
slightly in favor of his youth, was operative nonetheless. Alexander
Ulyanov and his four comrades died on May 20, 1887. A spasm of
fear and horror took possession of the student body of Saint Petersburg when he and three of his co-plotters were hanged. When the
rector of the University of Saint Petersburg sought to improve the
occasion by a sermon denouncing these "miserable creatures who
had insinuated themselves into our charming university family to
dishonor it," there were murmurs of indignation. The next day an
anonymous leaflet appeared saying that it was the university which
had dishonored itself by falling servilely at the feet of despotism.
The summer vacation intervened to stop the wave of muted protest.

In the autumn, the measures which the government took to control
the student body after the scare occasioned by the recent plot,
served to start a new wave of student protest, travelling slowly from
university to university, until it reached Kazan.

On December 4, of that same year, 1887, in which Alexander
died and Vladimir entered the university, the students of Kazan met
in assembly, drew up a series of demands, or rather respectful petitions, and sent a committee to invite the provincial inspector to
listen to their requests. Flanked by provosts, he ordered them to
disperse. For a while, they refused. The official eye was on the
alert for "ringleaders." In the front row it remarked the round head,
flat nose and Kalmuck eyes of the stocky little first-year student
from Simbirsk. As he walked out, he like the others was asked to
show his registration card. It bore the fateful name Ulyanov! That
very night police invaded the lodgings of young Vladimir Ilyich
Ulyanov and placed him under arrest.

No doubt the more active older students had tried to draw in
the boy who was surrounded by the aura of martyrdom as younger
brother of a hero who had just died on the scaffold. But apparently
Vladimir had had nothing to do with the calling of the assembly
or the drafting of demands. He had not said so much as a word
during the meeting, only sat "impudently" in the front row.[3] However, the authorities had been keeping their eyes on him from the
outset of his university career. The rector now sent in a report to
the effect that Vladimir Ilyich Ulyanov had conducted himself
during his brief three-month stay at Kazan "with deceit, dereliction,
and even discourtesy." The vagueness of the terms, their anticli-
mactic order, indicate that he had probably done nothing. "In view
of the exceptional circumstances surrounding the family Ulyanov,"
the report continued, "such attitude of Ulyanov in the meeting has
given the inspectors reasons to judge him quite capable of all sorts
of illegal and criminal manifestations." The young offender was
expelled from the university and ordered to leave Kazan. Because
of his three-month stay there, the university would one day be re-
christened with the name of Vladimir Ilyich Lenin, but of course,
only after his death, for he would never have permitted such self-
glorification while he was alive. Neither Simbirsk was renamed
Ulyanovsk, nor Petrograd Leningrad, nor the Rumyantsev Library

[3] A recent prize-winning painting in Russia portrays the freshman Lenin
organizing the whole demonstration and gathering students of all ages,
some heavily bearded, in a corridor to march at their head into the audi-
torium. (Water color by P. Alyakrinsky, reproduced in the Soviet Embassy
Information Bulletin, January 28, 1948.)

called Lenin State Library, nor the University of Kazan the Vladimir Ilyich Lenin University, until he was in his tomb.

According to an account of his official biographer, Adoratsky, accepted by Vladimir's sister Anna, the boy got into an argument with the policeman who supervised his expulsion from Kazan.

"Why do you revolt, young man?" the agent asked. "You are up against a stone wall . . ."

"A wall, yes, but a crumbling one, and one which will soon collapse," Vladimir is reported to have answered.

This anecdote, too, is probably apocryphal, but certainly the wall was there. Within a matter of some three months his university career had begun and come to an end. Thus did tsarism tend to drive young men into the profession of revolutionary by closing all other professions to them.

But Vladimir was only seventeen. His widowed mother, whose oldest boy was in his grave and whose oldest girl was in disgrace, had set her hopes on his career. He did not give up easily. During the next few years he made repeated attempts to gain readmission to the university, or, failing that, to get permission to take the professional qualifying examinations as a self-taught or external student, and thus win admission to the bar.

CHAPTER V

MATRICULATION IN MARXISM

> The very air of Russia seemed to be saturated with an in-
> tense desire for liberation. We became the enemies of the
> Autocracy almost as soon as we entered the university, and
> this seemed to happen naturally . . . there were no argu-
> ments among the students whether the Autocracy was to be
> fought or not . . . the only argument was as to where the
> real truth was to be found, with the Marxists or with the
> *Narodniki.*   — *Alexander Kerensky*

THE YOUTH who does equally well in all subjects is as yet lacking
in intellectual personality. It may be taken as a fair measure of
the slowness of Vladimir's spiritual development—as well as the
athletic prowess of his mind—that at seventeen he still liked Latin
and excelled in it; for in student circles at that time one's attitude
toward Latin was regarded as a reagent to test for the critical
spirit. The study of Latin had been deliberately enlarged by the
authorities to convert the schools into more suitable houses of
correction for the turbulent student movement. "Knowledge of the
dead languages"—the Minister had explained in his circular—"by
the very difficulty of success in its pursuit, gives a lesson in modesty,
and modesty is the first sign and prerequisite of a true education."
To the student generation just preceding Vladimir's, the idolization
of science and contempt for the dead languages were the badges
of enlightenment. But to Vladimir's robust and still undiscriminating
mind it was a pleasant exercise, a kind of linguistic chess.

As with his other subjects, young Ulyanov found the prescribed
pace too slow for him. When he tutored his sister Anna in Latin
during their enforced rustication in Kukushkino, he told her that
two years were more than enough to master the conventional eight-
year course in the language. Under his tutelage, two years seem
to have been sufficient. Some notion of how he might have gone
about it is suggested by an anecdote told by Albert Rhys Williams
apropos of Lenin's advice on the study of Russian.

Mr. Williams spoke to him at the historic session of the Constituent Assembly in the early winter of 1918, which ended with that
body's dissolution.

"And how goes the Russian language?" Lenin asked in the midst of all the turmoil. "Can you understand all these speeches now?"

"There are so many words in Russian," I replied evasively.

"That's it," he retorted. "You must go at it systematically. You must break the backbone of the language at the outset. I'll tell you my method of going at it."

In essence, Lenin's system was this: First, learn all the nouns, learn all the verbs, learn all the adverbs and adjectives, learn all the rest of the words; learn all the grammar and rules of syntax, then keep on practicing everywhere and upon everybody.

The advice seems humorously exaggerated, but Lenin mastered a number of living European languages, among them English, French and German, by some such method. When he tried to practise his attainments on the people he met in the streets of the various European cities, he was amazed to find that they did not understand a word he was saying. Yet his reading knowledge was excellent, his translations into Russian workmanlike, and he kept at it until he could make himself understood and understand spoken discourse also. The same direct and unsubtle but overpowering method of "breaking the backbone at the outset" he applied to the study of law, to the extrication of the socio-economic outlines buried in the maze of Russian statistics, to the works of the Marxists and their opponents, to philosophy when he found himself forced to concern himself with it, to the chaos that was Russia when he took over the helm of the Empire in 1917.

Expelled students were not allowed to live in university towns, nor in industrial centers. Mild cases were directed to go to their birthplaces, if these were rural, or to lesser towns and villages; severe cases were remanded to the wilds of Siberia. Vladimir was permitted to join his sister Anna in Kukushkino, both under police supervision. Their mother took the younger children with her and went to keep house for them. There the youthful state criminal concealed from himself his uncertainty and restlessness by long spells of chess with his younger brother Dmitri, with his sister Anna's fiancé, the insurance agent Elisarov, with such neighbors as could hold their own with him and were not afraid to visit the twice-accursed household. As these did not supply enough opposition, Elisarov arranged for his future brother-in-law to play chess matches by mail with a distinguished amateur named Khardin, a liberal attorney-at-law in Samara.

At Kukushkino they shared a large old house with the mother's sisters. Here Vladimir found a library which had been gathered by a deceased uncle, one of those miscellaneous libraries such as enlightened provincial gentlemen of the preceding generation were wont to acquire. The books teased rather than satisfied his appetite. He went through the collection of old reviews of the sixties and seventies, finding there obscure hints of the turmoil of discussion among the Russian intellectuals concerning their country's future.

By mail, he borrowed entire boxes of books from the library at Kazan. In a grove of linden trees outside the house he spent the long spring and summer hours, reading, making summaries in a neat, diminutive hand of the books that interested him, reflecting on their contents and their implications; thinking, planning, dreaming of his own future and more and more frequently, of the future of Russia. But he was not sure yet as to either.

Immediately after breakfast he would leave the family circle and work by himself until dinner—taken at three in the afternoon. After dinner he would read novels or poetry, take a walk or a swim—he was a powerful and effortless swimmer—exercise on outdoor crossbars which he built himself, tutor Anna in Latin, help the younger children with their studies. In the evening after a light supper there might be family singing or reading aloud, but more often than not the boy would return to his studies until bedtime. Unlike many of the thus early "ruined" intellectuals, he had no intention of giving way to despair or blind rebellion. He was not sure of his future, nor what he wanted to study or prepare for, but he was determined to keep fit in mind and body and to strengthen the powers of both. The good mother eyed him uneasily from afar, pleased with his serene self-discipline and composure, but deeply worried over his career. What, she wondered, would come of all this reading?

In his vexation and uncertainty, he took to smoking—like chess —as a way of quieting his nervous tension. Apparently it was an alien habit in this somewhat puritanical household. The mother first remonstrated with him on the grounds of health, then suggested that, since he was earning nothing, he should not increase the expenses of the household by such practices. Without a word he abandoned smoking, never to resume it. Thus, years later, when he was convinced that chess was absorbing too much of his energy, he abandoned that taxing game permanently also. The same strict power of self-discipline was to shelter him later from the chief vice of the Russian intellectuals, fruitless and endless discussion. Participating only when there was someone to be convinced or something to be clarified and settled, he saved much nervous energy by avoiding discussion for its own sake.

Five months after his expulsion from Kazan, he made his first application for reinstatement. The district inspector sent it to the Minister of Education along with a report which warned that "despite his remarkable abilities, Ulyanov cannot for the present be regarded as a reliable person either as to morals or as to politics." The Minister had no use for unreliable persons. Without even reading the report to the end, he began scribbling his objections: "Wouldn't this be the brother of the other Ulyanov? He too came from Simbirsk." When he read further, finding that it was indeed the brother of the would-be regicide, "It is not at all desirable to readmit him," he wrote.

Two months later the mother of the expelled student sent in a personal petition in his behalf, hoping that her widowhood and her husband's good name and career might avail in softening the heart of the Minister. Again the answer was negative.

Then Vladimir made the first of his applications (under the Tsars, as under the Bolsheviks, people could not leave Russia without permission) to go abroad "for his health." This petition, too, was rejected. Still the local police captain, who came to the house from time to time to interview the probationers Vladimir and Anna, continued to turn in uneventful reports. The boy's outward conduct was impeccable. Whatever might be transpiring in the household which could conceivably endanger the state, went on behind that brow which even then, in his eighteenth year, seemed to grow higher as the hairline began receding. In the autumn of 1888 he was allowed to return to Kazan, but was not readmitted to the university. Anna was not given the right to imperil Kazan with her gentle presence until sometime later. Her future, however, did not worry her mother, for she was engaged to her former schoolmate from the University of Saint Petersburg, Elisarov, and was making plans for her wedding. In Kazan, the boy joined a chess club, haunted the library, entered into an informal study circle for the consideration of social questions.

Maria Alexandrovna Ulyanova now went in person to Saint Petersburg to see if she could salvage the career of her son. She looked up the men who had known her husband. She begged one official after the other, pleaded her boy's youth, employed tears and whatever arguments a mother's heart could find. "It is a veritable torment," she wrote in one of her petitions, "to regard my son and see how the best years of his life slip unfruitfully away . . . such an existence must almost inevitably drive him to the idea of suicide." Nothing was farther from the boy's mind, but it was an under-

standable device, since the one thing that tempered the reactionary
régime was an occasional burst of sentiment.

While Maria Alexandrovna continued her importunings, she kept
an eye open for alternative careers for young Vladimir. Her widow's
pension was not much: twelve hundred rubles—six hundred dollars
—per annum. In addition she had the house they had lived in
during their years in Simbirsk, and her share in the paternal estate
at Kukushkino, which she had inherited together with her sister.
Remembering her childhood in a German farm community on the
Volga, she thought of making a farmer of her boy. She sold her
home in Simbirsk and perhaps her share in her estate, in one way
or another managing to assemble the necessary funds to purchase
a farm at Alakaevka, near Samara. The purchase price was 7,500
rubles.

Alakaevka was a miserable village of eighty-four families, nine
of which were without a single horse or cow, four without ownership of the huts they inhabited. The hamlet had no school. The
village was a faded remnant of a once-bright dream for Russia's
"redemption," part of a vast estate acquired many years back by
the wealthy mine-owner, Sibiryakov, who had planned to establish
modern model farms there. The venture had failed, leaving the
region as backward and the muzhiks as miserable as it had found
them. The new Ulyanov estate consisted of eighty-three dessyatins
(roughly 225 acres) with a mill and a "manor house" (our quotation marks are intended to prevent the reader from picturing too
much elegance).

Soviet biographers are strangely reticent about this little venture.
Anna merely records the purchase of "a little farm in the province
of Samara" and a request to the authorities that the young suspect
and his family be permitted "to go there to spend the summer."
An official biographer (Kerzhentsev) devotes to it only a tiny
phrase: "He spent the summer in the country, first in Kukushkino
and then in Alakaevka in the Samara *Gubernya*." Most official
biographers do not even mention Alakaevka.

What is the meaning of the taciturnity of these chroniclers concerning the several summers (at least three planting years) spent
by Vladimir Ilyich in this miserable village? The answer is suggested by a sentence in the memoirs of Lenin's wife, Krupskaya.
As brief as the others, her reference possesses a frankness and exactness lacking in the rest: "My mother wanted me to engage in farming," Krupskaya reports Lenin as saying. "I tried it, but I saw that

it would not work: my relations with the muzhiks got to be abnormal."

It is a pity that we do not know more, but it is evident from little scraps of information available that the farm possessed, aside from the mill, no implements for direct exploitation, and had to be worked by some form of sharecropping or rental to the necessitous villagers. In other words, the future Lenin went through a brief period as a landowner and exploiter of peasant labor. The biographers who speak vaguely and at some length on how Ulyanov "got to know the agrarian problem at first hand" by walks in the countryside around Simbirsk, by summers in rural Kukushkino, by eager questioning of chance muzhiks with whom he came into contact, are silent on this deeper insight obtained from personal experience during several critical, formative years as a young landowner. Yet, to one not a slave to official legend it would seem not at all discreditable that the young Ulyanov, in quest of a career, tried his hand at running an estate and found it distasteful, deriving therefrom a deeper understanding and a deeper detestation of the relations of rural exploitation.

Fortunately, there was no need for conflict with his mother on the abandonment of the career of gentleman squire which, in her desperation, she had chosen for him. In the summer of 1890, almost three years after his expulsion from Kazan, she at last secured the consent of the Minister of Education to her son's resumption of the study of law. He was not to be permitted to reenter a university, where he might "contaminate" other students, but he was authorized to take the law examinations given in Saint Petersburg whenever, after study by himself, he should feel ready for them. Thereupon, this vigorous and systematic student, who liked to "break the backbone of a subject" at the outset, easily made up the time he had lost through his almost three years of enforced rustication. In little more than a year he ranged through the four-year university course in Jurisprudence, passing the first group of examinations in the spring of 1891 and the rest of them in the autumn, all of them with the highest possible grade. On November 27, 1891, he was granted a diploma, once more with honors. He had come out first in the examinations.

After some five months more of his mother's dickering, he even succeeded in getting the requisite "Certificate of Loyalty and Good Character" without which he could never be admitted to practice. In January, 1892, shortly before he turned twenty-two, Citizen Ulyanov was apparently travelling the road back to respectability as a junior attorney, having secured employment with his old chess opponent, A. N. Khardin, in Samara. Lawyer Khardin was a political liberal who would later join the Constitutional Democratic Party when it was formed, the party led by Professor Miliukov, which Lenin would outlaw and then destroy after 1917. Thus for the second time was Vladimir Ilyich Ulyanov helped in his career by a liberal. And still later, yet another liberal, the Saint Petersburg lawyer M. F. Volkenstein, took him into his office, although Volkenstein must have known then that he proposed to use the title of attorney as a blind for other activities. As we see, the tale that Lenin detested all liberals from the day they deserted his family when Alexander was arrested, is a retroactive legend. That traumatic experience must have affected him deeply, but he did not break completely with the liberals as a political current until the Revolution of 1905. And even thereafter, he was helped with funds, meeting-places, and cover addresses by well-to-do liberals. But psychologically this legend is sound, and behind it lies a truth: the memory of the way in which so many of his father's old friends and colleagues had deserted his widowed mother and her twice-stricken family undoubtedly colored Lenin's feeling toward so-called liberal public opinion, predisposing him to a harsher judgment and greater irreconcilability than characterized most of his associates in the leadership of the Social Democratic Party in the early years of the new century. Even while he and his associates were in theoretical agreement on the need to turn to the liberal opposition for a common alliance against tsarism, Plekhanov was moved to say to him: "We want to turn our face; you your behind."

His actual career as junior attorney was brief and undistinguished. The year and a half he spent at it in provincial Samara yielded him ten minor cases of pitiful defendants: ignorant, poverty-stricken, degraded muzhiks who had robbed a bit of grain, held up a merchant, or stolen a few rubles, petty criminals all, the most serious complication being the additional charge of "breaking and entering" when three defendants opened a barn door to commit their thieving. All were clearly guilty, and all but one were charged with crimes against property. In one case, that of a wife-beater, he refused to plead mitigation for the client which the court assigned to him. In not one of the ten cases did he get an acquittal.

One case, however, he undertook without fee and without court assignment—a case that, like a flash of lightning, illumined the outlines of his future activities. In it he served as voluntary public prosecutor, at his own cost, for a public that had long accepted the abuse he challenged, and had neither fought it nor asked him to fight it. He and his sister Anna had tried to cross the Volga in a little boat, but a wealthy merchant named Arefeev was accustomed to collect tribute from all who crossed the river at that point, by forcing them to hire his steam launch. Arefeev's ship pursued the little craft the Ulyanovs had engaged and drove it back to shore. His sense of justice outraged, Ulyanov brought complaint against the merchant. The latter contrived to have the case tried in distant Syzran—a trip of nearly seventy miles from Samara for each hearing. He used all the devices of the law and all his influence with the local courts to have the case postponed and dragged out, hoping to weary the young plaintiff. In the end, Ulyanov won his suit—it was his only success as a lawyer!

The years 1886 and 1887 were the truly decisive ones in the life of young Vladimir Ilyich, though it would take a half-decade for the decision which they fostered to be transformed from an unconscious to a conscious one. During those two fateful years, the lad lost his father by sudden death (January, 1886), witnessed his brother's arrest, trial and execution on the scaffold (May, 1887), entered and was expelled from the University of Kazan (December, 1887), had his first run-in with the police, met his first arrest and rural, administrative exile. They were, too, the years in which he began to put questions to the world which he had hitherto taken for granted, the years in which he lost his faith in God and Church, in school and state authorities. They happened to coincide with the years in which the passivity and reaction of the eighties had reached their ebb and the outgoing tide of resistance was turning imperceptibly. The famine year 1891 once more started the whole of oppositional Russian society into movement. It was the same year in which Ulyanov passed his bar examinations. The rising tide soon covered the tiny spot of "respectability" on which he sought to stand, sweeping him along with the best of those who were coming to maturity in the early nineties, into open rebellion against the régime of "eternal stability" that Alexander III had erected.

"There can be no doubt," Alexander Kerensky has written of Lenin, "that it was the cruel execution of the noble-minded, brilliant Alexander which finally made Vladimir what he remained throughout his political career—an unsurpassed, sadistically revengeful cynic."

There can indeed be no doubt that the influence of Alexander's conspiracy and death was a profound one, and that Alexander's example imposed itself for several years upon the imagination of his younger brother, even deflecting him somewhat from the path

he was ultimately to follow. But the "vengeance on the Tsar" theory
is as dubious as it is simple and tempting. Vernadsky, not a friendly
but a more objective biographer, has outlined (in his *Lenin: Red
Dictator*) the obvious evidence against Kerensky's oversimplified
viewpoint. Lenin's detestation of capitalism, he points out, was no
less than his hatred of tsarism; he directed his blows no less against
the bourgeoisie than against the autocracy. During the seven years
that elapsed between the moment Alexander III signed his brother's
death warrant and the end of the Tsar's reign, Ulyanov does not
appear to have meditated any attempt on the Tsar's life. And when
Nicholas II, son and successor of the imperial executioner, fell into
Lenin's hands in 1917, "he showed no haste to square accounts so
long as it did not seem necessary for political reasons."

What then was the influence on the seventeen-year-old boy of
his brother's execution? It put him immediately before the dilemma:
to accept his brother's deed in his heart, or to reject it. What doubts
and struggles that may have meant we have no way of knowing.
The only seemingly reliable report that has come down to us
stems from the old family tutor of the Ulyanovs, Madam Kachka-
damova. "Well it seems," the boy Vladimir said to her, "that Alexander could not have done otherwise." The judgment was personal
and—at least in germ—social.

What Alexander's ardent, sincere and gentle temperament signified to all his brothers and sisters we can guess from Anna's letter
to him while they were both in prison. "There is no one better
than you, more noble on earth," she wrote to him. His forthright
acceptance of responsibility, his refusal to beg for mercy, all the
beautiful acts of his closing days and martyrdom, could only have
served to enlarge the impression he made upon the other children.

For Vladimir the shattering experience put a sudden end to a
hitherto joyous adolescence. At seventeen he was brought forcibly
into contact with heavy problems of maturity. Before that year was
out, in Trotsky's apt phrase, he had been expelled from the University of Kazan directly into the University of Marxism.

Yet the very spell of Alexander's person and example retarded
the boy's entrance into the current of Marxism. He found ready acceptance in Narodnik circles as the younger brother of a martyred
hero. He began his political thinking where Alexander had left off,
as a theoretical populist and terrorist, and far from leading—as
Soviet biographers invariably suggest—he lagged a year or two behind the sudden turn of the younger generation to Marxism.

For several years Vladimir Ulyanov continued to hold special
views on terror, and, even after he became an active opponent of

its employment, there was always a difference in his language from the more categorical condemnation of individual terror by most other orthodox Marxists.

> We have never rejected terror on principle—Lenin was to write in 1901—nor can we ever do so. Terror is a form of military operation that may be usefully applied, or may even be essential in certain moments of the battle—the point is, however, that terror is now advocated, not as one of the operations which the army in the field must carry on in close contact with the main body and in harmony with the whole plan of battle, but as an individual attack, completely isolated from any army whatever. . . . That is why we declare that under present circumstances such a method of fighting is inopportune and inexpedient; it will distract the most active fighters from their present tasks . . . and will disrupt not the governmental forces but the revolutionary forces. [*Iskra*, May, 1901. *Collected Works*, Vol. IV. Part I: *Where to Begin.*]

All his life Lenin regarded objections to individual terror *on principle* as "pedantic" and "philistine"—the latter adjective, in his special vocabulary, is the equivalent of unrevolutionary. And it was boldness in connection with deeds of individual terror that first attracted his attention to Joseph Stalin and caused him to advance the latter to posts of importance.

In 1891, as so many times before, famine swept over Russia. The black earth fields turned gray, then cracked, then became dust; the grain burned to tinder on the stalks; hunger took possession of Europe's granary. Whole villages took to the roads in quest of food or employment. Or, gathering their rags about them, died quietly in dark corners, as animals die. Cholera, typhus, typhoid followed in the tracks that hunger had smoothed.

They are wrong who believe that the starving revolt. The countryside suffered in apathetic silence; it was "society" in the towns that was stirred to its depths. Hunger that comes from scarcity, they said, was a medieval phenomenon (not to be compared with that modern want, proper to capitalism, which comes from abundance). In this, as in other respects, Russia remained "medieval" even into the twentieth century—and we shall have to take note of two such "pre-capitalist" crises under the "post-capitalist" Soviets.

If Russia's backwardness and social structure could not be blamed for the failure of the rain to come, they could be held accountable for bureaucratic incompetence, for callous indifference to mass suffering, for stubborn refusal to acknowledge the famine and enlist aid in time lest prestige suffer, for greed which set greater store by price current than by human life, for the policy of continued grain export, for the abominable transport system which prevented shipment of bread from more favored areas, for the normal starvation level of the "good years" which left the peasants without reserves for survival.

"The gravest, the deepest difference on which we opposed ourselves to Vladimir Ulyanov," wrote the populist Vodovozov some thirty years later, "turned about the attitude to take to the famine of 1891-2." All of Samara "society" occupied itself with giving aid "except Vladimir Ulyanov and his family and a little circle which followed him." These, according to Vodovosov, found a perverse pleasure in the suffering and saw in it a progressive factor which "by destroying the peasant economy . . . creates a proletariat and contributes to the industrialization of the country."

Once more we seem to be in the presence of a retroactive legend. The view ascribed to Vladimir (and to his mother, sisters and brother!) is a distortion of an actual dispute—or rather two disputes—then raging between the Marxists and the populists (Narodniki).

One, a theoretical question, concerned the perspective as to Russia's future. According to the populists, Russia had a special destiny and mission: to lead the world to socialism without ever going through the hell of capitalism at all. To them the city was an alien importation, an ulcerous excrescence on the countryside; the proletariat was but a symptom of a social disease that might be avoided; the peasants were all instinctive socialists; the rural communes and cooperatives of village artisans were the road to a new social order. But the Marxists insisted that Russia was even then becoming a land of big industry; that the village commune was in full decay; that the small peasant was being ruined and proletarianized; that the village was differentiating into rich and poor, exploiters and exploited; that the proletariat and not the peasantry was the main hope of a movement for socialism. The idea that famine would strengthen Russian industry, however, was on the face of it an absurdity and caricature of Marxist argument: a single uprooted peasant may become a proletarian, but starving millions are only paupers, while a ruined countryside destroys the market for domestic manufactures.

The second dispute concerned an immediate practical question: how should the revolutionists invest their energies in connection with the famine? Here the more revolutionary of the Narodniks were at one with the Marxists, the line of cleavage being rather between revolutionary and moderate, than between Narodnik and Social Democrat. Ulyanov was not making a policy of his own in any case, merely following his new leader, Plekhanov, of whom he was even then in the process of becoming a disciple.[1] The alternative which faced the intelligentsia was whether to offer their services to the government (which the government feared and rejected) or to bring pressure to bear upon the government and expose its culpability. "For a socialist," wrote Paul Axelrod, close associate of Plekhanov, "an effective struggle against famine is possible only on the basis of a struggle against the autocracy." And the aged Narodnik leader Lavrov declared: "Yes, the only good work possible for us is not philanthropic work, but revolutionary work."

When Vodovosov, as he himself records, was defeated by Ulyanov, it was in a circle of local Samara radicals where he had proposed to send a telegram of congratulation to the governor of the province for his noble aid to the sufferers. Further light on the accuracy of Vodovosov's account is thrown by the fact that Anna Ulyanov actually did volunteer her services as a nurse.

In the end, the liberals were not successful in ingratiating themselves with the government, which brought charges of profiteering in spoiled grain against the zemstvo of Samara. Nor did they win the confidence of the peasants, who responded to the measures of forced inoculation, hospitalization and quarantine by attacking doctors and nurses and accusing them of poisoning those who died of plague. When seven years later famine recurred, even the moderate liberals spoke of charity as a miserable palliative, regarded haphazard pilgrimage to the stricken areas as ineffective, and demanded a reorganization of the basic structure of Russia. The viewpoint of Plekhanov and his associates had by then become the viewpoint of all Russian intellectuals.

The famine of 1891 marked a fundamental turning point in Russian public life, and it coincided with a rising tide that had begun in Western Europe a year or two earlier. There, too, the eighties had been years of reaction. The First International, headed by Marx and Engels, had perished in the seventies in a fury of police persecution and internal dissension. When Karl Marx died in 1883—the same year which saw the death of the Narodnaya Volya—there was no great organized labor movement anywhere to mourn his passing. But late in the same decade, Marxism began to haunt the capitals

[1] Plekhanov enunciated his policy on the famine in two pamphlets: *The All-Russian Ruin* and *Tasks of the Socialists in the Struggle against Famine.*

of Europe once more. The French working class, prostrate since the fall of the Paris Commune, which had cost them a hundred thousand victims, raised its head again. German Social Democracy, which Bismarck had sought to outlaw and drive underground, found means of surmounting the barriers of the law and rolling up a million and a half votes in an election in which, as a party, it had no legal existence! The British trade unions broke through the crust of routine and narrow craft interest to embrace for the first time great masses of unskilled workers. In Russia, the name of Marx and the prestige of Plekhanov began to take possession of an entire generation of young intellectuals.

The reviving organizations of the principal European lands came together in international conclave in 1889 and the Second International arose out of the ashes of the First. The Congress met under the inspiring influence of the German Social-Democratic victory over Bismarck. Vladimir Ulyanov, like all the Russian youth of his generation, read with passionate interest the meager accounts of German working-class triumphs and Reichstag debates as they appeared in the Russian press. For young Ulyanov the mighty German movement was long to be the model party of the International. In controversy he would quote not only Marx and Engels, but Bebel and Kautsky with a disciple's awe, as authorities whose *ipse dixit* virtually sufficed to decide issues. In the German Social Democracy, with its hierarchical centralization and rigid discipline, he was to find the model after which he hoped to mold the diffused, slack and localized Russian movement; from it he was to derive theoretical conceptions and ideas on strategy and tactics; its workingman leader, August Bebel, was to be the prototype after whose image he sought to fashion Russian workingmen leaders; its outstanding theoretical spokesman, Karl Kautsky, was to be in his eyes the chief defender of the orthodoxy of the Marxist faith. Though he translated all these features into Russian according to his own requirements and strong sense of Russian realities, for a quarter of a century he never doubted this ideal working-class movement at all . . . until, in August, 1914, the news reached him, incredible, unassimilable, that it had voted support of the Imperial Government of Wilhelm II in the war that was just beginning!

At the First Congress of the Socialist International [2] the leading

---

[2] Its proper name is Socialist and Labor International. It regarded itself as the successor or continuator of the First International, founded in 1864 and disbanded in 1876. It came to be known generally as the Second International only after Lenin founded the Third or Communist International in 1919. Until then, it embraced all socialist parties and Socialist-inspired trade unions.

spokesman for Russia was George Plekhanov. An ex-member of the movement that had given birth to the Narodnaya Volya, he had been living in exile in Switzerland since 1881. If ever there was a movement which could be said to owe its origin to one man, Russian Marxism owed its origin to this one. In Geneva he had gathered around him Vera Zasulich, heroine of the attempted assassination of Petersburg Governor Trepov, Paul Axelrod, and Leo Deutsch, all veterans of the Narodnik movement, and in 1883 they had formed the first Russian Marxist or Social Democratic organization: the group known as Ozvobozhdenie Truda ("Liberation of Labor"). Until the revolutionary revival of the nineties, it had vegetated in obscure and lonely exile, a handful of neglected thinkers cut off from any connection with Russia. Under Plekhanov's brilliant intellectual leadership it studied Western Marxism, and, in its light, examined critically the assumptions that had actuated the Narodnik movement. In a series of closely reasoned studies (*Socialism and the Political Struggle*, 1883; *Our Differences*, 1884; *Toward the Development of the Monistic Conception of History*, 1895), Plekhanov subjected to "Marxist"[3] criticism the favorite populist dogmas; the doctrine that the peasant was the driving force of the revolution; the hope of a peculiar path of non-capitalist development for Russia; and the tactic of individual terror. These works, and others of the eighties and nineties from the same hand, contain, in the words of the Bolshevik historian Pokrovsky, "practically all the basic ideas that formed the stock-in-trade of Russian Marxism up to the end of the century." The works of Lenin prior to 1900—so often treated by his followers as if they broke ground for these ideas—were little more than many-sided expansions of hints, or detailed proof of generalizations, contained in the work of this master who, in Lenin's ungrudging acknowledgment, had single-handed served to "rear a whole generation of Russian Marxists."

When George Plekhanov addressed the foundation congress of the Socialist International in 1889, he told the delegates: "In Russia political freedom will be gained by the working class, or it will not exist at all. The Russian Revolution can only conquer as a working-

[3] If I have put the word Marxist in quotation marks here, it is because Marx himself was uncertain as to the possibility of a special non-capitalist path for Russia and warmly sympathetic to the Narodnaya Volya, whose recourse to terror he more than once justified as the only path open to it under then existing Russian conditions. And Frederick Engels, though he welcomed the foundation of the Marxist Liberation of Labor Group by Plekhanov and his associates and had anticipated many of their criticisms of the Russian Populists, yet deplored the intolerance with which *Our Differences* treated "the only people who are doing anything in Russia at this moment."

man's revolution—there is no other possibility nor can there be."

To the representatives of the Western workingmen's parties that must have seemed a trite commonplace. It passed unnoticed, or they wondered at the air of dramatic revelation with which it was delivered. But as the dictum seeped slowly into the Russian underground, it marked the end of an epoch. With the aid of the vast sounding-board of a world socialist congress, it proclaimed that henceforward the Russian intelligentsia was to turn its face from the village to the city. For an entire decade it was to remain a subject of voluminous, acrimonious, and ever more triumphant controversy. Yet, when the system of ideas it summarized seemed completely victorious, a new wave of peasant riots and uprisings in 1902 was sufficient to revive the oft-buried revolutionary populism in the form of the strong Social Revolutionary Party.

In the course of the nineties, however, spurred on by the negative experiences of the famine and the dark passivity of the peasants, and by a gigantic leap in industrialization and a wave of strikes in the cities, the majority of the radicals among the younger generation—Vladimir Ulyanov's generation—went over to the new creed. They conceived for Plekhanov an admiration without limit, an admiration which, in young Ulyanov's case, would amount to "respect . . . reverence . . . infatuation."

It was in Samara that the young lawyer, Ulyanov, first made his acquaintance with *Our Differences* by Plekhanov, and it was in Samara that he made the transition from populism to Marxism. The town of Samara was a provincial river port with no industrial proletariat and no university. Hence the police considered it safe for the residence of men and women who had served out their time in prison and in Siberia but were forbidden to reside where they might come into contact with students or workingmen. If our provincial lawyer, who was just acquiring an intense theoretical interest in the proletariat, could not observe genuine industrial workers there, he could the world of tramps, vagabonds, migratories, bargemen and boat-haulers down at the waterfront—the world from which issued his future friend, Maxim Gorky. If he could not meet students except for a few expelled university men, he could himself enroll as a student to those past masters of revolutionary conspiracy, the veterans of the Narodnaya Volya whom the police permitted to reside there.

They were aging men and women, survivors of a movement that had failed and perished. They came to life only in their memories. A good listener and a tireless questioner, Vladimir came to them with credentials of younger brother of one of their own hero-martyrs. What were the great days like? he wanted to know. How had they themselves come to the movement and how won recruits for it? What was their program, how had they expounded it, how circulated it, how had the masses responded? How did one "go underground" and what could they tell him of the technique of conspiracy? What of chemical inks, secret codes, signals, false pass-ports, jailbreaks, escapes from exile? How were the Narodovoltsi [4] organized, who chose the executive committee, what authority had it, how did it admit and instruct members, how limit their knowl-edge of each other to a minimum, how prevent the penetration of police spies? His questions were rigorous, searching, exact. He was not in quest of vicarious adventure, though his eyes must have burned when they told their heroes' tales. What he sought above all was information that might be useful in the future. Whenever he found that their answers lacked precision or that they were in-venting and covering vagueness by verbosity, he ceased to ques-tion. When they were sentimental and romantic and seemed to lose touch with reality, his eyes smiled while his face remained respect-fully impassive, as if he were the old one and these aging men and women the youngsters.

As his slowly changing views led to growing differences with them on theoretical matters, he abstained from argument. He was restrained by veneration for their heroism and distaste for exacerbat-ing and useless controversy with people not likely any longer to change their views. But it was not easy for him to break with them. He must have been speaking for himself, as well as for his genera-tion, when he wrote:

> In early youth they enthusiastically worshipped the ter-rorist heroes. It was a great wrench to abandon the capti-vating impressions of these heroic traditions, and it was accomplished by the breaking off of personal relations with people who were determined to remain loyal to the Narod-naya Volya and for whom the Young Social Democrats had profound respect.

Toward the end of his stay in Samara, he ceased to seek them out. Then young intellectuals who still followed in their footsteps found him, in his sister Anna's words, "an exceedingly presumptu-ous and rude young man."

With the same speed and thoroughness with which he had mastered Russian law and come out first among those taking the

[4] Narodovoltsi, members of the Narodnaya Volya.

examinations, the young attorney now absorbed Marxist theory. In Samara he sought out the forbidden works, mastered German to read the originals, obtained badly hectographed or handwritten Russian copies, tore out separate sections of outlawed books for more easy secreting. He plowed through the two volumes of Marx's *Capital* (the third was not yet published) and proceeded to apply its analytical method to Russian statistical material. He read all the government reports, all the economic studies, all the dissertations of liberal or populist economists and sociologists that he could lay hands on. During six silent years, he thought, studied, questioned, examined, soaking up knowledge like a sponge, organizing it in a mind as systematic as a library file, as dynamic and as sparely furnished as a power house. During all those years, except for notebooks, extracts, abstracts, brief or elaborate summaries, he wrote not a word. Not until 1893, during his last months in Samara, did he write anything intended to be read by others.

His first writing of which we have any record is a "book review" —itself almost book size—of a work on the agrarian question. The "review," loaded with statistics and written for legal publication, was rejected by the liberal *Russkaya Mysl* to which he submitted it, probably because it consisted too largely of quotation, paraphrase, tables and summaries from the already well-known book by V. E. Postnikov, *The Agricultural Economy of Southern Russia*. But he read the work aloud in the Samara study circle, where Postnikov's work was unknown. To the provincial circle it seemed a masterpiece of Marxist analysis by a twenty-three year old youth. It instantly established his authority. One of the two hand-written copies he prepared has come down to us thanks to those indefatigable collectors of manuscripts, the tsarist police. Not published until 1923, it takes up forty-six pages in the first volume of Lenin's *Collected Works*. The bulk of it was incorporated into his *Development of Capitalism in Russia,* written a half decade later, which also made liberal use of Postnikov's tables and analysis.

From the same last months in Samara dates another work which was circulated in handwritten copies among the youth of the town, but the police failed to preserve a copy for us. *Discussion Between a Social Democrat and a Populist* was its title. It took the form of a dialogue in which Vladimir rehearsed the arguments he had, first within himself, and then with young Samara populists. He wrote it out to clarify his own views, to seek for them a wider audience, and to compel his youthful opponents to listen to the end without interruption. He had too much confidence in his own ideas, even then, to tolerate disorderly and heated interruption by those

whom he deemed less informed and in need of listening and learning, not arguing. He was to have recourse to this monologue method
of "settling an argument" many times in his lifetime.

The theme of the two works was really the same: their personal
basis was Vladimir Ilyich's own break with the Narodniki, their
social basis the dispute that raged between the older and the
younger generation of revolutionaries throughout the decade of
the nineties. Whatever he was to title his future works, virtually
all of them until the end of the decade, including the fat *Development of Capitalism in Russia,* were one long "discussion between
a Social Democrat and a Populist."

As Vladimir Ulyanov became convinced that the proletariat was
to be the driving force of the struggle against tsarism and that the
industrial towns of Russia would be the directing center of the
revolutionary movement, he began to feel that he had exhausted
the possibilities of Samara. According to official biographers he
delayed his departure for Saint Petersburg during two years, 1891
to 1893, because he wanted to comfort his mother in a new grief
that had befallen her, the death of his younger sister Olga.

Yet the tale that he stayed two more years on the Volga to comfort his mother accords ill with the conception of devotion to duty
which he had derived from his father. It fits the facts less than does
the simpler, unsentimental explanation of his slow ripening to the
point where he decided to make revolution his profession. Moreover, only five months after his sister's death, he again asked the
government for a passport to go abroad. What was his purpose?
Health, he told the police; but actually he desired to drink wisdom
at the new source he had just discovered: George Plekhanov and
the Liberation of Labor Group in Switzerland. Permission to go
abroad was denied him.

What the young lawyer was like in the last months when he was
preparing to leave the Volga, on whose banks he had spent his first
twenty-three years, we can deduce from reminiscences of his contemporaries in Samara. "A profound faith in his truthfulness shone
through all his speeches," writes the none-too-friendly Vodovosov.
"Vladimir Ilyich was a stranger to all bohemianism," records
Semenov, a member of his circle in Samara. "In his presence, all of
us restrained ourselves . . . A frivolous conversation, a dirty jest,
were impossible in his presence." And young Samoilov, son of the
liberal justice of the peace of the locality, recounts the impression
Ulyanov made upon him when he visited the Samoilov household:

> When I went to greet the guests, my attention was sud-
> denly attracted by a new figure (brought by Elisarov): at

the table was seated at ease a very thin young man, marked with a lively red on his cheeks, his features somewhat Kalmuck, with sparse mustache and beard which had apparently not yet been in contact with the scissors, faintly touched with copper tint, looking at one out of deepset, lively, mischievous eyes. He spoke little but apparently that did not come from any feeling of being ill at ease in an unknown milieu. . . . On the contrary, I suddenly became aware of the fact that M. T. Elisarov, who ordinarily felt at ease among us, was not exactly upset by the presence of the new guest, but in some way intimidated. . . . In the midst of the conversation, after having made a deduction which seemed to him particularly well taken, he broke out suddenly in a little abrupt laugh, short, quite Russian. It was clear that in him there had just been born a thought, pregnant, piquant, which he had been searching for previously. That little laugh, healthy and not without mischief, emphasized by little wrinkles, equally mischievous, at the corners of his eyelids, remains in my memory. Everyone got ready to laugh, but he was already composed and once more listening to the general conversation, fixing on the speakers his attentive and slightly mocking gaze.

And in Krupskaya's memoirs we read:

Some comrades told me that a certain learned Marxist had arrived from the Volga. Then they brought me an exercise book containing an article *On Markets* which was being passed around for comrades to read in turn. The notebook contained the views of our Petersburg Marxist, the engineer Herman Krassin, and the newcomer from the Volga. The pages were folded in half. On the one side, in a straggling scrawl with many crossings out and insertions, were the opinions of Krassin. On the other side, carefully written and without alterations, were the notes and replies of our newly arrived friend.

CHAPTER VI

THE COMMON SOURCE

> In Marxism there is a sense of fatality, but also the exalta-
> tion of a will. Every time fatality comes before will, I am
> suspicious.   —*Kyo Gisors, in "Man's Fate."*

S UCH WAS Krupskaya's introduction to her future husband. She
was prepared to admire the man as soon as she had seen the
notebook, but a number of months elapsed before she met him in
person.

It was in the spring of 1894, five or six months after his arrival
in the capital, that Nadezhda Konstantinovna [1] met Vladimir Ilyich.
He was twenty-four and she twenty-six. They met at a pancake
party, a traditional holiday festival occurring on Shrove Tuesday
when the orthodox take their last fling with food and merriment
before going into the lean, sad days of Lent. Almost all of the
circle of Petersburg Marxists were there—intellectuals all, for there
was as yet not one workingman amongst these representatives of
the future "party of the proletariat."

The pancake festival maintained barely enough of a carnival
air so that if the police should break in, the celebrants might put
up the requisite show of gayety. The table was spread with the
traditional foods and drinks, but the solemn and unfestive talk
turned around questions of "revolutionary tactics." Nadezhda Konstantinovna could not keep her eyes off the new arrival from Samara.
What she saw was a serious young man with tiny, quizzical, ironic
eyes, a high, boxlike forehead prematurely bald, a solid figure that
was just beginning to grow stocky after a period of adolescent
leanness—unprepossessing enough, but with a quiet air of self-
confidence and self-mastery which she had already sensed in his
notebook.

---

[1] Nadezhda Konstantinovna Krupskaya, that is, Nadezhda, daughter of
Konstantin Krupsky. After her marriage to Lenin her legal name became
Nadezhda Konstantinovna Ulyanova. By those who knew her she was normally addressed, and referred to, by her given name and patronymic, as
Nadezhda Konstantinovna. Her immediate family and closest intimates, including Lenin, called her Nadya. Her first underground name was a nickname Lenin gave her, that of *Mynoga*, the Russian word for lamprey. Then
she switched to the *nom de guerre: Sablina*. In later years she was always
known simply as Krupskaya.

Vladimir Ilyich spoke little and was more occupied in contemplating those present. People who styled themselves Marxists became uncomfortable beneath his fixed gaze. . . . Someone was saying—I think it was Shevlyagin—that what was very important was to work in the Committee for Illiteracy. Vladimir Ilyich laughed, and somehow his laughter sounded laconic. . . . "Well," he said, "if anyone wants to save the fatherland in the Committee for Illiteracy, we won't stop him."

It was the same abrupt laugh that young Samoilov had noted in Samara; the same irreconcilability that Vodovosov had complained of during the famine. Nadezhda, who all her life loved children and untutored workingmen and took joy in teaching them, and who was working ardently in the Committee for Literacy (its proper title), was pleased with his scorn. It seemed to promise shorter and grander roads to the elevation of the masses. His contempt for their efforts to irrigate the desert of popular ignorance with spoonfuls of alphabet soup, completed the admiration that had been inspired by his notebook. His little, watchful eyes, searching the human material before him, must have noted the agreement and admiration showing in the face of the slight, large-eyed, snub-nosed girl, carelessly dressed, with hair cut almost boyishly short, as was the fashion with "emancipated" women. After the party, he walked home with her along the banks of the Neva. The walk is a lovely one; their talk did not make it seem less lovely. She told him about her evening and Sunday classes among the workingmen beyond the Nevsky gate. He spoke to her of his hopes and plans, and of the life and death of his brother Alexander. It was the first she had heard of the tragedy. Such was the beginning of their Marxist courtship.

Nadya was a typical representative of the female radical intelligentsia of the period. Both her parents were of noble birth, but orphans of families that had fallen into decay. Her father, Konstantin Krupsky, had entered the civil service, had risen to the rank of Collegial Assessor and been a provincial official in Russian Poland. There his liberalism took the form of attempting to shield the local population from Alexander III's policy of ruthless Russification. Charges of some sort were preferred against him and he was suspended from office. While his case dragged for ten years from court to court, he picked up his living as best he could as insurance agent, clerk, auditor, factory inspector. In the end, the charges were dismissed for lack of evidence. After his death, mother and daughter eked out the modest widow's pension by giving lessons. Thus her sympathy with the poor and the oppressed and her love of dispensing from her superior share of the world's cultural goods to the more needy, Nadezhda Konstantinovna had absorbed from the experiences of her childhood.

> We lived rather poorly, mother and I—she wrote in her memoirs—on what we could make by letting out rooms, copying work, and the like. Giving lessons took up all my time from morning to night, but all these lessons were but chance windfalls. The only regular work I had was an evening class at the *gymnazia*, but it prevented me from attending meetings and from working in the evening school, so I had to give it up.

This surrender of her one source of steady income in order to be able to give free instruction to the workers in the adult evening schools was typical of the abnegation that characterized her, as it did so many of the declassed nobility and radical intelligentsia. At the tender age of fourteen she had begun to teach. To get "to the people," she determined to become a village school teacher, but could not find a position. "It was only at the age of twenty-one," she wrote, "that I discovered that there was such a thing as social science . . . As soon as I began to understand the part that the workers must play in the emancipation of the working people, I felt an irresistible desire to be among the workers." Thus she became a member of the first Marxist circle in Saint Petersburg, two years before Ulyanov came from Samara. She continued teaching the workingmen common branches in the evening and Sunday schools, but increasingly her interest shifted from the mere spread of culture to making contacts for the Marxist intellectuals.

The Committees for Literacy, the free libraries and the adult education classes were a continuation of the *V Narod* ("to the people") movement of the preceding decades, with this noteworthy difference: that the "people" were now not peasants but workingmen. And with the further difference that among the latter was a readiness to receive the cultural ministrations of the intelligentsia, a deep hunger and thirst for knowledge.

At the end of 1891, when Krupskaya was preparing to join her first Marxist study circle, there were three free libraries in Saint Petersburg. Their readers were mainly skilled workers, artisans and poor students. Men and women trudged to the libraries from great distances, after long hours of labor and hastily bolted evening meals; sometimes they fell asleep in their weariness over books that seemed to promise unheard-of wonders. Most of them were but recently uprooted from the villages, newly freed from subservience to wind and weather and ancient communal tradition. The old rural content faded, but the mind, too, abhors a vacuum. Some, who performed the heavy labor, were likely to fill their few empty moments with drink. Others, generally skilled workers and artisans, stirred by the strange powers of the machines they tended, were beginning to have confidence in new laws of mechanism and power, of cause and effect, of man's dominion over the forces of nature. These drank as thirstily of science as the others of vodka.

Krupskaya's pupils watched their devoted school mistress with unlimited confidence shining from grateful faces. They told her everything. The usually gloomy workingman came beaming with the news that a son had been born to him; the consumptive girl from a textile factory brought her suitor along and demanded that he be made literate before she marry him; a Methodist artisan who had spent his whole life seeking God told her that "only on Passion Sunday had he learned from Rudakov (another pupil) that there was no God at all"; a conservative textile worker, wont to extol priest and Tsar, whispered: "Beware of that dark fellow there, as he's always prowling around on the Gorokhavaya." [2]

On Sunday afternoons Vladimir Ilyich would seek her out after the classes were over, and they would take long walks together. She would tell him what she had learned about conditions in the factories and the mood and outlook of her charges. He would question her minutely and exactingly, or sometimes talk to her of the latest book he was reading or the progress of his own thinking and writing. "Vladimir Ilyich was interested in the minutest detail of the conditions and life of the workers. Taking the features separately he endeavored to grasp the life of the worker as a whole." It was no easy plight this, to believe that the working class was the bearer of the future and yet not be one of them nor have any real knowledge of their lives. Later, Volodya, as she had begun to call him, gave her elaborate written questionnaires to guide her in eliciting information, got her to bring trusted workers home with her for questioning, made one of the chosen ones sweat (as the poor man afterwards recorded), while he plied him with interrogation after interrogation on which to base a leaflet to be distributed in his factory. Then Nadya and some other woman comrades, masquerading in working women's clothes, sought to slip the crudely hectographed leaflets, printed letter by letter in Ulyanov's own hand-lettering, into the workers' hands while shifts were chang-

[2] The name of the street where the headquarters of the tsarist secret police were located. Today men similarly refer to the G.P.U. or M.V.D. by the name of the street Lubyanka.

ing. Or they left them on work benches, in toilets, or wherever else the factory hands might find them. Thus with Krupskaya's aid, did Ulyanov embark on the long course of trying to unite the ideas of socialism with the spontaneously developing labor movement, an effort which was his central preoccupation for the next quarter of a century.

The Literacy Committees of which Ulyanov had been so scornful soon began to absorb much of his attention. The Saint Petersburg committee had about a thousand members. In more backward Moscow it numbered four hundred. They included Narodniks, Marxists, and all shades of democratic, liberal and radical opinion. They established free libraries and reading rooms, compiled bibliographies for popular education, taught common branches to the unlettered, published cheap books for workingmen. Their funds came from donations, dues, lectures, concerts, benefit performances. During the two years of Ulyanov's stay in Saint Petersburg they raised the not inconsiderable sum of 25,000 rubles ($12,000). Members gave their time and their money with no other compensation than that which came from their hope that they might thus serve the people and "redeem" Russia. Ulyanov, despite his scorn for cultural philanthropy, was not slow to see in these committees a cloak for his own activities: a means of getting contact with workingmen and their teachers and learning what these workingmen were really thinking; a means of recruiting a few of the teachers and their most advanced pupils into the Marxist movement; of getting social contacts with well-to-do and friendly disposed liberals. Thus he and his comrades "penetrated" the committees and made of them one of the first of the many "fringe" organizations to which we have since gotten so accustomed in connection with the Communist movement. Its leaders and most active members became the first "innocents," "sympathizers," "fellow-travellers" and "angels."

The most outstanding of these "angels" was Mrs. Kalmykova. She was a friend of Krupskaya's and, like her, had taught in the Sunday school classes in the Nevsky gate district. Her outlook was similar to what Nadezhda's had been before she fell under the spell of Vladimir Ilyich. A woman of wealth and the wife of a high official of the capital, she despised the upper social circles which her wealth and position entitled her to move in.

Mrs. Kalmykova opened a bookshop and publishing house which became the leading center for the distribution of cheap popular books and progressive literature, and, surreptitiously, of underground literature also. Under the wing of her official respectability, radicals foregathered to browse among the books, or engage in hurried conferences in the back rooms. Soon her importance to the underground movement was such that she acquired an alias in their correspondence, being referred to among them as "Auntie." "Auntie" gave generously of her own funds, and collected much more from her acquaintances in Petersburg society. This, too, became important enough to receive a code designation: "the bucket."

After two short years of Social Democratic penetration, the police, who had their spies among the Marxists, closed down the Committee for Literacy. Once more, as in the days of the *V Narod* movement, the efforts of the intelligentsia to share their burden of culture with the masses was thus blocked by the government, and once more some of the most idealistic among them took up a direct struggle with the government. Mrs. Kalmykova was one of these. In 1903, when the Social Democrats split into Bolsheviks and Mensheviks, the news of the split distressed her deeply. She wrote to her friend Vladimir Ilyich, rebuking him for his share in the responsibility for it, telling how it disheartened her, and asking what she should now do with the "bucket"—the funds she was collecting for *Iskra*, which had been the periodical of the united movement. Lenin wrote her two letters in which he sought to justify himself and persuade her to his side of the controversy. Despite her discouragement, she remained a revolutionary sympathizer, returning from long voluntary exile abroad after the Revolution of 1917. Until her death in 1926 she continued a warm and friendly correspondence with Lenin and Krupskaya.

Gradually a number of Nadezhda's workingmen pupils were recruited for secret Marxist study-circle work, under the direction of Vladimir Ilyich. He would read to his little group from a popularization of Marx's *Capital*, interrupting frequently to explain the text, ask elucidating questions, illustrate from Russian examples. Then he would expound orally, without notes, some idea connected with the text they were studying, clinching the application to Russian realities. The second half of the long evening—these Russians were used to late hours in the pursuit of learning—he would devote to answering his auditors' questions, and questioning them in turn about their problems and conditions of work.

> He frequently tried to provoke us to speak or arouse us to start a discussion—wrote the workingman Babushkin [3]—

[3] We are not here dealing with recollection embellished by knowledge of Lenin's subsequent victorious leadership; for Babushkin, one of the first work-

and then he would urge us on, compelling each to demonstrate to the other the correctness of his standpoint on a given question. Thus our lectures were made very animated and interesting, and we began to become accustomed to speaking in public. This mode of study served as an excellent way of clarifying a given question for the students. All of us greatly enjoyed these lectures, and were constantly delighted by our lecturer's power of intellect, it being a standing joke among us that an excess of brains had made his hair fall out. At the same time, these lectures trained us to do independent work, and to find material. The lecturer would hand us lists of questions which required on our part close knowledge and observation of life in the factory and workshop.

These Marxist study-circles, too, were largely attended by intellectuals. The workers who came to them were precious few, but to Ulyanov those few were indeed precious. He saw in them "the future Bebels" who were to lead the Russian working class, the realization of the hope which that same year he expressed in one of his illegally circulated notebooks:

"The role of the intelligentsia is to make special leaders from among the intelligentsia unnecessary."

The future of Russia would in large measure depend upon whether or not, or to what extent, this aim would be realized.

Ulyanov's chief work of the year 1894 was entitled *What Are the Friends of the People and How Do They Fight Against the Social Democrats?* For good measure it bore the subtitle: *Answer to the Articles in* Russkoye Bogatstvo [4] *Against the Marxists.* It circulated in three stout, carefully written yellow notebooks, the first of which he read aloud to the Marxist circle of which he was a member. The notebooks created a remarkable stir in the Marxist microcosm and were soon hectographed and passed from hand to hand anonymously, under the alias of "The Little Yellow Books." In truth, they were far from little; only the first and third parts have come down to us, but these occupy 170 pages in Lenin's *Collected Works.* One can imagine the labor, intellectual, statistical, and physical, which Ulyanov spent in writing all this out in his neat, tiny hand in the manuscript notebooks, and then, all over again, letter by letter according to the printed alphabet, on the hectograph sheets. Here

ingmen Bolsheviks, was shot and killed by General Rennenkampf in Siberia in 1906, when he was caught transporting arms.

[4] *Russkoye Bogatstvo,* "Russian Wealth," was the leading journal of economics, sociology, philosophy and literature. Its editor, N. K. Mikhailovsky (1842-1904), veteran Narodnik and their outstanding theoretical leader, had just opened an ideological crusade against Marxism.

was a warrior of the pen if there ever was one! "How proud we felt," wrote the engineer Krzhizhanovsky [5] "that such a man was marching in our ranks."

This, the first of Lenin's published volumes—or rather, of Ulyanov's, since the man Lenin did not yet exist—is a work of full maturity. In it are his mastery of Marxism, his ability to move familiarly in a maze of statistics and to distinguish the outlines of the basic structure of Russian reality without ignoring the multitudinous complicating detail. About it there is something of the freshness of youth, a bit of brashness, ever so light a touch of dreaming. Here, in germ, are many of Lenin's future deficiencies and weaknesses, but in full flower all his powers and sources of strength.

Unawed by the overpowering prestige of the venerable Mikhailovsky and his distinguished associates, this "presumptuous young man" studies and refutes their objections to Marxism, rectifies with caustic irony their misrepresentation of the views and aims of the Social Democrats, tears to shreds Narodnik theoretical conceptions and practical proposals. To their vagueness and sentimentality he opposes his rigorous exactness, to their wishful idylls his unvarnished description of the facts; the problems they talk around he carefully defines. He expends whole pages on wearisome *argumenta ad hominem;* but the next moment, in no greater scope of pages, he lays bare the skeletal structure of that vast architectural construction, Marx's *Capital,* and disposes easily of objections which have formed, and still form, much of the stock-in-trade of professional Marx-critics.

As the awkward title suggests, there is no concern for adornment. The style is severely logical with an austere attraction where the great generalizations are propounded, didactic in repetitive schoolmaster fashion where ideas are hammered home, applied to instances, drilled in and repeated again and again with only slight variations. It is ill-tempered and scolding, or amused and scornful, where he catches his distinguished opponent in unworthy tricks of polemics. Occasionally it indulges in high good humor, like that of a muzhik laughing at the blown-up words and pretensions of the gentry:

> Yes, Mr. Mikhailovsky, any idea will be too general if you first take all the insides out of it as though it were a dried herring, and then begin to play about with the skin . . .

[5] The *zh* which occurs twice in this, for us, so difficult name, is pronounced like the letter *z* in our word "azure." In the back of the book the reader will find some hints on the transliteration and pronounciation of Russian words.

> The lap dog must be very strong indeed if he barks at the elephant . . .
>
> Apparently he feels very much at ease in this not over-clean position: there he sits preening himself and splashing mud all around him . . .
>
> Naive attempts to make the bourgeois intelligentsia ashamed of being bourgeois remind me of the judgment of the pike which the court condemned to be thrown into the water . . .
>
> They are trying to devise arrangements whereby the wolves can eat themselves full, and the sheep remain uneaten . . .

Such are the simple and homely adornments of style with which the youthful combatant delighted his comrades, though the discriminating among them were more attracted by the austere rigor of the major outlines and the steamroller thoroughness with which the job was accomplished. Vladimir Ilyich was twenty-four years of age when he thus engaged in mortal combat with the great veteran publicist who for more than two decades had dominated progressive thought.

Plekhanov, too, had used his rapier-keen intellect in a duel with Milhailovsky, but he was content with a few thrusts that drew blood and exhibited his own duelist's superiority. Ulyanov preferred rather to go to work on the systematic demolition of the entire thought structure. Before he is finished he seems to have used axe, hammer, saw, chisel, plane, file, sandpaper, and everything else in the tool kit. Plekhanov was too much the intellectual aristocrat and too much the stylist to relish the task of going in detail after all the trivia and absurdities of his opponent. Not so Ulyanov.

"George [Plekhanov] is a greyhound," Vera Zasulich was later to tell Lenin. "He shakes and shakes his adversary, then lets go. But you, you are a bulldog; you have a deadly bite."

"A deadly bite, eh?" he repeated to her with evident pleasure.

The intellectual war between Marxists and populists (Narodniki) was really a battle between two rival varieties of socialism. Populism was the older and more indigenous, having arisen out of the "To the People" (V Narod) movement of the Russian intelligentsia. It was Russia's own native variety of socialism: a humanitarian, agrarian socialism, which pronounced with reverence the sacred word: people—meaning thereby not just city workers but primarily the vast majority of the Russian people: the muzhiks. It had preceded Marxism by several decades. Its leaders had translated and helped to popularize Marx's works, respected them as a powerful scientific critique of Western capitalism, but, still and all, a Western importation, not fully applicable to non-capitalist Russia.

More than either of the two contendants realized, they were complementary to each other, rather than irreconcilable rivals, since the populists based themselves upon the rural masses, the Social Democrats on the urban. Never could there be a truly democratic transformation of Russia unless these two classes should join forces in mutual and equal partnership, and, without either imposing itself upon the other. Since neither peasants nor workers were as yet stirring in response to the cries and conjurations hurled at them by the revolutionary intelligentsia, the actual struggle was not between those two classes, but between two little, all-or-nothing groups of intellectuals who were fighting for exclusive domination of the soul of the Russian intelligentsia, one trying to direct its attention to the working class, the other to the peasantry. Hence the ups and downs of the two tendencies coincided directly with the degree of stir in city and village. Whenever the peasants cut down forests, burned manor houses, drove out landlords or local authorities, as they had done for a decade before and a decade after the Emancipation of 1861, the hope of the intelligentsia in the peasantry flamed high, and the Narodnik movement became active and revolutionary. But for three decades, now, the village had been sullenly silent. It was despair at that passivity, even more than government brutality, which had driven the Narodniki to try individual terror. And, more than the police raids, it was the same despair which snuffed out the flame of the Narodnaya Volya in the eighties. What was left of populism became abstract and feeble and academically respectable.

Just at that moment, came the first great wave of industrial strikes of the middle nineties, turning the ever-hopeful attention of the Russian intelligentsia to the cities and the urban working class. The excitement caused by the great strike-wave was the emotional force that gave victory to the theoretical arguments of Plekhanov and his disciples, turning the attention of the entire younger generation, to which Ulyanov belonged, toward Marxism and Social Democracy. With characteristic Russian fanaticism, they excluded the peasantry from their thinking as a driving force of revolution.

Yet, early in the twentieth century, the village would awaken once more. Then the so-often routed Narodnik movement would rise again, phoenix-like, from its ashes, as the new Social Revolutionary Party. It would continue to grow in influence until, in 1917, its candidates for the Constituent Assembly would get 21,000,000 votes to the Bolsheviks' 9,000,000—indeed, a much larger vote than Bolshevik and Menshevik Social Democrats put together.

It was the doctrinaire, secretarian character of Russian disputation which turned these two groups, who might have been allies, into embittered enemies. Their theoretical controversy turned about this question: must Russia follow the course that the Western European nations have followed—from feudalism, through capitalism, and only then to socialism? Or might not Russia follow another road: from feudalism, by a "non-capitalist path," directly into post-capitalist socialism?

To answer this question it was necessary to know how long tsarism would last. More important, it was necessary to appraise the character of the peasant mind, and to estimate the nature and prospects of that peculiar Russian institution: the communal village or *mir*. The Narodniks contended that the communal village was "primitively socialist" in character and psychology, that it inculcated in its members the spirit of continuous redivision of property, of equality and fraternity, of collectivism and corporate feeling. The peasant mind, they held, was thus elementally or naively socialist, and well adapted—better even than the mind of the Western proletariat—to grasping the ideas and spirit of socialism. On the village *mir*, and the ideology it engendered, the Narodniks based their hopes that Russia might avoid the pangs of capitalism, and, shaking off the remnants of feudalism and absolutism, might build a socialist, free Russia. Was there an "iron law" which decreed that Russia must adopt a capitalism which was already showing its evils in the Western world? Or might not Holy Russia—the old messianic dream—from the last become the first, leading the whole world and showing it the way out of Western capitalism to a better and more humane order?

To these theoretical considerations, the Russian Marxists answered by making a banner of the name of Marx. They appealed to the schemata of Marx's *Capital*, which, they believed, "demonstrated scientifically" that all lands must "inevitably" go through the various stages from feudalism, through capitalism, to socialism. Moreover, was not industrial capitalism already developing with giant strides in Russia? Was not the village *mir* doomed? Was it not even then disintegrating into a "capitalist village"—extruding two new social classes: a landless, village "proletariat" and a rich-peasant, "capitalist farmer" class, or "village bourgeoisie"? This was the whole polemical point of young Ulyanov's first major theoretical work, his monumental *Development of Capitalism in Russia*. His examination of the real statistical trends of Russian economic development, an examination which was soon to win the admiration of all Russian Marxists, tended to prove that Russia was already taking giant strides along the path of capitalism, in agriculture, in industry and in trade.

But, most important of all—according to Lenin and his co-religionists—the mind of the Russian peasant was not "naively socialist" at all: but "naively bourgeois," or rather, "petty bourgeois," the mind of a small proprietor on-the-make. It was this distrust of, and unconscious antagonism toward, the peasant majority of the Russian nation which would, in the end, sterilize all Marxist protestations in favor of democracy. For, how can you have democracy where there is no trust in the majority of those who make up the nation?

Thus, with their characteristic thoroughness and abandon did the Russian Marxists unite statistical facts, theoretical logic, and temperament, to answer the over-all question concerning Russia's destiny. Yes, said they, Russia is fatally and inevitably destined to pass through the valley of the shadow of capitalism on its way to the heights of socialism! Moreover, such capitalism will be a step forward in Russia's march, a "progressive" development, both in that it will raise the productive powers of the nation and in that it will create an industrial working class or proletariat, which alone can be trusted and depended upon to develop a socialist ideology.

It is interesting to note that this view of those calling themselves Russian Marxists or Social Democrats was not necessarily the view of Karl Marx himself concerning Russia's "inevitable path." On the contrary, had he had to take his chances as a Russian in the midst of the Russian controversy, without the aura of authority that surrounded his name, he might well have been condemned by his Russian disciples as an indifferent and wavering Marxist, if not worse. In the last years of his life, he began to study the difficult Russian tongue, chiefly for the purpose of seeking light on this specific theoretical question, and he never could quite make up his mind as to which of the two alternative paths Russia was more likely to take. In 1877, he had written to a Russian magazine (*Notes on the Fatherland*) a letter in which he spoke of Russia's having "the best opportunity that history has ever offered to a people to escape all the catastrophes of capitalism." In 1881, only two years before his death, he had written to Vera Zasulich, associate of Plekhanov:

> The analysis given in *Das Kapital* offers no arguments either for or against the vitality of the rural commune

(*mir*), but the special study I have made of it . . . has convinced me that this commune is the *point d'appui* for the social regeneration of Russia. However, in order that it may function as such, it would be necessary first to remove the deleterious influences which are attacking it from all sides, and then to insure it the normal conditions of a spontaneous development.

And a year later, when he and Engels were called upon by Vera Zasulich to supply an introduction to her new Russian translation of the *Communist Manifesto*, they wrote:

In Russia, alongside the capitalist system (which is growing up with feverish speed) and the bourgeois landowning system (which is in its early stages of development), more than half the land is owned in common by the peasantry. The question we have to answer is: Will the Russian peasant communes (a primitive form of communal ownership which is already on the downgrade) become transformed into the superior form of communist ownership of land, or will they have to pass through the same process of decay we have witnessed in the course of the historical evolution of the West?

There is only one possible answer to this question. If the Russian revolution sounds the signal for a workers' revolution in the West, so that each becomes the complement of the other, then the prevailing form of communal ownership of land in Russia may serve as the starting-point for a communist course of development.

All these passages come at least as close to the hopes of the Russian Narodniki as they do to the asseveration concerning Russia's "inevitable path" made by those who called themselves Marxists and invoked Marx's name. Ten years after the latter's death, in 1893, his friend Engels drily refused to offer "authoritative opinions" on these Russian disputations:

If you have followed the writings of the Russian exiles during the last ten years, you will know yourself how the various groups among them interpret passages from Marx's writings and letters in the most contradictory ways, just as if they were texts from the classics or the New Testament. And anything I could say on the question you propounded to me would probably be used in a similar way, if any attention were paid to it. (Letter to I. A. Hourwich.)

It is noteworthy that, from the time they first became aware of the revolutionary movement in Russia until the day of their respective deaths, Marx and Engels held that revolutionary terror had a special justification in Russia, and that both the Narodnik and Social Democratic (Plekhanovist) movements were entitled to consideration as legitimate expressions of the needs of revolution in Russia. When Plekhanov published his *Our Differences*, Engels wrote to express his approval of the contents but his dislike of the intolerant attacks on the revolutionary wing of Narodniki, "the only people who are doing anything in Russia at present." And to Vera Zasulich he explained that it was immaterial which sect might set a revolution going for which every condition, material and psychological, was present. He was pleased that the Marxists accepted so much of his and Marx's doctrine, but he never ceased to disapprove of their relegating the courageous and revolutionary Narodniks to the lake of fire and brimstone "with other reactionaries." It might be that the Narodniks were prone to believe some fairytales concerning Russia's future, but they were superior to the Social Democrats in their positive activity and in their awareness of the importance of the agrarian problem and of the vast peasant population.

In the spring of 1892, Engels actually arranged a meeting in his home in London between the leaders of the two groups among the Russian socialist refugees, in order to unite Narodniks and self-proclaimed Marxists into a single party. But, what with the ardor of the Russian temperament in controversy, and the diffidence of Engels to intervene in a dictatorial manner, the plan fell through. Yet to Engels it seemed that it had failed only because these sectarians lived in the bitter "night of exile," in isolation from a mass movement. Thus his last word on the Russian question was a gently urgent plea for the unification of the Russian Marxists and the Russian populists, or, as they would later call themselves, the Social Democrats and the Social Revolutionaries. But, after his death, his name and Marx's were used as lance and pennant to smite the Social Revolutionaries. Not until the year 1914 did Lenin's old teacher, Plekhanov, seriously propose the unification of the two groups into a single movement. But by then it was too late, for the differences had gained enormous organizational and emotional momentum. As for Lenin himself, he would have no part of such unity.

Both Narodniks and Russian Marxists, then, were critical of capitalism, but with a fundamental difference. The Narodniks hoped that its "pitiless laws" could be avoided for Russia. "We have not yet seen anything good in Western capitalism," wrote Mikhailovsky. But the Marxists not only predicted a capitalist path for Russian development; they even regarded such a development as "progressive."

"Objectively" you are really apologists for capitalism, charged the Narodniks. You call it progressive, you get enthusiastic over every step in its infiltration of Russia, you celebrate its cruel triumphs. You need it so that you may have your proletariat, and you do not seem to care whether that involves the destruction of the village *mir*, the dispossessing of the peasants, their ruin and proletarianization.

"Objectively" you are no socialists at all, responded the Social Democrats. You glorify Russia's backwardness. You conceal from yourselves the fact that capitalism has already set in and is ruining the *mir* and sowing class differences in the countryside. You base your program upon the real or fancied needs of the peasants, who are not socialists but petty bourgeois. You want to defend the small producer against expropriation. Objectively you are the party of petty-bourgeois democracy and not a socialist party at all.

> The socialist ought to break *decisively and finally* with all petty-bourgeois ideas and theories—*that is the most important and useful lesson*—is Lenin's political conclusion from the chain of reasoning we have been outlining—. I ask you to note also that I am speaking of the necessity of a break with the petty-bourgeois ideas of socialism. The petty-bourgeois ideas I have examined are *unconditionally* reactionary *insofar* as they masquerade as socialist theories.
>
> But if we understand that there is really not the least bit of socialism about them, that really all these theories reflect and represent the interest of the small bourgeoisie, then we must have another attitude toward them. Then we ought put the question: *What attitude should the working class take toward the petty bourgeoisie and their program?* . . .
>
> This class is progressive insofar as it makes general democratic demands, i.e. fights against every remnant of medievalism and serfdom. It is reactionary insofar as it fights for the preservation of its position as a petty bourgeoisie, seeking to hold back, even turn backward, the general development of the country in the direction of capitalism. These two sides of the petty-bourgeois program should be sharply distinguished from each other and, while we must deny any socialist character whatsoever to these theories and fight against their reactionary aspects, we must not forget their democratic side . . . The rejection by the Marxists of these petty-bourgeois theories does not in the slightest exclude democracy from their [the Marxist] pro-

gram. [Lenin: *Collected Works,* Third Russian Edition, Vol. I, pp. 183-4. Emphasis, as throughout this book, in the original.]

Thus Ulyanov asserts that he does not want to destroy the Narodniki at all, only to put them in their proper place and force them to recognize that they are "not a socialist, but a petty-bourgeois democratic party." They attack Russian Marxism as he understands it, hence he refutes them. They term themselves socialist, hence he exposes them. They misjudge the peasant to be "naively socialist"; he insists that the peasant is a "naive petty bourgeois." They venture to include the working class in their general term, *narod,* "the people," hence he fights them; for only Social Democracy should have any right to appeal to the proletariat. Any other party seeking to trespass in that exclusive domain should be pitilessly denounced and forcibly ousted as an interloper. Yet, because the working class, too, needs democratic freedoms for its purposes, he would like to have an alliance with the Narodniki (once he has put them in their proper place), an alliance in a common struggle for democracy.

> The Social Democrats naturally regard the creation of such a democratic party as a useful step forward, and our activity against Narodnikism is intended to help in this, to contribute to the overcoming of all prejudices and myths, to the gathering of the socialists under the banner of Marxism and to the founding of a democratic party by the remaining groups . . . [It is] the direct duty of the working class to separate from this general democratic movement in order to organize a socialist labor party of its own . . . and then, to fight side by side with the radical democracy against absolutism and the reactionary estates.

All the Petersburg Marxists applauded the polemic of the young Marxist from the Volga. Soon young men and women of Vladimir's generation, and some who were considerably older, began to refer to this bald-headed young man of twenty-four as *Starik—*"The Old Man." They began to regard him as a *primus inter pares,* one of the first in a society of equals (there was no infallible-leader cult in those days), and the shadow he cast lengthened slowly over other parts of Russia. There was as yet no sign of the differences which would one day divide the Social Democrats themselves into angry and hostile factions. All were agreed in disputing with the Narodniki for leadership over the workers, which in practice meant no more than disputing for leadership over the revolutionary intelligentsia; sufficiently to direct the latter's gaze from the peasantry to the working class.

The "peasant socialist" movement did not end with the polemic of the nineties. The police thought they had put an end to it when they destroyed the Narodnaya Volya in 1883. Now the Marxists defeated its attenuated shadow in the nineties in theoretical disputations. Convinced by the continued quiescence in the village, by the giant strides which Russian industry was making in the cities, and by the first big wave of labor strikes, the whole younger generation let itself be persuaded by the arguments of the Marxists. But then, early in the twentieth century, the peasantry began to stir once more: riots, manor-house burnings, clashes with officials and police—and the ghost of peasant socialism arose from its ashes, mightier than ever, in the shape of the Social Revolutionary Party (founded in 1903). All through the first two decades of the new century—until 1917—the struggle between the "Westernizer" Social Democrats and the "Slavophile" Social Revolutionaries continued. Then suddenly, the same issues took on new and unexpected forms as a conflict between two wings of the Marxist Social Democrats: the Bolsheviks and the Mensheviks. The Social Revolutionary Party, too, split in the year, 1917, the larger branch allying itself with the Menshevik and the smaller with the Bolshevik Social Democrats.

For what was the theory behind Lenin's seizure of power in November, 1917, if not a new version of the theory that Russia (if aided by anticipated revolutions in the West) might leap over capitalism and follow a peculiar non-capitalistic path to industrialization and socialism? The village communal *mir,* too, was still there to build upon; its "naive peasant socialism," its primitive collectivist and corporate ideology, was used by the Bolsheviks to good advantage. The *mir* had not disintegrated as fast as the Marxists had anticipated, because its ancient roots were too deep in the Russian soil and because the tsarist government itself had kept it alive as a convenient unit for exacting collective responsibility for taxes.

If the Narodniki had underestimated the growing importance of the proletariat, the Marxists—deceived by the three decades of miserable quiescence in the countryside—had underestimated the revolutionary potential that was accumulating once more in the Russian village. But Lenin, almost alone of the Social Democrats, was to correct this underestimation early enough and completely enough to utilize that peasant discontent in 1917 for his purposes.

In the polemic we have been discussing Ulyanov assured the Narodniki that as "peasant socialists" they were really only petty-bourgeois democrats. Their views, he told them, "objectively led" to democratic capitalism, and once that was achieved these same views would "inevitably force them" to become opponents of socialism. This to men who sympathized with the lot of all the oppressed and exploited! To men who loved freedom, detested tyranny and bondage, abominated all forms of exploitation, not excluding the capitalist form to which, according to Ulyanov, their view "objectively led." Brashly, Ulyanov insisted that their "subjective desires" could be discounted, that he possessed an infallible science which enabled him to predict whither their wishes "objectively led."

But the discounting of subjective desires is a strange way of apprehending a historical process which is first of all a clash of subjective desires, a conflict of wills. And a clash in which the will of no single man or group ever wins through, be that man or group ever so great, or ever so sure that his will is based upon the most scientific analysis of history's possible or inevitable paths.

"People who imagined that they had made a revolution—Engels once wrote to Vera Zasulich—always saw next day that they did not know what they had been doing, and that the revolution which they made was nothing like the one they had wanted to make."

Suppose Lenin could look back now upon the subsequent career of the Narodniki and their successors, the Social Revolutionaries. To be sure, he might point out that from their ranks had come a number who would make their peace with capitalism. But so did the ranks of the Marxists beget such men in no less profusion. What he could never have foreseen in the nineties is the startling fact that in 1917 he would find it necessary to part company with all other Marxists groupings, but would form a coalition government precisely with the dissident wing of these "petty-bourgeois peasant revolutionaries"—the Left-Wing Social Revolutionary Party! Clearly, both in the Marxist camp and in the peasant socialist camp, subjective intention, subjective desire and will, in short, revolutionary temperament, would prove far more important than abstract formulae. And the actual formulae Lenin would act upon would turn out to be a peculiar fusion of elements of Narodnikism and Russian Marxism, while Bolshevism itself would take on aspects of Slavophile socialism.

The government Lenin was to set up was to call itself the Dictatorship of the Proletariat. But the leading organizations of the proletariat, the powerful trade unions, would oppose his seizure of power, while the land-hungry peasants, above all the peasant-in-uniform, the peasant-under-arms, would assure victory to his side. So would history turn out differently from that which the most self-assured "scientific analysis" and the most rigorous "objective logic" had predicted.

Was the peasant, as the Narodniks thought, an exploited toiler and a primitive socialist? Was his land-hunger the longing for security and the love of the soil which he must possess and till in order to live?

Or was he, as the Marxists thought, first of all a small proprietor, a petty bourgeois, an owner or would-be owner of property, longing to possess it *in extenso* and to exploit as many workers as possible upon it?

The Marxists in Russia, Bolsheviks as well as Mensheviks, tended to look upon the Russian peasantry with distrust and suspicion. Having set him down as a petty bourgeois, unconsciously the Marxist workingmen looked upon him as a potential enemy. Hence it became easy in Soviet Russia for the Bolshevik workingmen to sanction the use of force against the peasant majority and the use of police overseers over them: first to requisition grain and stop "profiteering" or private trading, then to police the planting and the harvesting and the marketing of the crops, then to marshal them in droves into the collective farms. But this same peasantry was really the overwhelming majority of the Russian people, so that to sanction a police overseership over them would inevitably exclude the possibility of democracy—in the simple sense of government of, for and by the majority of the people.[6] And a police apparatus huge enough to police the planting and harvesting all over vast, rural Russia, would it not tend to spill over into the very organizations of the advanced city workers who had sanctioned it: into their state, their unions and their party?

But none of this could be foreseen by either side in 1894. No man could know then whither this controversy "objectively led," when such Marxists as Plekhanov, Ulyanov and Struve, of the older and younger generations, joined forces for a victorious counter-offensive against the hitherto dominant, indigenous peasant socialism of the Narodniki.

[6] There are many forms and degrees of democracy but all include control of political and economic apparatus by the people, and not the reverse. Totalitarianism is not "just another form" of democracy any more than kicking over the checker board is "just another way of playing checkers."

CHAPTER VII

LEGAL MARXISM

Alekseev: If we go and ask for a rise in pay, they accuse us of making a strike, and they banish us to Siberia. That means we are still serfs. If the employers turn us out, and we ask for an account of wages due, they call out the soldiers . . . That means we are still serfs. We can look to no one to help us except the young intellectuals—

Judge: Silence!

Alekseev (shouting): But they will march with us until the day comes when a million sturdy workmen clench their fists—

Judge: Silence, I say. Silence!

Alekseev (shouting still louder): And despotism will be pounded to dust.

THE POLICE were by no means displeased by the strife between Marxists and populists. To them it was a simple case of "when thieves fall out." Still shuddering at the memory of the terrorists of the Nardonaya Volya, who had slain one Tsar and besieged another in his palace, the police tended to "sympathize" with the more academic and less dangerous-seeming Marxists.

That very year, 1894, in which Ulyanov's "Little Yellow Books" against the Narodniks were spreading painfully through the underground by hectograph, Peter Struve, another young Marxist of the same age as Ulyanov, tried submitting to the censors an academically phrased treatise against the Narodniks. To the astonishment of author and public, the police gave their approval to Struve's *Critical Notes on the Problem of the Economic Development of Russia.* With that, "legal Marxism" became a reality.

The same year, one Beltov submitted a work more openly Marxist, *Toward the Development of the Monistic Conception of History.* It, too, passed the censor. The writing had a familiar ring:

"I am a worm," says the idealist.
"I am a worm," says the materialist dialectician, "so long as I am ignorant. I am a god, when I know. *Tantum possumus, quantum scimus.*"

118

With great excitement, the Marxists recognized the slashing style of Plekhanov, who had been in exile abroad since 1881. The entire edition sold out in three weeks. It created as much of a sensation as would today the legal publication in Soviet Russia of a book *against* dialectical materialism. With these two works, the police had made Marxism respectable: the honeymoon of "legal Marxist" literature had begun.

Reviews and journals of Marxist trend sprang up in capital and provinces, carefully edited with one eye on Marx and the other asquint at the censor. Students, professors, members of the social elite, who but yesterday had called themselves liberals or humanitarians or Narodniks, began to flaunt the new, fashionable banner. Marx's *Capital* and *The Communist Manifesto* had always enjoyed great popularity among the Narodniks, having received their first Russian translation before they had been done into any other language. But now they were displayed in best-selling editions.

Finding Marxism a salable and distinguished commodity, publishers contracted for translations of the classics and of contemporary German and French Marxist books. They even offered advances for original works. To pass the censor these had to be couched in academic phrases; they had to be fat volumes (no pamphlets were tolerated); they had to avoid using language of battle or practical action. It was easier to get past the censor a whole volume which bombarded the Narodniki with statistics and formulae, than to say a single direct word of praise for their revolutionary struggle against autocracy. One might prove that the old agrarian village commune was destined to extinction, that capitalism was inevitable in Russia, that it was actually developing according to the general laws laid down by Marx, that as against feudalism it was a progressive force, that it brought into being new, progressive classes: the bourgeoisie and the proletariat. But one could not be too explicit on the fact that these new classes could only realize their destinies by uniting in a revolutionary struggle against feudal absolutism.

In common with the other Marxists, Ulyanov was pleased at this sudden break-through into legality. Yet, almost alone among them, he felt more uneasy than pleased. He at once began to work on a "legal Marxist book" and laid plans for a legal journal. But at the same time he began a polemic against the one-sided, non-revolutionary "reflection of Marxism in bourgeois literature," i.e. the dilution of its revolutionary content by its effort to maintain legality and pass the censors. And he redoubled his own efforts to reach the workers with the "illegitimate" portion of the Marxist message, multiplying the leaflets produced by pen and hectograph, casting about for means of acquiring or setting up an underground printing plant, for smuggling publications from abroad, for developing an underground newspaper.

At the end of that same year, with Peter Struve present in a Marxist circle to which they both belonged, Ulyanov entered into a sharp criticism of the latter's new book. He felt that Struve had been too easily carried away by enthusiasm for the expansion of capitalist industry. What angered Ulyanov most, however, was the fact that the book contained a first Russian example of what was later to be known as Marx-revisionism. According to Struve, Marx had "at times" thought of the collapse of capitalism as something abrupt and catastrophic, but "modern Marxists" thought of it not as a sudden revolution but as a gradual transition, through a series of reforms. "Reforms," retorted Ulyanov, "are not to be contrasted to revolution. The struggle for reforms is but a means of marshalling the forces of the proletariat for the struggle for a final revolutionary overthrow." This negative attitude toward improvements in the prevailing system remains to this day a distinguishing feature of all Communist parties.

To satisfy the requirements of the cenorship, and to prevent a break between himself and such "legal Marxists" as Struve, Ulyanov softened his critique somewhat when he sought to have it published legally as a lengthy review-article under the title: *The Economic Content of Populism and Its Critique in the Book of Mr. Struve. (The Reflection of Marxism in Bourgeois Literature.) In Reference to "Critical Remarks on the Question of the Economic Development of Russia," by P. Struve, Saint Petersburg, 1894.* Rather a sizable title for a book review! But the review itself is long enough to dwarf the title: it occupies 139 pages in Volume I of the Russian edition of Lenin's *Collected Works.*

It was the longest of a half-dozen or so essays intended for legal publication, as a symposium by leading Marxists, mostly using pseudonyms. The symposium, edited by Potresov, a friend of Lenin's, bore the general title: *Documents Concerning the Problem of the Economic Development of Russia.* Ulyanov signed his critique of Struve with the pen name of K. *Tulin.* Other contributors to the work were Plekhanov, Potresov, and, of course, Struve. Despite all the precautions taken, the police, guided by a spy or by a sensitive nose, detected the odor of brimstone from the Plutonic underground and confiscated the entire edition of two thousand copies. But a few dozen extra copies were "stolen" from the printing plant.

In the spring of 1895, after a severe case of pneumonia, Ulyanov again applied for permission to go abroad "for his health." This time it was granted. He took with him copies of the proscribed book as gifts for the leaders of the Group for the Emancipation of Labor in Switzerland, contact with which was the real object of his trip. Here is the account which Paul Axelrod has written of it in his memoirs:

> He introduced himself: "Vladimir Ulyanov. I have just come from Russia. George Valentinovich (Plekhanov), in Geneva, sends his greetings." The young man gave me a rather thick book . . . We talked about the situation in Russia and then the young man got up and said politely, "If you will permit, I shall come tomorrow to continue our conversation."
>
> During the night I looked through the volume . . . My attention was arrested by a long article by Tulin, whose name I was seeing for the first time. The article made an excellent impression . . . It was not very well constructed, perhaps even careless. But one felt in it a temperament and the fire of the spirit of battle; one felt that for the author Marxism was not an absolute doctrine but a weapon in the revolutionary struggle . . . But there were some tendencies in Tulin's article with which I could not agree . . .
>
> Next morning Ulyanov returned: "Have you looked at the symposium?"
>
> "Yes. And I must say I got great pleasure from it. At last there has awakened in Russia real revolutionary social democratic thought. The article by Tulin made a particularly good impression—"
>
> "That is my pseudonym," said the visitor.
>
> Then I explained where I did not agree with him. "You show," I said, "exactly the opposite tendency to the one expressed in the article I had prepared for the same symposium. [Axelrod did not finish it on time because of illness.] You identify your attitude towards the liberals with the attitude of the socialists towards the liberals in the West. And I . . . wanted to show that in the given historic moment the immediate interests of the Russian proletariat coincide with the vital interests of the other progressive elements of society . . . Both face the same urgent problem . . . the overthrow of absolutism . . ."
>
> Ulyanov smiled and observed: "You know, Plekhanov made exactly the same remarks about my articles. He expressed his thought in picturesque fashion: 'You,' he said, 'turn your behind to the liberals, but we our face.' . . ."

Thus early did his two mentors sense a difference in attitude towards liberals, democrats and other "allies" in the struggle against absolutism, in the young man who offered himself as a respectful, even worshipful disciple. Otherwise Axelrod found his visitor "a modest, businesslike, serious young man, without the slightest vanity." He felt sure that he and Plekhanov had instructed their disciple on his error and had convinced him of his need of correcting it. Ulyanov did indeed appear to defer for the next decade to these veteran leaders and their approach, but psychologically he was inclined to be of the same opinion still. Thus, in 1899, in a letter to Potresov, he ventures to criticize Axelrod for having written of "support for and alliance with" the democratic opposition to tsarism. "In my opinion," wrote Ulyanov, "*utilize* is a much more accurate and appropriate word than *support and alliance*." This attitude toward "allies"—the determination to "utilize" them rather than to give them mutual support and genuine alliance—remained a characteristic Leninist view for the rest of his life. And today, as in the past, it is a distinguishing feature of every united front or alliance entered into by any of the Communist parties.

In the course of the next five years, the "Legal Marxists," with Struve and Tugan-Baranowsky as spokesmen, actually went through the evolution which the young Ulyanov had so brilliantly sensed and foreseen: from demonstration of the inevitability and progressiveness of capitalism in Russia to apologetics and glorification; from a bowdlerized Marxism cut to measure for the censor as a matter of reluctant necessity, to a castrated Marxism robbed of its revolutionary vigor; and finally, to open opposition to Marxism. This early success as a prophet served to confirm the deep self-confidence of this "serious young man." In 1907, when Ulyanov had become Lenin, and was growing used to leading his own faction against all the old veterans at once, he would write:

> The old controversy with Struve furnishes an instructive example of the practical value of being uncompromising in theoretical controversy . . . It was useful to consider the situation as it was ten years ago, from what minor theoretical differences with Struvism as then visible—minor at first glance—the complete political demarcation of the Party has come about . . .

The closing words of Struve's book of 1894 had been: "Let us confess our lack of culture, and turn to capitalism for instruction." At the time, those words had infuriated Lenin. But a quarter-

century later, when he was head of the Russian state, striving to
combat economic inexperience, incapacity and chaos, he was to
use, word for word, exactly the same words!

Vladimir Ilyich spent four months in Western Europe during
the spring and summer of 1895. In Germany, he tried out his book-
learned German with disastrous results. ("I do not understand even
the simplest words—their pronunciation is unusual and they talk so
fast. I ask the conductor a question—he answers; I do not understand. He repeats his answer louder. I still do not understand; he
gets angry and goes away.") He made the personal acquaintance
of Karl Kautsky, editor of *Die Neue Zeit,* and his chief living idol
after Plekhanov and the aging Engels. He swam daily in the Spree,
took long walks about Berlin, spent as many hours as possible in
the *Koenigliche Bibliothek,* yielded to "the temptation to buy too
many books" and had to send twice to his mother for additional
funds. Among his most cherished purchases was the third volume
of Marx's *Capital,* just issued by Engels from Marx's posthumous
notes.

In France, as was characteristic of educated nineteenth-century
Russians, he understood the spoken language somewhat better. He
fell in love with Paris ("wide light streets, many boulevards, much
greenery"), piously sought out Marx's son-in-law, the socialist
leader Jean Longuet. In Switzerland he held long conversations
with Plekhanov, Vera Zasulich, and above all Axelrod, promised to
report to them regularly, laid plans for setting up an organization
in their name inside Russia, and for smuggling in their writings.
He yielded to the charm of the Swiss mountains and lakes, took a
cure for "my tiresome stomach trouble"—apparently a species of
colitis complicated by a "nervous stomach" whenever he was under
great strain—tramped the hills near Zurich with Axelrod, listening,
questioning, talking himself out.

"I must say," wrote Axelrod years later, after he had come to
detest Lenin, "that these discussions with Ulyanov were like a real
festival. Even now I remember them as one of the happiest moments in the life of the Group for the Emancipation of Labor."

Since 1883 these exiles had waited in Geneva in loneliness and
isolation; now their long effort promised to bear living fruit inside
the land which they longed to serve and transform.

Ulyanov took all manner of precautions, or at least so he thought,
but when he returned from abroad with his false-bottomed trunk
stuffed with illegal literature, the police rapped on the trunk while
his heart rapped at his throat. Then they let it through inviolate

and they detailed "shadows" to follow him and his baggage their separate ways. Apparently, Russian spies abroad had reported on his movements.

"Look," a cousin of Nadezhda Konstantinovna's heard a detective boast in the address bureau where she worked, "we've tracked down the important state criminal Ulyanov—his brother was hanged —he's just come from abroad but he won't escape us now."

Despite these suspicions, the "important state criminal" visited Moscow, Vilna and other nearby towns, to make contacts for the Union for the Emancipation of Labor. For the first time the veteran émigrés received reports from Russia and began to feel that they at last had the beginnings of an organization in the homeland.

The autumn of 1895 saw the first great wave of strikes in Saint Petersburg. Fat Marxist books were one thing to the police, and strikes another. They had not yet come to the idea of "legal" or "police unionism" which might keep the workers' wrath directed at the employers and deflected from the throne. That idea would come later.

Ulyanov, the like-minded Martov—who had learned to work in the labor movement within the Jewish pale—and some of their associates, now tried to inject themselves into the strike movement. They were the "party of the working class" but how could they make these striking workers aware of it? Vladimir's sweetheart, Nadezhda Konstantinovna, was of help to him now, thanks to the workingmen she had taught in the classes of the Committee for Literacy. With a vague feeling that he was being shadowed and working against time, Vladimir Ilyich cross-questioned the few workers he could get to, elicited facts concerning their grievances, drew up leaflets laboriously in his own hand with printed letters on the hectograph, or had them copied by hand in total editions of three or four copies. A few of his and Martov's leaflets were even printed in a secret printing plant of the Narodovoltsi. Apparently these were more friendly to the Marxists and the working class than accorded with Ulyanov's hostile analysis.

Of four copies of a leaflet distributed by the workingman Babushkin in the Semmyanikov works, two were seized by a foreman, but the other two passed surreptitiously from hand to hand. Next the women in the Laferme tobacco factory, the men and women in Thornton's textile works and the metal workers in the Putilov plant learned that there was such a thing as a "Petersburg League of Struggle for the Emancipation of the Working Class" which seemed interested in them, was informed about their needs,

knew how to express these in simple leaflets and link them up with
a vaguer, grander struggle for socialism and freedom.

At the same time, Ulyanov turned out two simple, repetitive,
didactic pamphlets: *On Fines* and *On the New Labor Laws*. Hand
in hand with the experienced young Jewish agitator Martov, he
sought to link all the dispersed study circles that were reading
Marx with the "League of Struggle for the Emancipation of the
Working Class," and to gather material for a paper to be called
The Workers' Cause.

All through the autumn, while these modest plans were matur-
ing, his sense of being spied upon continued to grow. To this problem, too, he turned his businesslike attention. He imparted to his
comrades his pitiful store of conspirative technique, which he had
acquired by interrogating the veterans of the Narodnaya Volya in
Samara. He showed them how to employ secret codes; how to put
names and addresses into cipher; how to mix invisible ink; how to
send messages in innocent volumes by putting tiny dots inside
letters which, sought out and combined, grew into words and sentences; how to paste letters inside the bindings of books; how to
use houses with through courtyards as a means of getting rid of
one's "shadow." Even to the veteran Axelrod in Zurich he wrote
detailed instructions:

> Add a crystal of potassium bichromate—$K_2Cr_2O_7$—to the
> ink; use thinner paper; use liquid paste, not more than a
> teaspoonful of starch to a glass of water, and potato flour,
> the ordinary flour is too strong . . .

All this seemed very wonderful to his associates. Among the most
attentive of his auditors was a "Marxist" dentist, Dr. Mikhailov,
who dutifully passed on all he learned to his superiors in the police
department.

December found *The Workers' Cause* ready to go to press, with
most of its articles written by the indefatigable Ulyanov. It was
to be printed by the underground press of his friendly enemies, the
Narodovoltsi. Two proofs were pulled, and sent to two different
addresses. One was carefully corrected by editor Ulyanov himself.
That very night, the police jerked the noose they had been spreading, hauling in both copies; the editor; his chief associate, Martov;
the engineer Krzhizhanovsky (one day to become head of the State
Planning Commission); Vaneev, who developed tuberculosis and
died in prison; Gutsul, who went mad and was released in the
custody of his parents; Starkov—in fact, practically all the members
of the little, new-born Petersburg League of Struggle for the Eman-

cipation of the Working Class. Of those Ulyanov had seen frequently, only Krupskaya, Potresov and Struve remained at large. The police were to pick the first two up later. Somehow, the workingmen with whom these intellectuals had been in contact discovered that Dr. Mikhailov was an *agent provocateur*. Soon after the big haul, Dr. Mikhailov was found murdered. And *The Workers' Cause* died at the hour of its birth while the entire Petersburg League transferred its domicile to Siberia.

CHAPTER VIII

PRISON AND EXILE

They make strange and very pleasant reading—these letters of Lenin from Siberia to his family. With the exclusion of but a few sentences they might be the letters of a delightful and indolent country squire of outdoor tastes but of a gentle epicurean philosophy which forbade him even to take such tastes too seriously—one whom wisdom had taught to turn his back upon the press of men and on the folly of affairs. Nor is there any reason to think that Lenin did not genuinely enjoy this quiet life just as he was quite certainly genuinely devoted to his family.   —*Christopher Hollis*

ULYANOV's first letter from jail served a double purpose. It was addressed to Mrs. Chebotareva, wife of one of his comrades, and it was approved by the prison authorities because he had taken his midday meal at her home and could pass her off as the mistress of his boarding-house. The letter was long, impersonal, free from any hint of self-pity. It did not read like the message of one who has been newly thrown into jail, or is uncertain of his fate, but like the missive of some medieval scholar who has retired to a cloister and writes to his former housekeeper to send his books. It spoke of "a plan which has been interesting me intensely ever since my arrest—the study of the marketing of goods produced by domestic manufacture." It asked her to send an enormous amount of material. More than three pages (with two precise footnotes!) outlined his plans for research on the development of the internal market; additional pages listed the titles of works he would need immediately.

"Perhaps you will not think it useless to hand this over to someone else to seek advice—while I wait for an answer." Reasonable enough, for how would the mistress of a boarding-house know how to procure all that? Mrs. Chebotareva showed it to the writer's sweetheart, to his sister Anna, and to a few other comrades still at liberty. These, his intimates, privy to every subtle allusion, pored over it for cryptic meanings in each deviation from the expected. They were struck by the fact that this always precise student with a prodigious memory for books and citations seemed uncertain of the titles of some of the volumes.

"As I am working from memory," he wrote, "I think I may have muddled some of the titles, and where I am not certain I have used a question mark."

One so marked was a work by Mayne-Read. Krupskaya perceived in it the anagram of Mynoga (lamprey), his nickname for her.[1] Mayne-Read, his sister answered, was available. Thus he knew that she was still at large.

In an inquiry whether "some writer or professor" could give him access to the books of the University Library and the library of the Ministry of Finance, they recognized the underground names of Struve ("The Writer") and Potresov ("The Professor"). They answered that a writer and a professor had been found who would help him. (Krupskaya and Potresov were not arrested until some months later. Struve not at all.) Thus the prisoner's theoretical work —for the letter as a whole was seriously meant—and his clandestine correspondence got started together before he had been a month in jail.

He had taken the precaution, as he explained, to discuss his research project with the Public Prosecutor. The latter, impressed by the scholarly interests of his charge, had "confirmed that there would be no limit set on the number of books permitted." He might keep a case of them in his cell with him, might borrow from friends and from libraries in the outside world, and return the books again after he had finished with them. He might buy from publishers and bookstores. Even the prison library, well stocked with the bequests of two generations of "politicals," contained much that was of use.

If, as Tolstoy said, "no one knows what kind of government it is who has never been in prison," the difference between the tsarist and the present Stalinist régimes inspire sombre reflections. The tsarist prisons were administered by educated and often scholarly officials. The jailers themselves ranged from the brutal to the mercifully venal and sometimes even the secretly sympathetic. By hunger strikes, by demonstrative suicides, and by the support of public opinion, a succession of martyrs had won a considerable range of privileges for political prisoners. It is ironical to contemplate that in lands where the dissenter is prosecuted in the name of the people, the category of political prisoner is often not a recognized one. But in autocratic Russia, when the accused was not

[1] The nickname was originally a teasing pet name. Krupskaya had large bulging eyes due, as it developed later, to exophthalmic goiter, which caused her friends to tell her she looked like a fish. Later she adopted Mynoga as her party name. When she was ill, she complained to Vladimir with mock indignation that his sister Anna said she looked like a smoked herring.

charged with some specific terrorist act, he was as a rule not sentenced to hard labor but permitted to spend his days, if he had it
in him, in scholarly pursuits. Moreover, this was the heyday of
"legal Marxism." The criminal seemed academic enough, and it was
obvious that he would be a model prisoner. During a little over a
year, he worked serenely in his cell. When they sent him to Siberia
for three years more, he said to his sister: "It's a pity they let us
out so soon. I should have liked to do a little more work on the
book. It will prove difficult to get books in Siberia."

But it did not prove so difficult. During his four years as ward of
the state, he bought and borrowed many hundreds of journals,
wrote articles for the legal press, even procured works which obviously subserved his activities as an opponent of the status quo.

The prisoner's plan for a study of the development of Russia's
internal market slowly grew in scope until it became the major
theoretical work of his lifetime: *The Development of Capitalism in
Russia*. Every bit of research, every line of writing and patient rewriting, all the negotiations for its legal publication (under the
pseudonym of V. Ilyin), took place while Vladimir Ilyich was a
police ward. The book appeared during the last year of his exile
in Siberia (1899) without any interference from the censor. When
the archives were opened by the first revolutionary government of
1917, it became clear that the police had known all along who "V.
Ilyin" was. It was they who had largely financed the first organ of
"legal Marxism," *Nachalo* ("Beginning"), and set up one of their
secret agents, a certain M. Gurovich, as "angel" and publisher. His
task was to find out the true names of all the Marxists writing under
pseudonyms. He reported that Plekhanov, Zasulich, Martov,
Potresov and Ulyanov were among those contributing. In the issues
of March, 1899, before Ulyanov submitted his big book to the
censors, he published in *Nachalo* a part of its third chapter, under
the title: "The Displacement of Feudal Economy by Capitalist
Economy in Modern Russian Agriculture." The article was signed
V. Ilyin, and carried a footnote to the effect that it was "a section
of a comprehensive investigation by the author of the development
of capitalism in Russia." Thus the police knew that the author was
their prisoner and the brother of a man who had conspired to
assassinate the father of the reigning Tsar. In 1907—after Russia had
gone through the general strikes and uprising of 1905, the government still permitted a second edition to be published. It carried a
new introduction with some fairly explicit political remarks. Today,
after we have come to accept a legendary conception of how com-

plete tsarist censorship was, it comes rather as a shock to read such passages as this and know they were legally permitted:

> Either the old landed economy connected by a thousand threads with serfdom will continue and gradually transform itself into a Junker economy [said the preface to the 1907 edition], or the revolution will destroy the old large landowning economy, annihilate every remnant of serfdom and, especially of large landownership. . . . Gentlemen like Stolypin work systematically, stubbornly and consistently for the completion of the revolution on the first model. The coup d'état [of Stolypin] of June 3, 1907, signifies the triumph of the counter-revolution which strives to assure to the landowners full predominance in the popular assembly. How long, however, this "triumph" will endure is another matter. The struggle for the second way out continues . . . Where this struggle will end, what outcome finally the first push forward of the Russian Revolution will have— it is still not possible to say. . . .

By actual count "Ilyin's" book makes use of 299 theoretical and statistical works in Russian, and 38 foreign studies in German, French and English, or in Russian translation. All these books, journals and reports Ulyanov purchased, or borrowed by mail from distant libraries, while he lived in prison and in Siberia. Terrible enough in their day, imprisonment and exile under the last Tsar, to some of its former victims, were to seem in retrospect like an intellectual's retreat, compared with the régime which one of their fellow-prisoners would one day set up for them in Soviet Russia.

Those who brought books to the Petersburg prison for Ulyanov were subjected to no interrogation. They could leave their packages of books—or food, or clothing, or other comforts—in the office any hour of the day up till five o'clock, and even at night with the watchman. No mere police censor or jail warden, but the Supreme Court Prosecutor or his delegate, subjected the packages of books to a superficial examination. The very next day they were in his cell. He received and dispatched such bundles at least twice a week all through 1896 and the first two months of 1897, while he waited for the authorities to decide further steps in his case. Every batch of books he received or sent back contained at least one volume with a letter hidden in the spine of its binding, or written in invisible ink between the lines of one of its pages, or coded by tiny markings within the printed letters. The two-way traffic enabled him to keep in touch with his organization, to write several strike leaflets, to draft and send out a proposed program for the Social Democratic Party, even to communicate with other comrades in jail. All through his stay in Siberia, books continued to come to him and return from him, carrying invisible letters to other exiles, to men and women in Russia, to Plekhanov and Axelrod in Switzerland. His foresight in having instructed his comrades in the lore of underground communication now served him in good stead. He could not secure the cobalt and sulphuric acid solutions such as were used outside. However, prison afforded homelier chemicals like milk and citric acid (lemon juice), which, to a casual inspection, left no marks upon the paper. But when they were heated, they turned a vivid brown. Milk was his chief writing fluid, and for inkwells he molded tiny cups of hard bread. If he heard footsteps, he could swallow ink and well together. "Today I have eaten six inkwells," reads the postscript of one of his secret communications.

Hints told him where to look for the answer. "The report of the Professional Congress in Moscow," he would say in a letter, "is very interesting," and they would know that he had found the letter concealed in the otherwise uninteresting work. Holding a match under the paper was a dangerous procedure, so he invented a new way of developing the invisible writing. He would tear the letter into thin strips, and when they brought him the boiling water for his evening tea, he made a strong infusion and immersed the strips in it; the tea made the milky letters a rich yellow brown.

Prison is a severe test of the will. Some never adapt themselves; their spirits are broken by ineffectual beating against the bars. Others, after the first restless weeks, get lost in a world of daydream, or in endless preoccupation with petty inconveniences. Still others let the hours pass idly like lizards dozing on a rock—but without the pleasant caresses of the sun. Most of the old Bolsheviks I have known seemed to me younger than other men and women of their years. They attributed it to the quiet parentheses of prison sojourn, where the flame of life burned slowly and the years slipped by without seeming to leave their usual mark.

Vladimir Ilyich settled down to the quiet of his prison cell almost with an air of satisfaction. Never was this orderly spirit's gift for planful expenditure of energy more in evidence. He had no labor to perform, beyond the cleaning of his cell, which he carried out with exaggerated meticulousness. He worked out a careful time schedule —so many minutes for physical exercise, so many for language study, so many for research and writing.

"I have everything I need," he wrote to his mother, "and even more than I need." They sent him so many dainties and comforts, that he told them he was playing with the idea of opening a prison store, and driving the official canteen out of business. The letters from prison to his intimates express a quiet, steady and deep affection, and assume sufficient interest on their part to make them carry out any number of burdensome commissions. Almost the only hint of inconvenience comes in the request to Anna that she procure for him a mechanical pencil because the rules will not permit him to keep a knife, while the warder grumbles and takes such an unconscionable time when he is asked to resharpen the prisoner's pencil. The letters to his mother perhaps have the special aim of reassuring her, who had suffered so much in her children. But those to his sisters and brother, and to Krupskaya and others, are no less cheerful. Once only does a note of loneliness creep into one of his messages to Krupskaya. Here is her account of it:

> But no matter how much he mastered himself, even Vladimir Ilyich was affected by prison melancholy. In one of his letters he put forward this plan: when they were taken out for exercise, it was possible through one of the windows in the corridor to catch a fleeting glimpse of the Shpalernaya pavement. So he suggested that at a definite time I (and a friend) should come and stand on this piece of pavement, and then he would see us . . . I went several days and stood a long while on that spot. Something went wrong with the plan, however, though I do not remember what.

Some notion of the routine of his planful prison days we can get from his letters of advice to his younger brother, Dmitri, when the latter landed in jail:

> First of all, is he keeping to a diet in prison? [writes Vladimir to his mother]. I am sure he is not. But in my opinion it is essential to keep to one there. And, second, does he do physical exercises? Again probably not. And yet, again, this is essential. I at least can say from my own experience that I derived great pleasure and benefit from doing exercises *daily* before retiring. They loosened my joints so that I used to get into a glow even on the coldest days, when the cell was icy cold; and one sleeps ever so much better afterward. I can recommend to him this as a fairly easy exercise, though a ridiculous one: fifty reverential prostrations! This is exactly what I made myself do— and I was not in the least disturbed that the warder, on peeping through the little window, would wonder in amaze-

ment why this man had suddenly grown so devout when
he had not once asked to visit the prison church . . .

When his younger sister, Maria, was imprisoned, and later Anna
and her husband as well, he again was detailed and exact in his
advice. He especially recommended language study, telling them
that his method of working without a teacher was to write out the
Russian translation of all the exercises, put them aside until they
grew "cold," translate them back into the foreign language and
check against the original. "My own experience has born out that
this is the most rational way of learning a language."

> I would again advise you to divide up your study periods
> according to the books on hand in such a way as to vary
> the subjects. I remember very well that a change of reading
> or work—from translation to reading, from writing to exer-
> cise, from serious reading to fiction—helped me enor-
> mously . . .
>
> In the evening, after dinner, for relaxation I remember
> that I would *regelmaessig* turn to fiction and nowhere did
> I appreciate it as much as in prison. But the main thing is
> not to forget your daily exercises, and to make yourself
> perform each exercise a score of times—without giving in.

Such, more or less, was the actual schedule of this redoubtable
mental and physical gymnast, whom no mere imprisonment could
break or even swerve from the pursuit of his aims.

Siberia! The name strikes terror into the hearts of lovers of freedom. All through the nineteenth century, the roster of its exiles
reads like a Russian *Who's Who*, in literature, thought, and public
life. Its marshy taiga, limitless steppes and frozen tundra, its polar
and sub-polar winters, its ice-locked river systems which empty
only into the Arctic, its successive generations of broken and forgotten men—these were Siberia to the nineteenth century. But as
the Transsiberian pushed its track eastward toward Port Arthur,
as the exile colonies increased in numbers until they were sufficient
to give each other moral sustenance, as the terms of exile shortened
and more and more prisoners returned, or, by incredible feats of
perilous overland journey, escaped to Western Europe, the picture
in men's minds began to change.

When on February 25, 1897, Vladimir Ilyich Ulyanov was conducted from his cell to the Prosecutor's office and informed that
two weeks earlier an administrative decree had been issued exiling
him to Eastern Siberia for the next three years, he sighed good-
humoredly at the interruption of his research. There had been no

trial; there rarely was in these political exile cases, just as there rarely is in analogous cases in Soviet Russia today. The political police had the right to give up to five years of administrative exile without trial. Today there is no such limitation. At the request of his mother—and with a little financial aid from her—he was allowed to travel to his remote place of exile at his own expense. Being an official's son and a hereditary nobleman had its advantages. They released him from the House of Preliminary Detention, let him spend almost a week in Saint Petersburg to say his farewells, consult his physician, gather things he would need for the journey, and even—though this was not comprehended in the authorization—hold conferences with the remaining footloose members of the League of Struggle for the Emancipation of the Working Class.

The prisoner journeyed freely to Moscow, spent a few days there with his mother, conferred with some of his comrades, then proceeded in leisurely fashion on the Transsiberian as far as Krasnoyarsk. There he waited for the spring floods to make river travel possible on the Yenissei, and for the authorities to notify him as to the exact spot of his final destination.

At Krasnoyarsk, provincial capital, he spent several weeks of the Siberian spring, walking two versts [1] out of town each day to visit the magnificent private library of the Siberian merchant and Bibliophile Yudin. There he found one of the best collections of eighteenth- and nineteenth-century periodicals in all Russia, and additional sociological works and statistical monographs for his book.[2]

Freed for the journey on February 26, he did not reach his final destination in the village of Shushenskoye near the headwaters of the Yenissei until May 20. The leisurely trip, the stopovers, the wide horizons, all left him refreshed after the confinement of his cell.

"I am not at all tired," he wrote his mother from Ob, "which seems strange, for a three-days' journey from Samara to Saint Petersburg used to knock me out. The fact is that without exception I sleep splendidly through each night. . . . The air is good; it's easy to breathe."

To be sure, those who could not afford a trip at their own expense or could not secure the permission did not find it so pleasant travelling under guard and being locked up on the way.

Yenisseisk Province is one of the healthiest and pleasantest regions of Eastern Siberia, far southward in the northern land of cold.

[1] A verst is about two-thirds of a mile.
[2] The Yudin library was sold to America in 1907 and forms the basis of the Slavic section of the Library of Congress in Washington.

Lenin's new home lay not far from Tannu Tuva, secretly annexed by Stalin in 1945 and now the site of Russia's most jealously guarded secret, its "atomic city." They call the region, Lenin wrote, "the Siberian Italy." His comrade Martov, because of official prejudice against a rebellious Jew, was exiled to lonely, frozen Turukhansk, some nine hundred miles farther north on the same Yenissei River, where it enters the Arctic Circle on its long course to the polar sea. Despite repeated petitions, Martov was kept up there during all of his three years of exile under conditions so hard that he found it impossible to do any systematic work. Krzhizhanovsky, Starkov, Vaneev, Lepeshinsky, Silvin, Lengnik, and Shapoval, were all sent to the nearby towns of Minusinsk, Yermakovsk, and Tessinsk, within a radius of less than fifty miles of Vladimir Ilyich. The Governor General of the Province assigned to each of them a monthly stipend of eight rubles (four dollars) for board and lodging, let them seek out their own homes within the prescribed village, wander pretty freely through the province on hunting expeditions, visit each other for as much as a week on end for Christmas and Easter holidays and on the occasion of weddings and funerals. Some brought their mothers out to Siberia to keep house for them, others sent for their wives; three weddings were celebrated among the Minusinsk contingent during Ulyanov's three-year stay. Those who could were allowed to get work to eke out their allowance, while the cost of living in Siberia was so low, and the purchasing power of a ruble so high in those days that even the eight rubles were sufficient for bare necessities, except where the upkeep of a family was involved. During the long visits to each other's villages there were days and nights of political discussion, of singing, of hotly contested chess games—with Vladimir the invariable victor— and long hunting expeditions with dogs and guns in the forests abounding with game.

The village was "not a bad place," although it was a little bare for all its fifteen hundred inhabitants, cold in winter as all Siberia is, torn at by great transcontinental winds in autumn and early spring, infested by clouds of mosquitoes after the melting of the snows. But there was the Yenissei to swim in, the forest for hunting, and, on clear days, the snow-capped Sayan range to lend magnificence to the horizon. Vladimir grew plump and forgot the very name of the mineral water he used to take for his stomach trouble.

Twenty years earlier, Prince Kropotkin, the anarchist leader, had spent his exile in this same "Siberian Italy." And thirty years after Ulyanov's stay, a letter smuggled out of here by anarchist opponents of the Soviet régime revealed that they had been sent there after their health had been broken by other, less healthful places. But they were receiving an allowance of only six inflation-weakened Soviet rubles a month, and were blacklisted against receiving work. Near them, under more comfortable conditions and with a considerably larger stipend, lived Smilga and other opposition communists, from whom the G.P.U. was then hoping to secure a "recantation." Thus does the pattern of Russian administrative exile of political opponents repeat itself under changing régimes, but with differences, especially during the later years of Stalin's rule, that it will not be pleasant to relate.

On his "salary" of eight rubles a month ("we receive the government allowance regularly,") Ulyanov was able to engage a furnished room in a peasant's cottage, get his food, and have his laundry, mending and cleaning done.

> One week they would kill a sheep and feed Vladimir Ilyich with it from day to day until it was all eaten up. When it was all gone they would buy meat for the next week, and the farm girl chopped up his supply in the trough where the cattle fodder was prepared. This mince meat was used for cutlets for Vladimir Ilyich, also for a whole week. And there was plenty of milk for both Vladimir Ilyich and his dog. [Krupskaya's *Memories of Lenin.*]

What he lacked was money for books. He set about to earn it by the translation of *The Theory and Practice of English Trade Unions* by Sidney and Beatrice Webb, by articles on economics and sociology, by book reviews and by the sale of the manuscript of his work on *The Development of Capitalism in Russia.* This he sold to the bookseller and publisher Alexandra Mikhailovna Kalmykova, whom we have already met as "Auntie," for the not inconsiderable sum of fifteen hundred rubles. His articles sometimes fetched him as much as a hundred or two hundred while the least of his book reviews was paid for in the form of books selected for him by the editor of the magazine, his old friend Peter Struve. He never lacked funds for the purchase of a steady stream of publications ordered from Moscow and even abroad, while his mother was ever ready to tide over a temporary shortage.

Life was lonely at Shushenskoye. With a little petitioning, he could easily have been transferred to one of the nearby towns, where his comrades lived in little collectives. But he refused to make the request, for he was afraid of the ingrown exile's squabbles, the endless hours of chess and disputation, the needless drain upon his sleep and working time. Here there were only two work-ingmen exiles: Prominsky, a Polish Social Democrat, a hatmaker by trade; and Enberg, a striking Finnish workingman from the Putilov works in Saint Petersburg, personally rebellious though lacking a Social Democratic outlook. Ulyanov tried to cultivate the local schoolmaster but found him interested only in drinking and cards. Then there was Zhuravlev, a consumptive peasant, formerly a clerk; and an old, thick-headed but devoted muzhik, Sosipatych. Through these two, says Krupskaya naively, "Vladimir Ilyich studied the Siberian countryside." The information he pumped out of them he supplemented by running on Sundays an unofficial law-yer's office for the peasants living nearby. The fame of this volunteer jurisconsult spread: muzhiks came from miles around with their quarrels about trespassing cows, unpaid wages, grievances against a brother-in-law who had failed to treat to ceremonial drinks.

For added company, there was a she-dog that the exile tried in vain to train for hunting, a little kitten, and Minka, the little son of an old Lettish feltbootmaker, all the rest of whose fourteen chil-dren were dead. When the prisoner left Shushenskoye at the end of his appointed time writes Krupskaya, "Minka fell ill with grief. Now he is no longer living, and the bootmaker has written asking for a piece of land over by the Yenissei—'for I don't want to go hungry in my old age.'" He got his piece of land from the Soviet Government as a reward for having befriended Valdimir Ilyich when the latter was his neighbor.

Exile had its sorrows, too. Vaneev, who had contracted tuber-culosis while in prison, slowly wasted away and died. Prominski, with a wife and six children, received at first a subsidy of thirty rubles a month, then was cut to nineteen. In vain did he try to make enough by selling hats to the villagers, so that he might return to Poland after his exile was over. Almost a quarter-century he spent there as a "free man," never accumulating enough to transport his numerous family. In 1923 the Soviet Government, under his old friend Lenin, arranged for him to return at last, but he contracted typhus and died on the homeward journey. Efimov, an exiled work-ingman at Tesinskoe, went mad with persecutory delusions. Julius Martov, in lonely northern exile at Turukhansk, petitioned in vain for transfer; a political prisoner he lived with quarreled with him so that they broke up their collective household. The ever high-strung Martov suffered a nervous breakdown, while his brilliant talents as student, writer and agitator went to seed.

"God preserve us from the exile colonies and the exile conflicts!" commented Ulyanov sadly in a letter to his mother. A bitter quarrel

broke out between the older Narodovoltsi and the younger Social
Democrats. Political issues, the conflict between generations, contempt of the terrorists for the opponents of individual terror, and
finally the escape of a Social Democrat which imperilled the privileges of those who remained, all mingled to exacerbate the quarrel.

> The scandal [writes Krupskayal] grew like a snowball.
> There is nothing worse than these exile scandals, Vladimir
> Ilyich said to me. They pull us back terribly. These old men
> have got bad nerves. Just look what they've been through,
> the penal sentences they have undergone. But we cannot
> let ourselves be drawn away by such scandals—all our work
> lies ahead. And Vladimir Ilyich insisted that we should
> break with these old people. I remember the meeting at
> which the rupture took place. The decision as to the break
> had been made beforehand. It was now a question of carry-
> ing it out as painlessly as possible. We made the break
> because a break was necessary. But we did it without
> malice, indeed with regret. And we lived afterwards in
> separation.

Such was Vladimir Ilyich's way. He was no friend of needless
fraying of the nerves. Whom he could not work with, he broke
with. Then, unless they opposed the things he stood for, he said
no more about them. Yet, the exiles' quarrels were to affect his
spirit, too. Both in Siberia and abroad in Western Europe, they
would work more ravages on the movement than all the persecu-
tions of the police.

But the police seemed to be doing well enough, too. The pitiful
stratagems of the few members of the Petersburg League still at
large availed them little. The hunt closed in; one by one they went
overland to Siberia, or, in milder cases, to provinces in the north
of Russia. Though the time seemed ripe for the fusing of the local
study circles into a single, all-Russian, social-democratic party, the
police appeared to know every secret move. Ulyanov and Martov
had been at work on this task when they were picked up. From
prison, Ulyanov smuggled out a draft program, but again and
again the constituent convention had to be postponed because
of fresh raids. By the time the "First Congress" was finally held,
in March, 1898, there were only four members left in Saint Petersburg to elect a delegate. Three of these were women, one being
Krupskaya, who had already been arrested but temporarily released under police surveillance while they determined her fate.
The police seemed to know about the secret congress, too. It gath-

ered in Minsk with representatives from Petersburg, Moscow, Kiev,
from the journal *Southern Worker,* and from the Jewish Socialist
League or Bund, of which Martov had been a leader before coming to Saint Petersburg. The gathering was poor in numbers and
in talents, hurried through its sessions in three days, failed to adopt
a constitution or a program. Its sole achievements were the issu-
ance of a manifesto, drafted by Peter Struve, the promulgation of
the idea of a nationwide party, and the election of a central committee of three. The manifesto was virtually.Struve's last act as a
revolutionary, already representing his past rather than his future.
It was notable chiefly for the sentence: "The farther east we go
in Europe, the weaker, more cowardly and abject does the bourgeoisie become politically, and the more do its cultural and political tasks devolve upon the proletariat." This thought was to have a
profound influence upon Leon Trotsky, who was just then becoming a socialist.

Eight of the nine delegates, and two of the three central committee members chosen by the congress, were picked up within a
few days of its adjournment. The victory of the police and the
rout of the new party seemed complete.

Eight months after Vladimir's arrest, Nadezhda Konstantinovna
was arrested. When one of the prisoners in the women's section
of the House of Preliminary Detention set fire to her own clothing
and perished in flames, the authorities released the other female
politicals pending official disposition of their cases. In due course
—the wheels of Russian bureaucracy turned very slowly—Krupskaya was notified that she had been sentenced by administrative
decree to three years' exile in Ufa in North Russia. She petitioned
to be permitted to go to Shushenskoye in Siberia instead, in order
to join her "fiancé," and asked that her term be shortened so that
she might accompany him back to Russia at the expiration of his.

The authorities agreed to the first part of her petition. Their
desire to see the lovers united however was not so strong as to
impel them to shorten her term. They allowed her to go to Shushenskoye at her own expense, and to take her mother along. They
warned her that if she did not get legally married "immediately,"
she would be sent to Ufa as originally provided.

Marriage had been unfashionable in certain revolutionary circles
—particularly among the nihilists and the anarchists—but among
Social Democrats a life-long union, with or without the ceremonial
forms, was the rule in those days rather than the exception. It is
clear that Nadezhda Konstantinovna and Vladimir Ilyich did not
object to the official proviso, and already regarded their union as

seriously as the most bourgeois marriage in all Russia. Living in that shifting world of prison, underground and foreign exile, a world in which a "Who with Whom" would have to be altered more frequently than a "Who's Who," their marriage was destined to be a true union for better and for worse until death should part them.

If one looks for it, one can detect the note of joy in Vladimir's unobtrusively affectionate letters when he learned that Nadya was to join him. But the actual words were merely a flood of instructions as to what his future wife should do, and what she should bring with her. She was to see Struve, who had become editor of a learned legal Marxist journal, and arrange with him for further articles and book reviews. She was to contract for a collection of articles by Ulyanov in book form. She was to subscribe to a number of periodicals. She was "to be loaded with as many books as possible," was to bring his straw hat, one of his chess sets (he had been playing with one he had carved himself), a penwiper to protect his coat lapel from further inking, graph paper in a dozen sizes, a pair of scissors for clippings (to replace the sheep shears borrowed from his landlord), picture books for Prominsky's children, new works for translation, grammars and dictionaries, a leather jacket for hunting, mountains of statistical reports. All the while that bureaucratic red tape kept delaying Nadezhda's departure, Vladimir continued to deluge her with additional commissions, so that when she and her mother finally left for Siberia they were loaded with a princely train of bags and boxes.

> At last [he wrote his mother in May, 1899] I have received the so long awaited guests . . . and just that day I got the bright idea of going hunting, so that they did not find me. Nadezhda Konstantinovna does not look well at all and will simply have to take care of her health. As for me, Elizabeth Vasilievna [Krupskaya's mother] said: "Gracious, how you've spread!" . . . Anyuta asks who I am inviting to the wedding. I invite you all . . . As you know, they have put to Nadezhda Konstantinovna the tragi-comic condition: either get married *immediately* (*sic!*) or go back to Ufa. I am not disposed to let her get away, and so have already begun the "moves" . . .

It was the officials themselves, however, who held up the marriage. Though he had lived more than a year now in Siberia, his record has not yet arrived from Petersburg, and without this "the local police chief doesn't know who I am and can't give me a marriage certificate!" Nadya arrived in May, but it was not until

July that the wedding was held. By that time they had been living together so long in the calm monotony of a Siberian village that they seem to have forgotten to communicate the news in their letters.

Nadya enriched his life by serving as wife, secretary, housekeeper, and devoted disciple. Her mother helped in the housekeeping, too, remaining a member of their household until her death during World War I. According to Potresov, Vladimir Ilyich "goodnaturedly carried on a daily struggle with his mother-in-law which was not without its comical side. She was the only person in his immediate circle who resisted him and defended her own personality." Krupskaya hints that the "resistance" turned about the clash between her mother's religious observances and Lenin's atheism. But the future leader of the Godless State was quite tolerant in personal relations, limiting himself to sly banter and comically assumed indignation.

The correspondence from Shushenskoye now took on a livelier, more personal tone. The envelope that carried Vladimir's concise communications bore "postscripts" from Nadya three or four times as long. Or she enclosed several sheets of her own, full of personal things and the breath of the Siberian countryside. Knowing his mother's interest in everything concerning Volodya, she rambles on for many pages about his hunting trips, his chats with the local folk, the children and animals, the antics of their "hunting" bitch, the preserves she and her mother put up, the walks they all take together in the woods, what they are reading, what he is writing, how they solve the servant problem (with a girl-of-all-work at two and one-half rubles a month plus shoes), how Volodya was commissioned to buy a blouse for Prominsky's little girl and instead of asking the size, wanted to know "how many pounds?"—all the intimate things that go into a warm and lively personal correspondence and help those far off to envisage the lives their loved ones are leading in an unknown place.

Vladimir was growing restless. While he had still a whole year to go, he had permitted himself to look at a map of Europe, in order that, as he wrote his younger sister, he might locate Brussels, whither she had gone to continue her studies.

> By stretching your hand you can touch London, Paris, Berlin . . . Yes, I envy you. During the earlier period of my deportation, I decided not for anything to look at maps of Europe or of European Russia, so deep was the bitterness I felt at unrolling the maps and seeing the various little

black spots on them. But now I am grown calm and can look tranquilly at maps. In fact, we often devote ourselves to dreaming in which of those spots it would be interesting to land after we leave here. Perhaps it is that in the first half of our exile we were looking backwards, and now we are looking forwards. Ah well, *qui vivra verra* . . .

As his final year crawled its interminable course, Vladimir found it harder and harder to work. His big book was done, except for Nadya's careful recopying. The Webb translation likewise. He was becoming uneasily aware of a change of mood in Russia. In but two years of exile he had lost touch with what was taking place over there. All the revolutionary Marxists of his generation—the *stariki* or "oldsters" they were called despite their youth—were in Siberia. The "youngsters" of all ages who had taken the places they left vacant, were leading the movement in quite another direction.

Even more disquieting was the news that in the very citadel of Marxism, the mighty German Social Democracy, a movement had arisen to "revise" and "modernize" Marxism. The "revision" seemed to Ulyanov a blasphemy, an attempt to cut out of Marxism its orthodox revolutionary heart. The leading Revisionist was no less a personage than Eduard Bernstein, friend of Engels and his literary executor. Engels had died in 1895. The very next year, Bernstein had begun his literary offensive in the pages of the theoretical journal *Neue Zeit*. Now, in 1899, the cautious series of articles had grown into a far from cautious book. In every letter, Vladimir pestered his sisters for a copy. When at last it arrived, he couldn't wait to finish it before he exploded.

"We have already read half of it," he wrote his mother, "and its contents caused us genuine astonishment. Theoretically it is incredibly weak. . . . It is not possible to doubt of his failure. The insinuation of Bernstein that there are many Russians who agree with him has filled us with indignation."

Alas for Ulyanov, he was to prove wrong on both counts. For him "it was not possible to doubt of Bernstein's failure" because Vladimir Ilyich was intellectually and temperamentally incapable of doubting the total soundness of Marxism, and he was no less incapable of doubting the essential health of the German movement, which led the Socialist International.

Contrary to the impression given by Lenin's official biographers, he played no international role in the titanic battle of the books which followed the publication of Bernstein's *Voraussetzungen des Sozialismus*. Never did he dream of making the claim, which since his death has been made for him, that there was a sort of

apostolic succession in Marxism: Marx, Engels, Lenin. . . . Nor did
he, as his disciples have since done, belittle the great galaxy of
Marxists who worked with Marx and Engels in their later years
and, after them, continued to lead the Socialist International. Until
the World War, Lenin cherished the profoundest respect for such
men as Kautsky, Mehring, Bebel, and—though he quarreled with
them on Russian matters—for Plekhanov, Parvus and Rosa Luxemburg. Even when he found that only Rosa Luxemburg and Mehring
agreed with him on the war, and while he was denouncing the
others as "traitors," he did not attempt retroactively to reduce the
importance of their earlier achievements in Marxist theory. Nor did
he believe, least of all in those humble days, that the Russian movement was capable of dictating to all the others. Or that, until the
war, he had ever been right against them all, except on peculiarly
Russian matters.

In the great polemic which raged around Bernstein's book, he
limited himself to combatting the Russian "Bernsteinians" and to
expressing agreement with Kautsky's works on the economic and
political aspects, and Plekhanov's and Labriola's on the philosophical aspects of the controversy. When Potresov, from Siberian
Vyatka, mailed him a copy of Kautsky's book against Bernstein,
he was so enthusiastic that he and Krupskaya dropped all other
work and scarcely slept for two weeks until they had completed its
translation into Russian.

To all appearances, Bernstein was easily worsted in the debate.
Almost every outstanding Marxist entered into the lists against
him. The convention of his party expressly voted to condemn his
views and stick to "the old victory-crowned tactics." But the defeat
of Bernstein proved in the end to have been merely a defeat in
words; for his book expressed in plain-spoken language what was
increasingly becoming the unconscious practice of his party.

The reason for Bernstein's hidden triumph lay in the changing
intellectual climate of Europe. His trivial remarks on economic
trends could not stand up against Marx's *Capital*. Though twentieth-century Europe was to assume a different shape from the
prophecies of either, it was to resemble far more the catastrophic
forecasts of Marx than Bernstein's optimistic predictions of an increasingly crisisless economy, an ever-wider diffusion of wealth
and an imperceptible growing of capitalism into socialism, without
convulsion or revolution. Yet Bernstein's views exactly suited the
prevailing mood of Europe as the nineteenth century set and the
twentieth rose bright with promise.

Marxism was the unacknowledged child of the stormy adolescence of capitalism. Politically it represented a series of deductions from the period of revolutions from 1789 to 1848. But Europe had known neither great wars, nor revolutionary upheavals, nor profound economic crises since the early seventies. Bernstein's generation knew of revolution only from the Marxist classics. They reserved their tribute to it for holiday occasions, and in their daily practice moved familiarly in the bustling, prosperous atmosphere of growing trade unions, improved labor legislation, mounting votes, increasing parliamentary representation, enlarging socialist newspaper circulation.

The sudden expansion of Europe overseas, the picking to pieces of the "dark continent" of Africa within a decade, the piling up of armaments, gave Europe a brief period of febrile prosperity. Railroad building, armament and capital export stimulated heavy industry. Monopoly profit and colonial profit seemed to offset Marx's dread law of the falling rate of profit. The capital plethora was taken up in stock speculation, in export to rapidly industrializing lands like Russia, and to colonies overseas. Crises diminished in intensity, recoveries soared to new heights.

In the face of these phenomena, "orthodoxy" held doggedly to Marx. Only Hobson, Parvus, Hilferding and Rosa Luxemburg—and later Lenin—ventured on any real investigation of these new phenomena. Nowhere but in Russia, where there was an absolute Tsar to fight, did a movement arise that was really based on a spirit of revolution. To the superficial observer it was far easier to believe in Bernstein's social meliorism than in grim prophecies of coming wars, social and political and economic breakdown, open struggles as to the nature of the future new order.

Even in Russia, things seemed quiet. The years of Ulyanov's exile were years of boom. The workingmen, largely with a leadership arising from their own ranks, were conducting strikes, many of them successful. The intelligentsia, tending, as is the intellectuals' habit, to elaborate temporary and superficial phenomena into deep and timeless generalizations, developed a new theory to fit the new situation. Because of the new theory's emphasis on economic struggle, rather than political struggle against the Tsar, it acquired the name of "Economism."

All that this new movement required—given the Russian tendency to worship authority—was encouragement from authoritative voices in the leading party of Western Europe. Bernstein was not bluffing when he claimed to have many Russian supporters.

Ulyanov's indignation at the claim yielded to white hot fury when he found that he and his fellow-exiles were in the minority in their own movement.

Indeed, a document had already reached remote Shushenskoye which Ulyanov had taken at first to be an individual aberration. The document, baptised by him "the Credo," was drawn up by Mrs. Kuskova. Its mere perusal, as he wrote to his mother, "infuriated" him.

The general law of labor activity, declared the "Credo," was for the movement to follow "the path of least resistance." In the West, where the bourgeoisie had conquered political rights for itself and for the proletariat, the working class had found it easier to go into politics than to build unions. But in Russia, where the Tsar represented a stone wall blocking political action, the path of least resistance was economic action against the employers and the attempt to organize trade unions. The Russian working class was too weak and backward anyhow for politics. All talk of an independent political party of labor was but an importation of alien doctrine based on different conditions. The duty of the socialist intellectuals was to support the workers in their effort to build unions, and support the liberal opposition against tsarism in its effort to democratize Russia. The workers would learn from their experience in strikes the necessity of supporting the liberal opposition on the political field also.

The "Credo" moved like a sword through the movement, dividing it into two quite unequal parts. Paul Axelrod had already warned against it in a pamphlet printed in Zurich and smuggled into Russia. Ulyanov now drafted a sharper and more irate rejoinder. Taking advantage of some festival, he arranged for all the exiles in the province to come together at a "party." He read the "Credo," analyzed it, read his answer. Seventeen exiles, including himself and his wife, the Finnish workingman Enberg, who had been studying Marxism with Krupskaya, Vaneev, who was dying of tuberculosis and had to be carried, bed and all, into the meeting, and the entire little group of the three nearby towns, signed the document. It became known by that fact as "The Protest of the Seventeen." Potresov, Dan and Vorovsky sent a similar document from Vyatka. Ulyanov mailed a copy of the "Protest" to Martov, who secured additional signatures in Turukhansk. It was smuggled out of Siberia for circulation in printed and hectographed versions. Thus began the counter-offensive of the revolutionary Marxist minority against "Economism."

From now on Ulyanov was like a bull that had felt the first thrust. He raged at the distance and the forced inaction, at the slovenliness of Russian thought, and at the slackness of Russian organization, which had landed every revolutionist in exile. He walked through the forest for hours with Krupskaya, or with visitors from the nearby towns, talking, talking, talking, confidentially, didactically, like a schoolmaster with his most advanced pupil, on what must be done. A plan was taking shape in his mind: a plan for an all-Russian underground newspaper, and a chain of secret agents who would smuggle it across frontiers and into cities and factories. The paper would lay the basis for fusing all the local circles into a nationwide organization. It would explain theoretical problems and make known practical tasks. It would educate and organize. It would defeat the "Economists" and take intellectual and organizational guardianship over the movement. Out of its pages would come the ideas, and out of its agents would come the organizational machinery, on which to base a unified, centralized, conspirative party, which the police could not break nor "liberal chatterers" weaken.

Vladimir Ilyich began to spend sleepless nights—writes Krupskaya—He became terribly thin. It was during these nights that he thought out his plan in every detail, discussed it with Krzhizhanovsky, with me, wrote about it to Martov and Potresov, discussed with them a journey abroad. The more time went on, the more Vladimir Ilyich was overcome with impatience, the more eager he was to get to work.

CHAPTER IX

LENIN'S ORGANIZATION PLAN

*Before we can unite, and in order that we may unite, we must
first of all firmly and definitely draw the lines of demarcation
between the various groups.—Editorial Statement of first
number of Iskra, drafted by Lenin*

AIDED BY CLEAR, frosty moonlight, the little party pushed on day
and night by sled down the frozen Yenissei. Nadya's mother
suffered from the intense cold, but the impatient Vladimir rode
through the sharp February air without his elkskin coat. He would
scarcely permit stops for adequate rest; yet, wherever there was a
chance to meet an exile or a little group of them, he halted to talk
over his plans for an all-Russian newspaper. He seemed bent on
knowing personally every Socialist in Siberia: later that knowledge would be useful to him. Many have left testimony of their
sudden sense of the bigness of his simple, practical-sounding
plans, and the potency of his concentrated will. As with a Loyola,
as with all outstanding organizers of parties of action, the force
of Ulyanov's personality, no less than of his ideas, was beginning
to bind men to him by ties that resembled those of disciple and
master.

His wife, whose term of exile had yet another year to run—this
was February, 1900—could not accompany him beyond Ufa in the
Urals, where she was to serve her final year. It did not enter into
his mind to remain with her there, though the big cities of Russia
were forbidden to him. He must get nearer to the capitals and
the frontier. He chose Pskov, a rail junction not far from the
border.

Ulyanov, Potresov and Martov, of about the same age (Potresov
was a year older and Martov three years younger than Ulyanov),
tacitly regarded themselves as the *troika*: a three-man team that
was to lead their generation and become the editorial board of
the paper they were planning. While in exile, they had carried
on a lengthy correspondence about it; who should write for it;
where it should be published; how be smuggled into the country;
what its position should be on a multitude of questions. The three
were so close that Ulyanov dubbed their union "the triple alliance" and referred now to one, now the other, in his code letters

147

as "Brother." Martov, his term of exile over, went to Poltava to get contacts in the south of Russia, while Potresov joined Ulyanov in Pskov. What talk there was between them we can guess from the way their host Radchenko's two little daughters used to tease them: "Placing their hands behind their backs the little girls paced solemnly up and down the room side by side, the one saying 'Bernstein' and the other replying 'Kautsky.'"

When the "brothers" applied for permission to go abroad in pursuance of their plan to found a paper, the government readily granted passports.

Before leaving, Ulyanov asked for permission to go to Ufa to see his ailing wife. While he was at it, he went to see his mother and sister in Moscow—and to pick up connections there. Then he made a tour of a number of lesser towns for additional contacts. Only impatience to get started on the paper itself made him give up a wild project of returning secretly to Siberia to see yet other exiles. Scarcely less reckless for police-dogged men was the decision of "Brothers" Martov and Ulyanov to visit Saint Petersburg together, a city forbidden to both. The very day after their arrival, they were arrested. Prisoner Ulyanov had on his person two thousand rubles, just received from "Auntie" (A. M. Kalmykova) to start the paper, a list of addresses, and a letter for Plekhanov. The letter and addresses had been written in invisible ink on old bills and notes. Still, the failure to travel "clean" in a forbidden city did not argue great skill in underground work on the part of the man who was about to become the teacher in such matters of a whole generation. But the police, who caught them easily enough, neither heated the scraps of paper, nor confiscated the considerable treasury of the future newspaper, nor detained more than a few days its would-be editors. Their arrest on this foolhardy mission constituted the first narrow escape for the unborn paper. The second came soon after from an émigrés' quarrel.

When Ulyanov crossed the frontier on July 29, 1900, he found a split situation bordering on hysteria. Potresov, who had preceded him, was plunged in gloom. He reported that Plekhanov and his veterans had quarreled with all the members of a recently founded Union of Social Democrats Abroad, the majority of whom were "Economists," and supporters of Bernstein against Plekhanov in the great debate then raging on "revisionism." The Union had held a Congress in April, where the scrap had been so bitter that the veterans had walked out and formed their own rival League of Revolutionary Social Democracy Abroad. Ulyanov went at once to Geneva to see Plekhanov.

> My conversation with him—wrote Vladimir Ilyich in a
> confidential report intended only for the eyes of Krupskaya,
> Martov, and a few close adherents—did indeed show that
> he was suspicious, distrustful and *rechthaberisch* to *nec plus
> ultra*. I tried to be cautious and evaded all the "touchy"
> points, but the constant restraint I had to place upon
> myself could not but affect my temper . . .

Plekhanov, he complained, had used "diplomacy" in dealing with
his future editorial colleague. But, from the above, we can see that
"diplomacy" was used by both. Ulyanov was angry that his old
master had split the émigré movement just when he was counting
on producing for it a journal which would guide and unite all
Social Democrats both abroad and inside Russia. The conversation
between master and disciple degenerated into a wrangle. Ulyanov
nourished the idea that the unborn journal could be the unswerving
champion of the revolutionary, orthodox Marxist viewpoint, which
he and his master, Plekhanov, held in common, could polemicize
against Liberals, "Economists," "Revisionists," and Populists, and
yet at one and the same time be everybody's paper, supported by
all, admonishing and instructing everybody, admitting all the warring opinions into its columns—in the form of contributions which
would be systematically criticized by the editors in accompanying
editorial notes. This peculiar notion, psychologically untenable,
Ulyanov derived as a logical corollary of his twin formulae: the
"alliance" of all opposition elements, and the "hegemony of the
proletariat" in the general struggle against tsarism. But Plekhanov,
opposing the admission of such contrary views altogether, "displayed a hatred toward 'allies' which bordered on the indecent—
suspecting them of espionage, accusing them of being *Geschaefts-
macher* and scoundrels, and asserting that he would not hesitate to
'shoot' such 'traitors.'"

Strange to hear the future arch-splitter complaining against
Plekhanov in the identical terms which would later be used against
Lenin by his opponents, including his present comrades-in-arms,
Martov, Potresov and this same Plekhanov.

Another and deeper, because less conscious, source of friction
was the older man's treatment of an editorial statement for the first
issue, which had been prepared by the younger. Plekhanov made
no objection to the ideas—which silence Ulyanov interpreted as
"intolerable diplomacy"—but condemned the declaration as too
commonplace, too lacking in depth, too pedestrian in tone, for a
would-be historic document. From his first meeting with Ulyanov,
he had conceived an admiration for this eminently businesslike dis-

ciple as a future practical organizer of the revolutionary movement
but had been unable to take him seriously as a writer and thinker.
"This is not 'written,' as the French say," he told the hurt author.
"This is not a literary work. This does not look like anything . . ."
As one reads Lenin's pedestrian manifesto, one cannot help but feel
that Plekhanov's criticism was justified. But style, too, is a matter
of temperament. Nor was the situation improved when the old
master took the document with the intention of "elevating the tone,"
and a few days later haughtily returned it unaltered.

In the course of the same week, Plekhanov, Axelrod and Vera
Zasulich met with Potresov and Ulyanov to negotiate an agreement
between the two "organizations," or rather, the two generations.
The strained relations between "master" and "disciple" flared into
open conflict:

> Now G.V.'s [Plekhanov's] desire to possess unlimited
> power became obvious . . . He stated that it was evident
> that we had differing views . . . he understood and re-
> spected our point of view, but could not accept it. It would
> be better if we were the editors and he a contributor. We
> were positively amazed, and began to argue against
> this . . .

The unstated source of the conflict was the question: whose leadership, Plekhanov's or Ulyanov's, the "older" or the "younger generation"? This was an issue that would never be clearly and consciously formulated, yet one that would never die down. But
Ulyanov could not then dream of leading the movement without
its most revered leaders, his own teachers. He stifled his indignation, and persuaded Plekhanov to reconsider. Immediately the
latter asked pointedly how voting would be conducted among six
editors, an even number. (The editors were to be Plekhanov, Axelrod, Zasulich, from the veterans, and Ulyanov, Martov, Potresov,
from the younger group.) On Vera Zasulich's motion, that question
was decided by giving Plekhanov two votes to break the potential
ties, and one apiece to each of the other five!

> On that—Ulyanov's confidential report continues—G.V.
> took the reins of management into his hands and in a
> high editorial manner began to apportion tasks . . . We
> sat there as if we had been ducked . . . we realized that
> we had been made fools of . . .
> My "infatuation" with Plekhanov disappeared as if by
> magic . . . Never, never in my life have I regarded any
> other man with such sincere respect and veneration. I

have never stood before any man with such "humility" as I stood before him, and never before have I been so brutally "spurned" . . . Since a man with whom we desire to co-operate intimately resorts to chess moves in dealing with comrades, there can be no doubt of the fact that he is a bad man, yes, a bad man, inspired by petty motives of personal vanity and conceit—an insincere man . . .

This discovery struck us both [Ulyanov and Potresov] like a thunderbolt because up to that moment both of us had been enamored with Plekhanov, and, as we do with our beloved, we forgave him everything, closed our eyes to his shortcomings . . . Our indignation knew no bounds. Our ideal was destroyed; gloatingly we trampled it under our feet. There were no bounds to the charges we hurled against him . . . Good-bye journal! We will throw up everything and return to Russia . . . Had we not been in love with him, our conduct toward him would have been different . . . Young comrades "court" an old comrade out of the great love they bear for him—and suddenly, he injects into this love an atmosphere of intrigue . . . An enamored youth receives from the object of his love a bitter lesson: to regard all persons "without sentiment"; to keep a stone in one's sling . . .

There are many more pages to this curious document which, under the title "How the 'Spark' was Nearly Extinguished," occupies fifteen pages of volume four of Lenin's *Collected Works*. From it we can learn little concerning the political differences which were to divide these two men in the future, but much concerning differences of temperament. No other document from Lenin's hand would ever again be as psychologically revealing. He soon learned well the lesson he here set for himself: "To regard all persons 'without sentiment'; to keep a stone in one's sling . . ." He taught himself to discipline severely the emotional side of his nature; to seek for and enlarge the political aspect of all future quarrels; to play down, even ignore where possible, the personal. But this document suffices to show us how far this self-disciplined, inexorably logical man shared the "peculiar soul" of the Russian intelligentsia whence he sprang. All this talk of boundless love, humiliation and disillusionment could well have come from a Russian novel; but it can not be matched in any political report from the labor movement of any other country. The historian is forced to the conclusion that, in the future quarrels, even when all sides are agreed that the issues are exclusively political, there remains a strong probability that the personal element has merely been "sublimated" or "rationalized" rather than altogether eliminated.

The quarrel ended, if not with mutual forgiveness and the joyful sobs of a "lovers' reconciliation," at least with a formal agreement to continue living together and to keep up appearances. The final negotiations were conducted "coolly, quite coolly." Potresov it was who proposed the compromise "so that a serious party enterprise might not be ruined by spoiled *personal* relations." (The emphasis, as always, is Lenin's.)

> We agreed among ourselves not to relate what had passed to anyone except our most intimate friends . . . On the surface everything appeared as if nothing had happened . . . But we felt an internal pang: instead of friendly relations, dry businesslike ones . . . We were always to be on our guard, on the principle: *Si vis pacem, para bellum.*

It is not too much to conclude that, from the disillusionment which ended his "youthful love affair," the thirty-year-old Vladimir Ilyich suddenly matured from Ulyanov to Lenin. Indeed, behind the whole "lovers' quarrel" was the fact, never consciously formulated, that Ulyanov was beginning to feel within himself the capacity to lead the movement, if necessary, without his master. When differences in temperament would ripen into differences in approach and formulation, Martov and Potresov, no less than Plekhanov, Axelrod and Zasulich, would remember the sudden anger and stubborn firmness which Ulyanov had displayed on this occasion. And they would find to their dismay that there was more than rhetoric in the conclusions about keeping a stone in one's sling and, while wishing peace, preparing war. Ulyanov immediately saw to it that the paper would be printed in Germany and not in Switzerland, so that Plekhanov would have to vote by mail. And he provided that all the machinery for underground distribution would remain in his hands.

> When I arrived in exile—Krupskaya writes—Vladimir Ilyich told me that he had succeeded in arranging that I should be made secretary of *Iskra* . . . This of course meant that contact with Russia would be carried on under the closest control of Vladimir Ilyich . . . He told me it had been rather awkward for him to have to arrange this, but that he considered it necessary for the good of the cause . . .

Now Vladimir Ilyich stopped using a different pseudonym for each article, and began to sign all of them with the single underground name: Lenin.[1] He was acquiring a serious view of continuity of leadership and of his own capacity to exercise it. His object was to build for the name Lenin a cumulative reputation, to make it stand for a set of systematic views on theory, politics, and, above all, organization. Whether signed or unsigned, his articles were supposedly an expression of a common view of all the editors, yet with a selfless intellectual self-love and an even profounder self-confidence he fought jealously for every fragment of his special viewpoint, even inserting it, often after shattering quarrels, as an interpolation into articles by the others. Most of his articles were unsigned, yet agents and readers became increasingly aware of the fact that a special set of ideas, presented in an especially stark, insistent, repetitive, unadorned and matter-of-fact way, kept recurring again and again over the same signature, or in the same style, from the same hand. Unlike the other editors, he would constantly refer to his own previous articles, expand them, gloss them, defend them, link the latest onto all the preceding ones in an unbroken chain.

The name Lenin passed from mouth to mouth in the underground. The police made increasing note of it. Exiles going abroad now often asked to meet Lenin as well as Plekhanov. In the obscure unconscious, Vladimir Ilyich was paving the way for its being known in separateness from and even against the fame-hallowed names of the "Oldsters" or the corporate name of *Iskra*. He began to sign it to personal letters to close followers, who looked to him within *Iskra* as they looked to *Iskra* within the less defined world of the labor and socialist underground. Sometimes his letters began with the impersonal "Lenin writing to . . ." or "Lenin speaking." And, despite his mere thirty years or so as against the more venerable ages of Plekhanov, Axelrod, Deutsch, Zasulich, he began

[1] Sometimes, N. Lenin. Between 1895 and the latter part of 1901, he had used the following names: K. Tulin, K. T——in, K. T——n, S.T.A., T.P., F.P., Petrov, Frey, T. Ch., T. Kh., Karpov, Meyer, Starik (in letters), Ilyin, V. Ilyin, Vl. Ilyin, and Vladimir Ilyin. The story told by Walter Duranty to the effect that he did not use the name Lenin until 1912, when he is supposed to have assumed it in honor of the Gold Strike on the Lena River, has no basis in truth. Beginning in 1901 he used the name Lenin or N. Lenin continuously, and over that signature even commented upon some of his earlier writings signed with his other pen names, thus tying them up with the set-of ideas to be associated thenceforward with his continuous signature. Prior to 1901, the name most frequently used had been Ilyin and its variants, V., Vl. and Vladimir Ilyin. Lenin is apparently derived from Ilyin, and Ilyin in turn from Vladimir Ilyich, his first name and patronymic, and from the "Ulyan" of Ulyanov. There is no basis for the American newspaper legend that the N. in N. Lenin stands for Nikolai. In European, and especially in Russian writing, N. or N.N. is a familiar symbol for anonymity, thus a kind of hint that Lenin is but a pseudonym.

some of them with "*Starik* speaking . . ." or ended them with the simple signature, *Starik* (in Russian, "The Old Man"). In a land soaked in patriarchal tradition, it was a nickname expressive of authority and respect, tinged with affectionate admiration. Stalin has since used all the overwhelming machinery of propaganda in vain to attach the nickname to his own person, but in their intimate moments his lieutenants still refer to him as *Khozyain*—"The Boss" —instead of *Starik*—"The Old Man."

It was unforeseen, yet inevitable, that this energetic, precise, schoolmasterly, youngish "Old Man" should dominate the new paper from the outset. It was his brain that had conceived it. He had found for it the name *Iskra*—"The Spark"—and for its masthead the Decembrists' longing, prophetic cry: "Out of the spark shall spring the flame." How could he fail to put his impress upon it when he attributed to it a role so much more ample than the others? To Plekhanov and his friends, and to Lenin's two "Brothers," it was just a revolutionary paper. That was no small thing, to be sure, in a country where all oppositional papers were forbidden. But to him it was more than that. It was to be a crusader against all forms of opportunism, revisionism, unorthodoxy, anti-Marxism. It was to encourage all the other oppositional currents against tsarism, yet criticize and expose them, too, and undermine their influence over the masses. It was not to serve a party but create a party, to unite Russia's scattered, narrow-visioned, short-lived, local circles into an All-Russian Social Democratic Labor Party. Its little band of secret agents, who would smuggle it across frontiers, were to form a close-knit company of schooled conspirators. They would penetrate everywhere, gather news, spy out information, report on moods, carry commands, recruit the best in every factory and locality and bind them closer to the movement. They would acquire influence over the working class and the whole revolutionary opposition; endow all spontaneous strikes and rebellions with socialist consciousness; teach the proletariat to look beyond the merely local to the nationwide and international; raise the workingman's eyes above the limited horizon of working-class concerns to those of all the oppressed and discontented. *Iskra* would be "the collective agitator and collective organizer," it would serve as "an enormous pair of bellows that would blow every spark of class struggle and popular indignation into a general conflagration." Its editors would be the ideological leaders of the future Party. Its agents would be the very framework of the Party, would, indeed, be that Party. And, as the Party, they would lead the proletariat, which in turn would lead all other oppressed, exploited and oppositional classes and strata of the population. Thus this group of *Iskra* editors, contributors, agents and organizers would form the skeletal general staff and officers' corps which tomorrow would mobilize and lead mighty armies into battle, hold them back from premature conflict, teach them to lay efficient, relentless, siege to the fortress of autocracy, and, at the right moment, go from siege to storm attack and victory.

There was poetry in this audacious conception of the role of a paper which, if it survived a few issues might consider itself fortunate, and which at best could hope to appear only irregularly, perhaps once a month or so, in an edition of a few thousand copies, more than two-thirds of which would be confiscated at the border. The other editors did not quite realize what thoughts their colleague was thinking. In the whole history of journalism, no other paper had been assigned quite so vast a role. Even if the careful Lenin had not taken the steps to bind the secret agents to him and get for his wife control of all the connections with Russia, his conception of *Iskra* as he expounded· it in article after article and as it gradually filtered into the Russian underground was sufficient to give readers and agents and supporters a sense of their own and the journal's importance, and to rally round the name of Lenin all those attracted to such audacious visions.

In the first number readers found an article, unsigned, bearing the title: "Urgent Tasks of Our Movement." Two ideas in it were momentous for the future history of Russia: (1) that the labor movement, left to itself without the guidance of the self-chosen "socialist vanguard," would "become petty and inevitably bourgeois"; and (2) that the vanguard in question would have to consist of people "who shall devote to the revolution not only their spare evenings, but the whole of their lives."

Only a few years before, Ulyanov had been proving that the peasants were "petty bourgeois" and that the peasant-socialist, Narodnik movement was "inevitably bourgeois," because they did not base themselves solely and exclusively upon the proletariat, "the class which alone can act as an independent fighter for socialism." Now he was taking a big step farther: the proletariat, too, would "become inevitably bourgeois" in its outlook unless it accepted the leadership and teachings of a self-appointed socialist vanguard of professional revolutionaries. If in the first contention was hidden the germ of a minority proletarian dictatorship over the majority of the Russian people, the peasants, in the second con-

tention was hidden the germ of a party dictatorship over the proletariat itself, exercised in its name.

This was a drastic departure from the much-quoted dictum of
Marx and Engels: "The emancipation of the working class is the
work of the working class itself." But the idea was not a new one
in Russia. More than a quarter-century earlier, Lenin's prototype
and predecessor, Tkachev, had written:

> Neither in the present nor in the future can the people,
> left to their own resources, bring into existence the social
> revolution. Only we revolutionists can accomplish this . . .
> Social ideals are alien to the people; they belong to the
> social philosophy of the revolutionary minority.

Lenin's sole change was to strike out the word "people" and substitute "proletariat." The spirit was the same. Questions still hidden
in the mists of the future were these: how were the members of the
revolutionary vanguard to be selected? how were they to know
what was best for the people, or for the proletariat? could they,
or would they, arouse it to take control of its own destinies, once
they had taken power in its name?

In the fourth number, Lenin returned to the same theme in a
longer article entitled "Where to Begin." Unsigned also, it pointedly
referred to the first article and promised to elaborate both into a
pamphlet. When the pamphlet, almost a year in gestation, finally
came out, it was a smallish book (160 pages in the English edition
of Lenin's *Collected Works*). It was entitled, after Chernishevsky's
famous novel, *What's to Be Done?*. It bore the signature, N. Lenin,
henceforth to be identified with these views.

Indeed, *What's to Be Done?* contained, some in germ, some fully
developed, virtually all of the ideas on politics and party organization which would later be known as "Leninist." It was destined to
mark the great divide down the opposing slopes of which would
flow separating waters. It was to become the gospel of all the
"hards" ("rock-hard" was the word they chose for themselves), to
whose only partly sensed ideas on leadership and control of the
nascent movement it gave a many-sided and sharply-chiseled formulation. And it was to possess a seductive attraction, too, for all
those "tender-minded" ones who mistrusted their own softness.
These might begin by opposing Lenin on one question or another,
but once they became convinced that they had been wrong and he
right in some conflict, they were likely to make complete surrender,
and become the most zealous of "Leninists." Thus, from the outset,

there were "repentant" Economists among the Bolsheviks. Other penitents would come with each new conflict. Together, these two types, the original "hards" and the "repentant softs" would make up the future Bolshevik leadership. That is why it could simultaneously harbor a Lunacharsky, who would shed tears and resign his commissar's post when he heard that the historic St. Basil's was under bombardment by the Bolsheviks, and a Stalin, whose self-chosen underground name suggested his steely core of hardness. As long as Lenin lived, most of his closest associates would be of the repentant soft type; under Stalin most of them would vanish from leadership altogether.

In intention, *What's to Be Done?* is a work of orthodox Marxism; not a mechanical copy or literal translation, but an attempt to assimilate the experiences of the Western labor and socialist movements and adapt them to the special conditions of Russian backwardness and lack of liberty. The profound respect for authority which characterized Lenin and his milieu caused him to "take counsel with Marx" (the words are his own), whenever some critical problem presented itself. Now as always he found quotations to fit his needs. But, of course, opponents searching so rich and varied a Scripture, could find quotations to fit an opposing viewpoint. In practical politics Lenin was too much a realist to rely on scholastic exegetics for the real outlines of his solutions. Sometimes the citations suggested a fertile line of thought; more often his line of thought suggested relevant quotations to lend authority to his solutions. In any case, to judge the present work by its quotations and professions alone is to miss its essence.

Thus the quotation which adorned its fly-leaf, if not from Marx or Engels, was at least from a letter to them from the hand of Lassalle. "Party struggles give a party strength and life . . . A party becomes stronger by purging itself!" These sentences, so alien to the real course of the unification of the Marxian and Lassallean movements in Germany, will bob up again and again in Russian labor history, taking on ever more sinister meaning with every split and expulsion, until they become the text of the great blood purges of the nineteen thirties. From all the voluminous writings of Marx, Engels and Lassalle, this was a strange choice to strike the keynote on the title page of a book intended to promote the "unification" of the still unformed Russian Social Democratic Party!

But Lenin did not mean the same thing as the others by "unification." His meaning was: the uniting of the autonomous local circles of the Marxist movement into a centrally controlled and ideologically homogeneous All-Russian party. Central control and ideological homogeneity: that was "unification." To secure it he was prepared to exclude all those who would not accept centralized organization; to force the merger of all papers into a single national organ; to exclude the Jewish Socialist Bund unless it was ready to give up its autonomy; to exclude Revisionists and Economists and all who were unready to accept without question the "orthodox" Marxist program, which he and Plekhanov and the other *Iskra* editors would prepare for the coming convention. There were some who thought that the first need of the still unborn party was a prolonged, full and free discussion of first principles. But to Lenin, as to Plekhanov, all that had already been settled, in Western Europe, by the works of Marx and Engels, and anew by Kautsky and Plekhanov in their still-raging controversy with Bernstein.

In Russia, the Bernsteinians, the Economists and Revisionists were already in retreat, defeated not so much by argument as by a deep change in mood. The economic boom which had given easy victory in strikes, had yielded to economic crisis. Storm clouds were gathering that three years later would burst out in revolution. Workers were even then beginning to go from petty economic demands to political demonstrations against the autocracy. Brooding students once more were meditating the assassination of tsarist officials. Manor-house burnings were beginning to illuminate the land. Even the liberal intelligentsia and bourgeoisie were drinking dangerous toasts at banquets, offering financial help to, and expecting political support from, the revolutionary movement, planning to participate in the socialist underground press or create an underground press of their own. All that the retreating Economists now asked before going into a unified party, which would apparently be led by Plekhanov and Lenin, was the right of continuing the discussion of those fundamental problems which they still regarded as unsettled.

But Lenin's conception of unification involved unconditional surrender or exclusion. The first chapter of his little book was one long attack on the very phrase "freedom of criticism":

> We are marching in a compact group along a precipitous and difficult path . . . surrounded on all sides by enemies . . . We have combined not to retreat into the marsh but for the express purpose of fighting the enemy. . . .
>
> Oh yes, gentlemen! You are free, not only to invite us, but to go yourselves wherever you will, even into the marsh. In fact, we think that the marsh is your proper place; and we are prepared to render *you* every assistance to get there. Only let go of our hands, don't clutch at us,

and don't besmirch the grand word *freedom;* for we too
are "free" to go where we please, free also . . . to fight
those who are turning towards the marsh.

Abandoning his opponents thus in the swamp, Lenin invites the
rest of his readers to scale heights from which is visible a vast
panorama. With Marxism as guide, the party can place itself at the
head of the proletariat, and the proletariat at the head of the
nation. And not only the nation!

> History has confronted us with an immediate task that is
> more revolutionary than all the immediate tasks that con-
> front the proletariat of any other country. The fulfillment
> of this task, the destruction of the most powerful bulwark,
> not only of European but no less of Asiatic reaction, places
> the Russian proletariat in the vanguard of the international
> revolutionary proletariat.

That is to be vanguard, indeed! Here in germ is the audacious
conception that inspired the Bolshevik revolution, of 1917, and the
founding of the Communist International.

Having disposed of peasant socialism, Economism and Marx-
Revisionism as "bourgeois," Lenin turns his attention to the nascent
trade-union movement. No flattery here either! The proletariat, left
to its own devices, without the benefit of direction by the Marxist
vanguard, becomes "bourgeois" too:

> The working class exclusively by its own efforts, is able
> to develop only trade-union consciousness . . . Modern
> socialist consciousness can only be brought to them from
> without . . . can arise only on the basis of profound scien-
> tific knowledge. The bearers of science are not the prole-
> tariat but the bourgeois intelligentsia. It is out of the heads
> of members of this stratum [Marx and Engels—and Lenin
> might have added himself and Plekhanov] that modern
> socialism originated . . . Pure and and simple trade union-
> ism means the ideological subordination of the workers to
> the bourgeoisie . . . Our task is to bring the labor move-
> ment under the wing of revolutionary Social Democracy
> . . . Working-class consciousness cannot be genuinely
> political consciousness unless the workers are trained to
> respond to all cases of tyranny, oppression, violence and
> abuse, no matter *what class* is affected . . . To bring po-
> litical knowledge to the workers, the Social Democrats must
> *go among all classes of the population,* must dispatch units
> of their army *in all directions.* The Social Democrat's ideal

should not be a trade-union secretary, but *a tribune of the people.*

The multiplying italics suggest the excitement with which Lenin presented his views and the importance he attached to them. Indeed, this vision of the role of Russian socialism brings us to the core of his political theories, and gives us his choice between the diverging crossroads at which the young movement was then standing.

Russian labor might choose to lay its major emphasis on immediate living conditions—wages, hours, dwellings, factory sanitation, social insurance. And it might limit its immediate political objectives, accordingly, to the legalization of the right of assembly, of the right of political party and union organization, and the securing of labor legislation. Or it might subordinate all these issues to the general revolutionary struggle against tsarism.

If the first path were chosen, it might lead to the gradual legalization of the labor movement, to the slow and at first precarious growth of autonomous, self-governing unions, the destinies of which would be directly determined by the workingmen who composed them. Later, it might lead to the development of a socialistic labor party formed on this trade-union foundation and controlled from below by the organized workers. In that case the professional revolutionaries of the intelligentsia, whose whole soul was concentrated on the struggle to overthrow tsarism, would find themselves still conspiring in a social vacuum, without a labor army over which to assume officership. Or this would-be general staff might change its course and offer itself to the labor movement as mere servitors, advisers, specialists, whose ideological views would be accepted only to the extent that they could convince the labor movement to adopt them.

However, if the second course, Lenin's course, were chosen, strikes and unions would be subordinated to the struggle against tsarism. The nascent labor movement would prolong its illegalization. Its transitory organizations would come under the control of the budding party of socialist intellectual conspirators, and these latter would determine labor's direction, its aims and its destiny.

Though it was never so clearly formulated, this was the real issue between "Economists" and Marxists, then between Mensheviks and Bolsheviks, then between Workers Opposition and Lenin, between Tomsky and Stalin, changing forms of the protean battle between Westernizer and Slavophile. One path led closer to the parties and trade unions of the West, which were democratically organized, comfortably adapted to the sizable legality permitted them, and long since devoid of insurrectionary spirit except as a banner for festal occasions. The other led to concentration on conspiracy and insurrection under the leadership of a self-selected, rigidly centralized, secret and conspirative band of revolutionary intellectuals under a self-appointed leader, formed on the pattern of the early "professional revolutionaries" of the Narodnaya Volya.

To be sure, Lenin did not feel the divergence of his path from that of the Western socialist parties and unions. They were right for the West because the West was "democratic, modern and progressive." But Russia was "Asiatic, barbarous, and backward." Into the holiday revolutionary phrases of the Western unions and parties, he read the meanings springing from the immediately revolutionary spirit of Russian life. Politically, Russia was still living in the eighteenth or early nineteenth century, still on the eve of its "1789" or its "1848." This it was that made the *Communist Manifesto*, issued on the eve of the European revolutions of 1848—now little more than a revered, if seminal, document in Western Europe—seem in every sense a contemporary document in Russia. How could Lenin know that the resounding phrases that issued from the tongues and pens of Western leaders on high holidays were but dimming reminiscences? For him, the West, above all Germany, was sweeping steadily toward social revolution. All that had held Western Europe back from successful revolution in 1848 had been tsarist Russia's intervention. Therefore, all that was needed to unleash the overdue revolution in the West, was to remove once and for all the threat of tsarist intervention. The overthrow of tsarism would start a socialist uprising throughout Europe, and even backward Russia might be dragged into socialism in its wake.

On Lenin's side was the newness and backwardness of Russia's working class, little suited as yet to organization in autonomous and democratically self-controlled unions and parties. On his side the narrow obstinacy of the Tsar and his closest advisers, who, while they yielded piecemeal to the demands of the "modern age," yielded too slowly and too little at a time. On his side the dark camarilla around the Tsarina, which was to take ever tighter control over affairs of state and seek the snatching back of every concession made to a slowly awakening people. On his side the conflict between the swiftly changing needs of modern industry and the slowly changing, ancient structure of the land. On his side the tremendous charge of energy which came from the so long overdue "bourgeois revolution," stepped up by the energy created by the modern, post-bourgeois movement for socialism. When a latecomer takes ideas from more advanced lands, it wants the "latest," freed from its origins, counterpoises and complexities. On his side, though he did not suspect it, was a coming crisis in the West itself, that would threaten the very existence of all its hard-won institutions of democracy and freedom. On his side, finally, was the simplicity, the fanatical ardor and fighting *élan* of a new, million-headed working class, yesterday's peasants in today's overalls and tomorrow's uniforms, just torn loose from their village ways of life and thought, open to whoever might present the simplest, most dramatic and most persuasive outlook to take the place of that which they had just lost.

On the surface, much of *What's to Be Done?* is an attack upon the intelligentsia, "careless and sluggish in their habits." Lenin's consuming "un-Russian" passion for system and order is largely explainable in terms of his reaction to the slackness of the human material with which he had to work. His book proposed a rigorously centralized hierarchical structure for the new party. The center would issue commands, the local organizations would carry them out, "discussing" them mainly in the sense of discussing how best to execute them. The center could draw people out of local work for its purposes, and would have the power to approve or reject the personnel of leading committees in the localities. The center would safeguard the purity of doctrine and action of the Party. This system he denominated "proletarian discipline," and castigated the intellectuals for their reluctance to accept it. The factory, Lenin asserted, accustomed the proletarian to such discipline; but it was alien and distasteful to the self-reliant, individualistic, slippered ease of the intelligentsia. The latter's opposition was therefore "petty bourgeois" and constituted "opportunism in the organization question." [2]

[2] It was not some spokesman of the "opportunists" but the leader of the revolutionary wing of the German Social Democracy, Rosa Luxemburg, who made the classic critique of this Leninist doctrine of "proletarian discipline":
"The discipline which Lenin means," she wrote, "is impressed upon the proletariat not only by the factory, but also by the barracks and by modern bureaucratism, in short, by the entire mechanism of the centralized bourgeois state. But it is nothing less than the abuse of a general term which at the same time designates as 'discipline' two such opposing concepts as the willfulness and thoughtlessness of a many-limbed, many-armed mass of flesh carrying out mechanical movements at the beat of the baton, and the voluntary coordination of the conscious political action of a social stratum; the corpselike obedience of a dominated class and the organized rebellion of a class struggling for freedom. It is not by making use of the discipline impressed upon him by the capitalist state, with a mere transfer of the baton from the hand of the bourgeoisie to that of a Social Democratic Central

Despite these strictures upon the intelligentsia, this book of Lenin's really assigns to them a larger role than does any other socialist work ever written. What were the "professional revolutionaries" if not revolutionary intellectuals, detached from "orderly society," breaking with family, friends and place in the social structure, and living in the Russian underground exclusively for the struggle against tsarism? All through the nineteenth century young men and women of generous vision had been abandoning other professions for this one of revolutionist, with its outlawry, its brief hide-and-seek with the police, its prison, exile to Siberia, flight abroad, or gallows. Every wing of the Russian revolutionary movement had been made up of such underground "professionals," and would continue to be. But Lenin alone, though he castigated them for their weaknesses, instilled in them a sense of their own importance and made a virtue of what had hitherto been a lonely necessity. Now that the masses were beginning to enter into motion on their own account, Lenin still proposed that the revolutionary party should be made up of professional revolutionists and that the masses and their wider, more elementary organizations should be directed and controlled by this underground party of professionals. As always when expounding his convictions, he was ruthlessly logical and unequivocal:

> I assert: 1. That no movement can be durable without a stable organization of leaders to maintain continuity; 2. that the more widely the masses are drawn into the struggle and form the basis of the movement, the more it is necessary to have such an organization and the more stable it must be; 3. that the organization must consist chiefly of persons engaged in revolution as a profession; 4. that in a country with a despotic government, the more we *restrict* the membership of this organization to those who are engaged in revolution as a profession . . . the more difficult it will be to catch the organization; and 5. the *wider* will be the circle of men and women of the working class or of other classes of society able to join the movement and perform active work in it.

Of course, Lenin did not object to workingmen being recruited into this classless company devoted to "their" class struggle—quite the contrary. But these would be only "exceptional workingmen," carefully selected by the professional revolutionaries, tested and

Committee, but it is only by breaking through and uprooting this slavish spirit of discipline that the proletariat can be educated for a new discipline: the voluntary self-discipline of Social Democracy."

trained for entrance into this élite of professional officers. Because of their lack of general culture, it would be harder for them than for the intellectuals to develop "full social-democratic conscious-ness" and Marxist theoretical knowledge, though they would pos-sess, in compensation, a closer knowledge of the psychology of the class from which they had come and which they were to lead in the future. But they, too, would have to be declassed, that is, cease to be workingmen, in order to make revolution their profession. Aside from the initial advantages in psychology and disadvantages in culture, no distinction would be made in the revolutionary movement between one who had been a workingman and one who had been an intellectual before he took up this profession. ("The organizations of revolutionists must be comprised first and foremost of people whose profession is that of revolutionist . . . As this is the common feature of the members of such an organization, *all dis-tinctions as between workers and intellectuals* must be dropped.")

In this kind of party, Lenin thought he had found not only the devices for protection against the police, but also a guarantee against theoretical weakness, lack of principle, opportunism, against the dilution of the revolutionary philosophy. Only those who had theoretically assimilated the whole range of Marxist thought and practically mastered the difficult technical arts of conspiracy were fit to make up the organization he envisaged. Such an organization, he thought, could not degenerate and could not fail. Its ideas, programs and decisions, given material force by the working class, and, beyond that, by all other discontented and aggrieved classes in tsarist society, would be able to destroy the old world and build a new. "Give us an organization of revolutionaries," exclaimed Lenin, Archimedes-like, "and we will turn Russia upside-down."

It must be clear that this "professional revolutionary" was some-thing quite different from the full-time paid official of the Western party or trade union. These latter are chosen by and responsible to the rank-and-file. Expertness, a "machine," or the passivity and inertia of the rank and file, might give them more or less permanent tenure. But always there remained the possibility of their being overruled, even removed by their membership. Lenin's plan, on the other hand, involved men who were self-chosen, who had chosen themselves as professional revolutionaries and professional leaders of a movement they were to create in their own image. At the top were the self-appointed *Iskra* editors. They, in turn, were to select their agents by careful winnowing and send them into the localities. These, in their turn, would select their local following with equal care. This organization constructed hierarchically from the top downward would set up or seek to control all broader organizations of actual workingmen, and, in the name of the workingmen, would attempt to assume leadership over the activities of other oppositional classes.

Nor were their lives as comfortable, or their "profession" as well-paid, as that of the full-time officials of other European organizations, not to mention the salaries of our American union leaders. Plekhanov, until his wife became a successful physician, earned his poor living by such mean tasks as copying and addressing envelopes; Axelrod by making and selling *kefir* ("yogurt" or "clabber"); Lenin did translations, placed an occasional article in a non-party magazine, got small sums from his mother; Trotsky, always an able journalist, gradually tapered off the receipt of aid from his family and earned his living by writing for non-party papers; Stalin worked as a night clerk in an astronomical laboratory, then lived by sleeping and eating around in the homes of members and sympathizers and collecting small sums from them. Only later did the movement, not through dues but through the donations and bequests of wealthy liberals, and, for a while after 1905, through the revolutionary holdups, acquire enough money to give these "professionals" a wage of anywhere from five or ten rubles to thirty to fifty rubles (fifteen to twenty-five dollars) a month.[3] Those who could get money from their families or from literary ventures often took nothing from the movement, even, like Potresov, contributing considerable sums to it.

What Lenin's theory of the centralized hierarchical organization of "professional revolutionaries" would mean in practice, what kind of party and general labor and revolutionary movement it would beget, what relations would obtain between the band of self-chosen, dedicated professionals and the still unborn mass organizations—all this was still hidden in the future. The immediate effect of the expression of this theory in *What's to Be Done?* and in the columns of *Iskra,* was to strengthen the latter journal in its feud with rival socialist papers, and to enhance Lenin's own rapidly growing reputation among the little band of professionals that made up the actual movement. The theory was truly Russian in that it was built upon the established tradition of the Narodovoltsi and other terrorists of the past: conspiracy, centralism, hierarchy, life-dedication, arrogant humility. The tiny band of *Iskra* agents were stirred by the vision

[3] "Those members of the Party who gave their entire time to the Party work got very small remuneration, sometimes as low as 3, 5 or 10 rubles, and never exceeding 30 rubles per month." Yaroslavsky: *History of the Communist Party,* English Edition, Moscow, 1927, Vol. V, Chapter X, p. 15.

of themselves as an officers' corps destined to lead mighty armies. Audacious yet detailed, the plan seemed to hold promise of overcoming the feebleness, slackness, local dispersion, transience and amateurishness which afflicted the movement. It gave new "Marxist" justification to the already traditional Russian revolutionary structure evolved by the old terrorist conspiratorial movement; it promised efficiency, uncompromising purity, ultimate victory.

While, in the underground, enthusiasm for *Iskra*, for its famous editors and its network of resolute agents steadily grew, clashes of temperament and unanalyzed differences of viewpoint slowly deepened the rifts among the editors themselves. In the painful vacuum of silence and exile, there was no superior force, no democratic rank-and-file organization to which they could submit their differences. Just because, to use Potresov's words, "we fought over special, individual, partial questions without as yet being able to catch the general sense of the differences which lay at the bottom of all these disputes," their clashes had a sharpness out of all proportion to the issues. Like the Russian intellectuals that they were, they tended to elevate every difference into a matter of principle.

Obsolescence, too, was doing its corrosive work. Not by quarter-centuries, as is the common reckoning, but by half-decades and less, did the revolutionary generations succeed each other. Plekhanov was forty-five when *What's to Be Done?* was written; Axelrod, fifty-one; Vera Zasulich, fifty. Theirs were names to conjure with, but they had been away from Russia for two decades. Lenin was thirty-one; Potresov, thirty-two; Martov, twenty-eight. Inside Russia, these three were already referred to as "the old ones." The Economists were the "youngsters." And from Siberia, a still more youthful Russian was beginning to send articles to *Iskra*, written with sufficient gusto to have earned for him the pseudonym of *Pero* ("The Pen"). This "Pen" was only twenty-two, far younger than the "youngsters"—herald of a new generation that was soon to give the Iskrists the victory over their Economist opponents. Already, Plekhanov with his mere forty-five years and his two decades of activity was alienating such young men when they disagreed with him by snapping: "Your fathers and mothers were still crawling under the table when I—" If Plekhanov was irascible, Axelrod was poor in health. Poverty and exile had taken their toll. The warmth with which Axelrod had first greeted the young Ulyanov back in 1895 had had in it an element of the feeling that at last there was something growing up inside Russia, and someone to hand over the burdens of organization. According to Krupskaya, Axelrod had "lost three-quarters of his working capacity . . . did not sleep for nights at a stretch . . . wrote with extreme intensity for months on end without being able to finish the article on which he had started." While Plekhanov was to waver for the next decade between bolshevism and menshevism, it was upon the ailing Axelrod that the task fell of working out the basic political and organizational conceptions that came to be known as menshevism.

If Plekhanov was the philosopher and Axelrod the political thinker of the old guard, the most picturesque and lovable of its members was Vera Zasulich. At the age of sixteen (that was back in 1867), she had been arrested for the crime of being acquainted with the conspirator Nechaev. From then on, she went into and out of prisons, into and out of administrative exile, until she acquired renown by shooting the Governor General of Saint Petersburg, Trepov, because of the flogging of an imprisoned fellow-student. Her trial—incautiously the government granted her a jury trial— turned into one long demonstration in her favor. Though her attorney had merely pleaded extenuating circumstances, the jury acquitted her. The crowd rescued her from police bent on her re-arrest. An "underground railway" smuggled her out of Russia. That was in 1878, when she was twenty-seven. During all the decades of her faithful discipleship to Plekhanov and Axelrod, she had longed with the deep longing of her warmly emotional being for another sight of her beloved country. Plekhanov and Axelrod had families but she had none. She lived in cheerful penury and bohemian disorder in a tiny, tobacco-dust- and stale-smoke-laden little room. Krupskaya tells how she used to cook her meat on an oil stove, clipping off pieces with a pair of shears. When some English ladies, to make conversation, asked how long she cooked it, she answered: "If I am hungry, ten minutes; if not, three hours."

More than once she spoke to Krupskaya of her loneliness. "I have nobody close to me." And then, to hide the poignancy of her feelings, "But you love me, I know. And when I die, you'll say—dear me, we're drinking one cup of tea less—"

Krupskaya did indeed love her, and so did Lenin. ("Wait till you meet Vera Ivanovna," he had written his wife, "there's a person as clear as crystal.") Yet, within a couple of years, he would be proposing to oust her and Axelrod from the *Iskra* editorial board so that he might be sure of a dependable majority.

Later a rift would grow up between Lenin and the other two members of his own "triple alliance," Martov and Potresov. But so far he thought of them as "brothers" and of all differences as something arising between the three of them and the older editors. It was his bloc against Plekhanov's. A tiny episode dramatized the growing tension. In 1902, young *Pero*, "the Pen" whose writings had attracted Lenin's attention, escaped from Siberia. He fled to London to drink wisdom at the fount of the famous six, and, having received the address from an underground *Iskra* agent, went straight to Lenin's lodgings. His knock waked the still-sleeping household, and he heard Krupskaya call up to her husband: "Hallo, *Pero* has come!"

Lenin examined the new supporter, took him walking, showed him London, discussed the "Leninist" views with him, decided that the bright but inexperienced young "Pen" must remain abroad for some time to be trained, and must be coopted onto the editorial board of *Iskra* so that a seventh man might break the frequent three-three deadlock. It was an astonishing proposal to add a mere youngster to the famous board of editors. Plekhanov, sensing an eclipse of the veterans by a lineup of four against three, developed an intense dislike for "The Pen," which that young man could not understand, for he had no more idea than the rest of the Russian revolutionaries of the secret antagonisms developing in *Iskra*. The new recruit was brought into the sessions, but without a vote because of Plekhanov's opposition. When he ventured to speak his mind in an insignificant controversy, Plekhanov poured upon his head the vials of his acid irony. Young "Pen" defended himself with spirit, and proved, too, to have an eloquent, ironical tongue, so that Lenin had to call him aside to teach him tact: "You had better leave it to Martov to answer Plekhanov. Martov will cement what you break. It is better for him to cement it." When Lenin submitted to the other editors an article from the newcomer, Plekhanov sent it back with the notation: "I don't like the pen of your 'Pen.'"

"The style is a matter of acquisition," Lenin replied, "but the man is capable of learning and will be useful."

Shortly thereafter, the young journalist abandoned the name that had given rise to these feeble puns, in favor of the name under which he was one day to become known throughout the world: Leon Trotsky.

CHAPTER X

LEV DAVIDOVICH BRONSTEIN

During a heated discussion at Karlsruhe in 1903, Medem asked his opponent Trotsky: "When it comes to classifying yourself, you certainly cannot ignore the fact of national allegiance. You consider yourself, I take it, to be either a Russian or a Jew."
"No!" cried Trotsky, "you are mistaken! I am a Social Democrat, and that's all."—*The Biography of Vladimir Medem*

UNTIL THE eighteenth century, the Ukraine—as its name implies— was a borderland or frontier. Only at the century's end, with the defeat of the Turks, the partition of Poland, and the dissolution of the free Cossack settlements, did Muscovy's power expand securely through the Ukraine to the shores of the Black Sea. The annexation of eastern Poland and Lithuania brought to the Tsars a considerable number of Jewish subjects, the largest and densest concentration of Jews in the world. They were desperately poor for the most part, making their living chiefly as innkeepers, petty merchants and artisans. By *ukaz* in the year 1804, Alexander I forbade his newly acquired subjects to continue in the liquor trade. But the *ukaz* opened to them a new avenue of escape out of the economic noose that had been steadily tightening about them: it offered state lands in the so-called "New Russia," the sparsely settled Ukrainian provinces of Kherson and Ekaterinoslav, for Jewish agricultural colonization. Thereby the course of history, which had been driving the Jews ever more completely out of agriculture since the decline of the Ancient World, gave promise of being reversed. Alexander's brother, Nicholas I, continued the Alexandrine policy, even granting exemption from the 25-year term of forced military service to Jews who would take up new lands and settle new villages in the midst of the steppes. In 1866, Alexander II put an end to the movement his father and his uncle had started. In 1872 much of the land was taken away from them. In 1882, after the assassination of Alexander II, in which several of the participants were Jewish, a new *ukaz* forbade Jews to rent, lease or buy further land. The noose was tightening again.

From one of these Jewish farms in the Province of Kherson, in the spring of the year 1879, a hardy, hard-working, well-built

farmer named David Leontievich Bronstein set out with his wife
and children to take up a larger farm in the same province, part
of a run-down estate of one Colonel Yanovsky, after whom farm
and village were known as Yanovka. Bronstein must have been a
second, perhaps a third generation farmer, a fact testified to by the
non-Jewish form of his patronymic, Leontievich, by his lack of
Yiddish and Hebrew, and by his skill in husbandry. Farmer Bronstein had been born in a little Jewish town in the Province of
Poltava, from which, as a small boy, his parents had taken him to
the open prairie in the Province of Kherson. He spoke a broken
mixture of Russian and Ukrainian, in which the latter predomi-
nated. Until he was an old man, and wanted to spell out for himself
the titles of his famous son's books, he was not able to read. But
he was a good judge of people, of hired help, of animals, of tools,
of markets and crops. The years of life in the open plains were
Russifying such families, ruralizing them, making them less and
less of a "peculiar people," more and more like the neighbors
around them. In spirit even more than in physical distance, Farmer
Bronstein was almost completely outside the invisible ghetto walls
that his grandparents had carried with them when they first entered
the steppes. As his prosperity grew with the years of his unremitting toil, the small store of his piety and conformity and Jewish
heritage continued to diminish. At first he kept up appearances
out of habit and under pressure from relatives and Jewish neighbors, continuing to make journeys on high holy days to the syna-
gogue in nearby Gromokley, four versts away. Mrs. Bronstein, being
town-bred and a woman, was a little more conservative in such
matters. She refrained from sewing on the Jewish Sabbath ("at
least," one of her sons would write, "within the sight of others"),
and, when that son was dangerously ill and had to be taken to the
doctor on a Saturday, she refused to ride with him, sending instead
a trusted Christian employee. Was it piety, or because the doctor
lived in the midst of a Jewish settlement? As the children grew
older, Farmer Bronstein spoke openly in their presence and hers of
his disbelief in the existence of God. And even Mrs. Bronstein,
though she prayed occasionally in moments of crisis, increasingly
neglected ritual prescription and prayer with the increasing tale
of her years.

The Bronsteins raised wheat and sheep and pigs, like their neighbors, and lived lives that were scarcely distinguishable from those
around them, unless by the fact that they were not so given to drink
as most, worked harder, were more foresighted, drove better bargains with the grain merchants, were able to make a go of it dur-

ing the prolonged crisis of the eighties, when the competition of American, Canadian and Argentine wheat ruined so many farmers of the steppes. But their thrifty German neighbors were as sober in their habits and did every bit as well. One other distinction—perhaps ascribable to their heritage as descendants of "the People of the Book," was the respect of this illiterate farmer and his barely literate wife for book learning, not merely as something practical to be used on the farm, but more as something desirable for their children, and elevating in whoever might possess it.

When the Bronsteins moved to their Yanovka farm from the Province of Kherson, in the spring of 1879, they brought with them two children, a son and a daughter, and left behind them the graves of two others who had died in childhood. In her womb, Mrs. Bronstein carried yet another child. It was to be a lusty manchild, born that same autumn, on October 26 of the Russian calendar, or November 7 on the calendar in use in the West.[1] They gave him the name of Lev or Lyova, the Russian word for "lion." Many in after years would feel the name's appropriateness. It would be translated into German as Leo, and into English, French and Spanish as Leon, and, coupled with the later pen-name of Trotsky, it would become known around the world.[2]

Thirty-eight years later, the boy's birthday would, by coincidence, become the birthday of the Bolshevik Soviet power. "Mystics and Pythagoreans," Trotsky comments in his Autobiography, "may draw from this whatever conclusion they like. I myself noticed this odd coincidence only three years after the October uprising."

For non-Pythagoreans it is more instructive to note two other calendar events of the year 1879 which were closely intertwined with young Bronstein's fate. Two months before he was born, the Narodnaya Volya passed its sentence of death upon the reigning Tsar. Two months after his birth was born one Iosif Vissarionovich

---

[1] The Russian calendar was twelve days behind that of Western Europe in the nineteenth century and thirteen days behind in the twentieth. On February 1, 1918, the Soviet Government adopted the Western or "New Style" calendar. In the present work, except as otherwise noted, the Western calendar is used throughout. The Bolshevik seizure of power took place on this boy's birthday, i.e. October 25, Old Style, November 7, New Style, 1917. It is referred to in Russian literature as the October Revolution, but, of course, it is now celebrated annually on November 7.

[2] As the son of David Bronstein, Trotsky's legal name was Lev Davidovich Bronstein. In childhood he was generally called by the diminutive Lyova. The pen-name "Trotsky," originally adopted for underground purposes, finally displaced "Bronstein" altogether, so that in 1917 he signed himself for legal purposes Lev Davidovich Trotsky. His admirers, and even his wife in her memoirs, generally refer to him merely by the initials "L.D.," and I have seen letters of his signed with that signature.

Djugashvili. The first of these events led to the assassination of Alexander II, with which began the black reaction of the eighties. As part of the reaction there was devious governmental encouragement of the first modern pogroms; the Jews were prohibited from further owning or leasing of land; the *numerus clausus* was introduced into higher education.[3] The second event, the birth of Iosif Djugashvili in Transcaucasia, was to provide David Bronstein with the chief antagonist of his closing years.

Yanovka was a lonely little village on a dirt road, scarcely distinguishable from the surrounding steppe, lost in sheep runs and wheat fields that spread in all directions to the horizon. The nearest postoffice was fifteen miles away, the railroad twenty-two; to see a doctor meant an overnight journey. Newspapers never reached this home; a letter was a rarity; a telegram, brought on horseback, could only signify calamity. The rest of Russia impinged on the closed life of Yanovka only to purchase wheat, levy taxes and conscripts, supply migratory workers for the harvest. Beyond Russia was a world which seemed to consist principally of two sinister places called Canada and Argentina, which, some years, dumped so much cheap wheat on the market that tight-fisted, hard-working landowner Bronstein could not make his cost of production, and his less thrifty and energetic neighbors were completely ruined. It seemed hardly likely that a lad born in this little village would ever acquire a world outlook or become a symbol of internationalism.

In the relentless language of status which his son's success would later make into a human touchstone, David Bronstein was a kulak. At the age of seventy, when that son was already in the seat of power, Old Bronstein was "menaced by the Reds because he was rich, and the Whites persecuted him because he was my father" (Trotsky, *Autobiography*, p. 19). By dint of parsimony and ambition and cruel, unremitting toil—his own toil and his wife's no less than that of his hired help—by paying no more wages than was customary or necessary, by adding kopek to kopek, building to building, animal to animal and acre to acre, he had come to own outright 250 acres of land and lease an additional 400. When, by the decrees of 1882 and 1887 the Tsar forbade Jews to buy or lease new land, he was well enough established and his neighbors friendly enough and sufficiently in need of his rubles so that subterfuge, palm-greasing, and extra tribute on each leased or purchased acre enabled him to continue to enlarge his farm. His long, open sheds were filled with wheat, which he could afford to hold until

[3] A decree of 1887 limiting the number of Jews to be admitted to state schools to 10 per cent of the total number of students.

the harvest dumping of the more necessitous was over. He had well-stocked stables, cowsheds, pigsties, chicken coops; a machine shop with a roof that did not leak like the one which sheltered his family; a mill with a ten-horse-power engine to grind his grain and, for 10 per cent in kind, that of all his neighbors for miles around. The mill made him more than the most energetic farmer, it made him the dominant figure of rural Yanovka.

As befitted an uncultured, middle-class family on the make, the Bronsteins lived in rude, self-denying simplicity. They knew no hunger nor want, but little luxury or leisure. Lyova, all his life an exaggeratedly neat dresser, remembers the agony he felt at his torn shoes when he was introduced to a revered older city cousin come on a visit. The barns might be wood with raised stone foundations to protect the harvest, the machine shop with its valuable machinery might boast a tiled roof, but all through his boyhood the family lived in a house of mud which they had found on the land when they purchased it from the Tsar's original beneficiary, Colonel Yanovsky. There were deep crevasses in the mud walls, where adders nested; the roof of thatched reed was aflutter with sparrows; the rain came through in summer storms, and pots and pans had to be set in strategic places to prevent the water from making mire of the earthen floors. Only two of the five little, low-ceilinged rooms had flooring of wood: the living room, which was sanded weekly, and the tiny parlor, where the wood was painted. Fleas nested in the earthen floors of the other rooms, as Lyova had cause to remember. In winter, the snow blowing from all the corners of the open prairie walled in the adders sleeping in the crevasses, closed up the cracks, piled up above the dingy windows, making the long winter evenings longer still, keeping the occupants—idle now—snug and warm. Not until Lyova was grown and had left his father's home for good, did David Bronstein take the time and substance necessary to build himself a house of brick with roof of tin. He built it sturdily—as was his wont—so that after the Revolution of 1917 it was taken over by the government and used as a schoolhouse. That was the first time there had ever been a school in Yanovka.

There was little time for display of affection or care in the gray-colored childhood of Lev Davidovich. Both of his parents were busy about the farm, except in mid-winter. The long summer days were spent with an older brother and sister, a younger sister, a visiting aunt or two, and above all with the help: a nurse, a chambermaid, a cook, a steward, a mechanic, a fireman, a shepherd, a stableboy, a number of permanent hired laborers. These were Lyova's principal companions and tutors. When crops were large and prices high there might be scores, even hundreds of temporary workers besides, from whom to pick up scraps of information and instruction, of amusement and discomfiture. His older brother, Sasha, and his older sister, Liza, taught him his first letters. As soon as he had a little additional schooling, he displaced them as his father's "accountant," talking down the sketchy and sporadic notations dictated to him by old Bronstein whenever they came into the farmer's head. The old man could neither read nor figure until his sixtieth year, when he began to wrestle with the mysteries of the alphabet to spell out the titles of his son's books and puzzle over their contents. Mrs. Bronstein could read, albeit with difficulty. When the snow walled in the old house and made work outside impossible, she loved to sit near the great stove in the living room, whispering loudly to herself the words of some Russian novel, which had been borrowed from a library many miles away.

An ink bottle, stoppered with paper, resting on the long, low rafter; a penholder with an old and rusty pen; a copybook to take down the notations dictated by the head of the house to his children; an old number or two of some rural magazine intended for the country gentry, probably acquired with the house; the borrowed novels read by Mrs. Bronstein; the tumble-down spinet bought for sixteen rubles from a bankrupt neighbor and repaired by the versatile mechanic; a bit of schooling and music lessons for the two older children while they lived with relatives near a schoolhouse—these would appear to represent the cultural aspirations of the Bronstein family. If you pressed old Bronstein as to why he worked himself and his wife so hard and why he continued to add to his wealth and cares after he had acquired a sufficiency of both, he might at first be at a loss to answer. But he would doubtless come to it in the end that he hoped to give his children an ampler life than he had known and endow them with that respected something called an "education." The important thing was the male children. Bronstein might be irreligious, but he wanted them to learn to read the Bible in the original Hebrew for that was part of his inherited concept of learning. When his older boy showed little aptitude for studies the farmer set his hopes on his younger son.

There was little in Lyova Bronstein's childhood of the sunny gaiety, the family warmth and closeness, the atmosphere of culture, the outdoor sports, which we noted in the boyhood of Lenin. Lyova never learned to skate or swim, never entered into tests of strength or physical skill. Though he was endowed with a good frame he never developed it until years later; it took Siberia to make him aware of nature and turn him into a passionate fisher and hunter; and it took command of the Red Army to give him his military bearing. Until he learned to read, the center of his world was the farm machine shop, his chief tutor in the ways of things and men being Ivan Vasilevich Grebin, the mechanic who presided there. It was Ivan Vasilevich who cut him out his cardboard train, let him blow the bellows and thread screws and nuts, showed him how to turn wooden croquet balls on the lathe; in later years even made him a homemade bicycle on which he learned to ride. It was from the lips of Ivan Vasilevich that he got his first inkling of the complexity of human conduct. When not with the mechanic, he would play games with his little sister Olya (Olga): "hide-and-seek" in the bins of wheat, or "house" with homemade rag dolls on the torn divan in the living room. Sometimes, of a winter evening, the whole family would play "Old Maid," the father joining in with the rest. As soon as Lyova learned to read and wield a pen, the new pursuits it opened to him crowded out all the others, until even the machine shop seemed to lose its attraction.

His pen became a sort of fetish with a power and will of its own. With the help of a table knife he carved himself a new one, using it to copy pictures of horses from an old magazine. On another occasion its magic powers impelled him to write down forbidden obscenities, heard in barn and fields but never in this puritanic household. He shed copious tears when his sister caught him at it and she and his mother tried to see what was on the secretive paper. Again the mysterious pen drew verses out of him, and his sister told the family, which thought him quite a poet. The boy knew better, somehow, fleeing in shame when his father tried to make him read them aloud to guests. With the pen's aid, he and his cousin played at editing a magazine. Clutched in his hand, it took down his father's mysterious gains and losses in contest with "Argentina," his debts and those his neighbors owed him, the calculations of the tithe for grinding at the mill, the miserable figures in kopeks and rubles that represented a summer's toil for his laborers—figures which gave the boy his first sense of the hardness of a system which left the rural laborer almost nothing to tide him over the enforced idleness of winter. The pen copied magnificent passages from the poets, eloquent speeches from the dramatists, then began to write original compositions that amazed and thrilled their author. When in later years he chose his first illegal name to throw the police off his track while he contributed articles to revolutionary journals, the name was *Pero*—"The Pen."

To the magic of the pen was closely linked the magic of the book. Books were the Arabian carpet that carried him far from drab Yanovka, lifted him aloft so that he could see great stretches of the world. From books, he learned of Russia's past and grandeur, of other provinces and kingdoms and ways of life more civilized than the rude ones his boyhood had so far known. He used books to show off, too, for he was always fond of displaying his powers. At school he deliberately read history books more advanced than the required text, and asked questions to show that he knew the answers, or to stump his teachers. In time he found that there were forbidden books: one on sexual crimes and perversions which his older brother brought home from the city and tried to hide behind other books out of reach; another by Tolstoy, called *Powers of Darkness*, which the censors had barred from the stage and which his learned cousin refused to read to him because he was "not old enough."

For a long time the world of reality around the village and farm and the world of reason, wonder and passion between the covers of books, were kept sharply separate in his mind. The farm had taught him many things, for he was curious and observant. He watched the hired help climb into the hayloft to make love, heard derisive stories about the gentry they had served, heard them berate his father with especial malice in his presence, spent so much time in kitchen, machine shop, barn and fields that he came to understand the point of view of the help and even take their side in controversies between them and his father. He found life around him hard, crude, occasionally cruel. But in the world of books he found people who were gentle and refined and exalted; they loved without evil words or haylofts or apparent physical basis; they spoke to each other in delicate, even poetic fashion of incorporeal, unterrestrial, inscrutable things. The ambit of his reading extended, his comprehension of the two worlds deepening until at last they began to merge and serve as counterpoint and clarification of each other. Where they differed, the world of books held him more closely.

> In my inner life—he wrote later—, throughout my youth, nature and individuals occupied a lesser place than books and ideas . . . The very word "author" sounded to me as if it was uttered from some unattainable height . . . From early years my love for words had been now losing, now gaining in force, but generally putting down ever firmer roots. In my eyes, authors, journalists, and artists always

stood for a world which was more attractive than any other, one open only to the elect.

These words are taken from his autobiography, written in exile in Prinkipo after Stalin had deported him from Russia. In the preface to the same work he wrote:

> A well-written book in which one can find new ideas, and a good pen with which to communicate one's ideas to others, for me have always been and are today the most valuable and intimate products of culture. The desire for study has never left me, and many times in my life I felt the revolution was interfering with my systematic work . . .

In the end, Death would catch him pen in hand.

Allied to the magic of book and pen was that of the theater. During Christmastide of 1886, when Lyova was seven and had barely learned how to write, a troop of mummers descended from nowhere upon the dining room while the family was at tea. The boy was so astonished that he fell on the divan from fright and remained rooted there spellbound while Tsar Maximilian declaimed till the rude living room became a realm of spendor. Imagine his amazement when he found that Tsar Maximilian was one and the same with the hired man Prokhor! Armed with pen and paper he penetrated into the servants' quarters, where Tsar Prokhor was at rest after dinner, and plagued him to dictate his monologue. When old Bronstein interrupted the eager boy and the reluctant Tsar at their "idle" task, Lyova was inconsolable.

His first visit to a real theater took place during his initial year in school in Odessa. "It was like no other experience and beggars description," he could still write fifty years later. "I sat pale as a sheet . . . and was tortured by a joy which was more than I could bear. During the intermissions I did not leave my seat lest—God forbid!—I might miss something." Then he planned, with a boy who had actually taken part in amateur theatricals, that together they would stage Pushkin's *The Niggardly Knight*. But his partner in the enterprise was tubercular and went off somewhere to die before their dream could become reality. An original play which he tried to write with another comrade a few years later also came to naught. After he had been in Odessa a while, he developed a fondness for Italian opera, spending every spare penny and even doing extra tutoring to earn money to go to the theater. He fell in love with a coloratura soprano "bearing the mysterious name of Giuseppina Uget, who seemed to me to have descended from heaven to the stage-boards of the Odessa theater." But since this was his third "love affair," it is clear that we are running a little ahead of our story.

Before we leave the subject of the stage, however, we must note that all his life this ardent follower of the theater retained a strong sense of drama. One could note it in his erect carriage on the public platform, in his scrupulous neatness and liking for being well dressed, in his boyish love of a student uniform, his later military outfit and bearing as War Commissar, his conduct of his own case in a tsarist courtroom in 1906, his blinding eloquence on the rostrum, his skillful dramatization of every role his highly dramatic life provided. His life possessed style no less than his writing, that touch of heightening which, when not carried to excess, makes for a compelling type of attraction and leadership while one has the center of the stage, and emphasizes the tragedy of a fall from high place. In his writings he would become one of the greatest stylists that the socialist movement had produced since the days of Marx. In the dramatization of his life none would equal him since the days of Marx's contemporary, Lassalle.

At the age of seven Lyova began his first schooling. For that purpose he went from Yanovka to nearby Gromokley, two and one-half miles away, to live with his Aunt Rachel and Uncle Abram near a Jewish village school. His teacher, a lean, apologetic, self-effacing man, plagued by a frolicsome wife, instructed him in Russian, arithmetic, and the Bible in the original Hebrew. With the other children Lyova had little to do, for their talk was in Yiddish, a language he did not understand. He became dimly aware here that the Jews were a people apart, held in some inferior status by incomprehensible forces. The village was divided by a ravine, on one side of which were prosperous German farmhouses, most of them with tiled roofs, on the other the dilapidated huts of the Jews. His most vivid memory of Gromokley was of the coercive force of the Ghetto when it turned out to drag a woman of evil repute through its miserable street, shouting at her, cursing, screaming, spitting. Later the community secured from the authorities the deportation of the young woman's father to far-off Siberia as an alleged horse thief. This "biblical" scene made a deeper impression on the boy than all the passages of ill-understood Hebrew shouted in chorus with his fellows. But, had his schooling ended with this meager year at Gromokley, as did that of most of his schoolmates, it would have left little mark upon him.

The peculiarities of that "peculiar people," the Jews, are largely a product of their centuries of intensive urbanization. Two or three generations of rustication had almost wiped out the influence of the city on the Bronstein family, but when the city came to Yanovka, adorned with gentleness and learning, in the shape of a scholarly cousin from Odessa, its appeal to young Lyova was instantaneous. Moisey Filippovich Shpentser was a man of book and pen, hence this unlettered family treated him with deference. He had come to the farm to drink fresh milk, eat fresh eggs, breathe fresh air, and fight off incipient tuberculosis. A *gymnazia* graduate, he had been excluded from the university for a minor political peccadillo. He made his modest living by free-lance journalism, writing children's books, preparing history texts, translating and annotating Greek classics, doing statistical work. He was shortly to open a little publishing house, which in later years would prosper. He was engaged to be married to the principal of a state school for Jewish girls, a fact which inspired even more awe in the Bronsteins than did his own learning. Finding no one else in Yanovka on whom to exercise his intellectual powers, he set to work on Lyova Bronstein, read to him, answered his incessant questions, taught him how to speak grammatically, how to hold a clean glass with the fingers outside, not inside, how to distinguish the Ukrainian part of his vocabulary from the Russian, and—more by example than by words—to feel a sense of revulsion at some of the cruelties and barbarities of the rude life of Yanovka.

In the spring of the next year, 1888, the Shpentser marriage having duly taken place, Lyova left his home in Yanovka to go to live with the Shpentsers in populous Odessa. He was fitted out with a new suit, a large trunk containing butter, jam and other rustic gifts for city relatives, and such clothing as the country might furnish to a future city-dweller. Though his autobigraphy complains of the "grayness" of the childhood years he was leaving behind him and the lack of attention and affection, when he left Yanovka he suddenly felt that it was very dear to him. His mother and sisters wept. He wept long and loud with them, continued sobbing all the way across the steppe until the cart came to the main road. Then he straightened up as befits a lad who is going to the big city to seek wisdom.

CHAPTER XI

LYOVA BECOMES A POPULIST

A shudder passes over us when we hear the terrible story of what happened in the theater. How do we Jews, who are likened to a little worm—the worm of Jacob—come to get messed up in such matters? How do we Jews, who, according to all sense and reason, are always obligated to pray for the well-being of the sovereign power, without whom we would long since have been swallowed alive—how do we Jews dare to climb to such high places and meddle in politics? Oh, beware, Jewish children! Look well what you are doing! God only knows what you may bring upon our unfortunate nation, upon yourselves, and upon your families. Our people always were proud of one thing—that they never had any rebels among them; and now you desire to wipe out this virtue too. We hope you will think well about all this and you will not wish to place in jeopardy the happiness of our whole nation, your own fate and the fate of your parents and your families.—*Sermon of the Chief Rabbi of Minsk in 1902 after Hirsch Leckert attempted to assassinate the Governor of Vilna.*

NOISY, COLORFUL, many-tongued Odessa was founded as a free port in 1794 by émigré Frenchmen. When Lyova Bronstein went there nearly a century later, it had great wharves and harbors and a turbulent waterfront, behind which rose on terraces a busy city, overlooking Odessa Bay and the Black Sea. It was a place where a boy could get the foundations of cosmopolitanism if not internationalism. Ukrainians, Great Russians, Jews, Italians, Germans, Frenchmen, Englishmen, Greeks, Armenians, Persians, Syrians, Turks, Tartars, rubbed elbows, drove bargains, exchanged currencies, goods, vocabularies, ideas, on the easy principle of live and let live. The Jews were the largest single group in Odessa, 30 per cent of the total population. Among so many urban, mercantile peoples from the Near East, they had not stood out especially nor felt any unusual discrimination. But, one year before Lyova's arrival, the *numerous clausus* decree limited Jewish students to 10 per cent of the student body despite the fact that Jews formed 30 per cent of the city's population. The nine-year-old candidate for learning was one of the first victims.

The Shpentsers chose for their ward the Saint Paul *Realschule,* founded by the local German colony for the education of its own children on the "progressive" and "practical" principle of mathematics, sciences and modern languages, rather than the classics. Shpentser chose it not out of admiration for the curriculum but out of consideration for the fact that the Realschule would be easier for a poorly trained rural Jewish boy to get into than the more crowded classical *gymnazia.* The entrance examinations, however, laid bare the gaps in the boy's training. A "4" in Arithmetic and a "3" in Russian—"3" being a bare passing mark under a system in which 5 equals 100—were not enough to win Bronstein a place among the top 10 per cent of Jewish applicants.

Thereupon, the Shpentsers, wise in the ways of the Odessa educational system, enrolled him in the Saint Paul preparatory class, thus giving him preference over outside Jewish applicants for the ensuing year. He was, after all, very young, his parents having falsified his age by a year to expedite his eligibility. Thus, despite the lost time, he actually entered the *Realschule* at the minimum age of ten. Nor was the year wasted, either. The low marks were a spur, so that the mediocre arithmetician of the year before became top man in mathematics and dreamed of taking up pure mathematics as a career. The year's training in discrimination between the Ukrainian and Russian elements in his vocabulary, and the increment of maturity in the ideas expressed in his compositions, helped to make him top man in the Russian class also. His teacher made a point of reading his compositions aloud to the class and rating them with the prideful mark of "5 plus." Thus the career of author continued to exert its rival attraction to the new dream of mathematician, while old David Bronstein hoped that his promising son would become an engineer.

There are those who would interpret the subsequent stormy life of this boy in terms of the Jewish rebel whose rebellion arises out racial persecution, or compensation for enforced inferiority. For this view, the year lost because of the *numerus clausus* is virtually the only point of support. In Yanovka, where David Bronstein was the leading farmer, respected by all his neighbors, the lad had known no discrimination. In Odessa, the growing trend to Russification which began with the accession of Alexander III (1881-94) weighed heavily upon Saint Paul's. But it was the Germans, who had founded and directed the school and made up the largest group of its pupils, that were the chief victims. Next in order came the Ukrainians, for whose land Odessa was the chief seaport. To guarantee the Russification of those who had gone through so German a school, the government obliged the students to spend their final year in a Russian state institution. The German Lutheran director, the German chaplain, and many of the teachers of German origin, were forced out during Lyova's seven years there. The Orthodox Russian priest who gave instruction in religion was patronizing to the boys who had to leave the room for other mentors, but his derogatory remarks were addressed to German Protestants and Roman Catholic Poles no less than to Jewish boys. The history teacher directed caddish questions concerning the reverses and "crimes" of their respective peoples at Polish and Ukrainian pupils. Bronstein, however, he treated with unfailing correctness as the star history student, even with a little fear, because Lyova would wade through the advanced books in Shpentser's personal library and use his extra knowledge to ask questions to which the instructor did not know the answers.

In this matter of nationality, like most of the Jews of the large urban centers of the Ukraine, the boy and his guardian unconsciously sided with the Great-Russian administrators and the superior Great-Russian culture as against the Ukrainian peasants and the handful of Ukrainian intellectuals who were striving to create a Ukrainian language and literature, and beginning to aspire to autonomy for their culture and their land. To Lyova Bronstein, all his life, as is revealed in his autobiography written in 1929, the Ukrainian tongue was no language, but a peasant "dialect" or "jargon." Insensibly, this would color his attitude towards the independent Ukrainian Republic which his armies would crush in 1919.

Far from giving him a sense of inferiority, his school triumph made the little lad from Yanovka vain and sure of himself. He never doubted for a moment in those days that he would get ahead in a world which he imagined to be very much like a greater classroom, where his compositions would always be good enough to be read aloud, where in the competitive struggle for marks his would always be "5" and "5 plus" and his place would always be at the "head of the class." Whatever the forces were that drove him during his sixteenth to eighteenth years to abandon thoughts of a career as mathematician or engineer—but never that of author—in favor of the profession of revolutionary, they were in the main the same forces that drove his entire generation of student youth in the same direction.

Important as the role of the Jew has been in the Russian revolutionary movement (there was no *numerus clausus* for intellectuals there), it has been much exaggerated and misinterpreted by Russian monarchist and German Nazi writers. In their zeal to expound the thesis of "Jewish Bolshevism," they have passed over in silence the role of Jews like Martov and Axelrod, the two leading ideologists of Menshevism, and made all they could and more out of the prominent place of Zinoviev (Radomyslski), Kamenev (Rosenfeld), and, above all, Trotsky, among the Bolsheviks. Actually there were many more intellectuals of Jewish origin among the Mensheviks than among the Bolsheviks and the few who were associates of Lenin, like Trotsky and his Russian Orthodox-born brother-in-law, Kamenev-Rosenfeld, were likely to be "unjewish Jews": non-professing, Russified, brought up outside the pale. The bulk of the Jewish masses, insofar as they were politically organized, were to be found in neither wing, but in specifically Jewish movements like the Jewish General Workers Union or Bund, and the Zionist organizations. In 1917, in the hour of Bolshevik triumph, there was not one among Lenin's associates with sufficient knowledge of the language of the mass of Jews, or sufficient understanding of their outlook, to start a paper in Yiddish. Only after a section of the Bund joined the Bolsheviks could that task be undertaken.

To understand the role of the Jew in the Russian labor movement we must bear in mind a few facts concerning his position in old Russia. There were more Jews there after the partition of the Kingdom of Poland and Lithuania, than in any other land on earth. In the course of the nineteenth century their numbers had grown by natural increase from a little less than a million to a round five million, while bit by bit the noose of closed areas of settlement and forbidden occupations was tightening around them. Herded into the teeming ghettos of the Jewish pale, they were reduced largely to trading with, and working for, each other under increasingly miserable conditions, like the legendary Chinese who lived by taking in each other's washing. Culturally, they tended to hold themselves superior to the Polish, Lithuanian and Latvian peasants around them, continuing to speak their German dialect—which developed into Yiddish—or adopting the superior, dominant culture of ruling Great-Russia. Thus, almost unconsciously, most of the Jews of the cities of Poland, Lithuania and the Ukraine tended to become opponents of the national separation movements that arose during the breakup of the empire in 1917.

More urban by far than the general population of Russia, they produced more than their proportionate share of the men and women of the professions, those who lived by ideas and ideals, those who engaged in that most urban of activities: politics. There was not a liberal, radical or revolutionary movement in Russia, from the Constitutional Democrats to the "peasant socialism" of the

Social Revolutionists, that did not have some Jewish intellectuals among its leadership. This was due to the double yoke of oppression which weighed upon them, and to the passion with which they delivered themselves to ideas. Doubtless their inherited background of urbanism, their wandering past, their sense of kinship with the fate of Jews dispersed through many lands, tended to promote cosmopolitanism and internationalism among them, an internationalism which sometimes took a socialist, some times a liberal-humanitarian and pacifist, sometimes a Zionist form. For, paradoxical as it sounds, Zionism, too, is a peculiar international nationalism.

Never numerous in absolute terms, or in comparison with the number of Great-Russians that figured in such leaderships, Jews nevertheless were to be found in the leadership of all Russian oppositional movements in larger numbers than the proportion their people bore to the total population. Five Jewish names among the doughty band that besieged and assassinated Alexander II were sufficient to cause Alexander III to visit the fury of his fright on "all their kindred," whence the first pogroms of modern times (1882), the *numerus clausus*, and the land exclusion law, which affected the lives of farmer Bronstein and his son.

If about 50 per cent of the Jewish population lived by small business and trade, about 30 per cent, more than is generally realized, were artisans and mechanics. More compact, more proletarianized, more influenced by Western socialist ideas than was the great peasant Russian mass, these Jewish artisans gave the first strong impulse to labor organization, in their own ranks, and then among the Russian workingmen. While the revolutionary movement of the Empire as a whole was still made up almost completely of intellectuals, the Jewish General Workers Union of Poland and Lithuania (the Bund) was not only working class in composition, but even in leadership. Of the Bund's thirteen founders, only five were intellectuals, at a time when in the leadership of the *Iskra* group there were no workingmen at all.

Deutsch and Axelrod, Russified Jewish intellectuals, were among the founders of Russian Marxism along with Plekhanov and Zasulich. Martov (Tsederbaum), after a brief period as a member of the Jewish Bund, broke with it to become Lenin's chief collaborator in the Petersburg League. Martov and Axelrod were two of the six editors of *Iskra,* and, when the Iskrists split into Mensheviks and Bolsheviks, they became the theoreticians of menshevism. Indeed, despite the Nazi-fostered legend of "Jewish bolshevism," Jews always played a much larger role in the "Westernizing" Menshevik wing than in the much more specifically Russian Bolshevik wing of the Party.

What is perhaps more surprising is that even the "peasant socialist" Social Revolutionary Party had a much higher proportion of Jews in its leadership than did the Bolsheviks: Gershuni, Mikhail and Abram Gotz, Fundaminsky, Rubanovich, Vishniak, Azev, Minor, Zhitlovsky, the two Rappaports, and later Kamkov, Natanson, and Steinberg, the Internationalist Left Social Revolutionaries who were to cooperate with the Bolsheviks in their dictatorship. Of course, as we survey the total list of leaders, the Jewish names prove to be no more than a minor fraction. But the propagandists of reaction, striving to create an abyss between the peasant-worker masses and the revolutionary intellectuals and to channel discontent into the by-pass of antisemitism, did their best to stress every Jewish name and make it appear as if all these opposition movements were "Jewish" and alien to Russia.

Outside the mass of artisans and workingmen who formed the Bund and the sprinklings of Jews that took part in other oppositional movements, there was a solid body of conservative Jewry. The bulk of the rabbinate and of the orthodox religious Hebrews, the bulk of those engaged in trade, the privileged whose privileges depended upon the favors of the government, the timid and conformist of all classes, that 2 to 3 per cent of Jewish farmers, most of those who were permitted to live outside the pale of settlement, were inclined to be conservative and to doubt, if not deplore, the activities of their oppositional brethren.

"Lyova," said Farmer Bronstein to his son, "this thing will not come to pass even in three hundred years." And when that son, as resident of the Kremlin, reminded his father of the prophecy, there was paternal pride and a core of still unbroken stubbornness in the old man's answer: "This time, let your truth prevail!" Having known persecution from his son's comrades for his wealth, and from his son's enemies for his paternity of the stormy petrel of revolution, he spent his last few years as a bewildered and unregenerate employee of the state his boy had helped to found: directing a little government-owned grinding mill near Moscow until typhus carried him off in 1922. As he lay dying, his son, at the height of his prestige and power, was delivering a report on the world situation at the Fourth Congress of the Communist International. Some of the bitterest opponents of what Trotsky stood for at that moment were to be found among Jewish intellectuals, Jewish organized workers, Jewish merchants. Hundreds of thousands of them had fled abroad rather than make their peace with bolshevism, while the latter had outlawed in Russia both the more largely Jewish Menshevik and Social Revolutionary Parties and the wholly Jewish Zionist movement and Bund. Later, Trotsky, Zinoviev, Kamenev, the few names that had been used to give a semblance of support to the legend of "Jewish bolshevism," were to disappear in the purges. The Bund lived on as a mass movement of Jewish labor in Poland, to give a heroic account of itself in the tragic Warsaw insurrections of World War II. The scattered remnant of menshevism abroad still has a fairly high proportion of Jewish names among its leaders. But in the immediate entourage of Stalin, only one, Kaganovich, is to be found whose parents accounted themselves Jews.

The boy from Yanovka slept behind a curtain in the dining room of the Shpentser home. He was held to an agreeable discipline, so different from the random life on the farm and so much more divorced from concrete physical things: homework, reading, being read aloud to, early bedding and early rising, proper language, elimination of "Ukrainian jargon" words from his speech, personal cleanliness, common courtesy, urbane social forms, humane and literate conversation, enthusiasm for fine sentiments, good books, and large ideas. Only the problem of getting the lad to bed with page or chapter unfinished, or the next one unread, required any exercise of constraint. In all other matters, example was more potent than prescript. Self-regard, vanity, the attractiveness of the things of the mind and the social graces which Yanovka had denied to him, made the boy a ready imitator of the superior models before him. Insensibly, too, the high examples of conversation, thought and conduct in the great classics of Russian literature sank into his soul. In after-years he would go from prison to prison, storm the heights of power, rush from front to front in the hard years of famine and civil war, but always he would care for his personal appearance, remain scrupulous to the point of prudery in his vocabulary, cherish the world of culture and books to which the Shpentsers were now introducing him. Shortly before his fall from power he would write a little brochure such as no other of his comrades could have composed, a series of homely lay sermons called *Problems of Life* (1923). In it he would urge upon the victorious proletariat, with its deep-rooted tradition of cursing and obscenity, the use of "cultured speech," the employment of "civility and politeness as a necessary lubricant in daily relationships," a "fight against bad language as part of the struggle for the purity, clearness and beauty of Russian speech."

Then, even as the ways were being greased for his disappearance from public life, he switched from homely sermons to some of the most audacious flights of fancy that socialist writing had offered since the days of Marx and Lassalle. The closing passages of his *Literature and Revolution* (1924) envisaged a future world where

> . . . the imperceptible antlike piling up of quarters and streets, brick by brick, from generation to generation, will give way to titanic construction of city-villages, with map and compass in hand. Around this compass will be formed . . . the parties of the future . . . Architecture will again be filled with the spirit of mass feeling and moods . . . Mankind will educate itself plastically, will become accustomed to looking at the world as submissive clay for sculpting the most perfect forms of life . . . Man will occupy himself with re-registering mountains and rivers . . . rebuilding the earth, if not in his own image, then at least according to his own taste . . . More than that, man at last will begin to harmonize himself in earnest. He will make it his business to achieve beauty by giving the movement of his own limbs the utmost precision, purposefulness and economy in his work, his walk, his play. He will try to master first the semiconscious and then the subconscious processes in his own organism. Social construction and psychophysical self-education will become two aspects of one and the same process. All the arts—literature, drama, painting, music and architecture—will lend this process beautiful form . . . Man will become immeasurably stronger, wiser and subtler; his body will become more harmonized, his movements more rhythmic, his voice more musical. The forms of life will become dynamically dramatic. The average human type will rise to the heights of an Aristotle, a Goethe, or a Marx. And above this ridge new peaks will rise.

It is not too far-fetched to see the elevating influence of the Shpentsers, the prophetic extremism of the Russian classics, the violence of the farm boy's reaction to the crudeness and spiritual poverty of life at Yanovka, still at work in this little series of Red sermons and in this audacious vision of the future. Our hardest task will be to keep in mind this side of his nature and to trace in the combative and often difficult personality of Leon Trotsky the subterranean line which leads from the boy who slept behind the curtain in the Shpentser home in Odessa to that rebel who could leave such a luminescent trail behind him in his fall.

Like every big seaport, Odessa had its rough and seamy side: its taverns, waterfront dives, sailors trying to crowd into a few brief days of shore leave all the things the land offers and the sea denies. But that side of the great port never entered into Lyova Bronstein's life. Though the sea danced and beckoned at the city's edge, he never learned to swim, nor went rowing or fishing as the other students did. No image of the sea ever seems to have figured in his writings. Taverns were "out of bounds" for the students, and Lyova, at least, did not enter one until it became part of the defiant routine of the day after graduation. It was as if mighty Odessa were some little inland town, made up of a school, a library, a theater, an opera house, a few friendly homes and familiar connecting streets. "The street" as such did not exist for him. Brawls, so common among the students, he detested. When a bully from another school tried to pick a fight about some of the meaningless things on which growing boys feed their combativeness, he disarmed the challenger by politely inquiring: "What is it you want of me?" so that the quarrel died in mutual bewilderment.

Athletic competitions and physical games held no attraction either. In recompense, he entered with a will into a different type of rivalry: to excel, to surprise the teacher, to lead the class, to talk well, to write well—these were his ambitions and in these he found his triumphs and pleasures. He would comb through books, fragmentarily for the most part, to garner a few elegant phrases and sparkling ideas to embed in his own compositions. He would read works intended for older heads than his in order to surprise his teachers with abstruse and difficult questions. He picked up easily viewpoints, attitudes, pieces of information, from the conversation of the Shpentsers and their guests or from random browsing through books. He possessed the gift of employing, combining, displaying his smallish acquisitions in the show window so that people would get the idea that behind it was a well-stocked store. But he was capable of a feeling of shame afterward and of fierce self-depreciation when he found that there were others who had really mastered the books he but pretended to know. The desire to shine was not altogether cut loose from the desire to know, to be able, and to excel. Yet it took many years before the latter dominated the former.

The infant publishing house which Shpentser founded about the time Lyova came to live with him, and which in later years grew to be the largest editorial enterprise in Southern Russia, took the place which the machine shop at Yanovka had earlier held in his affections. Here he learned type, make-up, layout, printing, paging, binding, made a pastime of the correction of proofs. This was his nearest connection in Odessa to actual, physical things. To happy hours spent thus he attributes his life-long love of the freshly printed page. In the years of the Civil War, one of his few pleasures was the printing press he carried with him on his armored train and the military newspaper and resounding proclamations he issued as he hurried from front to front. In the last years of his exile in Mexico, though he was surrounded by secretaries who would gladly have relieved him of such cares, he still insisted on going personally over the proofs of the articles, pamphlets and books which came from his pen.

His actual schooling, as distinguished from the cultural guidance of the Shpentsers and the personal adventuring in the world of books, left upon him a residual impression of grayness. The courses were routine and heavy with formalism and taboo, the texts dull and lifeless, the teachers petty, uninspiring and uninspired. The boy was not one to make personal attachments. At Yanovka only his younger sister Olga had been close to him, she who was afterward to become a revolutionary like her more celebrated brother and end up as the wife of the Bolshevik leader Leo Kamenev. At school there was not one outstanding teacher whom he could regard with gratitude and affection, or whose teaching he could carry with him consciously through a lifetime. Nor was there a single schoolmate whose friendship he would cherish after graduation. In his inner life, to use his own apt phrase, "nature and individuals occupied a lesser place than books and ideas . . . people passed through my mind like random shadows . . . " He was talking of his youth, but with rare and counted exceptions this was true of him all his life.

The "star pupil" was never late, did his homework assiduously, was quiet at his desk; listened attentively, learned quickly and precisely, answered—with invariable attention to what was expected —all the questions put to him; wrote well, recited well, easily led his class; was respectful to his teachers in the classroom, bowed deferentially when he met them on the street. Yet even so proper and bright a boy came into conflict with the régime.

The conflict arose out of a combination of accidental things with his own dawning sense of justice. The teacher of French, a man named Burnande, hated all German boys with a cold fury, and delighted in torturing the backward for their backwardness. His chief butt was one Wacker, a dullard and fawner for whom Lyova felt no liking. Yet he, along with many of his classmates, thought that Burnande was unjust to Wacker; with that rude sense of solidarity so common in schoolboys, they decided to teach the teacher a lesson. They planned a "concert," which consisted of "music" made by howling with shut mouth, to avoid detection, while the teacher was departing from the classroom. Inquisition yielded ten or twelve culprits for detention after school, though Lyova was not among them and felt no call to confess his complicity. During their detention, some of the worst and most backward boys, the ungrateful Wacker included, accused Bronstein of being a participant, even the ringleader. One added the terrifying information that Bronstein had proposed the writing of a joint letter to the Inspector General asking for Burnande's dismissal. In the petition—a neat conspirative detail that really suggested the head of the "star pupil"—each boy was to write a single character so that no one could be held responsible.

In vain did the Shpentsers intervene, urging their own experience as teachers, the boy's youth and record. A solemn trial was held by the faculty council, which considered three degrees of penalty: permanent expulsion from the school system, expulsion from Saint Paul's with no right of reinstatement, and expulsion with the right of reentry a year later if he could pass the requisite examinations. They adopted the mildest of the three measures. When Shpentser brought home to the waiting boy the fateful verdict of expulsion, he turned green, so that they thought he was going to faint. They were scarcely less frightened themselves, for Shpentser remembered his own blasted educational career. Nor did they know how to apprise old Bronstein.

Lyova stayed out the term in Odessa as if nothing had happened, then went on a visit to a friend's home while his older sister, tearful and frightened, was entrusted with the task of informing the stern old man. The boy returned to his home at last, to be greeted by stony silence. For three days not a word, then, in a moment of family reunion, Farmer Bronstein broke into hearty laughter, crying: "Show me how you whistled at your headmaster. Like this? With two fingers in the mouth?" Lyova tried to assure him that it was not whistling and not the headmaster. The mother burst into tears. The old man, as if the episode tickled his vanity, laughed harder than ever. Then he paid for a private tutor so that Lyova might make the next grade along with his classmates.

Even before the episode, the star pupil from Yanovka had based his friendships among the students on their acknowledgment of his own leadership. On reentering the class, to quote a self-revealing passage from his autobiography:

> ... I met most of the boys who had either betrayed me,
> or defended me, or had remained neutral. This determined
> my personal relations for a long time ... Such, one might
> say, was the first political test I underwent. These were
> the groups that resulted from that episode: the tale-bearers
> and the envious at one pole, the frank, courageous boys at
> the other, and the neutral, vacillating mass in the middle.
> These three groups never quite disappeared during the
> years that followed. I met them again and again in my life,
> in the most varied circumstances.

The reader will do well to bear this passage in mind when he
comes to Leon Trotsky's subsequent "political tests." It will help
us to understand the vicissitudes in the latter's relations with the
men and women he met in the revolutionary movement, above all
the astonishing ruptures and feuds that characterized Trotsky's
closing years in his personally led "Fourth International."

The episode of the "concert" for the French teacher was followed by a conflict of lesser scope with a new Russian teacher,
who failed to read and mark the themes he exacted from his pupils.
Both incidents suggest that in Lyova Bronstein there was growing
up a feeling of indignation at injustice. Imperceptibly this feeling
had been nourished by a whole series of childhood experiences at
Yanovka, experiences which were evaluated increasingly with the
criteria supplied by the attitude of the Shpentsers and the ideals of
the masterpieces of Russian literature. His contact with the servants
and laborers at Yanovka had made them aware of their humble
viewpoint. He remembered a woman's walking seven versts and
sitting submissively a whole day on his father's doorstep to collect
a ruble; the arrest of two peasants for their failure to renew their
passports; a sitdown strike of the farm help—no worse treated than
most—because they did not get enough to eat; a man pleading with
his father for the release of a cow that had trespassed on the Bronstein field; the shame he felt when old Bronstein failed to tip a
porter adequately and the latter cursed at him; the spectacle of an
overseer striking a shepherd with a knout because he had kept the
horses out late, with Shpentser standing by, face pale, hissing between clenched teeth, "how shameful!"

He began to contrast the more shameful things around him with
an ideal, imaginary world of Western Europe and America. In that
world there was literacy, culture, democracy, freedom of speech and
press, parliamentarism. Bit by bit he built up his picture of it from
conversations and fragmentary remarks in books, from the prevail-

ing "Westernism" of the liberal intelligentsia. If they were not permitted to criticize the Russian institutions, they could still describe
—and idealize—those which were found elsewhere. The boy from
Yanovka was becoming, without knowing the terms, a "Westernizer" and a rationalist. His inexorable rationalism made him believe
that consistency prevailed everywhere but in Russia, that whatever
was agreed to in principle was universally applied in practice.
Later he was astonished to learn that in Western Europe "people
could have superstitions and the Church exercise a great influence,"
that in the democratic United States there was race discrimination
against the Negro, that throughout the West there were whole areas
of culture and well-being closed to millions. The same rationalism
made him indignant when, on vacation in Yanovka, he could not
persuade his old hero, the mechanic, that perpetual-motion machines
were theoretically impossible, or could not convince the local
peasants that his methods of mathematical mensuration of their
fields were superior to their old, inaccurate rule-of-thumb methods.
He was indignant, too, when his classmates walked out of the
science class talking of the unlucky number thirteen. Every such
inconsistency made him feel as if human reason were being degraded and his own intelligence personally outraged. He felt capable
of doing any mad thing to convince those around him to be consistent.

It was largely via this abstract intellectual route of critical rationalism that he arrived at his ultimate revolutionary position.
Through all his writings runs the guiding thread of worship of reason: sometimes it takes the form of doctrinaire pedantry; sometimes vitriolic scorn of all waverings, half-measures, middle positions and inconsistencies; at its worst it degenerates into abstract,
diagrammatic sectarianism, impotent to obtain any purchase upon
the changing and complicated reality of a given moment; at its
best it gives his writing a tremendous intellectual sweep and
eloquence, enables him to grasp the most varied and random facts
on the wing and link them to the unifying thread of brilliant gen-
eralization. Unlike Lenin, whose long-run objective was the physical one of taking power, and who, never losing that end from view,
was a flexible tactician, a steersman changing the course of his skiff
with every hidden rock and every twist and turn in the rapids,
Trotsky early elaborated a single, unchanging, intellectual direction-
principle (that of "permanent revolution") and stuck to it, applying it well or ill on a national and a world scale, from 1905 to the
day of his murder. Other men might lose their vision of their distant goal in concentration on the next step of their march route; he

would be more likely to lose his sense of the next step with too-fixed gazing on the distant goal to perceive the broken nature of the terrain he was treading. "Without a broad political view of the future," he would write, "I cannot conceive either of political activity or of intellectual life in general." Socialism itself he was to envisage as an "effort to rationalize life, i.e. transform it according to the dictates of reason. . . . It is only socialism that has set itself the task of embracing reason and subjecting all the activities of man to it." During the leisure hours of his exile in Siberia, he would try to reorganize his personal life and attitudes, "to consider from the new viewpoint [of Marxism], the so-called 'eternal' problems of life: love, death, friendship, optimism, pessimism . . ." In a backward glance over his career up to his exile in Prinkipo in 1929 he would write:

> . . . the feeling of the supremacy of the general over the particular became an integral part of my literary and political work. The dull empiricism, the unashamed, cringing worship of the fact, which is so often only imaginary and falsely interpreted at that, were odious to me. Beyond the facts I looked for laws. Naturally, this led me more than once into hasty and incorrect generalizations, especially in my younger years when my knowledge, book-acquired, and my experience in life, were still inadequate. But in every sphere, barring none, I felt that I could move and act only when I held in my hand the thread of the general. The social-revolutionary radicalism which has become the permanent pivot for my whole inner life grew out of this intellectual enmity toward the striving for petty ends, toward out-and-out pragmatism, and toward all that is ideologically without form and theoretically ungeneralized.

That is Leon Trotsky's own conception of how he became a revolutionary.

It is instructive to compare the respective approaches of Lenin and Trotsky to this problem of the relation of the particular to the general. Both acknowledged the theoretical Marxist conception in which the general is derived from the particular and in turn applied to, tested by, and modified by further intercourse with the particular. But, in all his writing and thinking, Trotsky's emphasis is on "the supremacy of the general over the particular," whereas Lenin again and again emphasizes the view that "the truth is always and everywhere concrete." This difference in emphasis is in large measure the key to a difference in style, approach and political method.

The year 1896, at the end of which Lyova turned seventeen, marked a sharp break in his life. It was a year of important textile strikes and social agitation. (Lenin, Martov, and their associates spent it in jail, waiting for deportation to Siberia.) The strikes caused the intelligentsia, young and old, to become aware of the nascent labor movement and to go over in great numbers from theoretical populism to "legal Marxism."

At the year's opening, Bronstein completed his course at Saint Paul's. He left it without regret, to take his final year of secondary education elsewhere. Neither he nor the school authorities could imagine then that one day his stay there might be regarded as its chief glory, and that Saint Paul's name would be hauled down in order to put over it the name of L. D. Trotsky.

At home that summer he was especially restless and ill at ease. His book learning, which had given him all the little successes that fed his vanity, did not seem to impress anyone about his father's farm. More than ever he shrank from the crudeness with which social relations and the forces of life seemed to be laid bare. There was more than one useless argument between father and son on his still vague oppositionist and liberal leanings. The seven years in Odessa had made Lyova a stranger in the home where he had spent the first nine years of his childhood. Sensing the change, shrewd David Bronstein sought to keep a closer watch on his son by arranging for his last academic year to be spent at Nikolaev instead of Odessa.

Nikolaev was smaller and closer, a lesser seaport, also with a large Jewish population. The change meant that the lad had to board at a stranger's instead of with the Shpentsers. It meant separating him from his classmates and thrusting him, at a critical age, into an entirely new environment. Important in that environment was something old Bronstein had not reckoned with: as a smaller town, Nikolaev was a permitted residence for some of the old exiles of the Narodnaya Volya, who had completed their terms in Siberia. Radical talk—there was no such thing as organization—was more fashionable here than in Odessa. The mistress of Lyova's own boarding-house turned out to have several children, older than he, who professed to be socialists.

With the cocksureness of ignorance, the new boarder picked arguments with them, assuring them that their "utopias" were old stuff for him and that he, with his mellow seventeen years of wisdom, had long outgrown such childishness. A model for her own children, thought the mistress of the boarding-house! A dangerous model he proved to be, however, for the next few months found him fighting an unequal battle against being carried away by the over- whelming current of opposition which was once more taking pos- session of the student youth. Yet a few months more, and he would be swimming vigorously with the current, dragging her children after him.

Now the "star student" from Saint Paul's seemed to deteriorate. He neglected his homework, stayed up late, failed to hand in as- signments, played truant, got by on his past study. The transition from dutiful, neutral-minded grind to thinking person often mani- fests such contradictory forms. The chewed-out straw of the text- books, the daily minuscule pellets of unrelated fact and informa- tion, lost all savor. He hungered for stronger fare: for culture and wisdom rather than rules and facts, for understanding, rather than definitions. He wanted to begin his education—which is always self- education—but he found himself in an intellectual forest: so many promising titles, so many false trails, so many alluring perspectives. He did not come from a cultured home as Vladimir Ilyich had; nor did he possess the same plodding persistence and thoroughness, the same unwillingness to talk until he knew what he was talking about. Was there not some one work, or at least some one subject, which would be the key to everything? He wanted to become wise overnight, find answers to questions which he could not even for- mulate, grasp great systems of thought by violence, by an impetuous effort of the will.

He tackled Mill's *Logic*, lured by the promise of its title until its cool formalism disillusioned him. In like fashion he dipped into Lippert's *Evolution of Culture* and Mignet's *French Revolution*, only to abandon each of them unfinished. For several weeks on end he was a follower of Jeremy Bentham, assuring all who would lis- ten that the utilitarian calculus of pain and pleasure—which he would later refer to as a philosophy of social cookbook recipes—was the last word in human wisdom and the formula for all of man's problems. Before he could make a single convert, he himself had abandoned Bentham for an equally brief discipleship to Cherni- shevski. Each book was tasted rather than digested; each had a disparate existence for him. He strove, as thoughtful adolescents have done before him and since, to reduce his thought to a system. But Marxism—of which he knew nothing but the name—repelled him because its adherents alleged that it was systematic.

Looking for people to talk these things out with, Lev Davidovich found his way to the garden of Franz Shvigovsky, a Czech vegetable gardener, whose hut was the provincial "salon" of Nikolaev's radical

intelligentsia. In it foregathered the students who had no taste for
cards and drinking, a few young professional men, a few rusting old
political exiles. From Shvigovsky one could get forbidden books,
foreign newspapers, anecdotes about the great and near-great of
the vanished Narodnaya Volya. He had read some of the Marxist
classics in German, and reassured Lyova Bronstein by proclaiming
his own opposition to Marxism. The older visitors talked of Zhelyabov, Sophia Perovskaya, Vera Figner, not as heroic legendary
figures but as familiar personages. Bronstein now felt that he was
himself a populist, a "tiny link in a great chain." He talked populism
with no more knowledge of it than of the previous *isms* he had
adhered to. His quick mind, his skill in argument, his scornful
tongue and ready wit, his facile assimilation of ideas, his fiery
condemnation of Marxism, made him the immediate leader of the
coterie of students there. All the frequenters of the "salon" were
populists except one. "Wait till you meet Lev Davidovich," Ilya
and Gregory Sokolovsky told their sister Alexandra, the lone Marxist. "Such brilliance, such logic. No one can get the better of him
in an argument."

Alexandra Lvovna Sokolovskaya went to the Shvigovsky garden
from time to time because there was nowhere else to go in Nikolaev
for serious discussion. She was older than most of the frequenters
—she was twenty-two—simple, emotional, warm-hearted, single-
minded in her devotion to socialism. During vacation times she was
supported in her views by a medical student named Ziv, who was
studying at the University of Kazan, and who counted himself a
Marxist too, after having read Beltov's (Plekhanov's) *Monistic
Conception of History*. The rest of the time she held the fort alone
against the banter and onslaughts of her two brothers, of Shvigovsky himself, and all his company. Lev Davidovich prepared for his
arguments with her and Ziv much as he had previously prepared
for his recitations and compositions. He browsed around in legal
populist magazines and books, of which there were quite a number,
picking up fragments concerning Russia's "non-capitalist destiny,"
and random, fine-sounding strictures on Marxism. He memorized
strong, well-turned sentences, aphorisms, crushing arguments, covering up his uncertainties as sophomoric debaters are apt to do, by
a variety of rhetorical tricks. If we think of Vladimir Ilyich, patiently
plodding for years through stacks of statistical reports and the
major works of populism and Marxism before he could bring himself to utter a word, we see at once the difference between the two
generations and, no less, between the two temperaments. Ulyanov

worked out his whole chess game in theory before he moved his first piece; Bronstein improvised his game impulsively, even thoughtlessly, changing it for a while with each fresh move. With Ulyanov the hard thing had been to go over from study to public exposition and activity, and then from elaborate theoretical propaganda to simple, piecemeal agitation; with Bronstein both populism and Marxism were adopted impulsively and he began to agitate others before he had thought through whither he was going. He learned not so much from meditation and study as from contact with the people, the movements and the ideas that were swirling around him. For him the difficult feat was to continue to deepen his knowledge and revise his views, when in this garden of schoolboy debaters he so easily won first place and scored debater's triumphs without serious study. Both his populism and his early Marxism were superficial acceptance of what was in the air. As the atmosphere became more heavily charged, he would grow in stature— in 1905 and in 1917 to titanic proportions. Again and again we shall have to note the difference in the two "styles" that are two men.

Alexandra Sokolovskaya came to the garden to meet the new master of logical swordplay. She was astonished at the ignorance no less than at the self-assurance of the dynamic blue-eyed youth with the great shock of black hair, who was so confident that he could slay Marxism. All their meetings were combats, cheered on by a lively, one-sided audience. "I can't imagine how a young girl like you can stand that dry, narrow, impractical stuff," was his summing up at their first meeting—as she remembered it when interviewed many years later by Max Eastman. And, "I can't imagine how a person who thinks he is logical can be contented with a headful of vague, idealistic emotions," was her rejoinder. Between them arose a magnetic field of mutual antagonism.

The school inspector visited Lyova's boarding house to find out why he was so frequently absent. Next his father appeared. He stormed and threatened. The boy struck attitudes, talked incoherent mixtures of sense and nonsense, defended his right to intellectual independence, asserted the insignificance of university training and engineering in comparison with what he was doing.

But what was he doing, besides talking and groping? How could they understand each other, these two Bronsteins, when all they had in common was the strong will which separated them? David Bronstein presented an ultimatum. Lyova dramatized his defiance by refusing to accept further support. He abandoned the lodgings his father had been paying for, and went to live—with six other students—in a populist "commune" in the midst of Shvigovsky's garden.

At first the seven "communards" aspired to little more than plain living and high talk. They all slept without bed linen, wore blue workmen's blouses, carried mysterious black canes, lived on stews made from the garden's vegetables reinforced with chunks of cheap meat. Lyova, having managed to get his high-school diploma, applied his education to giving private lessons. The other students picked up the small amount of cash needed by similar devices. They read copiously and unsystematically, made the Shvigovsky "salon" more lively than ever, attracted the attention of the neighbors and the authorities by their "meetings," believed that they had seceded from the present and were already living in the future.

Before long, chiefly on Bronstein's impulsive prodding, they decided on "action." When the local library association raised the membership fee from five to six rubles annually, they flooded the library association with new members, captured the board of directors at the annual meeting, and restored the old fee. On the new board they elected the gardener Shvigovsky, the Russian novelist Osipovich, who had done time in Siberia, and other "persons of evil repute." Then the youthful Marx-slayer Bronstein circulated a petition to have the library cancel its subscription to the former populist magazine *Novoye Slovo*, because the "legal" Marxists had gotten control of it.

His impatience and brashness next inspired an attempt on the part of the "commune" to give Nikolaev society the benefit of their wisdom. With great fanfare, they announced public courses of lectures in which they were to be the lecturers, modestly titling the venture "The Universal Knowledge Association." Lev Davidovich's department was "sociology." He prepared for his course with all his powers, but his slender store of universal sociological knowledge petered out by the second lecture. Some of the other courses did not even get that far.

They formed a society to "distribute useful books among the people," collected funds, chipped in from their own meager earnings, reduced the already crowded space in their communal hut by acquiring bundles of paper-backed volumes. But where to go to find "the people"? Marxism would have suggested the workmen of Nikolaev, who were many of them literate and knowledge-hungry. But their superficial understanding of populism suggested that "people" meant peasants. Where, then, should they look for peasants to take their volumes? Thus, on a diminutive, ridiculous scale, they were recapitulating all the tragic experiences of the generations of the seventies and eighties, acquiring by their own efforts some smattering of the knowledge which censorship, deportation and the gallows had prevented from being handed down to them. During the vacations, returning university students brought to the vegetable garden the first news of the great wave of strikes among the weavers, not one word of which had been permitted to appear in the papers. Unconsciously, Lev Davidovich began to turn his face from "the people" in the villages to the workers in the towns.

Shvigovsky now hired a garden laborer and an apprentice, the better to devote himself to the activities of the "commune." At last, here were two people who might be viewed alternatively as workers or peasants. Upon them Shvigovsky and the six students fell with unrestrained ardor. What was their delight to find that the elder of the two was full of questions: about tactics, violence, terror, conspiracy, revolution. While the boys cudgeled their innocent brains, raced through their unresponsive books, talked the nights away in quest of answers, their interlocutor gave detailed, if confusing reports to the police chief of Nikolaev. It was this spy who made the first real recruit in the garden, for he succeeded before long in enlisting the apprentice into the police service also.

Lev Davidovich made a brief last visit to Yanovka. There he met with nothing but useless argument, and a lack of a common tongue for discussion. The father stormed, the mother and sisters wept, the boy held his uncertain ground. Everybody went around depressed. It was a relief to accept an invitation of an uncle in business near the University of Odessa, where, if so minded, Lyova might take courses in engineering or prepare for the career of mathematician. The uncle, a repentant liberal, hinted that he could bring the boy to his senses. Like many another oldster, he thought that radicalism was a mere infantile disorder, like teething, measles, growing pains, adolescent sexual turmoil. But Lyova could not find what he was looking for in Odessa. By the end of the year he was back in Nikolaev, in the communal garden once more and looking forward to fresh arguments with Alexandra Lvovna Sokolovskaya.

The crowded year 1896 ended with a New Year's Eve party at the garden. Shvigovsky had gone personally to invite Alexandra. "Congratulations," he said, "did you know that Lev Davidovich is back from Odessa and has become a Marxist?" She was sceptical, fearing to rejoice, but her two brothers assured her that the leading light of their circle had indeed been converted.

Her arrival was greeted with friendly raillery, suppressed gaiety, fresh congratulations, grave courtesy on the part of Lev Davidovich. At midnight, he arose from his place, a mocking smile on his lips, and proposed a toast:

"A curse on all Marxists, and on all those who want to bring into all the relations of life, hardness and dryness."

Laughter died as Alexandra Lvovna rose and walked out of the hut. Shvigovsky ran after her, assuring her that it was all a joke. "Some things are too sacred to joke about," she told him, "and as for Bronstein, you can tell him that I never want to see him again as long as I live."

CHAPTER XII

FROM POPULISM TO MARXISM

> The delegate from Nikolaev was Kalafati. Vladimir Ilyich
> questioned me in detail about him . . . and then he added,
> with a sly smile: 'He says he knew you as a kind of Tol-
> stoyan.'
> 'What nonsense that is!' I said almost angrily.
> 'What is the matter?' Lenin replied, half to calm me, half
> to tease me. 'You were then probably eighteen years old,
> and men are certainly not born Marxists.' —*Leon Trotsky*

IT WAS THE SPRING of 1897. Lev Bronstein and Gregory Sokolovsky, each aged seventeen, were walking solemnly along a Nikolaev street. The whispering gallery had brought to them the news that, in the fortress of Saint Peter and Saint Paul, a girl student, Vetrova, had committed suicide by burning herself to death.

"We must find some workers," said Bronstein.

"I used to know a workman," Sokolovsky answered. "He belonged to some Bible sect. Let's go look him up."

The Bible sectary no longer lived in his old lodgings, but a woman there told them the address of one of his co-religionists. That very evening the two boys met the electrician Ivan Andreevich Mukhin.

Their "find" introduced them to other sectarians. All were touched with opposition to the régime, an opposition which, in harmony with the unripeness of Russian political life, expressed itself as a religious dissent. They were primitive evangelical Christians, communing over the heads of the princes of state and Church, directly with their God. For the most part they were skilled workers, earning good wages, feeling no special trade grievances, only a thirst for knowledge, righteousness, and justice. They showed no surprise when the students came, for they possessed a simplicity of spirit which mated well with the naïveté of the young revolutionaries. The two explorers returned to the vegetable garden proud and excited. Reinforcements were called up from Nikolaev's radical society: Alexandra, the Marxist girl; her brother, Ilya, and younger sister, Maria; the medical student Ziv; the garden communards. Out of this innocent fusion of students and dissenting Christian workingmen was born the South Russian Workers' Union!

The large name was Bronstein's doing, but with unparalleled

energy and a flare for public activity, he set about to justify it. Each
week he took the night boat to Odessa, sleeping out on deck to
save money, and the night boat back the next evening, so that no
days were lost in travel. Before long he made contacts for the new
organization there, and in Yekaterinoslav and other Southern cities,
found his way to the experienced organizer of an underground
printing plant in Kiev, even returned from one triumphant trip to
Odessa with some literature that had been smuggled into Russia
from abroad. The grudging Doctor Ziv, whose subsequent memoir
is one long stricture on the mind and personality of Leon Trotsky,
concedes that "the lion's share of the success of the new organization we owed unquestionably to Bronstein, whose inexhaustible
energy, skill in plans and contrivances of all sorts and resistance
to fatigue, had no limits."

Alexandra Sokolovskaya welcomed Lyova's tacit acceptance of
Social Democratic methods without a word: her gentle heart was
no refuge for grudges, least of all against her attractive and valued
antagonist. To celebrate the foundation of the new movement, four
of its youthful leaders went to a Nikolaev photographer and had
taken for history (and the police) a collective photograph. Young
Bronstein is there, magnetic and proud, eyes slightly crossed because he has taken his glasses off, bushy haired and shaggy browed,
large featured, with thick, full lips and a strong jaw, despite the
suggestion of a dimple in the chin, later to be hidden by his beard.

Alexandra is next to him, with an air of dedication about her;
then her brother, Ilya, who later became editor of the *Odessa
News;* and the medical student Ziv, in European dress, collar and
tie, a stiff and solemn dress which Bronstein regarded as a lapse
from revolutionary purity. They autographed each other's copies
with appropriate sentiments. Because Ziv was soon to leave for
Kazan once more to complete his final year in the medical school,
Bronstein wrote on Ziv's copy words of implied scorn: "Faith without works is death." Alexandra, gentle and compassionate, insisted
on its erasure. Ziv treasured it along with other grievances, to
merge it later with his opposition to bolshevism.

The success of the amateurish organization was instantaneous.
The times, the reawakening public life, the longing of the sectaries
for greater human dignity, contributed more than the zeal of
these inexperienced youths. Even before their "unionization," most
of the dissenters were already on the road to a more secular opposition. Mukhin, their leader, had come to regard religion as a useful
cover. A cabinetmaker whom Bronstein enrolled in the library

filled out his faith in the application blank as *Ratiolist*—explained, it turned out to be *Rationalist*. The influence of the non-believing students and of young workers who had been trained in the technical school connected with the shipyards, pushed religious language, ritual and outlook more and more into the background, until even the aged evangelist member whom everyone called "grandpa" became apologetic in his references to the catacombs and the secret meetings of the primitive Christians.

The grievances which the South Russian Workers' Union publicized were in the main offenses against human dignity. On the positive side, their meetings were much concerned with the culture of the members. At the secret gatherings in the woods they would have talks on sciences; readings from a badly mutilated mimeographed copy of the *Communist Manifesto*, which Bronstein had obtained in Odessa; recitations, songs and poems, often of their own composition. The "ratiolist" cabinetmaker composed a "Proletarian March" in which his past found expression in such lines as "We are the alphas and omegas, we are the beginnings and the endings." Nesterenko, a red-headed carpenter, wrote a song in Ukrainian about Karl Marx, "Lo, a Great Prophet Comes." Out on the sand dunes, they sang it softly together.

In a closed room with blinds down and fire lit to burn the telltale evidence, or in Mukhin's home, specially rigged up with electric buzzers to warn of the police, Bronstein mixed gelatine and glycerine on a tin tray to make a hectograph pad for offset reproduction. It was a point of honor with Lev Davidovich to pen every letter personally in clear printed characters so that even the semi-literate should have no difficulty reading the leaflets. Two hours it took him—bent back never straightening for an instant—to pen a single page for the hectograph. Then they pulled two hundred or so beautiful copies in purple ink, more legible than the pallid, misprint-laden sheets being turned out by underground printing presses elsewhere in Russia.

To the workmen and the "public" of Nikolaev, the new leaflets were a sensation. Their neatness, their simple but eloquent language—the future "Pen" was learning fast—their mysterious air of knowing each foreman's rudeness, each act of outrage, what went on inside each factory, gave public and police the idea that there was behind them a mighty and experienced organization. Workmen did not have to be sought, they sought out the Union, offering help, information, enlistment. Lev Davidovich knew from his reading what a thanksgiving it had been to the older revolutionaries

when, after prolonged effort, they recruited one or two solitary
workmen. Yet here they soon found themselves at the head of a
loose organization of some two hundred! He was in a constant
state of exaltation and excitement. The Nikolaev police chief himself went from plant to plant in Nikolaev personally remedying
abuses complained of in the leaflets, so as to rob the mysterious
South Russian Workers' Union of its issues. This only increased the
organization's prestige.

The success of the leaflets led to a hectographed newspaper, *Our
Cause*, with Bronstein as editor. Now his aching back did not
unbend for days together. He wrote most of the articles, penned
every letter himself for the hectograph, ransacked the newspapers in the public library for cartoons, which he copied, combined
into new composites, adapted with new legends. Nikolaev was
proud of its underground socialist organ. Even in Odessa and other
towns there was talk of it.

The police redoubled their efforts. Spies multiplied. Shrentzel, a
mechanic who claimed to be an engineer, appeared from nowhere,
unprepossessing, furtive, inquisitive. (Later Lyova learned that he
had been driven out of Odessa as an exposed spy. Mukhin and
Bronstein staged a little comedy in the Café Russia to throw a scare
into him; he disappeared once more—until he was needed at the
police hearings.) Nesterenko, the red-headed carpenter who had
sung of Marx the Great Prophet, met Bronstein one winter midnight, near the end of 1897, in a graveyard to receive a roll of proc-
lamations. Out of the darkness loomed another figure, walked past
them, scrutinizing Lev Davidovich closely. Nesterenko, too, had
become a police spy.

Still the police withheld their blow, unwilling to believe that in
these boys and girls and simple religious dissenters they had found
the real leaders of the organization.

Not until January, 1898—when the Union was nearly a year old
and the third number of *Our Cause* had appeared, did the police
close in upon it. By then their information was detailed, their
dragnet thorough. Bronstein had gone out of town to visit Shvigovsky where he was working as a gardener, and to leave some papers
with him. A detective trailed Maria Sokolovskaya, Alexandra's
younger sister, who had come to warn him, so that all three were
arrested together. Alexandra was in Yekaterinoslav. With the
abnegation that characterized her, she came in to surrender so
that the workers should not think their leaders had deserted them,

and that the trial might be hastened when the police had all those they were looking for. Later such idealism in the conduct of political leaders would yield to more practical considerations of the continuing struggle. The medical student Ziv, identified from the collective photograph, was arrested when he returned from Kazan with his doctor's degree. All the papers which Shvigovsky had hastily hidden in the snow when the police came, turned up in the spring thaws, detailed, incriminating, so that Bronstein spent a good part of his time at the hearings accepting responsibility to exonerate the gardener. Virtually every workman who had had any contact with the organization was identified by the spies in their midst. All in all, there were some two hundred prisoners of varying degrees of complicity crowded into the moldering, foul, cold Nikolaev jail, never intended to house so many and with no tradition or resources for the special treatment of "politicals." One attempted suicide. Another went insane. Some were released without apology. Most held their tongues and took their punishment, or quixotically gave the police excessive evidence against themselves in the hope that they would thus shield others. There was no trial, no confrontation with accusers or with each other, no opportunity for counsel, only secret administrative hearings. Even these attentions were so rare that they were welcomed as a relief from solitary confinement.

This first prison, and its successor a few weeks later in Kherson, inured Lyova Bronstein, spending his nineteenth birthday in jail, against a lifetime in twenty prisons in a half-dozen countries. Prison, too, settled the question of engineering and mathematics, gave him time to think through the unthinking actions of the past year, took the place of the Tsar's universities. His father and mother were heartbroken when they learned of it, but to the boy, still held incommunicado, imprisonment was no disgrace, rather a badge of honor linking him up with the great names he had already learned to cherish. From the days of Nicholas I, the list of prisoners and exiles had read like a *Who's Who* of Russia's great men and women. It would continue to be so through all the years of tsardom. With the Tsar's fall, the prison and exile lists would empty for a brief season of their men of distinction, only to become a partial roster of anti-Bolshevik intellectuals a little later, and the completest *Who's Who* in Russian history during the high tide of the purges of the nineteen thirties. To the young prisoner, the consciousness of forming part of a distinguished company robbed imprisonment of one of its terrors, that of moral obloquy.

Cut off from contact with the outside world, unaware of who else had been arrested, housed in a large, cold reception room big enough for thirty prisoners, with only himself and a young Jewish bookbinder named Yavich as occupants, the lad had need of all his store of health and pride and idealism. The two boys slept on a straw mattress which, at six in the morning, was taken from them. Then they would sit on the bare floor—there were no furnishings—in hats, coats, galoshes, huddled close for animal warmth, hugging a stove which was barely warmer than they. There they dreamed away the timeless days, speculating on their future and their fate.

Three weeks slid by. He was transferred, alone this time, to solitary in Kherson. Still no word from the outside world, no parcels of food or clothing. For three months, no soap, no opportunity to bathe, or to wash clothes, no change of underwear. His body was consumed by vermin. He recorded later that he was able to judge the foulness of the air only by the grimace the warder made when he brought in the chunk of bread which had to serve for both breakfast and supper, and the prison stew which was his dinner. No pencil, no paper, no books, not enough bread to make him forget his continuous hunger. To distract his spirit he would pace the cell meditating on the problems of Marxism versus populism, trying to construct for himself a Marxian system of thought out of his own meager resources, composing verses and memorizing them for future commitment to paper. During the recent months before his arrest, he already knew that he was on the road from populism to Marxism, but he had been unwilling to give Alexandra the satisfaction of admitting it. Now, as a sign of his conversion he turned the peasant song "Dubinushka" into a proletarian "Machinushka" in exaltation of the machine. The verses, mediocre enough but "ideologically improving," lived to find their way into Soviet songbooks.

At the end of three months, the jailer entered one day with a clean pillow, a warm blanket, soap, a package of tea, sugar, cookies. Lev Davidovich may have renounced his father's aid, but father and mother were not so easily put off as an old suit or outgrown ideas. They had caught up with his whereabouts and had come to "save" and to help him. In fact, not until Lev Davidovich's fame had spread far in the Revolution of 1905 and the boy had become a man in his late twenties did stubborn old David Bronstein renounce the idea of someday winning him for respectability and engineering. Whenever the impecunious Lev Davidovich or his wife and children of a later date needed money, the Bronsteins were ready to help. But the connection was largely onesided; there

was never the intellectual understanding or the filial affection that
we have seen in the relations of Vladimir Ilyich Ulyanov to his
mother. Detachment from all but followers and friends-in-the-cause
was a striking aspect of this boy's character.

Soon after the parental visit, Lev Davidovich was transferred to
the so-called model prison—all steel and stone—at Odessa. Here
the Tsar's government recognized the "political" as a special class
of prisoner not to be grouped with common criminals. Bronstein
was allowed books from the prison library, and from outside, was
permitted to have paper and pencil, to make notes and write. He
was kept in a section with other politicals, could tap out messages
to cellmates which would be passed on to their destination, learned
how to code messages by little dots under letters in agreed books
in the prison library, even to circulate manuscripts of his own composition written in microscopic letters, then passed through a drain
or left in a matchbox in the toilet, to which the prisoners were taken
in a fixed order every morning. But this last method drove him to
desperation because the recipient could never comment on the
document or respond to it. Successive generations of political
prisoners had developed a whole technique of communication and
common life in prison.

He located one of the Sokolovsky boys, then Ziv, and Shvigovsky.
To each he announced his conversion to Marxism. Sokolovsky
agreed, Ziv was triumphant, Shvigovsky was cold and indignant.
Alexandra, when the news finally got to her by the grapevine telegraph, found in it cause for a deeper rejoicing.

With so much time on his hands, so many busy thoughts in his
head, Bronstein's pen could not long remain idle. The prison
library, being a prison library, was made up of edifying works on
theology, back files of a conservative historical journal and of the
Orthodox Review. He waded through them all, learned the lives
of the Saints, the ways of Satan and his devils, what was known of
the plan and structure of paradise, the Orthodox arguments against
Catholicism, Protestantism, Darwinism and the heresies of Tolstoy,
and Archbishop Nikanor's scientific proofs of such miracles as that
of Balaam's ass.

Then his sister Olga and the Shpentsers began bringing him
books: the New Testament in five languages, which enabled him
to study German, French, English and Italian; histories; Beltov
(Plekhanov) on the *Monistic Conception of History;* Antonio Labriola's *Essays on Historical Materialism;* Darwin's *Origin of Species*
and *Autobiography.*

Darwin stood for me—he wrote later to Max Eastman—
like a mighty doorkeeper at the entrance to the temple of
the universe. I was intoxicated with his minute, precise,
conscientious, and at the same time powerful thought. I was
the more astonished when I read that he had preserved
his belief in God. I absolutely declined to understand how
a theory of the origin of species by way of natural and
sexual selection and a belief in God, could find room in one
and the same head.

Much of Labriola's simple-seeming, gnomic observations on
Marxian philosophy still escaped him. He determined to master
historical materialism and test his mastery by an independent study
of an obscure phenomenon which had begun to intrigue him: the
social meaning of the strange history of Free-Masonry. He took
notes on the history of Masonry in a fat notebook of a thousand
numbered pages, writing with almost microscopic minuteness, in-
terspersing the notes with his comments. When any part of it
seemed complete, he copied it out on thin paper and smuggled it
to the other prisoners. Later he carried the fat notebook with him
to Siberia and had Alexandra Lvovna forward it to him in Switzerland, where it got lost, a loss he always regretted.

All through 1898 and most of 1899, he remained in the Odessa
prison, waiting for administrative disposition of his case. In November, 1899, he was informed that he had been condemned to four
years in Far Eastern Siberia. Alexandra and her two brothers were
also given four years, Dr. Ziv three, others lesser punishments. Now
the long monotony was relieved by preparations for the journey.
Those who had lovers proceeded to marry; those who had none
arranged fictitious engagements because fiancées and wives were
allowed special visiting privileges. Lyova Bronstein sent a proposal
of marriage to fellow-prisoner Alexandra Lvovna Sokolovskaya. But
as the would-be bridegroom was still a minor, having just turned
twenty in October, his father's permission had to be secured. Old
Bronstein was not minded to let his wayward son marry another
state criminal, who, he felt, had been the cause of his son's undoing.
Moreover, he thought the girl too old (six years older, according
to Max Eastman, who interviewed her, "at least ten years older,"
according to Dr. Ziv's memoirs) and the boy too young. The rage
of Lev Davidovich at this indignity to his independence knew no
bounds. But his father was armed with legal authority, backed by a
well-lined purse to convince any official inclined to sentimental
indulgence of the young lovers.

The prisoners were taken from Odessa to the transfer prison of Butyrki in Moscow, to wait there until a big enough batch should accumulate for shipment to Siberia. A group had just left, so that the prison was nearly empty. Once more the weeks passed into months while they waited. Now, however, their life changed completely. In place of solitary cells, the men were all kept together in the great clock tower, the women in another tower of the prison. There was company, talk, collective discussion. Here Bronstein first heard the name of Lenin as the prisoners read together his impressive economic work (published legally under the pseudonym of Vladimir Ilyin) *The Development of Capitalism in Russia.* They read and discussed Bernstein's revisionist critique of Marxism and decided for Marxist orthodoxy against revisionism. Lev Davidovich gave expression to his overflowing energies by leading a hunger strike; by writing and smuggling out of the prison a pamphlet on the labor movement in Nikolaev, which was published in Geneva; by beginning work on a Marxist propaganda novel, never destined to see the light of day.

Twice a week the prisoners were visited by their wives or fiancées, received books and packages, exchanged messages rather freely, held long interviews in a common room under the eyes of a single indulgent guard. Lyova gave Alexandra's name as his fiancée and she was conducted to the visiting room at the same time as the women from the outside world. "During those interviews," Ziv writes, "he showed a touching tenderness not only to his fiancée but also to all the other ladies who came to meet their husbands, brothers, etc., and charmed everyone by his chivalrous bearing." Old David Bronstein being far away now, Lyova soon succeeded in persuading the Butyrki prison authorities to allow the rabbi-chaplain to perform a marriage ceremony. His *Autobiography,* which is extremely reticent and dry in its few references to his relations with women, limits its account of his marriage to the following:

> There—in the village of Ust-Kut in northeastern Siberia—I was put ashore with one of the woman prisoners, a close associate of mine from Nikolaev. Alexandra Lvovna had one of the most important positions in the South Russian Workers' Union. Her utter loyalty to socialism and her complete lack of any personal ambition gave her an unquestioned moral authority. The work that we were doing bound us closely together, and so, to avoid being separated, we had been married in the transfer prison in Moscow.

One would never suspect the transports of a lover in this almost unfeeling suggestion of a party marriage of convenience. But Alexandra's own account (as told to Max Eastman), and Ziv's no less, carry the conviction that he ardently reciprocated the love which Alexandra Lvovna had long felt for him. In Siberia she was to bear him two daughters.

Not until May, 1900, after more than two years and three months in Russian prisons, did the Nikolaev criminal begin the journey to eastern Siberia. On the train to Irkutsk, "Bronstein," according to Ziv, "did not seem to interest himself in anything. He was entirely absorbed by A. Sokolovskaya." After a brief stay in the prison at Irkutsk on the edge of Mongolia, he and his bride, separated from their comrades, began a voyage in a convict barge down the Lena River to their final destination.

Ust-Kut was a solitary, vermin-ridden village of about a hundred peasant huts lying between the forest and the river. At night the cockroaches "filled the house with their rustling"; in the summer they were tormented by great swarms of midges. The beautiful countryside had no attraction for Lev Davidovich, wrapped up in his wife, his books, his writings, his plans for the future. "I lived between the woods and the river," he wrote later, "and I almost never noticed them . . ." With the passion for logic and consistency which we have already noted, he set out to revise his point of view on the personal problems of life: love, death, friendship, optimism, pessimism, in the light of his new-found Marxist *Weltanschauung*. Alexandra appears to have subordinated her life to his, following with anxious joy his excursions into the universal application of the philosophy she had urged upon him.

A daughter was born and named Zina, then a second, Nina, both destined to have a tragic end, as all those whose lives were linked with his. The Bronsteins' stipend from the government was raised to nineteen rubles a month, enough to pay for cooking, cleaning, rent and food. Books were another matter. To add to their income, Lev Davidovich got a job as a clerk for an illiterate but wealthy trader of Irkutsk. His heart, however, was not in his work. The billing of 40 pounds of red lead as 40 poods (i.e. 1600 pounds) caused him to lose his job. The family was sent back to lonely, frozen Ust-Kut once more.

Next he became local correspondent for the *Eastern Review*, a legal journal started by the older populist exiles in the Siberian provincial capital. At this work he was happy. His "local correspondence" developed into the familiar Russian essay type known as the

feuilleton analogous to the "column" that has become so popular
in recent American journalism. All the exiles of the Province of
Irkutsk read the paper and many of them contributed. His column
was well liked; before long his pay jumped from two kopeks a line
to four. The peculiar pen-name he had chosen, Antid Oto—the
Italian for "antidote"—achieved some local reputation.

The young columnist from Ust-Kut was proud of his first experience in non-political literature. He was to have recourse to this
method of making a livelihood again and again in his troubled
career. Still as *Antid Oto*—that slightly arrogant pen-name which
seemed to suggest that his writings might be an antidote to the
poison distilled by the rest of the paper—he wrote for many years
for the liberal democratic *Kievskaya Mysl* ("Kievan Thought"),
first from Vienna, then as war correspondent in the Balkans during
the "Little War" of 1912, and then in France during the "Great
War" of 1914. When the Soviet Government published both series
of *Antid Oto* essays in his collected works, he looked them over
and found them good. "Of course, I couldn't say all that I wanted
to . . . but I never wrote what I did not want to say." Many an
émigré revolutionary sought to eke out his living abroad by placing
less partisan writings in the general press, but none with such
genuine vocation for the writer's trade as he.

The Bronsteins received permission to move to Verkholensk,
where there were other exiles. In company with them, or in argument with them, Lev Davidovich settled accounts to his own satisfaction, with Revisionism, "legal Marxism," anarchism. His first
contact with an anarchist was with that romantic Russian type which
glorified banditry, a man who wounded a local police chief "not
that he had anything against him personally, but that he wanted,
through him, to strike at the tyranny of the state." A little later two
lengthy hectographed essays from the pen of their fellow-exile
Makhaisky reached the colony of Verkholensk politicals. The first
essay was a sharp critique of the political opportunism of the German Social Democracy. Coinciding as it did with their own opinions
of the opportunistic tactics being advocated in the book of Bernstein's they were then reading and discussing, the Makhaisky
pamphlet made a profound impression. Then the second hectographed volume arrived from the same pen, criticizing Marxism
itself and evaluating the socialist movement as one which would
lead to a social order in which the intellectuals (managers, technicians, bureaucrats, politicians, professional men) would be substituted for the capitalists as a new privileged class of exploiters
of the proletariat. For months the exiles discussed nothing but

Makhaisky. To Bronstein, this second essay was sufficient to "tear away the mask" from Makhaisky's face, and to inject into the young Marxist a "powerful inoculation" against anarchism, syndicalism and all related theories. Even in 1929—and to the day of his death —though Trotsky increasingly concerned himself with the bureau-cratization of the Russian state, it never occurred to him to re-examine Makhaisky's views; he always cited them as self-evidently monstrous. But we cannot dispose of them quite so easily, and shall have to return to them again for further examination.

Word came from Russia of Tolstoy's excommunication; then of the assassination of the Minister of Education, Bogolepov, by a student, and the Minister of the Interior, Sipyagin, by another. Obviously, the political cauldron was beginning to simmer. "All the exiles were as much aroused as if they had heard the bugle-call of alarm." They had heated discussions once more of the vexed question of terror as a revolutionary tactic, Bronstein siding with those who were against it.

Social Democratic organizations began to spring up among the railwaymen along the Transsiberian. He wrote leaflets and proc-lamations for them. Smuggled in the binding of books, arrived Lenin's pamphlet, *What's to Be Done?* and several numbers of *Iskra*. To Bronstein they were a summons. The mounting restless-ness among the exiles who sensed the growing movement in Rus-sia (the Revolution of 1905 was but three years away), was caus-ing a veritable epidemic of escapes. The numbers who wanted to risk the long flight were so great that they had to draw lots and take turns. Lev Davidovich consulted his wife. That devoted woman, though her younger daughter was less than four months old, did not hesitate for a moment. She met his objections with the two words: "You must."

His turn came. With another fugitive, a woman, buried in a pile of hay at the bottom of a peasant cart, he left Verkholensk. For four days the local inspection was staved off by Alexandra by means of a dummy lying upstairs in his bed, "too sick to be disturbed." In those trackless wastes, four days' head-start was enough. The un-derground railway was run by peasants whom the old populists had converted into sympathizers. Later, in starched shirt, collar, necktie, and European suit, and with a copy of the *Iliad* in Rus-sian, he boarded a train. In his pocket was a forged passport, which he himself had filled out in the name of *Trotsky*. It was the name of the chief jailer in the model prison of Odessa! Once on the passport, he was to use it, with occasional breaks, for the rest of his life.

In Samara he reported to someone using the name of "Claire" (or "Kler"). It turned out to be Lenin's old friend of the Samara days, the engineer Krzhizhanovsky, chief *Iskra* agent in Russia. The escaped convict from Siberia made an excellent impression on all the Samara comrades. "Claire" wrote a letter on him to Krup-skaya, secretary of *Iskra* abroad, in which he nicknamed him *Pero* —"Pen"—pronounced him a fervent supporter of *Iskra* and a young man of brilliant talents. "He is a real young eagle," the report con-cluded. The "young eagle" was sent around by Krzhizhanovsky on organizing trips to Kharkov, Poltava, Kiev, but the connections were unreliable; as organizer he did not distinguish himself. However, a brief negotiation on behalf of *Iskra* with the local illegal paper, *The Southern Worker,* elicited such a precise report on the pos-sibilities of joint work and the obstacles and grounds of possible difference, that Lenin was deeply impressed with the new recruit's political acumen. Before long, a summons came to him to leave for Western Europe and put his pen at *Iskra*'s service. Krzhizhanovsky supplied the necessary funds, and addresses for smuggling across the Austrian-Polish border. As he approached the frontier, a police official asked to see his passport. To the genuine astonishment of the newly christened Trotsky, the official found nothing wrong with it.

At the border, the usual smuggling difficulties, hiding in peasant huts, crossing a shallow river at night on another man's back so as to be dry on arrival, traveling hidden in a two-wheel cart with chickens as fellow-passengers, were varied only by the fact that the smugglers overcharged their inexperienced and spendthrift patron. Reacting against the hateful niggardliness of his father's household, he overtipped right and left, so that the money which was to carry him to London was gone by the time he reached Vienna.

Undaunted, this self-important young man who believed that the great parties of Western Europe were waiting breathless to welcome and to assist escaped Russian revolutionaries, demanded to see none other than the outstanding figure in the Austrian Social Democratic Party, Victor Adler. The good "Comrade Doctor" had a Russian daughter-in-law, and a sympathetic sense of humor, so that the impecunious young Russian refugee who disturbed his Sunday rest received better treatment than was to be expected. By the time he reached Zurich, he was broke again. In the same "uncivilized" fashion he woke Axelrod at 3 A.M., instead of waiting until dawn, and made him pay for the cab. It was almost the same story in London, where he knocked loudly at Lenin's door while the latter, always an early riser, was still asleep. Krupskaya, in dressing gown, hastened to answer the triple knock, an agreed sign, before the house should be roused by the knocking. "Hallo," she called up the stairs, "*Pero* has arrived." "The kindly expression of Lenin's face was tinged with a justifiable amazement," but he began forthwith to question the newcomer. Krupskaya had to pay for the cab.

CHAPTER XIII

LENIN PREPARES

> . . . The fact that all his powers and energies are concentrated upon one thing makes it easy for him to appear extraordinary in the eyes of the masses and become a leader, in the same way that those who really concentrate on God become saints and those who live only for money become millionaires.   *—Ignazio Silone*

IN LONDON young Trotsky, to use his own words, "fell in love with *Iskra*." Not with this shading or that, but with the whole board of editors, all the back numbers, viewpoints, formulations. When Lenin asked what he thought of the draft program which they had published for the consideration of the coming Party congress, his answer was wholesale endorsement. How could he dream that there were differences among those titans of orthodox Marxism, that the draft had been a product of bitter, dragging controversy, versions, counter-versions, ruptured relations, go-betweens, peacemakers, compromises? The newcomer was given a tryout as lecturer to the émigrés in London. His theme, derived from study in prison and Siberia, was a defense of historical materialism against the strictures of the Russian subjectivist school. The title was: "What is Historical Materialism and How Do the Social Revolutionaries Comprehend it?". The patriarch of Russian populist exiles, the venerable Chaikovsky, took the floor against him in the discussion period, as did the scarcely less venerable and distinguished anarchist leader Cherkesov. The young lecturer disposed of these great men so easily—to his own and most of the audience's satisfaction—that he returned to his lodgings "walking on air." Lenin fed his pride by suggesting that he write up the lecture notes as an article for the theoretical organ *Zarya* ("Dawn"), alongside of which even *Iskra* was but a "popular journal." But, as he wrote later, "I didn't have the courage to appear by the side of Plekhanov and the others with a strictly theoretical essay." He submitted instead a lesser article for *Iskra*, which Lenin, jesting the while, pruned of some of its literary adornments.

Next he was sent on a tour of the émigré colonies in Brussels, Liege, and Paris, to repeat the same lecture for a small admission fee and thus raise money for *Iskra*. In the diary of a young Russian

215

girl, Natalia Ivanovna Sedova, who served in Paris as a sort of
receptionist for visiting revolutionaries, his arrival merited a number of entries. She found a room for him in the cheap lodging house
where she herself lived. She marveled at the youth of the theoretician (he was twenty-two). She reported anxiously that when
she passed his door he was whistling instead of working on his
lecture. Blushing, she brought a message to him from an older
woman comrade that he was to work hard and not to whistle.
"The lecture," she recorded, "went off well and the colony was
delighted, as the young follower of *Iskra* exceeded all expectations."

That ordeal over, she presented herself as guide to the glories
of Paris, its boulevards in constant movement, its history-haunted
buildings, its galleries, museums, river banks, green gardens. But
the young man, resistant to being absorbed by anything that was
not politics or Marxism, fought against the contagion of her enthusiasm. "Paris resembles Odessa"—she reports his verdict in her
diary—"but Odessa is better."

Natalia Ivanovna was one of those devoted girls of the "repentant privileged classes," cultured, emotional, self-sacrificing, who had
early dedicated herself to righting the immemorial wrongs of
Russia. While still in a young ladies' boarding school she had been
a ringleader in introducing forbidden books. In the university,
first in Moscow, then in Geneva, she had joined rebel student circles. As "post-graduate" work, she unhesitatingly embraced exile
and the self-denying, anonymous role of a subordinate professional
revolutionist. All her thoughts were selfless, unless we except her
young girl's dream of finding some male comrade whom she could
love and learn from, and at whose side she could enrich her service
to the movement. To the self-assured, brilliant young visiting
lecturer, she made no secret of her admiration. With his usual reticence in affairs of the heart, he has left no record of his own feelings except to note in his *Autobiography:* "I was much more interested in learning about Paris than I had been about London . . .
because of the influence of N. I. Sedova."

In Siberia, while Trotsky as a new-baked Marxist was "considering from the viewpoint of Marxism the so-called 'eternal' problems of life: love, death, friendship," he had consciously rejected
any remnants of prejudice in favor of monogamy. Sex and family
life, like all things personal, would have to be subordinated to the
comings and goings required of him by the revolutionary movement. When his wife Alexandra had urged him to flee, she knew
that the task of supporting their two girls would devolve upon her,
that his escape to Western Europe would separate him from her

for an indefinite period. For years they did not see each other. When her children were in need, his old father helped. Toward the man she had married in prison, her loyalty never faltered. When she was over sixty, Stalin sent her to Siberia as part of the vengeance which cost Trotsky both his daughters and both his sons.

Though he set the demands of the movement above love or friendship, there was nothing of the puritan or ascetic about Leon Trotsky. In every period of his life—as young wandering revolutionary, as victorious War Commissar, as exile fallen from high station —this man was attractive to many women. He had little time for wooing; indeed, he would have fitted ill into the role of conventional suitor or ladies' man; but a number of "affairs," temporary and not engaging his spirit very deeply, came his way without much expenditure of effort.

His legal marriage to Alexandra, however, was different from these. And still more so his Paris idyll with Natalia Ivanovna Sedova. Natalia's affections clung to him, her admiration and comradeship were to sustain him all his life. She it was who would share the days of triumph in the Kremlin and follow him into exile into Soviet Asiatic Russia, then to Prinkipo, France, Norway, Mexico. Her love, like Alexandra's, was all giving and no demanding. Two children were born to her, too, both boys. Like the two daughters of Alexandra, they would know the bitter lot of having sprung from so ill-starred a father. Natalia Ivanovna was at his side when he died in a Mexican hospital. One of his last deathbed thoughts was of her lonely, uncertain future. She is today his literary executor and a revered symbol to the devoted remnant of his followers. Alexandra Lvovna retained the legal name of Bronstein, but Natalia Ivanovna is properly known today as "Mrs. Trotsky."

> I suggested to all the members of the Editorial Board— wrote Lenin on March 2, 1903—that they coopt "Pero" as a member of the Board . . . We *very much need* a seventh member, both as a convenience in voting (six being an even number), and as an addition to our forces. "Pero" has been contributing to every issue for several months now, works most energetically . . . gives lectures in which he has been very successful . . . Unquestionably a man of rare abilities, he will go much farther . . . Possible objections: (1) His youth; (2) his leaving for Russia possibly in a short time; (3) his pen [*pero*], this time without quotation marks, which shows traces of a *feuilleton* style and is excessively florid.

Lenin took up each of these possible objections. His youth? Time would remedy that, and already he was "a party man, a man of faction." He might leave for Russia? So much the better, for organized connection with the Board would be a plus for *Iskra*. The defects of style? He would outgrow them; in the meanwhile he accepted corrections, albeit reluctantly; if necessary, corrections could be made by majority vote of the editors.

The letter ended with a pointed postscript:

> I consider that it would be most inconvenient and awk-
> ward to put off cooptation, as it has become clear to me
> that *Pero is considerably* annoyed—though of course he
> does not show it openly—about being treated as a "youth."
> If we do not take *Pero* at once, he will slip away . . .

Far from resenting any alleged hesitancy to promote him to a full editorship, the innocent subject of this letter would have been flattered, and astonished, to learn that such a move was being proposed. The fiction had an element of verisimilitude, however, for Lenin, quick to size up the character of those he sought to utilize, had sensed the component of vanity in the young man's makeup. But why the fiction? Whose resistance was it designed to overcome? Not Martov's certainly, for the latter had answered that the proposed Board member showed "undeniable talent, is quite 'ours' in thought, wields considerable influence thanks to his exceptional eloquence . . ." Axelrod liked the newcomer sufficiently to spend long hours talking to and enlightening him. Potresov agreed with Martov and Lenin. Vera Zasulich, as women of all ages were likely to be, was enthusiastic about the proud and promising youth. But Plekhanov opposed Lenin's motion with ill-dissimulated fury. What, then, had happened to his dual vote which was to be exercised whenever there should be a three-three tie? Against what, if not his own leadership, would future four-to-three decisions be directed? What did Lenin mean by proposing a mere boy of twenty-two on the Editorial Board of *Iskra*? What could his object be if not to strengthen the "youngsters" against the "oldsters," and his own influence above all by the vote of an unconditional follower? Plekhanov countered with a proposal to wait with the reorganizing of the Editorial Board until the coming congress. A fateful motion it turned out to be!

Since coopting could only be done by unanimous agreement, Lenin's proposal to break the vexatious tie votes was blocked. To save face, he moved to invite young *Pero* to editorial meetings without vote. This elicited from Plekhanov a flood of sarcastic persiflage about the young candidate's "pen" and manners, until even the faithful Vera Zasulich was moved to declare, "I'll bring him, no matter what you say, to the next meeting." And to the next meeting she actually did bring him, proud and unaware of the atmosphere surrounding his invitation. But all his life he would remember "the studied coldness" with which Plekhanov shook hands with him.

From the worshipful distance of the Russian underground, or even from the closer vantage point of the new contributing editor, *Iskra* presented a solid front in political and organizational matters, a steadily advancing front that seemed to drive liberals, Revisionists, "Economists," anarchists, renascent populists (of the new Social Revolutionary Party), and all other rival opposition groups, triumphantly before it. Plekhanov expounded the major generalizations of Marxist doctrine, applying them particularly to the field of culture; Lenin discussed agriculture, cherished and enlarged upon every strike and riot, sharpened the edge of polemic against "Economists" and Social Revolutionaries, above all, laid down organization precepts; Martov, the most productive and speculative of the editors, wrote absorbingly on a wide range of happenings and problems. Potresov did not contribute much because he was going through an illness, and his few writings seemed to differ little as yet from Lenin's and Martov's. As he grew older, he was to reveal a political personality which would seem an anachronism in this new atmosphere of storm: a Marxist in ideas with the temperament of an intellectual of the Enlightenment of the eighteen-forties. Axelrod did not write often, but his fundamental political articles had a quality of durable solidity about them. Their full implications, like those of Lenin's articles, were to become clear only after the break between menshevism and bolshevism. Vera Zasulich contributed, as a woman, something lacking in the other editors: emotional expression, a lively psychological intuition, a capacity for seeing persons and programs in human, sentimental terms, and not as mere embodiments of political positions. To the Russian emigration and the Russian underground, the Editorial Board of *Iskra* seemed a closely knit team of champions, linking up the celebrated older generation with fresh blood and new energies for organization and combat.

Lenin, for his part, had displaced Axelrod as the organization theorist and organization agent for the group. Axelrod had yielded willingly, knowing that for the practical work of organization Lenin had both more talent and vastly more concern and energy. Vladimir Ilyich was the only man of high theoretical capacity which the

Russian Marxist movement produced, who possessed at the same
time the ability and the will to concern himself with detail organization work. This was at all times to represent his particular
strength and the strength of any faction he would build around
himself. This systematic attention to detail was the only un-Russian
feature in a political temperament that in all other respects was to
think and feel in more peculiarly Russian terms and traditions
than his more Europeanized associates.

He sent *Iskra* representatives hither and thither, made sure that
the corresponding secretary was always a person of his choice and
confidence, personally read every bit of mail and generally answered it in person or through his wife, Krupskaya. He invited
released Siberian exiles and escaped prisoners to come to stay
a while abroad, received them, gave them "inside information" on
all the groups and controversies, bound them firmly to him. He
drew promising men and women out of local work to use them
nationally; planted his agents in *Iskra's* name in cities where opponent views prevailed in the local committees; gradually weakened
localism of outlook and local initiative and autonomy, thus paving
the way for all-Russian organization under the centralized domination of *Iskra*. Until such a foundation should be securely laid, he
was opposed to the holding of a convention, which would adopt a
program, name a leadership (or rather confirm a self-constituted
leadership), and organize a national party. Thus the big battle for
the convention was planned as the culmination of innumerable
obscure skirmishes, both locally and—though this was less apparent
to the contenders—within the self-appointed general staff of the
projected party.

Rabochee Delo ("The Workers' Cause"), organ of the "Economists" and chief rival of *Iskra* for ideological leadership, tried to
head off the latter's growing domination by itself starting a drive
for unification. It, too, was published abroad, and was older than
Iskra. As late as 1902, it still had behind it more supporters both
in emigration and inside Russia. But it lacked the power instincts
and driving force of a Lenin and the prestige of a Plekhanov.
When it convoked a unification congress, the *Iskra* editors were as
one in opposing this threat to their hegemony. In view of the longing for unity prevailing in the Russian underground, they dared
not take upon themselves the onus of rejecting *Rabochee Delo's*
invitation. So they all journeyed to Zurich together, to lay down
what they hoped would prove unacceptable "conditions."

Akimov, Krichevsky, and the rest of the *Rabochee Delo* people argued until they were blue in the face—records Krupskaya—Martov became terribly heated . . . and tore his tie from his throat . . . Plekhanov bristled with wit. A resolution was drawn up (by the *Iskra* group) recording the impossibility of unity. It was read out at the conference by Dan in a wooden voice, accompanied by shouts of 'Papal nuncio!' . . . Plekhanov was in a very good mood, for he had dealt a knockout blow to an opponent he had fought so much. Plekhanov was both jolly and communicative . . .

Next the Jewish Socialist Bund, the best organized workingmen's body inside Russia, tried its hand at summoning a convention to unite the party. As was the case with the ill-fated first congress it had called at Minsk, this too was to be held secretly inside Russia, at Bialystok. The Iskrists, knowing that they could not dominate there either, sent Theodor Dan once more as "papal nuncio" to read a statement pronouncing the convention premature, improperly prepared, insufficiently representative (which last the Iskrists made sure of by keeping away the representatives of all the committees under their leadership). The statement ended with a demand that the Bialystok convention declare itself a mere "provisional conference" and limit itself to appointing delegates to serve on a wider committee to organize a real party congress. The Bialystok meeting did not feel equal to rejecting the ultimatum.

Meanwhile Lenin continued to work unceasingly to set up regular connections with the Russian local committees. His correspondence with them, and with the traveling and resident *Iskra* agents, was full of exhortations to write regularly and send detailed reports. The amateurishness of his letters from the standpoint of conspirative technique was equaled only by the amateurishness of the still inexperienced secret police. The letters spoke of "handkerchiefs" (passports), "barrels of beer" (shipments of *Iskra*), "warm fur" (illegal literature). It used Christian names beginning with the same initial letter to designate places (Ossip for Odessa, Petya for Poltava, Terenty for Tver); substituted women's names for men's and vice versa when dealing with persons; contained an amazing lot of nature-faking nonsense about animals like "the Snail," for Zinaida Krzhizhanovsky; "the Young Bear," for Lenin's sister; "the Horse," for Krassin, etc. It might seem plausible when "Papasha" (Pop) was used for Meyer Wallach, better known to history as Maxim Litvinov; but what censor could be so obtuse as not to see through a letter giving instructions to "Absolute" or "the Residue," both code names for Elena Stassova?

Small "barrels of beer" were sent through Stockholm destined for Saint Petersburg; through some misunderstanding they piled up in the cellar of the Stockholm People's House, where Lenin found them all several years later when he passed through bound for Russia. Other "beer" went through Marseilles, where a ship's cook carried it to Batum and threw it overboard at agreed spots at night in waterproof tarpaulin. Or through Alexandria and Persia, or through Galicia. "Probably not more than one-tenth of the literature dispatched," writes Krupskaya, "arrived at its destination." But "the Horse" (Krassin) and some local Georgians set up a secret printing plant at Baku, of which we shall hear more later, so that if a matrix or even a single copy of *Iskra* or some pamphlet got through, they could reprint it and spread it more widely.

Correspondence with Russia had a devastating effect on Lenin's nerves. He had to wait weeks and months for a reply, never sure whether a given matter had fallen through or whether the silence was due to shiftlessness, inertia, "the cursed Russian disorganization." His letters overflowed with scoldings and beseechings, fulsome praise for the slightest information, insults intended to prick a laggard into activity. He would spend sleepless nights waiting for answers, and still stormier nights when return letters did not carry the requested information. "Those sleepless nights," writes Krupskaya, "remain engraved on my memory." They preyed on Vladimir Ilyich's health, especially when they happened to coincide with periods of disagreement with the other *Iskra* editors.

As the long-awaited convention of the party finally drew nearer, he was so overwrought that he "developed a nervous illness called 'holy fire' [apparently shingles], which consists in inflammation of the nerve terminals of back and chest." Krupskaya looked it up in a medical handbook and consulted a Russian medical student. "We could not think of going to an English doctor, which would have cost a guinea . . . I painted Vladimir with iodine, which caused him agonizing pain." When he reached Geneva, a few months before the scheduled congress, he was in complete collapse and had to lie in bed for two weeks before resuming activity.

In April, 1903, the Editorial Board of *Iskra* was officially moved to Geneva. Lenin had been striving to keep the headquarters elsewhere, since he feared that Plekhanov would dominate the Board completely if it met in the city in which he resided. Vladimir Ilyich had gotten the paper out first in Munich, then in London. But early in 1903, by a vote of five to one, the paper was transferred to Geneva. Lenin's was the one negative vote!

He went to Geneva with mixed feelings. He had just gone through a second tremendous "lovers' quarrel" with his master, a quarrel which had raged in unabating fury all through 1902. At one point he had been moved to write:

> I have received my article—(on the *Agrarian Program of the Russian Social Democracy*)—with your remarks upon it. You have a fine idea of tact with regard to your colleagues on the Editorial Board . . . You do not hesitate to use the most contemptuous expressions, not to mention the matter of voting on suggestions which you did not even take the trouble to formulate, and voting even on style. I should like to know what you would say if I were to answer your article on the Program in the same way! If your aim was to make mutual work impossible—then the way you have chosen should help you to succeed very quickly. As for our personal, as distinguished from our business relations, you have finally spoiled them, or, more exactly, you have achieved their complete cessation. [Letter of May, 1902.]

The quarrel had begun early in January, 1902, and really, it was Lenin who had been the aggressor. It was he who had begun the motions on fine points of style and formulation, proposing to amend the draft program prepared by Plekhanov for the consideration of the coming party congress.

To everyone but Lenin, it had always seemed self-evident that Plekhanov must be the author of the program of the nascent party. From the day that he founded the Group for the Emancipation of Labor in 1883 until the congress now to be held in Geneva two decades later, he had been esteemed by all revolutionary Marxists as the founder, the outstanding leader, thinker and teacher of their movement. The men of Lenin's and Trotsky's generations alike acknowledged him as their master. His was a wide-ranging mind, at home in philosophy, esthetics, literature, as well as history, sociology, economics, and all the specialized subjects that went under the head of Marxism. His works were known and admired abroad, translated into French and German, formed part of the general treasure of Marxist theoretical writings. All Russian socialists admired him, and, when they had occasion to oppose him, were in awe of his flashing brilliance, his sharp, irrepressible wit, his habit of making sarcastic jests and quips at the expense of unclear or dull-witted opponents. As he had shown in his polemics first with the Narodniks and then with the émigré "Economists," he was, like Lenin, quick to split with those who could not be made to accept his ideas.

For more than six months of 1901, Plekhanov had labored on the program which was to serve as the permanent theoretical foundation for the coming party. When he completed it and it seemed good in his eyes, he submitted it as a matter of form for the ratification of the other editors of *Iskra,* in the name of which it was to be offered. Lenin took his copy and marked it full of underlinings, doubled and trebled question marks, exclamation points, suggestions as to style, proposed alterations at retail and wholesale. Not a sentence, not a clause escaped criticism. The elegant, compact and highly theoretical outlines of Plekhanov's program were dissolved and buried in a rain of specific, detailed counter-proposals. Some emendations dealt with scholastic trivia, anxious splitting of the finest of hairs. Others revealed unconscious differences of temperament, of attitude toward the movement and its doctrine, of approach to Russia's peculiar problems. Plekhanov's was the more European mind, Lenin's the more Russian. Plekhanov's draft sought first of all to teach Russia the theoretical generalizations of Marxism, and only in the tenth of twelve sections did it come to grips with special Russian peculiarities. Yet the real problem of Marxist politics lay in applying its brilliant generalizations concretely to concrete circumstance in each land and at each shifting moment. Plekhanov was all things the movement might require save only a politician, while Lenin's mind was political before aught else, and dipped into the body of Marxist generalizations only occasionally for guidance or for polemics.

Lenin now went so far as to draw up his own draft in rivalry to Plekhanov's. Viewed from the standpoint of intellectual esthetics it was a homely, inelegant thing. But it opened with the word Russia in the very first line, and determinedly if clumsily got down to practical business. The general Marxist description of capitalism it took for granted, focussing all its bare, clear light on the peculiarities of the Russian scene. And if Plekhanov's draft had more elegance, Lenin's had more pathos. Where Plekhanov had written of the "dissatisfaction" of the proletariat, Lenin wrote in the margin: "Instead of dissatisfaction—indignation!" Where Plekhanov wrote "labor," Lenin wrote "the laborer." Next to Plekhanov's "worsening of the lot," Lenin queried: "Would it not be better to indicate directly: unemployment, poverty?" These differences were characteristic. The inclination to analytical logic marked the teacher, the inclination to pathos marked the would-be agitator, the practical politician.

Finally, Lenin in his criticisms, and in his own counter-draft, insisted on his two favorite dogmas: (1) that the discontent of the workers would grow with the growth of capitalism, but not its socialist consciousness, "which must be brought in by us"; and (2) that Social Democracy aims "to create *an organization of revolutionaries,* which leads the struggle of the proletariat."

Latter-day Stalinist historians have stated that Plekhanov omitted the dictatorship of the proletariat from his draft program. This is not so, as an inspection of his draft will reveal. As a matter of fact, from the standpoint of "theoretical orthodoxy," there was no reason why either man could not accept the program of the other. Yet each produced a number of successive drafts and marked up the margins of his rival's with ironic and angry criticisms. Feelings became so outraged that an arbitration committee of the other *Iskra* Board members had to be set up to iron out differences and soothe ruffled feelings. In the end, Plekhanov's version, and not Lenin's, became the basis of the draft submitted by *Iskra* to the congress. Again the vote was five to one against Lenin! Yet, once he had cooled off, Vladimir Ilyich was quite pleased with Plekhanov's program and ready to defend it against all its critics. As a matter of course, Plekhanov reported on it at the congress. It actually remained the officially recognized program of the Bolshevik Party until after the Revolution of November, 1917!

Only in one respect had Lenin succeeded in amending it materially: he had added, and gotten accepted, a specifically Russian plank on the problem of the land and the peasants. When that codicile was later changed, the change, too, would be drafted and proposed by Lenin. Among the Marxists, he was almost alone in his sensitivity to the peasant question, and constantly engaged in thinking about it. It would be one of the secrets of his strength in 1917.

Before setting out for Geneva, Lenin once more sought to restore peace with Plekhanov. It seemed impossible to face Revisionists, "Economists," Bundists, and other assorted opponents at a congress without the agreement and support of the chief teacher and leader of revolutionary Marxism. Lenin wrote urging Plekhanov, who was on his way to an International Socialist Congress at Brussels, to cross over to London and visit him:

> Your report would be most useful here . . . But the main reason is that we have a number of things which need discussion . . . the measures to be taken for uniting the party . . . the agenda for the Congress, what reports are

to be delivered *by our people*, etc. . . . You know, I think
it would be a good idea if we were to begin (informally)
to be more friendly to the *Rabochee Delo* people . . . With
a firm handclasp, Your Lenin.

Yet, even as he was asking Plekhanov's opinion on the agenda
and related matters, he had already settled everything clearly in
his own mind, and had actually sent explicit instructions to his
Iskra agents in Russia. Thus, about the same time as the above
note, he had sent a letter to E. Y. Levin in Kharkov, urging that the
question of the attitude of the party toward the Jewish Bund
should be made "the first order of business," so that, if the latter
refused to yield its autonomy to a centralized party, it might be
ousted from the congress and not permitted to vote on other
closely contested matters. ("It is necessary to prepare everyone's
mind for this.")

The second order of business should be the program, to divide
the orthodox from the unorthodox on basic matters of principle.
The third order should be the question of a central organ, which
Lenin was convinced must be *Iskra*. It should have "ideological
leadership" over the party and should continue to be published
abroad. With this Editorial Board should be coupled a central committee, meeting inside Russia, to conduct the practical struggle.
"Then: as much centralization as possible. Autonomy of local committees in local matters, with the right of veto by the Central
Committee . . . District organization only with the agreement and
approval (of its personnel) by the Central Committee."

The letter admitted that his proposed order of business, running
on through eleven points, was subject to change. But "I consider it
important from the beginning to decide point 3, in order immediately to give battle to all opponents on a basic and broad question
of principle and to get a clear picture of the entire Congress: to
separate on a serious issue."

"*To separate on a serious issue!*" It is doubtful that Lenin actually anticipated a split, though the word he used, *razoitis*, literally
means to go apart; separate; sunder; each go his own way. Yet this
insistence on the readiness to oust the Bund, on the readiness to
"separate on a serious issue," is revealing as to the state of mind
and psychology of Lenin, and goes far to explain the air of fatality
with which a split did develop at the "unification" congress. (Incidentally, though Plekhanov's interests and insistences did not turn
so much around organization questions as did Lenin's, Plekhanov's
mood and temperament were otherwise similar. He too would be
ready to split with the Bund if it did not accept his views on the

"national question" and with the *Rabochee Delo* people and all
and sundry, if they were opposed to his program.)

These letters are interesting, too, for the light they throw on
Lenin's method of work, and how he prepared himself for battle.
Most men would come to the congress filled with a vague exhilara-
tion, prepared to trust much to its collective wisdom, to last-minute
inspiration and exchange of opinion, to proposals that would come
out of discussion and out of the spontaneous bright ideas of so
many devoted people. Plekhanov, too, was ready to do that on
everything but his pet project, the party program. But not so Lenin.
He was never one to leave anything to chance when he expected a
fight. He had little faith in collective discussion and spontaneous
improvisation. His days and nights were spent in trying to prepare
everything, anticipate everything, work out everything to the last
detail. "Do not fail to obtain from *each* Local Committee and
group," he admonished Levin with his usual underscorings, "an
official and *written* answer as to whether it recognizes the Organization Committee."

The Organization Committee, of which Lenin was a member, was
his, too. Not, to be sure, at the outset, when its members had been
named by the abortive Bialystok Conference. But, as luck would
have it, there had been a police spy at Bialystok, and when the first
committee was arrested, Lenin was quick to take advantage by
having *Iskra* agents named to replace them. To his old friend, agent
F. V. Lengnik in Samara, he had written:

> And so your task now is to create from *your own selves* a
> committee to prepare the Congress, to admit a Bundist into
> the Committee (after sizing him up *from all sides*—note this
> well), and to push your own people on to as many commit-
> tees as possible, guarding yourselves and your people more
> closely than the apple of your eye [against arrest] until the
> Congress. This is most important! Keep it in mind. Be in
> this bolder, more impudent and more ingenious, and in the
> rest quieter and more careful.
> Wise as serpents—and as gentle (with the committees, the
> Bund, and Peter[sburg])—as doves.
>
> All yours
THE OLD MAN

Petersburg is mentioned because the anti-*Iskra* tendency had a
majority there; the Bund because the Iskrists were determined to
put an end to its autonomy; the Local Committees because they
would elect most of the delegates. The letter is dated May 23.

1902, which shows how far back Lenin had been preparing for a congress that would not take place until the summer of 1903. There was not another man on the *Iskra* Board that could conceivably have written such letters. Nor was there any among his opponents. The injunction to be wise as serpents and gentle as doves had no sinister import in Lenin's mind, for he did not think of himself as a person looking for personal advantage or personal power, but as the selfless embodiment of a political line which was the only conceivably correct one. That unconscious conception of himself was as much a part of his strength as was the care with which he prepared the strategy, the tactics, the detailed deployment of forces and the general plan of every anticipated battle.

After taking care of the Russian Organization Committee and the Bund and the packing of the local committees in Russia with *Iskra* agents, Lenin turned his attention to the émigré colonies, where the opponents of *Iskra*, the *Rabochee Delo* supporters outnumbered the *Iskrists*. To Martov, who had gone to Paris because he could not stand the London climate, he wrote:

> The section of the Organization Committee abroad should be a section of the Russian Organization Committee—which should adopt an arch-important and an arch-severe attitude . . . either recognition of the Organization Committee and subjection to it, *or war. Tertium non datur.*

These prosaic preparations, this unblinking attention to organization detail, this predetermination of the selection of delegates and precalculation of the putative number of votes at the congress would be far more decisive than the debates, once the delegates should come together.

At the same time, Lenin did not neglect the preparation of his arguments either. He was already at work on the documents and resolutions he intended to present to the congress, the reports and speeches he intended to make there, even the refutation of anticipated objections. Night after night he paced the floor while poor Krupskaya tossed in their sleepless bed, whispering to himself, composing articles, resolutions, clauses, arguments, rehearsing reports, formulating precise phrases. When the parts of something had at last fallen into place in his mind, he would go for a walk with his wife and tell her about it.

Fearful lest the modest and laconic plank he had written as the agrarian section of the program might prove too difficult of understanding for the peasants, he was at the same time at work on one of the best pieces of popularization he ever did in his life, a pamphlet entitled *To the Village Poor.* In strikingly simple language it explained not only the immediate and long-range programs of the socialists for agriculture, but all the social, political and economic aims of socialism. The writing of this homely work was Lenin's diversion from the inexorable business of the preparation of the congress: it rested his torn nerves and restored his shattered health.

No sooner did he get out of the sickbed in Geneva than the delegates began to arrive. He greeted, sounded, walked, talked with each one personally. Martov was continually at the Ulyanovs now, and never tired of talking to the delegates either. They discussed program, party structure, theories, the role of the Bund. Martov's talk had the ampler sweep, but Lenin's was more sharply directed to the precise points that might become issues in the voting. When a doubtful delegate arrived from hostile Saint Petersburg, Lenin saw to it that he roomed with his young admirer, Trotsky, "for purposes of training."

"How Vladimir Ilyich longed for this Congress!" wrote Krupskaya a quarter of a century after it had taken place. "Longed for" . . . and prepared for it. "The general view was that there were no real differences and that everything would go swimmingly . . ." When it was too late, when the Congress had passed into history, one of the leaders of one of the defeated factions, Axelrod, would pay this reluctant tribute to the man who had tried to anticipate every eventuality:

> There is no other man who is absorbed by the revolution twenty-four hours a day, who has no other thoughts but the thought of revolution, and who, even when he sleeps, dreams of nothing but the revolution.

CHAPTER XIV

UNIFICATION CONGRESS

> Vladimir Ilyich and I recalled a simile that L. Tolstoy used
> somewhere. Once when walking, he spotted in the distance
> the figure of a man squatting on his haunches and moving
> his hands about in an absurd way. *A madman!* he thought.
> But on drawing nearer, he saw that it was a man sharpening
> his knife on the paving-stone.   —*Krupskaya*

CLOSE TO SIXTY revolutionaries, some from the underground and
others, the majority, from émigré colonies, gathered in Brussels
for a conclave that was to be kept secret from the Belgian police.
Four of the delegates were, or had once been, workingmen. The
rest were typical members of the intelligentsia, something we must
keep in mind if we are to understand the length, breadth, depth,
fanatical stubbornness and Byzantine subtlety of debates so heated
that they must have awakened policemen sleeping in the cemetery.
The injured self-love of men who identified self with their ideas
combined with a feeling of selflessness to make every defeat on the
minutest question a banner of conflict.

Those unfamiliar with Brussels were instructed to report to the
home of Koltzov, where they would be given connection with the
secret committee in charge of the Congress. After the first four
Russians had rung Koltzov's bell at odd hours, and engaged him
in intense and enthusiastic discussion, the landlady issued an ultimatum: "If one more Russian comes here, you will have to move!"
Poor old Koltzov and his wife took turns on the street corner, to
head off visitors and bid them go to the Coq d'Or. The first arrivals
became restless while weeks dragged in waiting for the representatives from underground Russia. Some of these did not arrive until
the congress was over. Delegates overran the hotel in noisy bands.
"Gusev, glass of cognac clutched in his hand," remembers Krupskaya, "sang operatic arias every evening in such loud tones that
crowds gathered beneath the windows. Vladimir Ilyich loved to
hear Gusev sing: 'We Were Wedded Out of Church' . . ."

By the time the sessions got underway all Brussels was aware of
the fact that some mysterious Russians were assembling for a secret
gathering that could bode no good for Belgium's foreign relations.
But what could be more secret than a Congress on whose organiz-

ing committee Lenin had named Dr. Zhitomirsky, Okhrana agent
delegated to shadow him, from 1902 to 1917? When the Congress
split, naturally Zhitomirsky sided with Lenin. In the scandals over
Bolshevik holdups and illicit funds (see Chapter XXII), Lenin
named this "man of confidence" to serve on a joint Bolshevik-
Menshevik investigating committee, and to block the inquiry "lest it
reach the police." The most secret of Lenin's secret committees, that
on finance, consisted of Lenin, Bogdanov and Krassin. When he
ousted the last two, he promoted Dr. Zhitomirsky to a place on it!

According to Lenin's account, probably the most accurate for he
was always one to check such things, there were forty-three delegates with fifty-one votes. Some of these, including Lenin and
Martov, were "two-handed" delegates with two votes apiece because they had secured mandates from both a Russian underground and an émigré organization. In addition there were fourteen "consultative votes," that is, fraternal delegates with voice but
no vote. These included Axelrod, Zasulich and Potresov of the *Iskra*
Board (Lenin and Martov had the two votes to which the Board
was entitled); Arkadi Kremer of the Bund; Noah Zhordania,
founder and outstanding leader of the Georgian Social Democracy
and future president of Georgia's short-lived democratic republic;
Hanecki and Warski of the Polish Social Democracy; and others
whose names need not detain us, since they will not play an important role in our story.

Of the fifty-one official votes, thirty-three, or a clear majority,
belonged to adherents of the *Iskra* faction. Lenin's careful preparations had made that certain. Among them were his younger
brother, Dmitri Ulyanov, some old friends from Samara and Siberian exile, and a number of *Iskra* agents that he had personally
sent to Russia. This did not necessarily mean that the local organizations which had sent them knew what issues might arise or what
Lenin stood for. Often an agent had been chosen because he had
demonstrated his ability to get in and out of the country, was possessed of the necessary funds and willing to undertake the hazardous
journey, whereas the local people lacked means and were bound to
the spot by employment and family ties. Thus, unwittingly, was
begun a fateful system in which a central body (or a leader) first
chose the local leadership and then the latter were designated as
convention delegates to choose the central body, that is, to confirm
the very men who had appointed them in the first place.

Iskra's chief rival, *Rabochee Delo*, possessed only three votes at
the Congress, two as a journal, and one, a delegate elected from

Petersburg! Yet they had the support of a good part of the emigration, and a decisive majority in Saint Petersburg, which Local Committee the Iskrists had just split so that the Congress might be made to seat one from each faction. From *Rabochee Delo* itself came the "Economists" Martynov (A. C. Piker), and Akimov (Vladimir Makhnovets), and from Saint Petersburg his sister Lydia Makhnovets. Even the powerful Jewish Bund, numerically the largest and best organized body of workmen in Russia, possessed only five votes, by no means representative of its actual strength in the total Russian movement. Six of the remaining delegates were faceless men and women who had not lined up on the anticipated issues, but had come to see and learn. These earned from Plekhanov and Lenin the derisive appellation of "the Swamp" because they voted now with one faction and now with the other. If the thirty-three Iskrists, most of whom had been conveniently planted by Lenin as local delegates, should•stick, all the others might talk themselves blue in the face, as they likely would, but *Iskra* would have its way.

The Congress opened at last on July 30, 1903, in a big flour warehouse festively draped with red cloth. The old edifice was infested with rats and fleas, while representatives of the Russian and Belgian police swarmed around nearby alleys and courts.

Georgii Valentinovich Plekhanov, who had waited twenty years for this occasion, delivered a moving opening address. There were tears in many eyes as the delegates, standing, sang with muted voices "The International." Out of respect for the still-born Minsk Convention of 1898, they called this the "Second Congress"; but really it was the first. They were coming together at last to found a party, adopt a program, draw up a constitution, unite the local committees, rival factions, warring papers and national and émigré groups, into a single, united, All-Russian Social Democratic Labor Party.

The exaltation soon gave way to wrangling over credentials. "The composition of the Party Congress," as Lenin put it bluntly, "was settled in advance by the Organization Committee." Still, if only as a matter of form, the convention had to set up a committee to pass on credentials. The committee included a Bundist whom Lenin denounced for "applying the strategy of tiring out the other members of the Commission, holding firm until 3 A.M., and still remaining in every question with his own 'special opinion.'" It is not hard to guess that his opinion was that the Congress was "packed" by the *Iskra*-controlled Organization Committee. Of course, the "pack" itself voted down all his protests.

Then briefly, the first puff of wind before a storm, Lenin and Martov clashed. It was a seemingly small matter, taking place not on the floor of the convention but in the "private" and "secret" (but of course quite generally talked about) sessions of the *Iskra* caucus. They were discussing the presidium of the convention, a directing body similar to an American steering or ways and means committee, plus the standing officers. If this were representative of all factions it could, and usually did, settle a great many matters by negotiation, without taking up the time of general sessions. Martov proposed such a representative presidium of nine members including one spokesman each for the Bund and *Rabochee Delo*. But Lenin was for a narrow presidium of three, Iskrists all, which should rule "with a firm hand, if necessary with an iron fist." Some uncomplimentary words about "hardness" and "softness" were exchanged. Lenin's steam-roller proposal won in the caucus; the caucus won in the convention. The presidium was Plekhanov, chairman, Lenin and Krasikov, vice-chairmen, all three Iskrists!

Exactly as Lenin had planned, the first full-dress debate took place on the question of the relationship of the Jewish Socialist Bund to the Party. The Bund was a product of the active awakening of the Jewish Pale in Russian Poland, Lithuania and White Russia, an awakening at once cultural, social and political. It is symbolic of this awakening that the Zionist movement and the Socialist Bund were born in the same year as rivals for the leadership of the masses in this, the largest concentration of Jews in the world. For a few years the Bundists, in their zeal to fight nascent Jewish nationalism, looked only to the Russian workers to lead in the solution of their special Jewish problems, and "forgot to maintain contact with the Jewish masses who understand no Russian." (It is from Martov, who was briefly a Bundist before he joined Lenin in Saint Petersburg, that these words are quoted.) But the Bundists soon discovered that the Jewish workers were far ahead of the Russian in organization and in consciousness. At the same time, their war with Zionism for the awakening Jewish communities compelled them not only to adopt Yiddish as their language but to recognize that "the growth of national consciousness and class consciousness must go hand in hand." Thus they came to this unification congress determined to demand continued autonomy in the handling of specifically Jewish problems, and to assert the claim to represent all Jewish socialists, not merely in the territorially compact pale of settlement, but in Southern Russia (where the Jews were more Russified), and wherever in the vast empire men might be found who suffered disadvantages as Jews or who, by reason of cultural or other considerations, classified themselves as Jews.

Behind this demand were both a theory of party structure and a theory of national self-determination. Its acceptance implied that, as the rest of the minority nationalities of the Empire awakened, they too would require similar arrangements of autonomy. Thus the Social Democratic Party would eventually become a federated party rather than a centralized one, with each nationality having its autonomous federation. And, if it should ever triumph, the state that would issue out of its victory would have to be a federalist rather than a centralized state. Lenin for his part held to the idea of a strictly centralized party in which national subdivisions would be no more than agencies for translating into their respective languages the slogans, program, decisions and will of the all-powerful Central Committee. And his conception of national self-determination was based upon territorial rather than cultural nationality, a difference which would become clear only a decade later.

Martov, the ex-Bundist, Trotsky and Axelrod, assimilated Jews, and the more or less Russified Jews of Southern Russia present at the Congress all lined up with Lenin and Plekhanov against the Bund. They were supported by the general desire for a centralized party, by the fear of fostering nationalistic separatism in this conglomerate of peoples, by socialist distrust of nationalism in the name of a supra-national internationalism, by the unconscious Great-Russianism of many of the delegates. "The Bund," wrote Krupskaya, "were brought to their knees." If they were, they found their feet again before the end of the Congress, and suddenly walked out, with unexpected results for the whole future of the Russian Social Democratic Party. Only Lenin, as we have seen from his letter to *Iskra* agent Levin (in the preceding chapter), was not taken by surprise but had actually based his calculations upon this secession.

Next the acknowledged founder of Russian Marxism, Plekhanov, rose to report on the projected party program. In 1929, Trotsky still remembered:

> With a clear, scientifically exact outline of the program in his mind, sure of himself, of his knowledge and of his superiority, with a gay, ironic sparkle in his eyes . . . with slightly theatrical but lively and expressive gestures, Plekhanov illumined the entire large gathering with a living fireworks of wit and erudition.

Given the composition of the Congress and the prestige of the reporter, adoption was a foregone conclusion. Yet a small determined minority, led by the "Economists" Akimov and Martynov, conducted a stubborn rearguard action. Every formulation was examined with subtlety. The debate raged through endless, round-the-clock sessions of a special Program Commission, and nearly twenty full sessions of the Congress itself! Akimov proposed no less than twenty-two separate amendments, every one of which was eventually defeated. He attacked the program wholesale and retail for its spirit of tutelage over the proletariat:

> The concepts Party and Proletariat are set in opposition to each other, the first as an active, causative, collective being, the second as a passive medium on which the Party operates. The name of the Party is used throughout as subject, in the nominative case, the name of the Proletariat as object, in the genitive case. (Laughter.)[1]

Some of those who laughed loudest at this "grammatical critique" of the program would live to wonder whether it had not touched on something symbolic, not of grammar, but of underlying sense.

But the main fire of the opposition was concentrated on a single sentence:

> The essential condition for the social revolution is the dictatorship of the proletariat, i.e., the conquest of such power by the proletariat as will allow it to suppress all attempts at resistance on the part of the exploiters.

How do you reconcile your endorsement of dictatorship, Akimov asked, with that part of your draft which comes out for a democratic republic? How do you square it with your demands for a constituent assembly elected by free, equal, direct, secret and universal suffrage? With your demand for freedom of speech, press, parties, organization, conscience, movement, occupation? for equality of all citizens regardless of status, sex, race, religion, nationality? Is not democracy an absolute good? Is it not a matter of principle? One of the desiderata for which we are fighting in every field? Shall we, representatives of those who suffer from dictatorship, countenance its use ourselves?

Trotsky rose to the defense of the program with a paraphrase from the *Communist Manifesto:*

> The rule of the working class was inconceivable until the great mass of them were united in desiring it. Then they would be an overwhelming majority. This would not be

[1] In Russian, masculine personal objects have the same form in the genitive as in the accusative.

the dictatorship of a little band of conspirators or a minority party, but of the immense majority in the interests of the immense majority, to prevent counter-revolution. In short, it would represent the victory of true democracy.[2]

Later, Stalinist historians would hold this speech against Trotsky, as a "repudiation of the principle of dictatorship." And he himself would abandon it in practice in 1917 . . .

Plekhanov brushed his unwelcome young defender aside. Akimov, Martynov and their supporters, he said, were confusing two distinct things: one was the immediate program of overthrowing tsarism and establishing a democratic republic; the other was the longer range struggle for socialism, which would not properly begin until the democratic republic had been achieved.

> Of course, we place universal suffrage in the foreground of our demands [he continued] but as revolutionaries we must say openly that we do not want to convert it into a fetish. It is not hard to imagine a situation in which the victorious working class may take away for a time the right of suffrage from its opponent, the bourgeoisie . . .
>
> The fundamental principle of democracy is this: *salus populi, suprema lex*. Translated into revolutionary language that means: *the health of the revolution is the supreme law* . . . If the safety of the revolution should demand the temporary limitation of one or another of the democratic principles, it would be a crime to hesitate . . .
>
> Some delegate has proposed that we amend our democratic demand for a parliament that meets at least every two years. He asks: Would not *every year* be even more democratic? But you must bear in mind, comrades, that the question of the term of parliament is for us revolutionaries a secondary one. If the people, in a moment of revolutionary enthusiasm, should elect a very favorable parliament, naturally we would try to make of it a Long Parliament. But if the elections should turn out badly for the working class, we might try to dissolve it, not at the end of two years, but in two weeks if possible . . .

Lenin said nothing in this debate, but his head must have nodded vigorous agreement, and the words of his master were a treasure in his memory. Fifteen years later he would quote them as he ordered the Constituent Assembly, elected by free, equal, direct and universal suffrage, to be dispersed!

[2] The minutes are not as a rule verbatim but represent summaries approved by an editorial committee and by the delegates themselves.

Plekhanov's remarks on the subordination of democratic principles to the needs of the revolution were interrupted by demonstrative applause. But there were hisses, too. Lenin, who was in the
chair, called the hissers to order. Rozanov cried out: "When in the
congress of a labor party such unheard-of words are spoken, it is
my duty to hiss!" Years later, still hissing these same ideas when
Lenin was putting them into practice, this same Rozanov would
be falsely accused of setting up a conspirative "National Center"
to "help Denikin overthrow the Soviet Government."[3] Sentenced to
death, he would be pardoned by Lenin's order and given employment in the Commissariat of Health . . .

"Abolition of the death penalty?"—Plekhanov continued imper·
turbably. "Very good! Still I am of the opinion that a few reservations are necessary. What do you think? Should Nicholas II be
permitted to live? I think we should reserve for him a death
penalty."

Martov was listening, too, with painful tension. One day he
would write a burning indictment of the Bolsheviks for restoring
the death penalty after the Revolution had abolished it. Listening,
he agreed with the general tenor of Plekhanov's remarks, but
thought them unnecessarily "hard."

Plekhanov could have avoided arousing indignation—he said—if
he had added that one could not imagine such a tragic situation in
which the proletariat would have to trample on such political rights
as freedom of the press in order to consolidate its victory . . .

To which Plekhanov responded by shouting an ironical *"Merci."*

The convention was bringing Plekhanov and Lenin closer. The
master dominated the public sessions, the disciple the private cau-
cuses of the *Iskra* faction; the one marshaled the arguments, the
other the votes. When the program was finally adopted, everyone
present voted for it except Akimov, who abstained. It seemed that
a united party must be assured since all had accepted a common
foundation of principle.

Yet there was an ambiguity in this common program, a program
which would serve Bolsheviks and Mensheviks alike until 1919.
It aimed at two successive revolutions: a "bourgeois democratic"
and a "proletarian socialist"—the overthrow of tsarism and the overthrow of capitalism. What was the relation between them? Would

[3] The "National Center" in question was that of the *Soyuz Vozrozhdenia*
("Union of Rebirth"), which aimed to unite the Right Wing of the Mensheviks
and Social Revolutionaries with the Left Bourgeois Liberals to reconstruct a
democratic Russia after the anticipated collapse of the Bolshevik dictatorship.
Perhaps this loose "union" included one of the ubiquitous Chekist "Denikin
officers." In any case, Rozanov's group did not.

the bourgeoisie, supported by the proletariat, make the first revolution? Would the proletariat make the "bourgeois" revolution, then hand over power to the bourgeoisie in order to go over into opposition? Or would the professional revolutionaries acting in the name of the proletariat take power and hold it in trust until both revolutions were completed? Would the one revolution flow over into the other, or would there be years, perhaps decades, between them? It would take the experiences of 1905 even to raise these questions. Meanwhile, the delegates voted unanimously, some of them with eyes fastened on the democratic republic, while proletarian dictatorship and socialism appeared some remote vision of the future; others strained in their thoughts, beyond an unsatisfying revolution that had not yet begun, toward another that was to follow after.

To no one present did it occur to ask the crucial question that the French socialist Charles Peguy had already asked in 1900: "I should like to know who will actually be the persons who will exercise the dictatorship of the proletariat." Nor to raise his corollary questions as to how the proletariat might dictate to its dictators, how determine the extent or duration of dictatorial powers, how liberate itself, if need be, from its liberators . . .

Thus far, the differences were more matters of temperament than doctrine. They were obscurely felt, rather than thought, which explains the passion that charged subtle debates and technical divergencies on all sorts of secondary things. Martov could only plead that "one could not imagine such a tragic situation in which the proletariat would have to trample on such political rights as freedom of the press." And the tougher-minded, more impatient delegates could only express their attitude and expectations by being ultra-orthodox in matters of theory and ultra-hard in matters of organization. In their hearts they unconsciously knew the answer to Peguy's crucial question. It was: "Such as we . . ." They were ready to give expression to that conviction by building a rigidly centralized, highly conspiratorial party to dictate, if not yet to an "enemy class," then to the "softs" in their own ranks. Repentant "softs" turned "hards" could only satisfy their own self-doubt by being hardest of all. Plekhanov's remarks on two revolutions, one for democracy and a second for socialism, Martov's plea to "imagine" or hope for the best, Akimov's opposition on principle to dictatorship, Rosanov's hiss—these lifted for a little moment a corner of the veil that hid future conflicts. But Marx himself had used the term *proletarian dictatorship* (in the sense that young Trotsky had rightly explained: "Not the dictatorship of a minority party, but of the immense majority in the interests of the immense majority, to prevent counter-revolution"). Who but Akimov wanted to be counted as not an orthodox Marxist? Unanimity, except for his vote, drew the veil down once more.

It is interesting to note how little part Lenin took in this great programmatic debate: only to explain and defend his small plank on agrarian matters, and to make one other brief, apparently insignificant remark. There was a sentence in the program which said that, as the contradictions inherent in capitalism continued to grow, with them would grow "the dissatisfaction, the solidarity and the numbers of the proletariat." The Program Commission brought in an amendment to add: "and the consciousness" before "proletariat." On this Lenin was moved to take the floor:

> This amendment would be a worsening—he declared. It would give the idea that the development of consciousness is a spontaneous thing . . . Aside from the influence of the Social Democracy, there is no *conscious* activity of the workers.

Here was something he could not leave to Plekhanov to say. Was it mere pedantry? This dogma, obscure as yet in its implications, was at the very core of "Leninism." From it flowed an attitude toward the working class, toward its ability to think for itself, to learn from experience, toward its capacities and potentialities for self-rule, toward its "spontaneous" movements such as might take place without orders and control from the party of socialist theoreticians and professional revolutionaries. From it would spring a special attitude toward trade unions, toward the impromptu strikers' councils or soviets, even toward two revolutions—in 1905 and the spring of 1917—that would come not on order but by surprise.

As one continues with the minutes of the congress one gets a growing impression of watching a congregation of somnambulists. The treasury—contributed by well-to-do ("bourgeois") sympathizers—dwindles to exhaustion. Agreement on fundamental principle seems virtually unanimous, yet nerves grow frayed with sleepless nights, endless wrangles, summer heat. Men squabble unceasingly over procedure. The discussions get tied up in knots. The delegates grow inordinately angry, gesticulate with inexplicable violence, lacerate each other's spirits.

In Russia at this very moment events are moving without the intervention of these men toward some unforeseen outcome. Here in an obscure chapel in working-class London, somnambulists are contending with each other impotently, as in a dream. All Russia's socialist leaders are here—prideful, strong-willed men, each sure that he is in the right, all comrades in a common cause with a common program and doctrine, contending endlessly over rules of procedure and niceties of formulation that seem infinitely remote from the first general strike in her history, at this very moment sweeping over south Russia and the Caucasus. The least of the somnambulists will be away for months; the leaders for years, decades . . .

The Russian and Belgian police swarm around the convention. They stick like autumn flies. They follow the delegates to their lodgings, sit at tables near them in the Coq d'Or, trail them into the park and along the lake shore, where, after midnight, discussions spill over in loud voices. They search rooms and baggage, rob the delegates' briefcases, intercept their correspondence. Finally, they seize pedantic-looking, tight-lipped Rosa Zemlyachka, an *Iskra* agent and one of Lenin's "hards," and deport her. They give several other delegates twenty-four hours' notice to leave the country. At this, the entire Congress packs up and takes train and boat for the freer atmosphere of London. All the way on the train, and on the boat over the Channel, the excited discussion never ceases. In London, they continue to meet, in a "socialist church," day and night in the midsummer heat, from August 11 to August 23.

The debate on the Party constitution began quietly enough. But now the Iskrists themselves were divided: Lenin and Martov had rival drafts. Lenin proposed that Article I should define a party member as one "who recognizes the Party's program and supports it by material means *and by personal participation in one of the party organizations.*" Martov proposed a substitute with the identical language, except that the final italicized phrase read: "*and by regular personal assistance under the direction of one of the party organizations.*"

The delegates were puzzled. Both formulations seemed substantially the same. Even Plekhanov, so close to Lenin now, was puzzled by the latter's excited insistence on the enormity of the difference.

Lenin explained his formulation. He took the floor again and again and again. Time would clarify the difference in approach, but for the present, all the delegates could make of it was that he wanted a "narrow" party of selected revolutionists, every one of them subject to control by the center, surrounded by broad circles of workers who obeyed the party without belonging to it.

> My formula restricts the conception of party member while Martov's broadens it . . . It is better that ten who actually work should not call themselves members (real

workers don't hunt for titles!) than that one who just talks
should have the right to be a party member . . .

Martov, too, took the floor again and again. He was for a centralized party but not one whose members "abdicated their right
to think." He wanted a broad party, not a party of professional
revolutionists alone, but one open to all workers and intellectuals
who believed in its program and were willing to work under its
direction. Party membership was not merely a "title" but the right
to a voice in the party's affairs. Those who carried out its directions
should have the right to influence its decisions, even if they did
not work for it full time. But how? Martov's formulation provided
no definite answer. He did not yet realize whither his divergence
with Lenin was tending, nor did he have the latter's skill in giving
organizational form to his approach. The delegates continued to
be puzzled.

Trotsky surprised Lenin by siding with Martov:

> I do not believe that you can put a statutory exorcism
> on opportunism. I do not give the statutes any sort of
> mystical interpretation.

Axelrod joined in:

> Is not Lenin dreaming of the administrative subordina-
> tion of an entire party to a few guardians of doctrine?

Plekhanov in turn rallied to Lenin, who seemed to be losing out:

> I have no preconceived idea, but the more I reflect on
> what has been said, the stronger is my conviction that the
> truth lies with Lenin . . . Intellectuals may hesitate for
> individualistic reasons to join the party, so much the better,
> for they are generally opportunists . . . for this reason if
> for no other, the opponents of opportunism should vote for
> his draft.

Two full sessions, many votes on procedure, and two time-con-
suming roll-calls on Article I alone! The vote: for Martov's formulation twenty-eight, for Lenin's twenty-two! Lenin was beside himself. Then and there he determined to split the *Iskra* caucus and
build up a "hard" faction of his own, to try to make every other
article in the Constitution ultra-centralist, "to bind up"—as he wrote
later—"the broken cask with double hoops . . . to load our weapons
with a double charge . . . to propose the limitation of the rights
of the majority" in the interests of his minority. In short, he prepared on the spot for a long, irreconcilable war against the Congress
decision, that had just been taken after a full and free debate.

The Iskrists gathered for what turned out to be their last caucus or faction meeting. The tension can be deduced from what Lenin wrote months later when he had cooled off:

> Lenin conducted himself like a madman. Right. He banged the door, that is correct. But with what result? . . . Only this, that out of the sixteen members of the *Iskra* organization present, after all, nine were with me . . . If there had been no "rudeness" perhaps more than nine would have been on my side . . .

Perhaps. But with four members of the old editorial board against his two, himself and Plekhanov, and with nine members of the larger caucus on his side against Martov's seven, Lenin called a new meeting of the "firm" Iskrists and posted guards outside the door with orders not to admit Martov, Axelrod, Zasulich, Potresov, or any of the other close comrades-in-arms who had voted against him. The excluded sent in a written demand to be admitted but it was denied. Vladimir Ilyich ceased to sleep at all by now, and, according to Krupskaya, was unable even to eat, which left him most of the twenty-four hours of the day to go after every delegate in person. Here is the account of one who up to that day had been known as "Lenin's cudgel"—his young disciple Trotsky:

> Lenin lost no opportunity to win me over to his side. He, Krasikov and I had a long walk together, during which they both tried to persuade me that Martov and I could not follow the same road, for Martov was a "soft" one. Krasikov's descriptions of the other editors of *Iskra* were so unceremonious that they made Lenin frown, while I shivered. My attitude towards the editors of *Iskra* was still touched with the sentimentality of youth. The conversation repelled me . . . Lenin made another attempt to win me over by sending a woman delegate, Z., as well as his younger brother Dmitri . . . The emissaries would not let me go. "We have orders," they said, "to bring you with us at any cost." In the end, I flatly refused to follow them.

And here is Lenin's own account of his talk with one of the delegates of the so-called "Swamp":

> "What a depressing atmosphere . . ."—he complained to me. "All this fierce fighting, this agitation one against the other, these sharp polemics, this uncomradely attitude!"
>
> "What a fine thing our Congress is,"—I replied to him. "Opportunity for open fighting. Opinions expressed. Tendencies revealed. Groups defined. Hands raised. A decision taken. A stage passed through. Forward! That's what I

like! That's life! It is something different from the endless, wearying intellectual discussions which finish, not because people have solved the problem, but simply because they have got tired of talking."

The comrade of the "Center" looked on me as though perplexed, and shrugged his shoulders. We had spoken different languages.

While Lenin was battling day and night for the soul of every delegate, the giddy wheel of fortune took an unexpected turn. The Bund delegates, who had been nursing their wounds apart since the blow dealt them on the question of autonomy, announced their withdrawal from the Congress—five solid votes that had been cast for the proposition of Martov! Following up this advantage, Lenin proposed a motion calculated to drive out another group of his opponents: he moved to dissolve the *Rabochee Delo* and give exclusive recognition to *Iskra* and its foreign organization as the only émigré body. Martov, as a loyal Iskrist, fell into the trap and voted in favor of the motion. Thereupon, two more delegates who had supported his draft of Article I of the Constitution withdrew from the Congress in a huff. Lenin's bloc was converted from a minority of five or six to a majority of two votes!

> It is incomprehensible to me why the *Bund* left the Congress under such circumstances—Lenin wrote later. It showed itself master of the situation and could have put through many things.

Since, all his life, Lenin attached a feeling of moral baseness to "opportunism," he found it hard to understand that these men of the Bund and *Rabochee Delo* could have firm convictions, principles of their own, and, defeated on them, would not content themselves with "putting through" what he regarded as opportunistic measures.

Now his keen sense of organization and power taught him that, with the aid of the slender majority handed to him by their withdrawal, he himself could "put through many things." The first of these was a moral advantage: the adoption of a name for his new caucus: *Bolshinstvo* ("Majority") or *Bolsheviki* ("Majorityites"). Though but yesterday he had been in a minority, and, more often than not would be in the minority in the future, he would never relinquish the psychological advantage of that name. A name, he knew was a program, a distilled essence, more powerful in its impact upon the untutored mind than any propaganda slogan. What pride it could give to his caucus, no matter how it might dwindle,

always to call itself "Majorityites." What conviction, what an air
of legality, of democratic, majority sanction, it would give in ap-
pealing to the rank and file and the non-party masses. If he had
remained in a minority, he would have chosen some other banner
name—like "True Iskrists" or "Orthodox Marxists" or "Revolutionary
Wing of Russian Social Democracy." But it is characteristic of the
ineptness of his opponents that they permanently accepted the
designation of Mensheviki (Minorityites) for their group.

His next move was to make sure that the new Central Committee
should be small, and contain a firm majority of "hards." He knew
that arrests and escapes might make it necessary for such a committee to add to its number by coopting, so he provided an elaborate machinery which would enable him to veto the coopting of
any unwelcome persons. Experience had taught him that the
police can break up Central Committees and that new men may
have other views. So, despite his predilection for centralism, which
should have subordinated a mere group of editors of a party paper
to the Central Committee in Russia, he put into the Constitution a
provision making the Central Organ, published abroad, dominant
over the Central Committee itself! The Board of Editors, which he
would control, should in turn control the Central Committee. Trotsky had an argument with him on the matter:

> "The Central Organ should be subordinate to the Central
> Committee."
> "That won't do," Vladimir Ilyich replied. "That is con-
> trary to the relative strength. How can they direct us from
> Russia? It won't do . . . We are the stable center and shall
> direct from here . . ."
> "But doesn't that mean complete dictatorship by the
> Central Organ?" I asked.
> "What is there bad about that?" Lenin answered. "In the
> present situation, it cannot be otherwise."

This was typical of Lenin. For all his dogmatic preaching of
organization principles, he always subordinated them to the prag-
matic realities of the specific power situation, and to his unalterable
conviction that his views were good for the Party and must, at all
costs, be made to prevail. If he was unsure of the Central Committee, he would give power to the Central Organ. If he lost the
latter (as he soon did), then he would give power to the Central
Committee. If he lost both (as he would within the year), he
would defy both and set up his own caucus committee of the
"hards" for whom he would still claim the suggestive name "Majority." Having managed to hammer out a majority of two for the

final days after the Bund and *Rabochee Delo* delegates withdrew
from the Congress, he would continue to claim that any caucus he
might form, however small, represented the "true majority" of the
Congress, even on issues which the Congress itself had not considered. While he himself had control of the leading committees,
however, he was remorseless in his denunciation of those who defied their discipline. This flexible inflexibility, which made his own
views the test of when it was a crime to break discipline and when
it was a crime not to, did not spring from hypocrisy or arrogance
or lust for power. It sprang from his unshakable conviction of his
own rightness. It was selfless in the sense that for Lenin the distinction between self and the movement had become completely
obliterated. It never occurred to him to say: *I am right* but only:
We are the stable center and shall direct from here. As Plekhanov
said to Axelrod in an aside of half-fearful admiration: "Of this
dough, Robespierres are made."

Lenin's next move with his exiguous majority stretched the bent
bow to the breaking point. He proposed that the old Editorial
Board of *Iskra* should be dismissed, and in its place should be set
up a new Board of three members, "with power to add to their
number." His candidates were Plekhanov, Lenin, Martov. When the
delegates realized that the veteran political thinker and organizer
Axelrod, and the movement's heroine, Vera Zasulich, were being
thrown out, a storm broke about Lenin's balding head. He wasted
many words, then and later, in trying to prove that he had not
sprung his proposal as a surprise, that he had discussed it in advance with all the editors and that the victims had agreed to their
demise. Against this we have not only the testimony of the other
editors, but that of Lenin's own wife:

> This was a very painful problem and nothing was said to
> the delegates about it. The fact that the *Iskra* Editorial
> Board as formerly constituted was no longer fit to carry on
> the work was too depressing to talk about.

And, in one of his innumerable polemics on the convention, Lenin
himself let slip the fact that his original plan, as revealed to Martov
and perhaps to a few other close cronies prior to the Congress,
had been more moderate: to set up an Editorial Board of the old
six plus one other—seven in all—and have them elect out of their
own number a small working sub-committee of three. "But," wrote
Lenin:

beaten in the question of Article I of the Statutes, I could
not help but try to get even in all the other questions which
were left for me and the Congress. I could not help but
try in the first place for a "strict" Iskrist Central Committee, and in the second for an Editorial Committee of
three . . .

Finally, we have the evidence of Krupskaya's psychological insight into the spirits of the two members of the Old Guard who
were being thus unceremoniously dismissed:

> P. B. Axelrod was particularly pained by the fact that
> *Iskra* was not published in Switzerland, and that the stream
> of communications with Russia did not pass through him.
> That is why he took up such an angry attitude at the Second
> Congress towards the question of the editorial triumvirate.
> *Iskra* was to be the organizing center, and *he* removed from
> the editorial board! And this when, more than at any other
> time, the breath of Russia could be felt . . .
> To her—Vera Zasulich—leaving *Iskra* would mean once
> more becoming isolated from Russia, once more beginning
> to sink in the dead sea of émigré life, that drags one to the
> bottom. It was for this reason that, when the question of
> the editorship of *Iskra* was brought up at the Second Con-
> gress, she revolted. For her it was not a question of self-
> love, but a question of life and death . . .

No, these two could not have accepted in advance their sentence
of extinction.

The air of the quiet Brotherhood Church rang with cries of "autocrat," "dictator," "martial law," "state of siege," "insult," "execution," "coup d'état." Delegates reminded Lenin that only a few
days back, they had voted unanimously—all but Akimov, who had
abstained—to endorse *Iskra,* which had meant to them not merely
a body of doctrine but its human incorporation in an editorial
board. Martov, who had learned to love and revere the veterans
Axelrod and Zasulich, threatened and pleaded, then served notice
that he would not make up part of any editorial board from which
they were absent. "In place of a period, but a tear in the minutes!"
shouted one of Lenin's "hards" after Martov's plea. When a motion
to reelect the old board was defeated, the outraged minority refused thenceforward to vote on any question. Plekhanov, Lenin and
Martov were elected editors of the Central Organ, regardless of
declination of the last named. Noskov, Krzhizhanovsky and Lengnik, "Leninists" all three, were elected as the Central Committee.
Each of these bodies was to name two men to a Party Council of

five, for which the Congress chose a chairman, Plekhanov. But the vote? Seven had already walked out of the Congress. Twenty more refused to participate in the balloting. In the voting for Plekhanov, who but yesterday had been the honored master of them all, twenty-two wrote his name on their ballots, two deposited blanks, twenty refused to vote! Twenty-two out of forty-four with twenty-two abstentions, and that after seven others had walked out—such was the celebated "Majority" (*Bolshinstvo*) out of which the Bolsheviks were born!

And even before the Congress was dispersed, a swing away from Lenin began to be perceptible once more. Topuridze, the "hard" delegate from Georgia, turned "soft" and joined the "Minority" as soon as the Congress adjourned. Plekhanov switched within less than six months, making Lenin a minority in the Editorial Board of three (which Martov had never consented to attend.) Before a year was out, the hand-picked Central Committee and the hand-picked Party Council, too, had turned against Lenin. Yet he never ceased to claim that he spoke for the "Majority" of the Party as expressed at the Congress, and that those who turned against him were revolting against the majority will.[4]

On Saturday, August 23, at five o'clock in the afternoon, the nightmare battle about the personnel of the leading committees, simply petered out. It had not been settled, since Martov had already announced that he would refuse to serve on the three-man Editorial Board to which he had been elected. It petered out more from exhaustion than from the conviction on any one's part that a workable conclusion had been reached. The exhaustion was general: funds, nerves, energies, throats, capacity to sit or listen. Lenin himself had spoken, according to the careful count of the Marx-Engels-Lenin Institute, approximately one hundred and twenty times, including reports, declarations, statements, interpolations, motions, etc. Of twenty-four points on the order of business, the delegates had thus far handled but four. After 5 P.M. on the last day, they began a desultory discussion of some of the resolutions on tactical questions: important matters like attitude toward the liberals,

[4] The official Party History of Emilian Yaroslavsky has this to say on Lenin's majority:

"The majority of the Congress (by 2 or 3 votes) upheld the Mensheviks. This should be borne in mind by those who believe that it was on this question (Article 1 of the Party Constitution) that we gained a majority at the Congress. No, Lenin gained a majority in the elections of the Central Committee and the Central Organ of the Party, when the most reactionary Economists and the Bundists had quit the Congress." (English Edition, Moscow, 1927, Vol. I, p. 87.)

toward the new, legally permitted, police-controlled "Zubatov" labor unions; toward the Social Revolutionary Party. In two hours they pushed through a half dozen or more resolutions, some of them (as in the case of two on the Liberals) even contradicting each other. Not even Lenin had the energy left to fight to a finish for the exclusive adoption of one or the other.

Feeling himself in control of the Party machine, he permitted his hopes to rise at the listless unanimity:

> The attitude toward the resolutions was so unanimous that we got the impression that a mood of conciliation had arisen . . . All resolutions were adopted in a peaceful and friendly fashion. [From Lenin's Report on the Congress.]

But the convention, which, after two decades of longing and two and one-half years of intensive planning, had been called for the purpose of unifying the movement, adjourned that same night *sine die*, hopelessly divided. It had been assembled to constitute a party. It would take at least ten years to realize that it had really constituted not one party but two.

CHAPTER XV

TAKEN BY SURPRISE

Member of the International Socialist Bureau: Do you mean
to say that all these splits and quarrels and scandals are the
work of one man? But how can one man be so effective and
so dangerous?
Axelrod: Because there is not another man who for twenty-
four hours of the day is taken up with the revolution, who
has no other thoughts but thoughts of revolution, and who,
even in his sleep dreams of nothing but revolution. Just try
and handle such a fellow.—*Dialogue at the International
Socialist Conference, Copenhagen 1910.*

THE FIGHT was the more bitter because it was rooted in differences
that had not yet become explicit. In time the two factions would
really diverge widely: in their estimates of the nature of the Russian Revolution and in consequent conceptions of grand strategy
and detailed tactics. Then the rupture and the sharpness of the
fratricidal struggle might be rationalized and systematized, or made
to appear acceptable to rational men. Moreover, factionalism has
a law of momentum of its own which tends to incubate difference,
exaggerate and systematically enlarge it, and minimize or ignore
agreement. But at the moment of this first split, springing thus unexpectedly out of a long labor for unification, all these divergencies
of the future existed merely in germ: incompatibilities of temperament ("softs" and "hards"), differences on personnel, and on questions of organization. Since organization itself seemed but ancillary
to common aims, a split on such secondary grounds could not be
accepted as natural. Agreed on Marxism, on socialism, on opposition to tsarism, disagreeing only on a definition in the Party Statutes,
and on the personnel of a committee—even to the combatants themselves it was altogether incredible that they should actually be
drifting toward irreparable estrangement.

Bolshevik historians have since sought to portray the split as a
brilliant anticipation on Lenin's part of all the subsequently engendered disagreements between bolshevism and menshevism.
There is a sense in which this is so, for politics is one of the arts,
and many of its profoundest decisions spring from deep, unconscious sources. But the actual outcome of the Congress—particularly

the rupture with Martov—had been as unexpected for Lenin as for any others, and his first efforts were directed to minimizing the conflicts. For several years thereafter, his writings were filled with assertions of the unnecessariness of the split. More than once, before their final divorce, the two factions would resume uneasy cohabitation in a common party.

No sooner had the Congress adjourned than Lenin sent the following personal appeal to Potresov, intending it for Martov's and Axelrod's eyes:

> And now I ask myself: why should we separate as enemies for the rest of our lives? I admit that I often acted and behaved with frightful irritation and rage. I am quite ready *to acknowledge to any comrade whatsoever this my fault* . . . But when I consider without any rage the results arrived at . . . I cannot see in the outcome anything, absolutely anything, harmful for the Party or hurtful or insulting to the Minority . . .

Of course, the letter may be interpreted as the calculated generosity of a victor, aware of his responsibility for the functioning of the Party, and eager to get all valuable forces to work once more. But this is something quite distinct from a sense of irreconcilable split. And how shall we explain, if not in terms of indecision, that Lenin's *Collected Works* for this period contain an unprecedented number of unmailed letters, undelivered statements and declarations, articles drafted and left unpublished? A month after the Congress he wrote to Central Committee Member Krzhizhanovsky:

> . . . write to Martov, appealing for the last time to reason . . . Act formally and prepare for a definite war with the Martovites . . . Let Krzhizhanovsky not look upon Martov as before. The friendship is at an end. Down with all soft-heartedness!

But after Krupskaya had taken down the letter and coded its names, he told her not to send it. It was not easy to decide to break with the comrade who had been closest to him.

Julius Martov (Tsederbaum) was three years younger than Lenin. Between them there had been a closer political partnership and intimacy than Lenin was ever to form with any man again, even with Trotsky in the crucial year of their common assault on the heights of power. Lenin had regarded Martov as a gifted younger brother. Together they had formed the Petersburg League of Struggle, together gone to prison, together planned *Iskra* (Potre-

sov was less important in their "triple alliance"). Together they
toured the underground on *Iskra's* behalf, together edited it abroad,
and together resisted the prestige and overbearing attitude of Plekhanov. Martov was unmarried, gregarious, bohemian in temperament, possessed of the Russian intellectual's hunger for impassioned
talk. Like Lenin he was wholly devoted to the movement, to the
exclusion of all other matters, ever ready to take upon himself the
most ungrateful tasks and carry them out conscientiously. He read,
wrote, conversed, speculated ceaselessly, kept up with all the news
and all the latest ideas, combined a far-ranging independence of
thought with an exceptional talent for taking the slightest hint from
Lenin or Axelrod, from his reading or from events, and giving it a
rich application and development of his own. This stoop-shouldered
Jewish intellectual, with the thin, ascetic face, the unkempt curly
hair and pointed beard, the slightly soiled and misted glasses
through which shone the dreamer's eyes of a ghetto seer . . . and
this stocky, bald-headed, solid, practical-looking Great-Russian, with
the high cheekbones and the twinkling little Tartar eyes: these
two had seemed till now to complement each other as the most
splendid of working teams. In the first forty-five numbers of *Iskra,*
Martov had written thirty-nine articles and Lenin thirty-two; while
Plekhanov had done twenty-four, Potresov only eight, Zasulich six,
and Axelrod four. The rest had been written by occasional contributors like Rosa Luxemburg, Parvus and Trotsky. Lenin and Martov
had done all the technical editorial work. Though their emphases
and approaches had been distinct, there had been no shadow of
political difference. To Potresov, the third member of the "triple
alliance," Lenin, so little inclined to sentiment, "spoke of Martov
with the unconcealed admiration of one who was quite carried away
by his feelings."

Yet, even before the break, in the rootless isolation and ingrown
intercourse of émigré life, they occasionally got on each other's
nerves. Martov became critical of the Lenin he admired when a
casual squabble about an *Iskra* agent "opened his eyes to the
amoralism in Lenin's makeup." He discovered that Vladimir Ilyich
was "uncompromisingly severe with 'strangers'" but was "prepared
to defend 'his own' agents with characteristic stubbornness, consciously closing his eyes to their personal misconduct." This conflict
had occurred, according to the memoirs of Potresov, a half year
before the 1903 Congress, as Lenin stubbornly opposed the investigation by the Editorial Board of an accusation made by a victim
against one of his appointees.

During the same period, Krupskaya notes that Martov's love of endless talk and too eager readiness to seize on new theories were making Lenin "quite ill and incapable of working." He even asked Martov to stop dropping in at all odd hours of the day and night, and arranged for Krupskaya to go over mail and manuscripts with his co-editor, to save wear and tear on his own nerves.

Might it have been that in a movement less ingrown and less torn up from its roots, these two could have continued to collaborate indefinitely despite differences of viewpoint and temperament? Certainly, in other parties that did not live under émigré conditions, parties in which all quarrels and differences had ultimately to be submitted to decision of the membership, such cohabitation was possible. Moreover, Lenin always retained in his own faction men who differed from him on critical occasions far more than Martov did, while the latter, for his part, was often in deepest conflict with his fellow-Mensheviks. Thus, in the crucial test of the World War, Martov remained, like Lenin, an internationalist, though many of Lenin's Bolshevik associates deserted him. After the seizure of power by the Bolshevik Party, which Martov naturally opposed, he nevertheless remained active in the congresses of the Soviets and defended the new government against all attempts at reactionary counter-revolution and foreign intervention. Indeed, so important did his support seem to Lenin in 1920 that he had Martov's speech in the Soviet Congress against the Polish attack on Kiev printed by the government, first in Russian and Polish, and then in German by the German publishing house of the Communist International.

When Martov at last could no longer stand the ever-growing terror and narrowing dictatorship and applied for a passport to go abroad, it was freely granted to him on Lenin's personal order. The days when even Bolsheviks would be executed *en masse* were still more than a decade and a half away. Before those days could come, death would long have removed Lenin from the scene. For, despite all his professed "rock-hardness," there was about him something of the inherited humane tradition of the Russian revolutionary intelligentsia, which he never wholly lost.

> It was exceedingly difficult for him to break with Martov—writes Krupskaya. Afterwards, Vladimir Ilyich fought the Mensheviks, but every time that Martov, even in the slightest degree, took the correct line, his old attitude towards him revived. Such was the case for example in Paris in 1910, when Martov and Vladimir Ilyich worked together on the editorial board of the *Social Democrat*. Coming home from the office, Vladimir Ilyich used to relate

in joyful tones that Martov was taking a correct line . . .
Later, back in Russia, how pleased Vladimir Ilyich was
with Martov's position in the July 1917 days; not because
it was of any advantage to the Bolsheviks, but because
Martov was acting worthily—as behooved a revolutionary.
When Vladimir Ilyich was already seriously ill he said to
me somewhat sadly, "Martov, they say, is dying too . . ."

With the shift in relationships attendant upon the split, all the
persons were revealed in a new light. Martov, not yet grown to
the full stature of independent leadership, fell for some years under
the sway of Axelrod and Martynov. Plekhanov, separated from his
associates of a lifetime, was clearly uneasy in the new partnership
with Lenin. Trotsky, too, seemed out of his natural element. By
temperament an imperious "hard," all his political instincts lay at
the opposite extreme of the spectrum from Martov and Axelrod
and Martynov, with whom he now found himself associated. From
his acid-dipped pen issued two sharp attacks on Lenin, the *Report
of the Siberian Delegation* and *Our Political Tasks*, the latter significantly dedicated "To My Dear Teacher, Pavel Borisovich Axelrod." In them, he portrayed Lenin as a caricature Robespierre,
talking socialism but modeling himself on the dictatorial bourgeois
revolutionary, setting up a pseudo-Jacobin dictatorship over the
masses, installing a committee of public safety over the Party, using
the "guillotine" to eliminate those he could not control, forming
local organizations on the Cartesian principle: "I am confirmed by
the Central Committee, therefore I am." Lenin's celebrated centralism, he said, was in reality "egocentralism" and one day it would
lead to a state of affairs in which:

> The organization of the Party takes the place of the
> Party itself; the Central Committee takes the place of
> the organization; and finally the dictator' takes the place
> of the Central Committee . . .

In 1917, when Trotsky and Lenin had "amnestied" each other
for all their past political and organizational differences and Trotsky was voluntarily assuming the unaccustomed role of disciple
once more, he would do his best to have these polemics against
Lenin forgotten. But how many times must he have thought of the
above prophetic words during the later stages of his struggle with
Stalin!

"How did I come to be with the 'softs,' " he asks himself in his
Autobiography:

> In 1903 the whole point at issue was nothing more than
> Lenin's desire to get Axelrod and Zasulich off the editorial
> board . . . My whole being seemed to protest against this
> merciless cutting off of the older ones . . . I did not fully
> realize what an intense and imperious centralism the revolu-
> tionary party would need to lead millions in a war against
> the old order . . . It is not without significance that the
> words "irreconcilable" and "relentless" are among Lenin's
> favorites . . .

Even more were those words to be among Trotsky's "favorites."
No, assuredly, his imperious spirit was not at home among the
"softs." His sojourn in their camp was one continuous quarrel. Before a year went by, not Axelrod nor Martov, but the brilliant and
gargantuan Parvus had become his guide; 1905 would find him and
Parvus deflecting menshevism politically in Lenin's direction, then
breaking with it and steering a course of their own.

Party quarrels have a momentum of their own. While Lenin was
still hesitating, it became his obligation to report on the Party Congress to the League of Revolutionary Social Democrats Abroad,
the foreign organization of *Iskra* which had elected him as its delegate to the Congress. He sensed that he would be outnumbered
there, that spirits would be exacerbated and the split needlessly
deepened, so he vainly tried to prevent the meeting. Immersed in
gloomy thoughts as he bicycled to this undesired conference, he
ran into the rear of a trolley car and was badly injured. In what
ways might the fate of his party and his country have been altered
if the crash had taken place with a few foot-pounds more of force?

He put in his appearance pale and swathed in bandages, but it
cannot be said that for this reason his opponents held their fire.
Who was this man, they asked, that he thought he could run the
Party without the rest of the historically developed leadership? The
debate was frenzied, people stood up, shouted with empurpled
faces, hurled epithets, came close to blows. Lenin made three
separate attempts to dynamite the conference by staging walkouts
of his followers. When it approved resolutions supporting the Congress Minority and adopted a constitution intended to safeguard
its independence of the Central Committee, he had Central Com-
mitteeman Lengnik summarily proclaim its dissolution. It refused to
be dissolved.

That very night, at a meeting of the Bolshevik caucus to consider
further strategy, Plekhanov broke down. "I cannot fire at my own
comrades," he declared, thinking of his lifelong association with

Axelrod and Zasulich. "Better a bullet in the head than a split. There are moments when even the Autocracy has to compromise . . ."

"Then it is said to be wavering," interjected the voice of a "hard."

Plekhanov was within his legal rights. The Congress, on Lenin's motion, had named a board of three editors, Plekhanov, Lenin and Martov, and empowered them to coopt additional editors. They had not done so merely because Martov stubbornly refused to attend any meetings of the Editorial Board until it should agree to coopt Axelrod, Zasulich and Potresov, thus restoring the original six. For three months after the Congress an appearance of continuity had been maintained by the cooperation of Plekhanov of the older generation with Lenin of the younger, to get out the paper between them. Now that Plekhanov demanded that the internecine war be ended by coopting the old editors *in toto*, Lenin stood utterly and nakedly alone. True, Plekhanov offered "to step out" but Lenin knew only too well that if Martov should be invited to attend a single editorial meeting under the new circumstances, Plekhanov's proposal would have a majority. Hence, he "stepped out" himself, to "give Plekhanov a free hand"—and to regain his own freedom from an impossible position. It was the only time in his life that he voluntarily relinquished a captured post.

From No. 53 on, the paper became to him the "new *Iskra*," an empty shell from which he, and with him the old spirit, had departed. He refused to serve now, as Martov had refused to serve before, but with the difference that he stood alone without any of the old guard in the camp of the sulkers along with him. All the guns of the "new *Iskra*" were trained upon its solitary ex-editor, exposed in no man's land, and upon his organization views, which formerly it had appeared to sponsor. Martov wrote on "the state of siege" in the Party; Trotsky on caricature Jacobinism; Vera Zasulich on the necessity of safeguarding the Party against the impatience of people who try to get rid of those who disagree. Plekhanov attacked Lenin's basic postulates in *What Should Not Be Done* (a take-off on *What's to Be Done*); *Centralism or Bonapartism; The Working Class and the Social Democratic Intelligentsia; A New Attempt to Bring to their Senses the Frogs Who Ask for a King.*

But the main theoretical attacks were made by two people of extreme opposite temperaments and, in most other respects, of opposing political conceptions: Paul Axelrod and Rosa Luxemburg.

Axelrod as usual, though unyielding in content, was gentle and impersonal in manner. In two articles, he sought to deepen the controversy from personalities to principles. Lenin's much-abused name did not even figure. The Russian Social Democratic Labor Party, he warned, did not yet consist of workers, but only of intellectuals who were "adherents in principle" of the working class. Russia faced not a proletarian but a bourgeois revolution. Unless these intellectuals sought to develop the initiative and self-activity of the masses, there was danger that the revolutionary intelligentsia would draw the workers into the coming revolution as a mere physical force—cannon fodder—as in so many revolutions of the past. Therein lay the danger of the traditional Russian conspirative organization forms: excessive centralism, hierarchical structure, ideological tutelage, the curbing of the self-activity of the masses, the discouraging of independent judgment and initiative.

Rosa Luxemburg's two articles for *Iskra* started where Axelrod's left off. Politically and temperamentally she was to stand at the extreme opposite pole ,from him and all the Mensheviks. A living flame of revolution, her frail body and mighty spirit were a force in three parties, the German, Polish and Russian, and in the leadership of the Socialist International. Where other "orthodox" Marxists were inclined to be mere scholasts, expounders of a closed system of thought, she was of that little band of original thinkers who would use the methods of Marx to tackle new problems in economics and politics. She was even then beginning her fight on bureaucracy and excessive centralism in the German Social Democracy, a fight which was to make her the outstanding advocate of revolutionary policy and the outstanding defender of democracy within the labor movement. Lenin, identifying his centralism with that of the leaders of the German Party, would side with them against her, and live to regret it, one day, with all his heart. Her entry into the lists was the more embarrassing to him since her temperament and her political views on the Russian Revolution were so far from Axelrod's and so close to his. Thus she represented a stumbling-block to his desire to identify menshevism symmetrically as "opportunism in the organization question" linked up with "opportunism in politics." Moreover, she was a harder hitter than Axelrod, while her belief in the creative initiative of the masses went far deeper than Axelrod's or that of any other recognized leader among the Marxists. It was, with her, a fundamental article of faith.

> Socialism—she wrote in *Iskra*—is the first movement in history to base its entire course on the organization and independent action of the masses. The ultracentralism advocated by Lenin is not something born of a positive creative

> spirit but of the negative sterile spirit of the watchman.
> His line of thought is cut to the control of party activity,
> not to its fructifying; to its narrowing, not its unleashing; to
> the role of taskmaster, not of gatherer and unifier. The
> Social Democracy stands on the eve of great revolutionary
> struggles [this was written in 1904] . . . in the midst of a
> period of the most intensive, creative activity in the field
> of tactics. The most important and fruitful tactical turns of
> the last decade in Russia were not invented by certain
> leaders but were the spontaneous product of the uncon-
> trolled movement itself. At such a time, to put hobbles on
> the initiative of the party's thought and to wall in its capa-
> city for expansion within a barbed wire fence would be to
> make the Social Democracy unfit for the great tasks be-
> fore it.

Even when Kautsky and Bebel, the two living socialists he most
admired, took sides against him, Lenin was singularly unable to
doubt the rightness of his views. He did not question their authority on anything else, but decided that they "did not understand
the Russian question." That capacity to stand alone against the
entire world of his peers, and that incapacity to think himself
wrong on any idea he cherished as fundamental, were to be two
well-springs of his strength in 1914 and 1917. To his opponents,
he seemed "organically incapable of assimilating opinions that differed from his own," so that every difference of opinion tended to
become the *casus belli* of a minor or major civil war. With him
the belief in a centralized, military form of organization had now
become as much a touchstone and article of faith or principle as
with Rosa Luxemburg her belief in the creative power of the
masses. Moreover, his organizational creed, if it was not in the
general tradition of European Marxism, drew strength from being
in the tradition of Russian revolutionary centralism and secret
conspiracy.

> The magnificent organization that the revolutionaries had
> in the seventies—he had written—should serve us all as a
> model . . . To regard it as something specifically Narodovo-
> list is absurd both historically and logically, because no
> revolutionary tendency, if it seriously thinks of fighting,
> can dispense with such an organization . . . The spontaneous
> struggle of the proletariat will not become a genuine class
> struggle, until it is led by a strong organization of revolu-
> tionaries.

Thus, though he stood alone, he had a better than even chance
to win a substantial following among the professional revolution-

aries of Russia against all his former co-leaders, for his views were
in the direct line of the Russian conspiratorial heritage which could
not but seem natural to that body of self-constituted "professionals"
or "functionaries" on whom the fate of the underground party was
most likely to rest. This almost unconscious Russianism was another well-spring of Lenin's strength. And with it went something,
harder to put into words, which his bitterest enemies sensed and
paid grudging tribute to. Potresov, after ten years of exile from
the land in which Lenin had taken power, would write of him:

> Neither Plekhanov nor Martov nor anyone else possessed
> the secret of the directly hypnotic influence exercised on
> people by Lenin, I should say, his power to dominate them.
> Plekhanov was respected, Martov was loved, but only
> Lenin was followed unquestioningly as if he were the sole
> undisputed leader. For only Lenin represented that rare
> phenomenon, rare especially for Russia: that of being a
> man of iron will, of indomitable energy, who combined
> a fanatical faith in the movement and the cause with no
> less faith in himself . . . Without wasting any superfluous
> words on it, Lenin always felt that the Party was he, that
> he was the will of the movement concentrated in one man,
> and he acted accordingly . . .

Deprived of his control of the Central Organ and the collaboration of all his old associates in leadership, Vladimir Ilyich displayed
amazing energy in the throwing up of new defenses and in the
improvisation of new methods of warfare. "Open letters" to *Iskra*,
confidential letters to his followers, detailed pamphlets, leaflets, public lectures, plans for a faction journal which would defy if necessary, the Central Committee, the Party Council, and the Central
Organ all at once, private discussions and public arguments, flowed
from him in an unending torrent. A whole volume of his *Collected
Works*, one of the stoutest, is all but filled with his writings on the
Congress and the split. One "pamphlet" alone, *One Step Forward,
Two Steps Backward*, constitutes a book of 250 pages, 75 of them
devoted to the single question of Article I of the Party Constitution adopted at the Second Congress! Tsarism, absolutism, capitalism, democracy, socialism, are forgotten or pushed into the remote
background. Now what is important is not the goal nor even the
road to be followed but the precise direction of the next step and
the nature of the military formation to be kept on the march. The
serene good humor, the confident sweep of thought that had characterized most of his work from *The Development of Capitalism in
Russia* to *What's to Be Done* are gone now. The polemic is arid,

irritable, nagging, and sags under a weight of detail which nearly obscures the outlines of its doctrine. It is written, so to speak, with a voice made hoarse by endless, fruitless argument.

The compulsive logic of factionalism now began to drive both groups toward ever greater one-sidedness. Martov, it was driving into a life-long association with some of the opportunists, like the "Economist" Martynov, whom but yesterday he had been fighting. Lenin, it impelled to the obdurate exaggeration of his centralism which had been suddenly called in question. No longer does that authoritarian centralism appear as one of the harsh compulsions of "our Asiatic and barbarous land." No longer does he clothe it in the merely practical justification that the police state and the hard necessities of underground conspiracy were what made it necessary and justified it despite the lack of democracy involved. Now centralism becomes a revolutionary virtue *per se* for all lands and all circumstances of struggle. One looks in vain in *One Step Forward, Two Steps Backward* for what was in the preceding works: some tribute to the desirability and corrective and educative force of democracy. On the contrary:

> Burocratism versus democratism, i.e. precisely centralism versus autonomy, such is the organization principle of revolutionary social democracy as against that of the opportunists. The latter principle strives to go from below upward, and therefore defends as far as possible and wherever possible autonomy and democracy . . . But the organization principle of revolutionary social democracy strives to go from the top downward, and defends the enlargement of the rights and plenary powers of the central body against the parts.

This is the most naked expression of faith in hierarchy and distrust of democracy to be found in all of Lenin's writings. Only the isolation from the criticism of equals and the stubborn tendency to cherish most what was most under attack could have wrung from him such an extreme statement. Later, under the fire of his opponents' arguments and the impact of the activity of great and uncontrollable masses, he would modify his doctrine from bare centralism to the more ambiguous "democratic centralism." But when we seek to understand the Russian state after Lenin came to power, and when we watch the formation of the Communist International, we shall have to keep this one-sided utterance in mind, for it takes an authoritarian party to make an authoritarian state.

Moreover, though Lenin might admit, as later he did, that he had exaggerated the value of centralism in this work in order to overcome the "anarchy" then prevailing in the leading circles of the Party, his followers would make this one-sided and embittered pamphlet the very gospel of their views on the organization question. Stalin, in his *Short History of the Communist Party*, published after the purges to replace all the other official party histories, would devote more space to it than to the ground-breaking, far richer and more balanced *What's to Be Done!* That is one of the difficulties presented by the varied works of any man whose every sentence becomes a canon of authority. Any partial polemical utterance of a moment can easily become the tangent of departure from the original curve.

For the moment, the most painful thing to Lenin was the lack of an organ in which to continue the unequal combat. Having lost control of *Iskra*, he had transferred all his forces to the Central Committee inside Russia. Forgotten was his few-months-old contention that only *Iskra*, because it was published abroad, could be trusted to provide a firm ideological leadership. The suppressed premise in that argument should have read: "because it is published abroad, and *because I am in control of it*." Now he tried to turn the Central Committee inside Russia into a fortress for blasting back at the paper. Though he was not in Russia, he asked them to coopt him, and several other dependables, onto the Committee, which they did.

But experience had taught him that it would be hard to control any committee from such a distance, and that arrests would sooner or later change its composition, weaken or destroy it. So, while the bewildered Russian members and local organizations were still trying to find out what had happened at the recent Congress, he made the following astonishing proposal to the Committee that had just coopted him:

> If we miss the opportunity and the right slogan for a · fight, then *complete* defeat is inevitable . . . *The only salvation is a Congress. Its slogan: war with the disorganizers.* Only this slogan will be able to get the best of the Martovites, attract the broad masses and save the situation . . . not a word *for the present* to anyone . . . *Move all our forces into the Committees and the Districts* . . . Resolutions of the Local Committees must fly to the Central Organ . . . we must push our people onto the shaky Committees in the name of the slogan: against disorganization . . . *A Congress is essential not later than January* . . . The worst would be *if the Central Organ would be theirs and the Council ours.* I repeat: either complete defeat

(the Central Organ will hunt us down) or *immediate prepa-*
rations for a Congress. It must be prepared secretly at first,
taking a month at the most, *then three weeks to collect the*
demands of half the Committees and to call a Congress.
Again and again I repeat: this is the only salvation.

The letter was written less than four months after the "unification" Congress had adjourned! And a few days later, he added by
way of argument:

> Arrest is inevitable, and will come fairly soon—it would
> be childish to ignore it. And what will there be for us after
> your arrest?
> . . . Do you think over the whole political situation, take
> a wider view, tear yourselves away from the petty every-
> day fussing over pennies and passports . . .

But Lenin was in for a rude shock. This habit of his of powerful
concentration on what at a given moment he deemed the main
chance, had carried him far from his followers. All the iterations
and underlinings were powerless to impress his will upon them.
They felt, as he did not, the loneliness of the isolation of his faction
from all the other leaders whom the Party had looked up to. They
were in Russia, where the confusion, the longing for unity, the impatience with the ill-understood controversy, were indescribable.
Wealthy sympathizers began to despair of this feud-torn Party's
ever leading a successful assault on tsarism. The "Bucket," the funds
gathered and contributed by Mrs. Kalmykova, became suddenly
empty. The "California Gold Mine," a mysterious source of funds
which to this day Party historians have not cared to elucidate,
ceased to produce. The millionaire manufacturer Morozov was
secretly contributing two thousand rubles (a thousand dollars) a
month to the Social Democratic Party through Lenin's close follower, the engineer Leonid Krassin, whom he hired to take charge
of one of his factories. But Krassin was soon to become a "conciliator," i.e. an advocate of Party unity, and Lenin would lose that
source of funds also.

Great numbers of intellectuals, who had thought of themselves
as Social Democrats, were alienated or discouraged, or switched
to the rapidly growing Social Revolutionary Party. Workers, too,
lost heart, or became bitter "anti-intellectuals" determined to ignore
a movement that did nothing but "split hairs" and to look elsewhere
to organization and leadership. Within the land was felt the ground
swell of great events, while the Party that should be leading and
strengthening the revolutionary upsurge lay helpless, tearing at its
own vitals.

Lenin's summons to his Central Committee to wage a fight to the finish fell on deaf ears. His demand for yet another convention—which might well mean a formal consolidation of the split—seemed to them monstrous. From a distance, with slow-traveling underground letters, Lenin pleaded, argued, urged, abused. Then he tried to stampede them by introducing his own resolution for a new congress into the Council meeting in Geneva. To his indignation, the Central Committee he had felt so sure of answered his action by a vote of censure of him, as its representative in the Council! And, under the leadership of the hitherto ever-dependable Krassin, the Committee opened negotiations with the Mensheviks for the cooptation of the latter and a conciliator's peace in the Party.

That splendid working and fighting machine, Vladimir Ilyich Ulyanov, seemed to have reached the end of its resources. "Do not bother me about leaflets—he wrote to them now—I am not a machine and cannot work in the present disgraceful situation." He resigned from all committees. He and Krupskaya took their knapsacks and went tramping in the mountains of Switzerland. They "selected the wildest paths and got far away from human beings." They tramped all day and slept each night where evening found them, too blessedly tired for thought. They subsisted on country bread, eggs, cheese, wine, spring-water. If they came to an inn, they dined cheaply and well at the servants' table. The fat French book and dictionary they carried with them for translation remained unopened during the entire journey. "After passing the time in this way for a month, Vladimir Ilyich's nerves became normal again," writes Krupskaya. Refreshed, he returned to the fray.

Unexpectedly at this juncture, fresh forces rallied to him, men of leadership caliber to take the place of those he had lost: Bogdanov, the able, independent philosopher; Lunacharsky, critic, writer, and future Commissar of Education; Bazarov, Olminski, Vorovsky. As in the beginning of his struggle with "Economism," he called together the remnant of the faithful. A pitiful twenty-two men and women, out of the whole active emigration, signed their names to a fighting platform drafted by him. In it this centralist denounced all three Central Bodies as having ceased to represent the will of the "Majority" of the Party, as expressed by the "Majority" which had elected them at the Party Congress. It branded Lenin's selectees of yesterday, the "conciliators" on the Central Committee, as worse than the "Minority" with whom they were trying to reconcile themselves. It appealed against the Central Bodies to the Local Committees, urging these to adopt resolutions in favor of the calling of a new congress. And it asked the Local Committees to elect delegates to a new, extra-legal, or illegal body, a "Bureau of Committees of the Majority," which Lenin now planned to set up in opposition to all the existing governing organisms. What then was left of his centralism if he fought all the Central Bodies? Only the political conception of how a party should be structured whenever its central bodies were acting in the way which seemed appropriate to him.

Most of the names of the little band of twenty-two who signed the document in emigration, and of the subsequent signatures secured in Moscow and Petersburg, are worth remembering, for out of them largely grew the general staff of the future Bolshevik Party. The signers included Lenin, his wife and his sister; Vorovsky, the future Soviet diplomat; Bonch-Bruevich, who opened a publishing house for Lenin; Krasikov, who was to be a member of the Soviet Commissariat of Justice; Lyadov; Zemlyachka; Lepeshinsky and his wife; Olminsky; Lengnik; Knuniyants and his wife; Essen; Baumann, who would be killed in the Revolution of 1905; Stasova, who would succeed Krupskaya as Party Secretary; Gusev (Drapkin); Litvinov (Wallach), who would one day be Commissar of Foreign Affairs; and Rykov, the youngest man to be put on the new Bureau, who would succeed Lenin as President of the Council of Commissars. With a few others who showed their mettle a bit later, most of these would make up a more or less permanent Bolshevik staff which would stick with Lenin through thick and thin and go with him into places of power in the Soviet Government.

By Christmas, operating through this extra-legal body, Lenin had succeeded in founding a new paper which should serve as organ of his faction in its fight to wrest the Party from the control of its leading committees. On Christmas Eve, 1904, cheerful once more, he wrote to Essen:

> An announcement about the publication of our newspaper, *Vpered* ("Forward"), came out yesterday. All the Bolsheviks are rejoicing . . . At last we have broken up the cursed dissension and are working harmoniously with those who want to work and not to create scandals! A good group of contributors has been got together; there are fresh forces . . . The Central Committee which betrayed us has lost all credit . . . The Bolshevik Committees are joining together; they have already chosen a Bureau and now the organ will completely unite them. Hurrah! Do not lose heart. We are all reviving now and will continue to re-

vive . . . Above all be cheerful. Remember, you and I are
not so old yet . . . everything is still before us.

Almost at that very moment, much to the astonishment of both
Bolsheviks and Mensheviks and without paying attention to the
prescriptions of either, revolution broke out in Russia!

CHAPTER XVI

POLICE SOCIALISM

> The air is heavy with ominous things; every day we see the
> glare of fires on the horizon; a bloody mist crawls over the
> ground; breathing and living have become difficult as before
> a storm. The muzhik is sullenly silent, and if he opens his
> mouth it is in such a way that one feels creepy all over.
> —*Letter of a Landowner of Voronezh, 1901*

FOUR EFFORTS were started simultaneously to inject some organization into inchoate Russian public life. The same years, 1901 to
1903, that had witnessed Lenin's attempt to constitute and "unify"
an All-Russian Social Democratic Party for the proletariat, were the
years in which were formed a Social Revolutionary Party, to give
leadership to the peasantry; a Constitutional Democratic Party, to
organize the liberal and democratic intelligentsia; and an amazing
series of experiments in police unionism and police "socialism." All
these were so many minor eddies in a swiftly rising freshet—signs
that the whole, long-frozen political structure of Russia was about
to go into a thaw. But none of the new organizations would prove
equal to the task it had set itself: to channelize the rapidly rising
flood.

In the countryside, sullenly silent since the flareup over Emancipation, the peasants began to harvest forbidden hay, cut forbidden
timber in the woods. Owners who resisted were found murdered
on the paths; mysterious fires destroyed their crops and manor
houses; they were driven from their estates by a foreboding fear.

In the cities, where there was as yet no organized labor movement
(unions were not legalized until 1906), strikes became more frequent, assuming unusual stubbornness. Demonstrations ceased to
be little, fugitive affairs manned only by intellectuals. They became
great presses of excitable workingmen, who jammed the squares,
protected the speakers, hurled missles and imprecations at the police, reformed after troops had passed through, held their ground
when blanks were fired, dispersed when the police shot to kill—
only to reassemble the next day in processions ten times as mighty,
to honor and bury the dead.

There was sudden talkativeness and courage and organization
among lawyers, doctors, agronomists, teachers, progressive land-

owners and civil servants of the zemstvos. The long-silent university halls rang again with speeches and the tumult of student strikes. As in the seventies, once more the student supplied their quota of "human bullets" for a direct critique of the bureaucracy by means of the terror. Student Karpovich murdered Minister of Education Bogolepov in 1901; Balmashev shot Minister of the Interior Sipyagin in 1902; Sazonov laid low Minister of the Interior Plehve with a bomb in 1904; Kalyaev killed Grand Duke Sergei of the royal house in 1905. From Minister of Education, who had direct power over students, to Minister of the Interior, who commanded the police, to the Tsar's own uncle, a Grand Duke of the Royal House —the terror rose in an ascending scale, to lap at the very feet of the throne. These were only the most startling of a series of such deeds which no longer seemed to alienate public opinion as in the past, but rather stirred it to its depths. All the survivors of these attacks, and all the young persons attracted by them, joined the "Fighting Section" of the new Social Revolutionary Party, in which Director of The Moscow Okhrana Zubatov, with Minister Plehve's approval, had recruited one of the most remarkable of his agents, Yevno Azev. To put a police agent in charge of the socialist terror organization, this was one aspect of the rash of experiments in police socialism, an aspect which, as we have already noted, cost Minister Plehve his life!

Even at the summits of society, there was self-doubt and dissent. The celebrated Count Leo Tolstoy, so long a troublesome critic, was now excommunicated by the Church. Two princes of the House of Trubetskoi and two of the House of Dolgoruki made public profession of liberalism. Prince Obolenski became one of the contributors to the columns of *Iskra* and then a founder of the new Constitutional Democratic Party. Millionaire industrialists like Morozov contributed regular and substantial sums to the underground. His own contribution from early 1904 until his death was two thousand rubles (one thousand dollars) a month, through his employee, the engineer Krassin. Was this contribution to bolshevism by one of Russia's richest industrialists a death wish for his class or for himself? Two days before he committed suicide in Cannes in 1905, he handed over a large sum in cash to Krassin for the Social Democratic Party. And the student Schmitt, heir to another branch of the Morozov fortunes, joined the movement directly. Dying in jail either of torture or as a suicide, he willed his estate to the Social Democratic Party. Bank directors and high state officials, writes Krassin in his memoirs, were among the regular contributors of monthly sums to the Party treasury. And once more, as in the middle of the nineteenth century, distinguished writers put pen and prestige at the service of the revolutionary movement.

At Court appeared would-be Neckers, Turgots, Calonnes: Bunge, Vyshnegradsky, Witte, Stolypin, who, given a wiser and stronger sovereign and a more peaceful international situation, might have succeeded in renovating the crumbling structure of the "Asiatic" state, with sounder finances, better and more honest administration and more scope to public opinion and the public will. Most important of these innovators at the turn of the century was Sergei Yulievich Witte. From his modest beginnings as a railway-station master Witte rose to the Directorship of the Southwestern railway lines, then to Minister of Communications, Minister of Finance, and in 1905, to the Presidency of the Council of Ministers and architect of the Constitutional Manifesto, with the title of Count.

He introduced the gold standard, secured foreign loans and investors, strengthened both private and state industry, set up Russo-Persian and Russo-Chinese Banks. Under him Russia's railways grew faster than those of any other country in Europe, faster than the Bolsheviks would ever build. Thus stimulated, Russian industry grew at a greater rate per annum than that of Germany, France, or England, and, during many years, than that of the United States. But he was more successful at modernizing industry than the regime. Working, as he had to, through favorites, subsidies, and ancient "Byzantine" intrigues, in these arts he was no match for his arch rival, Plehve. Witte's Transsiberian and Chinese-Eastern Railways, and his Russo-Chinese Bank, all of them in his mind projects for peaceful expansion and penetration of the Far East, actually put into his rival's hand that trump card of a "short, successful war" with Japan which was supposed to "unify the nation."

On all levels of the great bureaucratic structure, along with the corrupt, the complaisant and the brutalized there appeared civil servants and officials who led devoted and abnegated lives, sought to introduce local and departmental reforms, drew up illuminating reports, which, under the guise of warning and alarm, suggested the necessity of change. Contrary to the general impression, a reading of their reports suggests that no set of governing officials in history has ever given a clearer account of the situation facing it.

But at the very apex of the pyramid there existed a dangerous vacuity: a despotism-in-principle wielded by a man who lacked the strength and ruthlessness and understanding required for that ex-

acting trade. Until the very year of his accession, Nicholas Romanov
had been ruled like a child by his stern and atrabilious father.
Upon the latter's death, Nicholas entered, with ever-increasing
completeness, under the sway of the petty German princess who
had become his wife. Her victorian prudery, sickly mysticism, narrow obstinacy, her incapacity to believe evil of those who played
on her weaknesses or good of those who opposed her desires, were
poor equipment indeed for her constantly enlarging dominion over
the man who ruled the greatest land empire on earth. All her virtues, like his, were cut to a small domestic pattern. Her chief ambition was to provide the Tsar with a male heir. As buxom daughter
succeeded buxom daughter, she put herself in the hands of a succession of thaumaturges, charlatans and mystics, in the hope that
they would aid her to bear a son. When at last a Tsarevich was born,
she believed thanks to the intervention of one of them, that "miracle" served to confirm her in her superstitions. The boy proved
to be a victim of hemophilia, a weakness which does not show up
in females but has been transmitted through the female line to so
many males of Europe's royal houses. She blamed and reproached
herself and saw the visitation of hemophilia as some fault in her.
To do proper penance, and at every critical moment, to keep the
precious heir from bleeding to death, she put herself and her weak-
willed husband still more completely under the sway of her dark
camarilla, until the dissolute holy man Rasputin and the narrow-
minded Empress came to rule the Empire in the sovereign's name.
The demand for renovation, rising to the very feet of the throne,
but made her maternal will grow fiercer, narrower, more fanatical,
more concentrated on the single objective of transmitting to the
sickly heir the imperial power undiminished by a single iota.

> At the beginning of the nineties—writes an official popu-
> lar history of the Russian Revolution—there were in Russia
> 27,229 versts of railway lines, and at the beginning of 1900,
> 41,714 versts . . . The production of pig iron between 1890
> and 1899 increased in England by 18%, in the U.S.A. by
> 50%, in Germany by 72%, in France by 31%, in Belgium
> by 32%, and in Russia by 108% . . . The increase in the
> production of iron and steel during the same period, 1890
> to 1899, was as follows: England 80%, U.S.A. 63%, Ger-
> many 73%, France 67%, Belgium 48% and Russia 116%.
> Changes in the production of coal for the same period are
> as follows: in England an increase of 22%, in America of
> 61%, in Germany of 52%, in France of 26% . . . in Russia
> of 131%. In the production of oil Russia had only one

competitor, the United States . . . The Russian cotton industry at the beginning of the twentieth century was second only to that of England and America. [*Illustrated
History of the Russian Revolution*, English-Language edition, International Publishers, 1928, pp. 4-6.]

And in Popov's *History of the Communist Party*, printed in
Moscow in many languages in 1934, we read:

> The output of pig iron during the period 1890 to 1900
> increased by 220%, of iron ore by 272%, and of oil by
> 179%. [16th Edition, English, International Publishers,
> p. 33.]

These staggering figures, when checked against the statistical
reports compiled at the beginning of the century or more recently,
prove not to err on the side of overstatement. The startling difference between the first and the second is due to the fact that the
year 1900 was one of tremendous upsurge. They are analogous to
the ebbs and flows in increase during the Five-Year Plans and
show that Russia at the turn of the century was a sprawling giant,
just rising in its might, still a backward, but surely not a stagnant,
land. It was this tremendous expansion of Russian life, and not
stagnation, which made the Revolutions of 1905 and 1917 possible.
Today, such reminders of former bounding growth are no longer
to be found in government propaganda. We now have to dig them
out of heavier, more scholarly tomes like P. E. Lashchenko's *History of the People's Economy of the U.S.S.R.* But precisely because
they come from official histories they serve to give the reader a
perspective from which to view the present-day Five-Year Plans.

Then as now, islands of heavy industry thrust up everywhere out
of the vast peasant sea. Ancient "Asiatic" centers of bureaucratic
administration and marketing were transformed into modern European industrial cities. New metropolises sprouted on the steppes or
in the Urals, where there had not even been towns before. The
new-born industries exhibited a fantastic elephantiasis: giant factories succeeded by super-giants, as if to match the sweep of the
Russian plain and the reach of the Russian imagination.

The working class grew at a stormy and unprecedented pace. As
during the Five-Year Plans of the thirties, there was a shortage of
"living space" for the influx of new workers. Overcrowding and
slums increased; men lived in barracks erected by the enterprises,
dined in factory dining rooms, used communal kitchens. Whole
families and groups of unrelated persons of both sexes and all ages

crowded into single rooms. For the most part they were yesterday's peasants, their families often remaining in the village, themselves returning to it in periods of unemployment. Their outlook was a maze of their crumbling rural traditions and the unsettling experiences of their new city life.

As a land entering late into the current of modern industry, Russia found its capital ready accumulated in Western Europe, and in the taxing power of its own state. More important, it found its technique ready made. Frequently technicians, managers, funds, investors, owners were imported. Entire factory setups were shipped from Germany, or overseas from America, needing little more than a floor to be fastened down to, a roof to cover them and a labor force to operate them. The Girauds, Thorntons, Nobels, Maxwells, Urquharts, Rothschilds—the great oil, mining, metallurgical and textile companies of foreign ownership—would be at a special disadvantage once the native working class went into action against "foreign" exploitation.

When we examine the actual figures, we are astonished to find that this backward land with its hundreds of thousands of wooden villages now possessed if not the largest, yet the most highly concentrated industrial working class in Europe. In Germany at the turn of the century, only 14 per cent of the factories had a force of more than five hundred men; in Russia the corresponding figure was 34 per cent. Only 8 per cent of all German workers worked in factories employing over a thousand workingmen each. Twenty-four per cent, nearly a quarter, of all Russian industrial workers worked in factories of that size. These giant enterprises forced the new working class into close association. There arose an insatiable hunger for organization, which the huge state machine sought in vain to direct or hold in check.

In the bureaucracy there were striking differences of opinion on the attitude to be taken toward the nascent labor movement and the embryonic political parties. To Plehve, who as Minister of the Interior had charge of the secret police and public order, it seemed that the zemstvo liberals and Constitutional Democrats were the most dangerous, the Social Revolutionaries next, and the Social Democrats only in third place. His chief bugbear was the zemstvos, with their urge for local autonomy, their remonstrances and petitions reminiscent of the French Revolution's *cahiers de doléances*, their demand for a national council of zemstvo delegates or *zemski sobor*, that might easily become the germ of a parliament, another *Etats Généraux*. He feared and detested them because they represented socially the most exalted demand for constitutionalism, a species of treason to the autocracy amongst the landowners themselves.

Next came the manufacturers and financiers with their demands for subsidies, new tariff and taxation structures, a limited state budget, the transformation of the feudal-bureaucratic state in the image of modern capitalism. These, and the moderate zemstvo elements were the more dangerous because in the person of Witte they had their own advocate in the very Council of Ministers.

If the Social Revolutionaries came second in the order of Minister Plehve's attention, it was not by reason of their socialism nor their peasant committees, but because of their use of terror. Socialism never worried Plehve. With an inverted *narodnichestvo* common to many reactionaries in Russia, he looked on rural socialism as a kind of peasant communal village arrangement, not at all incompatible with the tasks of tax collecting, military levies, and absolutist dictatorship. The peasants he regarded as an unshakable rock of loyalty to the throne. Urban socialism he dismissed as a remote and impossible utopian dream, while Witte's projects for state ownership of railways and banks and the vodka traffic naturally troubled him not at all. The real problem was the owners of private industry whom Witte represented so ably at Court.

Plehve pondered much over a report made by the conservative Police Chief of Moscow, General Trepov, in 1898:

> In order to disarm the agitators—General Trepov had written—it is necessary to open and point out to the worker a legal solution of his difficulty, for we must bear in mind that the agitator will be followed by the youngest and boldest part of the crowd, while the average worker will prefer the less spectacular and quiet legal way. Thus split up, the crowd will lose its power.

The suggestion intrigued the Minister of the Interior. What were these restless workingmen, he asked himself, if not the same loyal peasants of yesterday, bewildered by the new industrialism, angered by the greed of the industrialists, led astray by revolutionary agitators from the intelligentsia? Why might the state not shepherd them and watch over them a bit more, weed out the hotheads, give the mass a chance to organize under the most dependable auspices, protect them by social legislation against the greedy and doubtfully loyal bourgeoisie, act as benevolent and impartial arbitrator in industrial disputes, avert strikes and disorders by friendly arbitration, bind them more closely to the paternal state and Tsar?

Would it not be a master-stroke of statesmanship to set the workingmen against the factory owners instead of against the government? And as a by-product, might not even a little carefully
directed labor disorder be a useful weapon on occasion to show
whither Finance Minister Witte's industrialization and liberal flir-
tations were leading?

The real architect of police-regimented unions in a police-
controlled paternal state was Sergei Vasilievich Zubatov, who now
became chief lieutenant of General Trepov in Moscow. It was
Zubatov, and not Plehve or Trepov, to whose name would be
attached the honor of the great experiment in police unionism,
destined to go down in history as the *zubatovshchina*. As a *gymnazia* student he had entered the Narodnaya Volya, enlisting with
the police almost simultaneously as a secret agent. Thereafter he
had risen rapidly in the service, being the sponsor of many progressive innovations: photography, fingerprinting, and a superior system of secret espionage on a scale hitherto unknown in Russia or
in the world. "You must look upon your colleague, the secret
agent," he once told the police, "as you would upon a woman with
whom you are conducting a secret love intrigue: one rash step and
you have dishonored her in the eyes of the world." Clearly a man
of sentiment and imagination!

His biggest achievement so far had been the nationwide simultaneous raids that smashed the beginnings of the Social Democratic
Party in 1897, rendering nugatory the efforts of their First Congress
at Minsk. Now he had risen to the headship of the Moscow
Okhrana or Secret Security Police, his only superiors being General
Trepov, in charge of all the police services of the Moscow Province,
and Minister of the Interior Plehve. This, his most ambitious plan,
was really the police counterpart of the general urge for organization that was beginning to take possession of all classes in Russia.
Against zemstvo intellectuals, students, Social Democrats and Social
Revolutionaries, he would offer his police unionism and police
"socialism."

In May 1901, he founded the Moscow *Society for Mutual Aid
for Workingmen in the Mechanical Industries*. As an experienced
secret agent, he tried to keep his guiding hand as unobtrusive as
possible, but his less subtle superiors, Trepov and Plehve, insisted
on tying up the Society with all sorts of rigid and too obvious safe-
guards. The by-laws and financial expenditures had to be approved
by General Trepov. The secret agents who were leaders of the

union were supplemented by uniformed police openly present at
each meeting.

But the Moscow workingmen, heirs to the ancient patriarchal
tradition and hungering now for organization, were more trustful
of the Tsar and his officials than either Zubatov or the revolutionaries had believed possible. Assured that a paternal government
was with them, they rushed into the strange union. Before it was
a year old, it was able to lead a procession of fifty thousand
workers into the Kremlin for solemn prayer before the tomb of the
Emancipator Tsar, Alexander II.

Intellectuals were barred from the organization, and "hotheads"
and "troublemakers" among the workingmen were arrested and
silently deported. Hence purists among the Social Democrats
wanted to limit their activity to denunciation and exposure. The
workers were too class-conscious, they contended, to continue to
have anything to do with such a monstrosity, once it was exposed
to them. But the more realistic knew that denunciation was not
enough.

> We must understand—Lenin wrote in *Iskra*—how to de-
> velop the struggle of the workers against every shameful
> intrigue and spy's trick . . . This struggle will develop the
> political consciousness of all who take part in the police-
> gendarme-and-spy "labor organization" . . . In the long
> run the legalization of the working-class movement will be
> to our advantage and not to that of the Zubatovs. . . .

This freedom from sectarian aversion to working wherever work
was needful, was not limited to Lenin. At the Second Congress,
one of the resolutions passed unanimously during the last session
provided that Social Democratic workingmen should join these
unions where possible, and try to defend and enlighten their members against the police. The startling successes even then being
achieved by police unionism made any other attitude impossible.

The Moscow Society for Mutual Aid began, with Zubatov's encouragement, by discussing economic and cultural questions and
formulating wage proposals. They chose as the first object of their
attentions a "foreign exploiter"—a French factory owner. But he
went crying to his ambassador, who in turn protested to Plehve
concerning this quasi-governmental action against one of his na-
tionals. The demands had to be dropped.

Zubatov's next idea was to help the union draw up proposals for
wages and working conditions, impartially for the whole of Moscow
industry. As head of the Okhrana he even went so far as to convoke

a meeting of the manufacturers, berate them a little, and insist upon concessions. With these first successes, the movement began to spread rapidly, from industry to industry, and then, on the wings of rumor and report, from town to town, until the newly industrialized factory centers of southern Russia were honeycombed with police unions.

While Zubatov supported labor legislation and repeatedly took the part of the workers against the employers, he simultaneously dispatched provocateurs into the rival revolutionary movements with an idea of "provoking you to acts of terror and then crushing you" as he said once in a moment of frankness. Chief of these agents was Yevno Azev, son of a poor Jewish tailor, who became a student spy, then, with Zubatov's aid, a Moscow engineer and one of the founders and the eventual leader of the Terror Section of the Social Revolutionary Party.

In Odessa a Doctor Shaevich appeared to start things moving. Colonel of Gendarmes Vasiliev, assisted by two Jewish women agents, even formed a "Jewish Independent Labor Party" in Kiev. A police-sponsored priest, George Gapon, offered himself as a leader of the working-class movement in Saint Petersburg. Police socialism was booming all over Russia.

In the spring of 1903, the new industrial regions exploded in a series of little strikes, that set each other off, merged with each other, began to grow into something too big for a police official to manipulate in comfort. In July, 1903, at the very moment when the Social Democrats at their Congress in London were adopting a resolution to send socialist workingmen into the police unions, Dr. Shaevich lost control of the Odessa movement. A general strike flared up there, then spread all over southern Russia and into the Caucasus, a dress rehearsal for the greater strikes of 1905. Zubatov, Vasiliev and Shaevich fell from grace, and were banished to their birthplaces, Zubatov was restored to the service in 1905, then dismissed again. But so loyal was he to the Tsar that when Nicholas abdicated in 1917, Zubatov committed suicide.

With the Odessa general strike ended the first phase of the experiment in police unionism. But in the capital, Father Gapon had not gotten started yet, nor was he under the Moscow jurisdiction of the disgraced Zubatov. Minister Plehve did not interfere with the priest's plans for a further experiment in clerical-police unionism.

Meanwhile, the border lands of the Empire, many of them economically more advanced than the Great-Russian central area, were also astir. The rapid industrialization of the nineties and the policy of Russification of the last two Tsars were rousing these non-Russian nationalities to fever heat. Here the Russian state had little opportunity to insinuate its control. The labor movement tended rather to submerge itself into a general nationalist struggle for independence. Where the working class was strongest and best organized, the nationalist movement in turn tended to take on a labor and socialist tinge. In Russian Poland, for example, the Bund became a labor movement with special views on Jewish nationality, while strong protagonists like Joseph Pilsudski and Rosa Luxemburg waged a war over the soul of the Polish proletariat, Pilsudski's nationalism tinged with socialism competing with Luxemburg's anti-nationalist or internationalist socialism.

The rise of the nationalist revolutionary movements in all the border regions suggested to the fertile mind of Plehve another experiment in "police socialism" of quite a different order. He would try playing the Mohammedan Tartar masses in Transcaucasia against the Christian Armenians, and, wherever there were Jewish settlements—most of them were in the borderlands—he would try playing Russians, Poles and other peoples against the Jews. His propaganda, spread by secret agents and government printing presses, emphasized the "socialistic" character of the enterprise. It sought to direct the existing mass anger not against landlords and capitalists in general, but against Jewish and Armenian merchants, Jewish estate managers and money-lenders. Like the "National Socialism" of Germany which later derived from it, the pogrom incitations simultaneously charged the Jews with being the moneyed and exploiting classes, and with being disloyal revolutionaries who would destroy Russia's unity and undermine her greatness. This experiment was more successful than the *zubatovshchina*, surviving its author, Plehve. Yet it too was to have unlooked-for results. In 1905 and 1906 it would provide the workingmen with one of their best reasons for demanding and bearing arms. In some of the affected regions, zemstvos, municipal councils, and even entire provinces of Transcaucasia would vote funds to arm workers' defense corps against the pogroms which a section of the government was secretly organizing.

On the night of February 8-9, 1904, Plehve's third dream bore fruit. Without prior warning, Japanese submarines attacked the Russian fleet in the harbor of Port Arthur, thereby overnight changing the relation of forces in the Far East. Plehve's "little successful war with Japan" opened up before him.

Witte's memoirs seek to put all the blame for the war upon the shoulders of Plehve and a little clique of Far Eastern speculators and adventurers who had the ear of the Tsar. But closer scrutiny reveals Witte as one of those statesmen who do not want war, yet want those things which lead to ever-sharpening conflict with the similarly "peace-minded" statesmen of other countries. His financial and railroad-building schemes for the penetration of China and Korea merit a closer examination for they present a startling parallel with the actions of the Soviet Government in the same regions in 1945. Indeed, they laid the foundations on which Soviet claims in Manchuria, Mongolia, Northwest China and Korea (and Iran, too) are based today.

Early in the nineties, Witte directed the attention of his government to Persia (Iran) and set up a Russo-Persian Bank under the control of the Russian Government. In 1894, when Japan defeated China in war and seized the Liao-Tung peninsula—on which Port Arthur stands—the main attention of the Russian state shifted to the Far East. Nicholas II, backed by Germany and France, forced Japan to relinquish the fruits of its victory and withdraw from the Chinese mainland. Witte negotiated a secret treaty of "friendship and non-aggression" with China, guaranteeing its territorial integrity and arranging to build a railroad through Manchuria to Port Arthur "to protect China from the aggressions of Japan." So deeply did the old Dowager Empress of China cherish this treaty of friendship that she hung the text (for a few years) in her bedroom.

Now Witte was able to extend his pet project, the Transsiberian Railroad, through China (Manchuria) to the sea. This "Chinese Eastern Railroad," as the extension was called, was nominally the property of a mixed company. But the controlling interest was in the hands of a Russian bank created by Witte for the purpose, and the Tsar's government got the right to "protect" and "police" the line. The railroad company soon entered into other industries (also claimed by Stalin today) and the economic penetration of Manchuria began to assume vast proportions.

The next move, made against Witte's advice, caused the Chinese Dowager Empress to tear up the framed document hanging in her bedroom. Still protesting friendship and giving as its purpose the protection of China's integrity, the Russian Navy steamed into Port Arthur, set up a naval base there, and, by a combination of bribery and coercion, forced the Chinese to agree to a twenty-five-year "lease" of the port and base. Simultaneously, the British moved in to take Weh-Hai-Wei, the Germans Kiao-Chow, the French Kwang-Chow, thus slicing off the choicest parts of the Chinese coast. Only

Japan, which had softened up the resistance of China by its attack, was left out in the cold. When the Kaiser used the murder of two German missionaries to extort a ninety-nine-year lease to Kiao-Chow from China, the Tsar, not to be outdone by his cousin, forced China to change his lease on Port Arthur to ninety-nine years also.

Now an aroused China attempted to drive out all the foreigners who were cutting her land to pieces (the Boxer Rebellion), whereupon all the Powers moved in with armies of occupation, the Russian Army occupying Manchuria. When the rebellion had been crushed, Russia pledged itself to withdraw its troops but continued to keep them there. It is on these foundations that the Soviet Government in 1945 based its claims to a naval base once more in Port Arthur, the right to police the Chinese Eastern Railway in Manchuria, and its other demands.

Meanwhile Japan was trying to get its share of the spoils by penetrating Korea, but here, too, the Tsar's government sent "police troops," arranged for a Russian gauge railroad, provided military and financial advisers. Korea negotiated anxiously with both countries in an effort to preserve its independence, while Japan tried to come to a peaceful agreement with Russia on the basis of a Japanese sphere in Korea and a Russian in Manchuria. This mutual penetration of Korea is the basis for Russia's present occupation of the northern half of that unhappy country. After several years of vain efforts at negotiation, the Japanese withdrew their envoys from Moscow, and three days later, without a declaration of war, smashed the Russian fleet off Port Arthur by a surprise attack. The date was February 9, 1904.

The internal struggle in Russia died down as Minister Plehve had calculated, submerged in a great wave of patriotic exaltation. But not for long. The Transsiberian, begun by Witte in 1891, had as yet but a single track, and at Lake Baikal there was a big gap which had to be covered by ferry in summer and sledge in winter. Yet this was the slender lane through which Russia's mighty resources would have to pass if they were to be brought to bear upon the far weaker but on-the-spot Japan. General Kuropatkin was for retreating inland into Siberia until Russia's slow-moving might could be brought up to crush his lesser adversary, but generals close to the Tsar disobeyed his orders and had them overruled in Court. For eight months the great Port Arthur fortress held out, falling at last to starvation, indiscipline and siege. As the Russian armies met reverse after reverse and the Court clique proved impotent to mobilize effectively Russia's vast resources for war, anger and shame and open defeatism took the place of the first patriotic

278 THREE WHO MADE A REVOLUTION

fervor. By the time the Russian war machine was really getting under way and the slender resources of Japan were showing signs of exhaustion, the threat of revolution had grown so great in Russia that the Tsar preferred to recall Witte to office (he had been dismissed for his wearisome admonitions against military adventures in the Far East, in 1903), and to send him to the United States to negotiate a humiliating compromise peace with Japan, so that the government's hands might be freed for the mounting war with its own people.

All through 1904, while millions of Russian workers and peasants were called upon to fight and die in the Far East for Port Arthur and Dairen, northern Korea and Sakhalin, and the Transsiberian Railroad, the faction strife between Lenin and his opponents so consumed their energies that they had little left over for reacting to the war, or even defining their position toward it. Incredible as it sounds, during the entire year 1904 there are only three sparse mentions of the war in Lenin's writings! The rest are concerned with his war on the Central Committee, the Council, the Editorial Board of *Iskra*. And the writings of his opponents show similar proportions. No wonder the revolution that began in January, 1905, caught them napping.

The few utterances on the subject made by all these leaders abroad are little more than passing references and casual slogans. There were differences of approach, but they did not achieve clear formulation. Trotsky and Martov regarded the war as an evil, and called for an immediate peace. Lenin, however, was inclined to regard the conflict with Japan as something positive since it would show up the weakness of the monarchy. He expected Japan to win, and thought that this would be an aid to the progressive forces in Russia in their own war with the Russian Government. When, in January 1905, the Japanese finally took Port Arthur, he wrote one of his few pronouncements on the conflict. Entitled "The Fall of Port Arthur," it is a scarce-concealed cry of exultation that "progressive Japan" had defeated "backward and reactionary Europe," and not merely Russian absolutism. His words are worth pondering, both because they contain within them the germ of his future "revolutionary defeatism" in World War I, and because they contrast so strangely with utterances on the same subject by his self-proclaimed "best disciple." Said Lenin:

> The proletariat has every reason to rejoice . . . The military goal of Japan is in the main attained. Progressive, advanced Asia has dealt backward and reactionary Europe

an irreparable blow. Ten years earlier this reactionary Europe, with Russia at the head, was made uneasy by the crushing of China by Japan, and it united to deprive Japan of the best fruits of its victory. Europe defended its prior and primal right, sanctified by centuries, to the exploitation of the Asiatic peoples. The reconquest of Port Arthur by Japan is a blow against the whole of reactionary Europe . . .

The war of a progressive land with a backward one has this time as so often in the past played a great revolutionary role . . . The proletariat is opposed to every bourgeoisie and every expression of the bourgeois order, but this opposition does not relieve it of the duty of distinguishing between the historically progressive and the reactionary representatives of the bourgeoisie. It is therefore entirely understandable that the most consistent and determined representatives of revolutionary international Social Democracy, Jules Guesde in France and Hyndman in England, have given expression without evasion to their sympathy for Japan, which is giving a beating to Russian absolutism . . .

Not the Russian people but Absolutism has suffered a shameful defeat. The Russian people has won by the defeat of Absolutism. The capitulation of Port Arthur is the prologue to the capitulation of Tsarism. The war is far from ended, but in its continuation every step strengthens the immeasurable ferment and indignation in the Russian people and brings us nearer to the moment of a great new war, the people's war against absolutism, the war of the proletariat for freedom. [*Vpered,* January 14, 1905.]

That "great new war" which Lenin spoke of, was actually to break out within a week, before even that issue of *Vpered* had reached Russia!

"The proletariat has every reason to rejoice . . ." Clearly, Joseph Stalin, if we are to credit his words of 1945, must have felt differently. In his "Victory Address" on the unconditional surrender of Japan, September 2, 1945, we read:

The defeat of the Russian troops in 1904 in the period of the Russo-Japanese War left grave memories in the minds of our peoples. It was a dark stain on our country. Our people trusted and awaited the day when Japan would be routed and the stain wiped out. For forty years have we, men of the older generation, waited for this day. And now this day has come!

Nothing could more sharply mark the contrast between the "master" and the "best disciple" than these two utterances on the fall of Port Arthur, the naval base which first the Tsar and then Stalin was to wrest from China.

The Japanese Government, for its part, felt that it might find interests in common with Russian "progressive forces." With admirable impartiality it offered money and arms to all shades and factions. Pilsudski journeyed to Japan to secure substantial help for his Polish Socialist Party. The Georgian Federal Socialists and the Finnish Activists accepted assistance. Rosa Luxemburg's Polish Social Democracy, however, rejected aid from such a source, as did Mensheviks, Bolsheviks, and Constitutional Democrats. It is characteristic of the Russian intelligentsia, from Lenin to Miliukov, that they thought it shameful to accept such support, and the fact of that rejection should effectively dispose of the slanderous view that Lenin's "revolutionary defeatism" converted him into an enemy agent of the government warring with his.

Since the Social Democrats, especially their foreign "general staffs," were too busy with their faction war, it was the liberals and democrats who first made their voices heard in opposition as misery mounted and the military reverses multiplied:

> Whose fault is it?—wrote Prince Trubetskoi in the Law Journal, *Pravo*, on the occasion of the defeat at Lao Yang — Is it Russian society's? Russian society was asleep, by order of the authorities. For years every measure has been taken to prevent its waking. If now and then someone tried to get up and stand on his two feet and say a human word, it was regarded as a disturbance of order and security. It called forth only a threatening snarl: *Mouth shut! Keep down there!* and a powerful hand would push down the lifted head. In recent years Russia has been like a dormitory in a police station . . .

On July 24, the already shaken bureaucracy was thrown into utter confusion by a bomb, thrown by Sazonov, in a plot directed by police-agent Azev, which tore the recently promoted Interior Minister Plehve to pieces. Without a strong adviser now, the frightened Tsar appointed a moderate liberal in Plehve's place with a program of "showing more confidence in society."

At that the liberal democratic movement found its tongue and burst into speech like a forest of birds at daybreak. Zemstvos adopted declarations of grievances and made open plans for a national conference of zemstvo delegates. Lawyers, doctors, architects, authors, journalists, engineers, economists, scientists, professors held public banquets, made speeches, memorialized, resolved, protested, demanded and respectfully suggested innumerable changes. Their staid professional conferences turned into political meetings and their professional societies into "unions." Then, under Professor Miliukov's leadership, these unions united into a *Union of Unions.* So powerful was the impression that these intellectual unions made upon the as yet unorganized workingmen that to this day the labor organizations of Russia are called "professional unions," generally shortened to *profsoyuzy,* "profunions."

The Social Democrats, as far as their faction quarrels permitted, followed these liberal oppositional activities with the deepest interest. But how to behave toward them? On this, as on other matters, Lenin and his erstwhile associates were of two minds. As Plekhanov had predicted, the Mensheviks were in favor of "turning their face; you your behind" toward the liberal democratic opposition.

Since we're all agreed that the coming revolution is to be a "bourgeois democratic revolution," reasoned the Mensheviks, such men as these are destined to lead it and form the future government. Let us give them courage and mass support. Let us call upon the workers to demonstrate in front of their zemstvo meetings, banquet halls, political demonstrations. And, in return for helping them win, let us exact promises from them for our own class: a truly democratic régime, universal suffrage, freedom of speech, press, organization, enlightened social legislation. After tsarism is overthrown, begins our fight with them. In the meanwhile, let us not burst into their meetings in disorderly fashion, make demands that will frighten them away, or split the opposition to tsarism before it has won its fight. "Before you divide the skin, first you catch the bear."

Lenin, for his part, waxed ironical at these proposals. True, he shared with the Mensheviks the common formulae: "alliance of all opposition forces"; "a bourgeois democratic revolution." But in his heart he was convinced that the bourgeoisie was too weak and cowardly to carry out its own historical tasks, that it was ready to "make a deal with the Tsar," that it was too crafty and Machiavellian to keep any promises made to the masses. "Promises," wrote Lenin in English, quoting one of his favorite English proverbs, "promises are like pie-crust—made to be broken." As for frightening away the bourgeoisie, you can count upon their being frightened away, all except the peasantry and the "radical urban petty bourgeoisie." The way to give these timid heroes courage is to set them an example of irreconcilable struggle yourself. If that frightens them off, so much the better: we shall know that we cannot count on them, and shall go on without them. You call upon the masses to demonstrate before their banquet halls and zemstvo meetings, to give them courage. But I call upon the masses to demonstrate before governmental buildings, palaces, prisons, police stations . . .

But the masses listened neither to Bolsheviks nor Mensheviks. Many of them followed the liberals directly. Even some of Lenin's Local Committees in Russia ignored his instructions, and gathered in liberal and democratic meetings, to cheer and support the most vocal opposition that had yet arisen. However, the bulk of the workingmen of the capital followed neither Bolsheviks, nor Mensheviks, nor Liberal Democrats, but swarmed into the organizations headed by the police.

Trotsky, who had joined the Mensheviks on the organization question, now fought them on what he contemptuously called their "banquet campaign." Alone of Russian Marxists, Trotsky was trying to break out of the hobbling circle of the formula that the coming revolution must be a "bourgeois revolution." The bourgeoisie, he asserted, will never carry their fight from the banquet hall into the streets, where along revolutions are fought and won. Once the police and the Tsar snarl a firm *no* at them, their flow of words will come to a stop. Before the end of 1904 this prediction at least, was verified.

"What next?" asked Trotsky in a pamphlet written near the year's end. His answer:

> A political general strike . . . A political strike of the proletariat, which ought to be turned into a political demonstration of the entire population . . . Not a local, but a general political strike all over Russia, with a general political slogan. This slogan: To stop the war, and to call a National Constituent Assembly . . . And the peasants ought to come together on the day of the strike . . . We ought to carry on the most intensive propaganda in the Army, in order that, on the day of the strike, each soldier should know that he is facing the people—who are demanding a National Constituent Assembly.[1]

Of all the formulae, plans, suggestions, slogans, and immediate proposals and analyses made in the year 1904, this one of Trotsky's on a general political strike was to come closest to realization in

[1] *Do Devyatago Yanvarya* ("Before the Ninth of January"). With an introduction by Parvus. Geneva, 1905. The pamphlet failed to get printed until after the stirring events of January 22, 1905 (January 9, Old Style), whence the title. Parvus's introduction contains the first exposition of the theory of "permanent revolution" (the proletariat begins by making a bourgeois revolution and continues it "in permanence" until it becomes a proletarian revolution), a doctrine which was to play such a central role in Trotsky's subsequent, life-long views.

1905. But history, as usual, was to prove sly and tricky, and reality was to turn out richer, more bizarre, more complicated than any formula derived from it and meant to describe it and prescribe for it. Not Marxian socialism but one of the experiments in "police socialism" became the bizarre starting point for a general strike. Or perhaps we should say "clerical socialism," for its leader was a priest of the Russian Orthodox Church!

Father George Gapon is one of the most interesting figures thrown up by the Revolution of 1905, and one of the most peculiarly Russian. Son of a Ukrainian peasant, at the time we meet him he was only thirty-two. He is described as intelligent, serious, meditative, energetic, strikingly handsome, an impressive orator and inspired leader of men. In his youth, one of his teachers, a Tolstoyan, had given him a clandestinely circulated manuscript tract by Tolstoy. The other main source of his inspiration was Zubatov and his experiment with police-directed unionism. The Saint Petersburg workers, more advanced than those of Moscow, had proved more suspicious of police direction. Father Gapon, who had already convinced his superiors of his ability to handle men as a prison chaplain, now suggested that the Petersburg workingmen could be better led in the direction of wholesome organization under "spiritual supervision" than under police control. His project for a "Union of Russian Factory Workers" with himself as leader and spiritual adviser received Plehve's ministerial approval shortly before the latter's violent death. The new Union's aims included "the sober and rational passing of leisure time," the elimination of drunkenness and gambling, the inculcation of religious and patriotic ideas, the development of a "prudent view of the duties and the rights of workers," and organized "self-activity for the legal improvement of the conditions of labor and life of the workers."

At first the workingmen kept away. The puzzled Gapon, torn between his Tolstoyan views and his moral and social ambitions on the one hand and his police instructions on the other, sought to increase the confidence of ordinary workers by getting active support and advice from the more advanced. After a few secret conferences with such people, he found his society flooded with applications for membership. More effective than their advice was the wartime rise in the cost of living. Before the year 1904 was over, his Union included practically all eligible workers engaged in the mechanical trades in Saint Petersburg, together with a sizable sprinkling of police spies and a few men under the influence of socialist ideas. There were no intellectuals. More successfully than

Zubatov, he seemed to be deflecting hostility from the régime to the employers. The great meetings sang "God Save the Tsar" with deep and genuine fervor, for had he not overruled his wicked officials and given them this sympathetic priest to guide their legitimate hope for organization and improvement?

In gauging the patriarchal backwardness of the Russian masses in the dawn years of the twentieth century, we must keep this picture clear in our minds. Nor was it only the unskilled workers, yesterday's peasants, who followed a priest and sang thus fervently, "God Save the Tsar." Actually, the main scene of our drama is the huge Putilov locomotive works and machine shops, the oldest and largest heavy industry factory in advanced Saint Petersburg, containing the largest number of skilled metal workers. Here Father Gapon had his greatest organization. Under his guidance, they formulated some moderate demands upon the enterprise. In December, the latter answered by firing the leading members of Gapon's committee. Thereupon, the entire force of the Putilov locomotive works walked out and urged Father Gapon to take them directly to the "Dear Father Tsar" that they might humbly lay their troubles at his feet.

Priest Gapon was scarcely less naive than the men he had brought together. He was influenced by the mass spirit quite as much as he influenced it. At first he was hesitant at the audacious idea of going directly to the "Father of the Russian people." Then he sanctioned it, finally was carried away by it. The movement was getting too big for its founder to control; its illusions, assuming independent life, were taking control of him. He began to avoid his superiors, the officials of the Police Department and the Ministry of the Interior. Like his followers, he too now sought to go over their heads and seek direct contact with Tsar Nicholas. On January 21 (January 8, Old Style), the eve of the projected procession to the palace, he wrote the following confidential message to the Tsar:

> Sire!
> Do not believe the Ministers. They are cheating Thee in regard to the real state of affairs. The people believe in Thee. They have made up their minds to gather at the Winter Palace tomorrow, at 2 P.M., to lay their needs before Thee. If Thou wilt not stand before them, Thou wilt break that spiritual connection which unites Thee with them . . . Do not fear anything. Stand tomorrow before the people and accept our humblest petition. I, the representative of the workingmen, and my comrades, guarantee the inviolability of Thy person.   (signed) GAPON.

Next morning, according to the common estimate, more than two hundred thousand men, women and children, workers and their families, gathered at many concentration points to converge in procession upon the Winter Palace. They were unarmed in keeping with Gapon's guarantee; the few terrorists, hot-heads, or police agents who had brought arms were searched by his ushers and their weapons taken from them. Their intention was pacific, even reverential. It was Sunday. Many bore ikons and pictures of the Tsar. This carrying of images of the ruler in procession is an ancient Russian custom that flourishes still today. As they marched, they sang as only Russian multitudes can sing, and over and over again their song was "God Save the Tsar."

At the head marched Priest Gapon with a scroll, a reflection of the medley in his mind and the variegated nature of his following:

> Sire—We workingmen and inhabitants of Saint Petersburg . . . our wives and our children and our helpless old parents come to Thee, Sire, to seek for truth and protection. We have become beggars; we have been oppressed; we are breathless . . . There has arrived for us that great moment when death is better than the continuation of intolerable tortures. We have left off working, and we have declared to our masters that we shall not begin to work until they comply with our demands. We ask but little . . . to diminish the working day to eight hours . . . minimum daily wage should be one ruble per day. To abolish overtime . . .
>
> The officials have brought the country to complete destruction, have involved it in a detestable war . . . We workingmen have no voice in the expenditure of the enormous amounts raised from us in taxes . . .
>
> These things are before us, Sire, and they have brought us to the walls of Thy Palace. We are seeking here the last salvation. Do not refuse assistance to Thy people. Give their destiny into their own hands. Cast away from them the intolerable oppression of the officials. Destroy the wall between Thyself and Thy people, and let them rule the country together with Thyself . . . Order immediately the convocation of a *zemski sobor* . . . order that the elections to the Constituent Assembly be carried on under the condition of universal, equal, secret voting. This is the most capital of our requests . . . the principal and only plaster for our painful wounds . . .
>
> Order and take an oath to comply with these requests and Thou wilt make Russia happy and famous and Thou

wilt impress Thy name in our hearts and the hearts of our
posterity forever.

If Thou wilt not order and wilt not answer our prayer,
we shall die here on this Square before Thy Palace . . .

So the people, finding their voice through a priest who had
picked up scraps of demands and slogans that were in the air,
marched to the palace of their Tsar, to lay their troubles at his
feet. But the Tsar was not in his palace. He had left the city hastily,
taking with him wife and daughters. In his stead he had left his
officials: generals, police chiefs, and his uncle, the Grand Duke
Vladimir.

Troops fully armed descended upon the marchers, surrounded
their separate detachments, fired at close range. Men, women, children fell. The crowds melted away. Crimson stains appeared on
the white snow. How many fell, no one knows, for the wounded
were treated in secret and the dead were withdrawn by their kin.
The common labor estimate is 500 killed, 3000 wounded. A public
commission of the Bar Association set the figures at 150 and 200
respectively. In any case, enough blood was shed to baptize the
day as "Bloody Sunday."

With it an epoch came to an end. It had been sufficient for the
masses to get the fearful idea of acting on a cherished fairytale for
it to be exploded forever. That day millions of primitive minds took
the leap from the Middle Ages to the Twentieth Century. In love
and reverence their best had come to lay their troubles at the feet
of the Dear Father Tsar. The bullets and the shed blood swept
away all vestiges of love and credulity. Now they knew themselves
fatherless and knew that they would have to solve their problems
themselves. Now their minds were opened at last to the teachings
of the republican and socialist intellectuals. Constituent Assembly
and Democratic Republic, General Strike and Armed Uprising
ceased to be phrases comprehensible only to the educated and the
specialists in revolution. They took possession of millions and
thereby became a material force for the transformation of Russia.

Father Gapon fled. With the aid of Social Revolutionaries he
escaped abroad. From hiding, he dispatched one more note to his
Tsar, this time without salutation or respectful capitals:

> The innocent blood of workers, their wives and children,
> lies forever between thee, oh soul destroyer, and the Russian
> people. Moral connection between thee and them may
> never more be . . . Let all the blood which has to be shed,
> hangman, fall upon thee and thy kindred!

CHAPTER XVII

1905 IN EXILE

Zhelyabov: History moves too slowly. It needs a push . . .

Semenyuta: What about a constitution?

Zhelyabov: All to the good.

Semenyuta: Well, what do you want—to work for a constitution or to give history a push?

Zhelyabov: Just now we want to give history a push.

THE MORNING after Bloody Sunday, the Ulyanovs were on their way to the Geneva Library when they were stopped by the Lunacharskys, who were hurrying to visit them. Mrs. Lunacharsky was so moved that she could not speak, only helplessly wave her muff. The four went to Lepeshinsky's restaurant, where they found other Bolsheviks, drawn to the familiar hangout as by a magnet. "The people gathered there hardly spoke a word to one another, they were so excited. With tense faces they sang the Revolutionary Funeral March. Everyone was overwhelmed with the thought that the Revolution had commenced."

Thenceforward, they would live in a dreamlike state, suspended between issue and issue of the daily papers. An irresistible force drew them one by one back to the land of their birth. With that controlled impatience which characterized him, Lenin alone resumed his daily trips to the library, until such time as it seemed possible for him to come out in the open in Russia. To his comrades on the scene of struggle he wrote ardent letters, full of suggestions, insistent yet tactfully tentative, because "from the cursed distance naturally one does not trust himself to take a definite position." Statistics began to gather dust once more on the peaceful shelves of the Geneva Library, for Lenin was disturbing other sections. He began to translate into Russian: *On Street Fighting, Advice of a General of the Commune.* Its author, General Cluseret, had first won distinction by the energy with which he had suppressed the revolt of the Paris workingmen in June, 1848. Later he had served with Garibaldi in Italy, then with the North in our

287

own Civil War (where he acquired his generalship). Returning to France he had joined the anarchist, then the socialist movement, becoming a socialist representative in the Chamber of Deputies, and finally a military leader in the defense of Paris during the Commune.

Vladimir Ilyich read everything he could find on military science in peaceful Geneva. He was the only exile who reacted thus to the news of Bloody Sunday. Besides Cluseret, there was Von Clausewitz *On War*, always the favorite authority on strategy in Russia. He "consulted" with Marx and Engels, as was his wont in each new situation, rereading and annotating everything they had written on military matters and on insurrection as an art.

The night-owl Martov had gotten the news earlier than Lenin. He had stayed up all night with his cronies, discussing meager dispatches, waiting for the morning papers. Trotsky, returning from a lecture and a sleepless night on a train, found them at dawn near the *Iskra* office. Their news convinced him that he must leave for Russia at once. More ardent and venturesome and younger than the others (he was now twenty-five), Trotsky was the first to go. In general, the émigrés were slower to recross the frontier in proportion to their age, the length of time they had been settled abroad, and the ardor of their temperaments. Lenin and Martov did not get back until the October amnesty, near the end of the year. Rosa Luxemburg, whose temperament was no less ardent than Trotsky's, was held back by her multiple activities in the German Social Democracy, so that she did not smuggle herself into her native Russian Poland until December. The death of Axelrod's wife detained him so long that by the time he set out, reaction was once more in full sway; he got as far as Finland, whither the others were already fleeing from Saint Petersburg. Significantly, all through the stormy years 1905 and 1906, Plekhanov did not return to his native land at all.

Natalia Ivanovna Sedova had just made the journey from Russia to Geneva in order to join Trotsky there, but the very next morning after the news came she accompanied him to Munich, and then went back to Russia to prepare things so that he might live clandestinely in Saint Petersburg. Her round trip was typical of her lifelong devotion to him as revolutionist and as man. While she went ahead to make arrangements for him Lev Davidovich stayed in Munich with Parvus and they talked themselves into agreement in what was to prove a fruitful partnership for the years 1905 to

1907. Parvus (Alexander L. Gelfand) was ten years Trotsky's senior and enjoyed an enormous reputation as a Marxist writer and political thinker. It fortified the young man's self-confidence, if that were needful, that Parvus should be greatly impressed by his still-unpublished pamphlet, even moved by it to fresh thought on Russia. "Why, events have confirmed your analysis," Parvus told Trotsky. "The twenty-second of January (Bloody Sunday) was that political general strike for which you have been calling, even if it was disguised under a priest's frock . . . All that is necessary now is to add that revolution in Russia may place a workers' government in power."

May place a workers' government in power! thus was outlined Parvus' introduction to Trotsky's pamphlet, and thus conceived the germ of the doctrine of "permanent revolution" which was destined to play such an important part in Trotsky's views and to sway Lenin's actions in 1917.

For the next decade, there would be three more or less clearly defined competing outlooks among Russian Marxists as to the nature and prospects of the coming revolution.

1. *That of the Mensheviks.* The coming revolution was a bourgeois democratic revolution. It would abolish feudalism, clear the ground for the free growth of capitalism, establish a democratic republic, bring the bourgeoisie to power. Under the republic there would be open political life, freedom to propagate socialist ideas, to organize the working class politically and economically and develop in it the culture, experience, self-consciousness and power necessary to prepare, at some future date, a second revolution, a socialist revolution. That revolution could be democratic only when the proletariat should become a majority of the population. But the proletariat in its present condition in this backward land could not dream of taking power, nor should the Social Democratic Party entertain the idea of entering into the provisional government. Since it could not secure the enactment of its own program in so backward a country, it would only compromise its program and itself by taking responsibility for the actions of a bourgeois government. To be revolutionary now meant to fight tsarism, to support the bourgeoisie in its struggle for power, to encourage it and push it and exact from it the promise of a maximum of freedom for the working class.

2. *The view of Parvus and Trotsky:* The first tasks facing the revolutionists were, to be sure, "bourgeois democratic" tasks, i.e. such tasks as had been accomplished in the West by the bourgeois revolutions. But the Russian revolution was taking place "too late"

in history to be a bourgeois revolution: the proletariat was already on the scene as an independent force, so that the two revolutions, the bourgeois democratic and the proletarian socialist, would tend to be "combined" or telescoped into one. Moreover, the Russian middle class was weak and cowardly. Equipped with the theoretical achievements and experiences of its Western socialist brothers and supported by the simultaneously developing peasant rebellion, the proletariat would have to do the job which the bourgeoisie was incapable of doing. "In Russia," wrote Parvus, in his introduction to Trotsky's pamphlet, "only workers can accomplish a revolutionary insurrection. . . . The revolutionary provisional government will be a government of the *workers' democracy.*" Thus the "bourgeois revolution" made by the proletariat, would tend to flow over into a proletarian revolution. "Once the revolution is victorious"—the words now are Trotsky's—"political power necessarily passes over into the hands of the class that has played the leading role in the struggle, the working class." And once in power? They would have to act like representatives of the class for whom they professed to speak: they would have to adopt, even if only in fragments, a working-class governmental policy. The line between their minimum democratic demands and their final socialist program would dissolve. Even if they started with the most modest working-class measures, say the enforcement of an eight-hour day or the obligation of the employers to support the unemployed, the latter would resist and shut down their factories. Would not the government then have to take over the factories? And would this not be a big step toward socialism? In short, wrote Trotsky, "the political supremacy of the proletariat is incompatible with its economic slavery." Similarly, in the rural areas, the proletariat in power would soon be impelled to undertake the collectivization of agriculture. There would be resistance to all these measures, from the enraged bourgeoisie, from the property-minded peasant masses, perhaps foreign intervention. But to offset this last, there was the hope that the Russian revolution would tend to spread to the West, already ripe and overripe, as everyone knew, for a socialist revolution. Thus the proletariat, once in power, might hold onto it and keep the revolution going "in permanence," transforming it from a brief upheaval into a whole epoch of revolution at home and abroad, combining the bourgeois and proletarian revolutions into a single, continuous process, dominated throughout by the proletariat. This "law of combined development," as Trotsky was to call it in his subsequent *History of the Russian Revolution,* he and Parvus now baptized with the name of "the permanent revolution."

3. *Lenin's position* which moved between these two polar extremes. In formulae, Lenin sounded much like the Mensheviks; in spirit he was forever attracted to the Trotskyist pole. With the Mensheviks, Lenin held that the economic level of a country determined whether or not it was ripe for socialist revolution. With the Mensheviks he asserted categorically that economically, politically, and culturally, Russia was ripe only for a bourgeois-democratic revolution. But with Trotsky and Parvus he held that the bourgeoisie was too weak and cowardly to be trusted to accomplish their own revolution, so that the leading role would likely fall to the proletariat. With Trotsky, too—and here we come to the dividing line in practical conduct—Lenin held that the Social Democratic Party must strive directly for a share in the political power, must strive to enter any provisional revolutionary government that might arise in the course of the struggle, and must strive to determine the policy of that government.

But how then could the revolution be kept democratic? For Lenin, in those days, was a convinced democrat, and the problem of political freedom concerned him deeply. Not only in those days, but until he seized power in 1917. "Not a single socialist," he wrote for instance in 1914, "unless he decides to pronounce the questions of political freedom and democracy as of no consequence to him, in which case, of course, he ceases to be a socialist . . ." His writings are full of such earnest avowals, and there can be no doubt of their sincerity. Even in 1917, he countenanced a "temporary" minority dictatorship in Russia only because he was convinced that the Russian example in the midst of war would end the war on all fronts by worldwide revolution, thereby solving the problems of Russia's backwardness by a solution on a world scale.

"But how then could the revolution be kept democratic?" Lenin asked anxiously in 1905. If the Social Democratic Party must strive directly to share in the power, to enter into any provisional revolutionary government that might arise in the course of the struggle, how could that government be prevented from degenerating into a minority dictatorship of the proletariat in a country where the proletariat itself was a hopeless minority? Here is where he differed sharply from Trotsky and Parvus. He answered his question to his own satisfaction by categorically rejecting the Trotsky-Parvus formula of a "labor government" or a "socialist government" or a "dictatorship of the proletariat." No, he was in favor of a democratic government by the vast majority of the Russian people. To insure this he advocated not a labor government but a two-class, or more than two-class, government, constituted by two parties or more than two parties. For this he coined the formula: "the democratic dictatorship of the proletariat and the peasantry." This was to be a coalition government of proletariat (through the Social Democracy), peasantry (through some peasant party, perhaps the Social Revolutionaries) and of the democratic sections of the bourgeoisie (through some bourgeois democratic party like the Constitutional Democrats). He regarded the peasantry as a "petty bourgeois class," the most revolutionary, though not necessarily the only revolutionary, section of the bourgeoisie. If a coalition government could be formed with them, with or without the collaboration of the "urban, democratic, petty bourgeoisie," such a government would be a temporary dictatorship against the Tsar's supporters, but only in the sense that every revolutionary government in history has been such. It would be a "democratic dictatorship" because it would represent the will of the overwhelming majority of the population, and could give rise to a genuine democracy as soon as the emergencies of civil war were over and the provisional government had given way to a constituent assembly which would draft a new constitution and create a new constitutional democratic government.

Hence, when Parvus wrote on behalf of himself and Trotsky: "The provisional revolutionary government will be a Social Democratic one . . . with a Social Democratic majority," Lenin answered sharply:

> That cannot be! It cannot be because a revolutionary dictatorship can endure for a time only if it rests on the enormous majority of the people . . . The proletariat constitutes a minority. It can only command a mighty overwhelming majority if it unites with the mass of the semi-proletarians, the semi-property owners . . . Such a composition will naturally reflect itself in the composition of the revolutionary government . . . It would be extremely harmful to yield to any illusions in this regard . . . Anyone who attempts to achieve socialism by any other route will inevitably arrive at the most absurd and reactionary conclusions, both economic and political.

Later that same year, Lenin returned to the attack on Trotsky and Parvus in almost identical language. He spoke of their view as

> . . . the absurd, semi-anarchist view that the maximum program, the conquest of power for a socialist revolution, can be achieved immediately. The present degree of econo-

mic development of Russia—an objective condition—and the degree of class consciousness and organization of the broad masses of the proletariat—a subjective condition indissolubly connected with the objective condition—make the immediate, complete emancipation of the working class impossible. Only the most ignorant people can ignore the bourgeois character of the present democratic revolution. Only the most naive optimists can forget how little as yet the masses of the workers are informed of the aims of socialism and of the methods of achieving it. And we are all convinced that the emancipation of the workers can only be brought about by the workers themselves; a socialist revolution is out of the question unless the masses become class-conscious, organized, trained and educated by open class struggle against the entire bourgeoisie. In answer to the anarchist objections that we are delaying the socialist revolution, we shall say: we are not delaying it, but are taking the first steps in its direction, using the only means that are possible along the only right path, namely the path of a democratic republic. Whoever wants to approach socialism by any other path than that of political democracy will inevitably arrive at absurd and reactionary conclusions both economic and political.

"Whoever wants to approach socialism by any other path than that of political democracy, will inevitably arrive at the most absurd and reactionary conclusions . . ."

Fateful, prophetic warning!

Ineluctably, it calls to mind that other prophetic warning which Trotsky had leveled at Lenin the year before. Indeed, the two warnings have an organic connection with each other, for Trotsky's had been a prevision of the dangers of minority dictatorship within the Party, while Lenin's was a prevision of the dangers of minority dictatorship within the State. To perceive the organic connection between the two prophecies, we need only ask the question: *what if the Party should become synonymous with the State?* With such a party ruling such a state, would not the two dangers reinforce each other and become one?

To perceive that connection in all its rigor, let us restate the pregnant syllogism, with the missing link in its place:

Trotsky's Warning: "The organization of the Party will take the place of the Party itself; the Central Committee will take the place of the organization; and finally, the Dictator will take the place of the Central Committee."

Connecting Link: "The Party will take the place of the government."

Lenin's Warning: "Whoever wants to approach socialism by any other path than that of political democracy, will inevitably arrive at the most absurd and reactionary conclusions, political and economic."

Thus, in 1904 and 1905, did the two future collaborators solemnly admonish each other of the dangers of minority dictatorship in the Party and the State. Who can doubt in the light of subsequent events that each of them at that moment had a brilliant prophetic vision of the dangers in the other's approach? But when they joined forces in 1917, each withdrew his warning against the other. Trotsky accepted Lenin's party machine; Lenin accepted Trotsky's "absurd, semi-anarchist view that the conquest of power for a socialist revolution can be achieved immediately," and Trotsky's conception of a minority "proletarian dictatorship," or more accurately, a single-party dictatorship. This fusion was the most natural in the world, for there is an indubitable structural and psychological connection between minority dictatorship in the Party and minority dictatorship in the State. Both are based upon the same assumption: namely, that a self-selected élite or vanguard, properly armed with expert knowledge (Marxism), and properly credentialed by a lifetime of experience and devotion, can dispense with the toilsome and hazardous democratic process, and still avoid the "absurd and reactionary conclusions," the dangers of "personal dictatorship," the pitfalls of totalitarianism, and the corrupting potentials of absolute power.

Thus, from 1905 to 1917, while there were two conceptions of party organization: Lenin's on the one hand, and that of Trotsky and the Mensheviks on the other, there were three conceptions of the nature of the coming revolution: the Menshevik at the one extreme; the Trotsky-Parvus or Trotskyist at the other; with the Leninist moving between them. The two extremes had a tidy air of logical consistency that was lacking to Lenin's intermediate view. The latter's apparent inconsistency was due to the conflict between his inherited Marxist formulae, which he shared with the Mensheviks, and the power-centered, self-confident, revolutionary will which he possessed in common with Trotsky.

But there was yet another reason for the lack of logical completeness in Lenin's formula: he was deliberately leaving one question open and unanswered. His whole conception was provisional in character. The "democratic dictatorship of the proletariat and the peasantry" of which he spoke was not a formula for a post-revolutionary government, but a formula for a "provisional revolutionary government." Its mission was to conduct the revolution, call a constituent assembly into being, and then let the constituent assembly decide upon a constitution and form of government. Once that was done, the provisional revolutionary dictatorship would hand over power to the new constitutional government.

When the Mensheviks reproached him with treason to Marxist orthodoxy by his proposal that a Marxist party should enter into a coalition government with the bourgeoisie, he answered: I am not talking of the permanent government of the new bourgeois democratic republic, but of the *provisional revolutionary government* of the period of revolution itself:

> The constituent assembly has to be convened by someone, he explained to the Mensheviks in his major work for 1905, *Two Tactics:* Someone must guarantee the freedom and fairness of the elections. Someone must invest such an assembly with full power and force. Only a revolutionary government which is the organ of an uprising can in all sincerity desire this and be capable of doing everything to achieve this . . .
>
> However—he adds, approaching closely to the Mensheviks once more, and giving a severe glance in the direction of Trotsky—the evaluation of the importance of the provisional government would be incomplete and erroneous if the class nature of the democratic revolution were lost sight of . . . This democratic revolution in Russia will not weaken, but will strengthen the domination of the bourgeoisie.

The last sentence seems to promise quite unequivocally that once the constituent assembly has done its work and the new, bourgeois democratic constitution is adopted, the Social Democratic Party will step out of power and go over to the position of an opposition struggling for the preparation of the next revolution, its own socialist revolution.

But on this point, the usually so precise Lenin grows indefinite. His forecast changes from page to page and from article to article, becomes a restless spark leaping up and back between the fixed points of his dogmas and his will. It is no longer a formula but a series of rival hypotheses, competing *perhapses:*

Perhaps "bourgeois domination" will indeed be strengthened, as he has just so categorically said, and there will be nothing to do but to go over to opposition.

Or perhaps the "provisional revolutionary government" will

achieve such miracles—are not revolutions the locomotives of history?—that another path may open out before it. Perhaps from the seats of power it may so transform the countryside, so expedite the organization and consciousness of the proletariat, release such revolutionary energies in the West, that the revolution in Russia may become the starting point of a whole era of revolution. (Now he is not frowning at Trotsky any more!)

The first "perhaps," part of his common heritage with the Mensheviks, is generally uppermost in *Two Tactics* and in all Lenin's writings between 1905 and 1917. But the second "perhaps," part of that charge of revolutionary will which he possesses in common with Trotsky, and in higher measure than Trotsky or any other man in Russia, pops out sometimes in language that is indistinguishable from that of Trotsky and Parvus:

> From the democratic revolution—Lenin wrote in *Proletarii* on September 14, 1905—we shall at once, according to the degree of our strength, the strength of the class-conscious and organized proletariat, begin to pass over to the socialist revolution. We stand for permanent revolution. We shall not stop halfway.

Recent translations by the Marx-Engels-Lenin Institute of this passage have attempted to conceal the identity of terminology with that of Trotsky and Parvus by substituting for the technical Marxian term "permanent revolution" the words "continuous revolution." (*Selected Works*, Vol. III, p. 145, and the Institute's *Lenin: A Political Biography*, p. 84.) Much as if some translator of Einstein would try to conceal his relation to Newton by substituting for the technical term "force of gravity" the words "force of heaviness"!

In short, Lenin's real answer to the question: what happens after we get power? is *Let's take power and then we'll see*. This readiness to "take power and then see" is the real core of "Leninism," separating him by an abyss from the Mensheviks, and blurring to the vanishing point the dogmatic line which divided him from Trotsky. "The seizure of power," he would write in 1917, "is the point of the uprising. Its political task will be clarified after the seizure." No one but Lenin among the Marxists could have written such a sentence. So, too, the last theoretical article he would ever write in his life would take as its text his favorite adage from Napoleon: *On s'engage, et puis . . . on voit*. Published in January, 1923, when he was already near death's door, it was his final attempt to answer the Menshevik reproach that he had seized power in a country unripe for socialism and in the name of a class insufficiently advanced in culture and organization to exercise power.

To Marx it might have seemed that "the forms of the state are rooted in the material conditions of life," that "the economic structure of society . . . independent of men's will . . . determines the general character of the social, political and spiritual processes," and that "no social order ever disappears before all the productive forces for which there are room in it have been developed." But to Lenin's political-power-centered mind, for all his Marxist orthodoxy, such formulae were intolerable fetters unless subject to the proper exegesis. And the exegesis literally turned Marx on his head until the Marxist view that "in the last analysis economics determines politics" became the Leninist view that, with enough determination, power itself, naked political power, might succeed wholly in determining economics.

In practice, the Menshevik view tended to fix Marxist formulae into dogmatic fatality, paralyzing the will to power and the very capacity to appeal to the masses when they were in an insurrectionary mood. In theory, Lenin's whole Marxist training and body of doctrine led him to accept the same formulae as Martov and Axelrod. He was as ready as they to give honest, unblinking recognition to the backwardness of Russia's economy, to the possibilities of its continued rapid expansion under a freer capitalism. He warned even more forcefully than they of "the absurd and reactionary" consequences inherent in minority dictatorship. And yet . . . And yet, the formula so piously repeated sat ill in his soul. It was modified by the concentration on power which had led him to form his hierarchical, power-centered organization. It was modified by the concentration on conspiracy and armed insurrection that had set him to studying Cluseret and von Clausewitz. It was modified by his Russian heritage of voluntarism from Pestel, Tkachev, Bakunin, Nechaev, the *Zemlya i Volya* and *Narodnaya Volya*. It was modified by his revolutionary impatience and longing, by his life-long absorption in the machinery of power, and the seizure of power. He did not expect to live to see the day when power would fall into his eager hands, but if that day should come to him, there could be no doubt but that he would repeat with Napoleon: *On s'engage, et puis . . . on voit.*

Thus when Trotskyists and Stalinists, after Lenin's death, would contest the heritage of the Master and comb his writings for confirmatory texts, it would be as possible to find scriptural authority for the one view as for the other. The Mensheviks, too, would be able to find ground for reproaching him for having abandoned what "once he so well knew" and so categorically asserted in common with them.

What actually happened would not fully justify any one of the three positions. History, a sly and capricious wench, would show that she had yet other tricks up her sleeve. The unity of all oppositional forces would indeed suffice to overthrow the Tsar and set up a democratic republic (the formula of the Mensheviks plus Lenin). But Lenin, who in 1905 had been in favor of entering a "provisional revolutionary government," would refuse to enter: and the Mensheviks, who had regarded such a coalition with the bourgeois parties as impermissible "ministerialism" or opportunism, would take a leading part in the Provisional Government. Further, revolutionary will and a power-centered party organization would suffice to overthrow the republic and set up a minority dictatorship (the formula of Trotsky). But it would not suffice to bring into being a world revolution and a socialist society (the further expressed calculation of Trotsky and Parvus, and the unformulated hope of Lenin). In short, History—with that capital H which these men who knew her every intention were prone to use—would decide neither for Axelrod-Martov, nor for Trotsky-Parvus, nor for Lenin-Trotsky, but for yet another variant, undreamed of by any, the chief embodiment of which would be that third one of our protagonists, Joseph Stalin, whom we are shortly to introduce into our story.

And Parvus in 1917? His strange destiny by then will have carried him far from the others. A Russian Jew of the generation of Lenin—he was born a year earlier—A. L. Gelfand (Helfand) was a cosmopolitan internationalist, at home wherever fortune drew him. He had emigrated from Russia at the beginning of the nineties, soon abandoning the ingrown Russian émigré colony to acquire fame under the pen-name of Parvus in the German Social Democracy. There, at the side of Rosa Luxemburg, he fought for a left-wing revolutionary position against the growing bureaucratic stiffening, centralism and opportunism of the German official leadership. He wrote articles for *Neue Zeit*, edited the *Saechsische Arbeiterzeitung*, founded a paper of his own, characteristically called *Aus der Weltpolitik*. His most important writings—*On the World Market and the Agrarian Crisis, General Strike, Russia and the Revolution, Colonial Policy, Socialism and the Banks*—show the scope and bent of his interests. He dreamed constantly of turning his knowledge of economics and world affairs to "practical account" in some colossal speculation which might make him a fortune to found a "great daily of revolutionary Marxism to be published in three languages." In 1904, as agent for the performance of Gorky's "Lower Depths" in Germany, Parvus made 60,000 marks "for the movement," but did not turn over a cent. Bebel and Kautsky hushed the scandal. (See report of Ladyshnikov, summarized in 3d Rn. ed. Lenin, VIII, p. 494).

The year 1905 revived Parvus's interest in Russia and he hastened to follow Trotsky there. Together they edited the Menshevik legal organ, *Nachalo,* deflecting the Menshevik schemata in the direction of their views. Parvus took over the tiny *Russkaya Gazeta,* turning it into a journal with hundreds of thousands of readers. Both Parvus-Trotsky papers gained much larger circulations than the legal Bolshevik organ, *Novaya Zhizn,* founded by Minsky and Gorky, then taken over by Lenin. The low price of their paper, one kopek, the business skill and journalistic flair of Parvus, the extremism of Parvus and Trotsky ("down with the Tsar, up with a Labor Government," "permanent revolution"), the mounting personal prestige of Trotsky, made theirs the most popular of legal revolutionary journals.

Banished to Siberia in 1906, Parvus, like Trotsky, soon escaped to Western Europe. From 1910 to 1914 he was in the Balkans as correspondent for the German Socialist press. Here he became interested in the "Young Turk" movement and wrote for its paper. In that world of tangled intrigue, Parvus's knowledge of affairs made him the adviser of diplomats, politicians, businessmen, government officials—a role he hugely enjoyed and profited from. One day, a tip picked up from a Turkish official in a Constantinople café and turned over by him a few minutes later to a speculator at another table in the same café, started Parvus on the road to wealth. The "Little Balkan War" of 1912 found him trafficking in war supplies. The Great War of 1914 expanded his traffic, his wealth and his flare for intrigue in proportion. In 1915, he went from Constantinople to Stockholm, where he made money in coal and steel and other supplies needed by wartime Germany. He tried to renew his collaboration with Lenin, Trotsky and Rosa Luxemburg, but all three refused to have anything to do with him. The paper which he founded, *Die Glocke,* combined the criticism of opportunism and reformism with "revolutionary" support of German arms. This he justified after his fashion by asserting that the German armies would shatter tsarism, unleashing a revolution in Russia which would in turn make possible a revolution in Germany and the birth of a democratic, socialist German republic. Thus he completed the swing from Left Wing conscience jogger to that of a most subtle revolutionary apologist for the Right Wing of the German Social Democracy in its support of the war.

When, in 1917, the charge was made that Lenin had been sent back to Russia as a German agent, the enigmatic figure of Parvus loomed in the background as the alleged go-between. It is almost the last we hear of A. L. Helfand-Parvus, except that, after Lenin's rise to power, this revolutionary speculator made one more attempt to act as "broker," for an alliance between the German Social Democracy ruling in Germany and the Communist Party ruling in Russia. When that "deal" fell through, he applied to the Soviet Government for repatriation to Russia, stating that he was willing to accept the judgment of its tribunals on his career and to take any work assigned to him. His grown son, who applied at the same time, was admitted to Russia but he was refused. Thereafter he stuck pretty closely to his business affairs, taking time out to advise Social Democrat Ebert, who had become president of the German Weimar Republic, and to make generous donations to German socialist papers. In 1924, the year of Lenin's death, he too died of the same cause, the bursting of a blood vessel in the brain.

But we must return to Leon Trotsky. In February, 1905, he crossed the frontier into the region he knew best, the Ukraine, where he took up a hunted existence in Kiev. As a "retired corporal," as an "eye patient" in a hospital directed by a sympathetic doctor, and under various other guises from various hiding places, he wrote articles, issued leaflets, sought contact with such strikers and revolutionists as he could find. One of the latter turned out to be the engineer, Leonid Krassin, of the Bolshevik Central Committee, a man of organizing genius who continued to work as a first-rate technician and factory director while he founded and supervised a clandestine printing plant in the Caucasus, collected funds from wealthy liberals, arranged meetings of secret committees in the most elegant and improbable homes, organized the smuggling of literature and later of arms, and worked in his own laboratory on bombs. One of Krassin's dreams was to perfect a pocket bomb "the size of a walnut" with the explosive power necessary to become a real weapon in street fighting. His other dream was to reunite Mensheviks and Bolsheviks, and such footloose revolutionaries as Trotsky, into a single organization. Despite Lenin's indignation at such "conciliationism," the latter valued this indefatigable, efficient, noiseless organizer most highly.

Now Krassin came to Trotsky's assistance, printed his leaflets in a clandestine printing plant, facilitated his journey to Saint Petersburg, absorbed some of his doctrine of "permanent revolution," and helped introduce it into Bolshevik theses. When scandalized Leninists heard of this, they complained to their chief. But Lenin had already become aware of a new voice in Russia. In his articles, he publicly praised the writings of Parvus. When there were objections to offer, Lenin advanced them with the greatest respect. ("We don't stress these little errors out of a desire to nag but because from one to whom much is given, much is also demanded.") Trotsky he was slower to forgive because of the latter's defection in 1903 and the stinging phrases of his blast against Leninist organization views. But Vladimir Ilyich was never one to let resentment stand in the way of recognition of a capable comrade-in-arms. To a complaining Bolshevik he wrote:

"So they are printing Trotsky's leaflets . . . Dear me! There's nothing wrong in that, provided the leaflets are tolerable and have been corrected. I shall also advise the Saint Petersburg Committee to reprint his writings after they have been edited, let's say by you." (Letter of September 14, 1905.)

After Lenin got to Saint Petersburg and could watch Trotsky at work, in mass meetings and in the Council of Workingmen's Delegates, he was ungrudging in his recognition that his erstwhile disciple had grown up and could now teach him as well as be taught by him. Indeed, in 1905 the master would learn more from the former disciple than the disciple from the master, for 1905 would be Trotsky's year.

In Saint Petersburg, Trotsky lived with the passport of a landowner, working under the name of "Peter Petrovich." "Peter Petrovich" found the local movement fighting under second-string leaders and nameless rank-and-filers, while the top leadership of both Social Democratic factions still continued to remain abroad. In increasing demand as a swift, clear-headed thinker, a writer of short, trenchant leaflets with a spark of fire in them, an amazingly eloquent speaker, he enjoyed the advantages of his interfactional position in the midst of a newly awakening mass of workingmen. These knew nothing of the old controversies and cooperated with each other—regardless of the faction they chanced to enter into, regardless, too, of the continuing émigré feuds and long-distance paper instructions. Working through Krassin with the Bolsheviks, Trotsky at the same time assumed leadership of the local Menshevik group. Thus the Petersburg Mensheviks began noticeably to follow policies which set them into opposition to the views of Axelrod, Martov and Martynov, and which elicited Lenin's praise.

There was the inevitable police agent among them, one Dobros-

kok, nicknamed "Gold-spectacled Nikolai." Natalia Ivanovna was
soon arrested at a secret May Day meeting in the woods. One by
one other active workers were picked up. "Peter Petrovich," known
by sight to the gold-spectacled spy, left for the comparative peace
and safety of a summer resort in nearby Finland. There he spent
several peaceful, solitary months, reading, writing, thinking through
his views, watching the course of events. The September-October
strike brought him back to Saint Petersburg, this time under the
name of "Yanovsky," reminiscent of the Yanovka in which he was
born.

While unknown men of the masses inside Russia were leading
strike waves, peasant insurrections, mutinies in the armed forces,
in closest cooperation between adherents of menshevism, bolshevism and the Social Revolutionary Party, the leaders in exile continued their battle of factions. When Father Gapon reached Geneva,
he tried to use his prestige to unite all revolutionary parties.

> Being first of all a revolutionist and a man of action—
> he wrote in an "open Letter"—I summon all the socialist
> parties to enter immediately into agreement and to begin
> the business of armed uprising against tsarism . . . Bombs
> and dynamite, terror by individuals and by masses—every-
> thing which may contribute to the national uprising. The
> first aim is the overthrow of the autocracy. The provisional
> revolutionary government will immediately proclaim am-
> nesty for all fighters for political and religious freedom,
> immediately arm the people, and immediately convoke a
> constituent assembly on the basis of universal, equal, secret
> and direct suffrage . . . Every delay or dispute is a crime
> against the people whose interests you are defending . . .

A Social Revolutionary woman came to Lenin to tell him Gapon
wanted to see him. The interview was arranged for late at night in
a café—"neutral territory." Unlike Plekhanov, who was cold to
Gapon, saying, "No good can come of a priest," Lenin was excited.
To him Gapon promised more instruction than thousands of letters
from backward workers; he was a part of the living revolution,
expressing the million-headed illusions, the new-found enlightenment and wrath.

The interview left Lenin with no doubt as to the priest's sincerity. "I said to him," he told Krupskaya on his return, "don't you
listen to flattery, little father; study, or that's where you'll find yourself—and I pointed under the table." That was typical for Lenin:
in that sentence was his faith in the power of the classics to illu-

mine, his dislike of flattery, his eagerness to utilize and train all those who showed promise. Father Gapon dutifully took up the works of Plekhanov, which—despite his differences with the latter— Lenin had recommended. The ex-priest tried to penetrate the mysteries of dialectical materialism, revolutionary disputations and feuds, but they seemed to him utterly alien to the force which had caught him up and flung him into the camp of uprising. He spent more time learning to ride and shoot. Distinguished gentlemen and ladies lionized him; famous world newspapers sent representatives to interview him and buy articles from him; funds poured into his hands for the purchase of arms.

On April 2, representatives of eighteen socialistic parties were summoned together by his "open letter." The list will serve to give us some notion of the state of the revolutionary movement at that moment. There were Social Revolutionaries, Bolshevik and Menshevik Social Democrats, the Polish Socialist Party, the Social Democratic Party of Poland and Lithuania, the Polish Socialist Party "Proletariat," the Jewish Socialist Bund, Armenian Social Democracy, Armenian Revolutionary Federalists (Dashnakists), White-Russian Socialist *Hromada*, Lettish Social Democratic League, Lettish Social Democratic Labor Party, Finnish Labor Party, Finnish Party of Active Resistance, Georgian Socialist Federal Revolutionaries, Ukrainian Socialist Party, Ukrainian Revolutionary Party, Lithuanian Social Democratic Party.

Gapon came to the meeting with an exalted conception of his role as a leader. He was to be a channel to unite all these rivulets into one mighty torrent to overwhelm the Tsar. But the Social Democratic delegates came full of suspicions concerning the language of his call with its mention of "dynamite and bombs." The Lettish Social Democratic Labor Party entered the hall only to deliver an ultimatum. The Lettish Social Democratic League, they said, was non-existent in their land and its so-called representative must be excluded or they themselves would withdraw. When, after an interminable wrangle, their demand was rejected, they walked out and with them walked out the Jewish Bund, the Bolsheviks, and the Armenian Social Democrats, all before the conference had so much as begun. Poor Gapon! This was quite another matter from simple indignation and the calling down of God's curse on the head of the Tsar.

Gapon's role dwindled steadily. Not at home in the emigration, this "revolutionist and man of action" engaged in gun-running, chartering in England the ship *John Grafton*, with a load of arms. Gapon found that Lenin had the best smuggling apparatus and it was the Bolsheviks, through either Litvinov or Krassin, who supplied him with a passport and addresses in Petersburg. But the *John Grafton*, which was to land its arms on a frontier island, ran aground, then blew up near the Finnish coast. The former mass leader was lost as an isolated, hidden and hunted man of the underground. Without the stimulus of crowds, he was reduced to nullity. Returning to Russia, he reentered the service of the police. In April 1906, his body was found hanging from the rafters of a little cottage at Ozerky. The masses who still revered him believed that the police had murdered him. Years later it came out that Pincus Rutenberg, the Social Revolutionary who, together with Gapon, had led the fateful January march and then helped him to escape and flee Russia, had been solicited by him to become a police spy. Aided by workers who had marched with Gapon, Rutenberg had personally directed his execution. Rutenberg's subsequent career included an official post under Kerensky, prison under the Bolsheviks, voluntary exile, service with a British electric company in Palestine, and a number of years as a leading Zionist. Gapon's life and Rutenberg's and Parvus's are alike symbols of the bizarre complexity of the pattern through which we are trying to follow a few guiding threads.

As the archaeologist attempts to reconstruct from a few shards the whole of a vanished civilization, so Lenin was forever on the lookout for the slightest clues that might lead him to an understanding of the Russian peasant. Knowing that Father Gapon was of peasant origin and had retained much of the mentality of a muzhik, Lenin observed him most attentively. Almost accidentally, as Krupskaya reports it, Vladimir Ilyich made his first real discovery of the peasant as a concrete revolutionary force through this intercourse with Gapon. Not that the most Russian of Russian Marxists had ever left the peasantry out of his calculations: more than any other Social Democratic leader he had kept them steadily in mind. But he had thought of them up till now as a class, essentially conservative in character, which would have to be set in motion by extremely moderate slogans, which he and his fellow-revolutionaries would have to invent and indoctrinate into them. As in dealing with workingmen he had found it fitting to go from such petty beginnings as fines and hot water for tea to the larger general ideas of class struggle and socialism, so by analogy he conceived that the peasant could only be moved in the beginning by some petty, elementary demand. For this purpose he hit upon the *otrezki*, lands formerly worked by the serfs but kept by the landlords during the Emancipation. Since no other Marxists had any definite ideas on the question, Lenin had succeeded in getting the demand for the return of the *otrezki* written into the program adopted by the Second Congress. The trouble with this was that the Russian peasant was by nature an extremist. The very rhythms of his life were determined by the severe alternations of the Russian climate, which for many months of the year prevents any useful outdoor work at all, then calls for prolonged bursts of extraordinary effort. So too his social history was a record of long periods of abject passivity alternating with extreme attempts to turn the world upside down.

One day Father Gapon came to the Ulyanovs to read the text of his latest manifesto. "We do not need a Tsar," it said. "Let there be but one master on earth: God. And you will all be His tenants." Vladimir Ilyich laughed heartily, much to the priest's discomfiture. But beneath the unfamiliar veil of religious formulary, he recognized the authentic voice of the Russian peasant. It was but a variant of that age-old subversive utterance: "The land is God's and the Tsar's," a saying which left the landowners out of the picture. Only now the Tsar was excluded also.

While Lenin was still pondering this he chanced to come upon Matushenko (a sailor of peasant origin who had escaped from the mutiny of the battleship *Potemkin*), when the sailor was engaged in an apparently heated discussion with Father Gapon. Overhearing their angry voices, Lenin paused to listen. He discovered that they were not arguing but agreeing with each other in a heated denunciation of the Social Democrats for the miserable character of their agrarian program. They were denouncing one of Lenin's proudest contrivances: the demand for the return of the *otrezki*. "No!" he heard them shouting, "not the cut-off pieces, but *all* of the land to the muzhiks!" With only such pitifully meager evidence to go by, this man who lived so far away from his country but was so close to it in spirit, humbly recognized that his pet peasant plank was hopelessly inadequate. He decided to seize the first opportunity to change the program so as to include in it a demand for the nationalization of all the land, and its renting out by the state or its distribution integrally to the peasants. That same summer he called a congress abroad, which was attended only by the Bolsheviks. He had no trouble in getting them to drop his *otrezki* in favor of "all the land." A year later, in a united congress of both Bolsheviks and Mensheviks, he fought in vain to put through the same program.

Lenin had been learning, too, from the merciless bombardment to which his organization views had been subjected by Plekhanov, Trotsky, Parvus, Rosa Luxemburg, Axelrod and Martov. His resolute and tidy mind, reacting as always against the slackness and disorganization of the Russian intellectual, was still attracted to centralism and direction from above. He was still sure that the top leadership was somehow guaranteed to be the most devoted, the most skilled in Marxian science, the most fitted to decide issues and pick subordinates. He still insisted as before that the Central Committee should have the power to select or add to the Local Committees and confirm or reject all local selections. But the mass stirrings in Russia, no less than the bitter debate, had schooled him in the necessity of giving ground on the questions of democracy, the elective principle, the safeguarding of some measure of local autonomy, the right of opposition, the protection of a minority. He felt now that his rigid organization must be loosened up to admit thousands and tens of thousands without such close scrutiny as in the past. In short, his one-sided emphasis on centralism was now reformulated as the bifurcated term: "democratic centralism." How much of democracy and how much of centralism would go into the compound was a question which would be answered differently in differing periods. The time would come when democracy would be once more swallowed up in centralism, but for the moment his problem was to reeducate the "hards" and authoritarian centralists he had indoctrinated and gathered around him, and to persuade them to accept some measure of democracy.

Once more he had recourse to a Party congress, that is, a convention of his own faction posing as the leadership of the entire Party. There he could convince and reorient his own followers, correct the agrarian program, amend the Party constitution to correct the error Martov had written into it as *Article I* at the Second Congress, renew his contact with Russia, put the idea of armed insurrection on the order of business, rearm his faction and the Party for the new day of open mass activity of millions.

"The Congress," Lenin wrote, "must be simple—like a war council—and small in numbers—like a war council. It is a Congress to organize war." Whatever his followers may have thought, he did not mean war against the Mensheviks. It took place in London from April 25 to May 10, 1905, with only Bolsheviks, conciliators and neutrals present. The Mensheviks held a simultaneous "conference" in Geneva.

Lenin prepared for his Bolshevik convention with his characteristic thoroughness, as indeed, he had need. The "Leninists" he him-

self had trained in centralism, professional revolutionism and
"hardness" had learned his dinned-in formulae by rote. Many of
them had been attracted by the very authoritarian rigidity of those
formulae. Now, in the name of "the traditions of Bolshevism" and
"true Leninism," they resisted all his sweeping proposals for change.
Lenin would have to refight this ominous battle again and again
at every critical juncture in the history of his party, for, while it was
easy to teach definite formulae, it was not easy to impart the spirit
of realistic flexibility with which he himself approached the changing world. What would happen to a party thus nurtured when its
authoritative leader was not present, or when his voice should be
stilled forever? But since, as Freud has put it, "in the unconscious
every one of us is convinced of his immortality," it never occurred
to Lenin to pose such a question.

To him, the organization changes he now advocated were important not so much to meet the Menshevik criticisms half way as
to prepare the Party for open public life and imminent revolution.
For months he had been firing away at the premature sclerosis
which seemed to have taken possession of the Bolsheviks in Russia.

> Really, I often think that nine-tenths of the Bolsheviks
> are really formalists—reads a typical letter—. . . One must
> recruit among the youth more magnanimously and boldly,
> more boldly and more magnanimously and still more mag-
> nanimously and still more boldly, without fearing them.
> Forget all the old cumbersome ways, the respect for titles,
> etc. . . . Give every subordinate committee the right, with-
> out many conditions, to write leaflets and distribute them
> (it is no great misfortune if they make breaks: we will
> "gently" correct them in *Vpered*) . . . The events them-
> selves will teach *in our spirit* . . . Organize, organize and
> once again organize, hundreds of circles, push the usual
> hierarchical committee follies entirely into the background.
> It is wartime . . . Else you will perish with the honors of
> Komitetchiki ["Committeemen"—the word of scorn in later
> years would become *Aparatchiki*, "Apparatus Men"] with
> the official seal imprinted upon you . . . [Letter of February
> 4, 1905.]

At the Congress his forebodings turned out to be more than justified. He stormed at his erstwhile followers, took the floor again
and again and again, employed irony, ridicule, indignation, interrupted others while they were speaking, made a general nuisance
of himself.

> I could not sit still—he explodes at one point—and hear it said that there are no workers available who are fit to be committee members. The question is being postponed. Plainly there is a sickness in the Party . . .

At another point:

> The Party does not exist for the Party Council, but the Party Council for the Party . . . In all constitutional lands the citizens have the right to express lack of confidence in this or that official or official body. This right cannot be taken from them . . . Who is the judge in the handling of a dispute between the Party Council and the Local Committees . . . Under free political conditions our Party can and will be built completely on the principle of election . . . Even under absolutism the application of the electoral system in much greater measure than at present would have been possible . . .

His old followers could not recognize him! Almost single-handed he succeeded in introducing a number of sweeping changes into the Party Constitution. The first was of course the repeal of Section 1, the celebrated "loose" definition of membership which Martov had succeeded in putting through at the Second Congress. But the others were all in the spirit of those who had been his critics at that Congress: the safeguarding of the autonomy of the locals against Central Committee alteration of their composition; approval of the widespread introduction of the electoral principle; the protection of minorities; their right to oppose and criticize the Central Committee; their right to issue oppositional literature and have it circulated by the Party smuggling apparatus, provided one-sixth of the locals requested it.

But when Lenin pointed out that at this Congress of the "party of the proletariat" there was only one delegate who had ever worked in industry, and he proposed to pump fresh blood into the local organizations by making mandatory a majority of working-men on each local committee ("I would greatly favor a rule that in our committees for every two intellectuals there should be eight workingmen") his astonished following of professional revolutionaries or *komitetchiki* voted down his proposal as impractical, and likely to dilute the revolutionary clarity of the Bolshevik organization. Vladimir Ilyich was in a towering rage, which diminished only after a few days of reflection had persuaded him that the bubbling, overflowing life that was churning up the stagnation of ages would likely wash this incrustation away also.

The Mensheviks, too, were almost wholly professional revolu-

Lenin as a student in Samara 1893

Trotsky at eighteen

Trotsky when arrested as chairman of Petersburg Soviet

Trotsky at the time of his last exile by Stalin

Father Gapon, the Police Chief of St. Petersburg, and members of Gapon's labor union

Stalin's mother

Stalin as a boy of fifteen

Bukharin in 1917

Stalin in 1917

Lenin's family

Portrait of Alexander Ilyich
Ulyanov, Lenin's brother, taken
shortly before he was executed

Lenin as a child

Krupskaya when Lenin first met
her

Lenin in 1895

Martov, Lenin's closest associate
until the split

Plekhanov, Lenin's teacher

(left) Lenin as a teenager.

(right) Lenin after the assumption of power, 1918.

(left) Lenin in Krakow before the onset of World War I.

(above) Stalin at the time he was opposing American "exceptionalism."

(left) Stalin as Field Marshal during World War II.

(right) Stalin applauding himself.

(left) Stalin in his Kremlin office under a picture of Marx.

Leon Trotsky when he was head of the Soviet Army and Navy.

Trotsky in his Mexican exile.

Police pictures of Kamo, hero of the Tiflis holdup

Police pictures of Litvinov at the age of twenty-five (1901)

Police picture of Kras-
sin at age twenty-five

Molotov at
thirty-five

Police picture of
Dzierzinski, founder
of the Soviet secret
police

Police pictures of Roman Malinovsky, Bolshevik leader and agent
provocateur

Tomsky as Soviet Union
Leader

Rykov as Premier

Police pictures of Trotsky at time of first arrest at age nineteen

Police picture of Sverdlov in 1910

Kalinin as "Head" of Government

Stalin, Rykov, Kamenev and Zinoviev in 1925 when they were "The Big Four" ruling Russia

Police pictures of Zinoviev at age twenty-four when first arrested

Police pictures of Kamenev. Date uncertain

Police pictures of Bogdanov taken shortly before he became a member of Lenin's *troika*

Police pictures of A. V. Lunacharsky

Police pictures of Lenin taken after his first arrest

tionary intellectuals, but their theory predisposed them to look upon the new period as one which would bring millions into "public life" and lead to the formation of a "broad, non-partisan or supra-partisan organization of the working masses," out of which a new and broad and truly working class socialist party might grow, to replace the narrow conspirative organization of intellectuals. It was this predisposition of the Mensheviks which gave them a decisive leadership in the Soviet of 1905 and in the new trade unions which sprang up.

On the other subject close to Lenin's heart: the technical prepa-rations for an armed uprising, his followers gave him no trouble. Lunacharsky made the report, but the thought that went into it was largely Lenin's. ("Vladimir Ilyich provided all the essential theses for my report. Further, he insisted that I should write down my entire speech and give it to him to read in advance.")

Why then, it might be asked, did he not make the report him-self? Unlike his successor in the leadership of his party, Lenin was ever anxious to avoid the appearance of one-man rule of personal dictatorship. With more moral authority and less opposition than Stalin would ever know (until the latter had executed all who might challenge him) Lenin sought to maintain the appearance and as far as possible the reality of a collective leadership in his party. When he could prepare a Lunacharsky to give the report on armed insurrection or a Stalin to write on the national question, it seemed to him to be a positive gain in the broadening of the circle of lead-ership. Even when someone opposed Lenin and was defeated by him in debate, he often arranged for his defeated opponent to re-port on the very thing which the latter had opposed. Thus the man's prestige was preserved after defeat, for Lenin knew from bitter experience how hard it was to gather together and build up this handful of persons to the stature of revolutionary leadership, and how easy to tear down and destroy them.

Lenin's other proposals: the new and more sweeping agrarian program; the question of participation in a revolutionary provisional government, like the resolution on armed uprising, went through without serious opposition. For these were measures congenial to the temperament of the men he had been welding together into a faction.

At the Congress, Lenin had to agree to considerable relaxation of control from abroad. The new Central Committee was made up of Lenin, Krassin, Bogdanov, Rykov, Postalovski, with Essen, Rumyantzev and Gusev as alternates. Of all these, only Lenin remained in Geneva as "Foreign Representative" and editor of the official organ, *Proletarii*. Two secretaries were chosen, Krupskaya for the Foreign Center and Stasova for the Russian.

If we are to believe the official Bolshevik biographer Kerzhentsev:

> The small apartment of the Ulyanovs in sleepy petty-bourgeois Geneva was the headquarters of the Russian revolution . . . Each day, Lenin viewed, as it were, the map of military operations of the revolution and gave instructions directing the struggle of the different detachments.

But in actual fact, events were moving so rapidly, and Lenin's knowledge of them, based on Swiss and other West European news dispatches, was so meager and inaccurate, that any attempt to guide things from Geneva with the aid of belated letters and smuggled copies of *Proletarii* had become impossible. Lenin could not even get reports from the busy, self-confident Central Committee members in Russia. On events in the homeland he now exerted no influence at all. Even they, on the spot, were finding it easier to follow the mass upsurge than to direct it. "Ilyich," writes Krupskaya, "became very nervy" (i.e., irritable). He made futile attempts to convince his Central Committee to cross the frontier for a conference with him. Then, the same autumn strike wave that had brought Trotsky back from Finland to Saint Petersburg convinced him that he, too, should and could go to Russia.

Krupskaya followed him and Elena Stasova left Russia for Geneva to keep the "foreign office" open, virtually alone. Before Lenin left, he wrote a friendly, flattering letter to Plekhanov, telling him how essential he was, how the Bolsheviks admired him, how small all past differences were in the face of the great events now transpiring, urging him to return also and become one of the editors of the new "legal" paper which the Bolsheviks were founding. Plekhanov did not answer. By the time Lenin reached Saint Petersburg, the Tsar had been forced to issue a pledge of liberties, a promise of a constitution and a parliament, and an amnesty. It was late November. The great Russian cauldron was boiling over.

CHAPTER XVIII

1905 IN THE CAPITALS

*I would delay the uprising until next Spring. But we shan't
be asked.*   —*Lenin*

LENIN FAILED to get to Russia while the great October general strike
was on. The agent who was to meet him in Stockholm with a
forged passport did not show up. Storms delayed the steamer on
which he wanted to sail to Finland. During the two fateful weeks,
while he fumed and fretted in enforced idleness with even the post
and telegraph on strike so that he could neither send nor receive
word from his followers, the strike wave was spreading over the entire country; Saint Petersburg was setting up its "Soviet" and forging
its leadership in the struggle; critical questions were being settled
without so much as a by-your-leave. Worst of all, his comrades on
the scene were committing blunders in the name of what they conceived to be his teachings, blunders which would deprive his faction of the hoped-for post of leadership at this most crucial moment
in the country's history.

The farther we get from the original documents (and from the
comparatively reliable party histories written while Lenin was still
alive), the more difficult it is to make head or tail out of the famed
Soviet of 1905 and the relations of the Bolsheviks to it. Thus in
Stalin's history of his party (1939) we read:

> As we know, Lenin had not yet arrived in Saint Peters-
> burg; he was still abroad. The Mensheviks took advantage
> of Lenin's absence to make their way into the Saint Peters-
> burg Soviet and to seize hold of its leadership.

If the expression "took advantage of Lenin's absence" reveals the
habits of thought fostered by the Stalin cult of personal dictatorship
and one-man factotumship, the phrase concerning the Mensheviks'
making their way into the Soviet is contrived to conceal completely
the fact that it was the Mensheviks who gave the initial impulse to
the Soviet's formation, while the Bolsheviks at first opposed it as
an unreliable and uncontrollable substitute for the Party. In fact,
during the first few sessions, the Bolshevik Petersburg Committee
went so far as to advocate its boycott!

To understand why the Mensheviks favored, and the Bolsheviks in Russia opposed, the formation of such a general Council of Workingmen's Representatives (the word *Soviet* is merely the Russian word for "Council"), we shall have to go back to a series of theoretical disputes between the two factions that had been going on since their respective conferences of the spring of that year.

Since spring, the Mensheviks under Axelrod's leadership had been groping their way toward two new and related formulations for broader public life in a time of growing revolution. One was a call to Russian workingmen to form a "broad non-partisan labor organization"; the other a call to the entire people to set up in the course of their struggle "local and municipal revolutionary self-governments."

To Axelrod, in whose mind these ideas were born, the underground Social Democratic Party as it had developed in Russia was no labor party in the West European sense at all, but a conspiratorial circle of intellectuals who in principle espoused the cause of the still-unorganized working class, a conspiratorial circle which professed to act in labor's name. The new freedom that was being won in the course of the present struggle, he thought, would at last give the workingmen a chance to come together, form their own trade unions and their own party, select their own leadership, draft their own program, become aware of their own existence and interests as a class. This genuine workingmen's party could then supplant and absorb the narrow, conspirative cadres of professional revolutionary intellectuals, who had hitherto acted in its name and who, *faute de mieux*, had passed themselves off as "the party of the proletariat."

Parallel with Axelrod's advocacy of this "broad labor organization" ran his agitation for the creation of "broad democratic organizations" of the people as a whole. These were to assume the powers of local autonomy and local self-government, seek to displace and challenge the local bureaucratic apparatus, and, in due time, send delegates to an all-Russian congress which would convoke a constituent assembly, or perhaps act as one. Axelrod conceived these by analogy with what had happened in previous revolutions: the Jacobin clubs and Communes of France; the Committees of Correspondence and Continental Congresses in America. For a people without organs of self-expression these "village and municipal revolutionary self-governments" would become means of organizing and expressing the popular will.

While Axelrod was developing these ideas in *Iskra*, Lenin kept subjecting them to ceaseless criticism. He was a Party Man in the strictest sense of that expression. These formulations seemed to him to displace "*the* Party" and abdicate its superior knowledge, its right and duty of assuming a leading role. To him Axelrod's formulations were a mixture of utopian nonsense and downright treason. To the notion of "local revolutionary self-governments" gradually growing into a national congress, he opposed the concept of a centrally led and directed uprising which would call into being a national revolutionary provisional government. This would be made up not of representatives of the unorganized masses and local communes, but of representatives of the already organized revolutionary parties. Under the armed shield of this centralized leading body the constituent assembly would be convoked and the local governments of the future created. Thus Lenin's conception was that of a centralized revolution, which would seize power in the capitals, then create the new local administration from above, while Axelrod's was that of a movement starting from below and culminating in a national representation. For Lenin the Party as it already existed was the leader and directing force and nucleus of rule; to Axelrod it was but a group of volunteers who would now put themselves at the service of broader organizations more truly representative of the working class and the Russian people as a whole.

In Axelrod's "broad, non-partisan, democratic organizations" Lenin scented the heresy of subordinating the Social Democratic Party to the democratic bourgeoisie. And his "broad labor congress" or "labor party" was both senseless and dangerous. Senseless, since no broad organization of labor could be formed until after the autocracy had been overthrown. Dangerous, since to advocate a "non-partisan" (i.e. a multi-partisan or supra-partisan) labor organization was to call in question the fact that the Social Democratic Party had already worked out the true program for the working class. If the Party itself set up broader organizations, these should serve only as a wider sphere for its own operations, a recruiting ground and preparatory school, more muscle behind itself as fist. And if broader organizations should spring up without party initiative, it was the Party's duty to penetrate them, control them, get its program and leadership accepted by them. If it could not win control of the broader organization, then it should destroy the latter as harmful to the true interests and true program of the proletariat.

In this theoretical dispute, neither side foresaw the speedy emergence of the Petersburg General Strike Committee or Soviet of Workingmen's Representatives. They were straining their eyes to see into the future with the aid of the past. But each based himself on a different past. Axelrod kept his eyes fixed on the West: England, Germany and France. His thinking was predicated on the expectation that Russia, too, would go through a democratic capitalist stage after a successful bourgeois revolution, and that all its local communities and its labor movement would eventually develop the tradition of self-government, so far lacking in Russian public life. But Lenin thought rather in terms of the historic Russian revolutionary conspiracy in a land which had been so long centralized that every impulse was wont to come from above. His views were in the tradition of all past Russian movements for reform from the palace coup d'état to the conspiracies of the Narodnaya Volya. All his hopes were concentrated on the speedy victory of a centralized uprising and then the organization and education of the working class and peasantry afterwards, from above, from the vantage point of the summits of power.

Since Axelrod's "Westernizer" views required a long period of development in the tradition of self-government, a tradition which was lacking in Russia, the advantage lay in Lenin's traditional Russianism. It was this that made his simple slogans and proposals so accessible at critical moments to vast numbers of backward but aroused workingmen and—more important for the immediate party struggle—it was this that attracted to his banner the more "Russian" of the Russian revolutionary intellectuals.

If we call the roll of Menshevik and Bolshevik leaders, this "national" difference is immediately revealed. The core of the Bolshevik leadership in 1905 was Lenin himself, a Great-Russian from the heart of the Volga; Rykov, Bogdanov, Krassin, Postalovski —Great-Russians all. But the Menshevik camp was led by Axelrod, Martynov (Piker), Martov (Tsederbaum), Dan (Gurvich), all four of them Russian Jews of Westernized thought. Only Plekhanov and Potresov in the Menshevik top leadership were Great-Russians, and it was the fate of the first to vacillate for years between bolshevism and menshevism, and the second to be forever seeking an alliance between the Social Democracy and Russian liberalism. Indeed, Potresov was a strange anachronism: in temperament a liberal Westernizer of the eighteen forties with a Marxist theoretical equipment.

On the other hand, Trotsky, Parvus and Rosa Luxemburg—all three of them Jewish, and the last two with years of experience and activity in the West European movement—combined a revolutionary temperament with a Westernizing outlook, vacillating between criticism of Lenin's organizational centralism and attraction to his organic Russian revolutionism. In the light of these personal back-

grounds, how fallacious appears the Nazi legend of "Jewish bolshevism." Indeed, the virtues and defects of bolshevism alike come
from its deep roots in the national heritage of Russia, and—despite
all international and Western modification and theoretical embroid-
ery—bolshevism expresses fundamentally the national peculiarities
of the Russian revolutionary tradition.

That centralizing tradition possesses both advantages and dangers. It tends to concentrate initiative and power in a top leadership, even in a single leader, and requires from the rank and file not
so much initiative and understanding and democratic control over
the leadership as loyalty and energy in executing the latter's decisions. To understand enough to grasp the leadership's understanding and expound and act on it, is understanding enough. This gives
the multiplied fighting power of a disciplined army capable of
carrying out orders swiftly and with a minimum of disputation;
it relieves the common man of the painful duty of thinking out
difficult problems; but it leaves the rank and file at the mercy of
an error of the leader, and makes them less capable of reacting
with new appreciations to sudden turns of history, if the leader
happens to be mistaken, or cut off from them.

The Council of Workingmen's Representatives of Saint Petersburg was the child of an unforeseen and unprecedented general
strike. Though its nucleus was formed by Petersburg Mensheviks
and its appearance was in harmony with the idea of initiative from
below that Axelrod had been groping toward, the Soviet was not
called forth by anybody's theoretical formulations, nor could it be
conjured away by boycott or theoretical exorcism. With the flexibility and realism which characterized Lenin whenever he was
faced by important new phenomena, he was quick to realize that
the general strike and the general strike committee it called into
being represented something new and magnificent in Russian life.
But he was cooling his heels in Stockholm, while the distrust he
had inculcated toward broad organizations not controlled by the
Party seemed to his followers to be directed against just such
bodies as this creation of the Mensheviks and non-party masses.
Lenin's last attack on "broad non-partisan labor organizations" and
"local revolutionary self-government" had appeared in the *Proletarii* of October 17—at the very moment when the Soviet was coming into being! On the other hand, all the recent articles of Axelrod,
Dan, Martov and Martynov had predisposed the local Mensheviks
to welcome the Soviet as something which seemed to fit to perfection their two favorite formulae of the moment.

Trotsky, too, hastening back from Finland to participate in the general strike, had brought with him a plan for a representative labor body to run the strike, with one delegate for every thousand workers. When he got off the train at the Finland Station in Saint Petersburg, he learned that the Mensheviks in various factories and unions had proposed such a delegate body (with one delegate for every one hundred workers) and that elections were already taking place.

From the outset, and at all times thereafter, the Mensheviks had a majority of the politically affiliated among the delegates and possessed overwhelming influence in the Soviet. They elected one of their own number, Zborovski, as its first Chairman. A few days later, in pursuance of their own formula of "broad, non-partisanship," they had him step down in favor of the non-party lawyer, Georgii Nosar—better known under the pseudonym of Khrustalev—who inclined toward menshevism. Avksentev was made a vice-chairman for the Social Revolutionaries and Trotsky for the Mensheviks. Before the fifty-day Soviet was over, Trotsky was its outstanding leader. His leadership was primarily due to his exceptional eloquence, his swiftness in forming plans, proposing motions, drafting resolutions, inditing stirring manifestoes, but he was undoubtedly helped by his immediate and unreserved espousal of the Soviet and by his relatively interfactional position.

Lenin's writings have suffered a strange fate. Where every word is sacred, to quote the wrong passage at the wrong time may nevertheless get a man into trouble. Official interpreters stress now one part, now another, as political convenience dictates, explain away what is momentarily or permanently inconvenient by editing and footnotes, go slow with the publication and translation of things they think the canonized leader might better have left unsaid. To this day, two decades after his death, the "Complete Works" are not really complete. Here, for instance, are Volumes VIII, IX and X, dealing with the Revolution of 1905 and containing, supposedly, all that Lenin had to say on the 1905 Soviet. A dozen passages seem to attack the whole idea of the Soviet before it was born, but the document which presents his mind in the noblest and most inspiring light as that of a swift thinker reacting to sudden innovation on the part of history, is not here.[1] Without explanation it was withheld

[1] References here as throughout, are to the Third Russian Edition of Lenin's Collected Works, the most complete so far published. As this book goes to press, various volumes of a Fourth Edition are beginning to appear. In some ways more complete than the earlier editions, it, too, is incomplete. It suppresses certain writings of Lenin which are uncomplimentary to Stalin or in

from publication until 1940, then, once more without explanation, it appeared in the Russian theoretical magazine *Bolshevik*. Was it lost all these years? Was it found suddenly in time for the twenty-third anniversary of the October Revolution? Where? How? Was it withheld because of the vested interests of faction? *Bolshevik* offers no explanation. It is vastly superior to anything else Lenin has written on the Soviet of 1905, to his discussion of the Soviet's exclusion of the anarchists, for example (in which he declares that "the Council of Workingmen's Deputies is not a parliament of labor and not an organ of proletarian self-government, not an organ of government at all but a fighting organization for the achievement of definite aims"). Or to his thesis on the Soviet prepared for the 1906 Congress of the united Social Democratic Party, in which he returns to his old distrust of broad organizations.

From the internal evidence it is clear that this remarkable document, unpublished until 1940, was written in Stockholm early in November, 1905, while Lenin had nothing to go by but foreign press reports and a few issues of Russian newspapers.

> I am giving my views—it begins with becoming modesty and tact—as a "foreigner" still forced to write from the accursed distance, the disgusting "beyond-the-frontier" of the émigré . . . without having seen a single session of the Soviet of Workingmen's Delegates, without having had an opportunity to exchange opinions with my comrades . . . Comrade Radin in *Novaya Zhizn*[2] is wrong to pose the question:
>
> The Council of Workingmen's Delegates *or* the Party. It seems to me that the solution ought to be:
>
> *both* the Council of Workingmen's Delegates *and* the Party . . .
>
> Who conducted the strike and conducted it victoriously? The *entire* proletariat, among whom—fortunately in a minority—there were also Social Democrats. What were the aims pursued by the strike? Economic and political at the same time. The economic aims touch the *entire* proletariat

too obvious contradiction with the present official version of Party history. There has been an especially ruthless suppression of some of the illuminating footnotes prepared by the Marx-Engels-Lenin Institute for the Second and Third Editions.

[2] Radin is the pen name for Knunyantz. His view was the basis of the Bolshevik boycott of the Soviet and then the ultimatum that it recognize the Social Democratic program and "join" the Party. The local Bolshevik leaders changed their mind in two days under the pressure of mass enthusiasm for the Soviet.

. . . the political aims the *entire* people . . . The Soviet ought to *aspire,* to include deputies of *all* the workers, office employees, domestics, unskilled laborers . . . *all those* who want to fight in common . . . all who possess elementary political honesty . . . It does not seem reasonable to me to demand of the Soviet (as the Bolsheviks had just done) the adoption of the Social Democratic program and entrance into the Party . . . Soviet and Party are alike absolutely indispensable . . .

Maybe I am wrong, but it seems to me (on the basis of the incomplete and exclusively "paper" data that I possess) that politically one ought to consider the Soviet as the germ of the *provisional revolutionary government*. It seems to me that the Soviet ought to proclaim itself as quickly as possible as the provisional revolutionary government of all Russia or (what amounts to the same thing under another form) ought to *create* the provisional revolutionary government . . . The Soviet ought to choose a strong nucleus of a revolutionary provisional government and complete it with the representatives of all the revolutionary parties and all the revolutionary democrats . . . We do not fear broadness and difference of shadings . . . rather we desire it, for without the unification of the proletariat and the peasants, without the fighting union of social democrats and revolutionary democrats, complete victory is impossible . . .

In its program ought figure . . . complete realization in fact of the political liberty so hypocritically promised by the Tsar: abolition of all restrictive laws against the freedoms of speech, conscience, press, union, strikes, the suppression of all institutions [such as police, army, censorship] which restrict those liberties . . . convocation of a truly general constituent assembly supported by the free armed people . . . real and complete freedom for oppressed nationalities . . . transfer of all the land to the peasants . . . support of all the measures the peasants themselves have taken to seize the land, formation everywhere of revolutionary peasant committees . . .

The word *Soviet,* which has come to be charged with special meanings and emotional overtones, is, as we have said, merely the Russian word for "council." It is no different in original intention and flavor from the same word when found in our familiar "Central Trades and Labor Council." Had there been such a Central Trades Council already in existence, it might conceivably have taken charge of the Petersburg General Strike. Even then, it would have had to be enlarged by numerous delegations from hitherto unorganized groups, it would have assumed new powers and functions and been transformed from a routine body handling day-to-day union matters into a general staff for an all-inclusive political general strike. When, in the twenties on our own continent, general strikes broke out in Seattle and Winnipeg, the participants found it necessary to displace the workaday Councils by special emergency general strike committees. Labor actions of such magnitude require unified direction. An authority must be created enjoying the confidence of the strikers, empowered to spread or limit the strike, to determine its strategy and tactics. Decisions must be made from hour to hour, even minute to minute. What services shall be continued so that friendly sections of the public and the participating workingmen and their families may suffer as little as possible? What trucking and shipping shall be exempt so that food and milk may be delivered to the workers' homes, so that garbage may be disposed of, hospitals continue in operation? (In Seattle and Winnipeg it was a familiar occurrence to see a garbage truck bearing the placard: "Exempt by decision of the General Strike Committee.") There are some aspects of public order to maintain; strike bulletins must be printed to take the place of struck newspapers; negotiations must be conducted with other sections of labor, with employers, the public, the authorities; aims must be defined and redefined; decisions must be made on behalf of the entire labor movement. In proportion as the strike is truly general must it assume all sorts of communal, public, governmental and quasi-governmental functions. In Russia, the lack of existing union organization, the political character and the all-inclusiveness of the strike, its spread to every industry, trade, profession, branch of public service and to some 120 cities and towns, the centralist tradition which made the whole country look to Saint Petersburg for leadership, the paralysis of government and the revolutionary mood which expressed itself in the ambition to displace the government altogether—all these gave a magnificent sweep to the functions of the Council of Workingmen's Delegates of Saint Petersburg. It was at once general strike committee, communal administration, organizer of nationwide revolt, temporary parliament of labor in particular and the Russian people in general, rival governmental power. With a little more time at its disposal it would have called into being peasant councils (some sprang up during its existence). Before its fall it was dispatching delegates over the countryside to form additional Soviets (scores had sprung up spontaneously; several had assumed complete local governmental powers) and was

issuing a call for an all-Russian Soviet congress. All it lacked was
soldier delegates (sporadically a few of these were already appearing) to become a decisive political power, as in 1917.

This all-national general strike had no parallel in labor history.
Even before October, the year 1905 had been the greatest year of
strikes in the life of Russia (more strikers in one month after
"Bloody Sunday" than in the ten preceding years put together).
Yet, what occurred now took the government, the socialists, the
participants themselves by surprise. A little strike of compositors
in Moscow, demanding a few kopeks more per thousand letters
set, with pay for punctuation marks, spread by spontaneous com-
bustion through the inflammable materials that had been accumulating for many comparatively quiet months. The war had just
ground to a close. Millions of dispirited soldiers were waiting at
railroad sidings to be shipped home and demobilized. Many still
bore arms and nursed grievances that were soon to flare up in military and naval mutinies. The movements of grain for export were
at their height, ships waiting expectant for their freight in the harbors. From printers to bakers to railway shopmen the strike spread;
from shopmen to general railway personnel, until 26,000 miles of
line and 750,000 rail employees were tied up in the space of ten
days. Thereafter, pay for punctuation marks and suchlike economic
demands were lost sight of in the general nature of the strike and
the political aims it set itself. With the stoppage of the railroads,
the whole industry of the country stopped still. Sympathy and
necessity combined to close steel mills, textile mills, metallurgical
factories, industrial establishments of every kind: such was the
strategic nature of railways in the life of a modern country. For
the first time in many decades there was no factory smoke on the
Russian horizon.

Even "middle-class" intellectuals, professional men and liberal
industrialists joined the strike. The Constitutional Democratic
Party, assembled in its first national convention, gave its endorsement. The Union of Unions, made up of intellectuals and professional men of all descriptions, refused to enter law courts, laboratories, hospitals, universities, business offices, government offices,
declaring themselves on strike like ordinary workers. Most of the
employers looked upon the movement with friendly eyes. Some
gave their strikers half pay or full pay. After the strike was over, a
number of industrialists continued to pay wages to delegates from
their factories for the time taken off to attend the further sessions
of the Soviet. Wealthy capitalists contributed most of the money

for the legal Bolshevik daily, *Novaya Zhizn*, the first number of which appeared on November 9, 1905, and for similar Menshevik and Social Revolutionary journals.

No strike in history in any land has ever been as "general" as this one. On the 23rd, the whole of Moscow, Kharkov and Reval were out; on the 24th, Smolensk, Koslov, Yekaterinoslav, Lodz; on the 25th, Kursk, Samara, Poltava; on the 26th, Minsk, Kremenchug, Simferopol, Petersburg. With the entrance of the capital into the strike it assumed a leadership so decisive that we will have to neglect the explosions spreading elsewhere, to concentrate on St. Petersburg and its Soviet.

On the 26th, the day the first delegates to the Council of Workingmen's Deputies were being elected, the strike embraced, besides the factory workers, drug clerks, court clerks, bank clerks. On the 27th, lawyers, doctors and civil service men declared themselves on strike. On the 28th, the employees of post and telegraph, state banks and finance ministry joined the strikers; the *corps de ballet* of the Marinsky theater walked out; house servants, janitors (*dvorniki*), cab drivers, retail clerks and many storekeepers struck. On the Bourse there were neither demands nor offers. Water supply was partially maintained by locking in the workers under armed guard. At night the city was in darkness save for the blinding glare from a solitary searchlight on the Admiralty Building anxiously sweeping the Nevsky Prospekt. For three days there were no newspapers while the city was given over to the wildest rumors. On the 30th, only the official paper of the strikers (the *Izvestia*, or Bulletin of the Council of Workingmen's Delegates) and the official government gazette (*Pravitelstvennie Vestnik*) appeared, the latter printed by soldiers.

The government seemed to have been seized with paralysis. The Tsar's ministers could not even get to him at Peterhof until they secured a river launch. In widely scattered regions of the country, peasants began "joining the strike" by burning manor houses, seizing crops, moving in on lands. Soldiers "joined" by mutinying against the slowness of demobilization, the conditions of service or the unpleasant duties of punitive expeditions.

On October 30 (October 17, Old Style), the Tsar announced a Duma, civil liberties and a constitution. Here is his own account in a letter to his mother:

> You remember, doubtless, those January days—after "Bloody Sunday"—when we were together at Tsarskoe— they were miserable, weren't they? But they are *nothing* in

comparison to what has happened now. . . . It makes me
sick. . . . The Ministers, instead of acting with quick decision, only assemble in council like a lot of frightened hens
and cackle about providing united ministerial action. . . .
One had the same feeling as before a thunderstorm in summer. . . . There were only two ways open: to find an
energetic soldier and crush the rebellion by sheer force.
. . . That would mean rivers of blood, and in the end we
should be where we had started. . . . The other way out
would be to give the people their civil rights, freedom of
speech and press, also to have all laws confirmed by a
State Duma—that would of course be a consititution. . . .
We discussed it for two days and in the end, invoking God's
help, I signed. . . . There was no other way than to cross
oneself and give what everyone was asking for. . . . We
are in the midst of a revolution with an administrative
apparatus apparently disorganized, and in this lies the main
danger. . . .

In such mood, debating the two ways out, accepting the one and
longing for the other, the Tsar signed the Manifesto known as that
of October 17, charging Witte with the task of executing it and
winning the confidence of the people. At the same time there were
in his entourage men who thought they understood his inmost
desires, as once an English king had been understood by those
who murdered Thomas à Becket. Advocates of firmer police rule like
D. F. Trepov and Durnovo went into action at the same time as
Witte, aided by the fact that the Tsar, like Witte, was of two minds.

The next month and a half were known as the Days of Freedom.
More apt would have been, Days of Deadlock. Though the strike
could not long survive the Tsar's Manifesto, the "Strike Committee"
did not cease to function. Though a constitution had been promised and with it all sorts of freedoms, the Autocrat, the police, the
prisons, the censorship, continued to operate. Lenin (still not in
Russia) welcomed as an analysis of "astonishing clarity" Trotsky's
characterization in *Izvestia* of the roles of Witte on the one hand
and Durnovo-Trepov on the other:

So a constitution is granted—wrote Trotsky.—Freedom of
assembly is granted but the assemblies are surrounded by
the military. Freedom of speech is granted, but the censorship exists after as before. Freedom of knowledge is granted,
but the universities are occupied by troops. Inviolability of
the person is granted, but the prisons are overflowing with
the incarcerated. Witte is given us, but Trepov remains to

us. A constitution is given, but the autocracy remains. Everything is given—and nothing is given. . . . The proletariat wants neither the police hooligan Trepov nor the liberal broker Witte—it wants neither the wolf's mouth nor the fox's tail. It does not want a *nagaika* wrapped up in a constitution. [*nagaika*, whip.]

In general, it should be noted that the whole attitude of the Bolsheviks toward Trotsky was changing as it became apparent that this twenty-six-year-old stormy petrel had become the outstanding figure of the Soviet, was writing all the most admirable documents on the spur of the moment, preparing all the most welcome motions, making the most moving speeches, doing much of the quick thinking that guided the life of the Soviet in the face of kaleidoscopic change. When the first number of the Menshevik popular daily, *Nachalo*, appeared, the Bolshevik *Novaya Zhizn* wrote: "We welcome a comrade in the struggle. The first issue is notable for the brilliant description of the October strike written by Comrade Trotsky." And Lunacharsky records in his memoirs that when Lenin heard someone say: "The star of Khrustalov is setting; today the strong man of the Soviet is Trotsky," he responded after a moment: "Well, Trotsky has won this by his tireless and striking work."

A general strike cannot continue indefinitely. At best it can only paralyze a government, but, except it develop into armed insurrection, it cannot overthrow it. Meanwhile, prices rise, food grows scarce, wages cease, the strikers themselves suffer. And men can not live forever at fever heat.

The Tsar's Manifesto (drafted by Count Witte) was calculated to separate the more moderate sections of the population from the compact mass of striking workingmen. It accomplished its purpose. Nor were the strikers themselves exempt from pleasant illusion that they had won the freedom they had been fighting for. In vain did the Soviet leaders, Trotsky in the van, seek to instil in them suspicion of the "*nagaika* wrapped up in a constitution." The day the Manifesto became public, tens of thousands of the celebrating population gathered before the building in which the Soviet was meeting. Trotsky stepped out on the balcony, uttered his ringing warning, then, with his flair for the dramatic, he tore up a copy of the Tsar's Manifesto before their eyes. Tumultuously they cheered the act, yet the strike fever at once began to ebb. On October 31, Moscow called off its strike. Next day the Petersburg Soviet had the good sense to set November 3 as the day for orderly return to the factories. The workingmen, loyal to the end, went back impressively in disciplined ranks on the appointed day and hour.

The Soviet's further strategy was directed to the conquest by direct action of the liberties which had been promised. Their first objective was amnesty. Preceded by crimson banners and led by a committee from the Soviet, a mighty procession—unarmed and uneasy—wound through the city with the intention of emptying the prisons. Behind the walls of jails and fortresses, Trepov lined up his men fully armed, while in the palace Witte negotiated anxiously with the Tsar. The news of the signing of an amnesty decree arrived melodramatically at the last possible moment: the unequal test of strength between Trepov and the marching mass was postponed.

Using the printers as spearhead, the Soviet turned next to the conquest, once more by direct action, of freedom of the press. Ignoring the Tsar's censors, they even set up a censorship of their own, refusing to put into type attacks upon the Soviet itself, or slanderous pogrom appeals for the murder of Poles, Armenians and Jews. Then the Soviet took a graver step, prohibiting the printing of a political manifesto of the liberal Zemstvo Congress. The majority of the zemstvo delegates had welcomed the October Manifesto and adopted a declaration against "further disorders." We must leave it to the reader to ponder the problems of "legitimate" and "illegitimate" censorship and the true meaning of freedom. To Trotsky, prime mover of these actions, the case seemed clear enough. "Obviously," he wrote, "they were not hurting in the least the freedom of the press when they refused to print reactionary or liberal slanders." Here was a foreshadowing of the future censorship under the Soviet dictatorship, which would stretch the elastic term "reactionary or liberal slanders" until Trotsky's own writings would be embraced in it. This business of "protecting" the masses against clashing views and the need to think, is an inclined plane down which "progress" is rapid.

The next step in the battle with the Tsar's censors was an announcement by the printers' union that they would not set in type any newspaper which submitted its copy to the government officials for approval. The publishers were delighted to be forced into taking their freedom. All papers, conservative ones included, now appeared with a boxed notice that the issue in question had not been submitted to censorship. They agreed to print touchy items in identical language and if one were suspended therefor, all would suspend. The Soviet had won another round in the conquest by direct action of promised liberties. For six weeks the Russian press was freer than it had ever been in its history, or would ever be again, except for the eight-month period between the first and second revolutions in 1917.

Having won so much by direct action—freedom to assemble, freedom to organize and to strike, freedom of speech and press, and political amnesty—the Soviet now set out to conquer by the same methods the eight-hour day. The Soviet leaders were hesitant; the initiative came from below. This time, however, they could not count on the benevolent cooperation of the employers. To the latter, this was no conquest of freedom but the crossing of the proverbial borderline which is supposed to separate liberty from license. Now they felt sudden closeness to the state, any state. Moreover, was not their man Witte, the man of industrialization and liberal subsidy, quite visibly at the helm?

On the appointed day, November 13, the workingmen quit work in a body, exactly at the end of eight hours. No strike this, just the revolutionary enactment of a more human working day. They had come to work at the accustomed hour of 6:45, had refused the time-honored hour and three-quarters for lunch, staying away from their machines a bare thirty minutes.[3] At the sunlit hour of 3:15 they left their posts, fresh and exhilarated, roaring "The Marseillaise," marching from factory to factory in a body, pulling out the reluctant. Hereafter the workingmen would have time for rest and recreation, for home and family, for meetings and discussions, for culture and education, for politics and training in the use of arms.

But the employers, with few exceptions, refused to increase the hourly and piece rates to maintain the none-too-big take-home wage. With the same speed as the workingmen had organized previously, now their employers built up associations—directed not against the Tsar but against the workers. Led by the great workshops and offices of the state, they posted notices of dismissal and lockout of those who should take the liberty of deciding their own working hours. The unity of the entire people against the Tsar was at an end. While the Soviet delegates and workingmen were pondering this new turn of affairs, the eight-hour fight got lost in something bigger, for the Soviet voted another general strike.

The issues were once more political. The "constitutional" government of Witte had just declared a state of siege in Poland. At the same time, a short-lived revolt of the soldiers and sailors of Kron-

---

[3] The average working day in the capital at the time was ten hours with an hour and three-quarters for lunch, i.e., those who started at 6:15 A.M. got off at 6 o'clock at night.

stadt (the chief harbor fort defending Petersburg) was put down and the leading participants handed over to a summary field court-martial for trial. Moved by a desire to demonstrate the unity of all the nationalities in this "prison-house of people," and long in quest of some way of binding together the discontented army and the rebellious civilian masses, the Soviet appointed November 15 for a second general strike. Although only two short weeks had elapsed since they had last resumed work, and although the eight-hour fight was still unsettled, the workingmen set out again with amazing unanimity. If anything, their response was more immediate and universal than before. But the employers now exhibited a sullen hostility; the storekeepers, *droshky* drivers, retail clerks, government employees, white-collar workers, ballet dancers, and most of the professional men and technicians were nowhere to be seen. The mechanism of economic, and especially of government life was less paralyzed, the government less frightened than before. On November 17, the executive committee of the Soviet voted nine to six to call off the strike, but was reversed by the general council. But the next day it was so clear that the strike was ebbing that the same general council set its end for the 20th. Still the retreat was in good order and the strike elicited some concessions from the government: the Kronstadt mutineers were transferred from the field courts-martial (in practice mere firing squads) to the regular military courts, and in Poland the state of siege was revoked. Lenin's verdict, written in Stockholm on the day of the Tsar's Manifesto, still seemed to hold good: "Tsarism is no longer able to suppress the revolution; the revolution is still unable to destroy tsarism." But both sides were preparing, according to their resources and vision, for an early day of reckoning.

Attempting to return to their factories, the workingmen found them closed against the resumption of work, on the old issue of the eight-hour day. Confusion set in. Before long the Soviet found itself obliged to let each trade and workshop decide for itself and make such terms as it could for the resumption of work. The weapon of strike was being blunted by too frequent use; the power behind it was being diminished by weariness and hunger in the working-men's families, and by the growing isolation of the workingmen from other sections of the population. Yet they had reached out toward closer union with the all-important armed forces and had reason to hope that they had made some impression on the soldiers. Many felt that the deadlock must soon be broken somehow, by recourse to arms.

During this time of uncertainty, the forces of reaction were not idle. On the very day that the Tsar granted a constitution, they had rallied around him to defend his throne against his own yielding. Unsure of its troops, the government began to make hasty concessions: increases in pay, extra rations, rounds of vodka, confinement to barracks in moments of stress, shifting of regiments to regions where they were alien to the populace and its aspirations, premium pay for punitive expeditions. Most important of these devices was the playing of one nationality against another—indeed, whenever a government finds it necessary to use troops of one region against the people of another, it is a fair assumption that its case will not bear popular examination. Simultaneously with these measures, the reaction began to organize extra-legal armed forces as shock troops for the impending struggle, forces that were precursors of the secret military groupings, the Blackshirts, Brownshirts, and Storm Troopers of Italy and Germany in the twenties. Under the banner of Holy Russia was gathered together a most unholy and variegated band: the backward, the degenerate, the brutalized, the bewildered, the enraged, the entrenched, the ruined: officers, landowners and gilded youth, demobilized old soldiers and personal servingmen to whom loyalty to the master was the sum of all loyalties, criminals whose police record made them amenable to any instructions, ruined artisans and shopkeepers who were persuaded that the strikes and the eight-hour day were the cause of all their woes, hungry, degraded slum proletarians from the human scrapheap of the great cities, the more illiterate and credulous among the workingmen and peasantry. To the familiar compound of rabid nationalism and national antipathies and social demagogy was added the peculiar Russian component of the Orthodox religious banner and the deep susceptibility to legendary rumor of an illiterate, and credulous people. The extra-legal groupings were armed by the police, transported to regions where they were unknown, inflamed with drink, protected in their acts of assault, pillage, rape, murder. Their marching song was "God Save the Tsar," their banner the Tsar's image or the holy ikon, their organizations bore such titles as Union of the Russian People, Union of the Russian Land, Russian Orthodox Committee. Their leaflets, printed sometimes in church offices, more often in the secret chancelleries of the police, proclaimed that the war with Japan had been lost because the socialists had been bought by the Japanese and the Japanese by the Jews, that "the Tsar would divide large tracts of Crown lands among the peasants if he could only get rid of the Jews and the Poles," and "Saint Vladimir, who first baptized the people of Russia [in the year 998], has risen from the bowels of the earth and weeps because of the Fatherland brought to shame by Poles and Jews." This last, issued by the Russian Orthodox Committee, bade each recipient make three copies and send them to other villages. "Who has not fulfilled this order within six days will be stricken by grave sickness and affliction, but whoever spreads more than three copies will be granted recovery from incurable disease . . ."[4]

The workers responded by forming fighting companies of armed men. Funds were collected, many employers contributing. Sporting goods stores were emptied of their rifles and pistols, solitary policemen were disarmed by force. On November 11, in response to the rumor of a pogrom, a veritable fever for arming took possession of the Petersburg proletariat. In the factories they forged "cold arms," daggers, pikes, brass knuckles, wire whips, iron bars. According to government reports, in a few weeks there were some six thousand Petersburg workingmen organized in motley armed companies, of whom some three hundred formed a better-armed fighting corps, patrolling meetings and the workingmen's quarters in groups of ten. Police raids were organized to confiscate the weapons. In Moscow, by December, there were some hundreds of indifferently armed workingmen, destined to play a fearful and heroic role. In many cities, notably in the Caucasus, the local governments aided directly in the arming of bands for self-defense. There the armed bands were to have a special history of their own.

On December 9, the government, cautiously feeling its way toward the offensive, arrested Georgii Nosar, who, under the name of Khrustalev, presided over the Petersburg Soviet. The Soviet had no answer ready: It could only choose a provisional presidium of three, Yanovsky (i.e. Trotsky), Vvedenski and Zlydnev, and vote "to continue to prepare for an armed uprising." Parvus drafted a Financial Manifesto, issued in the name of the Soviet, of the Peasant League, and the Socialist Parties, calling upon the masses:

> To refuse payment of government land installments and all other payments to the government.
> To demand all wages and salaries to be paid in gold. . . .

[4] The spiritual leader of this proto-fascist religious organization was the priest Evlogi. Forty years later, on September 2, 1945, Ambassador Alexander Bogomolov sat in the first row in the Orthodox Church in Paris while this same Evlogi, a Metropolitan now, said a solemn mass and blessed the new ruler of the Russian state, Marshal Stalin. (New York *Times*, Sept. 3, 1945).

To withdraw all deposits from the banks . . . demanding payments in gold.

   . . . We decide not to acknowledge the debts which, in the form of loans, the government of the Tsar has contracted while it has been carrying on open war against the whole people.[5]

Eight newspapers published the Manifesto and were suspended by the government. Next day one hundred newspapers did the same, constraining the government to refrain from further confiscations. There was a run on the banks. Abroad, government credit toppled. The government responded by arresting the entire Executive Committee of the Council of Workingmen's Delegates on December 16. Their last act under Trotsky's chairmanship, as the police were putting them under arrest, was to vote a new general strike and to smash their pistols so that they should not fall into the hands of their captors.

More workingmen struck in Russia during this single turbulent year than in any other country in any year up to that time. The government estimate is 2,800,000 workingmen involved, more than the entire number of industrial workers in the country, meaning that many workers must have struck more than once. The metal workers struck on an average more than three times during the year. In this as in other things, Saint Petersburg had led the nation. But now its workingmen were weary and exhausted. Besides, its most advanced workers knew only too well that this time the strike must end in armed insurrection or not be undertaken at all. They looked at their miserable weapons, and knew they were not prepared. Fresher, more backward Moscow, where the garrison was seething with unrest, picked up the challenge with yet another general strike. The railwaymen joined once more, but—a fateful fact—this time the railroad from Petersburg to Moscow did not close down.

The Moscow general strike, intended as part of an all-Russian general strike, began peacefully enough. The top leadership there had hesitated and had been pushed forward from below. But that leadership, lodged in a Moscow "federal council" of united Bolsheviks and Mensheviks, was arrested the very day the strike began. The national leaders of the Bolsheviks were taken by surprise by what followed, too. They had just called a conference in Tammerfors, Finland, and all during the fateful days while Moscow

---

[5] This warning to those who might lend money to the Tsar was the basis of the Bolshevik repudiation of tsarist debts in 1918. The repudiation also included the loans made by the Tsar's government during the World War.

was in general strike and armed insurrection, they were not in Russia proper. Second-string Moscow leaders and a few from other parts of the country—Bolsheviks, Social Revolutionaries and Mensheviks—directed and organized as best they could what was in reality a spontaneous eruption. None of the men whose names we have become acquainted with were on the spot at all.

The moral responsibility if not the direct initiative for what happened in Moscow, was above all Lenin's and that of his party, and they did not reject it. From the day he first heard of the fate of Gapon's procession he had been studying military tactics, writing detailed instructions on bombs, pistols, tacks and broken glass to disorganize the mounted Cossacks, barricades, propaganda in the armed forces, the acquisition of arms, the necessity of an armed insurrection. The Mensheviks, a little more hesitantly, had followed suit and *Iskra* had carried precise instructions on barricade fighting. The Social Revolutionaries had added proposals for individual terror. Troop mutinies and naval mutinies and peasant insurrections had contributed to the spirit of rebellion. The great general strikes had given the masses confidence in their power, shaken the government, spread the feeling that perhaps one more exertion, one extra push, might finish the job. Pogroms and defense groups and sporadic armed clashes had added to the fighting mood.

In Moscow, moreover, the garrison had been rife with discontent for some days. Soldiers, even officers, had appeared at workers' meetings to pledge their support. The government had rushed Admiral Dubassov there, fresh from punitive expeditions in other parts of the country. He was one of the die-hards of the stamp of Durnovo and Trepov, spoiling for a showdown by physical force which would terrorize the masses, discredit the Witte arm of the government and undo the Constitutional Manifesto.

The Moscow insurrection had no strategic plan, no plan to assume the offensive, to seize key places, no set date or fixed intention. The strike began peacefully on December 20 and in the first days there were sporadic attempts to woo the excited troops. One regiment left its barracks singing "The Marseillaise," but before anything could be done about it, the regiment was surrounded, returned to barracks, disarmed, and plied with vodka, promises and concessions. Twice Cossack bands were persuaded to disobey their officers and ride off, amid the cheers of the populace. The first sniping shots at troops were possibly fired by provocateurs in an effort to inflame them. The first barricade on the Tverskaya was put up by a jovial population including respectable burghers in fur coats. On the third day there were bloody clashes: barricades began springing up in earnest.

The insurrection was never more than defensive. Barricades were built, but behind them men had almost no arms—perhaps 200 pistols and some hunting rifles to defend a line over ten miles long, against some 100,000 regular troops. Behind the 200 with pistols was a larger number with improvised cold arms, and five or six thousand ready to take up the arms of those who fell. Much of Moscow's population, especially its workingmen, aided with food, barricade construction, information, and sanitary support. The barricades were little more than obstructions to prevent cavalry charges. Fighting was hit-and-run, from doorways and windows and rooftops, around corners and out of courtyards through which retreat was secure. Men fought in detachments of twos and threes and fives and tens, avoiding pitched battles, vanishing swiftly, giving the impression of great numbers. However, once it had become clear that the troops would not join and that the general strike in Saint Petersburg had failed, not for a moment was there any doubt of the outcome. Still, for more than a week, in the Presnya District, the insurrection held out.

Admiral Dubassov was afraid to use his own troops. Two-thirds of them he considered so unreliable that he kept them confined in barracks; the rest, some five thousand, seemed inadequate to crush the movement. Twice he sent urgent calls to Petersburg for help. Only when it arrived—the crack Semenevsky Guard on the open railway line between the capitals, and other troops that had just been used in punitive duty in the Baltic Provinces—was he able to go over to the offensive. On the 27th, with the new troops, Dubassov managed to clear the center of the city and confine the guerrilla bands to the Presnaya district, a workingmen's quarter. Then, for three days he bombarded the Presnaya with artillery at long range, indiscriminately. Factories were destroyed, houses set in flames, men, women and children suffered alike. How many were killed and wounded is unknown, perhaps a thousand all told, among them a hundred-odd soldiers and police and eighty-six children. On December 31, when the mopping-up squads went through the Presnaya district, they found that most of the armed fighters had made good their escape. They had to wreak their vengeance on the non-combatant population. Thus the year 1905, which had opened with the Tsar's firing on his petitioning children, closed with the forces of the Holy, Orthodox, Autocratic Government systematically destroying by artillery bombardment an entire quarter of the holy city that had been the traditional capital of Old Russia.

CHAPTER XIX

TROTSKY'S ROUND TRIP

Simpletons and hypocrites urge us to keep within legal
limits . . . One would think our lungs infected with an
irresistible desire to breathe the atmosphere of solitary
dungeons . . . We love our underground as little as the
drowning person loves the bottom of the sea . . . But it
will not choke us . . . History is a tremendous mechanism
serving our ideals. Its work is slow, barbarously slow, implacably cruel, yet it goes on. We believe in it. Only at moments, when this voracious monster drinks the living blood
of our hearts as its nourishment, we wish to shout with all
our might: *What thou dost, do quickly!—From the Preface
to Trotsky's* My round Trip

T HE RAID on the Soviet Executive netted three hundred prisoners,
the most prominent being the acting Chairman, Yanovsky (Leon
Trotsky). It is significant of the weakness of the Bolsheviks in the
Soviet that there was not one of their leaders among the arrested.
For a long time the fate of the prisoners was clouded in uncertainty. While the authorities wondered how the workers would
answer the raid on their "parliament," the Minister of Justice was
profuse in assurances that they would not be put on trial but had
been arrested purely as a "preventive" measure. When the strike
called to force their release fizzled, and Moscow's working-class
quarter had been reduced to rubble, the government hinted at
summary execution. In April, 1906, during the honeymoon period
of the convocation of the First Duma, there was talk of immediate
amnesty. Thus the fate of Trotsky and his fellow-prisoners wavered
between firing squad and freedom until June of 1906, when formal
charges were rather hastily drafted against them as fomenters of
armed insurrection.

A special high court was set up in medieval fashion out of representatives of the Estates into which Russian society was still officially divided. Before this anachronistic court over two hundred
witnesses paraded in motley procession: high military men, officials,
workingmen, muzhiks, apartment house *dvorniki* (janitors, used by
both the tsarist régime and the present GPU or MVD as spies),
provocateurs, tramps, policemen. There were witnesses whose main
target was Count Witte rather than the accused; witnesses who

took the stand to denounce the government and to call upon the proletariat to free the prisoners and try their prosecutors. Every latitude was allowed in the courtroom.

Inevitably, the young Social Democrat who had begun 1905 by predicting a general strike and closed it by presiding over the last sessions of the Soviet, became the outstanding defendant. With mother and father in the courtroom, the twenty-six year old Lev Davidovich Bronstein addressed his judges for several hours in a "defense" that was an exposition of Social Democratic views and an indictment of the régime which had put him on trial:

> The strike threw hundreds of thousands of workers out of the factories, awoke them to open political life. Who could undertake the leadership of these masses, who bring discipline into their ranks? The police, maybe? or the gendarmes? or the Security Section? . . . No one but the Council of Workingmen's Deputies. . . . Under such conditions the Council of Deputies was neither more nor less than the self-governing organ of the revolutionary masses, *an organ of state power.* . . . The historic force in whose name the state prosecutor speaks here is only the organized violation of the majority by the minority. The new force, however, represents the organized will of the majority. . . . This difference provided the Council of Deputies with its revolutionary right of existence. . . .
>
> Yes, Messrs. Judges and Representatives of the Estates, we realized *de facto* freedom of speech, press, assembly, inviolability of person—all the things which under pressure of the October strike were promised to the people. But the government apparatus gave signs of life only when it was a matter of tearing the legal conquests of the people to pieces. . . .
>
> Under what circumstances, in our opinion, could the uprising lead to victory? If the troops sympathized with us! So above all the Army had to be won. . . . What is necessary for that? Machine guns and rifles perhaps? Naturally, if the masses had machine guns and rifles, they would have possessed enormous power. But the masses had not, and even today do not have nor can they have, weapons in great numbers. . . . Yet, however important weapons are, Messrs. Judges, not in them does the greatest power lie. No! Not the capacity of the masses to kill others but their great readiness to die themselves—that, my Judges, assures in the last instance the success of a popular uprising. . . . When the troops come to the conviction that the people are ready to fight in bloody earnest and carry the

struggle to the end, then the soul of the soldier will and must experience, as in all revolutions, a profound commotion. . . . Even barricades, apparently a mechanical element of the uprising, are of significance in reality above all as a moral force. . . .

The prosecutors demand that you, Messrs. Judges, recognize that the Council of Workingmen's Deputies armed the workers for the direct struggle against the existing form of government. If you ask me categorically: *Was that so?* I answer: *Yes, indeed!*

When he ended, his lawyers crowded around to congratulate him. His mother wept openly, proud of this eloquence which she had but dimly understood, naively sure that acquittal must follow, even some sort of honors for her son. But he and fourteen others were condemned to life-long exile in Siberia; two additional defendants were given short prison terms; two hundred and eighty-four of the three hundred were set free.

In prison once more, Leon Trotsky settled calmly down to work. Outside, rebellion and repression raged: pogroms, punitive expeditions, field courts-martial, mass floggings, firing squads, peasant riots, holdups of government banks, military mutinies, disarming and slaying of police. But the tsarist prison régime continued astonishingly liberal for all "politicals" who could not be directly connected with acts of terror. Trotsky received all the books he wanted, wrote, smuggled out articles in the brief cases of his lawyers, was allowed two visits a week from Natalia Ivanovna, who claimed to be his legal wife. For fifteen months, before, during and after the trial, amidst muted alarms and rumors of mortal danger, he lived the life of a studious anchorite. It was a pleasure, he assured Natalia, to work in this quiet place "without any danger of being arrested." For relaxation he devoured French novels. The love for the French novel born in this succession of jails would remain with him to the end. It would be his refreshment on forced journeys in an armored train during the Civil War and a solace in exile in Turkestan, Prinkipo, France, Mexico. One of the last essays from his pen would be a generous appreciation of the then little-known young Polish-French novelist, Jean Malaquais, who had sent him a copy of his first novel, *Les Javanais* ("Men from Nowhere").

In his cell he studied the third volume of Marx's *Capital* and wrote an essay on the Marxian theory of ground rent—token of his deepened interest in the peasant and the land. He analyzed the role of the Soviet and the driving forces that would shape the next

Russian revolution. These essays were calculated to defend, deepen, strengthen his conviction of the rightness of the theory of *permanent revolution*. Except for the one on rent, which went astray during a prison transfer, all his writings of this period constitute parts of his *The Year 1905*, published a few years later. It proved to be the most brilliant account from any hand of that memorable year, and one of the greatest examples of eyewitness-participant reporting in all historiography. Published originally in German in Vienna in 1909, it was reprinted in 1922 by the Soviet Government and translated in whole or in part into innumerable languages to serve as a textbook for the study of the year that began with Father Gapon's pilgrimage and ended with the arrest of the Soviet Executive and bombardment of Moscow. After Lenin's death and Trotsky's fall from grace, *The Year 1905* was made the target of elaborate polemics against "Trotskyism," and finally placed on the Index and burnt. But subsequent Soviet historiography has been unable to produce anything to replace it.[1]

Fifteen months after his arrest, Trotsky started on a journey to "perpetual exile" in Obdorsk up near the Arctic Circle. Fifteen hundred versts (about a thousand miles) separated Obdorsk from the nearest railway line, eight hundred from the nearest telegraph— a remoteness of which the convict would be glad. The prisoners and their heavy military guard, traveled from the last railroad stop in forty sleighs, which carried them daily some ninety to one hundred versts toward the north. "Every day," he wrote to Natalia Ivanovna, "we ascend one degree farther into the kingdom of cold and barbarism."

Almost at the very end, when the distance seemed infinite from the nearest telegraph from which an alarm might be sent, he escaped across the snow. Wearing two fur coats, fur stockings, fur boots, fur cap, fur gloves—the outfit of a Siberian *Ostyak*—armed with some bottles of vodka against the dreaded cold and some gold pieces which had been concealed in the heels of his boots, he hid in a reindeer sleigh under a load of hay and was driven by a drunken Zyryan guide. A local exile broke a long false trail through the snow for the police to follow, thus giving him several days' head-start. When he reached more traveled trails he posed as a member of a polar expedition, then as a petty official. At last, the

[1] The complete version is available in German, French and Russian (outside of Russia, of course). Some of the preliminary sketches for it were translated by Moissaye J. Olgin under the title *Our Revolution* (Henry Holt, 1918). All versions are at present out of print. Unaccountably, the Trotskyist organizations, usually so pious in the handling of his literary remains, have not reprinted this, his masterpiece.

Urals, the railway, the Great-Russian frontier, and the comparative safety of semi-autonomous Finland. Here he wrote *There and Back* (known in English as *My Round Trip*). With the money earned by its publication he went on to Stockholm. Natalia and her child joined him in Vienna in October, 1907. He would not return to Russia until the next upheaval in 1917.

CHAPTER XX

THE TRIAL OF VLADIMIR ILYICH

> Is everything that is gathering force, underground, in the
> dark, in the night, in little hidden rooms out of sight of
> governments and policemen . . . is all this going to burst
> forth some fine morning and set the world on fire? Or is
> it going to sputter out and spend itself in vain conspiracies,
> be dissipated in sterile heroisms and abortive isolated move-
> ments? —*The Princess Casimassima*

MEN CANNOT LIVE forever at fever heat. Even in victory, as the
years after 1917 would prove, the fever of social unrest has a
way of burning down and leaving the frame exhausted. Those who
are dedicated to the single goal of revolution may continue with
their self-appointed tasks, though even they will show signs of
lassitude. But the common man who lives for the day's bare existence must return to his personal cares.

While the wave was rising it swept all before it, bringing together
the most diverse classes, groups, factions, temperaments. As it
receded, spent swimmers found themselves in ridiculous postures
far from their accustomed or intended haunts. Only the most determined and powerful could feel themselves being swept away by
the current, yet still face upstream and keep thrusting toward the
receding goal.

Lenin was an unusual compound of revolutionary temperament
with an acute sense of actual reality. He was more reluctant than
the Menshevik leaders, and slower by many months, to realize that
the fortress could not be taken by storm. When he did recognize it,
he found himself almost alone in his own camp. For several years
he had to conduct a struggle with the majority of his colleagues
to make them grasp the true state of affairs and abandon slogans,
tactics, gestures, appropriate only to a time of open warfare.

All through 1906 and early 1907 he vacillated between sturdily
realistic appraisal and too easily reviving hope. A big Socialist fraction in the Second Duma (although almost three-quarters were
Mensheviks); strikes among backward workers who had not participated in the earlier ones; peasant riots, more numerous in the spring
of 1906 than in 1905; a belated mutiny of peasants-in-uniform at
Kronstadt and Sveaborg; all the lingering fires that flared in the

peripheral regions of the great empire when the blaze at the center had died—each of these in turn was taken by Lenin as a sign of renewal. By temperament, by creed, by obligation, he would rather err on the side of hope than miss an opportunity because of too easy despair.

> Revolutionary Social Democracy—he wrote in the middle of 1906—must be the first to enter on the path of the most decisive and relentless struggle, and the last to have recourse to methods which are more roundabout.

So his creed. But still his sense of reality bade him prepare for the resumption of the roundabout path.

It is not hard, with benefit of hindsight, to note the main steps in the reconsolidation of governmental power. The ending of the war with Japan freed the government for war with its own people. The abortive eight-hour strike by the workers and the promise of Duma and Constitution by the Tsar, combined to separate liberals and moderates from revolutionary socialists. The arrest of the Executive Committee of the Soviet and the crushing of the Moscow uprising gave the officials new confidence, strengthening the physical force wing in their camp as against the moderate constitutional tendency represented by Witte.

As Russia's greatest industrializer and financier, and as a constitutional monarchist, Count Witte alone enjoyed the confidence of foreign banking circles. With a devotion to his sovereign worthy of a better fate, he now negotiated a foreign loan to make the Tsar independent of the coming Duma. The bankers demanded constitutional forms as a means of conciliating public opinion in France and guaranteeing greater stability to the régime. It was Witte's mistake to believe that such forms of government would make him indispensable to the Tsar. He was a sort of "Menshevik" of government circles, too much the "Westernizer," too alien to Russia's historic peculiarities, to win out at Court, any more than the Mensheviks could in the long run win out with the Russian masses.

Secretly, with false passport, M. Noetzlin of the Banque de Paris et des Pays-Bas came to Petersburg during the October days to discuss terms for a 2,250,000,000 gold franc loan. The last act of the Soviet before its dispersal was to warn prospective creditors that a loan to the government for war on its own people would never be honored by the latter should they come to power. Fair warning! But the Banque de Paris was playing for bigger stakes than could be measured in per cent. The Algeciras Conference was in session. "Our representatives," recorded Count Witte, "were directed to vote for France."

Thus Witte was able to dump a huge pile of gold at the Tsar's feet, and the Tsar was enabled to dispense with Witte and ignore the coming Duma. Yet the loan was to be fateful for the dynasty. Its negotiation completed the long process begun when Bismarck chose Austria as against Russia in his scheme of alliances and instructed the Reichsbank to accept no more Russian bonds as collateral for loans. Now the last strand was broken which, for a full century—since their common complicity in the partition of Poland—had tied Russia to Prussia and Austria. Instead, a new chain of gold was forged to link millions of Tsarist bayonets to billions of French francs for a war which, narrowly averted at Algeciras, was less than a decade away. That war would give Lenin the chance which the Russo-Japanese War had fallen short of providing.

During the autumn and winter of 1905, Bolsheviks and Mensheviks had been almost indistinguishable. Lenin had moved closer to the Mensheviks by abandoning his opposition to the non-party soviet, to broad, non-controlled, mass organizations, to local autonomy and initiative, to democratic process in the movement that had conquered legality in despite of the law. The Mensheviks, for their part, forgot their distrust of conspiracy and of "planned" uprising, their misgivings about power's falling into their own reluctant hands, their eagerness to avoid clashes with the bourgeoisie before the latter had become the ruling class. While the masses were storming forward with irresistable élan, Mensheviks were swept along and as much attracted as Bolsheviks by the "Russian" as against the "Western" way of political struggle.

But at the beginning of 1906, Axelrod, who had stayed abroad during the great year and was thus exempt from its contagion, noted with a sense of shock what Lenin had already recognized with satisfaction: that Mensheviks and Bolsheviks had been fighting side by side in ways that implied the unconscious acceptance of a number of Lenin's views and tactical methods. In the cold outer darkness after the flames had died down, many a Menshevik decided that the Revolution of 1905 had failed because the working class had gone too far with its own independent tactics (strikes and the Moscow uprising), with the arbitrary dictation of its class will (the eight-hour decree of the Petersburg Soviet), with its own special demands as against those of the opposition as a whole. Thus it had frightened away the bourgeoisie, which, according to the Menshevik formula, should have been inspirited, encouraged, if necessary pushed, into taking power. The crisis in menshevism was the deeper for the fact that it was the Petersburg Soviet, an organization which they dominated, that had carried them away with it into pressing the extreme program. And it was their own daily, *Nachalo*, under the dynamic editorship of Parvus and Trotsky, which had advanced the wholly un-Menshevik idea of immediate working-class seizure of power and proletarian-socialist dictatorship —an idea still combatted even by Lenin. What could be more demoralizing than the fact that the Menshevik organ had advanced ideas which Lenin could praise and the Mensheviks could not choose but condemn. Martynov, as Menshevik spokesman at the unity congress of the two factions, summed up their conduct in 1905 in this fashion:

> We said to ourselves then: *Le vin est tiré, il faut le boire.* —Since the wine is poured, it will have to be drunk.—At decisive moments one is forced to act firmly, with no time to analyze. . . . The difference, however, was that we considered our situation as one forced upon us, while the Bolsheviks strove for it and regarded it as natural.

A strange spirit in which to have entered into general strikes, an uprising, and a struggle for power! So deeply did they repent now of their ideological sins, committed when the revolutionary tide had swept them off their feet, that henceforth the Mensheviks were to become increasingly passionate pedants in their insistence that the working class must thrust the power into the hands of the bourgeoisie, though the latter was losing its appetite for rule without the security of a Tsar. The active paralysis of the will which the Mensheviks were to show in 1917, the dogmatic, even frantic way in which they would fight off power with both hands and feet when there was no other real center of power in the country, are largely attributable to the inner crisis of remorse which they went through during the years of reaction.

Martov no less than Axelrod was oppressed by a growing uneasiness as soon as he saw the proletariat—in the eight-hour strike and Moscow insurrection—fighting in isolation from the bourgeoisie and frightening and enraging the very ones who, according to Menshevik theory, were their natural allies and the legitimate claimants to power. As early as February, 1906, Martov wrote in a tortured letter to Axelrod:

> For two months now I have been unable to finish any of the writing I have started. It is either neurasthenia or mental fatigue—but I cannot gather my thoughts together.

Trotsky for his part drew his conclusion from the phenomenon of close Bolshevik-Menshevik unity in the time of actual revolution. The differences that had grown up in more peaceful times between the two factions had thus proved artificial and unreal. Whenever there was a chance for action, their common program, their common desire for socialism, their common loyalty to the working class would sweep aside all the pedantic and dogmatic cobwebs of their differences. For most of the next decade, from 1907 to 1917, he berated them both for quarreling so furiously with each other, and sought to make himself the champion of unity between them. Since Lenin was invariably the aggressor in the splits, he directed his main fire against the latter. After he became a Bolshevik in 1917, however, he thought otherwise. "Martov did not know what to call his illness in 1906," Trotsky wrote after 1917, when the private letter to Axelrod had become public, "but it has a quite definite name: menshevism."

At first, Lenin drew the same conclusion as Trotsky from the union of Bolsheviks and Mensheviks in 1905, for, like Trotsky, he was impressed by the way the Mensheviks had accepted the Trotsky-Parvus thesis of general strike, armed uprising, proletarian dictatorship.

> Indeed—wrote Lenin in April, 1906—if we look at the matter from the point of view of the departure of the Social Democrats from their "normal" road, we will see that a period of "revolutionary whirlwind" shows *more* and not less closeness and ideological unity in the social democracy. The tactics of the epoch of "the whirlwind" did not increase the distance between the two wings of social democracy but brought them closer together. In place of the former differences there arose unity of views on the question of the armed uprising. The Social Democrats of both factions worked in the Soviet of Workers Deputies, those unique organs of embryonic revolutionary power. They appealed together to the soldiers, the peasants, to enter into the Soviets. They issued revolutionary manifestoes together with the petty-bourgeois revolutionary parties. The previous controversies of the pre-revolutionary epoch gave way to agreement in practical matters. The rise of the revolutionary wave removed the differences, compelling the acceptance of fighting tactics, brushing aside the question of the Duma, placing the question of an uprising on the order of business. . . . In the *Northern Voice,* Mensheviks and Bolsheviks together called for a

strike and an uprising, together called upon the workers not to give up the fight until the power was in their hands. The revolutionary situation itself suggested the practical slogans. Differences of opinion concerned only details in the estimate of events. For instance, *Nachalo* regarded the Soviets as organs of revolutionary self-government, while *Novaya Zhizn* looked upon them as embryonic organs of revolutionary power, uniting the proletariat and the revolutionary democrats. *Nachalo* inclined to a dictatorship of the proletariat; *Novaya Zhizn* stood for the democratic dictatorship of the proletariat and the peasantry. [Lenin: *Collected Works*, Third Russian Edition, Vol. IX, pp. 123-4. This article was originally published legally in Saint Petersburg in April, 1906.]

That was the high point of friendliness on Lenin's part. But the same actions which had called forth Lenin's enthusiasm had awakened Axelrod's chagrin, Martov's abulia, Plekhanov's doubts and Martynov's remorse.

Whatever Bolshevik and Menshevik leaders may have thought, the demand for unity in the ranks had acquired so great a momentum that neither side dared oppose it. Both factions had been overwhelmed by an inrush of new members who knew nothing of the ancient quarrels. All over Russia, the organizations fused without waiting for the leaders. Around them was the whole newly awakened working class, demanding that their would-be leaders stop quarreling over bygones and "fine points." If we cannot get together, they said, how will we lick the Tsar?

Despite misgivings as to recent tactics, the Mensheviks were by conviction and dogmatic formula responsive to the popular will, and therefore they became champions of unification for the next decade. They did not renounce their theoretical position, but proposed to argue it out in a united party. Unlike the Bolsheviks, they even permitted their separate faction organization to disintegrate. Not so Lenin. At all times he strove to keep his faction apparatus tuned up for possible rupture, or alternatively, for the more effective imposing of his views upon the united party. Yet he too felt the force of the demand for unity, and became for the nonce in his own fashion that, to him, most detestable of political beings: a "conciliator."

By the end of 1905, finding their lower units everywhere fused, the two leaderships set up a provisional "Parity Executive Committee" with an equal number from each side, to prepare a joint unification congress. Krassin, Lalayants and Rykov represented the

Bolsheviks; Krokhmal, Taresevich and Jordanski the Mensheviks. When the government suppressed their two daily papers, they set up a common daily with a joint editorial board: Lunacharsky, Bazarov and Vorovsky, Dan, Martynov and Martov.

Inside the fused locals Bolshevik and Menshevik leaders presented rival platforms and ran rival sets of delegates for the unification congress. Thus they would determine its decisions, and their relative shares in the united leadership.

But now a new sector of "public opinion" appeared on the scene, not sewed up in either faction. The special language groups, and the socialist parties of the subject nations and borderlands, seeing the prospect of a united party, sent fraternal delegates to see if they too could not enter into one all-Russian body. These included the Jewish Socialist Bund, the Social Democratic Party of Poland and Lithuania; those of Latvia, Armenia, and the Ukraine. Significantly, the overwhelming majority of the Georgians were in the Russian Menshevik faction as an integral part of its leadership, and the minority, in which Djugashvili was soon to figure as a leader, was an integral part of the Bolshevik faction. Other Georgian parties, more nationalist than socialist, did not apply for affiliation.

The fraternal delegates from the borderland parties came to the 1906 Stockholm unification congress empowered only as observers, but by the London Congress in 1907 they were full-fledged members. This time, it almost seemed as if the process of forming a single, All-Russian Social Democratic Party, which had miscarried in 1903, would be brought to completion. For the next four or five years, Bolsheviks and Mensheviks were on the whole so evenly balanced in the united organization, that the Poles under the leadership of Rosa Luxemburg and Jan Tyszka, the Latvians, and the Jewish Socialist Bund held the balance of power in the united committees and sought to exert it now this way now that, to keep the precarious see-saw in balance and themselves at the fulcrum as balancing force. Though the Poles and Latvians inclined toward Lenin most of the time, it infuriated him to be so dependent upon forces which he did not control and which might fail to see eye to eye with him on matters which seemed to him most precious. At the Stockholm Congress of 1906 he was in a minority. It elected a Central Committee of seven Mensheviks and three Bolsheviks. Hence he secretly kept his faction apparatus alive, though he had just voted for the motion to dissolve both factions. At the London Congress in 1907, where, with the aid of the Poles he got a majority on the Central Committee, five Bolsheviks, four Mensheviks, and two each from the Poles, Bund and Latvians, he felt the majority to

be so slender and unreliable that still he kept his caucus. Too often
when he was sure that he was right (a conviction that was always
with him), the Poles, Letts and Bundists, holding the balance of
power, voted against him, or sought a "despicable compromise."
As we know his character, we need not be surprised to find that
this ultimately became intolerable to him. For, whatever he was
thwarted in was likely to assume the guise of a shibboleth, distinguishing Ephramites from the true followers of Gilead. This was
one of the reasons why in 1912, after six or seven years of uneasy
unity, he would once more split the united organization and proclaim his own faction to be the Party.

After the two unity congresses, the movement was to decline so
rapidly that it would become incapable of holding another. All its
subsequent quarrels, growing more ferocious as the movement
dwindled, were fought out in lesser conferences, joint central committees, joint editorial boards, rival faction papers.

Indeed, there were signs and omens of disunion from the outset.
Professional politicians differ considerably from the constituents
who elect them. Though they bear the latter's mandate, they bear,
too, longer memories, completer systems of views, more deeply ingrained attitudes. A young delegate named Voroshilov (future
Commissar of War) came to Stockholm bearing the pseudonym
Volodya Antimekov, a cryptogram for Anti-Menshevik, while Kater-
ina Samoilova sported the *nom de guerre* of Natasha Bolshevikova.
Though the local elections had been held under joint parity auspices,
the credentials committee of the Congress became a battlefield.
Krupskaya, for instance, sought to enter as a delegate from Kazan
but, in her own words, "was short a small number of votes," i.e.
her comrades had attempted to set up an *ad hoc* local but could
not show enough members. She was accepted as a "consultative
delegate," with voice but no vote. But, at the end of four additional
days and nights of wrangling in the credentials committee, when
a Georgian calling himself Ivanovich presented himself as a fictitious delegate from Tiflis, where the Bolsheviks had no organization
at all, the credentials committee was so exhausted and the Mensheviks so sure of their majority that the Transcaucasian delegation
(Mensheviks all) declared: "For the sake of peace and unity, we
will not challenge Comrade Ivanovich's mandate." As victors foreseeing the difficulty of leading so ill united a party, they were inclined to be generous. Upon the defeated would fall the burden
of reluctant subordination, or of finding the means to keep the fires
of faction smoldering. At the Stockholm Congress, the Georgian

Ivanovich attracted no further attention, but we shall soon have
reason to keep an eye on him.

The final count of delegates to the Stockholm Congress was
sixty-two Mensheviks to forty-six Bolsheviks. The Bolsheviks had
lost the main working-class center of the country, Saint Petersburg,
largely because of the inglorious role they had played in the Petersburg Soviet. They were hurt, too, by their opposition to taking
part in the Duma elections. As the question of attitude toward the
Duma was long to be a critical one, let us examine it in more detail.

During the General Strike ot October, 1905, when the Tsar had
issued his Manifesto promising a legislative Duma, all socialist
parties had impulsively decided to boycott the elections. They did
this because they were under the excitement of the October days,
because they did not trust the Tsar to carry out his promise, and
because they did not like the undemocratic electoral procedure of
plural voting for the wealthier classes, and of indirect elections. The
electoral law was drafted by S. E. Kryzhanovsky, then modified
by Witte to give more representation to the "tsar-loving" peasant. After the October Manifesto, suffrage was extended to all
males. But this suffrage was hedged by a plural weighting of the
vote of the propertied classes, and by indirect elections. Following medieval Russian traditions, the voting was to be done by
estates or classes. Peasants and workingmen voted in separate
bodies, apart from landowners and urban property owners. Perhaps
this division of the population into *soslovie* was intended to separate the masses from the influence of the radical intelligentsia.
Moreover, Witte believed that the Zemstvo liberals were too radical and the peasants were by nature conservative. He hoped
to bind them still closer to the throne by a sweeping program of
land reform, but Witte's influence with the Tsar was too weak
to get this part of his program through. All that remained was
a voting scheme admirably adapted to promote class consciousness
among workers and peasants. In factories employing more than fifty,
the workingmen voted directly in their factory, an arrangement which tended to bring out a maximum working-class vote
and develop a maximum of working-class consciousness. In each
such factory (or group of smaller workshops), they chose delegates
to a higher voting body, which in turn chose delegates to the
"Workers' Curia" of the general electoral college of the city, which
in turn chose deputies to the Duma. Thus the famed system of
the Soviet Government, with voting by classes, "functional" representation by factories, and three- or four-stage voting, which was
offered to the world in 1918 as something new under the sun, was

really an invention of Kryzhanovsky, based on Russia's medieval heritage. But in 1906, Lenin joined with all other democrats and socialists in denouncing this indirect three- or four-stage voting as undemocratic. He denounced, too, the unequal representation of different classes, not according to their numbers but according to their "political reliability" or "stake in the state." Instead, he demanded what he called the "four-pronged democratic formula: *universal, direct, equal, and secret suffrage.*" Which did not prevent him in 1918 from adopting unequal, indirect, limited, and unsecret suffrage, as devices to maintain a Bolshevik majority in the Soviets though they were a minority in the country.

Both Mensheviks and Bolsheviks had accepted the idea of boycotting the elections when the Tsar first spoke of a Duma, but the Mensheviks soon decided that they had made a mistake. When the Bolsheviks, more stubborn and ardent boycotters, tried to use this "treason" as a talking point in the elections to the Stockholm convention, the Mensheviks registered gains instead of losses. For the rank and file of the Petersburg party membership, sensing that the period of direct assault was over, were beginning to turn their hopes to the Duma.

The Bolsheviks and the Social Revolutionaries, and—at the other extreme of the social spectrum—the Black Hundreds and the Union of the Russian People, continued to urge the masses to refuse to vote. Neither of these political extremes wished to accept the compromise of a constitutional monarchy, the Black Hundreds because they opposed any concessions by the Tsar, the Bolsheviks and Social Revolutionaries because they still hoped to overthrow him and call their own constituent assembly.

By the time the Stockholm Social Democratic Congress was assembling, voting for the Duma had already taken place in most parts of the country. To Lenin it was obvious that the Mensheviks had been right, and he and his group wrong. Ignoring the cries of boycottists, both of the Right and of the Left, the masses had voted in overwhelming numbers. In default of Social Democratic and Social Revolutionary candidates, they had voted for the most advanced personages available: for Constitutional Democrats, independent liberals and radicals, non-party labor men, individual Social Democrats who ran in defiance of party instructions, and (in the rural areas) for peasant and agrarian intellectuals who pledged themselves to demand a redistribution of the land. Thus the Constitutional Democrats (popularly known as Kadets from the initials *Kah Deh*) had changed overnight from an insignificant group of doctrinaire intellectuals into the largest party in the Duma, with 190 mandates. No less revealing to Lenin was the news that there was a group of 94 agrarian laborites, calling themselves Trudoviki (from *trud,* meaning "labor"). As the Kadets under the leadership of Miliukov had swept the cities in default of Social Democratic candidates, so the Trudoviki under the leadership of Kerensky had swept the countryside in default of Social Revolutionary candidates.

When the Stockholm Congress assembled to take stock of this staggering news, elections were still to be held in Transcaucasia. The Menshevik delegation proposed that the Party give up its boycott and nominate candidates there. Indignation possessed the Bolshevik faction at this "betrayal" of the "revolutionary" position, but the indignation changed to consternation when Lenin deserted his faction and cast his vote for the Menshevik motion. The motion carried. Instructions to nominate a ticket were telegraphed to Transcaucasia, with the result that the Social Democratic Party carried not only the Workers' Curiae but the whole of Transcaucasia. All of its deputies to the Duma were Social Democrats of the Menshevik faction.

For several years—the next four, to be exact—the Duma question would overshadow all others, and would put Lenin into opposition both to the majority of his own faction and, for different reasons, to the Mensheviks. His faction were in love with that splendid moment when they had appealed to the masses to ignore the Tsar's concessions and, by insurrection, convene a constituent assembly. In Trotsky's tart words, they had observed that lightning is accompanied by thunder, and therefore concluded that if they kept making a noise like thunder, the lightning would strike again. Lenin's stern sense of realism told him that the days of direct storm were over, which alone could justify the departure from the Marxist tradition of participating in parliamentary elections. Hence he voted with the Mensheviks for participation, though it threatened to separate him from the faction he had formed.

Yet he could not agree with the Mensheviks either, for it seemed to him that they set too high a value on the Duma. He would make it a mere sounding board for revolutionary propaganda, a forum where revolutionists, clothed with special immunities and powers of attracting national attention, could denounce the Tsar's "parliamentary comedy" and could talk over the heads of fellow-deputies and ministers to the masses outside the Duma, rallying them to extra-parliamentary actions, strikes and demonstrations. The Mensheviks, however, took the "parliamentary comedy" as serious drama.

They wished to propose genuine legislative measures in the interests of the working class; they sought to form a bloc with all oppositional parties, including the Kadets, against absolutism; they hoped to win genuine powers of legislation for the Duma, perhaps even a responsible ministry, which would take its instructions from the legislature and not from the Tsar: in short, they hoped to convert the Duma into a "Western" parliament. They ascribed to the Duma potential revolutionary significance, too, looking forward to the day when it might rally the whole nation behind it against absolutism, as once the French Estates General had rallied the French nation against Louis XVI. Finally, they saw in the Social Democratic Duma deputies one more chance to get out of the to them hateful blind alley of underground, conspirative revolutionary parties. The Social Democratic deputies, openly and democratically chosen by the masses, would provide, they hoped, a democratically elected socialist leadership to replace the self-appointed professional-revolutionary leaders.

Lenin held these views to be opportunistic, as he held the views of his own faction to be foolish and self-defeating. His own comrades' boycott would isolate the Party from the masses, who were interested in the Duma, and would voluntarily relinquish a weapon useful to expose "the parliamentary comedy." But Menshevism would lead the masses into the false path of parliamentary illusions, and away from the path of revolution. A party such as he believed in, a self-chosen "vanguard" of underground conspirators and professional revolutionaries, could not develop primarily out of peaceful election campaigns, nor nominate its real leaders for public office, nor permit the "backward mass" to choose its leadership for it. If any Bolsheviks were elected, he thought they would be simple workingmen and not career leaders. His underground committee, or he himself, would draft speeches for them, and tell them what to say so that the parliamentary rostrum could become a splendid sounding board to train the masses and summon them to struggle.

Even in 1905, when the boycott tactics were first adopted, Lenin was reluctant to accept them. But at the Bolshevik Conference which was held at Tammerfors, Finland, in December, 1905, he was startled to find his whole faction lined up against him! Here is Joseph Stalin's report of that episode, as given to a little party in 1920 to celebrate Lenin's fiftieth birthday:

> The debate—at Tammerfors—opened, and the provincial members, Siberians and Caucasians, led the attack. What was our astonishment when, after our speeches, Lenin in-

tervened and declared himself in favor of participating in
the elections. But then he saw his mistake and took his
stand with the faction. We were stupefied. The effect was
electric. We gave him a great ovation.

Lenin did not reply at his birthday party but during the course
of that same year, 1920, he took occasion to make it clear in a pamphlet that he thought that not he but "the Siberians and Caucasians"
had been mistaken at Tammerfors.

Why then had he gone along? Was it because he feared to be
cut off from his followers? That was part of it. For the next four
years that fear would make Vladimir Ilyich tread warily, until
he had mustered enough strength for his conception of Duma activities so that he could expel (and he actually did expel) all the re-
calcitrant revolutionary romanticists from his faction.

But in December, 1905, at Tammerfors, there had been special
reasons for yielding to the "Siberians and the Caucasians." At that
moment, the Duma was to Lenin a very secondary matter. He let
himself be persuaded by the very unanimity of his conference
delegates that they were expressing—how he longed to believe it!—
the temper of the masses themselves. If it were but so that the
masses had no faith in the Tsar's Manifesto, with its promises of
Duma, Constitution, and civil liberties! Perhaps his followers were
so unanimous because they had come right from the localities
where the masses were planning, arms in hand, to overthrow the
Tsar and write their own constitution. This attractive idea was the
easier to accept because, even while the Tammerfors Conference
was in session, the Moscow insurrection began. It was the crack
of pistols and rifles there, and not the "attack of Siberians and Caucasians," by which Lenin had let himself be seduced. But by the
time he got to Stockholm for the unity Congress he knew he had
been mistaken to yield.

First he had noted with chagrin that the Black Hundreds, too,
were for boycott. Next, that all the efforts of himself and his faction
had failed to persuade the masses from voting. The Kadets and
Trudoviki were benefiting thereby, while the Social Democrats
were isolated. Moreover, his own followers showed him the dangerously undemocratic abyss toward which the boycott tactics led,
when they came to him with a proposal that the Bolsheviks should
use force against the "unheeding" masses to disperse the electoral
meetings in which the workers were to choose their electors to
the Workers' Curiae. The Bolshevik resolution on the First Duma,
voted over Lenin's protest, read:

> . . . to declare everywhere a general political strike, hold
> manifestations, demonstrations, and utilize every means to
> the end of preventing elections from taking place, not hesi-
> tating if necessary even at the violent breakup of the
> electoral meetings. . . .

It was impossible for Lenin to imagine then that he too would
one day use similar tactics against a constituent assembly, called
into being by a successful revolution.

Most disconcerting of all to Vladimir Ilyich was the realization
that he had utterly misjudged the peasantry. Unconsciously he had
assumed—as had the government itself—that the "petty-bourgeois"
peasant as voter would choose conservative rural leaders to represent him. But with simple, single-minded doggedness, they everywhere voted for the spokesmen who promised the most radical
solution of the land question. Since the Social Revolutionaries, although they had a better understanding of the peasant, had also
made the mistake of boycotting the Duma, the muzhiks were voting
for unattached and independent village radicals, for the more
articulate of their own people, or for radical members of the local
zemstvo intelligentsia. Thus the Trudovik Party suddenly appeared
in the Duma with ninety-four deputies, spiritually close to the
Social Revolutionary Party.

> We are told—said one of the new peasant spokesmen in
> his maiden speech in the Duma—that property is sacred,
> inviolable. In my opinion it cannot possibly be inviolable;
> nothing can be inviolable, once the people will it. . . .
> Gentlemen of the gentry, you have stolen our land. . . .
> This is what the peasants who sent me here say: "The land
> is ours, we have come here not to buy it, but to take it."

What a golden opportunity for Lenin, who had been looking
everywhere for a peasant movement with which to negotiate his
alliance for a "Democratic Dictatorship of the Proletariat and the
Peasantry"! This was not the Social Revolutionary Party, which also
appealed to the working class and therefore had to be fought. This
was a true peasant party such as he had dreamed of. And here
he had left it alone in the Duma with the Kadets! Only four months
had elapsed since Tammerfors, where, according to Stalin, he
had "seen his mistake and taken his stand with the faction." But
everything that had happened in those four months had convinced
him that the Tammerfors Conference had been wrong and that
he had been wrong to yield to it. That is why, at whatever risk,
he broke with his faction at Stockholm, and voted with the Mensheviks on the Duma question.

The next six months were a particularly difficult time for Lenin. Never did he seem more irresolute, inconsistent, specious. On the one hand he was trying to hold onto his followers and maintain the prestige of the Bolshevik faction, on the other to force them toward the viewpoint which he felt was the only right one. In the face of his own better judgment, he continued stubbornly to maintain that the boycott, up to that very moment, had been correct. (Not until 1920 did he make public acknowledgment that the Bolsheviks had been wrong from the outset when they boycotted the First Duma. Then he did so for pedagogical purposes in the pamphlet *"Left" Communism: An Infantile Disorder,* directed against a faction in the Communist International that was in favor of boycotting parliamentary elections in imitation of the Bolshevik "model.")

The greater Lenin's logical entanglement, the more fiercely did he attack as "parliamentary opportunism" every utterance and action of the Mensheviks in connection with the Duma. The secret doubt that enmeshed him was whether he could or should risk an all-out attack on the stand of his own faction, so long as there was the slightest chance that the period of armed uprising was not over. If it was not over, the Duma was secondary and not worth a scrap with his faction. If it was over, then such a scrap was unavoidable. It was the government that finally resolved Lenin's difficulty by dissolving the First Duma.

Lenin had been expecting quite another outcome. He had calculated that the Tsar would ask the Kadets to form a ministry and that the Kadet Duma majority would make its peace with tsarism as a contrived deception of the masses. In this Lenin misjudged both the Kadets and the Tsar. The former were not unwilling to compromise with tsarism, but only on their own terms: a responsible cabinet government, limitation on the monarchy's powers, parliamentary control of budget, taxes, and legislation, end of the arbitrary régime of police violence and *ukaz.* If the Mensheviks overestimated the fighting spirit of this moderate democratic party, Lenin was no less wrong in imputing to them lack of principle and a mere desire to contrive maneuvers to cheat the masses. Now that the full record is available, it is clear that Miliukov and his associates in the leadership of the Kadets were a would-be loyal opposition to His Majesty within the framework of a limited monarchy. On the one hand they feared the people, the revolution and socialism; on the other they opposed absolutism and arbitrary government by camarilla. In short, they cherished a doctrinaire belief in moderate constitutionalism as that narrow strait between the twin rocks of absolutism and "anarchy" through which the ship of state must be cautiously steered to bring it into the safe harbor of "Western" ways.

Still wider of the mark was Lenin's estimate of the mentality of the other party to the anticipated "deal." Lenin always regarded the governing apparatus too schematically as a conscious, united and coldly calculating instrument of a conscious and united ruling class. It never occurred to him that the gulf between Black Hundreds and Kadets might be as wide as the gulf between Kadets and Bolsheviks, or that the Tsar's opposition to the responsible parliamentarism the Kadets worshipped might also be a matter of principle.

"One of the last of the Narodniki," G. P. Fedotov has shrewdly called Nicholas II, mindful of the fact that *narodnichestvo*, more than a definite economic-political program was a philosophical-emotional attitude toward "Holy Russia" and her destiny and toward the Russian muzhik as the primitive and undefiled repository of all Christian and Holy Russian virtues. The modern bourgeois world of Western Europe, worshipped by the Kadets and yearned for by the Mensheviks, was deeply repulsive to Nicholas. All that Lenin himself called backward, barbarous, Asiatic in Russia, was sacred to this romantic on the throne. The "dark peasant" whose entry on the stage of history inspired terror in Plekhanov, Miliukov, Martov, even in Maxim Gorky, was to Nicholas the guarantor of the throne and the source of Russia's strength and peculiar mission. Not even the shocks of peasant riots and mutinies could shake his faith in them. His "democratic" bearing with servants, grooms, common soldiers and muzhiks, testified to by all who were close to him, was undoubtedly genuine and spontaneous. But with advisers like Witte, Rodzianko and Stolypin he was always ill at ease. As his reign drew to a close he would increasingly dispense with such would-be councillors to take counsel with upstarts sprung from the folk, ignorant muzhik monks and "holy fools." In the end he would reject even the advice of reactionary nobles and grand dukes of the royal house, putting instead the fate of his family and the destiny of his empire into the hands of a coarse, lewd, mad, magnetic, "holy muzhik," whose shrewd and earthy judgments on matters of state were to the Tsar at once the voice of the people and the voice of God. The few courtiers whom he really trusted were men who shared his romantic, inverted-Narodnik views, or assumed the pose of sharing them. This brought him in principle and conviction far closer to the Union of the Russian People and the Black Hundreds than to the moderate reformers, the Wittes and Stolypins and Guchkovs, who sought to become his ministers and advisers, or the liberals who sought to set up a constitutional monarchy to limit his powers. And the Black Hundreds, as we have already noted, were as irreconcilable boycotters of the First Duma as were the Bolsheviks.

If the Tsar had no intention of letting the Duma control his policies or appoint his ministers, yet he had given his solemn word to permit its existence and he had no intention of going back on it. When the First Duma ventured to take up the land question in July, 1906, the Tsar ordered it dissolved. The entire opposition wrongly imagined that he was returning to the pre-1905 state of affairs. Haunted by reminiscences of the famous French Tennis Court Oath of 1789, the democratic and socialist deputies fled to Vyborg, Finland, the autonomy of which was still respected by the Russian police. From there they issued a manifesto calling upon the people to refuse to pay further taxes or furnish military recruits until the Tsar should permit them to reconvene. For good measure, the Social Democratic Party (led at the time by the Menshevik Central Committee Majority) followed this up with a call for a general strike to defend the Duma.

What should the Bolsheviks do who had just been denouncing the Duma as a government device for deceiving the people? And how would the masses themselves react to an appeal to defend the institution of which they had heard so much denunciation? To Lenin this exposed in a more glaring light than before the impossibility of the tactics his faction had forced upon him.

As was to be expected, the workingmen, exhausted and confused, remained passive. But again the peasants, and above all the peasants in uniform, furnished the surprises. They had set high hopes on the big Trudovik delegation, and on the land reform proposals of Kadets and Trudoviks, which had led to the Duma's dissolution. They responded with riots in many provinces and mutinies in the fleet and garrison at Sveaborg and Kronstadt.

The government was strong enough, however, to keep the initiative. It suppressed the disturbances, executed a few of the ringleaders, "pacified" the insurgent rural areas by punitive expeditions, disbarred the signers of the Vyborg Manifesto from running for office, and then—contrary to expectation—issued a call for elections to the Second Duma.

> History has shown—wrote Lenin in October, 1906—that the convening of the Duma brings with it the possibility of useful agitation . . . that inside we can apply the tactics of an understanding with the revolutionary peasants. It

would be ridiculous to close our eyes to reality. The time
has come now when the revolutionary Social Democrats
must cease to be boycottists.

"History has shown"—that was Lenin's way of admitting that he
had been proved wrong and learned something. But his followers
were never so ready as he to go to school to Mistress History. Once
more he had to fight on two fronts: against the irreconcilable
among his followers (and that meant most of them), to drag them,
reluctant, into the election campaign; and against the Menshevik-
controlled Central Committee, which proposed an electoral bloc
with the Kadets against the Rightist parties.

After the Unity Congress at Stockholm, Lenin had lost not a day
in trying to mobilize the Party membership against the new Menshevik-controlled Central Committee. Now, when it was time to
nominate Duma deputies from Saint Petersburg, he found himself
with a majority in the capital, but not in the Petersburg Province
as a whole. As so often happens, matters of principle got inextricably tangled with a petty organization question—whether Petersburg city should hold a nomination convention separate from the
Province as a whole, or whether there should be a single, inclusive
provincial convention. In the one case the Bolsheviks would control the city nominations, in the other the Mensheviks. We could
well afford to ignore this squabble were it not for the fact that it
nearly wrecked the new-found "unity" of the Party, and elicited
from Lenin one of the most self-revealing documents that ever
came from his pen.

In secure control of the city convention, Lenin put through a
proposal there for "a Left Bloc" in the elections, a block of Social
Democrats, Social Revolutionaries and Trudoviki *against* the Kadets.
Obeying the instructions of the Menshevik-controlled Central Committee, thirty-one Menshevik delegates walked out of the city convention and held a separate provincial convention, which decided
for a bloc *with* the Kadets as well as the more Leftist parties
against absolutism and the parties of the extreme Right.

"Good-bye to unity," thought Lenin, whose mind was ever attuned to the idea of split. He proceeded on the assumption that the
rift in Saint Petersburg was the beginning of a fresh split in the
Party as a whole. Always ready for the offensive when battle was
to be joined, Lenin promptly issued a pamphlet accusing the
seceders of negotiating with the Kadets "for the purpose of selling
the votes of the workers" and "bargaining to get their man into the
Duma in spite of the workers and with the aid of the Kadets." This

was not merely a charge against the seceders but also against the Central Committee of the Party, to which Lenin owed disciplined obedience according to his own theories of organization.

But the Party was not ready for a split, so that Lenin's calculations miscarried. Before long he found himself on trial before a democratically set-up Party court, charged with "conduct impermissible in a Party member." Lenin was allowed to name three judges, the Central Committee three judges, and the Lettish, Polish and Jewish Bund organizations, as neutrals, named one judge each. This was a species of democracy in Party trials which Lenin never allowed in the organization when he had majority control. The trial itself need not concern us, since it was interrupted by a new Party congress which upset the Menshevik majority and put Lenin in control.

But Lenin's remarkable speech in his own defense must concern us, for it throws a glaring light on his entire conception of how to conduct polemics with rival working-class groups and parties.

As the trial opened, Lenin calmly acknowledged that he had used "language impermissible in relations *between comrades* in the same party." He confessed that there were politically more accurate ways and more fraternal ones of designating the efforts of the Central Committee to unite all oppositions against the Tsar than that of charging them with "selling workers' votes." His choice of obnoxious phrases, he admitted, was

> . . . calculated to evoke in the reader hatred, aversion and contempt . . . calculated not to convince but to break up the ranks of the opponent, not to correct the mistake of the opponent but to destroy him, to wipe his organization off the face of the earth. This formulation is indeed of such a nature as to evoke the worst thoughts, the worst suspicions about the opponent and indeed, as contrasted with the formulation that convinces and corrects, it "carries confusion into the ranks of the proletariat." [The words in quotes are taken by Lenin from the Central Committee accusation against him.]
>
> I may be asked [he continued], Well, do you admit that such formulations are *impermissible?* I shall answer: Yes, certainly, *but only with the following little proviso:* impermissible among members of *a united party.* . . .
>
> A split means the rupture of all organizational ties, the shifting of the struggle of ideas from the ground of influencing the organization from within to that of influencing it from without, from the ground of correcting and per-

suading comrades to that of destroying their organization,
to the ground of inciting the masses of the workers (and
the masses of the people generally) against the seceded
organization. . . . It is wrong to write about Party comrades in a language that systematically spreads among the
working masses hatred, aversion, contempt, etc., for those
who hold different opinions. But *one may and must write*
in that strain about a seceded organization.

Why must one? Because when a split has taken place it
is one's duty to *wrest* the masses from the leadership of the
seceded section. I am told: you carried confusion into the
ranks of the proletariat. My answer is: I purposely and
deliberately carried confusion into the ranks of the section
of the Saint Petersburg proletariat which followed the
Mensheviks who seceded . . . and *I shall always act in
that way whenever a split occurs*. . . . Against such political enemies I then conducted—and in the event of a repe-
tition and development of a split *shall always conduct*—
a fight of extermination. . . .

Are there any limits to permissible struggle based on a
split? There are no limits to such a struggle set by any
Party standards, nor can there be such, for a split implies
the cessation of the existence of the Party. . . . The limits
of the struggle based on a split are not Party limits, but
general political limits, or rather general civil limits, the
limits set by criminal law and nothing else. . . . [All italics
in the original speech as published by Lenin. Full text in
English in *Selected Works*, Vol. III, pp. 486-498.]

Three times, in a speech that could not have lasted an hour, did
Lenin pledge himself that he should *always act thus*, whenever a
split was in prospect. It must be recognized that he kept his word!
Hence we shall always have to bear in mind this frankly avowed
view that all things are permissible in polemics between competing
parties. It will help us to understand the polemical documents from
Lenin's hands, directed against Mensheviks and Social Revolutionaries, against the Second International and its parties after he split
from it to form the Third, against Bolsheviks differing from him
sufficiently to secede or be expelled from his faction. But this will
not exempt us, in any case, from a concrete analysis of his polemical
writings to determine how much of each is objective truth, and
how much deliberately "calculated to evoke hatred, aversion, and
contempt . . . to evoke the worst thoughts, the worst suspicions
about the opponent . . . not to correct his mistake, but to destroy
him, to wipe his organization off the face of the earth . . ."

We shall have to bear in mind, too, that Lenin is not always as "rock-hard" as he would like to appear. There were times when he would restrain his polemical language out of other considerations than "the limits set by criminal law." Chief of these other considerations would be the feeling, often neglected but never fully abandoned, that the working class must in the long run be educated by political controversy to a deeper understanding of its position and tasks. As for the restraints of the criminal law, these would vanish when his party became the government and made the law. We shall have to ponder then what would happen to this doctrine, especially when the doctrine was taken up by lesser men with less ingrained humaneness and less concern for the long-run effect of polemics upon the understanding of the masses. Or when it was adopted by the leaders of other Communist parties, lacking the counterbalancing humane tradition of the old Russian revolutionary intelligentsia.

CHAPTER XXI

LENIN AND STOLYPIN

What they want is great upheavals; what we want is a great
Russia.   —*Peter Arkadyevich Stolypin*

IN PARTY POLITICS as in statecraft generally, the sovereign can do
no wrong, nor be sued without consent. Lenin's trial for "conduct
impermissible in a Party member" came to an abrupt end when,
at the London Congress of the United Party (April-May, 1907),
Lenin achieved a slender numerical majority. The new Central
Committee simply forgot the charges against its now dominant
figure.

But that did not put an end to the nagging Duma controversy.
All through the years from 1906 to 1912 Lenin had to continue his
war on two fronts: with the Bolshevik boycotters for their "infantile leftism"; with the Mensheviks for their "parliamentary opportunism." His need to keep the boycotters with him sharpened his
fight against the "non-revolutionary" use of the Duma by the Menshevik deputies, while his need to join with the Mensheviks against
his own boycottist faction embittered relations inside the Bolshevik
group. In the years of lowest ebb in the revolutionary movement
(1909 to 1911) this tangled controversy, conjoined with other issues, called forth splits in both factions. The general confusion
was fantastic. Everyone became short of temper and long on
vituperation.

In the year elapsing between the Stockholm (1906) and the London (1907) Congresses, it looked as if Lenin's authority would win
over, or at least overawe, the majority of his faction on the Duma
issue. But in the summer of 1907, just as Lenin seemed to be making decisive progress, the government under Premier Stolypin reopened the whole question in a much more drastic form. On June
16, 1907, Premier Stolypin peremptorily dissolved the Second Duma,
using as a pretext a circular planted by a police agent, and the revolutionary speeches concerning armed insurrection in which Lenin
and his fellow-Bolsheviks had indulged at the London united party
congress. Duma deputies had participated in these conspirative discussions, Stolypin declared (they happened to be Menshevik deputies, opposed to Lenin's viewpoint!), and he demanded that these

conspirers be expelled from the Duma. When the latter body hesitated to deprive them of their mandates and immunities, Stolypin dissolved it. Then, by simple *ukaz*, the government revised the electoral laws so that they would not again give a majority to the oppositions, as they had in the First and Second Dumas. The new *ukaz*, known as the *Coup d'état of June 16, 1907*, cut the value of a peasant's vote in half. Labor electors were cut by one-third. Poles and other deputations from the border countries were greatly reduced. The Third Duma was thus packed with landowners and their agents, priests, great-Russian nationalists, state officials, and other conservatives. All the radical oppositions: Kadets, Poles, Social Democrats, Social Revolutionaries, Trudoviks, etc., were cut to an insignificant minority.

A new cry arose for boycott of the Duma. The Social Revolutionary Party reverted to boycott, while Lenin's faction overwhelmed him once more. This was a "cardboard, comic-opera Duma," they cried, and the Constitution was now a mere fraud. What self-respecting revolutionary could so humiliate himself and so deceive the masses as to participate in such undemocratic elections, play a role in such a farce, pretend that anything could be accomplished in such a travesty on the idea of popular representation?

But Lenin knew no finical pride as to the kind of institution in which he would work if he could thereby serve the revolution. "In a pig-sty if necessary," he told his comrades. Moreover, he had been studying Stolypin and his maneuvers with increasing respect. Here was an opponent worthy of his steel, a man who, with opposite intentions, but from similar premises, was doing much what Lenin would have done had he been a champion of the existing order and an enemy of the revolution.

Stolypin's policy as Premier combined measures to diminish the franchise of "unreliable elements" and to repress open revolutionary activity, with a series of bold positive schemes for modernizing Russian life, reforming agriculture, and stabilizing the tsarist régime. As if he had studied Lenin's *Development of Capitalism in Russia* and all Lenin's writings on the agrarian question, Stolypin proceeded now to foster capitalism in agriculture, to promote class differentiation in the village, to break down the communal *mir*, to secrete out a new class of property-minded individual peasant proprietors as a rural support for the existing order. ("I put my wager not on the needy and the drunken, but on the sturdy and the strong.")

The trouble with the Emancipation of 1861, reasoned Stolypin, was that it actually preserved and fostered the peasant commune instead of setting up a class of individual proprietors. Each communal village had received the entire area of land allotted to its members as a communal holding under a system of collective responsibility for the redemption payments of all its members. The commune itself then divided the land for tilling among its members according to the size of the families, fresh subdivision taking place every few years to keep up with population changes. Hence there was no inducement to improve the land, and no sense of private ownership such as characterized Western farmers and tended to make them socially conservative. The system conserved communal or corporate ideology. It preserved the memory of serfdom, and reminded the former serfs that they had gotten on the average only half of the land they had tilled for their lords before emancipation. Thus it kept alive the idea that the halfway job might be completed by adding the rest of the land of the big landowner to the communal village land fund.

Now Stolypin set about to create in Russia a class of individual small proprietors. He abolished the *zemski nachalnik* who kept the village in tutelage; he instituted equal civil rights for peasants with the rest of the population; he inaugurated a series of land and loan laws which would encourage all the more energetic to withdraw from the communes and become individual owners of their share of the land. "The natural counterweight to the communal principle," he said, "is individual ownership; the small owner is the nucleus on which rests all stable order in the state." In short, he tried to create the conservative, property-minded class that the Marxists had wrongly imagined the Russian peasant to be. This was sound reactionary politics, Lenin told himself with ungrudging admiration.

And no less sound was Stolypin's *ukaz* limiting the voting power of elements opposed to the régime while he enlarged the voting power of its supporters. So Lenin, too, would act in 1918, when he made a worker's vote equal to that of five peasants.

Between 1907 and 1914, under the Stolypin land reform laws, 2,000,000 peasant families seceded from the village *mir* and became individual proprietors. All through the war the movement continued, so that by January 1, 1916, 6,200,000 families, out of approximately 16,000,000 eligible, had made application for separation. Lenin saw the matter as a race with time between Stolypin's reforms, and the next upheaval. Should an upheaval be postponed for a couple of decades, the new land measures would so transform the countryside that it would no longer be a revolutionary force. How near Lenin came to losing that race is proved by the fact that in 1917, when he called upon the peasants to "take the land," they already owned more than three-fourths of it. According to Nicholas S. Timasheff, "the increase in the area tilled by the peasants (after the revolution) did not exceed 8 per cent; for an additional 8 per cent, the peasants no longer had to pay rent. The rest was not arable land." (*The Great Retreat*, p. 107.)

> The Stolypin Constitution—wrote Lenin in 1908—and the Stolypin agrarian policy mark a new phase in the breakdown of the old, semi-patriarchal and semi-feudal system of tsarism, a new movement toward its transformation into a middle-class monarchy. . . . If this should continue for very long periods of time . . . it might force us to renounce any agrarian program at all. It would be empty and stupid democratic phrase-mongering to say that the success of such a policy in Russia is "impossible." It is possible! If Stolypin's policy is continued . . . then the agrarian structure of Russia will become completely bourgeois, the stronger peasants will acquire almost all the allotments of land, agriculture will become capitalistic, and any "solution" of the agrarian problem—radical or otherwise—will become impossible under capitalism. [*Proletarii*, April 29, 1908, reprinted in *Collected Works*, Third Russian Edition, Vol. XII, p. 193.]

Thus the two men had opposing purposes, but in premises, in analysis of the possibilities, in tactical methods, they understood each other. It almost seemed as if Premier Peter Arkadyevich were addressing Bolshevik leader Vladimir Ilyich directly when, from the rostrum of the Duma, he made his famous declaration:

"What you want is upheavals, what we want is a great fatherland."

Would a fresh upheaval come before the new régime could complete its self-reform and consolidate its new foundations? "I do not expect to live to see the revolution," said Lenin several times toward the close of the Stolypin period.

But the dark forces which Plehve had created and which Stolypin continued to use to spy upon the revolutionary movement were the forces which struck him down. On September 14, 1911, in the presence of the Tsar and two princesses, at a gala performance in the best theater in Kiev, an assassin's bullet put an end to the career of Peter Arkadyevich Stolypin. The murderer was a Jewish lawyer named Dmitri Bogrov, who seems to have been simultaneously an agent of the police and of the terrorist wing of the Anarchist movement. The assassination was never fully cleared up. Cir-

cumstances pointed to the possible complicity of the Department
of the Interior, whose secret police were guarding the Tsar, or, at
the very least, to the guilty negligence of the Kiev police authorities. The specters of *agents provocateurs* like Ryss and Azev
must have haunted Stolypin as he lay dying. The Tsar and Tsarina
did not mourn the loss of the man who had tried so hard to save
them. They never even understood what he was doing. The great
state that he had hoped to reinforce and modernize by the combination of police force, legislative manipulation, and enlightened economic and political measures, was taken over increasingly thenceforward by the dark and backward forces around Rasputin. Yet so
well had Stolypin done his work that the agrarian reform continued
to develop after his death. It was the sudden coming of war, and
not the failure of his plans, which brought the fresh upheaval in
time for Lenin.

The Central Committee (under Lenin's control since the London
Congress) called an All-Russian Conference in July 1907 to consider Stolypin's coup d'état and prepare for the elections to the
Third Duma. Though he had just captured the Central Committee,
Lenin again lost control of his own faction. Out of fifteen Bolshevik
delegates, fourteen were for boycott! The lone dissident was Lenin.
They deposed him as spokesman and chose Bogdanov to report for
them. Once more, as at Stockholm, Lenin voted with the Mensheviks. Poles, plus Bundists, plus Mensheviks, plus Lenin, outvoted
the Bolshevik delegation.

All through 1908 the conflict smoldered in the faction, in forms
too complicated to follow in detail. At times it seemed as if Lenin
had persuaded a majority to participate in the elections. But then
the fight broke out in a new form because they wanted to recall
those Deputies who were chosen (14 of the 18, Mensheviks) for not
acting in a sufficiently intransigeant fashion. This trend Lenin
dubbed *otzovism* ("recallism," from the Russian word for recall).
Or they wanted to present an ultimatum to the socialist Duma
Deputies, which could only lead to the resignation of the Deputies
either from the Party or from the Duma. This trend received the
name of "ultimatism."

All these boycottist and semi-boycottist trends rallied around the
personality of the philosopher Bogdanov, who had succeeded
Krassin as the number-two man in Lenin's *troika*, and who now
threatened to oust Lenin from domination in his own faction.
Among those who sided with Bogdanov were Lunacharsky, Gorki,
Krassin, Bazarov, former Bolshevik Duma leader, Alexinsky, the

historian, Pokrovsky, the future GPU chief, Menzhinsky, the historian of the Party, Lyadov, the future Comintern leader, Manuilsky, and many others whom we shall meet again. Not until the middle of 1908 did Lenin win a slender majority (eighteen to fourteen) in Moscow, and as late as 1909 he was still in a minority in Petersburg. Only when he felt strong enough and had built himself a new *troika* (the first three-man leadership had been Lenin-Krassin-Bogdanov; then Lenin-Taratuta-Dubrovinsky; Lenin-Malinovsky-Zinoviev; Lenin-Zinoviev-Kamenev; then, in wartime, Lenin and Zinoviev), did he expel without ceremony or any constitutional warrant all the boycottists, recallists and ultimatists from his faction. Under what conditions we shall see in a succeeding chapter (Chapter XXIX, "Lenin as Philosopher").

Ultimately, all but two of these dissenters returned to the fold as more unconditional followers than before. Only Bogdanov remained aloof because of his independent temperament and deep differences on philosophical matters. The other permanent loss was Alexinsky, who became a bitter enemy of Bolshevism. However, at the high tide of the boycottist movement in 1907, Lenin had been so alone that even the future constituents of his *troika*, Zinoviev and Kamenev, were lined up for a while against him.

Once more, in this uncanny ability to appraise Stolypin correctly and to adapt his tactics to the hard realities of revolutionary decline, Lenin proved so superior to his faction that, as one by one, they returned rather sheepishly to the fold, they were more like sheep than before in their readiness to follow the leader. Here, for instance, are the words of the outstanding Marxist historian M. N. Pokrovsky:

> There was above all, his enormous capacity to see to the root of things, a capacity which finally awakened in me a sort of superstitious feeling. I frequently had occasion to differ from him on practical questions but I came off badly every time. When this experience had been repeated about seven times, I ceased to dispute and submitted to Lenin even if logic told me that one should act otherwise. I was henceforth convinced that he understood things better and was master of the power denied to me, of seeing about ten feet down into the earth.

If we bear this strange, freely made confession in mind, bear in mind, too, that it is the utterance of an original thinker whose histories are monuments of research and rational and logical interpretation, we get an insight into the mind of the Russian intellectual and into some of the sources of Lenin's power over his followers.

We get some insight, too, into how the power of Lenin came to be transformed into the quite different power of Stalin.

If the Duma question had been the only controversy at the Stockholm and London Congresses, Lenin would scarcely have dared to side with the Mensheviks on it, since it would have meant rupture with his faction. But, actually, it was overshadowed in all minds by a number of other issues which were to keep the united party in turmoil until it split forever six years later.

At the Stockholm Congress of 1906, as we know, the Bolsheviks were in a minority. Yet, except on the Duma and on the ticklish business of revolutionary holdups of banks and merchants, Lenin managed to retain the offensive and, in no small measure, impose his views upon the majority.

The Mensheviks were still too much under the spell of 1905 to say straight out what they thought of the Moscow uprising and of armed insurrection in general. Lenin pressed his advantage.

On the land question, too, as always throughout the history of Russian Social Democracy, he took the initiative. He it was who had written for the original Party program of 1903 the demand for the return of the *otrezki*—the pieces of common land cut off from the peasant estates at the time of the Emancipation. He had thought that a realistic, "immediate demand," but 1905 had taught him how inadequate it was and how little in tune with the mood of the peasantry.

> Our mistake—he declared boldly—consisted in under-estimating the breadth and depth of the democratic, or rather bourgeois-democratic, movement among the peasantry. It is stupid to persist in this mistake now when the revolution has taught so much.

Lenin thus criticizing his own errors, Lenin learning from "History"—here is Lenin at his best and greatest. Once more he caught the Menshevik majority at Stockholm off guard by proposing a new agrarian program, with two sweeping alternative or complementary proposals: support of the peasants in any attempts they might make at direct seizure of the land, or, as a more desirable variant, complete nationalization of the land by a victorious revolutionary government, which might then rent it, or if need be distribute it, to the peasantry. Lenin's predilection for strengthening the future revolutionary state power made him prefer nationalization to disorderly seizure from below, and state control to general distribution. Yet he knew—better than any other leader except Rosa Luxemburg

—that a revolution is infinitely more complicated and disorderly and chaotic than any preconceptions and tidy formulae for channeling its torrents. Hence he thought of these alternative proposals not as in sharp opposition to each other, but as varying aspects of one general process which should break the power of the landowners, smash the old régime, win the support of the peasants for the workers' party. In mid-1917 it would be charged against him that he suddenly "stole" the land program of the Social Revolutionary Party; but those who made the charge were too short of memory. The program on which the Social Revolutionaries claimed exclusive copyright was one of the related alternatives which he kept in mind from 1906 onward.

Russian Marxists, both Bolshevik and Menshevik, tended to view the peasantry with strong reserve as a backward, property-loving, potentially hostile "petty bourgeoisie." In this all Marxists, Lenin included, differed from the Social Revolutionaries. But, unlike his comrades, Lenin could not forget that the peasants were in a majority and discontented, and that no revolution could be made without them or against them in the Russian land. Moreover, deep within him there was a substratum of peasantophile tradition inherited from the older Narodnik fighters. In the peasant question as in the terror, there was something, hard to put one's finger on, which distinguished his interpretation of their common formulae from that of all the rest of his Marxist brethren—including those in his own faction.

Instinctively, the Menshevik majority at Stockholm felt an aversion to Lenin's plan for seizure and nationalization or division of the land. Instead, Maslov and Plekhanov offered a proposal for "municipalization." Lenin's nationalization assumed a victorious revolution; his proposals for peasant seizure of the land were calculated to promote such a victory. But on what was their "municipalization" based? It reflected their longing for local self-government and their fear of centralization. It assumed somehow the emergence of democratic local governments. It was silent on the status of the national government during this period of emergence. And it was insistent that the peasants should wait in orderly fashion until the properly constituted municipal authorities were ready to rent the land to them. But behind this utopian plan lay not so much positive vision as instinctive dread. These men feared the peasantry in action, dreaded the prospect of anarchic, uncontrolled uprisings of the "dark folk." They sensed that Lenin's plan was tied to the heretical doctrine of seizure of power by the Party. Above all they feared—and this was a truly brilliant premonition on Plekhanov's part—that nationalization of the land would bind the peasant to the state afresh, to any state that might hold in its hands the weapon of overlordship of the soil, thus continuing the age-old servile "Asiatic" tradition which had always bound the rural masses to the ruling power. And if the peasant majority were bound, could the urban population be free?

> The situation in our country—ran Plekhanov's prophetic warning—is such that the land, together with the tillers, was held in servitude to the state. And on the basis of that servitude, Russian despotism developed. . . . There is not and cannot be, any guarantee against restoration. Remember the history of France, remember the history of England: in each of them, the wide sweep of the revolution was followed by restoration. . . . True, not the restoration of the remnants of feudalism. But in our country we have something that resembles these remnants, to wit, the fact that the land and the tiller of the soil are tied to the state, our own peculiar form of "land nationalization"! And, by demanding the nationalization of the land, you are making the return to this type of nationalization easier, for you are leaving intact this legacy of our old, semi-Asiatic order. . . ."

Thus was lifted for a moment the curtain that obscured the future. It was a prevision as brilliant as that of Lenin when he warned Trotsky of the consequences of an undemocratic revolution and minority party government, and that of Trotsky when he warned Lenin of the dangers inherent in his hierarchical, centralized, undemocratic party structure. They were like the three blind men who grasped three different parts of an elephant. Marxists contend that their method of sociological analysis enables them to predict the future. If these three Marxist prophecies could but have been added together, and acted on together, they would indeed have constituted a brilliant example of foresight and forewarning.

The curtain that was lifted a moment dropped again, for Plekhanov was no match for Lenin in debate on the agrarian question. Both camps were divided internally. Most Social Democrats knew so little about the countryside that the issues eluded them. The debate became more and more confused. Most Bolsheviks, too, faced the muzhik with ignorance, and a vague, unconscious dread, or with contempt, enclosed in the formula: "property-minded, petty bourgeois." Some delegates thought that the whole question of land proprietorship was alien to the workers. Others that nothing could be done until "after the revolution," and then there would be "immediate and total socialization of the land" in the form of big "agricultural factories" owned and controlled not by the vast majority of peasants but by the small class of hired help or "rural proletarians." Some abstained from voting. Others held that the question was "a bridge to be crossed when you come to it." Yet others thought up *ad hoc* motions, new and fantastic alternatives, which might satisfy their revolutionary feelings and give them something for which to cast their vote and yet evade the issue which eluded their understanding. In the end, Lenin's resolution, although in a diluted form, was the only one with a solid bloc behind it. He emerged once more as the expert on the question which was the key to popular revolution in Russia, and to the kind of state which would emerge from it. After all, Lenins were as rare in the Social Democratic camp as were Stolypins in the camp of tsarism.

At Stockholm, too, and more sharply at the London Congress, emerged the first outlines of two additional controversies which would tear the Party once more asunder. They were concerned with the two extremes of the variegated spectrum of popular organizations which had sprung up during the Days of Freedom in 1905: the open or legal mass organizations on the one hand and the illegal fighting companies or armed guerrilla bands on the other.

As we have already noted, the Mensheviks were inclined by temperament and conviction toward the trade union, the mass organization, the broad party *of* the working class; the Bolsheviks toward the conspirative underground, the armed group, the uprising, the narrow, self-selected vanguard party *for* the working class. The difference in attitude of the workingman toward his union, and of the outlawed conspirator toward his underground and his armed band, would determine real differences in spirit, relative staying power in the period of reaction, aptness for legality and for conspiracy, varying loyalties and degrees of devotion, attitudes toward autonomy, Party control, labor democracy, and a host of other divergencies. If we keep this fundamental difference of approach in mind, then many of the controversies which we are to consider in the next few chapters lose their apparent hair-splitting character and fall into place as parts of a pattern.

Outwardly the Stockholm Congress was full of confidence, in the spring of 1906, for the Party membership was still growing. But already the wider world of open and public activity and independent mass organization was being cut to pieces by the sabre blows of triumphant reaction. How the Mensheviks shuddered at the prospect of being driven back once more into the narrow cellars of the conspirative, "professional" underground! To stave it off, they revived Axelrod's proposal: the calling of a broad, non-partisan or multi-partisan labor congress, which should absorb all existing parties and mass organizations into a federated party of the entire working class.

Lenin was no less saddened than the Mensheviks by the disappearance of one after another of the new mass organizations. But he thought of it chiefly as the loss of the wider arena in which the Social Democratic Party had been able to operate, win converts, influence and control. Reluctantly, but with no severe jolt, he reverted now to his older conception that such open organizations as might still be maintained or set up should serve as mere "covers" or spheres of operation ("front organizations"—to borrow the terminology of a later day). In Axelrod's proposal he saw a heretical attempt to dilute socialist doctrine from the highly developed theoretical system of élite specialists in Marxism to the confused and "anti-proletarian" (i.e. incompletely socialist or anti-socialist) notions of an ignorant and backward working class. Against Axelrod's talk of control of the proposed new party by the mass organizations, he favored the control of the mass organizations by the vanguard party. Axelrod's "broad labor party" would be a "bourgeois labor party," he maintained, amorphous in structure, eclectic in doctrine, reformist and unrevolutionary in aim, and even—he was convinced—incapable of existence under an autocratic government. In the "right of the working class to self-determination" as urged by the Mensheviks, he saw only a "democratic superstition" that heads should be counted regardless of their individual capacity for determining matters which could be properly determined only by those who devoted their lives to the study of Marxist theory.

Even before the Mensheviks were quite sure what they were proposing, Lenin was denouncing its proponents as "liquidators" of the revolutionary party. Every time the proposal bobbed up, in whatever protean form, Lenin was ready with his epithet of scorn. As with other cherished phrases, he would hammer away at it for five years, until the entire Party began to feel the overtones of betrayal with which he endowed it, and until some of the "liquidators" defiantly accepted the epithet.

On the question of the Soviet, too, Lenin now reverted to his older conception, never altogether surrendered:

> The Party—he wrote in a polemic against the Stockholm majority—has never renounced its intention of making use

of certain non-party organizations like the Soviets in order
to extend the influence of the Social Democrats in the working class. At the same time the Social Democratic organizations must bear in mind that if social democratic work
among the masses is properly and widely organized, such
institutions may actually become superfluous. . . .

"*Actually become superfluous!*" This single statement, even if not
matched by others of similar import, should be enough to destroy
the sedulously nourished official legend that Lenin "instantly appreciated" the Soviets from the day the first Council of Workingmen's
Deputies was formed in 1905. In the above quotation there is no
room for the conception of the Soviet as a broader, more democratic workers' parliament, superior to the Party because more
inclusive and more representative. Rather does such language fore-
shadow the wasting away of the Soviets once the growth of the
influence and power of the Party might make them "actually
become superfluous."

At that very moment, Trotsky in prison was writing:

> The Soviet was in reality *an embryo of a revolutionary
> government.* . . . Prior to the Soviet, there had been rev-
> olutionary organizations among the workingmen. . . . But
> these were organizations *in* the proletariat; their immediate
> aim was to *influence the masses.* The Soviet is an organi-
> zation *of* the proletariat; its aim is to fight for *revolutionary
> power.* At the same time, the Soviet was an organized
> expression of the will of the proletariat as a class. . . . The
> Soviet is the first democratic power in modern Russian
> history . . . the organized power of the masses themselves
> over their component parts. This is a true unadulterated
> democracy, without a two-chamber system, without a pro-
> fessional bureaucracy, with the right of the voters to recall
> their deputy at any moment and to substitute another for
> him. . . . There is no doubt that *the first new wave of the
> revolution will lead to the creation of Soviets all over the
> country.*

In this remarkable passage from Trotsky's *The Year 1905*, rather
than in anything that Lenin was writing at the time, is the germ of
the doctrine concerning the Soviet as labor parliament and proletarian government, which Lenin and Trotsky were to expound
jointly in the autumn of 1917. Thus the Soviet idea has a peculiar
history. It was conceived in the matrix of the Menshevik "autonomous local revolutionary self-administrations" and Axelrod's "broad,
non-partisan (or rather, multi-partisan) labor congress." It was

nourished by Trotsky's and Parvus's doctrine of "permanent revolution." In 1917 it was to mature, as Trotsky had predicted, from "an organization of the proletariat fighting for revolutionary power" into "the organized power of the masses themselves over their component parts . . . and the embryo of a revolutionary government." And it was to go into decline after 1918, in accordance with the Leninist formula of a single party that controls all mass organizations and ultimately renders "such institutions actually superfluous." Thus the Menshevik conception was closest to the origins of the Soviet of 1905; Trotsky's to the high role assigned by him and Lenin to the Soviets in the autumn of 1917; and Lenin's to their ultimate destiny as mere instrument or transmission belt of the controlling party. Once more, three blind men, each gifted with a highly developed sense of touch, had grasped three parts of the elephant, and each described it as if it were the whole.

CHAPTER XXII

ARMS AND THE MAN

An oppressed class which does not strive to learn to use arms, to obtain arms, deserves to be treated as slaves.—V. I. Lenin

DURING the storms of 1905, all parties had sanctioned defensive arming: for the protection of meetings, leaders, racial minorities. But there agreement ended. The Mensheviks were slower to advocate the formation of armed bands when the tempest was rising, more insistent on their purely defensive function once they came into existence, swifter to demand their dissolution as soon as calm returned. But for Lenin they were an object of passionate absorption, central to his whole idea of revolution.

Not that he was one to play with armed insurrection in season and out. Yet, as soon as events permitted him to think—or hope—that an uprising might be on the order of business, he would give to the question of arms first place. From the day that the followers of the priest Gapon fell bleeding upon the snow, arms and armed bands or fighting companies were never absent from his thoughts.

"The arming of the people," he had written in his very first article after the news of Bloody Sunday reached him in exile, "the arming of the people has become an immediate task . . ."

Martov had spoken of arms, too, but Lenin had only scorn for Martov's twice-removed formula for "arming the people with the burning desire to arm themselves." Martov soon ceased to speak of arms even in such fashion. After the ill-prepared Moscow uprising of December 1905, he and his associates became convinced that it had been a mistake to form little armed bands for insurrection, or "conduct the struggle for democratic demands within the framework of a political conspiracy."

"They should not have taken up arms," said Plekhanov categorically.

> On the contrary—answered Lenin—they should have taken to arms more resolutely, energetically and aggressively. . . . Those who do not prepare for armed uprising must be ruthlessly cast out of the ranks of the supporters of the revolution and sent back to the ranks of its enemies, traitors or cowards. . . .

371

In the exciting weeks and months after Bloody Sunday, Lenin had spent day after day alone in the library in Geneva, studying military tactics and translating General Cluseret on barricade fighting. In the summer and autumn, he had sent from Switzerland endless streams of instructions:

> I see with horror, real horror, that we have been talking of bombs for more than a half year and not one single one has been made. . . . Don't demand any formalities, for God's sake spit on all schemes, send all "functions, rights, privileges" to the devil. Don't demand of people entrance into the Party—in an armed uprising that's an absurd demand . . . the only condition, dependability against the police and readiness to fight against the Tsar's troops. . . . [Letter of October 16, 1905.]

He had worked out the most detailed practical directions:

> Give every company short and simple bomb formulae. . . . They must begin their military training immediately in direct connection with practical fighting actions. Some will immediately kill a spy or blow up a police station; others will organize an attack on a bank, in order to confiscate funds for the uprising. . . .

That last sentence was to open a gulf between him and the Mensheviks over which there would never be a dependable bridge again!

A few days later he had written on weapons: "rifles, revolvers, bombs, knives, brass knuckles, clubs, rags soaked in oil to start fires with, rope or rope ladders, shovels for building barricades, dynamite cartridges, barbed wire, tacks against cavalry . . ."

There were further precepts concerning passwords, the value of mobility and surprise, relations with friendly officers and soldiers, use of women, children and old people, duties of unarmed contingents, who might disarm a lone policeman or climb roofs and shower troops with stones, acid, boiling water.

No other leader, not Trotsky, who was to organize the Red Army, nor Rosa Luxemburg, who was to lead the Spartacan uprising in Germany, and certainly no Menshevik spokesman, could conceivably write such instructions. If we would understand Lenin as revolutionist, we must never let them slip out of our mind. Such letters might alienate, indeed did alienate, many leading Bolsheviks, but in compensation the faction began to attract all the fighting types, of which this land of extreme passivity and bursts of sudden energy had so plenteous a share. During 1906 and 1907, Lenin would gather unto himself those who had put themselves outside the law by engaging in insurrection or acts of terror, and those hardy persons who hoped by supreme acts of individual will to hold back the ebbing tide and reverse its flow. This was what it meant to be a "hard" in a time of open combat. At the Bolshevik Conference in Tammerfors in December, 1905, news came that Moscow had risen. To express their feelings and continue the discussion in practical fashion, the delegates used the intervals between sittings in revolver practice (Krupskaya: *Memories*, Vol. I, p. 157). A year later, in defiance of the decisions of the Stockholm Congress and the instructions of the Central Committee, Lenin called a second conference at Tammerfors, this time a secret "military-technical" conference of a few kindred spirits, together with delegates from fighting companies and from sympathetic groups inside the armed forces. The government learned more than the Central Committee about what transpired there, since once more it had an agent among the participants.

The fighting companies or guerrilla bands were not Lenin's exclusive monoply nor invention. They had sprung up spontaneously in all parties and factions and among many non-party groups. They became most numerous in the borderlands: in Poland, where they were affiliated with Pilsudski's Polish Socialist Party and distinguished themselves by the great numbers of police officers and government officials that they killed; in the Baltic countries, where they produced crack riflemen and snipers and merged with such Robin Hood bands as the "Forest Brothers"; in the Urals and the Caucasian mountains, where they had roots in an ancient heritage of banditry, smuggling, guerrilla warfare, and blood feud. In all these border lands they were sustained by the populace and nourished by general nationalist movements for independence.

But in Saint Petersburg after the general strikes, and in Moscow after the insurrection, armed bands began to grow, too, just as the revolutionary wave was beginning to recede. Workmen who had left homes and jobs to participate in barricade fighting; strikers blacklisted by their employers or sought as ringleaders by the police; revolutionaries who had been away from home when the gendarmes called, and who no longer dared to return; men who had acquired arms by attacking police posts, robbing sporting goods stores of rifles, breaking into arsenals; soldiers and sailors who had deserted; escaped mutineers; all the hunted and proscribed who had been thrust by circumstance or had thrust themselves by fearless deeds outside the law; energetic men of the people for whom life had, for the first time, taken on broader scope and deeper meaning—such were the recruits who swelled the ranks of the fighting bands at the very moment when the great grey mass was returning to sullen quiescence.

And, precisely because other forms of public activity were diminishing, the armed bands assumed a new importance to Lenin's movement. Funds were dwindling to a trickle when funds were needed more than ever. The working class was too new, the Party too little rooted in the masses and too little belonging to the masses, for them to finance it by regular dues. The well-to-do liberals, oppositional manufacturers, parlor pinks, who had contributed most of the funds up to now, were losing their taste for revolution. Insensibly, the fighting detachments began by financing themselves and ended by financing the Party, or rather Lenin's faction. The money came from raids on state and private banks, holdups of mail coaches and trains, and, since it was easier to "expropriate" individuals than well-guarded institutions, the robbery of merchants and manufacturers. Having failed to expropriate the bourgeoisie wholesale as a class, they began "expropriating" it at retail, using the word quite solemnly and unhumorously, until in Party literature and debate such robberies came to be known for short as "exes." This method of financing was to make the Party leadership more than ever independent of the rank and file.

The armed bands began to attract all sorts of men who had a stomach for such things. Moreover, even the most idealistic were forced to keep increasing sums from the holdups for themselves— how else could one live in this illegal underworld?—and to seek relaxation from the strain of such a life in carousal and the pleasant, protective cover of personal luxury. If one dressed well, one was safer from police suspicion than a ragged man haunting the slums. Besides, there is something in the hunted man's way of life which makes a moment's respite and physical ease seem intensely precious. Thus the dual process—from above, the incipient degeneration of idealists; from below, the recruiting of submerged, demoralized, declassed and criminal elements, the "Lumpen" or "slum proletariat." These last joined now the Church-blessed, pro-tsarist Black Hundreds, now the revolutionary fighting *druzhini* or *boyeviki*,[1] finding in both extremist movements ideological banners and moral sustenance for activities which formerly had been shamefaced and desultory, and had been frowned upon by the decent men and

[1] *Druzhini* means *"companies," "bands," "brotherhoods"; boyeviki* are "fighters."

women who now gave warmth and significance and the courage of conviction to such deeds.

> Ordinary bandits—wrote Rosa Luxemburg in the recoil of horror—stand side by side with revolutionary workers before the courts-martial. They attach themselves to the class movement of the proletariat, enter into the common statistical figure of the victims of the counter-revolution, fill the same prison cells and die on the gallows with the song of the "Red Flag" on their lips. A large part of the bandits consist of former revolutionary workers and members of the various socialist parties. . . . How could this community arise between the drama of the proletarian revolution and the guerrilla struggle of the Lumpenproletariat against private property, a community so hurtful to the revolution?

Lenin, too, was not unaware of the danger. Yet, in autumn, 1906, after the Stockholm Congress had specifically forbidden armed bands and "exes," he wrote:

> The partisan struggle is an inevitable form of struggle at a time when the mass movement has already matured for an uprising and longer or shorter pauses occur between great battles.

And in 1907, when he already rejected the boycott of elections on the ground that there was no longer any prospect of an early "widespread revolutionary revival," he still continued secretly to direct "armed actions" and "expropriations," permissible only on the basis of the expectation that a "widespread revival" and a "major engagement of civil war" were imminent. How shall we explain this glaring contradiction? I think psychologically rather than logically. For his attitude toward parliamentarism he held as a derivative of the formulae of his international Marxism, while his attitude toward the terror was an unconscious heritage from the tradition of Russian conspirative technique and organization. Not in the realm of logic, but in the realm of practical organization, there was a connection between these two tactical measures. For Duma elections it was necessary to reach great numbers, and the "exes" gave him the wherewithal. When he thought of parliamentary activity he predicated it on the end of the period of direct assault. But when he thought of the armed bands, he estimated the same period as one of a "longer or shorter pause between great battles." A fascinating example of how the most logic-worshipping mind can harbor logic-tight compartments.

If it were indeed a pause between great battles, he reasoned, then the evil excrescences would be sloughed off. A growing social movement would bring them under control, the armed groups would coalesce, enlarge, be joined by contingents of the Tsar's armies and whole layers of the civilian population, merge into a general struggle for power. But if the revolution were on the downgrade . . . ?

The Mensheviks grew more and more alarmed and indignant. Sensational robberies, played up in the press of the world, began to compromise the Party in the eyes of a public opinion already weary of strife. The government used the holdups as a pretext for raids on unions and it added a fabricated conspiracy of its own to dissolve the Second Duma. Thus the whole system of open and legal organization was jeopardized by this return to the terror. Nor was their indignation lessened by the fact that the "exes" secretly directed by Lenin brought funds to the Bolsheviks, enabling them to maintain newspapers in the field, to pay the expenses of delegates to the united congresses, thereby giving Lenin's faction the upper hand. Henceforth the secret Bolshevik Center, and the still more secret "military-technical" center, became far richer and more powerful than the regular Party committees.

At Stockholm in the spring of 1906, the Mensheviks, with the support of great numbers of Bolshevik delegates, put restrictions upon Lenin's armed bands. The Congress forbade "expropriations," ordered the dissolution of all bodies engaged in such activities, and the expulsion of all "expropriators." Lenin was not afraid to face the issue, but was astonished to meet strong opposition in his own camp. He withdrew his own motion, the prohibition passing by a vote of sixty-four to four, with twenty abstentions. The twenty were Lenin's diehards. He himself stayed away from the session in which the vote was taken!

But the majority, still under the spell of the great year, felt obliged to accept his amendments to their resolution. The amendments sanctioned defensive actions against the Black Hundreds and the governmental terror. That was all Lenin needed. When the new Central Committee, with its Menshevik majority, set up a military-technical bureau" to handle these confidential matters, Lenin easily won control of it. Was it not his special field and the field of men who would naturally be attracted to his position? In defiance of Congress decision and Central Committee discipline, he now used the military-technical bureau to call a conference in Tammerfors in November, 1906. Thenceforth the Party possessed a legal Central Committee, with a Menshevik majority and an almost non-existent treasury, an extra-legal Bolshevik Center, and an illegal secret finance and military affairs committee of three: Lenin, Krassin and Bogdanov, which was more powerful than either of the other two, since it alone possessed funds. Even the Bolshevik Center, which was financed by it, did not control it or receive reports on its activities. Lenin's reasons for this were simple: the fewer there were who knew about such confidential matters, the less the danger of police agents getting in on the secrets. He picked "men of confidence" and they in turn other men of confidence, who engaged in the preparation and procurement of arms, and in border smuggling. These in turn chose traveling agents and regional agents, who selected local men of confidence to plan and execute the hazardous deeds for which the arms were supplied. Once more, Lenin was in possession of a complete apparatus built from the top downward. It was a party within the Party and a faction within his faction: the faction of the desperate, the hardy and the reckless. When Party members prepared to engage in big holdups, disciplinary requirements were met by the simple expedient of having them resign from the Party. But they continued, nonetheless, to receive instructions from the secret finance committee. By the time the second congress of the unified party was held in London in the spring of 1907, Lenin's financial resources were such as to give him the upper hand. The Mensheviks were outraged. They had a majority in the trade unions and mass organizations and official Party bodies, but Lenin turned up with a slight majority of the delegates. Part of the secret was the support of the border parties, and part his ability to pay the expenses of delegates for the journey.

> The famous "majority of the London Congress"—Martov wrote—was manufactured. . . . "Voting units" were hastily formed with the aid of enormous pecuniary resources acquired by the editorial board of *Proletarii* [organ of the Bolshevik Center] in part by expropriations, in part by "confiscation" of funds intended for the general aims of the Party—and these "voting units" each gave the right to send a delegate.

When Martov first made his charges concerning the "enormous pecuniary resources" obtained "in part by expropriations, in part by confiscation of funds intended for the general aims of the Party," he did not have the details to prove his accusations. Lenin guarded secrets well, and it would take a better sleuth than the solitary theorizer Martov to disentangle them. During the next few years, however, the evidence slowly leaked out: the complaints of the female heirs of a wealthy manufacturer whose estate was left to the Party but confiscated by Lenin for his faction; the arrest of prominent Bolsheviks abroad trying to cash a huge quantity of five-hundred-ruble notes stolen in a celebrated bank robbery in Tiflis; the charges of fighting bands in the Urals, who had paid Lenin's secret committee for arms out of the proceeds of their holdups and then failed to receive the arms; finally a break of the other two members of the secret committee of three, so that Krassin and Bogdanov, who knew all that Lenin knew, could bear witness against him. By 1910 the scandal had grown so great that confidential committees of the Socialist International were forced to concern themselves with it, and Lenin had to hand over certain "dirty monies" (the phrase is that of his friend and admirer, Klara Zetkin, one of the founders and leaders of the Communist International) to a "Committee of Honor" of three German Marxist leaders, Franz Mehring, Karl Kautsky and Klara Zetkin. In 1910, too, Lenin had to face a "Court of Honor" in his own party, a conference of the leaders of all factions, which ordained a cleanup in the organization. When Lenin was thus brought to bay, the final split into two parties became inevitable.

In 1911, when Martov saw that Lenin was not abiding by the agreement of the 1910 "disarmament" conference, he published all the patiently gathered evidence—as far as it was available and might safely be revealed to the police. His *Spasiteli ili uprazdniteli* ("Saviors or Destroyers," Paris, 1911) is one long documented indictment of Lenin's "fund-raising" methods. Its truth was never challenged by Lenin. In general, in all his fights against Martov on strategy and tactics, Lenin never cared to challenge the latter's personal honesty and veracity.

The pamphlet, given Lenin's temperament, made a final split inevitable. Yet, in 1912, when the split did occur, it was, as usual, on Lenin's initiative. He coolly summoned a conference of his faction in Prague and called it a Party Congress. It "expelled" Martov and his associates for refusing to recognize its discipline, and for "plotting to liquidate the Party." Ideological and political issues were so intertangled with moral ones, and the rank and file in the dispersed underground knew so little of the facts, that Lenin's separate party did not fare badly. On the contrary, his sense of timing and of issues, and his choice of the organizational form for the break enabled the Bolsheviks to forge ahead of the Mensheviks at the moment of rupture, although all through the years 1906 to

1911 the latter's supporters were in a majority in trade unions, legal organizations, Duma elections, and all tests of strength.

In *Saviors or Destroyers* Martov told, among other sensational things, the tangled story of the "expropriation" by Lenin of funds intended for the general Party treasury. In 1906, Nicholas Schmitt, member of the millionaire Morozov family and owner of a Moscow furniture factory which had served the insurrectionists as a fortress, was jailed on the charge of financing the purchase of arms for the Moscow uprising. In prison he committed suicide, leaving his estate to the Party. Since this occurred between the Stockholm and London Congresses, while the Mensheviks controlled the Party machinery, Lenin attempted to arrange the diversion of the sum to the "Technical Military Committee," where he did have a majority. The "legal heirs" were two unmarried sisters. Lenin's first emissary, a Bolshevik lawyer, married the older sister to establish a legal claim, but then handed over to Lenin only a small portion of her share. Vladimir Ilyich now sent one of his boldest and most unscrupulous agents, "Victor" (Victor Taratuta). Seeking a legal counterclaim to pose to that of the older sister, he became the lover of the younger one. But, being himself "illegal" he could not marry her to acquire a legal claim on her heritage. So he arranged a fictitious marriage between his mistress and Ignatiev, another member of the Bolshevik fighting detachments who somehow had escaped a police record. Mr. and Mrs. Ignatiev now claimed her share, and handed it over to her lover. But Taratuta was not satisfied. He threatened the older sister and her husband with a visit from the Caucasian fighting detachments unless they, too, handed over the remainder.

It was at this point in our novelesque tale that the Mensheviks became sufficiently aware of the whole "confidential" operation to put in a claim on behalf of their section of the Party. This was the "dirty monies" to which Klara Zetkin had reference, and which Lenin was compelled in 1910 to turn over (insofar as it was unspent) to the Court of Honor of the International Socialist Bureau, Mehring, Kautsky and Zetkin. But in 1912, when Lenin's rump convention in Prague declared itself to be "the Party," he managed to persuade the Court of Honor to turn the remainder over to him.

> The Bolshevik Center—wrote Dan in the Martov-Dan *Geschichte der russischen Sozialdemocratie*—supplied each month to the Petersburg Committee 1000 rubles and to the Moscow Committee 500 rubles. During the same period

the Central Committee of the Party did not have an average income of so much as 100 rubles a month.

This assertion is confirmed by a number of Bolshevik documents. Thus, in the summer of 1908, when the movement had so far declined that income from dues had ceased, Lenin wrote to Vorovsky, living in Odessa:

> We absolutely count upon your coming as a delegate. . . . We will send money to all the Bolsheviks for the journey. . . . We beg you to write for our paper. We can pay now for articles and will pay regularly.

To this letter Lenin's wife, Krupskaya, appends the explanation that the funds came from the fictitious marriage which Victor Taratuta had arranged between his lover, Elizaveta Pavlovna Schmitt, and the Bolshevik Ignatiev (*Memories of Lenin*, Vol. II, p. 25).

And there are the memoirs of Sulimov, who participated in the Ural "exes" or holdups. In *Proletarskaya Revolutsia* (Moscow, 1925, No. 7), published under Bolshevik auspices, he writes:

> During the years 1906 and 1907, we sent to the District Committee of the Party (Bolshevik) some 40,000 rubles and to the Central Committee—i.e. Lenin's Secret Center—some 60,000. With these resources the District Committee issued three papers: *The Russian Soldier, Proletarii,* and a paper in the Tartar tongue. Besides, money was provided for the journey of the delegates to the London Congress, for the support of the school for military instructors in Kiev and the Bomb-throwing School in Lemberg, as well as for the arrangement of border crossing for the smuggling of publications and fugitives.

Lenin himself, though he might use deceit freely against the police and his comrades in rival factions, was never one to shrink from the defense of the things he believed in. Hence his writings give more than one hint on the source of his funds. In a remarkable theoretical defense of *Guerrilla Fighting* (not available in English but translated into German under the title *Der Partisanenkampf, Saemtliche Werke*, Band X, pp. 113-26), written just prior to the London Congress, he declared:

> The armed struggle pursues two *different* goals . . . in the first place the goal of the killing of individual persons, higher officials and subalterns in police and army; second, the confiscation of funds both from the government and from private persons. The funds seized go in part to the Party, in part for the arming and preparations of the up-

rising, in part for the support of the persons who conduct the struggle. The funds which have been seized in the great expropriations—more than 200,000 rubles in the Caucasian, 875,000 rubles in the Moscow expropriation—have gone in the first place to the revolutionary parties. Lesser expropriations have served above all, sometimes even exclusively, for the maintenance of the expropriators.

This he published in his underground paper *Proletarii*, No. 5, in the issue of October 13 (Old Style, September 30), 1906. The statement must have been as interesting to the police as to the Mensheviks, who, with much Bolshevik support, had prohibited just such operations only a few months before, at the Stockholm Congress. At the London Congress, scheduled for the spring of 1907, the Mensheviks would demand a reckoning. But at the London Congress, aided by just such funds, Lenin was to have a majority of the delegates!

The London Congress (April-May, 1907) marked the highest point ever reached by the "united" Party. Not one delegation appeared but five: Bolsheviks, Mensheviks, Polish Social Democrats, Lettish Social Democrats, Jewish Bund. Leon Trotsky, just escaped from Siberia, tried to form yet another faction of the "non-factional" but he could find only three. Almost everyone was already lined up in a disciplined caucus. On most issues, his four votes swelled Lenin's majority. The student Angelica Balabanoff, future secretary of the Communist International, and the writer Maxim Gorky, each visiting a Party congress for the first time, saw a festive and brilliant gathering: the venerable but still vigorous founders, Plekhanov, Axelrod, and Deutsch; their renowned disciples who had laid the cornerstone inside Russia, Lenin, Martov, Dan; the disciples of these in turn, young men of the generation of Trotsky and Stalin; the founders of the Jewish Bund and the Polish and Lettish Social Democracy; and, most impressive of all, a great flux of newcomers, genuine workingmen who had been brought to the surface by the storms of 1905. The Congress statistics listed 116 workingmen and 196 intellectuals and professional revolutionaries, further noting that 118 delegates were "living at the expense of the Party," a truly impressive officer apparatus. With no less pride the delegates recorded the number of centuries of prison and exile that they had already collectively undergone. As we shall not again be able to see so many and such distinguished revolutionists assembled together, we might take advantage of the occasion to look at the Congress as it appeared to the eyes of Angelica Balabanoff and Maxim Gorky.

Around Lenin were gathered many of his present and future lieutenants: the philosopher-economist-scientist Bogdanov, who in 1904 had replaced Krassin as second man in Lenin's inevitable *troika;* Zinoviev and Kamenev, who would make up the *troika* after he had broken with Bogdanov; Tomsky, who would lead Bolshevik trade union work from 1905 until the purges of 1937; Litvinov, who would one day be Foreign Commissar; Voroshilov, who would be Commissar for War; Bubnov, who would be Commissar for Education; Yaroslavsky, future leader of the Atheist League; Pokrovsky, the historian; Alexinsky, Bolshevik spokesman in the Second Duma; Rykov, who would be Vice-Chairman of the Council of Commissars while Lenin was its Chairman, and Chairman of the Supreme Council of Economy; Nogin, who would lead the Moscow uprising of November, 1917; Victor Taratuta, who had just brought the Bolsheviks a pretty penny through the Schmitt legacy.

Besides the Mensheviks whom we have already met, there was a large and brilliant delegation from Transcaucasia, henceforward to be the chief popular base of Menshevism and of its bloc of Duma deputies. At the head of that delegation were Tseretelli of Georgia, leader of the Social Democratic Fraction in the Duma; Zhordania, who would one day be President of the Democratic Georgian Republic; and Noah Ramishvili, future Minister of the Interior.

And yet another Georgian, with whom we must concern ourselves from now on, appeared in the humble role of fraternal delegate, silent because he was not yet quite sure of himself in these fine-spun debates, without a vote because in all of Georgia he had not been able to muster the five hundred Bolshevik supporters, or major fraction thereof, which would have entitled him to a voting mandate. As at the preceding Stockholm Congress, the Menshevik Transcaucasian delegation again challenged his credentials, this time successfully because they showed that the Borchalo District, from which he professed to come, did not have a functioning branch. He attracted the notice of neither Balabanoff nor Gorky nor Krupskaya nor any other memorialist of the Congress. Official legend today makes him out to have been Lenin's right hand since the beginning of the century, but as late as this Congress in 1907 he was not yet important enough to be named as member or alternate for the Central Committee (the Bolsheviks named five members and ten alternates)[2] nor one of the secret committee of seven-

[2] Those named by the Bolsheviks as their members and alternates on the Central Committee were Lenin, Bogdanov, Krassin, Zinoviev, Rykov, Nogin, Dubrovinsky, Goldenberg, Roshkov, Teodorovich, Shantzer, Zommer, Leiteisen, Smirnov and Taratuta.

teen which was set up as an extra-legal Bolshevik Center to run the affairs of the supposedly dissolved faction. Yet, for reasons which will appear later in this chapter, he was beginning to attract Lenin's attention as a trustworthy lieutenant for some particularly difficult and dangerous tasks which required the highest secrecy and conspirative skill.

There were 91 Bolsheviks and 89 Mensheviks at the Congress (according to other accounts, 106 and 99), of whom we have named but a few of the outstanding. And there were 55 representatives of the Bund, of whom we must note at least Rafael Abramovich and M. I. Lieber (real name Goldman), who would be elected by the Congress as the two Bundist members of the Central Committee. Long after Martov was dead and Martynov had become a Bolshevik and Dan a "Menshevik fellow-traveler," Abramovich would become the outstanding leader of menshevism in the days of its post-1917 exile, when it had been reduced by defeat and persecution and despair to a pitiful remnant, dispersed to the far corners of the earth.

Of the forty-four Polish Social Democrats, the most impressive were Rosa Luxemburg, frail and dynamic, fresh from prison, and her close comrade in leadership and personal companion, Jan Tyszka (Lev Grozowski or Leo Jogiches), who had just escaped from Siberia. He was the organization man of the Polish Social Democracy and she was the strategist and theoretician, as if Lenin's two roles in the Bolshevik faction had gotten incarnated into two separate persons forming one indivisible union. Though she might excoriate Lenin for his excessive centralism. his penchant for splitting and expelling and his "night-watchman discipline," her co-leader Tyszka ran the Polish Party with a similar hand of iron, drawing her into the complicity of justifying his acts with her pen. Both internationalists in a sense that the Russian leaders were not, they were active in three parties and they would ultimately lead the Spartacan uprising in Germany and perish in it. Around them in the Polish Party had already gathered an able group, of whom we must note at least Warski (real name Adolf Warshawski), who would be elected to the Central Committee in London along with Tyszka; Dzierzynski, Unschlicht, Radek, and Hanecki. All of these would become Bolsheviks in 1917. Dzierzynski would lead Lenin's Cheka and later Stalin's GPU while Unschlicht would become its Vice-Commissar. Radek, like Tyszka and Luxemburg, would be active in three parties and become an outstanding journalist for the Comintern and the Stalin régime, only to end up in the purge trials. Warski would become the leader of the Communist Party of

Poland and would be killed along with all other leaders of that party who sought refuge in Russia, during the same great purges. Hanecki we shall meet again because he figures in the celebrated charges that Lenin was a German agent during the war.

Of the Letts we need note only Comrade "Hermann" (real name Danishevsky), one of the two elected to the Central Committee, to become celebrated later in connection with the crackshots of the Lettish Rifle Corps, which furnished such important contingents to the Cheka and GPU and to the Bolshevik armies in the period of civil war. Danishevsky was to become an important aide of Trotsky's when the latter was Commissar of War.

So vast an assemblage, so noisy and quarrelsome, including Caucasians in sheepskin hats and bearded workingmen in Russian blouses and ten Deputies from the Second Duma, over 300 delegates in all, representing over 150,000 members, could not contrive to meet in secret in some tiny cellar hole, unbeknown to the police. First the whole variegated army filtered into Denmark with the intention of meeting in Copenhagen. But the democratic city fathers took fright and banned their meeting out of deference for Denmark's ruler, who was uncle to Russia's Tsar. London was their next choice, but how to get funds to transfer three hundred-odd people to England? Angelica Balabanoff and Gorky proved to be more than interested spectators now, for the former secured a substantial donation from the German Social Democratic Party and Gorky raised additional funds in London.

The ousted Congress found shelter in the Brotherhood Church in Whitechapel belonging to a Christian Socialist group under the leadership of Ramsay Macdonald, a church—as Gorky noted— "unadorned to the point of absurdity."

Having lent their building for what they conceived to be a convention after the British fashion—two or three days to settle all issues—the congregation spent the next three weeks trying to get this convention-in-permanence to adjourn, if not *sine die*, at least long enough for Wednesday evening prayer meeting and Sunday service.

But these Russians had never had an opportunity to talk themselves out. Now they were going to say all that the censorship and the vicissitudes of prison and exile had forced them to leave unsaid. They were going to settle all the past; appraise the experiences of two years of revolution; apportion the blame for defeat; resolve all the problems of the unforseeable future. The debate was a full-dress affair, alternately on a higher level than that of any other movement in the world, then as suddenly on the lowest plane of faction bitterness and calculation. To make matters worse, the heart of the Congress, the Russian delegation proper—180 strong—was almost evenly divided between Bolsheviks and Mensheviks: of the former 91 to 89 of the latter. Every debater had not only to pour out all that was on his heart, even if it meant repeating what a score had said before him; he must also say that unsaid word which he hoped would convince and reconvince the last man in his faction, win away some waverer from the opponent group, persuade the little reservoir of neutrals, Poles, Bundists Letts, whose votes would break the deadlock. Every resolution had to be dickered over in caucus, compromised, blurred, until it could command somehow a slender majority. Everyone who abstained from voting felt an irrepressible urge to explain his abstention.

The election of chairman (Lenin won over Plekhanov by a few votes) "provoked a debate that covered practically every issue with which the Congress itself was to deal . . . raged for over a week with a ferocity which I felt sure must have exhausted the entire stock of polemics as well as the strength of the delegates" (Memoirs of Angelica Balabanoff).

Naturally, the funds ran out once more. Maxim Gorky was pressed into service to convince some wealthy London admirers to finance the further deliberations. A Mr. Joseph Fels (whose name the reader may recognize in the Fels-Naphtha soap trademark) was prevailed upon to make a loan of three thousand pounds sterling against a note signed by all the leading delegates. The Party would soon fall on evil days and be unwilling or unable to honor its note, but when the Bolsheviks took power Mr. Fels would dig it out of his bank vault and present it, and it would be paid. When last I was in Moscow, it lay on velvet in a glass case, a curious memento of an infinitely remote and incomprehensible day when the Revolution was not a state power but an inspiration.

Gorky had come from self-imposed exile in Italy, hungry for a Russian face, the sound of the Russian tongue, a glimpse of the "giants" of the movement.

> My festive mood lasted only until the first meeting when they began wrangling about "the order of business." The fury of the disputes chilled my enthusiasm. . . .
> When we were introduced, Lenin shook my hand heartily and looking me over with his keen eyes and speaking like an old acquaintance, he said jocularly: "So glad you've come. I believe you're fond of a scrap. There's going to be a fine old free-for-all here."

I hadn't expected Lenin to be like that. Something was lacking in him. He rolled his *r*'s gutturally, and had a jaunty way of standing with his hands poked up somehow under his armpits. He seemed too ordinary, did not give the impression of a leader. . . .

He began at once to speak about the defects of my book, *Mother*—evidently he had read it in the manuscript in the possession of S. P. Ladyshnikov.[3] I was hurrying to finish it, I said, but did not succeed in saying why. With a nod of assent, Lenin himself offered the explanation: Yes, I should hurry up with it, such a book was needed, for many workers who take part in the revolutionary movement do so unconsciously and confusedly, and it would be very useful to them to read *Mother*. The very book for the moment.

Thus began a friendship which, thanks to Lenin's special attitude toward literary talent and Gorky's admiration of a man in whom his soft, romantic temperament sensed strength and greatness, was able to outlast many bitter differences.

Martov, too, made an admirable impression on Gorky, as he did on everybody. But not so the rest of Lenin's opponents:

Plekhanov, in a frock coat closely buttoned up like a Protestant pastor . . . spoke like a preacher confident that his ideas are incontrovertible, every word, every pause, of great value. . . .

Little Theodor Dan spoke like a man whose relationship to the authentic truth was that of father to daughter. . . .

Martov, this amazingly attractive man, spoke with the ardor of youth and was evidently most deeply affected by the tragic drama of the dissension and split. He trembled all over, swaying backward and forward spasmodically, unfastening the collar of his starched shirt and waving his hands about. . . . Martov did not give so much the impression of arguing as of urging and imploring. . . . At times he sounded almost hysterical. . . .

But now Vladimir Ilyich hurries to the pulpit and cries *Comrades!* in his guttural way. He seemed to me to speak badly, but after a minute I and everybody else was absorbed in his speech. It was the first time I had heard complicated political questions treated so simply. . . . No striving after eloquent phrases . . . but every word uttered distinctly, and its meaning marvelously plain. . . .

He was interrupted by shouts of hatred. One tall, bearded individual kept jumping up from his seat and stuttering:

[3] Probably an error on Gorky's part for *Ivan* (not S. P.) Ladyshnikov.

> *Little p-plots . . . p-playing at little p-plots! Blanquists!*
> These hostile thrusts had no noticeable effect on him. I
> learned what this external calm had cost him a few days
> later. . . .

The debate which Gorky remembered so vividly two decades
after it occurred was the one dealing with armed uprising, armed
bands, "expropriations." As we have already seen, the bearded
heckler had some grounds for excitement. The supreme body of the
Party, the Congress at Stockholm, in the spring of 1906, had forbidden the "exes"; but all through that year notorious robberies
continued. And in the autumn, Lenin had written the defense of
such actions which we have already quoted. He had even hinted
that he knew where the funds were going. ("The funds which have
been seized in the great expropriations, more than 200,000 rubles
in the Caucasian and 875,000 rubles in the Moscow expropriation,
have gone in the first place to the revolutionary parties. Lesser
expropriations have served above all, sometimes exclusively, for
the maintenance of the expropriators.") There is a curious vagueness about one of the two large sums mentioned which tempts us
to pursue the subject a little farther.

The Moscow "ex" referred to was the work of Maximalist Social
Revolutionaries, the Caucasian "ex" of Federalist Socialists; yet
Lenin's secret bureau undoubtedly had a hand in the second and
probably in the first. At any rate, it is a matter of Bolshevik record
that Lenin's group did help the Social Revolutionaries in two other
resounding exploits of the same year 1906. We can find evidence of
this in the memoirs of Leonid Krassin, and in recollections concerning him published shortly after his death. Typical is this sentence from the essay of the Communist party-historian Lyadov:

"The contrivance which blew up Stolypin's villa and the bombs
thrown in the Fonarny Pereulok [Fonarny Alley] were made under
Nikitich's supervision. Nikitich was a party pseudonym of Krassin."

Before we go into these celebrated holdups—and others still more
celebrated—we must look into this peculiar *de facto* alliance between Lenin's secret bureau and the Social Revolutionary Maximalists. The Social Revolutionary Party, the reader will remember,
was an offspring of the old Narodnaya Volya, inheriting along with
the latter's devotion to the peasantry and democracy, its inclination
toward acts of terror. In an undemocratic land where the government employed organized violence against all dissent, violence
must be met by violence. Thus assassination and, by extension,
"expropriation" were matters of principle.

At the other extreme of the socialist spectrum were such men as Axelrod and Martov, who favored "European," "civilized" mass and class methods, and rejected acts of terror by individuals and small bands—also as a matter of principle. They looked on holdups and assassinations as demoralizing adventurism, unworthy, degrading, self-defeating for an idealistic movement that was seeking to raise the level of social life. Such acts would give supremacy inside the movement to the desperate, secret and conspiratorial, and would alienate the broad mass of workingmen and all liberal and democratic public opinion.

In between these "Westernizing" Mensheviks, who thought their movement should, politically speaking, learn to "talk German," and the Russian Social Revolutionaries, who wanted their movement to "talk Russian," stood Lenin. In periods of lull he would have it "talk German" and in periods of storm "French" (France has more of a tradition of violent insurrection). But, more than he was himself aware, at all times he was building a movement that would "talk Russian"—the Russian of the old Narodnaya Volya and the Maximalist wing of the Social Revolutionary Party. He rejected individual terror only and exclusively on the basis of expediency. The main point of his article on *The Partisan Struggle*, from which we have quoted his figures on the size of certain "expropriations," is that a movement which aims at nothing less than the overthrow of the autocracy and the social order, cannot be choosy about the means it employs, nor reject on theoretical or moral grounds any means of fighting which arise out of the struggle and seem to further it.

In the autumn of 1905, the Tsar's promise of a constitution had caused a division of the various revolutionary groups according to temperament and principle. The Social Revolutionaries, in love with democracy, had always said they would abandon the terror if a democratic way of transforming Russia were offered. When the elections to the First Duma were being held, they publicly renounced the use of terror. Only after the Duma was dissolved did they resume it as a method of political agitation. But Lenin deduced from the same Manifesto of the Tsar that the autocracy was feeling weak and was therefore engaging in a deceptive retreat, a mere maneuver. Hence the use of direct force and the blows of the armed bands should be redoubled. Thus Lenin became more "terrorist" than the terrorist Social Revolutionaries. Both the Social Democrats and the Social Revolutionaries split on this issue. While the Mensheviks and Social Revolutionary majority were for giving the Constitution and the Duma a reasonable trial, and avoiding acts which might give the government an easy pretext for return to unlimited absolutism, Lenin chose this moment to issue his precise and detailed instructions to the armed bands. At the same time, a Left Wing group of the Social Revolutionary Party, calling themselves Maximalists, decided to continue the terror in defiance of their party's decision. The secret fighting groups of Lenin and of the Maximalists moved closer together. All through 1906 they cooperated in the manufacture of bombs (in Krassin's laboratory) and in a series of holdups and assassinations. In return for Krassin's preparation of the munitions of war, Lenin's group received some of the proceeds from Maximalist "exes." More than has been generally realized, this rapprochement paved the way for the united action of Leninists and Maximalists or Left Social Revolutionaries in 1917. The first Soviet coalition government was an alliance of these two tendencies.

The Moscow "ex" which Lenin referred to was one of a series of celebrated robberies of the years of 1906 and 1907. Twenty Maximalist *boyeviki* held up the Bank for Mutual Mercantile Credit in March, 1906, disarmed four guards and made off with 875,000 rubles. In October, the Maximalists held up the Mutual Credit Bank on Fonarny Pereulok in Saint Petersburg, and a treasury truck laden with funds for the State Bank. The explosives for Fonarny Pereulok and for Stolypin s villa came from Krassin's "Technical Bureau."

By virtue of his duties as an engineer, Leonid Krassin found it easy to travel. During 1906 he took several trips to Baku and Tiflis to "activate" the work of seizing funds in the Caucasus. At the same time, the third member of Lenin's secret *troika*, the philosopher Bogdanov, was given charge of operations in the Ural Mountains. There the guerrilla chieftain was a daring, capable fighter named Lbov, and the proceeds, as we have seen from Sulimov's memoirs, were for a while considerable. However, one of the chief confidential gun-runners recruited by Krupskaya, Kommissarov, turned out to be a man who had been planted in Lenin's immediate circle by the secret police so that when Kommissarov's wife transported guns to the Urals the entire shipment was seized there together with everybody with whom the police agents had contact (Krupskaya: *Memoirs of Lenin,* Vol. I, pp. 173-4).

But it was the Caucasus, with its mighty mountain ranges, embattled races and peoples, and long tradition of banditry, smuggling and guerrilla warfare, that proved to be the ideal center for these activities. The *boyeviki* could count on the sympathy of the common people and even of men in high official position. According to the memoirs of the Bolshevik Makharadze (*Twenty-Five Years of the Struggle for Socialism*, Tiflis, 1923) published by the Soviet Government while Lenin was still alive, 1150 acts of terrorism, large and small, were carried out in the Caucasus between 1904 and 1908.

Though the Bolsheviks were not numerous in Transcaucasia, they possessed a few men exceptionally qualified for the conspirative planning and execution of this kind of enterprise. These cooperated at first with other groups. Then, appetite whetted by some small successes, they organized on their own the most active and celebrated fighting band of all. Krassin conferred with them in Baku and Tiflis. The actual captain of their armed band, known as Kamo, made several trips in 1906 and 1907 to see the *troika* in Saint Petersburg and Finland. He came back with his head full of limitless admiration for the wisdom of Lenin, Bogdanov and Krassin, and with his suitcase full of dynamite, revolvers, munitions and bombs. For reasons which have never been clarified, Kamo's immediate superior, Joseph Djugashvili, also made two trips to see Lenin during 1907 and 1908, trips on which, despite his efforts to prove an early kinship with Lenin, he has been virtually silent.[4] We can only conjecture that they dealt with the question of continuing the "exes" after two Party congresses had forbidden them. (Since many details of these operations are to this day shrouded in mystery, our parenthetical notes and footnotes in this chapter are fuller than elsewhere, and the reader will be well advised to note where the sources are Bolshevik publications, where those of the police or partisan opponents, and where there is an element of conjecture. One of the unusual features of the passage from Lenin on the Caucasian "expropriation" (quoted above) is that he is both vague and incorrect as to the amount involved, though the daily papers were full of stories on the matter. He writes, as if with purposive inexactitude, "more than 200,000 rubles." Other Bolshevik sources specifically state: 315,000 rubles.[5] This raid on the Dushet treasury was not carried on by Bolsheviks, yet according to the memoirs of the Bolshevik historian Lyadov both Krassin and Kamo had a hand in it. The actual holdup was the work of six Federalist Socialists (a Caucasian revolutionary party) disguised in the uniform of soldiers of the 263rd Regiment garrisoned there. They deposited

[4] The only mention of them came in his interview with Emil Ludwig: "Whenever I visited him abroad—in 1907, 1908 and 1912—I saw heaps of letters he had received from practical workers in Russia." (English language edition of the interview, Moscow, 1932, p. 18.)
[5] See for instance note 71 in Vol. X of Lenin's *Collected Works*, German translated from the Second Russian edition.

the huge sum with a "reliable person," whence, according to a later complaint, it somehow found its way not into their party's, but into Lenin's coffers.[6]

So skillful and secretive was Stalin that few Bolshevik memoirs, even those of eyewitnesses and participants, recognize his directing part in these celebrated affairs. All of them, however, are aware of the exploits of Kamo, and the remoter superintendence of Krassin and Lenin. The first to give direct credit to Stalin is Tsintzadse, who knew whereof he spoke because, like Kamo, he was a leader of the Caucasian guerrilla bands. But the real connecting link between the "exes" and Stalin is to be found in the person of Kamo.[7]

The *boyevik* known as Kamo was the proto-hero of all these holdups. Brave as a lion and crafty as a fox, simple, big-hearted, sentimental, worshipful of those whose leadership he accepted, ruthless in action and saintly in his selflessness, Kamo was a type of Robin Hood revolutionary scarcely to be conceived of in the Socialist movements of Western Europe and America. (The nearest comparable figure is the German revolutionary, Max Hoelz.) Even the Bolshevik historian Lepeshinsky expresses a sense of strangeness in paying tribute to him as a "medieval hero."

His real name was Semyon Arshakovich Ter-Petrossian. He was the son of a moderately well-to-do Armenian merchant of the town of Gori, which is also Stalin's birthplace. The two were chums in

[6] Souvarine: *Stalin,* p. 93. The reader will find the following partial studies of the question of expropriations readily available in English: Souvarine: *Stalin;* Levine: *Stalin;* Pope: *Litvinov;* Trotsky: *Autobiography* and *Life of Stalin.* The best of these is Souvarine's. All of them make use of original Soviet sources. To fortify the reader's belief in these fantastic facts, I have, wherever possible, traced their statements to the original sources, and, except for Martov, have given in general only sources published under Bolshevik auspices. My chief debt—a matter of lesser interest to the reader—is to Souvarine, who, in the French edition of his work, gives an excellent bibliography. He failed, however, to document the most striking statements by specific notes, merely giving references *en bloc* at the end of the chapter. The American publisher, without his consent, made the matter much worse by throwing out the bibliographical notes altogether, thus weakening the authority of a really solid and carefully documented work.

[7] The memoirs of Tsintsadze were published in *Revoliutsiis Matiane,* Tiflis, 1923 and 1924, Nos. 3, 4, 9, 10. Most of the documents out of which the details of this obscure matter are pieced together were published during those two years either in Tiflis or Moscow (i.e. in both cases under Soviet auspices) as part of the voluminous literature attendant upon the celebration of the twenty-fifth anniversary of the foundation of the Russian Social Democratic Party. All the material was written in 1922 and 1923 and has the special authentication of having been approved for publication by the Soviet Government while both Lenin and Krassin were alive as well as many of the active participants in the events described.

boyhood, Stalin, as the older and brighter, being the leader even then. When Semyon was early expelled from school for some "offense against religion," Djugashvili was engaged to tutor him. The ascendancy intensified: he converted his pupil to socialism, taking him along in due course into the Bolshevik faction. The very nickname, "Kamo," came from Stalin. One day when Semyon came for orders, speaking in Russian with his strange Armenian accent, he asked: "*Kamo?*" (meaning *komu?*, "to whom?") and Stalin teased him, "Hey you, *kamo, kamo!*" The name stuck and he became known by it throughout the movement.

When a bodyguard was required, or a spy was to be done away with, when heroism and loyalty and tight-lipped secrecy was needed, Kamo could always be depended on. His first successful "ex" at Kutais netted fifteen thousand rubles, but he continued to allow himself and the members of his band exactly fifty kopeks (twenty-five cents) a day for maintenance. When he was caught after several such exploits, he made a daring escape from the Tiflis jail and went to Lenin, then in hiding in Finland. Lenin sent him to Belgium to aid "Papasha" (Litvinov) in gun-running. The future Commissar for Foreign Affairs, posing as an officer in the Ecuadorian Army, then as a Belgian, ordered arms from the State Munitions Factory of Denmark (Denmark's King was the uncle of Nicholas Romanoff!) and from Schroeder and Company of Germany. Thence the diminutive Litvinov and his giant Armenian companion went to Bulgaria, where they let on that the arms were intended for Macedonian and Armenian revolutionaries fighting for freedom from Turkey. Litvinov purchased a small yacht in Fiume and engaged its entire crew to sail from Varna across the Black Sea to the Caucasus. But the yacht ran aground, Rumanian fishermen stole the arms, and Kamo and three associates were arrested and sent to Constanza. The sources for this strange story are Litvinov's own memoir on Kamo for a biography written by Bibineishvili and published in Moscow in 1934, and an entry in the archives of the tsarist secret police which reads:

> With money stolen from the revenue department of Kvirili in 1905, Kamo and the emigrant Meyer Wallach (Litvinov's real name) . . . bought arms abroad and wanted to bring them on the yacht *Zara*, bought for this purpose, from Varna to Russia. . . .

How the police department knew about it we shall learn later. Released from the Rumanian jail, Kamo returned to the Caucasus, stopping on the way to get bombs from Krassin. The bombs could not have been very good, for Kamo's wife, Medvedyeva Ter-Petrossian, records that they were serviceable only for a few days, so that he had to rush into holdups without proper planning. He made two unsuccessful attempts. In the second, one of his own bombs wounded him in the face so badly that he nearly lost his sight in one eye. Securing fresh explosives, he began planning more carefully what turned out to be the most famous of all revolutionary robberies.

On the morning of June 26, 1907. a cashier and a bank clerk drove through Erivan Square accompanied by a guard of two policemen and five Cossacks. In the carriage, according to an advance tip received by Kamo (the revolutionaries had spies in the government just as the government had spies among the revolutionaries) was more than a quarter-million rubles from Saint Petersburg, destined for the State Bank in Tiflis. Ten members of his band, two of them women, stationed themselves at various points in the Square. He himself, in the uniform of an army officer, had been circulating around the populous Plaza all morning, warning bystanders away in cryptic commands. On one side was his own coach. As the government mail coach drove in, bombs were hurled. Two policemen and a Cossack were killed and about fifty persons wounded, most of them but slightly. The frightened horses dashed off with the money still in the carriage till a bomb hurled at their legs put an end to their flight. The "army officer" Kamo, shouting and uttering fierce oaths, dashed up and "arrested" the member of his band who had seized the bags of money. The booty turned out to be 341,000 rubles,[8] nearly all of it in 500-ruble notes. Kamo hid it in a couch in the study of the director of the Tiflis Observatory. The hiding place assumes a special interest when we find that a few years back a police report had contained the following entry: "Joseph Djugashvili, employed at the Tiflis Observatory, intellectual, has connections with railwaymen . . ." (The police reports published in this chapter and throughout the work are those published by the Soviet Government after it opened the tsarist police archives.)

Four weeks later, once more disguised as an army officer and carrying a hat box crammed with 500-ruble notes, Kamo set out for the frontier. High in Lenin's confidence in Berlin was a Russian police spy, Dr. Jacob Zhitomirsky, entrusted by Lenin with all sorts of "confidential" tasks. He it was who notified the Russian and

---

[8] The above figure, higher by almost a hundred thousand rubles than that given in most accounts, is taken from Lenin: *Collected Works*, Vol. XII, Third Russian Edition, 1936, p. 566.

German police when Kamo arrived in Berlin, arranging that the Armenian should be arrested when he was carrying a suitcase laden with dynamite. In December, 1907, Lenin set a given day on which various agents should try simultaneously to exchange the 500-ruble notes in banks scattered all over northwestern Europe. Dr. Zhitomirsky was in charge of the agents entrusted with the "hot" money! Police and state banks in each country were supplied with a list of the serial numbers and descriptions of the persons involved. A Lettish Bolshevik was arrested in Stockholm; Olga Ravich, future wife of Zinoviev, and two Armenians, were taken with part of the *corpus delicti* in Munich; Maxim Litvinov, future Foreign Commissar, was picked up by the Paris Security Police with a huge sum in these stolen bills on his person.[9] There is a touch of irony in the fact that the new Minister of Justice in France, Aristide Briand, saved him from extradition to Russia by a decision that his crime was "political." Most unjust was the arrest of N. A. Semashko, future Commissar of Health in the Soviet Government, who had bitterly fought against Lenin on the question of the robberies. He fell under suspicion because some woman wrote a postcard to one of the would-be passers of the stolen funds, and addressed it care of Semashko. "It was the most absurd event in my life," he would write in his memoirs.

Further raids on addresses supplied by Dr. Zhitomirsky resulted in the capture of a supply of fresh banknote paper. From photographs, the paper firm identified the purchaser as the dignified representative of the Allgemeine Elektrische Gesellschaft, the engineer Krassin. Part of it had already been shipped to Lenin while he was still in Finland, through the transport facilities of the German Social Democratic daily, *Vorwaerts*. They thought they were handling Russian underground literature, and were furious to learn that they had been made unwitting accomplices in a counterfeiting ring.

The scandal in Social Democratic circles was enormous. The Swiss party adopted a resolution protesting the abuse of their country's cherished right of political asylum by "common criminals." Men high in the Swedish and French parties rallied to the defense of the arrested. Axelrod wrote to Plekhanov suggesting that this was the time and the issue for discrediting Lenin once and for all.

[9] For confirmation of these arrests and the reason for them see Krupskaya: *Memoirs of Lenin*, Vol. II, pp. 11-14. As this volume was published while Litvinov was Foreign Commissar, it omits his name. But Litvinov's own memoir on Kamo and other Bolshevik documents of the twenties, give him a leading role in the attempt to dispose of the 500-ruble notes, as do the tsarist police archives and the records of the French police.

Yet, despite their indignation, the Mensheviks were too decent in their common feud with the tsarist police to arrange for any but highly secretive party investigations. From the standpoint of party welfare as they understood it, and certainly from the standpoint of elementary party discipline, they had grounds enough. Had not the Stockholm Congress of 1906 ordered the dissolution of the bands and the termination of the "exes"? And in 1907, had the vote not been even more overwhelming in London, where on most matters Lenin had a majority? Lenin, taking advantage of his place in the Chair, had avoided registering his vote. But a majority of Bolsheviks had voted with the Mensheviks. And, when delegates shouted from the floor: "What does Lenin say? We want to hear Lenin!" he only chuckled, "with a somewhat cryptic expression." (Trotsky: *Autobiography*, p. 218.)

Then, only a month later, with the Mensheviks still smarting at their defeat, due in part to his "superior finances," his secret committee had carried off the Tiflis holdup, provoking a scandal which cost the whole movement dear in public sympathy. By the year's end, with the arrests all over Europe of the stolen banknote passers, the scandal had become international.

Several investigations were set on foot at once: one by the Central Committee, which named a tribunal under the upright chairmanship of Chicherin (Litvinov's future chief as Foreign Commissar); another by the Transcaucasian Party Committee; a third by the International Socialist Bureau. Chicherin's probing began to point to the conclusion that Kamo had been planning to rob the banker Mendelssohn in Berlin (Bolshevik writers have denied this and assert that Kamo was planning to take explosives with him to the Caucasus), and that the banknote paper had been ordered by Krassin for counterfeiting Russian rubles. (This last takes on a special interest in view of the seizure of GPU agents in the United States in the nineteen thirties, when they were transporting counterfeit American dollars so perfectly printed that only the duplication of serial numbers confirmed their falsity. And still in 1946 the same story repeated itself when the Korean Communist Party was caught counterfeiting money in the American zone of occupation.[10]

To block further exposure, Lenin managed to use his majority in the Central Committee to transfer the investigation from Chicherin's court of honor to a more "confidential" and more malleable sub-committee. In Baku and Tiflis, where the members of Kamo's band were found to have "resigned" from the Party prior to the raid, the finger of suspicion now began to point a little higher, at

[10] New York *Times*, May 11, 1946.

Kamo's superior, Joseph Djugashvili. Here it was impossible for
Lenin to block the investigation, since the Mensheviks completely
controlled Transcaucasia. The local committee continued to press
its inquest until Djugashvili was either expelled, or else circum-
vented the dishonor of expulsion by timely resignation.[11]

But neither resignations in the Caucasus nor the sidetracking of
the Chicherin Committee abroad could stop the slow accumulation
of knowledge by Lenin's opponents. By the beginning of 1910 the
scandals concerning the Schmitt estate, the "expropriations," the
counterfeit banknote paper, and the arrests for attempting to convert the proceeds of the Tiflis "ex" into foreign currency, made
such a clear picture that Lenin at last was brought to bay. The
Mensheviks and those Bolsheviks who were shocked by the things
done against their will and behind their backs by Lenin's secret
committee, forced him to agree to a joint party conference (held
in January, 1910), which attempted to bring order out of chaos,
disarm the factions, restore the Party as a united organization,
abolish the faction organs, set up a single paper with a joint editorial committee of Bolsheviks and Mensheviks, and, in general,
clean up an unhealthy mess. One of the first acts of the conference
was to compel Lenin to burn the remaining 500-ruble banknotes
(over 200,000 rubles' worth) and all the blank banknote paper
intended for counterfeiting. But, even while he was at bay and on
the defensive on these "technical" matters, Lenin pressed as best
he could the beginnings of a fresh political offensive against the
"boycotters, recallists and ultimatists" from his own faction, and
against the "liquidators" in the Menshevik camp, who wished to
liquidate the underground party in favor of legal trade unions and
a legal party.

On February 1, 1910, Lenin wrote from Paris to his sister Anna:

> Darling Anyuta,
> We have had a very "stormy" time lately, but it has ended
> in an attempt at peace with the Mensheviks. Yes, yes,
> strange though it may seem; the factional organ (*Proletarii*)
> had been closed down and we are trying hard to move
> towards union. We shall see whether we shall succeed. I
> freed myself recently from very urgent matters in view of
> these changes. . . .

But we are running a little ahead of our story. . . .

In his German prison, Kamo's lawyer brought him a secret message from Krassin giving him a fresh assignment: he was to say

[11] For the evidence on this matter see Chapter XXVII.

nothing, but feign insanity. With amazing fortitude he carried out the order. Here is Souvarine's moving summary of what followed:

> He stamped, shouted, tore his clothes, refused food, struck his keeper. He was shut up naked in an icy cell . . . put under observation, subjected to horrible tests; he stood upright for four months, refused food, was forcibly fed at the expense of several broken teeth, tore out his hair, hanged himself counting on intervention at the last moment, opened blood vessels with a sharpened bit of bone and lost consciousness in a flood of blood. . . . To test his pretended insensibility, needles were stuck under his nails and he was touched with red-hot irons. . . .

At last the German Government deported him to Tiflis, where he underwent a fresh series of tortures. In August, 1911, after four years, he achieved a perilous escape, aided by his fellow *boyevik*, Tsintsadze. We cannot follow his incredible career further, except to note that he was heartbroken to find that the revered *troika* had broken up, that Krassin had dropped out and that Bogdanov and Lenin were fighting each other on incomprehensible political and philosophical issues.

Lenin's repentance, or caution, did not prevent his sending Kamo once more from abroad in 1912 to attempt another highway robbery in the Caucasus. Caught and sentenced to death, his sentence was miraculously commuted to life imprisonment as a result of a general amnesty order issued that year, as part of the tercentenary celebration of the Romanov dynasty. Released by the Revolution of 1917, he died when an automobile driven by a Soviet official struck his bicycle on a mountain road in Tiflis. In Tiflis today this loyal and gentle and formidable bandit of the Revolution has a street, a hospital, a steamboat, and a children's park named after him. Not to know the career of this twentieth-century Robin Hood Bolshevik is to miss an essential element in the understanding of the Russian movement and the Caucasian scene, out of which Joseph Stalin emerged to leadership of an empire.

The expulsion, or resignation under fire, of Djugashvili in connection with the Tiflis "ex" did not lower him in Lenin's eyes. Rather was it dating from this time that Vladimir Ilyich began to take note of him as an agent at once circumspect and audacious. In 1912, while the Party was still ringing with the scandals that Martov had just made public in his *Saviors or Destroyers*, Lenin coopted "Koba" (Stalin's nickname at that time) onto the Bolshevik Central Committee. In 1913, he called Koba to him in Cracow, Austria, for training. He needed some spokesman of one of Russia's minority nationalities to present the Marxist—or better, the Leninist—view of the national question. To Gorky, who had just rebuked him for neglect of that burning issue, Vladimir Ilyich replied:

> As to nationalism, I am fully in agreement with you that it is necessary to pay more serious attention to it. We have here a wonderful Georgian who is writing a long article for *Prosveshchenie*, for which he has gathered all the Austrian and other material. We are applying ourselves to the question. . . .

CHAPTER XXIII

The Youth of Soso Djugashvili

If there are no separatist tendencies at present on the part of the various nationalities, neither are there any on an all-Caucasian scale, because all the nationalites of the Caucasus are at loggerheads with one another and submit to cohabitation only under the influence of the Russian Government, without which they would plunge at once into bloody rivalry.
— *Report of Vice-Roy Vorontsov-Dashkov to Nicholas II, October 1912.*

THE BLACK SEA is half European, the Caspian all Asiatic. Between them lies a broad peninsula that would be a natural bridge uniting the continents, were it not for the Caucasian range, one of the mightiest mountain chains in the world. West of the range lies Turkey; east, the desert-steppe; south, the tableland of Iran; southwest, Asia Minor. Thus on three sides lies Asia, but on the northwest, Europe begins.

From before the dawn of history innumerable waves of migration, conquest, flight, have broken over these crests, leaving in high-hung valleys and inaccessible gorges fragments of all the passing peoples. There they have remained lost to time in little pocket-worlds of their own.

When the third of our protagonists was born in the mountain town of Gori, in the most important of these little "pockets," the ancient Kingdom of Georgia, this region was, as it still is, a veritable museum of history. The Soviets found it necessary to divide the area into some seventeen Autonomous Areas, Autonomous Regions and Autonomous Republics; the North Caucasian; the Adygeisk; the Cherkess; the Karachaevsk; the Kabardino-Balgar; the Northern Ossetian; the Southern Ossetian; the Chechen-Ingush; the Abkhaska; the Adzharskaya; the Nagorny Karabagh; the Yakhichev; the Orjonikidze; the Armenian; the Daghestan; and the Georgian. Nor does the above list complete the complexity of this patchquilt of peoples. Thus, to take only one of the Autonomous Republics: in 1945 the Council of People's Commissars of the Daghestan Republic included among its twenty-two members three Avars, five Kumyks, four Laks, two Lesghians and two Darghins.

Stalin in *Marxism and the National Question,* written in 1913, would poke much fun at the Austrian Marxist notion that the way of maintaining the integrity of a multi-national state was the way of "cultural autonomy," but that is the solution he has adopted today for his homeland, insofar as there is any autonomy at all.

In 1913, too, he had the notion that there was no such thing as Georgian nationalist antagonism toward the Great-Russian rulers, only toward the neighboring nationalities:

> There is no serious *anti-Russian* nationalism in Georgia [he wrote] primarily because there are no Russian land-lords there or a Russian big bourgeoisie to supply fuel for such nationalism among the masses. In Georgia there is *anti-Armenian* nationalism; but this is because there is an Armenian big bourgeoisie there which, beating the small and still unconsolidated Georgian bourgeoisie, drives the latter to anti-Armenian nationalism.

But the formation of a separate Georgian Republic in 1918; the repeated revolts against Soviet rule in the twenties, the vast numbers of soldiers of Georgian origin in displaced persons camps after World War II who refused to return to their homeland, tell a different story.

In his childhood, Joseph (Yosif) Djugashvili [1] rubbed shoulders with representatives of all these peoples, as well as with Turks, Tartars, Persians, Greeks, Kurds, Jews, Moldavians, Esthonians, Czechs, Poles, and, of course, the Ukrainians and Great-Russians who dominated the administrative centers and made up the majority of the newly forming industrial proletariat and technicians in the oil and machine industries. A perfect living laboratory for a future Commissar of Nationalities to be born into!

A child born in Transcaucasia might be born historically into almost any century, culture and code, or, indeed, into several at once. On feast and market days tribesmen came down to Gori from the higher ranges, resplendent in silver filigree, a slotted cartridge belt and a long-tongued dagger in a silver sheath. Hidden in the wilder gorges were such "museum" peoples as the Svanethians or Khevsurs (from the Georgian *Khevi,* "gorge" or "cleft"), numbering perhaps eight thousand, who, on festal occasions, still dressed in helmets, chain mail, greaves, shields, swords, the full panoply of the medieval crusaders who left this little time capsule as they passed through on their way to or from the Holy Land.

---

[1] Pronounced *Jugashvili.* I have used the *Dj* instead of plain *J* merely because this has become conventional in English, but the Russian *Dzh* is exactly equivalent to our *J* in *Joseph.*

Nansen in 1925 found all these mountain peoples quarrelsome and quick-tempered, addicted to blood feuds in which a man's relatives and friends were subject to vengeance for his deeds. Feudists went armed even when they worked in the fields. "Just think," Stalin was to write in the polemic of 1913 from which we have already quoted, "just think of 'preserving' such 'national peculiarities' of the Transcaucasian Tartars as self-flagellation; or 'developing' such 'national peculiarities' of the Georgians as the vendetta!"

The legends of innumerable nations cluster round these peaks. On Ararat (16,916 feet high) on the Turkish slope, the Ark of Noah came to rest. Where the flank drops to the Black Sea is Colchis' strand, where Jason sought the Golden Fleece and modern Argonauts found oil. On Kazbek (16,531 feet) the father of the Greek Gods chained the revolutionist Prometheus. On the summit of Elbruz (18,480 feet above the level of the sea) there is today a statue of Joseph Stalin, bearing the legend: "On the highest crest of Europe we have erected the bust of the greatest man of our time."

When the boy Soso (diminutive for Joseph) chanced to lift his eyes above the roofs of Gori, he beheld Kazbek thrusting its peak more than 16,500 feet into the sky. Along its flank lay the famous military highway through the Dar-y-al Gorge (*Dar-y-al*, "Gate of the Alans"), reminding us that before the beginning of history the Alans from the Russian steppes went through this high-flung pass. To note the armies which have traversed it since would be to list almost all the conquering peoples of Eurasia. The tale of endless clashes would continue into Soso's childhood, when Slav and Turk fought south of the Caucasus wall; into his manhood, when in the winter of 1915, the Turks tried to force the frozen passes, leaving behind them 30,000 frozen corpses; on to 1921, when his friend, Sergo Orjonikidze, would lead a ragged band of the Red Army over the Dar-y-al Highway in a surprise attack upon the Socialist Republic of Georgia; and on to the year 1943, when the Wehrmacht stormed through to hold for a while the key town of Vladikavkaz, "Lord of the Caucasus."

Georgia is a land of ancient civilization. From Egypt and Mesopotamia, the smelting and forging of metals spread to Armenia and Georgia more than two thousand years before the Christian Era, while the Eurasian plain lived, for many centuries more, in the Stone Age. Two of the oldest Christian kingdoms in the world, Armenia and Georgia, were converted more than a half-millennium before Kievan Russia forsook its heathen gods.

But if Georgia entered earlier than Russia into history, it left it earlier too. From the late Middle Ages until the spouting of the oil gushers at the beginning of the present century, the land almost ceased to develop. Lying for centuries "between the hammer of the Turk and the anvil of the Persian," it had finally sought protection from Russia, which, converting "protection" into conquest, had detached it from Asia and incorporated it into Europe. Yet this age-old connection with Turkey and Iran was deeply to influence the Russian foreign policy of the Georgian who is today ruler of Russia. Few aspects differentiate more sharply the days of Lenin from the days of Stalin than the differences in their attitudes toward Turkey and Iran. Lenin was tireless in his denunciation of the tsarist government for its drive toward the Dardanelles and its efforts to subject northern Iran. Against the Kerensky government one of Lenin's bitterest accusations was that it still coveted these areas.

> The Provisional Government—he wrote in July, 1917—has not even published the secret treaties of a frankly predatory character, concerning the partitioning of Persia, the robbing of China, of Turkey, the annexation of East Prussia, etc. . . . It has confirmed these treaties concluded by tsarism, which for several centuries has robbed and oppressed more peoples than all other tyrants and despots . . . disgracing and demoralizing the Great-Russian people by transforming them into an executioner of other peoples.

When Lenin came to power, one of his first acts was to renounce all claims to those areas of Iran and Turkey which Stalin is pressing for at this moment. Thereby he won the support of Turkey and Persia, an admiration and gratitude and close alliance which outlasted all vicissitudes of Soviet relations until the moment of the Stalin-Hitler Pact of 1939.

Transcaucasia is a Mohammedan stronghold too. Two decades before Djugashvili's birth there came to an end a twenty-year-long Mohammedan holy war of the Cherkess (Circassian) Moslems against the Russian conqueror. A year before Soso was born, they rose again.

On January 5, 1943, in the midst of the Second World War, the Soviet army journal, Red Star, startled many of its readers by announcing with approval that the Moslem Ingush tribe of the Caucasus had proclaimed a "holy war" against the Germans, and Red Star reported a rush of volunteers from the mountain heights—a report with a strange sound in a land that had had two decades of anti-religious campaigns and military conscription. That there was more to the story than appeared in *Red Star* became obvious later when an *ukaz* of October 17, 1945 revealed the summary extinction of both the Chechen-Ingush Autonomous Socialist Soviet Republic and the Karachaev Autonomous Region, their "self-determination" having been cancelled and their remains apportioned to the Georgian and other republics. It was reported that this was a punishment for "collaborationist tendencies in these districts at the time of their occupation by the German army." (New York *Times*, November 30, 1945.) To wipe out the very memory of their "autonomous" existence the names of some of their principal towns were changed from their tribal language to the Georgian tongue. As I write, eighty thousand former Soviet soldiers of Caucasian origin in displaced persons camps refuse to return to their homeland and families. They are all that are left after battle and labor battalion loss, forcible return, and execution of some four hundred thousand Red Army Caucasian troops who surrendered to the Germans and in some instances fought on their side (New York *Times*, December 15, 1946).

Stalin's later life, spent in industrial centers and among Russian Marxists, has not fully obliterated the marks left by his boyhood mountain home upon his character and thought. In his youth he assumed the nickname of Koba, derived from a celebrated guerrilla fighter for Georgian freedom. Says his schoolmate, Iremashvili:

> Koba became a divinity for Soso. He wanted to become another Koba, a fighter and a hero as renowned as Koba himself. . . . His face shone with pride and joy when we called him Koba. Soso preserved that name for many years, and it became his first pseudonym when he began to write for the Party. . . .

Like all revolutionists, he took many names to cover his traces: David, Nizheradze, Chichikoff, Besoshvili, Ko., K. St., K. Kato, Vasilyev, Totonyantz, Ivanovich, and others. But those which remained his favorites throughout were revealing: that of the romantic guerrilla fighter-bandit Koba and that of Stalin, Man of Steel. When the writer met him in the twenties, though Djugashvili had been using the name of Stalin officially for over a decade, he still delighted in having his intimates call him Koba. His most important theoretical work, *Marxism and the National Question* (1913), was signed K. Stalin, combining the two names.

It was this mountain background with its tiny pockets of national or tribal feelings which caused Lenin to encourage him to write on the national question in 1913, and to report on it at many subsequent Party conferences. This led to his appointment as Commissar of Nationalities in the first Soviet Government. If, as head of the state, this man from anti-Russian Georgia was to become more of a Russian nationalist than the Great-Russian Lenin, the sources of that transformation are to be sought in the same psychological well-springs that made Napoleon, the Corsican, the symbol and architect of Imperial France; Hitler, the Austrian, the protagonist of the greater German Reich; Charles, the Fleming, the greatest instrument of Spain's world empire.

It would be false to look for a one-to-one correspondence between a given aspect of Stalin's character and the characteristics of the peoples among which he was born, yet again and again we will get sudden insights if we bear those Georgian origins in mind. The difference between Stalinism and Leninism is as much explainable in terms of their differing backgrounds as in their differing personal characters. Without that key, the whole trend of Stalin's independent leadership after Lenin's death is incomprehensible. The successive displacements in leadership from 1917 on are a symbolic epitome of the long struggle between Russophiles and Westernizers that marks the dualism in the Russian soul: first Kerensky, Miliukov and the Mensheviks, extreme Westernizers all; then Lenin, the Great-Russian from the Middle Volga, blend of Westernizer and Slavophile; finally the elimination of all of Lenin's westernizing comrades by this Georgian from the Caucasian mountain ranges.

By Lenin the word "Asiatic" was frequently used as a term of opprobrium concerning Russia's past and institutions: "Asiatic despotism," "Asiatic bureaucracy," the "Asiatic humiliation of the individual." But by his Georgian disciple, except in the one article he wrote under Lenin's direct personal guidance in 1913, the word is never used thus. And it would be strange if it were.[2]

In April, 1941, when Matsuoka for Japan and Stalin for Russia signed the non-aggression pact that set Russia free to face the West and Japan free for the attack on Pearl Harbor, Matsuoka raised his glass to express the hope that the treaty would be kept.

---

[2] It is interesting to note that the classic Marxist classification of societies into "Asiatic, Ancient, Feudal and Capitalist" has been completely abandoned in all present-day Stalinist literature. Since Russia has taken on afresh some of the essential aspects of "Asiatic Despotism," the very words have disappeared from historical and sociological literature published by Stalinist "Marxists." For the profound social implications of this omission, see the forthcoming work: Russia's Asiatic Restoration, by Karl A. Wittfogel.

"If not," he added with the institution of hara-kiri in mind, "I must give my life, for, you see, we are Asiatics."

"We are both Asiatics," was Stalin's retort.

Strange fact: in none of Stalin's biographies does he come to life! Whether official and authorized like Yaroslavsky's, Beria's, Barbusse's and that of the Marx-Engels-Lenin Institute, objective and critical like Souvarine's, or frankly hostile like Trotsky's and those of the Georgian Mensheviks who were the companions of his youth, there is a shadowy and insubstantial character to them all. So silently did he rise to power that he seems hardly to have attracted the attention of his contemporaries until he was already in the Kremlin. We know nothing about his father, of whom he has always been reluctant to speak. We have no such accumulation of memories from wife, brothers, sisters, neighbors, childhood friends, as in Lenin's case; no such collection of intimate and revealing personal and political letters; no self-revealing autobiography as with Trotsky; nothing to tell us what manner of boy, and little beyond public actions and dictated documents to tell us what manner of man he was. Every foreign observer has commented upon the secretiveness that envelops him. On his fiftieth birthday even *Pravda* took notice of this in an article entitled: "Stalin the Enigma." Official biographers, men who have worked and feasted with him (Enukidze, Beria, Yaroslavsky) write strangely as if they were reconstructing the life of a man long vanished from the scene. Their works are more notable for what is left out than for what is put in, and what is put in has the studied air of being manufactured to fit a prescribed pattern. We are beset with obscurities and contradictions at every step. The succession of "memoirs" and official biographies published since the "enigma" article of 1929 have served not to dispel but to increase the mystery, and to blot out the few fixed points of the earlier framework of fact.

When one writes of a still living man it would surely seem a simple matter to put moot points up to him, and then, since no man is to be fully trusted as to his own opinion of himself, to check his answers against records, the testimony of neighbors, friends, associates, opponents. But in Stalin's case this is not as simple as it sounds. The versions he himself has dictated sometimes contradict each other concerning even elementary facts. Records have been destroyed, altered, suppressed. Many of those in a position to speak—not only opponents but even comrades of a lifetime—have been silenced by fear or purge, or made to say what on the face of it cannot be so. Stalin has been made the object of an amazing cult which leaves no room for fallibility or common humanity. Mountains of documents, general histories, Party histories, memoirs, have been banned and burned. There was more barbarous bravado about German book burning, but far less thoroughness in the elimination of essential records. In the Soviet Union, state agencies are the sole publisher, entrust the task, direct the writing, dictate the approach and conclusions, censor, edit, correct, publish, market at wholesale and retail, purchase for schools, libraries and institutions, reward, recall, condemn, replace, destroy. Account after account has received the *imprimatur* and been declared official, only to be publicly denounced, or quietly withdrawn in favor of a different version within a year.

In 1935, to give only a single instance, the Ninth Congress of the Communist Party of Georgia concerned itself at some length with the rewriting (and not the first official rewriting nor the last!) of the history of the Transcaucasian revolutionary movement.

> Noting the distortions of the history of the Party and of the revolutionary movement in Georgia and Transcaucasia occurring in the works of a number of Communist historians, the Congress deems it necessary to concentrate still greater attention against attempts to falsify the history of Bolshevism.

On July 21 and 22, 1935, Lavrenti Beria—shortly to become head of the All-Russian *GPU*—delivered a two-day-long address on the execution of that instruction. The address was later printed in many languages under the title *On the History of the Bolshevik Organizations in Transcaucasia,* alternatively titled *Stalin's Early Writings and Activities.* Previous histories and memoirs, many published when Stalin was already the head of the state, or as faction documents serving his rise to power, were declared by Beria to be false. He publicly warned the aged Philip Makharadze, until then regarded as the leading Communist historian of Georgia, that he had better revise all his writings afresh:

> As for the expositions of the struggle of the Transcaucasian Bolsheviks given in the writings of Ph. Makharadze . . . they contain a number of errors in principle and of a historical nature, distort historical facts and events and present a number of points in the history of the Party *dishonestly.*
>
> So far [added the future head of the GPU ominously] Comrade Makharadze has not taken the trouble to revise

his works and correct the mistakes and distortions they contain.[3]

The meaning of Beria's admonition is made clearer by a sentence inserted at this point in a later edition:

> A. Enukidze and M. Orakhelashvili, since exposed as enemies of the people, smuggled deliberate distortion and falsification of the history of the Transcaucasian organization into their books.

Enukidze was executed; Orakhelashvili has disappeared without a trace. Yet Enukidze had been for over a third of a century an intimate friend of Stalin's. By 1930 he had sufficiently revised his always Stalin-loyal memories concerning the early history of the Transcaucasian movement so that he was selected by his Leader to be one of the four official birthday memorialists whose collective *Life of Stalin* was printed by the government in all the tongues of the Soviet Union and in many other languages for distribution by the Comintern throughout the world. (The other three co-authors were Kaganovich, Voroshilov and Orjonikidze.) To make matters worse, essential sections of Enukidze's earlier memoirs, now officially declared false, are confirmed precisely where they had been challenged—confirmed, that is, by a host of earlier published documents and by the memoirs of Krupskaya and Krassin, which are still officially declared true.

In view of this difficult state of affairs, we shall have to have recourse to the methods of the "archaeologist," who, by collating successive layers of myth and legend, seeks to arrive at the historical truth. Where there is doubt, we shall simply range the versions side by side, with due attention to antiquity, surrounding circumstances, and presumptive social meaning of each, leaving it to the reader to evaluate the evidence and draw his own conclusions as best he may.

---

[3] It is interesting to note the dates of the various writings of Makharadze referred to by Beria. These dates reveal the length of time that some of them were considered authoritative and the fact that the later ones were actually written for the exaltation of Stalin. But, alas, Stalin's stature continued retroactively to grow! *The Dictatorship of the Menshevik Party in Georgia* (Moscow, 1921) and *On the History of the Communist Party of Transcaucasia* (Tiflis, 1923) were written while Lenin was still alive. *Outlines of the Revolutionary Movement in Transcaucasia* (Tiflis, 1927), *The Best Disciple of Lenin* (an article in *Zarya Vostoka*, No. 293, Tiflis, December 21—Stalin's fiftieth birthday—1929) and *Outlines of the History of the Workers' and Peasants' Movement in Georgia* (with G. Lachapuradze, Moscow, 1932) were faction documents serving the cause of Stalin's rise to power. But these, too, had lost their virtue by 1935!

Iosif or Joseph Vissarionovich Djugashvili was born at Gori, Georgia, on December 21, 1879. Leon Trotsky was then a month old, and Lenin a boy of nine. Gori was a town of perhaps five thousand, pleasantly situated on the River Kura. Soon after Soso's birth, the railroad was to link it to Tiflis, changing its ways, uprooting many of its inhabitants, the boy's family among them.

Soso, as he was called throughout his childhood, was born in a modest two-room house, now a national shrine, with walls and floor of rough native brick and a large window running the length of one side, as in an old-fashioned country store. The larger room, with its small table, rope-seat stool, sofa and built-in bunk covered with a straw mattress, served as living room, bedroom for the whole family, and cobbler's shop. The other room was a kitchen. Poverty and disease were familiar visitants. Soso's three brothers died in childhood, leaving him the only child. At seven he contracted smallpox, which left his swarthy skin oily and pockmarked. According to police records of 1903, which noted the pockmarks, his other distinctive mark was the joining together of two toes of one foot. In addition, some accounts say that his left arm was slightly atrophied. Leon Trotsky has suggested that the atrophy was a degeneration of congenital alcoholic or syphilitic origin, but this is pure speculation. It is too suspiciously frequent a phenomenon, this attributing of syphilis, congenital or otherwise, to detested men: a kind of folkloric vengeance. At the time of Lenin's death a number of circumstantial stories as to the "syphilitic origin" of the latter's final paralysis were spread, yet all the evidence, hereditary and medical, is to the contrary. Trotsky has also written that in sessions of the Political Bureau, to which they both belonged, Stalin frequently wore a warm glove on his left hand, alleging rheumatic pains. I have watched Stalin at close range, in meetings and in more intimate conversations, but aside from a comparative immobility of the left arm and a tendency to thrust it into the breast of his jacket—which may be a mere habit of posture—I never noted anything unusual. Its supposed immobility and imperfect growth, if such exist, suggest a mild attack of infantile paralysis in childhood more than anything else. It is a matter of record that in 1916 either this deficiency or the imperfect foot caused him to be pronounced physically unfit for military service after he had been called up in general mobilization. The police records, so far as I have been able to examine them, say nothing about an atrophy of the arm.

Joseph's father, Vissarion Djugashvili, is listed in police accounts as a peasant from the nearby town of Didi-Lilo. In biographical notes stemming from Stalin himself in the early twenties, he set down his father as "of peasant origin." Later, when the faction fight for the succession to Lenin was at its height and great store was being set by the "social origins" of the candidates for leadership (these origins were supposed to determine the "hereditary" social psychology and even the propensity to "deviations"), Stalin recorded himself as the "son of a factory worker."[4]

At the end of the thirties, when his leadership was secure and when social classes and class distinctions had been "abolished," a biography issued by the Marx-Engels-Lenin Institute combined the two versions. Actually, both are correct. Vissarion was a hereditary peasant, but, like so many of that class, he belonged to the category of peasant-artisan. For generations his family had engaged in cobbling. He intended his son Soso to be a cobbler, too, but died before he could instruct the boy in the trade. During his last years, the elder Djugashvili took employment in the Adelkhanov shoe factory, thus becoming "proletarian," without ceasing to be a peasant in the records of the state. Beyond that we know little concerning Vissarion Djugashvili. According to Iremashvili, boyhood friend and later political opponent, Soso's father was given to drinking and to beating the boy unmercifully. Stalin himself said to Emil Ludwig: "My parents did not treat me badly by any means." Beyond that he has never mentioned his father unless the following solitary passage may be regarded as a mention:

> Imagine [Stalin said] a shoemaker who once had his own tiny workshop, but being unable to stand the competition of the big man, is forced to close down and ta a job, let us say with Adelkhanov. But he goes to work in Adelkhanov's factory, not with the idea of becoming a permanent wage worker, but in order to pinch and squeeze and save up enough money to open his own workshop again. As you see, the status of this shoemaker is already that of a proletarian; his mentality, however, is not yet proletarian, but thoroughly petty bourgeois. . . . It is the external condi-

---

[4] At Party congresses it was the custom for delegates to fill out questionnaires in which they gave a brief *curriculum vitae:* date of birth, social origin, date of entrance into the movement, posts held, arrests, length of time in prison and exile, etc. Such information then served as the equivalent of a Russian *Who's Who* and for biographical footnotes in other publications. There are in addition a number of brief biographies of Stalin, written by men close to him or by men who were permitted to interview him to secure some of their material. Finally, there are two brief autobiographical speeches in which he told the assembled hearers the story of his life, a biographical chronology prepared by Stalin for his *Collected Works* and an official biography issued by the Marx-Engels-Lenin Institute, all of which derive their frequently contradictory data from Joseph Stalin.

tions, the mode of life of men, that changes first; then their mentality changes in conformity with the changed conditions.[5]

Vissarion Djugashvili died when Soso had reached eleven. Thereupon, his mother, devoutly religious and with no one to devote herself to but her sole surviving child, determined to prepare him for the priesthood. In Georgia, the ambitious were likely to select that career, for there was no other in which a non-Russian plebeian might easily rise. Along with service to the Church, it was, of course, a career of service to the Russian state.

Ekaterina Djugashvili (*née* Geladze) came from a family of peasant serfs of the village of Gambareuli. Soso, her fourth and last child, was born when she was twenty. Until he left her side as a grown man, widowhood was consecrated to supporting him and giving him the chance to prepare for something better in her eyes than the trade of cobbler. She was strong and industrious. Even while her husband lived she had eked out the family income by taking in washing and hiring out for housework by the day. She kept the boy from physical want, and it was not her fault that he did not realize her ambition.

At seven, according to one of the latest official biographies, that of Yaroslavsky, Soso "began to study the alphabet, and within a year was able to read, first in Georgian and then in Russian." Here, as throughout Yaroslavsky's account, the writing seems purposively or ineptly obscure. It is doubtful whether his mastery of Russian followed immediately, "within the year," his mastery of Georgian. More likely it came only with arduous study in the church school, where Georgian was forbidden as the language of instruction. Certainly, the latter tongue remained his language of preference and the one in which he habitually thought on homely topics for many years. The fact that his power to express himself in Russian got its first development in the theological seminary left a life-long mark upon his style, which tends to dry, categorical and dogmatic assertion and the brief question-and-answer method of the catechism. To this day his Russian is spoken slowly with a distinct Georgian accent. A certain bareness of vocabulary and lack of imaginativeness remind us that it is not his native tongue, nor the language of his childhood thoughts and dreams.

In the autumn of 1888, when he was nearly nine, he enrolled in

[5] E. Yaroslavsky: *Landmarks in the Life of Stalin*, p. 38. Yaroslavsky uses the quoted anecdote not to throw light on Stalin's father but to exhibit the young Soso's ability "to explain the most difficult and intricate questions to the workers in a clear and comprehensible way."

the church-controlled four-grade elementary school of Gori, where he remained until 1894. Then, being nearly fifteen, he entered the Tiflis Theological Seminary on a free scholarship providing uniform, clothing, meals and lodging. The studies were dull, dogmatic, repetitive. The discipline was that of a spiritual barracks, loyalty to God and the Tsar (the order is not certain) being the overriding consideration in determining the content of all subjects. The students were immured within the walls except for a brief leave on Sunday afternoons, were spied upon and regimented from matins to lights out. Stalin thus described his seminary life in his interview with Emil Ludwig:

> *Ludwig:* What drove you to become a rebel? Was it, perhaps, because your parents treated you badly?
> *Stalin:* No. My parents were uneducated people, but they did not treat me badly by any means. It was different in the theological seminary of which I was then a student. In protest against the humiliating régime and the jesuitical methods that prevailed in the seminary, I was ready to become, and eventually did become, a revolutionary, a believer in Marxism. . . .
> *Ludwig:* But do you not grant the Jesuits any good qualities?
> *Stalin:* Yes, they are methodical and persevering in their work. But the basis of all their methods is spying, prying, peering into people's souls, to subject them to petty torment. What is there good in that? For instance, the spying in the dormitory. At nine o'clock the bell rings for tea, we go to the dining hall, and when we return we find that a search has been made and all our boxes have been turned inside out. . . . What is there good in that?

Whatever freedom of spirit might be instilled was by reaction against the régime and studies. The faculty were wont to express contempt for the Georgian language and culture. This was a frequent source of disorder in nationalistic Georgia. In 1873, six years before Soso's birth, students had been expelled for Georgian nationalism. Again in 1885, a decade before his matriculation, circles sprang up among the students, mixing nationalism and socialism. When the rector expressed contempt for the national heritage, Sylvester Jibladze, who was to be one of Stalin's first Marxist teachers, arose from his student bench and struck the rector, to the fiery applause of his fellows. He was condemned to three years in a military disciplinary corps, and the seminary was closed. A year later, in true Georgian fashion, the rector was stabbed to death. The seminary was closed again. From the dispersed and expelled divinity students sprang up the first circle of Georgian Marxism, tinged with the colors of the national independence movement. Their spirit still hung over the place when, in 1894, young Soso entered.

In the 1930's, the seminary still stood, though put to other uses. On its façade was a plaque recording that Joseph Stalin had studied there "from September 1, 1894, to July 20, 1899," that is to say from a little before he turned fifteen until he was going on twenty. Those dates, presumably based on the school records, raise the first of a series of obscurities in Stalin's early career.

According to the Lenin Institute biography (1939), Djugashvili was expelled not on July 20 but on May 29, 1899 for "secret revolutionary activities." The date is almost two months earlier, and does not coincide with the end of a school year. In 1931, Stalin wrote in a questionnaire, after the word: *Education?*: "Turned out of a theological seminary for propagating Marxism." Henri Barbusse, who did an authorized biography in 1935, based on interviews with Stalin, declared that his protagonist was expelled for "a lack of 'political balance.'" Kaganovich, Voroshilov, Orjonikidze and Enukidze in their joint *Life of Stalin* state that he was expelled "as politically undesirable" (1930). Earlier, Enukidze had written in an adulatory biographical note that he "flew out of the seminary." In a series of tributes on the occasion of his sixtieth birthday (1939), Kalinin says: "He turned his back on the seminary." The *Small Soviet Encyclopedia*, in its article "Stalin" (Vol. VIII, 1930), writes: "In the seminary Stalin became 'suspect' and was soon expelled for 'infidelity.'" Other accounts, no less official, have him expelled for reading forbidden books. Yaroslavsky (1940) grows prolix on this point, as if he were trying to reconcile all the variants into a concordance. In direct quotation marks he gives a number of synthetic-sounding and mutually contradictory "entries in the conduct book of the Theological Seminary" concerning the offenses of pupil Djugashvili. The first, dated September 29, 1898, reads:

> At 9 P. M. a group of students gathered in the dining hall around Joseph Djugashvili, who read them books [*sic*] not sanctioned by the seminary authorities.

Yaroslavsky does not tell us how many books nor which ones Djugashvili read to them on that occasion, but other "entries" charge the boy with belonging to the "Cheap Library," possessing a library card, being caught reading Hugo's *Toilers of the Sea* and

Ninety-Three, and Letourneau's *Literary Evolution of the Nations.* Two entries deal with defiance of authority:

> In the course of a search of students of the fifth class made by members of the board of supervision, Joseph Djugashvili tried . . . to enter into an argument with them . . . declaring that such searches were not made in other seminaries. Djugashvili is generally disrespectful and rude towards persons in authority and systematically refuses to bow to one of the masters. . . .

When one Father Dmitri entered Stalin's room, reports Yaroslavsky, the student kept on reading. "'Don't you see who is standing before you?' the monk demanded . . . 'I don't see anything except a black spot before my eyes.'" As this is not quoted from the records, the account of demonstrative rudeness must have come from Stalin himself.

Finally, on May 27, 1899, this Father Dmitri proposed to the seminary council "to expel Joseph Djugashvili as politically unreliable."

> The proposal—continues Yaroslavsky, interspersing his own comment with quotations from the records—was approved. Officially, Comrade Stalin was expelled from the seminary for failing to pay tuition fees and for "not attending examinations for reasons unknown." But the real reason was his political activities. He was expelled from the seminary as a person who harbored views dangerous to tsardom.

Not paying his fees, not taking the examinations, rudeness, political manifestations, religious infidelity, reading forbidden books, to himself, to others, harboring dangerous views, actively propagating Marxism—that would seem to be at least a half-dozen reasons for being expelled, some mutually contradictory and most of them put into direct quotation as from the "records" of the school. Yaroslavsky advances all these reasons within two pages (English Edition, printed in Moscow by the Foreign Languages Publishing House, Moscow 1940, pp. 15-17). The more we collate the successive and simultaneous versions, the less certain we are whether Stalin left without taking his examinations or failed to pay tuition fees (he was a free scholarship student!) or was expelled. To add to our bewilderment, we have his mother's statement, made to reporters in the year 1930:

> Soso was always a good boy. . . . I never had occasion to punish him. . . . His father, Vissarion, wanted to make of Soso a good shoemaker. But his father died when Soso

was eleven. I did not want him to be a shoemaker. I wanted only one thing, that he should become a priest. . . . He was not expelled. I brought him home on account of his health. When he entered the seminary he was fifteen and as strong as a lad could be. But overwork up to the age of nineteen pulled him down, and the doctors told me that he might develop tuberculosis. So I took him away from school. He did not want to leave. But I took him away. He was my only son. . . .

In 1946, all these contrary versions having been subjected to merciless textual criticism by Souvarine and Trotsky in their respective biographies of Stalin, the protagonist set about to produce some order out of the chaos by preparing his own biographical notes to his *Collected Works*. According to these, he entered the Gori, "four-year church-run elementary school" in September, 1888, and graduated in July, 1894, "in the first category," i.e. with high marks, among those of the uppermost section of the class (*Collected Works*, I, 415). As no light is shed by Stalin on the apparent contradiction between graduating "in the first category" and taking six years for a four-year course, we may conjecture that he was either held back by his early difficulties with the unfamiliar Russian tongue or by illness.

On September 2, 1894, according to the same note, he entered the Tiflis Priestly Seminary, where he claims to have, from 1896 on, "led Marxist study circles of the students," himself studied Marx's *Capital*, the *Communist Manifesto*, "and other work of K. Marx and F. Engels." In January, 1898, he "began to lead a workingmen's circle in the main Tiflis railway shops." In August, he "entered the Georgian Social Democratic organization Mesame-Dasi," where, apparently at once, "I. V. Stalin, V. Z. Ketskhoveli and A. G. Tsulukidze formed the kernel of the revolutionary minority of Mesame-Dasi." It is Stalin himself that puts his own name first as against that of Ketskhoveli, whom he had earlier acknowledged to have been one of his teachers in Marxism. On May 29, 1899, the account continues, "I. V. Stalin was excluded from the Tiflis Priestly Seminary for the propaganda of Marxism."

Except for the light it throws on formative influences and on the difficulties of our "archaelogical" research, the whole matter would seem to be of small importance. A little earlier or a little later, in one form or another, for one reason or another, Soso Djugashvili did undoubtedly break with the seminary and all it stood for. Whether he left or whether he was expelled, whether he lost interest, failed to present himself at an examination without excuse, read forbidden books by Marx or Victor Hugo, or both, whether he read them by himself or to others, did not pay his fee, was withdrawn for reasons of health, was expelled for holding undesirable views or teaching undesirable views or for being rude or irreligious or politically unreliable, does not alter that fundamental fact. His life would seem to be full enough of the honors that accrue from being expelled, jailed, hunted, persecuted, so that expulsion from a seminary would be a minor increment to the sum.

But if we try to represent him as "the best disciple of Comrade Lenin" and to present all other leading "disciples" as weaklings and foul and unfaithful traitors; if further we wish to portray him as "Lenin's closest collaborator throughout the history of our Party . . . from the very inception of bolshevism, Lenin's co-worker in the building of the Party" (Molotov); if, despite the ten years of difference in their ages, we would picture Stalin as advising Lenin from the start and "having no little influence on Lenin" (Kalinin); if, moreover, he is indeed "the greatest of our contemporaries" (Barbusse, Mikoyan, Beria, and others); "the most profound theoretician of contemporary times" (Beria); "no one so able to penetrate into the most secret recesses of the human heart" (Shvernik); "the God-appointed leader of our military and cultural forces" (Patriarch Sergius); "the father of us all" (Yaroslavsky); "the greatest man of all times, of all epochs and peoples" (Kirov)—then the need to establish the precocity of his genius and the vast sweep of his early rebelliousness becomes more understandable.

If we arrange all his successive official, officious and authorized biographies and birthday eulogies in chronological order, we observe a persistent process of enlargement of the precocity and scale of his theological seminary rebellion, along with a steady pushing back of the date when he first became active in the revolutionary movement and a continual enhancement of the scope of that early activity.

In the earliest editions of Lenin's *Collected Works*, the mention of Stalin brings a footnote, presumably stemming from his Party questionnaires, which records him as "member of the Party since 1898." In 1932, he told Emil Ludwig: "I joined the revolutionary movement at the age of fifteen (i.e. in 1894), when I became connected with certain illegal groups of Russian Marxists in Transcaucasia." Of course, these two accounts are not necessarily incompatible since he might have entered an illegal study circle at the first date and a membership organization on the second, and not left the seminary for yet another year. But soon after the Ludwig interview,

Yaroslavsky and Beria went to work on the enlargement of the idea
that Stalin became a Marxist at fifteen and they produced a number
of improvements. Thus Yaroslavsky writes that in Gori (i.e. before
he entered the seminary):

> While still a schoolboy he would explain to the workers
> and peasants the causes of their poverty . . . and got his
> first acquaintance with Marxist ideas. . . . When he left
> the seminary he already had had four years of experience
> in secret Marxist circles and had published his first illegal
> periodical.

Yaroslavsky, Beria, and the Lenin Institute all quote a memoir
which pictures him as having read his first Lenin article in 1898
while a student at the seminary, and having said: "I must meet him
at all costs." According to Beria, young Djugashvili was then "conducting two revolutionary Marxist circles of the students" and
eleven or more "Social Democratic workers' circles" outside the
school. The text, as so often in Beria's and Yaroslavsky's accounts,
seems deliberately vague. On page 21 Beria writes, referring to
"the period of 1898-1900," that "Comrade Stalin alone conducted
more than eight Social Democratic workers' circles." But a footnote lists "two student circles . . . in 1896 and 1897" and "at the
same time in 1898" eleven workers' circles plus others "at small
workshops, printing plants, etc." It seems likely that activities of
the years 1901 and 1902 are here condensed and set back several
years. Both Yaroslavsky and Beria picture the eighteen-year-old
seminarist as having led a big railway strike in Tiflis in the last
years of the nineties, while he was leading all these classes and
study circles. More than mere precocity of genius, this begins to
suggest an astonishing ability to get around, the more astonishing
when we consider that he himself has recorded that he and his
fellow-students lived in a barracks atmosphere, spied on in all
their movements.

> Life in the school was sad and monotonous—writes his
> classmate Iremashvili—Locked in day and night within bar-
> rack walls, we felt like prisoners obliged to spend years
> there.

Iremashvili's memoirs, more than a decade earlier than Beria's
second-hand account, speak of one such circle in place of Beria's
dozen. His account tallies closely with one given by Stalin himself
in 1926, nine years before Beria's lecture on "Stalin's Early Writings
and Activities." It is interesting to compare the statements of the
two classmates concerning the same episode. Writes Iremashvili:

One evening Koba and I secretly made our way from the seminary to a small house, which stood leaning against a cliff and which belonged to a worker of the Tiflis railway. After us, secretly arrived others from the seminary who shared our views. There also met with us a Social Democratic labor organization of revolutionary workers.

Said Stalin, speaking in Tiflis in 1926:

I recall the year 1898, when the first circle from the railway shops was assigned to me. I remember how in the home of Comrade Sturua, in the presence of Sylvester Jibladze—he was at the time one of my teachers—and of other advanced workers of Tiflis, I received lessons in practical work. . . . Here in the circle of these comrades, I then became a pupil of the revolution. . . .

The words "assigned to me" would give more importance to Stalin than Iremashvili's account written three years earlier, but neither version squares with the idea that the young student was conducting two student and eleven or more workingmen's Marxist circles at the time. Nor does it square with the picture Yaroslavsky gave to the Academy of Sciences of the USSR on Stalin's sixtieth birthday when he said:

Beginning with the end of the nineties, Lenin and Stalin became for the development of the revolutionary movement of the new epoch . . . what Marx and Engels were for the previous century.

Finally, there is yet another version of Djugashvili's break with the seminary. According to Dr. Gogokhia, another classmate of Soso's whose memoirs received the official accolade of quotation by Yaroslavsky in the latter's biography of Stalin:

Joseph stopped paying attention to his lessons, studied no more than to get passing marks, so as to pass examinations. The ferocious monk Abazhidze guessed when the talented, well-developed Djugashvili, who possessed an incredibly rich memory, studied only for passing marks and he (the monk) succeeded in obtaining a decision to expel him from the seminary.

With this passage we leave to the reader the problems and a consideration of the documentation. More interesting to us than the actual facts is the phenomenon of their retroactive "editing" and the social meaning of that method of writing history.

CHAPTER XXIV

BIRTHPANGS OF
GEORGIAN BOLSHEVISM

Oh if the World were but to recreate,
That we might catch ere closed the Book of Fate,
And make the Writer on a fairer leaf
Inscribe our names.   —*Omar Khayyam*

WHEN Djugashvili left the seminary, he tried private tutoring. It was as a tutor that he won his influence over Kamo, the Transcaucasian Robin Hood. So miserable were his earnings that he had to be helped by comrades still at the seminary. This is affirmed both by Iremashvili, who was a fellow-student, and by Barbusse. But his poverty did not trouble him. Then as later, he lived simply and dressed modestly.

> He was not in the least concerned with his personal welfare—testifies the politically hostile Iremashvili—He demanded nothing from life, for he thought such demands incompatible with socialist principles. He had enough integrity to make sacrifices for his ideal.

Even when he had become lord of the Kremlin, he continued to dress plainly: an unobtrusive semi-military tunic, trousers stuffed into soft knee-high boots, peaked cap, alike for every day and state occasions. Only in the forties, when he had introduced gold braid and epaulettes for civil officials as well as military, to set the hierarchy once more apart from common mortals, did he don a marshal's uniform, shoulder-wide golden epaulettes, gold-braided cap, self-bestowed medals, decorations, ribbons, orders, a jeweled star. In the Teheran and Yalta Conferences, though his power was never greater, his rugged figure seemed somehow to have lost in magnitude now that the trappings had enlarged.

To his brief period of tutoring attaches the first of many evil rumors concerning his relations with comrades. According to the Social Revolutionary, Vereshchak, who was soon to be Stalin's cellmate in prison and would one day be chairman of the Tiflis Soldiers' Soviet:

> Stalin's comrades in the seminary circle say that soon after his expulsion, they were in turn expelled [as] the result of a denunciation made by Stalin to the rector. He did not deny the accusation, but justified the deed by saying that the expelled students, having lost their right to become priests, would become good revolutionaries.

What credence shall we give to this? *Pravda* has set a perilous example in two articles by Demyan Bedny on Vereshchak's memoirs, under the title "Certified Correct," in which Bedny extracted all items favorable to Stalin. Still, the charge does not seem to be justified. It is contradicted by the declaration of Iremashvili that Stalin's fellow-students contributed to the expelled Djugashvili's maintenance. Moreover, if it were true, some official account would surely have boasted that Soso "took a group of students with him" when he was expelled from the seminary.

In December, 1899, Soso got his first and only "respectable" job. Vano Ketskhoveli, also a former seminary student, was about to resign from a minor post in the Tiflis Observatory, and apprised Djugashvili. The position required a literate person with a bit of education, but, as it paid poorly, was open to unskilled Georgian intellectuals. For the better part of a decade it was a monopoly of such "unfrocked" seminary students: first Ketskhoveli, then Djugashvili, then Davitashvili, then Berdzenishvili. Such was the continuity of the succession, that in 1907 Kamo was able to hide his booty of more than a quarter-million rubles in the couch of the director of the observatory.

Djugashvili's duties were not arduous. He had to make observations at night with the help of various instruments. But he did not last long as a scientific worker. On May 1, 1901, some two thousand Tiflis workingmen paraded through the streets in defiance of the police. They were fired upon, fourteen being wounded and fifty arrested. Then the police went round the city arresting all Social Democrats on the lists supplied by their spies. When they visited the observatory to pick up Djugashvili, he was not there. Nor did he report again for work, but hid in his native Gori. Thus began his career as professional revolutionary.

When the excitement blew over, he returned to Tiflis, where he lived, like a lay preacher in some poor sect, on the hospitality of comrades. He lasted thus for a year before the police got him and set him down as "without written documents or definite occupation and without lodgings of his own." Of his life during that year we have only sketchy indications, but they suggest that he was a center of Party quarrels and labor demonstrations, first in Tiflis, then in Batum, where he was staying at the time of his arrest.

In the autumn of 1901 he became a member of the Local Committee of the Tiflis Social Democrats. After attending only two sessions, he left for Batum. Official accounts picture him as having been "sent there" by the Tiflis Committee. *Brdzolis Khma* ("Echo of the Struggle"), a Georgian Menshevik paper published in Paris (No. 3, 1930) paints a less flattering picture of the motives for his journey:

> From the earliest days of his activity among the workmen, Djugashvili attracted attention by his intrigues against the outstanding Social Democratic leader, Sylvester Jibladze. He was warned but took no notice, continuing to spread slanders with the intention of discrediting the recognized representatives of the local organization. . . . Brought before a Party tribunal, he was found guilty of unjust slander and was unanimously excluded from the Tiflis organization.

But, as if made to order to refute this charge, Lavrenti Beria in the middle thirties published a newly discovered letter purporting to be from the chief of gendarmes of Tiflis to the assistant chief in Kutais, dated July 1, 1902: "At the end of 1901 Djugashvili was sent to Batum for propaganda work . . ." Beria's *Stalin's Early Writings and Activities* (1935) contains a number of such pat finds of old police records which fit like hand to glove for the refutation of the unfavorable memoirs of Georgian Mensheviks in exile, or of Georgian Bolsheviks whose reminiscences had been published by the Soviet Government while Lenin was still alive. Among such newly discovered police entries, we find:

> As a result of Djugashvili's activities Social Democratic organizations headed in the beginning by the Tiflis Committee began to spring up in all the factories of Batum.
> Djugashvili has always occupied extremely prominent positions. . . .
> Djugashvili headed the Batum, Tiflis and Baku Social Democratic organizations at various times. . . .

One wonders why these reports were not discovered in the twenties when the police archives were opened and every scrap of paper bearing on Party history was duly published. One is moved to wonder, too, that these new finds tell a different story and even speak another language from all police documents and Bolshevik reminiscences published in the years 1919 to 1923, while Lenin was

alive and the memoirs of countless old Bolsheviks still fresh and
free.

The language sounds uncommonly like Beria's own. The Tsarist
Secret Service is actually exhibited as no less anxious than the
GPU to make clear the young Djugashvili's unique leading role
and to confound all his critics. Indeed, the excerpt which makes
Djugashvili "head" all three city organizations proves too much,
since it overlooks the fact that there was no "head" to any Social
Democratic organization in those days. If outstanding leader was
meant by the term, then there were men like Zhordania, Khets-
khoveli, Jibladze, Isidore and Noah Ramishvili, Chkheidze, Topuridze, Shaumyan, and others who were more prominent than Djugashvili, not to mention members in Transcaucasia of the All-Russian
Central Committee like Krassin and Nogin. The very idea of a
personal and individual "head" is an anachronism borrowed from
the language and thought of a later day, when Stalin had had himself proclaimed *Vozhd*, or Leader (the Russian analogue of Duce
and Fuehrer) of Party, Army, Government, Comintern, the peoples
of the Soviet Union and of the World.

To be sure, the authenticity of any particular document can be
neither proved nor disproved in any final sense so long as free
research is not permitted. Such research would require an examination of the paper, ink and type, a comparison with other documents
from the same hand, the use of X-ray, and all other methods that
are employed when the authenticity of a painting has been called
in question. Until such an opportunity presents itself, we are limited
to such tests as are offered by comparisons of style and subject
matter, collating of earlier and later reminiscences, and occasional
check against objective fact.

To return to the charges of intrigue against Djugashvili which
the police record so patly refutes, we must note that such charges
surround his personality at many points in his life. So far we have
seen that he was accused of denouncing fellow circle members to
the rector of the theological seminary and of having been forced to
leave Tiflis because of intrigues against Jibladze. The same *Brdzolis
Khma* makes yet a third charge to the effect that after he got to
Batum he became jealous of the more prominent Shaumyan there
and was suspected by the workers of denouncing Shaumyan to the
police. His own arrest and exile is supposed to have prevented an
investigation. Beyond the assertions of the Georgian Mensheviks in
exile, there is no evidence that any of these grave charges are true.
Still there are so many accusations against him (there are more to
follow in our story) that it is important to note that men who

worked with Stalin should have thought him capable of framing up his comrades to advance himself or his party's interests as he conceived them. Lenin and Trotsky, too, made bitter enemies and were subject to savage attacks by the defeated and the exiled. Yet in all the polemical literature against them, there is a notable absence of charges such as these.

"Before Stalin came to Batum," writes Beria, "there was no workers' Social Democratic organization whatever." On his arrival, he called a conference disguised as a New Year's party, at which he "delivered four or five brilliant talks" and set up "a leading Party group headed by Comrade Stalin." Within the next two months "eleven Social Democratic workers' circles began to function actively under the leadership of Comrade Stalin." On February 27, a strike broke out in the Rothschild plant in which "Comrade Stalin himself led the work of the strike committee, drew up the demands . . . wrote the leaflets and organized the printing and distribution of them." On March 8, thirty-two strikers were arrested for deportation to their native villages. "Comrade Stalin retaliated" with a demonstration which ended in three hundred arrests. An attempt was made to storm the jail: fifteen workers were killed, fifty-four wounded, five hundred arrested.

Yaroslavsky's account, less dry than Beria's, treats us to a vivid picture of the storming:

> Comrade Soso stood in the midst of the turbulent sea of workers, personally directing the movement. A worker named Kalanadze who was wounded in the arm during the firing was led out of the crowd and afterward taken home by Comrade Stalin himself. . . .

During all this feverish activity, according to Beria, "Comrade Stalin maintained close contact with the Tiflis organization, often visited Tiflis, and directed the work of the Tiflis Social Democratic organization." Such remarkable labors could not go unnoticed forever, least of all in the hitherto somnolent Batum. On April 18, 1902, Djugashvili "together with others" was arrested "at a meeting of the leading party group." Thus began his first prison experience.

An *Iskra* account of the Rothschild strike and storming of the Batum jail, printed at the time, makes it appear more spontaneous and fails to make the usual claim to socialist leadership. It mentions two workingmen by name as having led the affair; Stalin does not figure by implication or under any of his aliases. Menshevik sources, however, confirm Beria's assertion that he was the secret promoter of the attack on the prison, nay more, they reproach him for the "senseless adventure and useless shedding of blood." Without accepting the officious and official version which makes the young Djugashvili do everything, lead everybody, be everywhere at once, we can be sure that the twenty-two-year-old professional revolutionary took as active a part as he could in the turbulent strikes and demonstrations that shook sleepy Batum shortly after his arrival. We can be certain, too, of the date of his arrest, though not of the manner. Beria makes it "at a meeting." The Lenin Institute has him picked up during a general search. Barbusse pictures him as calmly facing the police during a raid on another's home, while "talking to Kandelaki and smoking a cigarette." These discrepancies are the more puzzling in that all three versions are based on the research of those who had the benefit of personal guidance from their protagonist.

For a year and a half Djugashvili was in the prisons of Batum and Kutais awaiting an administrative disposition of his case. Then he and fifteen others were exiled to Eastern Siberia. Among them were Lenin's friend Kurnatovsky and another veteran Social Democrat from Central Russia, Franchesky. These were given four years each. Djugashvili and the remaining twelve, possibly as first offenders or as natives "misled" by the two Russians, were given only three years. At the end of November, 1903, the exiles started out on slow stages for the long journey to Eastern Siberia. Soso's destination proved to be the lonely outpost of Novaya Uda, a tiny village in Irkutsk Province, not far from Lake Baikal. Quite a hard journey in the dead of winter, yet, within a month and eight days of his arrival, on January 5, 1904, he escaped, reappearing in his accustomed haunts in Tiflis and Batum in February.

While Djugashvili was still in prison, according to the inimitable Barbusse, he heard "a great piece of news": that the congress called to found an all-Russian party had not ended in the longed-for unification, but in a split. To most, this was a bewildering calamity. The differences, so far as anyone yet knew, turned about a single clause in the statutes and the personnel of the Editorial Board of *Iskra.* All the memoirs of old Bolsheviks concerning that period testify to their dismay when the tidings first reached them. Thus, the future Commissar of Education, Lunacharsky, remembers his "embarrassment at the insignificance of the reasons which led to the split." Piatnitsky, Lenin's faithful man Friday, "could not understand why such petty differences should keep us from working together." Krzhizhanovsky "found the idea of Martov's opportunism far-fetched." Trotsky saw "nothing more than Lenin's desire to get

Axelrod and Zasulich off the Editorial Board." Plekhanov took Lenin's part but was sure that the issues were too small to keep the groups separated. When he came to the conclusion that Lenin's stubbornness concerning the composition of the Editorial Board was the chief hindrance to unity, he forced the admission of the candidates of the other side. Even Lenin himself, as we have seen, did not consider it "great news" but a matter for doubt and anguish. The very Bolshevik majority he set up in the Central Committee soon deserted him in favor of reunification ("conciliation"). The upsurge of 1905 forced reunification, a unity which Stalin hailed as the principal achievement of the London Congress of 1907. "The actual unification of the advanced workers of all Russia into a single all-Russian party under the banner of revolutionary Social Democracy," wrote Stalin in 1907, "that is the significance of the London Congress."

The period of decline after 1907 brought new squabbles, but not until 1912 was the split made permanent, and even after that Lenin sought unity, now with Plekhanov, and again (more than once) with Martov. Yet Barbusse pictures the twenty-three-year-old Djugashvili as seeing far beyond Lenin and welcoming the unexpected split as "a great piece of news," not "hesitating for a moment when, like Hercules at the beginning of his career, he was compelled to choose between vice and virtue." Without Barbusse's ornaments of style, all subsequent biographers, not excluding Stalin himself, have sought to give the same impression, which brings us to another problem requiring "archaeological" investigation.

> I first became acquainted with Lenin in 1903—Stalin declared in 1924, one week after Lenin's death, in a memorial address to the students of the military academy in the Kremlin.—True, it was not a personal acquaintance; it was made by correspondence. But it left an indelible impression upon me, one which has never left me throughout all my work in the Party. I was an exile in Siberia at the time. My knowledge of Lenin's revolutionary activities since the end of the nineties, and especially after 1901, after the appearance of *Iskra*, had convinced me that in Lenin we had a man of extraordinary caliber. I did not regard him as a mere leader of the Party, but as its actual founder, for he alone understood the inner essence and urgent needs of our Party. When I compared him with the other leaders of our Party, it seemed to me that he was head and shoulders above his colleagues—Plekhanov, Martov, Axelrod and the others; that, compared with them, Lenin was not just one of the leaders but the leader of the highest rank, a

> mountain eagle who knew no fear in the struggle and who led the Party boldly forward along unexplored paths. . . . This impression took such a deep hold on me that I felt impelled to write to a close friend of mine who was living as a political exile abroad, requesting him to give me his opinion. Some time later, when I was already in exile in Siberia—this was at the end of 1903—I received an enthusiastic letter from my friend and a simple but profoundly expressive letter from Lenin to whom, it appeared, my friend had shown my letter. Lenin's note was comparatively short, but it contained a bold and fearless criticism of the practical work of our Party, and a remarkably clear and concise account of the entire plan of work of the Party in the immediate future. Only Lenin could write of the most intricate things so simply and clearly, so concisely and boldly that every sentence did not so much speak as ring like a rifle shot. This simple and bold letter strengthened my opinion that Lenin was the mountain eagle of our Party. I cannot forgive myself for having, from the habit of an old underground worker, consigned this letter of Lenin's, like many other letters, to the flames. My acquaintance with Lenin dates from that time.

The more we examine this spiritless memorial address on the beloved leader but a few days dead, the more questions it raises. Stalin assures the military cadets that he burned the letter: but where is Krupskaya's copy? It was written at a time when the Ulyanovs had a settled address in Geneva, and during the period immediately following the split, a period for which Krupskaya has conserved complete copies of all letters and notes which Lenin dictated to her, or wrote himself, including even letters drafted but not sent. And "this profoundly expressive letter contained a remarkably clear and concise account of the entire plan of work of the Party for the immediate future." Neither in Krupskaya's files, nor in her memoirs, is there any trace of this letter to Djugashvili in Siberia.

A more cogent question: by his own account, Stalin did not get to Novaya Uda until November 29, where he stayed a month and eight days, fleeing on January 5, 1904. There was thus no time for a letter from Geneva, or even from Russia proper, to reach him there in the dead of winter. As prisoners were never told their final destination until they were deep in Siberia, he could not even have had time to send his address home, still less to a friend abroad. In short, the facts as given are self-refuting, as Trotsky has fully demonstrated in his posthumous *Stalin*.

By now it should be clear to the reader that we are dealing with the most striking example in all history of a man who has succeeded in inventing himself. The entire governmental apparatus, the printing press, cinema, textbooks, schools, paintings, etc., of a great and centrally directed nation have been employed in the task of remolding its ruler's past closer to his heart's desire. There is none to challenge, for textual criticism is "treason" and challenger and evidence are destroyed together. This retroactivity concerns itself even with minuscule details, for the larger facts—that he early became a Leninist, early became important in Caucasian bolshevism, that his importance grew steadily until he became the most powerful man on earth—these facts are beyond dispute. It is fruitless, therefore, for us to follow this process in detail. It will interest us only where it throws, as it sometimes does, a strong light on the real events of Stalin's life and the social meaning of one or another emendation. As we shall see, his self-created or imagined life is usually a projection backwards in time of his real place in later life. Thus the biographer is faced with the unprecedented task of translating shadow into substance. In some ways this shadow life becomes as important a key to this man's true place in history and actual character as the real life that it retroactively transforms.

If we look into Krupskaya's records of Lenin's correspondence and literary activity during the period in question, we do find a document having a possible connection with Stalin's tale to the military cadets. At the moment to which Stalin's speech refers, Lenin was republishing in Geneva as a printed pamphlet a prior "Letter to a Comrade on Our Organizational Tasks." Written originally in September, 1902, to A. A. Schneierson, Lenin considered it important enough to circulate to other comrades in hectographed form. Then, in June, 1903, it was republished in Siberia by the Siberian Committee of the Party. It is not impossible that the Siberian hectographed copy was given to Stalin in exile by a fellow-deportee. It does indeed "contain a remarkably clear and concise account of the entire plan of work of the Party for the immediate future." If this conjecture—and it is no more than a plausible conjecture on my part—is correct, it would suggest that from that period dates Stalin's discipleship.

However that may be, the problem remains: what were Stalin's motives for predating his first *personal* acquaintance with Lenin, a predating accomplished exactly one week after Lenin was dead? One reason will become abundantly clear when we come to examine the strained relations between Lenin and Stalin during the last year or so of Lenin's life. And another when we examine the ensuing struggle for the succession. We cannot help but be struck by the long-range planning and meticulous attention to detail which Stalin showed thus early in the struggle for power.

A motive of a different order may possibly be supplied by an examination of the one police entry concerning Joseph Djugashvili which neither Beria nor any other official biographer has ever referred to:

> According to information recently received from our agents—reads a report of the Tiflis Chief of the Secret Police, Karpov—Djugashvili was known in the Organization under the pseudonyms of Soso and Koba. He has been working in the Social Democratic Party since 1902, first as a Menshevik, then as a Bolshevik, as propagandist and director of the first section (railways).

This item, like all the police archives in Georgia, fell into Bolshevik hands in 1921, after the Red Army overthrew the Georgian Republic headed by Zhordania. It was published for the first and last time in the Soviet Union, in the Georgian Bolshevik paper *Zarya Vostoka* ("Dawn of the East"), journal of the Communist Party in Tiflis, on December 23, 1925. It was one of a number of items from police records, reminiscences of old Georgian Bolsheviks, etc., published to honor Stalin on his forty-sixth birthday. For reasons which may not seem too clear to a disinterested Western reader (one would think that more than two decades of unquestioning discipleship as a Bolshevik would be enough for any man), this item did not seem to Stalin to honor him. He made no public comment on the implication that he was in his youth, as all Georgian Social Democrats were, for a while a follower of the main body of Georgian Social Democracy, whose outstanding figure was Noah Zhordania. No attempt has ever been made to refute the item, to examine or explain it. Nor was it denied. It was simply never referred to in print again. Whoever had been responsible for its publication has doubtless long ago gone the way of all flesh.

Once started in the nineties, Georgian socialism expanded with amazing rapidity in the political vacuum of Transcaucasia. Tsarist officials had looked with complacency on its early growth. Just as they gave a certain legality to Marxism in the nineties in Central Russia because they saw in it a useful counterweight to the more dangerous Narodnik terrorism, so they gave even greater legal freedom to Georgian Marxism, because they hoped it would sow divisions within the nationalist movement. Even after the brief honeymoon of legality was over in Russia as a whole, it continued in Transcaucasia. By the time the authorities began to doubt the wisdom of their maneuver, it was too late. Georgian socialism had developed into a mighty mass movement and there was no forcing it back into the womb of time. Unlike Marxist organizations elsewhere, it enjoyed a great following among the peasantry as well as among the numerically weaker working class and intelligentsia. It became the first open mass party of Social Democracy anywhere in Russia. During the revolutionary days of 1905-1906, it ruled over whole districts, had mayors and deputies and Georgian princelings in its ranks, enjoyed the support of peasant villages and city Dumas, and of the nascent middle class and intelligentsia. Municipal councils voted funds to arm its Red Guards. The Tsar's Viceroy, Vorontsov-Dashkov, even asked it to intervene to stop the Armenian-Tartar massacres which less enlightened officials had encouraged, and he provided a thousand army rifles for the purpose! (Chavichvili: *Patrie, Prisons, Exil,* p. 132). In 1906, the authorities deliberately postponed the national Duma elections in Transcaucasia until other provinces had voted, lest the expected Social Democratic sweep should set an undesirable example.

The mass character of the movement helps to explain the slower ripening of bolshevism (which slowness Stalinist historiography would now conceal as something shameful), and the comparative freedom from splits and fine-spun theoretical debates such as possessed the narrow underground and émigré circles of Russia. When, during 1905 and 1906, the Social Democratic movement became a mass party in Russia proper, unity was forced upon the factions in Central Russia, too.

Lenin's principal ideological stock-in-trade after the 1903 split—"opportunism in the organization question"—could find no echo in a movement organized so differently. The word "opportunism," moreover, sounded strange in the ears of a party which was unanimous in favoring armed conflict with tsarism.

The real father of Transcaucasian socialism was Noah Zhordania. Of the same age as Lenin, this Georgian intellectual first participated in the Central-Russian underground, then went abroad as Lenin did to work with Plekhanov. Zhordania and his close associates and disciples remained all their lives orthodox Marxists in the sense that Plekhanov was such. And, like him, they sometimes assumed a position between the two factions.

In 1897, Zhordania had returned from his stay abroad to take over the editorship of the progressive journal *Kvali* ("The Furrow"), which he transformed at once into the Georgian-language organ of "legal Marxism." So complacent were the tsarist authorities about Georgia that long after "legal Marxism" had been forgotten in Russia, *Kvali* continued to appear freely. It was not suppressed until 1904! During more than six years it carried on a notable work of polemic, exposition, education, adaptation of Marxism to the regional characteristics of Transcaucasia. In it Zhordania wrote personally all the major programmatic documents of the movement. The paper helped to form many men of such ample caliber that when, following Plekhanov, the Georgian Social Democracy went over to menshevism, it was able to supply leaders of national standing for the Menshevik faction. Thus, the leader of the Social Democratic deputation in the Second Duma was that body's youngest and most able Deputy, the twenty-six-year-old Georgian, Hercules Tseretelli. ("A mad man," wrote the arch-conservative *Novoe Vremya*, "a mad man, but the most brilliant Deputy in the Duma.") When the government jailed Tseretelli and barred his further candidacy, it was another Georgian, Nicholas Chkheidze, who assumed leadership of the entire Social-Democratic fraction in the Third and Fourth Dumas. In 1917, Tseretelli was to become a member of the Provisional Government, and Chkheidze the first Chairman of the Petrograd Soviet and then of the All-Russian Soviet Executive. So much had their influence become national.

It was from the journal edited by Zhordania and his associates that Soso Djugashvili got his first taste of Marxism. For any Georgian Marxist to fail to acknowledge an indebtedness to Zhordania would be a mark of ingratitude equivalent to a failure on Lenin's part to acknowledge indebtedness to Plekhanov. Such acknowledgement Lenin gave in full measure. So did Trotsky, despite Plekhanov's openly expressed antagonism toward him. But neither Stalin nor his official biographers are willing to admit that he owes an iota to *Kvali* and Zhordania. Factional differences are extended backward retroactively to make the youthful Soso spring fully armed out of the high, bald forehead of Vladimir Ilyich.

It was the government that sowed the first seeds of the future Bolshevik movement in Transcaucasia by its deportations and administrative exilings. Since the nineties they had been sending "released" Russian politicals to this "safe" and distant march to live "under police observation." Along with them, it sent a number of native Georgians, arrested in Central Russia, back to their homeland. Two of these rusticated Georgians would become leading Bolsheviks, Lado (Vladimir) Ketskhoveli and Abel Enukidze.

Here are four typical Great-Russian newcomers to Georgia for the year 1900. Leonid Krassin, engineer, was brought in to manage the power station in Baku. Michael Kalinin, machinist, and Sergei Alliluev, locksmith, were hired by the Tiflis railway shops. Victor Kurnatovsky, close friend of Lenin, received police permission to work in Tiflis as a chemical engineer. All four were to play important roles in the life of Soso Djugashvili.

Engineer Krassin managed the power company until late in 1904. In his office he met with trustworthy Georgian leaders, arranged the smuggling of literature, forging of passports, raising of funds, carried on his duties as a member of the Central Committee, contrived to expand the local clandestine printing plant into one serving all Russia. Of this printing plant, we shall hear more.

So well did the chief engineer lead his double life that, even to the day when he was promoted to a higher post in Central Russia, neither management nor police nor workers suspected his underground role. Four years of such intense activity without discovery was rare indeed in the annals of the movement. The workingmen under him went so far during one of their strikes as to demand his removal as manager! No wonder Lenin set a high value upon him.

The reader will remember that this man, who during his four years in Tiflis, was the most influential Leninist in the whole of Russia, became a "conciliator" shortly after Lenin contrived his election to the Central Committee. He was unconvinced of the seriousness of the split of 1903, and sceptical concerning the need of devoting one's major energies to internecine rather than anti-tsarist struggle. Thus his influence helps to explain why a split was retarded in Transcaucasia and why the Tiflis printing plant, the largest underground plant in all Russia, kept right on printing the works of both factions until 1905. And in that year, as the reader may remember, it was Krassin who arranged for the printing of the leaflets of the Menshevik, Leon Trotsky. Yet another member of the Lenin-selected Central Committee of 1903, Victor Nogin, who lived for a while in the Caucasus, was also a "conciliator."

If Krassin's influence was a retarding one, what of the other three Great-Russians we have mentioned? Though Michael Kalinin probably met Stalin at this time, he did not stay long in the Caucasus. After a few months he took part in a railway shopmen's strike there and then returned to Central Russia. Twenty-one years later, he would become "President of the Soviet Union," i.e. President of the All-Russian Executive Committee of the Soviets, an honorific but otherwise unimportant job. A man of limited horizon

and simple, homely ways, he would remain high in the façade of
government as a symbol of the proletarianized peasantry whence
he had sprung. And he would remain close enough to the favor
of Joseph Stalin to attain to a ripe old age and die a natural death
in office in 1946—of all deaths the most unnatural for members of
the Bolshevik Old Guard of his generation.

Kalinin's fellow-shopman, Alliluev, settled down permanently in
Transcaucasia and married a Georgian woman. He was not important politically but of personal importance in the life of Soso Djugashvili by reason of a bilingual daughter born of his Georgian marriage. In 1918, when Soso became Commissar for Nationalities of
all Russia, he engaged this girl, Nadezhda Allilueva, as his secretary.
A year later, she became his second wife, she then being seventeen
and he forty. She was the mother of his son Vasili and his daughter
Svetlana.

The fourth of the 1900 immigrants from Great-Russia, Victor
Kurnatovsky, was a lesser figure than Krassin but a more unconditional follower of Lenin's. It is probable that Kurnatovsky first
apprised Djugashvili of *Iskra's* and Lenin's existence, and gave him
his first push in the direction of "irreconcilable bolshevism." In
Beria's biography of Stalin (1935), the relationship between the
two is described in this fashion:

"After Kurnatovsky's arrival at Tiflis, he established close contact with Comrade Stalin and became his intimate friend and co-
worker."

This would imply equality, or perhaps the subordination of
Kurnatovsky to Stalin. But on the next page, the Tbilisi (Tiflis)
Branch of the Marx-Engels-Lenin Institute is quoted as recording:
"All the comrades went to Kurnatovsky with their disagreements
and disputes. His opinions and conclusions were always accepted
without objections."

The spirit of that sentence, so different from the democratic and
turbulent spirit of the early Georgian movement, is a result of the
retroactive injection of the idea of personal leadership and blind
obedience. But it is interesting to note that, in contradistinction
to everything said by Beria in the rest of the book, the absolute
leader is clearly not Stalin here, but Kurnatovsky as the emanation
of the spirit of Lenin.

In the autumn of 1904, the Bolsheviks Vladimir Bobrovsky and
his wife were sent to the Caucasus by Lenin, as was Lev Borisovich
Kamenev to fill the vacancy left by the arrest of Kurnatovsky and
the transfer of Krassin. Kamenev had spent his childhood in Georgia

and knew the region. He worked hard to bring about a split in the solidly unified and strong Georgian movement. By ones and twos he gathered them, no doubt Soso Djugashvili among them, but he has since been purged, so no trace of his activity is any more permitted in official historiography. If we limit ourselves to it, we can no longer explain such passages as this in the memoirs of Victor Taratuta (the Victor whom the reader has already met in the chapter on expropriations): "I first met Comrade Kamenev, Lev Borisovich," writes Taratuta, "in his capacity as leader of the Caucasian Bolshevik organizations . . ."

Strangely, Taratuta, like Krassin, mentions innumerable Caucasian Bolsheviks, but the name of Koba-Djugashvili-Stalin is not among them. Still harder to reconcile with Beria's and all post-Berian biographies, are the simple memoirs of Mrs. Bobrovsky, whose book, written in 1934, was published in Russian, and then by the Comintern in various languages. In the autumn of 1904 she worked in Tiflis and Baku, was coopted into the newly formed Bolshevik Committee for Transcaucasia, became Secretary of the Baku Committee, reorganized the underground printing plant, which she found running "on too large a scale and with too little secrecy," and broke it up into two separate plants for greater safety. She notes the activities of her husband, of Tskhakaya, Japaridze, Tsulukidze and others. Concerning Djugashvili, who, according to Beria, was then running the whole district committee of the Bolsheviks and indeed the whole activity of the entire party in the Caucasus, she has nothing to say with the exception of the single reference to him as "the still quite young Stalin (Soso)" on page 113! When she describes the great strike of 1904, which, according to official historiography, Stalin is now alleged to have led, she says quite simply and frankly that it was led by the Mensheviks. This she explains by

> . . . the exceptionally talented demagogic oratory of their mass leader, Ilya Shendrikov. . . . The error of the Baku (Bolshevik) leadership in their approaching the masses not quite correctly, somewhat academically. A special role was played by the fact that we had not one single agitator who could compare with Ilya Shendrikov's fiery talent as a speaker.

She pictures the Bolsheviks as trying to criticize him at a meeting, and being heckled by the workingmen. "We left the meeting not exactly with light hearts." They tried a rival meeting, but Shendrikov prevented its success by the simple device of pro-

longing his own speech so that the workers did not leave his meeting in time to go to theirs. Except for the half-sentence about
Soso's "youth," he does not figure in her memories at all. Having
been published in 1934 with the approval of Stalin's apparatus, it
undoubtedly represents a true picture of the state of affairs in the
autumn of 1904 and the spring of 1905. But that was before
Lavrenti Beria got to work on the remaking of the past and the
memories of men. Today, Mrs. Bobrovsky's book has been burned
in Russia along with countless other pre-purge accounts.

According to Beria, the great movement created by Zhordania
was limited to "legal Marxism," and "the minority of the Mesame-
Dasi, headed by Comrades Stalin, Ketskhoveli and A. Tsulukidze"
began a struggle for an illegal paper with the result that "the
minority headed by Comrade Stalin adopted Lenin's position, the
position of bolshevism."

But if we turn to Volume XIX of the *Big Soviet Encyclopedia*,
which volume was published in 1930 under Stalin's dictatorship,
we find a different order of names and a different story:

> At the head of the revolutionary Leninist tendency—we
> find on page 578—stood M. Tskhakaya, F. Makharadze, Soso
> Djugashvili [Stalin], A. Tsulukidze, and others. . . .
> The Social Democratic movement from the beginning of
> the nineties developed simultaneously on a legal and illegal
> basis. . . . In the journal *Kvali*, the editor of which from
> 1898 on was N. Zhordania, were printed the articles of both
> tendencies. . . . The articles of the advocates of revolu-
> tionary Marxism were also printed in the pages of *Kvali*.
> These, as far as that was possible in the legal press, ad-
> vanced a clear class ideology. Such, for example, were the
> articles of F. Makharadze. At the end of 1898, one of the
> future leaders of Georgian bolshevism, A. Tsulukidze, came
> out with a protest against the position of Zhordania in
> *Kvali*. . . . At that time [in 1903] all Transcaucasia, in-
> cluding the Georgian Social Democratic Organization, stood
> on the platform of *Iskra*. Economism had no open support-
> ers. In 1904 *Kvali* was closed. There was felt a great need
> of an illegal organ. . . . The Bolsheviks, with Lado Kets-
> khoveli at the head, organized in Baku an illegal journal,
> *Proletarii Brdzola*. . . . The situation changed at the be-
> ginning of 1905 when the majority of the Georgian Social
> Democrats stood on the position of menshevism. . . . Dur-
> ing the course of 1905 there developed a bitter struggle
> between bolshevism and menshevism. . . .

From all this dull and contradictory evidence, a few essentials begin to emerge. First, it is clear that Stalin was not born number-one man in the Caucasus but apprenticed himself to others and learned from others. Second, that a Bolshevik group was formed in the Caucasus in 1904, after Kamenev was sent there to call into being an organization, but it developed under the imposing shadow of a mass organization and large Georgian figures, and did not make a sharp break with the general organization there. It was in this little circle that Stalin got his first training as a faction fighter.

The official biographies assure us that Stalin immediately converted Transcaucasia into "a stronghold of bolshevism," but mountains of evidence testify to the contrary. At the two united congresses of Bolsheviks and Mensheviks (Stockholm, 1906, and London, 1907), the Caucasian Bolsheviks were not able to muster up enough votes to entitle them to a single uncontested delegate. In all four Duma elections, while the Social Democratic Party won many Transcaucasian seats, all the Deputies were Mensheviks, no single Bolshevik appearing among them. Whatever tendency to bolshevism may have developed in 1904, once more in 1905, according to the *Big Soviet Encyclopedia,* "the majority stood on the position of menshevism." In 1906, Bolsheviks and Mensheviks continued to form part of a single unified movement. Thus in *Sotsial Demokrat,* published in Petersburg with Lenin as one of its editors, the issue of October 13, 1906, page 7, carries a report from Transcaucasia, which reads:

> Within the last few days ended the Fourth Congress of the Caucasian Social Democratic organization. Forty-three delegates attended with one vote for every three hundred members of the Party. About ten were there with voice but no vote. In the number of the former there were six Bolsheviks, the rest being Mensheviks. . . . The greatest number of delegates were from Tiflis—twenty-two—where at present there are six thousand members. . . . The elections were direct, almost all members took part in them. Baku sent four delegates. All were Mensheviks. . . . The Bolsheviks did not put through a single Bolshevik resolution. . . .

Thus neither Tiflis nor Baku, where Stalin had worked, was in Bolshevik hands, and the Bolshevik total was less than one in seven.

Skipping to 1910, we once more find a report in *Sotsial Demokrat* (now published in Paris), this time signed "K.S.," i.e. Koba Stalin. It is dated Baku and says that there are not more than three hundred members in the Baku organization of Bolsheviks.

They are in a majority there but are trying to unite with the Mensheviks ("about one hundred members") but "unification with the Menshevik comrades has not yet been realized, since mere wishes alone do not liquidate a split."

Skipping again to 1912, we find that the Bolsheviks have still failed to break for good with the Transcaucasian Regional Committee led and controlled by the Mensheviks! Even Beria involuntarily testifies to the fact of this being the first attempt at a "disrecognition" of the Transcaucasian Committee:

> In April, 1912—he writes on page 150 of his book—the Tiflis Bolshevik organization came out against the Transcaucasian Regional Committee of the R.S.D.L.P. which was led by the Menshevik-Liquidators . . . and called upon the Social Democratic organizations to boycott the Transcaucasian Conference being called by the Regional Committee. . . .

Again I sought the real outlines of the event in contemporary papers. In *Sotsial Demokrat* No. 32, there is a report from the Caucasus signed "Sr.," which reads:

> At the Regional Conference were present delegates from seven localities. Baku was not represented. From the group of Tiflis Bolsheviks also no one was present since it was proposed to the latter to take part only with an advisory vote—and our people completely refused. The chief and most important point was the question of Party work. A report was given which was based on the idea that the legal organization ought to work under the control and leadership of the illegal. The conference approved and accepted the report. . . . There were present Liquidators of the first water, but they hid their character. . . . In the newly elected Organization Committee was elected one Bolshevik and one who strongly vacillates between Caucasian menshevism and our position. . . .

This report is dated December 15, 1913! Still no clean and clear break!

As long as Lenin was alive—and even three years after his death —the leading Communist historian, Philip Makharadze, could write without challenge:

> In the Transcaucasian Social Democratic movement of that time [1897-1904], opportunist and revisionist tendencies were rarely encountered in general. We may even say that they did not exist at all. . . .

In the Revolutions of 1917, the Georgian Mensheviks, unlike their Russian counterparts or associates, had no misgivings about taking power locally and had sufficient following to set up an independent democratic republic with Noah Zhordania as President. In accordance with his doctrine of self-determination and his quest for desperately needed peace on his frontiers, Lenin was in favor of recognizing the Georgian Republic. So too, as it appears from his still unpublished papers, was Trotsky. (Some evidence on this point is to be found in the posthumous *Stalin*, by Leon Trotsky, Harpers, 1946, pp. 266-8, and confirmatory documents were found by the editor, Charles Malamuth, among Trotsky's papers in the Harvard Library.)

But Stalin felt otherwise, as did his bosom friend Orjonikidze. Covertly they arranged an invasion by troops of the Red Army in 1921. Zhordania's government was ousted. Thereupon Lenin sent Orjonikidze the following significant instruction:

> Gigantically important to seek an acceptable compromise for a bloc with Zhordania or Georgian Mensheviks like him, who even before the uprising were not absolutely hostile to the thought of a Soviet structure in Georgia under certain conditions. [*Collected Works*, Third Russian Edition, pp. 187-88, dated March 2, 1921.]

Two things are notable in this message: the recognition of the strength of Zhordania with the Georgian masses ("gigantically important") and the recognition of the exceptional political character of Georgian menshevism. Even in 1924, the Zhordania forces were still strong enough to stage a general uprising. Publicly, Stalin characterized it as a "comic opera uprising" but in the Politburo, he said: "All Georgia must be plowed under." Apparently poor Makharadze was not so wrong after all in the histories against which Lavrenti Beria in 1935 began thundering his anathemas.

Why we say "poor Makharadze" will appear in the next chapter.

CHAPTER XXV

HOW HISTORY IS MADE

"Paper will put up with anything that is written on it."
—*Joseph Stalin*

NOTHING in the preceding chapter should surprise us were it not for its conflict with the new Russian historiography, for it is only natural that Lenin's break with the other Iskrists at the 1903 Congress should have taken some time to penetrate into the Caucasus. And no less natural, when even Lenin's decorative key figure, Plekhanov, and his loyal Central Committee partisans deserted him, that the rank and file inside Russia should have been puzzled by the split and hesitant to take sides. Then from 1905 to 1912, the whole movement was to some degree reunified, so that in the Caucasus, where there was a powerful, orthodox, Left-Plekhanovist mass movement, not Bolshevist nor yet Menshevist in the same sense as in the rest of Russia, the little Bolshevik faction of which Stalin was a part should have continued within the general organization. All memoirs written while Lenin was alive, all Party documents and reports of pre-revolutionary days, all evidence that can stand the test of ordinary historical investigation, have had to be ignored, explained away, supplanted, suppressed, destroyed, before a new version could be established. The decisive turning points are: the year 1929, the first of Stalin's absolute rule and of that cult which required the bringing of every moment of his past into accord with his present infinite glory; the year 1935, when Lavrenti Beria, then head of the Georgian GPU or Secret Police, went to work on the streamlining of the new history; the years 1936-38, when the purges persuaded innumerable memorialists to lose or revise their memories; the year 1938, when Stalin himself took over the task of writing history in the originally anonymous official *History of the Communist Party of the Soviet Union*, which now forms Volume XV of Stalin's *Collected Works*; and the year 1946, when those *Collected Works* began to appear with biographical and other notes under Stalin's own supervision.

What this has meant in human terms can be seen by following the fate of Stalin's old friend, Abel Enukidze. Enukidze was one

of the best of that corps of second-string leaders recruited from
the working class, which made up the most dependable strength
of Lenin's party. Unlike the intellectuals who followed him, these
professional revolutionaries from the working class essayed little
independent thinking, vacillated less, more seldom questioned or
broke with him. They found the meaning of their lives in carrying
out the orders of the machine. A proletarianized son of peasants,
two years older than Djugashvili, Enukidze early left Georgia for
Central Russia, where he learned a skilled trade and got his first
training in Marxism. Deported from Central Russia in 1897, he
entered the railway shops in Tiflis. In April and September, 1902,
he began an endless round of arrests and escapes interspersed
with brief periods of underground work. He escaped from Siberia
in 1903, spent a long period living literally underground and
working in the sub-cellar printing plant in Baku from 1903 to 1906.
His record then continues: arrest 1907, escape; arrest 1908, deportation to Archangel, escape; arrest 1910, escape; arrest 1911,
escape; arrest 1914, deportation to Turukhansk whence he was
drafted into the Army. In 1917 he appeared at the First Congress
of Soviets as a soldier delegate, reached high positions in the
Soviet Government and became a member of the Central Committee of the Communist Party. So close was this solid, dependable
Georgian to Stalin that in 1929, on the occasion of the latter's
fiftieth birthday, he was one of four friends considered intimate
enough to contribute to a symposium called *The Life of Stalin.*
The other three were Orjonikidze, Voroshilov, and Kaganovich,
which last was later to become Stalin's brother-in-law and chief
industrial trouble-shooter.

Nineteen twenty-nine was the year of the first great glorification of Stalin and the first attempt to bring every moment of his
past into accord with his present glory. Enukidze's contribution
was an effort to link Stalin's name with the Baku underground
printing plant, with which, as Krassin's and Enukidze's earlier
memoirs had amply demonstrated, Stalin had not had the slightest
connection. That celebrated printing plant had been discussed in
innumerable memoirs in 1923; whole books had been published
concerning it and everybody connected with it. Not a single
memoir so much as mentioned the name of Stalin! Enukidze was
handicapped by too much knowledge of the past and too much
respect for facts to do a job such as Beria would attempt a few
years later. Enukidze's efforts to enlarge Stalin's past were therefore strangely destined to contribute to his downfall. His fateful
contribution began:

> Today Stalin is fifty years old. How quickly time flies!
> I see quite clearly before me the young Soso Djugashvili
> at Tiflis, where I had my first business interview with him
> . . . Vladimir Ketskhoveli was organizing a small illegal
> printing press at Baku. He wanted two reliable compositors
> and type for them. The then existing Tiflis Committee of
> the R.S.D.L.P. was prepared to give all this on condition
> that all publications and the whole work of the Baku print-
> ing press . . . be subjected to the control of the Tiflis
> Committee. . . . Ketskhoveli sent me for the second time
> to Tiflis for the type and compositors. "Try and find Soso
> Djugashvili, he's a good chap, tell him everything and he'll
> help." After a short conversation with Soso I obtained every-
> thing. . . .

This obliging invention contained one fatal implication: either
Djugashvili was not a member of the Tiflis Committee, or, being
a member, did not control and head it, or else, far from "instructing" Ketskhoveli to set up the Baku plant, opposed him when he
learned of the latter's initiative, even withholding support in an
effort to get control. All the voluminous literature on the plant
published in 1923, while Lenin and most of the veteran participants
were still alive, makes clear that Tiflis had no control over Baku
at the time, that Ketskhoveli did indeed start the plant on his own
initiative, did meet jealousy from Tiflis, and that eventually, with
the support of Krassin, the plant came to service not only all of
Transcaucasia but all of Russia.

However, Lavrenti Beria, as Stalin's agent and inquisitor, wanted
to paint another picture. According to this picture, the Caucasian
organizations were born fully centralized: Batum and Baku had
no organizations and did nothing except when Tiflis ordered something or sent someone there. Enukidze's standing declined steadily
as Beria forced him to explain away his own earlier memoirs. The
process is pitiful but worth following for the indirect light it
throws on Stalin's past, on its revision, and on the major event in
Stalin's subsequent life, the great purge of the later thirties. Here,
then, are the successive versions of the origin and activity of the
celebrated Baku printing plant. The first version carries us back to
the year 1903.

In that year, Lado (Vladimir) Ketskhoveli, the most important
of all those arrested in the raids of 1902, was shot dead in his
prison cell on secret police order. In honor of the martyred leader,
the Party issued a pamphlet, containing the following eulogy:

> Lado was the *first* to create a Georgian revolutionary
> literature. He was the *first* to organize a revolutionary print-

ing plant here, the *first* to sow the seeds of revolution among the Baku workers. . . .[1]

This then, is the first reference to the great printing plant. In 1923, when the Bolsheviks were celebrating the twenty-fifth anniversary of the founding of the Social Democratic Party, a voluminous literature appeared dealing with the most notable of all underground presses. Here is Leonid Krassin's own account:

> The most important printing plant was our press in Baku. This press was planned in 1901 by our Georgian comrade, Lado Ketskhoveli, who died prematurely. . . . Comrade Lado solved the problem [of a government permit to buy a press] very simply. He issued an authorization in his name, forging the governor's signature . . . then got a notarized copy of the false document. . . . The successor to Lado in the direction of our plant was Tifon Timurazo-vich Enukidze [underground name "Semion," not to be confused with Abel Enukidze]. He who at present, 1923, is the director of our plant for printing paper money. . . . Semion installed the press in the Tartar quarter, so well hidden that even if the entire personnel, with A. S. (Abel) Enukidze at the head, had been arrested, the printing plant would have been safe. . . . In 1904 Comrade Semion handed all the affairs of Baku over to A. S. Enukidze and went to Moscow. . . .

If we turn to Abel Enukidze's memoir on the printing plant, published the same year as Krassin's, and collate it with the statements of others who worked in the plant, we learn many additional details. Ketskhoveli had first run a legal print shop. When he decided to devote himself fully to underground printing, he got two hundred rubles from his wealthy, conservative brother, on the pretext that he was going to give up revolutionary activities and needed the money to aid him in establishing a "respectable" career. From various sources in Tiflis he collected an additional hundred rubles. Krassin got together eight hundred rubles from

---

[1] From *The Life and Revolutionary Activity of Lado Ketskhoveli*, Tiflis, 1903. Italics in the original. The revolutionary paper referred to is the clandestine *Brdzola* ("Struggle"), which Ketskhoveli founded and edited. *Kvali*, edited by Zhordania, was the legal Marxist paper. The pamphlet from which we quote was issued by a united party prior to the split in the Caucasus and therefore expressed the opinion of both future Bolsheviks and Mensheviks. In his "Biographical Chronological Data" to Vol. I of his *Collected Works* Stalin now writes: "Sept. 1901. In Baku appears No. 1 of the illegal paper *Brdzola*, founded on the initiative of I. V. Stalin." Here, however, Stalin makes no claim to having founded the Baku printing plant in 1901 but merely to having organized a lesser plant in Batum in January, 1902.

wealthy liberals and finally even a loan of two thousand rubles from the municipality of Baku, at the head of which was the old Narodnik, A. I. Novikov. Under Krassin's financial tutelage the plant expanded until it covered a vast area underground and contained a cutting machine, type in several languages, presses, binders, even a casting machine for using stereotype mats. Krassin personally designed a disappearing trapdoor. In this steadily enlarging plant underneath the houses of Tartar Baku, first two, then five, then seven selfless printers worked and lived together like friars in a cloister. They worked ten hours a day, and in emergencies, hours without limit. The plant was without heat or ventilation; windows leading to the street were sealed with brick and mortar. To avoid notice, no one ever emerged during the day. At night they took turns going up for air for three-hour periods. All got the same food; each received twenty-five rubles a month; they read and discussed the same books. First Ketskhoveli, then Semion, then Abel Enukidze became the contact man with the outside world.

Krassin arranged for Krupskaya to make a mat of each issue of *Iskra* abroad, and send it to him bound in a scientific book. From the mat they made castings. Suddenly the police were astonished to find that, despite their skill in stopping *Iskra* from being smuggled over the borders, a flood of copies was issuing northward from the Caucasus. They doubled and trebled their guards on the Persian frontier, but to no avail. The secret plant printed ten thousand copies of *Iskra;* the *Communist Manifesto;* Kautsky's *Erfurt Program* (of which one hundred copies were done on de luxe paper, one being sent to Kautsky and the others sold by the ingenious Krassin to liberal sympathizers for large donations); Parvus's *War and Revolution;* Trotsky's first 1905 pamphlet; Lenin's *What's to Be Done* and *To the Peasant Poor;* and countless other things—over a million copies in all of leaflets, pamphlets, periodicals. "Among us," wrote Enukidze in 1923 (i.e. while Lenin and Krassin were still alive), "the Bolsheviks were in a majority but there were some Mensheviks in the plant, too. Our differences did not affect our work at all." Not until 1905, after the Bolshevik Third Congress, did it become an exclusive Bolshevik plant. At that time Krassin had ceased to be a "conciliator" and had become once more a 100 percent Bolshevik, while the Third Congress itself had adopted a decision for negotiating unity with the Mensheviks. All the memoirs of 1923 substantiate this general picture in all its circumstantial details.

As late as 1926, Volume IV of the *Big Soviet Encyclopedia* carried the following account of the Baku printing plant:

> The initiator and organizer of the Baku printing plant was Ketskhoveli. . . . In 1903 the director of the plant was T. T. Enukidze (Semion) . . . the general direction and financing was transferred to the Central Committee represented by L. B. Krassin. . . . During the time between the beginning and liquidation of the Baku printing plant, I. Bolkvadze, V. Dumbadze, S. Todria, K. Josha, I. Sturua and A. Enukidze worked in it.

But, at the beginning of 1935, Lavrenti Beria, head of the Transcaucasian GPU, went to work on the printing plant's story. His first step was to force Enukidze to write a "confession" of inaccuracy in *Pravda*. His next was to summon a Conference of Party Functionaries in the Caucasus on July 21 and 22, 1935, and deliver his two-day lecture *On the History of the Bolshevik Organizations in Transcaucasia*, later printed in Georgian, Russian, and all leading languages of the world, in various, frequently revised editions, both under the above title and under the alternative title of *Stalin's Early Writings and Activities*.[2] The two titles are properly interchangeable for the Bolshevik organizations in Transcaucasia are reduced to emanations from the early writings and activities of Joseph Stalin.

According to Beria, the Baku plant was established by Ketskhoveli, but "on the initiative of Comrade Stalin and under the direction of the Tiflis Committee headed by Comrade Stalin." And Stalin had caused the leading group to "supply Comrade Ketskhoveli with the type, equipment and money."

Ketskhoveli, who had cozened the first two hundred rubles from his brother and secured the type and press by forging the governor's signature, was dead. So was Krassin, who had raised the major sums. But not so Abel Enukidze. Therefore the readers of *Pravda* were treated on January 16, 1935, to the public prologue of this drama, the spectacle of Enukidze's self-denunciation, the purpose of which was not to establish the outlines of the "new truth" but to discredit the old truth and himself, and muddy the waters of public memory. The performance was the more startling because he had always been looked up to as one of the most

---

[2] The "American" edition is issued under the imprint of the Communist publishing house, International Publishers, from sheets printed in Moscow and bound here. It bears both titles and was translated from the fourth Russian edition, which edition reveals the further workings of the process of revision of history by some significant alterations of the "truths" established in the first.

dependable of the veteran fighters, a distinguished Central Committee member, and a bosom friend of Joseph Stalin.

> Unfortunately—Enukidze now found himself obliged to write—until the present these questions have not been sufficiently and not always accurately elucidated. . . . I too must correct the errors I have admitted into the *Encyclopedia Granat* and the *Big Soviet Encyclopedia*. There the story of my life is told as if I had founded in Baku the Social Democratic organization. This is untrue. . . . The outstanding role was played by Lado Ketskhoveli, sent to Baku by the Tiflis Central Party Group made up at that time of Jibladze, Tsulukidze, Ketskhoveli, Stalin and others. . . . Lenin maintained connections with the Baku Party organization through Comrade Ketskhoveli. . . . Along with a number of other comrades, I merely helped Ketskhoveli. Therefore, it is completely unjustified to reduce in any way the role of Comrade Ketskhoveli in the creation of the Baku Committee and in giving of a Bolshevist Iskrist face to this organization. I did relatively little work in comparison with Ketskhoveli. . . .

This peculiar breast-beating continued through six columns of *Pravda*, making a half of one of that paper's oversized pages. The reader will note that while Enukidze is made to denounce himself as a liar and a boaster and throw doubt on all his memoirs, the account he gives is still substantially the one just quoted from the *Big Soviet Encyclopedia* and the one he gave in 1923. There is, indeed, a tendency in Enukidze to boast of his long and honorable record and perhaps to enlarge somewhat his services to the printing plant. But those who suddenly began to denounce him as a boaster were not engaged in restoring the exact outlines of that record: rather was their interest that of arrogating to Stalin the credit for initiating and directing everything that had happened in the Caucasus. Not the human weakness of boasting was Enukidze's crime, but the setting down of facts that stood in the way of the credibility of Stalin's claims.

Before Enukidze submitted his article to *Pravda*, he negotiated with Beria concerning every sentence and secured the latter's approval for its publication in the official Party organ. But for Beria that was just the beginning. Once a man is made to discredit himself by a public confession, the drama of his inexorable downfall has begun.

Six months later, when Beria got around to delivering his celebrated lecture *On the History of the Bolshevik Organizations in*

Transcaucasia, the fallen leader's comparatively innocent crime of "boasting" had been transformed into:

> A. Enukidze, deliberately and with hostile intent, falsified the history of the Bolshevik organizations of Transcaucasia . . . cynically and brazenly distorted well-known historical facts, crediting himself with alleged services in the establishment of the first illegal printing shop in Baku. . . . In view of the imminent danger that these fallacies and distortions of his would be exposed, A. Enukidze was obliged to admit these "mistakes" in the columns of *Pravda.* . . .

Next Beria had the compositor V. Tsuladze (who, incidentally, is not so much as mentioned in the earlier memoirs as having worked in the plant) make the following declaration:

> During its entire period of existence, no one worked in the printing shop besides Comrade Ketskhoveli, myself, and one other compositor.

Thus Enukidze's very participation, vouched for by Krassin, is officially effaced, although it thereby becomes obvious that Tsuladze's "memory" is false, since it reduces the total number of workers in the great plant to only three (one mysteriously nameless), and eliminates all but one of the names which figure in Krassin's account and that of every other participant.

Less than three years later, when the Fourth Edition of Beria's fateful lecture appeared, the sentence on Enukidze bore a new note. "A. Enukidze," it read, "since exposed as a mortal enemy of the people . . ." "Mortal" indeed, for by that time he lay dead with a GPU bullet in the base of his brain.

The text of this Fourth Edition, the one chosen for translation into all the major tongues of the civilized world, bristles with such ominous sentences. On page 9 is still repeated the warning to Philip Makharadze, which we quoted in Chapter XXII. It is repeated without the awful footnote, which means that at that moment the seventy-year-old Georgian historian and one-time Communist Chairman of the first Provisional Council of Commissars of the new-formed Georgian Soviet Republic, was still alive. But how much more fearful it sounds now when we read the words, "so far Comrade Makharadze has not taken the trouble to revise his works and correct the mistakes and distortions they contain"! For now we must read them in the context of such footnotes as "A. Enukidze, since exposed as a mortal enemy of the people" (p. 35). So, on page 155 we read:

In their articles and reminiscences T. Zhgenti, B. Bibineishvili and others [!] maintained silence about the great historical significance of the struggle of the Transcaucasian Bolsheviks against the Mensheviks . . . under the leadership of Comrades Stalin, Orjonikidze and Spandaryan. . . . Is it not clear that Zhgenti and Bibineishvili slandered the Bolsheviks of Georgia and unceremoniously falsified and distorted the history of our Party?

Once more there is a footnote: "In 1937, B. Bibineishvili was exposed as an enemy of the people."

On page 168, Makharadze's name is brought in again, this time not to be charged with "distorting historical fact dishonestly," but as one of a group of "national deviationists" who in 1922 thought it preferable for Georgia to enter directly into the Soviet Union as an autonomous republic, in place of entering indirectly through a Transcaucasian federation which would affiliate directly with the Soviet Union.

The leading group of the Georgian national deviationists [says the text] included Ph. Makharadze, B. Mdivani, S. Kavtaradze, M. Okujava, M. Toroshelidze, and K. Tsintsadze.

And a footnote writes finis to four of the names thus grouped:

In 1936, B. Mdivani, S. Kavtaradze, M. Toroshelidze— and K. Tsintsadze at an earlier date—were exposed as enemies of the people.

In 1907, the Koté Tsintsadze thus disposed of had been immediate director of the great expropriations carried out by Kamo. In Lenin's day he too had written memoirs which "boasted" of his role in starting the terrorist and expropriation groups in the Caucasus ("Our prominent comrades, especially Koba-Stalin, approved of my initiative"). And in Lenin's day he had been entrusted because of that past with the direction of the Tiflis Cheka (future GPU) and then of the All-Caucasian Cheka. In other words, he had been Beria's predecessor in office. But in 1931, after a faction quarrel with Stalin, he had been exiled to Siberia, where he died. Budu Mdivani and Sergei Kavtaradze, like Philip Makharadze, had been successive Chairmen of the Council of People's Commissars of Soviet Georgia. Like Lado Dumbadze, Chairman of the first Bolshevik Soviet in Tiflis, like Misha Okujava and Misha Toroshelidze, members of the Presidium of the Tiflis Soviet Congress of 1922, their memories have been silenced by the successive refutations of prison, exile and death. Only the aged Makharadze, stubbornly "refusing to correct his errors" and effectively silenced, so far as I know is still alive.

This "Georgian national deviation" referred to by Beria in his lecture of 1935 has an interesting past, and was destined to have an interesting future. In 1923, when Lenin lay paralyzed, too ill to participate in political life, he became increasingly alarmed at what Stalin and Orjonikidze, aided by the GPU Chief Dzierszinski, were cooking up against the local Georgian Communist Party, the Georgian Soviet Government and its leaders. On March 5, 1923, Lenin dictated the following note to Leon Trotsky:

> Strictly Confidential. Personal.
> Esteemed Comrade Trotsky:
> I earnestly ask you to undertake the defense of the Georgian matter in the Party Central Committee. It is now being "prosecuted" by Stalin and Dzierszinski, so that I cannot rely on their impartiality. Indeed, quite the contrary! If you would agree to undertake its defense, I would rest easy. If for some reason you do not agree, please return all the papers. I shall consider that a sign of your disagreement.
> With best comradely greetings,
>
> LENIN.

And the very next day, he wrote to

> Comrades Mdivani, Makharadze and Others: (Copies to Comrades Trotsky and Kamenev.)
> Esteemed Comrades:
> I am with you in this matter with all my heart. I am outraged by the rudeness of Orjonikidze and the connivance of Stalin and Dzierszinski. On your behalf I am now preparing notes and a speech.
> With esteem,
>
> LENIN.

As in other matters, Lenin has been censored by his "best disciple" and neither of these notes is now reprinted in the *Collected Works,* the *Selected Works,* or the *Letters* of V. I. Lenin. But their genuineness is attested to by each of Lenin's three secretaries of the period, Miss Glyasser, Miss Fotieva, and Miss Volodicheva. To the first of these he said that he "was preparing a bombshell for Stalin at the Twelfth Congress." But two days later, Lenin suffered his third stroke and was unable to attend the Congress, which took place in April. There is reference to these notes in the minutes of the Central Committee meeting of April 16, 1923, in remarks of Stalin made at that meeting, in a note of Trotsky to

Stalin dated April 18, and another to the Central Committee dated April 17, and in a speech of Stalin's at the Congress itself on April 23. However, it would now be a form of suicide to so much as refer to these matters in the Soviet Union. Officially, they have no longer happened.[3]

The death of Tsintsadze in 1931 and of Mdivani, Kavtaradze and Toroshelidze in 1936, did not end this affair. There is another note on page 178 of the same Fourth Edition of Beria's book which reads: "In 1936, R. Akhundov was exposed as an enemy of the people." Akhundov is not a Georgian but an Azerbaijanian. In 1922, Azerbaijan, too, or at least its Communist leadership, had opposed Stalin's scheme for incorporation in a Transcaucasian federation and had preferred direct entry into the Soviet Union as an Autonomous Republic. It is this crime that Stalin and Dzierszinski were "prosecuting" as alleged Georgian and Azerbaijanian "nationalism"—a prosecution which gives us an indirect insight into Stalin's conception of the famous right of national self-determination.

But the ironical climax to this list of "national deviationists" who had been "exposed as enemies of the people" is that the "crime" alleged against them in the First Edition of Beria's book was actually consummated by Stalin himself in the year after their liquidation. But GPU Chief Beria was nothing if not a flexible prosecutor. The same Fourth Edition which announces their fate comes to a conclusion on page 190 with the news that Stalin now considered "the conditions ripe for the abolition of the Transcaucasian federation and the incorporation of Georgia, Azerbaijan and Armenia into the Union of Soviet Socialist Republics in accordance with the great Stalin Constitution."

"Paper will put up with anything that is written on it," Stalin once wrote (in *Marxism and the National Question*). Need we wonder then that so valuable a historian as Lavrenti Beria should in 1938 have been promoted from Transcaucasian to all-Russian historical activities as the All-Union chief of the GPU or NKVD, now MVD? Or that, in the course of Beria's historical revision, the broken Enukidze, the broken Mdivani, and all the others, including many whose passing was not marked by so much as a footnote, should have perished with bullets in the base of their brains, sure end to all undesirable memories?

[3] The texts can be found in English in Trotsky's "Letter to the Party History Bureau," October 21, 1927, subsequently republished in *The Stalin School of Falsification*, by Leon Trotsky, Pioneer Publishers, 1937, pp. 69-70, and in Trotsky's *Stalin*, Harpers, 1939, pp. 361-62.

CHAPTER XXVI

DJUGASHVILI BECOMES A DISCIPLE

"And make it his mature ambition
To think no thought but ours,
To hunger, work illegally,
And be anonymous.

—*W. H. Auden*

WHEN Djugashvili fled from Siberia in early 1904, he returned to his native Georgia. This would suggest that he was either not yet marked as a well-known figure, or had peculiar talents for acting secretively. Probably both, for we have already notice that the Mensheviks held him responsible for the attack on the Batum jail, while the police did not. This talent for discreetly moving other actors while remaining invisible will appear many times in our story.

That he returned implies, too, that the Georgian tongue and scene were most natural for him. He had not yet sufficiently attracted the attention of the national leaders to be invited abroad for conference, training, reassignment elsewhere in Russia. Not for another seven years—a long time in the life of a revolutionist—would he undertake activities in Saint Petersburg which indicated that he had become part of the national leadership. And it would be nine years before Lenin would call him abroad for theoretical training in connection with the national question. It is probable that jealousy of those of his own generation who earlier went abroad—Trotsky, Kamenev, Zinoviev—figured in the subsequent official belittling of all those who "did not stick to the Russian underground." Actually Kamenev, for example, spent quite as much time in the underground as Stalin, a good part of it in Georgia, too. Born in 1883—four years later than Stalin and Trotsky—he graduated from a Tiflis *gymnazia*, was arrested while a student at the Moscow University, served a brief sentence, and then was deported back to Tiflis. There he taught a circle of railway workers and another of shoemakers, until the middle of 1902, when he went abroad to live near Lenin. In Paris he met Olga Bronstein, Trotsky's younger sister, whom he later married. After the Second Congress, Lenin sent him back to Georgia, where he organized the Bolshevik faction. His activities in a strike on the Transcaucasian railway caused a police search for him in January 1904. He fled to Moscow, where he was arrested and deported once more to Tiflis in July, 1904. After the years of the 1905 revolution he went abroad again only to be sent back to Russia by Lenin in 1913 to take charge of *Pravda*. Most of the World War, like Stalin, he spent as a deportee to Siberia. Such comings and goings were natural events in the life of all professional revolutionaries.

A more serious target of Stalin's envy was the career of the young man of like age with himself, Leon Trotsky, for in the year 1905 this young revolutionist attained nationwide prominence as the outstanding figure in the famed Petersburg Soviet. In October, 1917, and the years succeeding until Lenin's death, the name of Trotsky was always linked with that of Lenin in inseparable union. It was largely to bury the memory of the duality Lenin-Trotsky, and substitute therefor the duality Lenin-Stalin that the peculiar revision of history was first undertaken.

Shortly after his flight from Siberia, Joseph Djugashvili set up his own home. The date of his marriage, like all aspects of his life, is cloaked in secrecy. His boyhood chum, Iremashvili, gives it as 1903, which would imply that the marriage took place while he was in prison. Others make it 1904, immediately after his escape from Siberia. Trotsky maliciously suggests that the latter date would account for his comparative inactivity in politics during 1904, owing to the counter-attractions of the first year of married life. Iremashvili, certainly not friendly but generally well informed, is most likely right.

Djugashvili's wife was a Georgian girl, Ekaterina Svanidze, sister of a comrade whom Stalin would one day make president of the Soviet Bank for Foreign Trade. But she herself was not a revolutionary. From all accounts, she appears to have been a girl of simple, domestic, peasant mentality, devoted to her husband, deeply religious, submissive, loyal, unquestioning. Trotsky construes this marriage to a religious girl as a sign of Djugashvili's indifference in matters of Marxian theory. There is perhaps some justification for this view, but we must understand the marriage in terms of Djugashvili's Caucasian origins and environment. The Georgian organization did not consist of a small and doctrinaire band of professional intellectual revolutionaries like that in Central Russia. It was already a broad mass movement, influencing great numbers and being influenced in turn by the attitudes of the masses which followed it. Moreover, there was lacking in Georgia that close comradeship between men and women and that sense

of equality which was part of the tradition of the Russian parties,
inherited from several generations of idealistic terrorist bands, recruited from both sexes. The Caucasus produced no Sophia
Perovskaya, no Vera Figner, no Vera Zasulich, or—to select at random from the women that people these pages—no Nadezhda
Krupskaya, Angelica Balabanoff, Rosa Luxemburg, or Alexandra
Kollontai. Nor was it likely to, for among the mountain tribes,
amidst the Mohammedan city dwellers, even among Georgian and
Armenian Christians, women were subordinate creatures, kept close
in the home. Few indeed were the Caucasian revolutionaries who
found their mates in the course of the struggle, in underground
meeting, prison or exile; few were the unions in which love and
comradeship-in-struggle were inseparable.

Iremashvili has this to say on Djugashvili's relations with his
wife:

> His marriage was a happy one. True, it was impossible
> to discover in his home that equality of the sexes which he
> advocated. . . . But it was not in his character to share
> equal rights with any other person. His marriage was a
> happy one because his wife, who could not measure up to
> him in intellect, regarded him as a demi-god. . . . Being
> a Georgian woman, she was brought up in the sacrosanct
> tradition which obliges a woman to serve . . . With all her
> heart she served her husband's welfare. She passed her
> nights in ardent prayer waiting for her Soso, who was busy
> at his meetings, praying that he might turn away from
> ideas that were displeasing to God and turn instead to a
> quiet home life of toil and contentment. . . . This man,
> so restless in spirit, could find love only in his own impov-
> erished home. Only his wife, his child and his mother were
> exempt from the scorn he poured out upon all others.

The child was Yasha (Jacob) Djugashvili, born several years
after their marriage. When Stalin left the Caucasus in 1911, his
wife was already dead and he did not take his child with him.
Jacob remained either with Stalin's mother or his mother-in-law.
We hear nothing more about the boy until 1919, when Iremashvili became a teacher in a Tiflis secondary school and found Jacob
Djugashvili among his pupils—not, according to the teacher, a particularly bright one. That was in Social Democratic Georgia. When
it became Soviet Georgia, Stalin sent for his son and installed him
in his apartment in the Kremlin. There he began to study railroad engineering. According to the frequently fanciful account of
the Czech journalist Kurt Singer, "he proved himself a poor student . . . At last Stalin lost patience and ordered Yasha home

from college saying: 'If you can't be an engineer, you can at least
be a shoemaker.' But Yasha disobeyed [sic]. He ran away to the
Caucasus, where he worked as an electrician."

In 1942, a German communiqué reported that the Wehrmacht
had captured one "Jacob Djugashvili, Stalin's son." The Soviet
press, usually so attentive to everything concerning the *Vozhd,*
said nothing. In 1944, sources close to the Vatican gave further
details:

> Jacob was a lieutenant in the Red Army when he was
> taken prisoner near Lesno by the Germans on July 24, 1941
> . . . The Vatican has a report on the conversation between
> Goering and young Mr. Stalin in September 1941. . . .
> Goering, in his discussion with the then 24-year-old Com-
> munist, tried to impress him with Germany's military and
> industrial power . . . to convince him also of the supe-
> riority of Western civilization as a whole. Jacob was not
> only not impressed but expressed contempt for all that was
> non-Russian. Moscow, he told the astonished Nazi leader,
> would become the mightiest political, scientific and eco-
> nomic center of the world. As far as his private career was
> concerned, Jacob said, he saw his father rarely and had no
> personal privileges at all because he was the Premier's son
> . . . [New York *Times,* Oct. 4, 1944.]

The difficulty with this story is the age given to Jacob, 24 in
1941. Actually he was then closer to 34 than 24. On May 1, 1945,
the *New York Times* carried a dispatch from Dachau, Germany,
concerning the liberation of 32,000 inmates by American troops.
"These were said to have included Premier Stalin's son, Jacob,
who was captured in 1941." Again no comment in the Russian
press. A possible explanation of the discrepancy in age lies in the
existence of yet a third son, illegitimate, by a Siberian peasant
woman of Turukhansk, where Stalin spent a term in exile. According to Anton Ciliga, Yugoslav Communist deported to
Turukhansk by Stalin, he met such a son there who boasted of
his paternity and was 20 in 1935. (A. Ciliga: *Siberie.* Plon, 1950,
p. 287.)

On June 30, 1945, Edgar Snow wrote in the *Saturday Evening
Post:*

> His one daughter, Svetlana, an attractive girl of 18, is
> perhaps closer to him than anyone else. . . . Stalin used
> to call her his "housekeeper," but recently she married and
> went to live elsewhere. . . . Stalin also had two sons, both
> in the Red Army. The elder, Jacob, by Stalin's divorced
> [*sic*] wife, fell into the hands of the Nazis early in the war,

and is reported as having committed suicide in a prison camp near Berlin. The other son, Vasili, by Stalin's second wife, is a bomber pilot and has been awarded the Order of the Red Banner and the Order of Suvorov, Second Class.

On Vasili, son of Stalin's second marriage in 1919 to the young Nadya Alliluyeva (also the mother of Svetlana), the Russian press has not been so reticent. On October 9, 1944, as Colonel Vasili Yosifovich Stalin, he was given honorable mention along with a number of other officers, in his father's Order of the Day. On May 30, 1945, Colonel Stalin was one of seventy-six officers awarded the Order of Suvorov, Second Class. On March 2, 1946, Generalissimo Joseph Stalin signed a decree promoting his son Vasili from colonel to major general. Then it was recorded that he had won the Order of the Red Banner in 1942 and that of Suvorov in 1945 for "skilled and courageous leadership." In May 1948, *Ogonek* released a picture of "Major General Vasili Stalin, son of Premier Stalin, at the controls of his plane in command of the air section of the May Day parade in Moscow." More honors have been heaped on him since.

It is worth noting that Jacob, son of the simple Georgian peasant woman Svanidze, bears the name Djugashvili, while the son of the Party comrade, Allilueva, bears the proud name Vasili Yosifovich Stalin (Basil, Son of Josif Stalin). Jacob, and the son Ciliga found in Siberia, seem less eager to be known as sons of Russia's ruler, while the tight silence of the Soviet press on their very existence suggests that their father has been no more anxious to be known as the sire of these sons. If Vasili has received a big share of publicity, the dictator's daughter, Svetlana, has not. Even when she married, there was no public announcement, and the very name of Svetlana's husband has been preserved a state secret.

During the course of the years 1905 and 1906, the boyhood friends Soso Djugashvili and Soso Iremashvili drifted apart as the Caucasus began belatedly to feel the rift between Bolsheviks and Mensheviks. It is no doubt to this period that the *Little Soviet Encyclopedia*'s remark under "Stalin" begins to have application: "For the Mensheviks, Stalin was the most hated of all Caucasian Bolsheviks."

This is confirmed by Iremashvili:

> The brunt of his struggle was henceforth directed against us, his former friends. He attacked us at every meeting and discussed matters in the most savage and unscrupulous manner, trying to sow poison and hatred against us every-

where. He would have liked to root us out with fire and sword. . . . But the overwhelming majority of Georgian Marxists remained with us. That only angered and enraged him the more.

About the time these debates were getting fully under way, Djugashvili lost his beloved wife Ekaterina. The already alienated Iremashvili went to her funeral for old friendship's sake. He gives this account of the occasion:

> He was very downcast, yet he met me in a friendly manner as of old. This hard man's pallid face reflected the heartfelt anguish caused by the death of his faithful companion. . . . When the modest procession came to the cemetery gate, Koba firmly pressed my hand, pointed to the coffin and said: "Soso, this creature softened my stony heart. She is dead and with her have died my last warm feelings for all human beings." He placed his right hand over his heart: "It is all so desolate here inside, so unutterably desolate!" . . .
> From the day he buried his wife, he indeed lost the last vestige of human feeling. His heart filled with the unutterably malicious hatred which his cruel father had already begun to engender in him while he was still a child. . . . Ruthless with himself, he became ruthless with all people. . . .

It was while Djugashvili was in prison awaiting deportation to Siberia that the unexpected split had occurred at the Congress called to form a unified party. Lenin, as we already know, soon proposed a "Third Congress" to settle the crisis arising from the Second. By the time Djugashvili resumed activity in the Caucasus in 1904, Lenin's movement to force a Third Congress was already in full swing. In November, 1904, that is, ten or eleven months after Djugashvili's return from Siberia, the Bolsheviks succeeded for the first time in setting up a faction in Georgia, and held their First Conference at Tiflis. To this conference came fifteen delegates from four local Caucasian organizations in Tiflis, Batum, Baku and Kutais. They met under the chairmanship of Leo Kamenev, whom Lenin had dispatched to Transcaucasia to build his faction. Startling as the fact may seem if we permit ourselves to be persuaded by the official version of Stalin's early and primeval prominence, Djugashvili was not even a delegate. Either he was not yet prominent enough to be one of the first fifteen Caucasian Bolsheviks, or in November, 1904, he had not yet made up his mind between Lenin and the Mensheviks.

Naturally, present-day hagiography can accept neither of the two possible explanations. Hence the Marx-Engels-Lenin Institute biography of Stalin discreetly ignores this conference, though it gave birth to Georgian bolshevism. Beria, however, in his *History of the Bolshevik Organizations in Transcaucasia*, finds it impossible to ignore it. He gives the number of delegates, reports on the election of a leading committee to continue the struggle, but, in a book peppered with names of great and small, carefully avoids giving the names of the delegates or those elected to the committee. Yaroslavsky's *Landmarks in the Life of Stalin*, published yet a few years later, when the purges had enormously furthered the science of rewriting the past and revising one's memories, brazenly states that the First Conference was "presided over by Stalin"!

Actually, a complete list of delegates is available in older Party histories and records and in various memoirs by participants in the Conference, written while Lenin was still alive. In no case is Stalin's name among them. Moreover, all memoirs written in Lenin's day, or indeed until the purges had finished with most of the participants, specifically declare that Kamenev presided. Not only did Djugashvili fail to attend the Conference or to get elected on the leading committee it set up, but he was not chosen, either, as a delegate from the Caucasian region to the national faction leadership which Lenin was then constituting under the name of "Bureau of the Committees of the Majority." The Caucasian Conference chose Kamenev to represent it on this Bureau. There were seventeen in all, constituting Lenin's general staff in 1904. Djugashvili was not among them. Yet, according to the Marx-Engels-Lenin Institute biography, Stalin was already "Lenin's faithful lieutenant in this campaign for the Third Congress, the leader of the Transcaucasian Bolsheviks." And at the same time, according to the same work, he was "the virtual director" of the Caucasian Federal Committee of the Russian Social Democratic Party, which committee was under the control of the Mensheviks whom Lenin was fighting! Obviously, the two claims contradict each other, while there is ample evidence that both are wide of the truth.

Finally, when the Caucasian Bolsheviks came to choose their delegates to the Third Congress itself, they selected Kamenev, Tskhakaya, Japaridze, and Nevsky. (According to some accounts the fourth man was not Nevsky but Lehmann.) But once more, the name of Djugashvili is missing!

All Party histories and memoirs written while Lenin was alive, or indeed throughout the twenties, give the above four names, differing only as to whether the fourth man was Lehmann or Nevsky.

All histories written in the first half of the thirties, as weapons in Stalin's faction war on his associates, are purposely evasive on the makeup of the Transcaucasian Delegation to the Third Congress. Thus Popov's History (Moscow, 1934) gives a list of leading members of the Third Congress, including among them the Caucasian representatives Tskhakaya, Kamenev, and an unnamed "Baku Worker." Knorin's history (Moscow, 1935), though it gives names of delegates for all other congresses, avoids a list for this one. Stalin's own history (Moscow, 1938) omits any list of delegations. Nor does a single memoir written while Lenin was alive give Stalin the remotest connection with the organization of the Third Congress, with the fight for its convocation, with its actual guidance, or the Central Committee of Bolsheviks elected by it. Even as late as 1935—when Beria was already getting busy with his major operation on men's memories—the faithful Piatnitsky, writing on the occasion of the thirtieth anniversary of the Third Congress, had not one word to say of Stalin. None of these omissions would appear in the least remarkable, were it not for the effort, begun with the purges, to make it appear that from the beginning Stalin was the leading Bolshevik in the Caucasus and one of the two nationwide leaders of bolshevism. To make that legend stick, the mighty Russian state would have to undertake one of the greatest book-burning operations in all history, not only burning, as the Nazis did, the works of opponents but with no less zeal, all the records of their party published prior to Stalin's own history. Not only the writings of Lenin, but even Stalin's, have been censored wherever they might contradict the present official tale. To give only one example:

On December 31, 1910, Stalin wrote a letter from his then exile in Solvychegodsk to Paris. It has been published many times in Russia, and always, until the purges, it began: "Comrade Semeon! Yesterday I received from a comrade your letter. First of all, warmest greetings to Lenin, Kamenev and the others . . ."

But after the purge of Kamenev, the letter was quoted by Beria, and by Stalin himself in his *History*, without any salutation whatsoever. Semeon's name disappeared along with Lenin's and Kamenev's and the letter began with the second paragraph. Finally, in 1946, the letter was published once more "in full" (in Stalin's *Collected Works*, Russian Edition, Vol. II, p. 209) but it now read: "Comrade Semeon! . . . First of all, warmest greetings to Lenin and the others . . ."

Thus the effort is made to cover the fact that Leo Kamenev was in 1910 Lenin's closest associate in Paris, and, because of his prior

leadership of the Bolsheviks in the Caucasus, the most important
Bolshevik that Stalin knew intimately.

Before we leave the subject of the Third Congress, we should
note that Krupskaya's *Memories of Lenin* throws an ironic side-
light on the state of organization of the Caucasian Bolsheviks at
the time it was held:

> Four delegates came from the Caucasus—she writes—but
> there were but three mandates. Vladimir Ilyich inquired
> as to which of the four were entitled to the three mandates.
> "Who received the majority of the votes?"
>
> Mikha [Tskhakaya] replied in consternation: "Why, do
> you think we put things to a vote in the Caucasus? We
> decide all matters in a comradely way. They sent four of
> us, and it's not important how many mandates there are."

During 1946 Stalin began to publish his *Collected Works*. From
a source which must remain nameless I learned that Beria directed
the preliminary gathering of the material, and put it into his chief's
hands as early as 1935. In that year, Beria himself used the early
writings which now appear in the first two volumes of Stalin's
Collected Works for his own *Stalin's Early Writings and Activities*.
Stalin hesitated from 1935 to 1946 before he released the first two
volumes of his early writings! Volume III, however, represented no
problem since it contains pretty largely only material much published and republished before. The suspicion is inescapable that
the long delay between Beria's editing and Stalin's releasing of
the early work is due to hesitation on Stalin's part as to which
of his early writings should, and which should not, see the light of
day in permanent form. When it finally appeared it contained
three pieces (originally unsigned) dated 1901 and then nothing
until late in 1904. Moreover, the articles dated 1901 present several
problems of content and style to the biographer.

The initial piece is an anonymous Editorial Statement of Policy
for the first issue of the underground Georgian paper, *Brdzola*
("Struggle"), dated September, 1901. As we have already seen, it
was Lado Ketskhoveli, two or three years older than Djugashvili,
who founded the underground printing plant and paper for which
Stalin's biographers now assign him the credit of "initiator, inspirer
and director." There is, of course, nothing inherently impossible
in the claim that Djugashvili and not Ketskhoveli wrote the editorial statement for the first issue. The ideas are manifestly drawn
from *Iskra* and the style is quite different from that of Stalin's
later, signed writings. The style may conceivably be explained by

the fact that it was a general editorial statement, and may have been gone over by several people.

But when we come to the second article in the *Collected Works,* the problems of both style and content become more complicated. It is a longish article, written, judging from internal evidence, by a rather soft-spoken, humane person who is much influenced by Western Europe and thinks very highly—too highly—of the Russian student movement and quite disparagingly of strikes in Russia whether as economic or political weapons. None of the easily identifiable characteristics of Stalin's style or thought, as manifested in all his signed articles, is to be found here. There is none of the catechism type of self-answering questions, no mixed figures of speech such as we will find in all Stalin's efforts to attain pathos in print. The style is more conventional, smoother, more lyrical, more bookish, less combative, less energetic, lacking in rudeness toward opponent classes or viewpoints. The phraseology and ideas are rather Plekhanovist than Leninist. In it the student body is assigned an excessively important role and represented as "entering the social movement at the present time almost as the conductor, the vanguard . . . To the students we ought to be grateful for the lesson they have taught us: they have shown what a great significance is possessed by the political street demonstration in the revolutionary struggle." Follows an exaltation of street demonstrations and a disparagement of strikes:

> In the present political conditions an economic struggle [strikes] cannot give anything essential. Strikes even in free countries are two-edged weapons. Even there, despite the fact that the workers have the means of struggle— political freedom, strong unions, rich treasuries—strikes often end in defeat. . . . But with us, where strikes are a crime bringing arrest, suppressed by armed force, where all unions are forbidden—here strikes have only the significance of a *protest.* As a protest, demonstrations are a much stronger weapon. . . . The organization of general strikes is very difficult even in Western Europe but with us it is altogether impossible. But it is in the street demonstration that the workers at once unite their forces. . . . [Stalin: *Collected Works,* First Russian Edition, p. 29.]

This article is supposed to have been written by Stalin at the very moment when he is likewise supposed to have been organizing the Mantashev and Rothschild factory strikes! Its attitude toward strikes is so different from that of Stalin and the Bolsheviks generally that either someone else wrote the article "The

Russian Social Democracy and its Immediate Tasks," here printed in his *Collected Works,* or in December, 1901, the youthful Djugashvili was far from being a Leninist and a strike leader. Whichever horn of the dilemma the reader prefers, the fact remains that after 1901 Stalin wrote nothing more or did not choose to reproduce anything written between 1901 and the end of 1904. Significantly, Beria in his *Stalin's Early Writings and Activities* actually quotes from the first of the two articles cited above but does not claim it as having been written by Stalin! In fact, the implication is that it was written by Ketskhoveli (see Beria, English-language edition, pp. 34-37).

During the course of the year 1905 we gradually move onto firmer ground. Now we have definite records showing that Djugashvili has joined the Bolshevik faction and become one of its outstanding propagandists in the Caucasus. By the end of 1905 he rates high enough to be one of the delegates to the Bolshevik Conference at Tammerfors. Whereas all earlier evidence is equivocal and vanishes into thin air as soon as we apply ordinary methods of historical verification, now we can find documents, articles, facts, which are clear in their significance and incontrovertible. In 1906 and 1907 Djugashvili becomes a fairly frequent and consistent expounder of Lenin's Doctrines in Georgian in polemical articles signed at first I. (Iosif) Bibineishvili, and then with such names as Koba, Ko. K., K.Ko, Comrade K., K. Kato, Ivanovich, Koba Ivanovich. In 1908 he begins to experiment with the names K. Stefin, K.S. and K. St., and, after ringing the changes on K. Solin and K. Salin, in 1913 signs the name K. Stalin to his article on "Marxism and the National Question." This represented a combination of the name Koba, under which he became known on a Georgian scale, and the name Stalin ("Man of Steel") which was destined to become world-famous.

During the years 1905-07 there is also manifest a ripening in knowledge, abilities and self-confidence in the still young (twenty-six to twenty-eight) Djugashvili. A number of causes contributed to this. One was the death or departure of those who had been his superiors in experience and capacity: Ketskhoveli was assassinated in 1903; Tsulukidze died of tuberculosis in 1905; Kurnatovsky was exiled to Siberia; Krassin and Nogin, reconciled with Lenin, worked in 1905 in Central Russia, as did Kamenev and the two Enukidzes; Zhordania returned to Geneva. Djugashvili's path was further cleared by the fact that most prominent Georgian leaders now aligned themselves definitely with menshevism, including all three delegates to the Second Congress (Topuridze, Zurabov and Knunyantz), and such future leaders of the Georgian masses as Tseretelli and Chkheidze. Nascent Transcaucasian bolshevism had to develop a new leadership in the persons of Tskhakaya, Nevsky and Japaridze (the three delegates to the Third or Bolshevik Congress of 1905) and the already well-known Shaumyan and Makharadze. Among these the young Koba Djugashvili was perhaps still not the first, but certainly no longer an obscure figure.

It is from the year 1905 that are to be dated the first articles with a definite Stalinist style. Thenceforward, signed or unsigned, there is no mistaking their authorship, or their Bolshevik intention. Except for occasional leaflets, they are invariably exegetical, taking some proposition of Lenin's and translating and expounding it in Georgian. Their style tends to quasi-religious characteristics: ". . . only the proletariat can lead us to the Promised Land . . ."; "the Government has trampled on and mocked our human dignity, our Holy of Holies . . ."). They make frequent use of the catechetical method: dogmatic questions and answers. They are full of such expressions as: *kak izvestno* ("as is known"); *vsem izvestno* ("it is known to all"); *kak yasno* ("as is clear"), etc., precisely at those critical points where, for all but the already convinced, some solid proof is necessary. Since Stalin has become the undisputed leader of his land, this characteristic has become so widespread in his agents that there is not a diplomat of top rank from England and the United States who has not known moments of speechless fury when Molotov or Gromyko or Vishinsky or Manuilsky trots out a *kak izvestno* ("as is well known") as a surrogate "proof" of the most controversial assertions.

As "style is the man," it might be well to examine this question a little more closely. On January 19, 1905, there was issued in Georgian a leaflet, anonymous save for the words "Union Committee," with the title: *Workers of the Caucasus, It Is Time for Revenge!* The style is undoubtedly Stalin's. Beria, in an effort to make it appear that this January leaflet was Stalin's contribution to the leadership of the 1905 Revolution, a call for an armed insurrection in response to the events of "Bloody Sunday," deliberately left the leaflet undated (Beria, pp. 62-64). Trotsky, in his posthumous *Stalin*, relying on Beria, commits a serious injustice by contrasting Lenin's strong indignation at the massacre of January 22 ("make way for the anger and hatred . . .") with Stalin's bureaucratic cold calculation ("Rally round the Party committees . . . only the Party committees can lead us . . . to the Promised Land"). But an examination of the leaflet reveals that it was written before the events of Bloody Sunday and printed a day before the massacre of the people marching to the Winter Palace. Its main fire is directed not so much against tsarism as against "the liberals." It accuses them of "extending a helping hand to the Tsar . . . soliciting alms from him . . ."

> Yes, gentlemen—his leaflet continues—your efforts are in vain! The Russian revolution is inevitable, and it is just as inevitable as the sunrise! Can you stop the sun from rising? That is the question! The chief force of this revolution is the urban and rural proletariat, whose standard bearer is the Social Democratic Labor Party, and not you, Messrs. Liberals! Why do you forget this obvious "trifle"? . . .

> Russia is a loaded gun at full cock, liable to go off at the slightest concussion. Yes, comrades, the time is not far off when the revolution will hoist sail and drive the vile throne of the despicable Tsar off the face of the earth! . . . Let us join hands and *rally round the Party committees*. We must not forget for a moment that *only the Party committees can lead us as we should be led, only they* will light our way to the "Promised Land" called the socialist world! The Party which has opened our eyes and shown us our enemies, which has organized us into a formidable army . . . which has never deserted us in joy or sorrow and which has always marched in front of us . . . And it will continue to lead us, *only it!* A constituent assembly, elected by universal, equal, direct and secret suffrage, is what we must fight for now! . . .[1]

The mixed figures concerning the liberals whose outstretched hand simultaneously sustains the tottering throne and begs for alms, concerning the revolution that is a gun at full cock, hoisting sail and driving the vile throne from the face of the earth, are typical of the ornamentation that bedizens Stalin's writings wherever feeling and eloquence seem called for—as if there were a lack of real depth of feeling, or some barrier denying expression to it. Whenever Stalin attempts to express any other emotion than personal anger, this hollow rhetoric appears. The rhetorical question which reduces the political issue between liberals and socialists to "Can you stop the sun from rising? That is the question!" is typical too.

And the words in italics in the original (*"rally round the Party committees . . . only the committees can lead us . . . only it . . ."*)

[1] Beria: *Stalin's Early Writings and Activities*. English language edition, p. 63; Stalin: *Collected Works*, Vol. I, pp. 74-80; all italics are in the original.

are no less typical. They give us a key to Djugashvili's career and to the things that attracted him to Lenin. Of the old *Iskra* leadership, Lenin was the organization man *par excellence*, the one who insisted on the Party as leader rather than servant of the labor movement, on organization as the key to victory and the brake against opportunism, on control of the Party by the Central Committee and of the masses by the Party.

Did these ideas mean the same thing to master and disciple? Many fateful issues in our story will turn about that problem. For the moment, it is sufficient for us to note that when Lenin was taken by surprise by the initiative displayed by the masses themselves in 1905, he began to belabor his own followers for trying to force that great initiative into the constricting molds of the old Party committees and the underground, narrow-circle and close-control Party structure.

> This is wartime—he reminded his committeemen followers in letter after letter from his 1905 exile—Push the usual hierarchical committee follies entirely into the background . . . Else you will perish with the honors of *Komitetchiki* ["committeemen" or "committeeites"], perish with the official seal imprinted upon you. . . .

And again in the stormy year 1917 he would have to war against his routine-incrusted lieutenants with their fetishistic cult of the Party organization. He would remind them of 1905 and of "those 'Old Bolsheviks' who have more than once played a melancholy part in the history of our Party by repeating mechanically a formula which they have learned by heart, instead of studying the special character of the new and living reality . . ."

"*Grau, teurer Freund, ist alle Theorie, und gruen des Lebens goldner Baum,*" he would cite them from Mephistopheles. That was the strength of Lenin as revolutionist that, despite his passionate and dogmatic attachment to centralized organization and its rigid control of the masses, he could thrust both into the background whenever the foaming, tumbling, creative and uncontainable life of the million-headed mass in motion made their doctrinaire application dangerous to the Party's life.

One searches in vain through Stalin's writings of 1905 or 1917, indeed through all his writings of a lifetime, for any analogous flexibility in his attitude toward his master's organization dogmas. In fact, Stalin's main programmatic writings of 1905—their total volume is not large—are nothing more than exegesis of quotations from Lenin's writings of the pre-revolution years on the need for the Social Democratic Party to control and lead the masses and "import socialist consciousness into the spontaneous labor movement."

If Stalin was attracted to Lenin as the creator and glorifier of a strong centralized party machine, it was this aspect of "Leninism" which alienated Trotsky for many years. He did not scorn to use the machine dictatorially once he was in the Kremlin at Lenin's side, but his distaste, or incapacity, for building himself a party organization was to cost him dear in the struggle with his great opponent after Lenin's death. Perhaps in some obscure way Trotsky's Jewish heritage as a descendant of "the People of the Book" and, more directly, his Marxist heritage as a disciple of the greatest sociological thinker of modern times; his literary heritage as a lover of the Russian tongue and master of the written word; his revolutionary heritage as the pre-eminent tribune of the people able by flaming eloquence to stir the masses and lift them outside their petty, personal concerns to the level of action in the arena of history—all these combined to make him set the highest possible value upon ideas, originality and clarity in their formulation, exactness in their expression, eloquence in writing and in speech, contagious personal magnetism and attractive force. Deceived by Stalin's inept and awkward writing and lackluster public speech, Trotsky, insofar as he was compelled to notice his rival at all, set him down as "a gray and colorless mediocrity." As writer, as orator, as theoretician, Stalin was and remains a mediocrity. But first as a subordinate part in Lenin's machine, then as an appropriator and transformer and enlarger of that machine, Stalin has few equals. Nineteen five and nineteen seventeen, the heroic years when the machine was unable to contain the flood of overflowing life, would bring Trotsky to the fore as the flaming tribune of the people, would show Lenin's ability to rise above the confining structure of his dogmas, and would relegate Stalin, the machine-man by antonomasy, to the background. But no people can live forever at fever heat and when that day was over and Lenin was dead, the devoted machine-man's day would come.

I do not mean to imply that only Djugashvili thus absorbed the organizational fetishism and Leninist formulae, against which Lenin himself had to fight in 1905 and 1917. Nor to imply that the indignant letters of Lenin's in 1905 were addressed principally, or at all, to Djugashvili, of whose very existence he was as yet scarcely aware. It was this side of Lenin, which Vladimir Ilyich himself could slough off at need, that attracted to him all the "hard" professional revolutionaries who, by natural selection, came to make up the bulk of his permanent officer staff. Had Djugashvili been alone in this regard, it would be impossible to explain how he could one day assume the driver's seat when Death had compelled Lenin to vacate it.

> He was the *komitetchik par excellence*—Trotsky wrote in his posthumous *Stalin*—Lacking the personal qualifications for influencing the masses directly, he clung with redoubled tenacity to the political machine. The axis of his universe was his Committee—the Tiflis, the Baku, the Caucasian, before it became the Central Committee. In time his blind loyalty to the Party machine was to develop with extraordinary strength; the committeeman became the super-machine-man, the General Secretary, the very personification of the bureaucracy, its peerless leader . . .

True enough. And Trotsky might seem to have the right to be critical, since he alone of the Bolshevik leaders who made the October (1917) Revolution had held out for fourteen years against Lenin's machine and been critical of it. Had he not written with Cassandra-like prevision the warning with which we are already familiar:

> The organization of the Party will take the place of the Party; the Central Committee will take the place of the organization; and finally, the dictator will take the place of the Central Committee?

Was ever prophecy more fatefully fulfilled by history? And yet, as we read Trotsky's strictures on the *komitetchik par excellence* based on Stalin's sparse and dreary writings of the memorable year 1905, we are reminded that Trotsky too came to accept Lenin's machine in 1917. Once he had swallowed Lenin's conception of the machine, was it not increasingly inevitable that that machine in turn might swallow him, verifying with himself as object lesson all his earlier forebodings? Yet even to the day when an agent of that machine buried an Alpine pick in the back of his skull, his criticism would never again be of the machine as such, but only of Stalin's use or abuse of it. In the unfinished life of Stalin thus terminated by death, Trotsky would approach perilously close to a new fundamental critique of the Leninist conception of organization, then shy off, squidlike in a flood of his own ink:

> It is rather tempting—he says at one point—to draw the inference that future Stalinism was already rooted in Bolshevik centralism, or more sweepingly, in the underground hierarchy of professional revolutionaries . . .

Rather tempting—but he refuses to be tempted. Throughout that pathetically unfinished last book of his, nowhere does he dare to subject Lenin's machine to genuine reexamination, that machine which, in Trotsky's words, "was not created by Stalin but created him," which lent itself so easily to "the usurpation of the driver's seat" by the absolute, personal dictator. For, once having accepted Lenin's machine and organization doctrine, Trotsky thenceforth reduced himself from the role of a genuine critic of "Stalinism" to that of a pretender denouncing a usurper.

CHAPTER XXVII

STALIN AND LENIN

Dressed in Caucasian costume, with rows of white-tipped
cartridge cases, he carried some spherical object in a napkin.
Every one in the restaurant left off eating . . . 'He has
brought a bomb!' . . . But it turned out to be a watermelon.
Kamo had brought the melon and some sugared nuts as a
present for Ilyich and me. 'My aunt sent them,' he explained rather shyly. This fighting man, with his colossal
courage . . . seemed at the same time an extraordinarily un-
sophisticated and gentle comrade. . . . Kamo often travelled
between Finland and Petersburg, always going fully armed.
Mother used to tie his revolvers on his back each time with
particular care. *—Krupskaya:* Memories of Lenin.

IN DECEMBER, 1905, Stalin first met Lenin, at the Tammerfors
Conference. Koba does not seem to have made much of an impression on Krupskaya if we are to judge from her memoirs, published when Stalin was already ruler of Russia:

> It is hardly likely that any of the delegates to that con-
> ference could ever forget it. Among those present were
> Lozovsky, Baransky, and Yaroslavsky. I remember those
> comrades because their reports from their localities were
> so enthralling.

But neither does Djugashvili seem to have been much impressed
by the man whose leadership he had accepted:

> I was hoping to see the mountain eagle of our Party—
> Stalin told the Kremlin cadets a week after Lenin's death.
> —I was hoping to see a great man, great not only politically
> but, if you will, physically, for in my imagination I pictured
> Lenin as a giant, stately and imposing. What, then, was
> my disappointment to see a most ordinary-looking man,
> below average in height, in no way, in literally no way,
> distinguishable from ordinary mortals . . .
> It is the accepted thing for a "great man" to come late
> to meetings so that the assemblage may await his appear-
> ance with bated breath; and then, just before the great
> man enters, the warning goes up: "Hush! Silence! He's
> coming!" This rite did not seem to me superfluous because
> it creates an impression, inspires respect. What then was

465

> my disappointment to learn that Lenin had arrived at the
> conference before the delegates, had settled himself some-
> where in a corner and was unassumingly carrying on a
> conversation, a most ordinary conversation with the most
> ordinary delegate . . . I will not conceal from you that
> at that time this seemed to me to be rather a violation of
> certain essential rules.

During sessions of the Comintern and its Executive, and on
public holiday occasions, I had many occasions to note that Stalin
himself was careful not to neglect this "rite." The words tell us far
more of Stalin than of the "great man" he had come to wonder at.

In the Stockholm Unity Congress of 1906, Djugashvili saw Lenin
again, this time "in defeat."

> I remember the Bolshevik delegates gathering together
> in a small group gazing at Lenin and asking advice . . .
> I remember Lenin saying sharply through clenched teeth:
> "No sniveling, comrades . . ." Hatred for sniveling intel-
> lectuals, confidence in one's own strength, confidence in
> victory—that is what Lenin talked to us about at that time.

Djugashvili may well have joined those who gathered around
the defeated leader, but, for some reason, he did not sign the
manifesto which Lenin drew up in criticism of the Stockholm
Congress. Issued in the name of "Delegates Belonging to the Former Bolshevik Faction" ("former" because all groups had been
"dissolved"), it bore twenty-six signatures, including Krassin,
Rykov, Bubnov, Taratuta, Voroshilov, Yaroslavsky, Krupskaya, and
Lenin. But Stalin's name, for reasons never explained, is missing.
(The complete list may be found in the Third Russian Edition of
Lenin's *Collected Works*, Vol. IX, p. 521.) Yet, the sharpest of the
issues arising at the Stockholm Congress, an issue still more acute
a year later in London, would bind Stalin to Lenin with bands of
steel and make Vladimir Ilyich appreciate the qualities of his
Caucasian adherent. It was the issue of the "exes."

At the Stockholm Congress the Bolsheviks were allowed only
three members on the incoming Executive of ten. They named
Krassin, Rykov, Desnitsky. At the London Congress, they won a
total of fifteen members and alternates. These included Lenin,
Bogdanov, Krassin, Zinoviev (a newcomer at this congress), Nogin,
Rykov, Taratuta. The Bolsheviks also chose a secret faction center
of seventeen. Besides those mentioned above, it included Kamenev,
the Marxist historian Pokrovsky, and others of lesser interest to us.
But neither on the three, the fifteen, nor the seventeen, do we find

Koba-Djugashvili. Once more, the omission is surprising only if we take seriously the Beria, Yaroslavsky and Lenin Institute biographies, which make the still immature Stalin, already then, Lenin's chief adviser and second-in-command.

At Stockholm, Djugashvili differed with Lenin on the peasant question. As the reader may remember, Lenin was for "nationalization" of the land and Plekhanov and the Mensheviks advocated "municipalization." Djugashvili, along with the majority of the Bolsheviks, rejected both Lenin's and Plekhanov's proposals:

> Since we are making a temporary revolutionary union with the fighting peasantry—said Djugashvili—we ought to support their demands, provided they do not by and large contradict the tendency of economic development and the course of the revolution. The peasants demand division. Division does not contradict the above phenomena. That means that we ought to support the full confiscation of the land, and its division. From this point of view, both nationalization and municipalization are alike unacceptable. [Minutes of the Congress, p. 59.]

It was Djugashvili's view that prevailed. And in 1917, the Bolshevik seizure of power was aided, just as Djugashvili had foreseen, by accepting the peasants' demand for partition instead of nationalization. One would think, then, that Stalin biographers would give great space to this example of political originality and prevision. But not a word!

If it was Lenin's theory of party organization that proved most fitted for the seizure of power; if it was Trotsky's theory of immediate "proletarian dictatorship" or "permanent revolution" which provided the formula for the minority, one-party government that emerged; it was Stalin's proposal to "support the real demands of the fighting peasants" by "division of the land" which drew the peasants into benevolent neutrality toward the new Bolshevik power. The impartial biographer must recognize this as Stalin's contribution.

But not a word! And that for two reasons. The first, because Stalin professes that until Lenin's death he was no more than Lenin's "best and most faithful disciple." Originality could and did come later. Between Lenin's death and Stalin's final attainment of uncontested power (i.e. between 1924 and 1929), it was the "best disciple's" proudest boast that all his rivals had at some time opposed or differed with Lenin, but he never. "Of all the Old Bolsheviks," he once declared to admiring Comintern leaders, "my vest is the cleanest."

And the second reason: that, in due course, Stalin himself shifted from "supporting the peasants' desires" to enforcing the state's desires upon the peasants, i.e. he undid the one great achievement of the Revolution so far as the peasants were concerned, substituting, even as Plekhanov had feared, direct state ownership of the land and fixing the once freed peasants once more upon the land as appurtenances thereto. This "collectivization" is really a more total "nationalization" than Lenin advocated or Plekhanov could imagine in his nightmare prevision of total statism. And it was, indeed, as Plekhanov had foreseen, the real economic and political foundation for a "Restoration"—of personal absolutism, labor fixity, purges, forced labor, bureaucratic privilege, police rule—a swelling of the state that would make Tsarism seem a limited state by comparison.

Today, Stalin claims credit for the "collectivization" as one of his greatest achievements, a claim incompatible with emphasis on his earlier proposal of a democratic way to win the support of the peasantry. But the biographer not guided by reasons of state can note this speech of Djugashvili's in 1906, and two expository articles of the same year on the same theme, as the first fruits of Stalin's independent thought and social foresight in the field of the seizure of power of November, 1917. It is a contribution no other biographer friendly or hostile has noted!

When Djugashvili returned to the Caucasus in 1907, he wrote in Russian, in the *Bakinskii Proletarii*, a "Report on the London Congress." Two things are worth noting in this report, both of them in the nature of rather clumsy jests.

> Not less interesting—reads the first—is the composition of the Congress from the standpoint of nationalities. Statistics showed that the majority of the Menshevik faction consists of Jews—and this of course without counting the Bundists—after which come Georgians and then Russians. On the other hand, the overwhelming majority of the Bolshevik faction consists of Russians, after which come Jews —not counting of course the Poles and Letts—and then Georgians, etc. For this reason, one of the Bolsheviks observed in jest (it seems, Comrade Alexinsky) that the Mensheviks are a Jewish faction, the Bolsheviks a genuine Russian faction, whence it wouldn't be a bad idea for us Bolsheviks to arrange a pogrom in the party. [Stalin: *Collected Works*, Vol. II, Russian Edition, pp. 50-51.]

We leave it to the reader to judge the factional purpose of this coarse-grained jest and its possible effect in a Russia that had just gone through three years of pogroms. In passing we might note that this same Alexinsky whom Stalin was citing against the Mensheviks would one day point to Zinoviev, Kamenev, and Trotsky as evidence of the number of Jews in the leadership of the Bolshevik Party![1]

The second "jest" dealt with the question of the "exes" or revolutionary holdups. Djugashvili might easily have ignored this question, as he did a number of others. Or he might simply have reported that the "exes" were condemned by the Congress, by a vote of all the Mensheviks and an overwhelming majority of Bolsheviks. Instead he reported:

> Of the Menshevik resolutions the only one to pass was the one dealing with guerrilla crimes, and that passed only by accident: the Bolsheviks for this once did not give battle, or rather, they did not want to carry it through to the end, simply out of the desire to give the Mensheviks at least once something to be happy about . . .
> [Stalin: *Collected Works,* Russian Edition, p. 52.]

This is a strange picture of the Bolshevik faction and its methods of deciding matters of principle! Moreover, it is simply not true. Lenin, as we know, failed to give battle on this issue because he did not think it politic, and still more because he had been defeated on it within his own faction. But Djugashvili chose to report it thus because he was even then intending, with Lenin's approval, to ignore and violate the decision. And he wanted to inspire in his determined partisans, Tsintsadze, Kamo, and their band, contempt for the decision of the Congress, by portraying it as having passed "only by accident" and for a ridiculous reason, "to give the Mensheviks for once something to be happy about."

Back in the Caucasus from his secret conference with Lenin on the question of the "exes," Djugashvili found that Zhordania had come home after a two-year stay abroad, and was earnestly trying to liquidate the widespread banditry which by then involved members of all factions and parties. The Social Democratic Party set

---

[1] This same Alexinsky invented the story of Lenin's "affair with Elizabeth K.," and produced a poem he claimed Lenin wrote in 1907. Lenin did it to show a comrade that it was not harder to write poetry than prose. Compare this with Gorky's report of Lenin's words: "I couldn't write two lines of poetry if you flayed me alive." The poem bears marks of Alexinsky's style. A French translation is in *L'Arche,* Paris, Feb., 1946. Alexinsky offered to sell Lenin's letters to Elizabeth K. to the Soviet Government, then to the Columbia Library. To prove their authenticity he finally "confessed" that Elizabeth K. was his own wife. No sale!

up a committee to disarm the partisan detachments, and threatened with expulsion anyone who should continue to play the role of revolutionary highwayman. The result was an accession, for the first time in Transcaucasia, of some real strength to the Bolsheviks, a natural selection of all those who were already too far outside the law, or too enamored with the life of revolutionary adventure, to lay down their arms. Whenever conditions required it, these would formally resign from the Party (to "preserve discipline" and prevent expulsion), but would maintain contact with a secret center now set up in Baku, whither Djugashvili had gone. This was the first "Caucasian Center" that he really led, as contact man between Lenin's secret Center in Saint Petersburg and the local bands under Tsintsadze and Kamo. Skillful and conspirative, he worked behind the scenes. The exact degree of his participation has to this day remained unclarified.

The London Party Congress decisions were but little more than a month old when the Tiflis "ex" shocked the world. The flurry of investigations which followed led ever closer and closer to the person of Koba Djugashvili. As all the findings had to be veiled in mystery lest the police get wind of them, the full details may never be known. But on March 18, 1918, Martov lifted the veil a little. In his Moscow paper, published legally under the Soviet Government, he wrote:

> That the Caucasian Bolsheviks attached themselves to all sorts of daring enterprises of an expropriatory nature should be well known to that same Citizen Stalin, who was expelled in his time from his Party organization for having had something to do with expropriation.

When this appeared, Citizen Stalin was the powerful Commissar for Nationalities, and Citizen Martov the leader of a barely tolerated Menshevik opposition. The Commissar had Martov and fourteen colleagues indicted for "criminal libel of a Soviet official and slander of the Soviet Government." Stalin's chief lawyer was *Pravda* Editor Sosnovsky, subsequently to perish in Stalin's purges. Martov chose Lapinski (Pavel Lewinson), Polish Left Socialist lawyer, subsequently to be a leader in the Comintern, and then also to perish in the purges. As "lay defender," something permitted then by Soviet judicial procedure, Martov chose Rafael Abramovich. But chiefly in his own hoarse, barely audible voice, he conducted his own defence, as if it were a prosecution of plaintiff Stalin. Martov demanded a jury trial. Stalin, alleging his high office and the implication of the good name of the government, insisted

on a Supreme Court hearing, before three Bolshevik judges. This
was before the days of bureaucratic privilege, and the Commissar
winced as Martov denounced him for refusing to take his chances
with a democratic court and jury of his peers. But Stalin had his
way.

> Never in my life—Stalin swore—was I placed on trial
> before my party or expelled. This is a vicious libel . . .
> One has no right to come out with accusations like Mar-
> tov's except with documents in one's hand. It is dishonest
> to throw mud on the basis of mere rumors . . .

The defendant asked for a postponement to produce the documents. He asked that summonses be issued to Isidor Ramishvili,
chairman of the Transcaucasian Party court that had tried Stalin;
to Shaumyan, Caucasian Bolshevik leader; Soviet Finance Commissar Gukovsky (Bolshevik), under whose chairmanship, according to Martov, there had been an investigation of an attempt on
the life of one Comrade Zharinov for exposing Stalin's part in an
expropriation; and various other members of the Caucasian District Committee for the years in question. Stalin objected on the
ground of "the difficulty and unreliability of communication with
the Caucasus." He said nothing about the qualifications of the proposed witnesses, and nothing about the new charge concerning the
attempt to assasssinate Zharinov. "I was never tried," he repeated
doggedly in the first day's summary. "If Martov says so, he is a
vicious libeler."

The court granted a postponement and Boris Nikolaevsky, who,
though no Bolshevik, was in 1919 made Director of the Historical
Archives of the Revolution, was sent down to the Caucasus on
Citizen Martov's behalf. There he gathered affidavits from Sylvester
Jibladze, Isidor Ramishvili, and others who had taken part in the
Tiflis Court of Honor. The Second session was to be a consideration
of this documentation, and cross-examination on it. But there never
was a second session! When the matter came before the court
again, all the records of the first session had somehow "disappeared." Martov was dismissed with a mere "social reprimand"
for "insulting and damaging the reputation of a member of the
government."

As the records are gone, I have reconstructed the trial from
interviews with Rafael Abramovich, Boris Nikolaevsky, and Samuél
Levitas, all of whom were present in the courtroom. Perhaps I might
add as a gloss a conversation which Gorky reports he had with
Lenin, precisely during the period in question: "I am sorry, deeply

sorry, that Martov is not with us. What a splendid comrade he was, what an absolutely sincere man."

In all his bitter feuds with Martov, feuds in which he aimed, as he had once promised a Party court, to "bring his opponent into public contempt," Lenin could never bring himself to impugn directly Martov's personal honesty. This was the more remarkable because all Martov's attacks upon Taratuta, Djugashvili, and other accomplices in the holdups invariably laid the real responsibility at Lenin's feet.

After the Tiflis "ex," the lean years set in, years of stubborn self-delusion for a few, of decay, despair, renegation for many, years for Lenin of returning to the picking of agents by ones and twos where formerly there had been thousands. It was at this moment that Lenin came to put a high value on Joseph Djugashvili. Since Vladimir Ilyich had approved, even directed, the deeds with which his lieutenant was charged, he saw no dishonor in the cloud under which the latter moved. When, amidst the general decay, the rift between Bolsheviks and Mensheviks deepened until they became two separate parties, Lenin placed the expelled or self-dismissed Stalin directly on his Central Committee. Peculiarly, he was not democratically elected by the Bolshevik Prague Congress (1912). Was it because Lenin did not want to stir up old rancors among those of his followers who had opposed expropriations? Or because Stalin was not generally known in the faction? At any rate, Lenin did not propose his name to the Congress, but, as soon as it adjourned, proposed that the newly elected Central Committee should coopt Djugashvili. Since the Congress had already elected Orjonikidze, that made two Georgians to carry the war into the Menshevik stronghold of Transcaucasia. Moreover, as part of that war, Lenin needed some Georgian to become his spokesman on the national question. It was with this promotion in mind, that Lenin applied to him the term in his letter to Gorky of February, 1913: "a wonderful Georgian." It is interesting to note that in all his articles and letters, this is the only time that Vladimir Ilyich ever referred to the nationality of any Party member. Daring and secretive agents, spokesmen from minority peoples who were immune to their compatriots' nationalism, Georgians to carry the war into the fortress of menshevism in Georgian—such disciples were precious few now. He would have need of them in the lean years that had set in.

That the picture we have painted of Stalin's early development is closer to the truth than the official versions of Beria, Yaroslavsky

and Company, has received confirmation on at least one occasion
from the lips of Joseph Stalin himself. The time was 1926. Lenin
was dead. The hero cult was just beginning and its object was not
yet used to incense and adulation, nor dreaming of the destruction
of almost all his associates and of all contrary evidence. He revisited
Tiflis that year and addressed a gathering of its workingmen. After
listening for hours to sycophantic speeches from some future priests
of his cult, he replied:

> I must in all conscience tell you, comrades, that I have
> not deserved half the eulogy that various delegates have
> given me . . . This is mere fantasy, comrades, and a per-
> fectly useless exaggeration. That is the way one speaks at
> the grave of a revolutionary. But I am not preparing to
> die. Therefore I must give you a true picture of what I
> once was and say to whom I owe my present position in
> the Party . . .
> I remember the year 1898, when for the first time the
> workers in the railway workshops put me in charge of a
> club . . . In comparison with these comrades (Jibladze
> and others) I was then a tyro . . . Here, among these
> comrades, I became an apprentice of the revolution . . .
> My first teachers were the workers of Tiflis. Allow me to
> express to them the sincere gratitude of a comrade.
> Then I remember the years 1905 to 1907, when at the
> desire of the Party I was thrown into the work at Baku.
> Two years of revolutionary work among the oil workers
> made me a practical fighter and a practical leader . . . I
> learned for the first time what the leadership of great
> masses of workmen really meant . . . I became a journey-
> man of the revolution . . .
> I remember 1917, when by the decision of the Party,
> after prison and deportation, I was thrown into Lenin-
> grad. There, among the Russian workers, in close contact
> with the great educator of the proletariat throughout the
> world, Comrade Lenin, in the storm of the mighty struggle
> between the proletariat and the bourgeoisie during the
> World War, I learned for the first time to understand what
> it meant to be one of the leaders of the great working-
> class party . . . There, in Russia [as opposed to Trans-
> caucasia], under Lenin's direction, I became a master-
> workman in revolution . . .
> From apprentice at Tiflis, to journeyman at Baku, to
> master-workman in our revolution at Leningrad—such,
> comrades, is the course of my apprenticeship to revolution.
> Such, comrades, is the true picture, honest and without
> exaggeration, of what I was and what I have become.

These appear to be substantially the outlines of the truth. Many present at that meeting in Tiflis were able to judge of its correctness from their own knowledge. Since then, some have risen to high place by testifying to quite another picture; others have been cowed into silence or acquiescence; yet others, with too stubborn a regard for the facts, or unfortunate enough to have published reminiscences before they knew what to remember, have vanished from the scene. Today, no one any longer dares say that Djugashvili was a mere tyro in 1898, an apprentice until 1905, a journeyman revolutionist on a provincial scale from 1905 to 1907, on a national scale to 1917, and a master-workman only during 1917, as part of the collective leadership of many such "master-workmen," under Lenin's overseership.

CHAPTER XXVIII

NIGHT OF EXILE

"If a tooth could feel after being knocked out, it would probably feel as lonely as I did . . . 'Everything is lost,' people said, 'they have crushed, annihilated, exiled, imprisoned everybody!' . . . I often felt as if a pestilential dust were blowing from Russia."
— *Maxim Gorky*

"EMIGRANT LIFE is now a hundred times more difficult than it was before the Revolution of 1905," wrote Lenin to Gorky. In his first emigration he had stayed abroad five years, but they were years of confidence and hope. This second exile was a flight from failure. For most of the decade that followed, Lenin felt sure that he would die abroad.

Revolutionists who but yesterday had stood at the head of millions saw the bonds which linked them to the mass dissolve without a trace. Driven to impotent fury by each day's increment of evil, they fell to quarreling among themselves, meanly, bitterly, denouncing error in each other, apportioning blame for defeat. The isolation which seemed the more silent for the tumult that had just been stilled, they filled with the sound of their own quarrels. No secret admiration sustained them, no generous contributions nor general sympathy nor public expectation followed them as they returned to alien places.

Only now did the self-exiled know the full misery of the émigré's estate: separation from family, friends, country, from all the round of activities that go with belonging to some land's daily life. Exile may be "the home of the virtuous" but too often it is likely to be short of the homelier virtues: tolerance, humor, proportion, charity, love. The very principles which raise the refugee above the ordinary citizen serve also to deprive him of organic relation either with the land of his longing or the land of his exile, contracting him to something less than the ordinary citizen's estate. This lack of a place in the society with which they are at war throws these lonely, high-minded groups utterly in upon themselves, turning their talents to controversy, recrimination, intrigue and schism.

Even Vladimir Ilyich, more rugged, more self-sufficient, more sure than most, was not exempt from the ravages of the émigré's malady. In keeping with the slow, contradictory nature of his spiritual retreat from the certitude of a new uprising, he withdrew by stages. Since the Tsar's Government showed enormously more respect for the autonomy of Finland than would today be conceivable for the "autonomous republics" of the Soviet Union (or even for the still "independent" Finland of today), Lenin was able to work openly there, less than two hours by train from Petersburg. Within the Empire but free from imperial persecution, he lived with the Leiteisens, Krupskaya, her mother, his younger sister Maria, the Bogdanovs, and Dubrovinsky, all in the Leiteisen home. By a simple raid, the government could have captured this entire Bolshevik general staff.

Each morning Krupskaya, known to the police, left by early train for Saint Petersburg, with articles, proofs, instructions, returning each night with news, arrangements for appointments, questions to be resolved. But the government, though it shot batches of men caught in open rebellion, in acts of terror or robbery, gave even the Executive Committee of the Soviets a public trial. For a year the authorities debated the right or expedience of making arrests for plots against the régime on "autonomous" Finnish soil.

> At that time—writes Krupskaya—the Russian police had decided not to meddle in Finland and we had considerable freedom there. The door of the house was never bolted, a jug of milk and loaf of bread were left in the dining room overnight, and bedding spread on the divan so that in the event of anyone's coming on the night train he could enter without waking anybody, have some refreshments and lie down to sleep. In the morning we often found comrades in the dining room who had come in the night.

To grasp this situation fully, we need only try to imagine centers of open plotting against the Stalin régime, functioning, let us say, in Soviet Karelia or in the "independent" Finland of today, sending messengers, instructions, legal literature (if we can imagine such) and illegal, across the frontier from Karelia to Leningrad. Yet, despite the daily contact, Lenin began to feel the demoralizing effect of the declining movement and growing isolation.

> He could not help getting into such a mood sometimes— writes Krupskaya—that he needed some distraction. Thus it was that the inmates of the great house would sit down to play the game of "dunce." Bogdanov played with calculation, Ilyich both calculated and gambled, Leiteisen became greatly enthralled. If at such moments someone happened to come from the District Committee on an

errand, he would generally display annoyance and bewilderment. Fancy Central Committee members playing
"dunce" for money!

Though less ruthless and thorough in the suppression of opponents, and enormously less numerous than the GPU to which we
have become accustomed, the Okhrana was second to no other
secret political police of its day. Where peasant risings and mutinies
gave it the pretext, it proclaimed martial law and used gallows
and firing squad. In other provinces, it made use of the power of
administrative deportation without trial, up to a maximum of five
years in Siberia. But a roster of millions of prisoners in concentration camps would have seemed an incredible nightmare to this little
band of routine-incrusted police officials. According to the testimony of its chief, Vasiliev, at the height of its power it never had
more than one thousand secret agents in all Russia, nor more than
one hundred in the capital. He complains that he had "very few"
operatives abroad and, every time a congress was held in foreign
parts, had to further debilitate his Moscow and Petersburg forces
by sending some of his best agents.

But, with its years of political experience, the Okhrana sensed
earlier than Lenin the nature of the new political situation, and
prepared, too, to "go underground" once more. With forces that
seem numerically so modest today, it now developed a system of
espionage that eclipsed even the Zubatov and Gapon experiments.
If, at every stage of our story so far we have found a police agent
in the midst of each fairly numerous gathering, now we shall find
them penetrating into the topmost secret hierarchies of the Social
Revolutionary Party and the Bolshevik faction of the Social Democratic Party.

Krupskaya got her first taste of the new brew when she set up
machinery for smuggling Lenin's newly revived *Proletarii* from
Finland into Russia proper. Lenin had resuscitated it even while
there was still a legal, i.e. police-sanctioned, Bolshevik paper in
Saint Petersburg. Two members of the Petersburg District, husband
and wife, named Komissarov, presented themselves.

> The first moment a strange feeling came over me, a kind
> of acute mistrust. I could not think where this feeling came
> from and it soon disappeared. Katya Komissarov proved to
> be a very business-like assistant, did everything quickly,
> accurately, and with secrecy . . . After smuggling arms into
> Petersburg, Katya took them into the Urals . . . Her hus-
> band became caretaker for Simonov, owner of a house at
> 9 Zagorodny Prospekt . . . During the years of reaction,

Komissarov put up any number of illegal comrades in that house, supplying them with passports.

The trip of Katya Komissarov to the Urals was followed by the arrest of all concerned, the confiscation of the arms and breakup of the armed bands. The comrades whom Komissarov supplied with shelter and false passports always seemed to come to grief while crossing the European frontier.

Spies entered the military organization of the Bolsheviks so that after the mutinies at Sveaborg and Kronstadt (in 1907) all the secret organizers were arrested (but not executed, one more evidence of the sporadic and often surprising liberality of the tsarist police régime).[1] They permeated all the local committees, none in the end remaining exempt, so that "every man regarded his comrade with suspicion, was on guard against those nearest to him, did not trust his neighbors." As the movement declined, the shortage of qualified people made it easier for secret agents to rise in the underground hierarchy. They hastened their own promotion by causing the arrest of those whose posts they coveted. By a series of such carefully planned arrests, the provocateur Kukushkin rose to the very summit of the Moscow organization in 1910. The curve of Moscow membership reflects alike the general decay and the success of Kukushkin's career: end of 1908–500; middle of 1909–250; end of 1909–150; 1910–all threads fall into the hands of Kukushkin and the Moscow District ceases to exist.

Nor was this, the headship of the second most important district, the highest post which a police spy attained. Abroad, as we have seen, it was Dr. Zhitomirsky who took care of Kamo, arranged for the carrying of explosives and the storing of banknote paper for counterfeiting, took charge of the disposal of the five-hundred-ruble notes from the Tiflis "ex."

In 1912, when the legal Bolshevik daily, *Pravda*, was founded in Saint Petersburg, two police agents, Miron Chernomazov and Roman Malinovsky, were on its editorial staff, the former as a regular editor and chairman of the Board and the latter as contributing editor and treasurer. A legal Moscow paper was founded for the Bolsheviks by a police agent. One of these agents, whose story we shall consider separately in Chapter XXXI, was so admired by Lenin that he was called abroad for the smallest and most confidential meetings and made privy to the most secret and dangerous

[1] Compare the account of Krupskaya (Vol. I, p. 170) of the arrest of the Bolshevik military organization, including its head, Vyacheslav Rudolfovich Menzhinsky, with the fact that he lived to become Commissar of Finance (1917) and first vice-president (1923), then president (1926) of the GPU.

matters. He became a Central Committee member and, for several years, the leading authoritative spokesman for the Bolsheviks inside Russia.

This fantastic state of affairs found its counterpart in the case of Yevno Azev of the Social Revolutionary Party. The son of a poor Jewish tailor and an informer since his student days, Azev actually became the top leader of the Social Revolutionary Party's dread Terror or Fighting Section. For the last five of his fifteen years of political life (until the middle of 1909, when his dual role was exposed), Azev was the actual director of the entire work of the Fighting Section. In this post he took funds both from police and revolutionaries, deceiving and cheating both. He betrayed the plans for many acts of terror, prevented many intended assassinations, delivered many of his comrades into the hands of the authorities. But other projects he permitted to be carried out, even planned some and saw to their success. His motives? To raise the price of his services to the police, to retain the confidence of his associates, to serve the obscure intrigues of one official against another, to settle grudges, even to satisfy his own strangely ambivalent personal convictions. In the end he scarcely knew himself whether he was a terrorist spying upon the government or a police agent spying upon the terror. In varying degrees he was responsible for the assassination of at least one Minister of the Interior, Plehve (1904); one of the Tsar's own uncles, the Grand Duke Sergei (1905); for the wounding of General Dubassov, after the latter had suppressed the Moscow insurrection (1906); the execution of two of his fellow-agents, including Father Gapon when the latter re-entered the service of the police in 1906. Apparently as an act of vengeance for the Jewish pogroms which Minister of the Interior Plehve fomented, Azev actually organized all the details of the latter's assassination in 1904, leaving the throne without a firm and trusted adviser when one was needed most. And it is probably not Azev's fault that a plot against the Tsar himself miscarried at the time when Azev's double role was being exposed. But Yevno Azev's strange life lies outside the scope of the present work, while the story of Lenin's lieutenant belongs to a subsequent chapter.

When Lenin returned from the London Congress in the summer of 1907, mustache clipped, beard shaved off and wearing a huge straw hat by way of disguise, Krupskaya found him extraordinarily fatigued, and unable to eat. She packed him off to the pine forests of Stirsuden, deep in Finland, where "Little Uncle" (Lydia Knippovich) was living.

The first few days he kept dozing off to sleep. He would sit under a fir-tree and immediately drop off. The children called him "old sleepyhead." Those were wonderful days at Stirsuden: the woods, the sea, the wildest of the wild . . . "Little Uncle" fed Ilyich assiduously on omelettes and reindeer-ham. He got steadily better and became his old self again.

So Krupskaya. But it was evident that he was not his old self. The isolation grew. He retreated from current politics to more theoretical reading and writing, another form of relief for his exhausted spirit. Then he went to Oglbu, Finland, where he could no longer maintain day-to-day contact with his followers. In Petersburg the police had picked up Zinoviev, Kamenev, and Roshkov, three of his most important lieutenants. Rumors reached him that they were beginning to search for him, despite Finnish autonomy. (Actually, they were hunting, on a tip from Azev, for one Karl Trauberg and his "Flying Terrorist Detachment of the Northern Region," responsible for the death of General Pavlov and now plotting to blow up the State Council and execute the Tsar.) Not until December 5, 1907, did they venture to violate Finnish autonomy in order to raid Trauberg's apartment. News from the Okhrana had entered Finland made up Lenin's mind to go abroad once more.

But if the police were indeed looking for him, it would not do to board the little steamer at Abo which, following a channel cut by icebreakers, made weekly winter trips to Stockholm. Abo would be the place the police would most likely be watching. He engaged a guide to conduct him over the ice to an island—three versts, about two miles, out over the frozen sea—a port of call for the same steamer. The journey was undertaken at night, without lights. The guide proved to be drunk, the way perilous. Somewhere in the darkness, near the channel, the ice began to crack and move under Lenin's feet. " 'Oh, what a silly way to die,' I thought," he told Krupskaya later. It teases the imagination to contemplate how the history of Russia in the fateful year 1917, indeed, how the history of Europe and the world might have been altered, if Vladimir Ilyich Ulyanov had gone under the shifting ice near the channel over the open sea, that night at the end of 1907.

Krupskaya joined him in Stockholm and then went on to Berlin. It was Christmas Eve but they felt anything but festive. The comrade who met them warned them not to go to the home of any Russian émigré, since the German police were engaged in widespread raids. All day they were led around the cold streets, from café to café. In the evening they went to the home of Rosa Luxemburg, whose future was to be so fatefully linked with theirs. Vladimir Ilyich felt very close to her at that moment, despite their old quarrels over the question of organization. At the London Congress she had taken a position close to Trotsky's on the forces and perspectives of the Russian revolution. Though the Mensheviks had repeatedly challenged Lenin to attack Trotsky's and her theory of "the permanent revolution," he had refused. Rosa and her Polish delegation in turn had supported him, if not on the organization question in principle, yet on the organization question that mattered most to him: the proportion of Bolsheviks on the Party Central Committee. Thereafter, he had met her again at the International Socialist Congress at Stuttgart, and they had joined forces to draft a resolution on war which was very close to both their hearts and deeply significant for their common future. "For that reason," writes Krupskaya, "their talk that evening was particularly friendly."

From Berlin they went to Geneva, home for so much of their happy first emigration. But they arrived there now (January 20, 1908) sick from eating bad fish, then caught a chill. "Geneva looked cheerless . . . dead and empty. While we walked along the empty Geneva streets which had turned so friendless, Ilyich murmured, 'I feel just as if I had come here to be buried.'"

His letters home, hitherto so unfailingly cheerful, were gloomy and complaining. "For several days now," ran his first letter to his sister Anna in 1908, "I have been stuck in this damned Geneva. A sordid hole, but it cannot be helped. We will adapt ourselves."

And planning to leave for Paris a year later, he wrote his mother: "We hope that a large city will cheer us up a little; we are sick of sitting in a provincial backwater."

Yet another year later, at the end of 1909: "Paris is a rotten hole . . . I have still not been able to adapt myself . . . All the same, I feel only special circumstances could drive me back to Geneva."

In the autumn of 1911, when his second exile had run for almost four years, his sister Anna went to visit him in Paris. He could not conceal from her that the second emigration had been excessively painful and remained so. "His state of mind was noticeably less gay . . . One day when we were walking together, he said to me: 'Will we be able to live until the next revolution?'"

But Lenin was not one to waste time in self-pity. In Geneva he found an old Party printing press which had been forgotten in the excitement of the departure for Russia in 1905. He started up *Pro-*

letarii afresh. Of the first issue, only thirteen copies reached Russia, of the second, third and fourth, only sixty-two. But Lenin wrote to Gorky and Lunacharsky in Italy and to Trotsky in Vienna, urging them to contribute. He sent letters to Russia, too ("but we waited for the answers more than we received them"). He drafted leaflets, started work on pamphlets and books, analyzed Stolypin's new agrarian policy and the unexpected development of a conservative constitutional monarchy; studied every word of the Duma proceedings; gathered statistical reports; engaged in polemics on the Duma and on philosophy—the bitterest in his whole life with the people who had been and were closest to him. He still spent his days in the library, though he no longer knew what to do with his nights. He kept up with national and international affairs. He struggled to train new people to replace those who were deserting and those he was breaking with and driving away. In short, all his activities had the same external appearance as before, the old habits serving as a protective armor for his spirit. But everything was emptier, less satisfying, less absorbing. He was irritable, restless, frequently melancholy.

> Watching him closely from day to day—writes Krupskaya—I noted that he had become more reserved . . . more reflective, and when interrupted in reveries one seemed to catch a glint of sadness in his eyes . . .
>
> We found it difficult to get accustomed again to life in exile. Vladimir Ilyich spent his days in the library, but in the evenings we did not know what to do with ourselves. We did not feel like sitting in the cold, cheerless room . . . we longed to be among people, and every evening we would go to the cinema or to the theater, although we rarely stayed to the end but left in the middle of the performance and would go wandering off . . .
>
> During those most difficult years of the reaction, years about which Ilyich always spoke with such pain even when we were back in Russia—he sustained himself by dreaming . . .

Such passages testify to the effect of those bleak years upon him who was perhaps the most robust of the émigrés. They supply one key, hitherto neglected, to the character of the new round of polemics into which he now entered. They left permanent scars on Lenin's spirit which we will have to bear in mind when we consider his influence as Russia's leading figure in the years after he came to power.

Among the few inside Russia who remained with him, or indeed with Social Democracy at all, there grew up during these difficult years a tendency to safeguard themselves from all the new quarrels and make light of them and of the "make-work" activities of the second emigration abroad. In 1912 this attitude nearly provoked a break between Lenin and the editors of the legal Bolshevik daily *Pravda*, founded that year in Saint Petersburg. To answer the scoffers, he wrote:

> Yes, there is much that is hard to bear in the émigré environment . . . more want and poverty here than else-where . . . a high percentage of suicides . . . [Yet] only here and nowhere else have been posed and considered the most important and fundamental questions of the entire Russian democracy during these years of confusion and interregnum.

He himself did not have to endure physical poverty. His sister relates that he lived badly, ate poorly, dressed shabbily, spent parsimoniously, suffered from restlessness, insomnia, recurrence of his old stomach trouble, headaches, and more frequent spells of ill-ness than before. But Party wages, small earnings from writing, occasional help from Krupskaya's mother or his own, provided all that was needful. Except for the purchase of cheap tickets to cinema, theater and music hall in the working-class district, and walking trips, cycling trips, long summer stays by the seashore in modest housekeeping quarters, his expenditures were as frugal and ascetic as ever. Even in Paris he drank no wine, for a time went without meat, not on principle or for economy, but for health's sake.

> Such poverty as when one has not the wherewithal to buy one's bread, we never knew—writes Krupskaya.—Our life, it is true, was simple. But does the joy of life consist of eating one's full and living in luxury? Vladimir Ilyich knew how to take pleasures from life.

Even now he could laugh heartily at times and stir others to hearty laughter. This is testified by all who came in contact with him. In this ability to snatch moments of unrestrained joy and laughter out of a tragic existence, he was a true son of the Russian people.

"As at every new stage of the Revolution," Krupskaya informs us, "he turned to the masters for advice and consolation." He was especially attentive to the public utterances and private letters of Marx and Engels to each other during their own "sleepless night of

exile" after the collapse of the Revolution of 1848, a long night
which ended only with their death. They, too, had been dominated
for a time by an illusion, bred of revolutionary ardor, that the uprisings of 1848 could not be over for good. But when the sober
examination of key political events and underlying economic trends
had convinced them that a new revolution was only possible as the
result of some new crisis, they broke with the romantic Left that
could not cure itself of unjustified hope.

> You make sheer will instead of real conditions the
> driving force of the revolution—Lenin read in Marx's de-
> bate with his opponents in the Communist League (1850).
> —While we say to the workers: you have fifteen or twenty
> or fifty years of bourgeois and national wars to go through,
> not merely to alter conditions but to alter yourselves and
> make yourselves fit to take over political power, you tell
> them on the contrary that they must take over political
> power at once or abandon all hope. Whilst we point out
> how undeveloped the German proletariat still is, you flat-
> ter the nationalism and craft prejudices of the German
> artisan in the crudest fashion . . .

Those words Lenin could understand and take to his heart, to
fortify himself for the coming struggle with the romantics in his
own faction.

But there was another side of Marx's and Engels's reaction to the
defeat of 1848 which was alien to Lenin's nature. On Marx's motion, the famous Communist League, progenitor of the *Communist
Manifesto,* had declared itself dissolved as "no longer opportune."
The two friends, distressed by the madness that seizes defeated
émigrés, had breathed a sigh of relief as they separated themselves
from the intrigue-ridden foreign colony, its disintegrating organizations and outbreaks of romantic folly. Never again in their lives did
they consent to belong to a German or international conspirative
organization. They were convinced that such a secret league was
appropriate only to the circumstances of imminent revolution, that
broad, legal workers' unions and parties had become feasible, that
underground conspiracies could serve only as breeding ground for
self-deception and police espionage, that they themselves could do
more to build the real movements of the future by engaging in
theoretical labors than by participation in organizations inappropriate to the emerging times.

Lenin felt, however, that his times were different. The conservative constitutional monarchy of Stolypin seemed to be stabilizing
its existence, so that there were moments when he despaired of

living to see a second upheaval in Russia. But Europe did not seem to him, as it had to Marx in 1850, to be on the eve of a long epoch of relatively peaceful expansion. On the contrary, capitalism had reached a stage that smelled of imminent decay: a world war was in the offing which might call forth a crisis greater than that brought on by the Russo-Japanese War of 1904-05. A half-century had elapsed since Marx had spoken those words, a half-century which had brought into existence solid, mighty, permanent-seeming parties. These, in Lenin's estimation, had made the workers "fit to take over political power." The "fifteen or twenty or fifty years of bourgeois and national wars" had been a bit slow in coming or drawing to an end, but the general upheavals might soon begin. From the great international socialist movement and from the Russian socialist movement, thought Lenin, convinced socialists could not now dissociate themselves if their actions squared with their theories and beliefs. Moreover, at heart, he was a man of organization, a man of action; for all his display of theory, a man in whom there was a primacy of will. Of all his writings, there is not one which was not dedicated by some practical need of the immediate struggle. Never could he feel himself, as Marx had felt in 1850, pregnant with a work of such great theoretical import that it might justify his withdrawing from the broken party and its spasmodic struggles. Whether party meant the narrow circle of conspirators, the mighty movement of great masses, or the tortured, inbred, defeated émigré cliques and quarrels, Lenin was always and above all a man of party. Though it might dwindle to the point where the very name would seem a tragic jest, yet to whatever he should call "party," to that he would remain attached. He could never have written as Marx to Engels in 1851:

> I am much pleased with the public and authentic isolation in which we now find ourselves, you and I. It perfectly corresponds to our principles and our position. The system of reciprocal concessions, of half-measures tolerated only in order to keep up appearances, and obligation to share in public with all these asses in the general absurdity of the party—all that is done with now. [Letter of February 11, 1851.]

Nor as Engels in his answer to Marx:

> We now have a chance again at last . . . to show that we need no popularity, no support from any party whatsoever . . . from now on we are responsible only to ourselves, and when the moment comes that these gentlemen

need us, we shall be in a situation to be able to dictate our own terms. Till then we shall at least have peace. To tell the truth, even a certain loneliness . . . How can people like us, who avoid official positions like the plague, ever find ourselves at home in a "party"? . . . The principal thing for the moment is: some way of getting our ideas into print . . . What will all the gossip and scandal mean which the whole émigré pack may circulate against you, once you answer them with your political economy? [Letter of February 13, 1851.]

Lenin was not critical of that withdrawal, for to it he owed such works as Marx's *Critique of Political Economy* and *Capital*. But he could not follow their example. When he learned of the double suicide of Marx's daughter and son-in-law (the Lafargues, in 1909), he said to Krupskaya: "If one cannot work for the Party any longer, one must be able to look truth in the face and die the way the Lafargues did."

In that utterance is the core of Lenin. By 1909 the Party had crumbled away until Krupskaya could write "we have no people at all." In retrospect, Zinoviev, very close to Lenin then, would say, "at this unhappy period the Party as a whole ceased to exist" (*Lectures on Party History, 1922*). In Russia, spies and apathy would combine to decimate and destroy. Abroad, the majority of his collaborators would desert, or be read out of the faction by him, in a succession of tactical and ideological quarrels of incredible bitterness. Yet through it all this man who first came to leadership on the basis of an organization doctrine would remain the man of party, and "party" would continue to mean to him wherever he and even two or three might foregather together to serve as a leading committee for whatsover adherents might be induced to follow its lead. This selfless egocentrism, held unconsciously, rooted in the inescapable conviction of the rightness of his views, would sustain him even when he was most shut off from Russia and from his fellow-émigrés.

Trotsky's spirit seemed less bruised than that of the others. His previous stay abroad had been too brief to have any effect upon him. Younger than most of the leaders—he was only twenty-eight when this second emigration began—he was happy to have escaped from perpetual exile in Siberia to a Western Europe which possessed for him many attractions. His theories as to the nature of the Russian revolution made him sure that he would live to see its triumph and that that triumph would not be too long delayed. Like

Marx and Engels before him, he sought for some correlation between the ebb and flow of economic crises and the rise and fall of
the revolutionary spirit, coming to the conclusion that not depression and misery but a rise in all the indices of economics and employment would restore self-confidence and militance to the Russian working class. (The year 1907 was a year of world depression.)

Always of a self-confident temperament, his belief in his own
destiny had been enhanced by the events of 1905. On the public
stage of the fifty-day Petersburg Soviet he had acquitted himself
with distinction, becoming despite his youth its outstanding and
most popular leader. During the trial of the members of its Executive Committee for high treason, he had further enlarged his reputation. And the events of the year 1905 had fortified his theoretical
self-assurance. At the year's beginning he had published his first
sketchy outline of the doctrine of "permanent revolution"; at its
end he had witnessed what seemed to him the doctrine's fulfill-
ment and verification in the springing into being of the Soviet
and in the powers which that "embryonic workers' parliament" had
taken unto itself. In prison he worked serenely on a series of pamphlets, each of which was to form a chapter in his subsequent
work, *The Year 1905*—the greatest piece of writing from any hand
to come out of that memorable year.

His escape from Siberia brought him to London in time to attend
the Unity Congress of 1907. There he found that the overall unity
of the year 1905 was already dissipating and the Party disintegrating
into factions once more. He was pleased to note that Rosa Luxemburg, who like him had gained enormously in prestige during the
past year, stood close to him in her conceptions as to the nature of
the Russian revolution, and that Lenin did not stand sharply against
him. To his profound surprise, the great political gulf was that
between him and the Mensheviks, despite the fact that he and
Parvus had been editors of their journal, *Nachalo,* and that he had
risen to leadership in the Council of Workingmen's Deputies with
their support. This discovery led him to the conclusion which was to
be the principal determinant of his conduct for the next five years.
Since Bolsheviks and Mensheviks had fought so bitterly from 1903
to 1905, then united in common action when the opportunity for
action presented itself, surely the next wave of revolution would
bring them together once more. Then the clear need and demands
of the awakened working class would again overwhelm these Byzantine disputations and faction animosities. Again the mighty power
of the millions would overcome Lenin's organization narrowness
and the Menshevik mistrust of power. Again great general strikes

would call into being Soviets or Councils more inclusive, more
authoritative, than any faction or party. Again the class would find
its voice and drown out the petulant quarrels of groups and sects.
From this position, neither argument nor event could dislodge him
until "the next wave of revolution" brought him to a different conviction.

Hence the ever angrier and ever more bitter quarrels of those
unhappy years from 1907 to 1914 found him at his self-chosen station in the no man's land between the contending bands, exposed
to cross fire from both. Much of the official literature of "anti-
Trotskyism" published in Russia today consists of quotations from
Lenin's indignation at his supra-factional stand during this period.
They could be matched by no less indignant denunciation from
the pen of Plekhanov, Axelrod and Martov. As he self-confidently
berated now one side, now the other, as if he stood far above all
their little quarrels, he infuriated both at once. His aloofness from
issues looming ever larger in their eyes seemed to them either
vanity or unprincipled indifference. His vain attempts to form a
faction of his own on the basis of his "non-factional" platform,
they deemed ambition. His claim to speak for party while they
each spoke for group, was intolerable arrogance. If he sought to
give his platform more positive content by stating his organization
views, he found himself against Lenin and with the Mensheviks.
If he injected his political perspectives, he was forced inevitably
in the direction of Lenin. Leaving aside defects of personality and
temperament which made it hard for him to form a collective
leadership in which he would have been at most *primus inter
pares*—and there were such defects in his makeup—how could
he possibly form a successful faction on the narrow basis of
"unity," where everyone was agitated precisely by the divisive
matters of organization and politics which he was forced to
ignore? And if he did not ignore them, how could he form a faction either, when his message to others was *peace* while inwardly
he was at war with himself? As an orator, a pamphleteer, a tribune
of the people, this young man had been splendid during the
culminating moments of the year 1905. But as an organizer of a
group and as a club to force the contending factions into unity
he was to be an ignominious failure.

> What has the split done for you?—he challenged both
> sides at the London Congress.—To do the same thing side
> by side, to march on common ground, but mutually tread
> on each other's toes? And what is the result? You are

compelled to reunite, first on a federative basis and now here in a unity congress.

There would be further splits, he warned them, if they did not morally disarm, moderate the spirit of faction, dissolve the groups into the single unified party they were supposed to be. Small consolation to see the prophecy of further splits verified beyond the scope of his imagining!

On the whole, his position brought him closer to the Mensheviks during the ensuing five-year period than to the Bolsheviks, for, in the matter of splitting, Lenin was invariably the aggressor. In 1910, when Lenin's spirit of faction was temporarily brought to bay by a combination of Mensheviks of all shades with those Bolsheviks who believed in party unity (the so-called "Party Bolsheviks" or "Conciliators"), the Conference of the United Party declared Trotsky's personal organ, the Vienna *Pravda*, the organ of the Party. And in August, 1912, while Lenin was openly reading his opponents out of the organization and proclaiming his faction the legitimate party, Trotsky became the rallying center once more for "Party Mensheviks," "Menshevik Liquidators," "Party Bolsheviks," "Bolshevik Vperyodists." This so-called "August Bloc" was Trotsky's last effort to unite all the other groups against "the aggressor," to force Lenin to keep the peace, or at least confine the controversies and methods of struggle within the bounds permissible to comrades in a single organization and a common cause.

> In a large Marxist community embracing tens of thousands of workmen—Trotsky proclaimed—it is impossible that divergences and discords should not exist. Every member of the community has not only the right but the duty of defending his point of view on the basis of the common program. But in fulfilling that duty none should forget that he is dealing with differences among a band of brothers . . . Discipline and cohesion in the struggle are inconceivable without an atmosphere of mutual esteem and confidence, and the man who fails to observe these moral principles, whatever may be his intentions, is undermining the very existence of Social Democracy.[2]

If this conception could have been adhered to, how different might have been the fate of the Russian Revolution, of the Soviet Government, of Trotsky himself! But could it? The question would obtrude itself again in 1917. This time, Trotsky would be as insistent as Lenin that they were not "dealing with differences

---

[2] Cf. Engels to Bebel: "The greatest party in Germany cannot exist without allowing full play to all shades of feeling in it."

among a band of brothers." He would deny that there could be
"an atmosphere of mutual esteem and confidence." Later he
would deny too that "every member of the community has not
only the right but the duty of defending his point of view" within the Bolshevik Party. Later still, too late indeed, he would take
the road back toward the conception of party structure proclaimed
above. Then the fateful years between 1907 and 1917, when he had
struggled for the unity of the Party and proved unable to build
a faction of his own would cost him dear.

His aloofness from the issues dividing the emigration was emphasized by physical detachment. Instead of going to Paris,
Berlin, Geneva or Zurich, where most of the Russians were, he
chose Vienna. There, in 1908, he founded an organ of his own, the
Vienna *Pravda*, which made itself fairly popular inside Russia by
its insistence on unity and its extreme political radicalism ("permanent revolution"). For three and one-half years, he got it out as
a bimonthly, almost single-handed. He wrote most of its articles,
arranged for its smuggling through the Sailors' Union of the
Black Sea, carried on correspondence with adherents of his non-
factional faction. But the police had their agents in the Sailors'
Union, too, and shortly before the World War—when it would
have been most important to have such a smuggling apparatus—
they bagged all the leaders and broke up the union.

Trotsky's chief editorial aid was A. A. Joffe. Joffe suffered from
a nervous or psychic disorder which caused him to submit to
psychoanalysis by Alfred Adler. The Adlers became household
friends of the Trotskys, and from this dates his interest in Freud.
When Trotsky sent Joffe to Russia as an underground organizer,
the police got him immediately; he did not emerge from Siberia
until 1917. As Soviet Ambassador to Germany, he was the first to
breach the *cordon sanitaire*. In 1927 he committed suicide as a
protest against the expulsion of Trotsky by the Party he had helped
to victory.

Other friends of Lev Davidovich in Vienna included Riazanov,
also a unity advocate and trade union organizer, who by then
was by way of becoming the leading Russian Marx scholar; Skobelev, a revolutionary student who would later become Minister
of Labor in the Kerensky Government; and Kopp, who, like Joffe,
would become a Soviet diplomat. Skobelev, Kopp, Joffe—that was
about all there was to the staff of Vienna *Pravda*, aside from the
indefatigable editor.

While he lived in Vienna, his second son, Sergei, was born, and
his older son, Leon (Lev, Lyovik) got his early schooling.

> When Lyovik entered school—writes Natalia Ivanovna
> Trotsky—the question of religion came up. According to
> Austrian law, children had to have religious instruction in
> the faith of their parents. As none was listed in our docu-
> ments, we chose the Lutheran for our children, because
> it seemed easier on the children's shoulders as well as their
> souls . . .

Trotsky's aging mother and father came to visit him. They
brought his daughter (by his first marriage). In Berlin his mother
underwent a kidney operation and treatment for actinomycosis,
which burdened the last decade of her life. She and her husband
seemed reconciled at last with their son's radicalism. ("The final
argument," Trotsky writes in his autobiography, "was probably my
first book in German.") After their visit in 1910, his mother, aged
sixty, went home to Yanovka, where she had borne him, and died
the same year.

During his second exile, the young man who had once used the
Party name of *Pero*—"Pen"—earned his living by the use of that
implement. He became correspondent for *Kievskaya Mysl* ("Kievan
Thought"), a legal journal with a socialistic tinge. He wrote on
literary subjects, German and Austrian affairs, economics and politics. Later the Soviet Government republished the essays. The
writing brought him enough money for his modest needs, except

> . . . when he was too busy with *Pravda*. Then my wife
> learned the road to the pawnshops, and I had to resell to
> booksellers books bought in more affluent days. There were
> times when our modest possessions were confiscated to
> pay the house-rent. We had two babies and no nurse; our
> life was a double burden to my wife. But she still found
> time and energy to help me in revolutionary work.

During all this time Trotsky dedicated some of his vigor to
studies of the correlation of economic crises and political upheavals,
to national and labor questions as they presented themselves in
the Austro-Hungarian Empire (three-quarters of the population
of which were Slavs!) Eloquent in any language that he mastered,
he was soon addressing meetings of Vienna workingmen.

It is worth noting that of the émigrés from the Tsarist Empire, the
four who were able to feel most nearly or completely at home in
the parties of other lands—Rosa Luxemburg, Angelica Balabanoff,
Parvus and Trotsky—were all of Jewish origin. There seemed to
be something in that heritage (something too in their temperaments
and views) which made them less concentratedly Russian or

Polish, more European, more instinctively and radically international in outlook, than most of the other émigrés. This did not
automatically follow from "Jewishness," for Axelrod, Martov,
Zinoviev, Kamenev were Jewish too, yet they never entered into
the life of the parties and lands of their emigration. Nor did Plekhanov, Zasulich and Lenin ever become part of the movements in
the capitals in which they lived, though Lenin spent fifteen years,
and the others their entire adult lives, in exile. Parvus was a
leader in the German Social Democracy; Rosa Luxemburg in three
parties; Angelica Balabanoff became more deeply identified with
the Italian working class than with that of her native land. Trotsky
was somewhat less "international" than these. Russia always took
first place in his thoughts until the day of his death. But he
became a brilliant orator in German and French and an intermittent participant in the affairs of the Austrian party. It helped preserve him from the émigré inbreeding and despair.

In the unwonted stillness of Vienna after the turbulence of
Saint Petersburg, he turned to Marx and Engels, as Lenin did. He
read the Marx-Engels letters, and their effect upon him is worth
quoting, not for what it tells of them but of him:

> The correspondence was for me not a theoretical but
> a psychological revelation. *Toutes proportions gardées*, I
> found proof on every page that to these two I was bound
> by a direct psychological affinity . . . Their attitude to
> men and ideas was mine . . . Marx and Engels were revo-
> lutionaries through and through. But they did not have
> the slightest trace of asceticism or sectarianism. Both of
> them, and especially Engels, could say of themselves that
> nothing human was alien to them. But their revolutionary
> outlook lifted them always above the hazards of fate and
> the works of men . . . What philistines and vulgarians
> considered aristocratic in them was really only their revo-
> lutionary superiority . . .

Like Lenin, Trotsky turned, too, to the Marx pamphlets of the
immediate post-1848 period. But he did not find his wisdom in the
call to retreat, but in Marx's last enunciation of a program for a
new wave of revolutions. Written early in 1850 while Marx still
clung to the delusion that a new uprising was on the way, it said:

> While the democratic petty bourgeoisie would like to
> bring the revolution to a close as soon as their demands
> are more or less complied with, it is our interest and task
> to make the revolution permanent, to keep it going until
> all the ruling and possessing classes are deprived of power,

the governmental machinery occupied by the proletariat
. . . the more important forces of production concentrated
in the hands of the proletarians . . .

Besides the official government, the workers must set
up a revolutionary workers' government, either in the form
of local executives and communal councils or workers'
clubs or workers' committees, so that the bourgeois democratic governments not only lose immediately all backing
among the workers, but from the commencement find
themselves under the supervision and threats of authorities behind whom stand the entire mass of the working
class . . .

In order that this party, whose betrayal of the workers
will begin with the first hour of victory, should be frus-
trated in its nefarious work, it is necessary to organize and
arm the proletariat . . . with their own chiefs and general
staff, to put themselves under the order not of the government but of the revolutionary authorities set up by the
workers . . . They must not be diverted from their course
in proletarian independence by the hypocrisy of the democratic petty bourgeoisie. Their battle cry must be: *The
revolution in permanence!*

The reader will perceive in these words the schematic outlines
of the program on which both Lenin and Trotsky sought to act in
1917. In this "Address to the Communist League" of March, 1850,
we can find, too, Lenin's attitude toward independent parliamentary
action of labor, a source of his attitude toward the liberal Kadets in
the Duma elections, an outline of the agrarian expropriation program he favored, an injunction "to concentrate as much power as
possible in the hands of the central government," and much else
that is regarded as characteristically Leninist. There can be no
doubt that Lenin no less than Trotsky drank deeply at this source.

Because of Trotsky's seven years in Vienna, because of his aloofness from the émigré struggle and its issues, and because his subsequent wanderings will carry him to the Balkans as a war correspondent, then to Spain and far-off America, we shall lose sight
of him for long periods between 1907 and 1917. Before we permit
him to vanish thus from our view, it would be well to examine the
brilliant portrait done by the sensitive pen of Anatole Lunacharsky,
future Commissar of Education of the Soviet Government:

I first met Trotsky in 1905, after the January events
. . . Trotsky was then unusually elegant, in distinction to
all of us, and very handsome. That elegance of his, and

especially a kind of careless, high-and-mighty manner of talking with no matter whom, struck me very unpleasantly. I looked with great disapproval on this dude who swung his leg over his knee and dashed off with a pencil an outline of the impromptu speech he was going to make at the meeting. But Trotsky spoke mighty well . . .

I remember how somebody said in the presence of Lenin: "Khrustalev's star has fallen and the strong man of the Soviet now is Trotsky." Lenin seemed to darken for a moment, then he said: "Well, Trotsky has won that with his tireless fine work . . ."

Trotsky's popularity among the Petersburg proletariat up to the time of his arrest was very great, and it increased as a result of his extraordinarily picturesque and heroic conduct in court . . . Of all the Social Democratic leaders of 1905 and 1906 Trotsky, in spite of his youth, undoubtedly showed himself the best prepared. Least of any did he wear a certain stamp of emigrant narrowness which impeded even Lenin at that time. More than any other did he realize what a broad struggle for power really is. And he came out of the revolution with the greatest gain in popularity. Neither Lenin nor Martov made any essential gain. Plekhanov lost much . . . Trotsky stood from that time on in the front rank . . .

Trotsky succeeded very badly in organizing not only a party but even a little group . . . A tremendous imperiousness and a kind of inability or unwillingness to be at all caressing and attentive to people, an absence of that charm which always surrounded Lenin, condemned Trotsky to a certain loneliness . . .

For work in political groups Trotsky seemed but little fitted, but in the ocean of historic events where such personal features lose their importance, only his favorable side came to the fore . . .

I believe that Lenin never looks at himself, never glances into the mirror of history, never even thinks of what posterity will say of him—simply does his work. He does his work imperiously, not because power is sweet to him but because he is sure that he is right and cannot endure to have anybody spoil his work. His love of power grows out of his tremendous sureness and the correctness of his principles, and out of the inability, if you please—an inability very useful in a political leader—to see from the point of view of his opponent . . .

Unlike him, Trotsky looks at himself often. Trotsky treasures his historic role and would undoubtedly be ready to make any personal sacrifice, not even excluding that of his life, in order to remain in the memory of mankind with the halo of a genuine revolutionary leader . . .

These observant and prophetic words were written while Lenin was still alive and published in the first edition of *Revolutionary Silhouettes*, Moscow, 1923. In that edition there was no silhouette of Stalin, not because Lunacharsky had anything against Stalin, but because in 1923 it still occurred to no one to consider the latter as a figure of the first rank. The sketch of Trotsky was omitted from later editions as part of the general conspiracy to substitute in the public mind another picture of him and remove all traces of his part in the Revolution. But in justice to Lunacharsky it must be said that the omission was made under compulsion and not by any choice of his.

CHAPTER XXIX

LENIN AS PHILOSOPHER

The belief in an external world independent of the percipient
subject is the foundation of all science. —*Einstein*

POLITICS as the cure for the sickness of Russian society having
been tried and found wanting, men withdrew from the political
arena or limited their vision to the narrow horizon of constitutional
possibilities. As after Spartacus came Christ, after Muenzer and embattled Tabor the sword-rejecting Mennonites and Brethren, so
after Gapon, Khrustalev, Trotsky, Lieutenant Schmitt and the Man-
with-the-Leather-Belt[1] came the day of Bulgakov, Berdyaev and
Tolstoy. Hope of changing the world dwindled, the minds of men
turned inward: to self, to personal cares, searching of the spirit,
anodynes, individual salvation.

The period of reaction is generally presented as if all the movements which possessed it arose directly as a result of the defeat of
1905. Actually, Tolstoy's doctrines were formulated in the eighties
after the failure of the Narodovoltsi terror. Bulgakov and Berdyaev
abandoned Marxism for Christian Socialism around 1900. Symbolism, frantic hedonism, "art for art's sake," all were subordinate but
persistent currents at the turn of the century. They had almost
been overwhelmed by the rising revolutionary tide. Now that it
ebbed, they appeared to dominate the desolate scene.

The exhaustion and follies that characterized the period known as
"the decadence" possessed high and low from working class to court.
In 1904 the Tsarina Alexandra gave birth at last to a male heir,
thanks to the intercession of Saint Seraphim, a thaumaturge who
had been irregularly canonized on the insistence of Nicholas II.
The child of this miracle was cursed with the hereditary curse of
hemophelia, which had been transmitted by so many women
of royal households to their male children. A deep sense of personal
guilt took possession of Alexandra, and she had need of daily

---

[1] The Man-with-the-Leather-Belt is an almost legendary figure reported by
many witnesses to have directed the Moscow uprising; Lieutenant Schmitt
was the leader of the Black Sea mutiny; Khrustalev and Trotsky were successive chairmen of the Soviet which called for general strike and armed
uprising.

miracles to keep this precarious life in being. She delivered herself into the hands of a succession of quacks and wonder-workers, then wholly into the keeping of the shrewd and mystical, dissolute and holy "Man of God," the muzhik Rasputin. At first it was only the affairs of the household, then of the Court, then the affairs of state that were entrusted to him. The ascendancy of Rasputin is as truly a phenomenon of the post-1905 decadence as is the wave of drunkenness and gambling among workingmen or the cult of Saninism among students. While the Bolshevik armed bands degenerated into banditry and the underground crumbled and became honeycombed with spies; while students forgot politics and turned to purely academic concerns or the tavern and the brothel, the Court was taken over by the corrupt camarilla around Rasputin. A whole society was moving toward its end.

Among the young, eroticism and suicide became mass phenomena, embraced with the same headlong extremism that had been given to revolution. The brief celebrity of Artsybashev's *Sanin* (published in 1907) was due to the fact that it combined both themes in one. Two suicides, two seductions, a glowing description of nudity, a toying with incest; the glorification of bodily strength, voluptuousness, physical joys; the ridiculing of those who waste their time on politics or knowledge; the admonition to live like animals, follow instinct and impulse, abandon principles, plans, regrets, and to use reason only as devil's advocate and instrument for liberating oneself from all codes, conventions and principles—such is Saninism. It was as symbolic of its moment as the nihilism of *Fathers and Sons* had been for the sixties of the preceding century.

Among the older intelligentsia, many who had been sucked into the radical movement from their student days paused for the first time to examine its premises. Some shrank shuddering from the abyss over the edge of which they had just peered. Even those ardent men of action, the terrorists, found themselves, amidst forced inaction, reflecting over the meaning of their deeds. How did I get to this pass that my ideals and my life are dedicated to executing sentence of death upon my fellowmen? Boris Savinkov, one of the assassins of Minister of the Interior Plehve, gave expression to this wonder in two novels: *Pale Horse* (1909) and *The Tale of What Was Not* (1912):

> Why shouldn't one kill?—asks the protagonist of *Pale Horse.*—And why is murder justified in one case and not in another? People do find reasons, but I don't know why

one should *not* kill. And I don't understand why to kill in the name of this and that is considered right, while to kill in the name of something else is wrong . . . I am on the boundary between life and death, and there where death rules, there is no law, for law relates to life alone.

Terror is a creed to live and die by, a religion in which love, and sacrifice, and . . . damnation, are inextricably linked together:

> Just remember the words: *Greater love hath no man than this, that a man lay down his life for his comrades.* And he must lay down more than his life—his soul!

Still expressing the ambiguities of Savinkov's own inner debate, one of the terrorists in *The Tale of What Was Not* cries in anguish:

> Where shall we find the law? In the Party program? in Marx? in Engels? in Kant? . . . Neither Marx, nor Engels, nor Kant ever killed anyone. They never killed, do you hear me? They do not know, they cannot know what you and I know . . . Whatever they may have written, it still remains hidden from them whether we may or may not kill . . .

Nor did Russian Marxism's greater certitudes, its denser body of doctrine and higher degree of extroversion, immunize it against the epidemic of self-examination. Because of the recent international socialist controversy on "revisionism" versus "Marxist orthodoxy," the argument largely turned about the question: is it permissible, is it "orthodoxy" or "revisionism," for a Marxist to take any significant ideas from the prevailing fashion of neo-Kantian revival?

This debate, too, had started before the 1905 defeat. In 1900 and 1901, Bulgakov and Berdyaev, two leading Russian "neo-Kantians," had broken completely with Marxism and gone over to religion. Whereas the German and Austrian neo-Kantian Socialists had fought to retain their places inside the movement and had won recognition as a legitimate tendency, the Russian revisionists soon flung themselves passionately into the path of schism. Bulgakov became a leading theologian of the Orthodox Church, spending the last twenty years of his life (1924-44) as the director of its theological seminary in Paris. Berdyaev developed into one of the outstanding religious writers of our time, preaching a synthesis of socialism, personalism and corporate Christianity. In this, as in all things, the intensity of Russian thought made for extremism. German revisionism was a reformist dilution or an apologetic "modernization" of Marxism; Russian revisionism was a heterodoxy, a fanatic schism, a *raskol*. And the impulse of Russian "orthodoxy," particularly as embodied in Lenin, was to resort to excommunication.

The year 1904 had marked the hundredth anniversary of the death of Kant. For several years thereafter there was an intense discussion of Kantian ethics, and of "neo-Kantian" epistemology as it figured in modern scientific thought. In this discussion, the acknowledged leader of the forces of orthodox Marxism was Plekhanov. Lenin longed to support him, but refrained at first because he "did not know enough about philosophy" (Letter from Siberia to Potresov). Later he became silent for another reason: in 1904 he made a bloc with Bogdanov, who was the chief target of Plekhanov's philosophical attack! Lenin had to keep silent thereafter for five years, until he was ready to break that bloc. This enforced and humiliating abstinence explains much of the violent intensity with which he finally expressed himself when the restraint was removed.

It is hard to explain why Plekhanov (and Lenin following in his footsteps), reared as he was in a land where every question tended to be viewed as a question of ethics, should insistently have ignored the ethical aspects of this great controversy on "neo-Kantianism." For it was a two-pronged controversy, dealing as much with ethics as with epistemology. To both Plekhanov and Lenin, however, ethics itself was preconscious, as religion is for most men: something which has been acquired once and for all in one's youth, or at the moment when one made his decisive choice. Thereafter, rules of personal conduct, relations to others, and moral problems of means and end, were assumed to be settled self-evidently by one's cherished total belief. Socialism was the end which determined and sanctified the means by which it was to be arrived at. The central means was the movement to which one had dedicated one's life. Even to discuss that self-dedication seemed to these men a little "philistine" or in bad taste. Hence Plekhanov, and Lenin after him, ignored the ethical aspect of neo-Kantianism and limited their contributions to epistemology.

It was not till the period of reaction that the debate on epistemology and Marxism took full possession of the defeated movement. What was left of the Marxist intelligentsia found a measure of distraction and solace in these theoretical pursuits. Though they might seem disparate phenomena, Krassin's ceasing to make bombs in his laboratory and his gradual withdrawal from socialist activity to devote himself to engineering; Riazanov's abandonment of trade

union work and of his struggle for Party unity, in order to become
the greatest Marx scholar and textual critic of his generation;
Lunacharsky's growing preoccupation with literature and religion
and Bogdanov's with proletarian culture; and Lenin's "shameful
neglect of my work on *Proletarii*" in order to immerse himself in
philosophy—are all related symptoms of the deep crisis that had
set in within the Social Democratic Party.

At the home of Maxim Gorky on the idyllic island of Capri, all
the Bolshevik tendencies opposed to Lenin foregathered to set up a
training school for Russian workers. It was by Lenin's choice, not
theirs, that Gorky's home became an "opposition school" for "ultra-
Leftist" Bolsheviks. Repeatedly they urged him to become one of its
teachers, but he stayed away from Capri for reasons which will
appear in the course of this chapter. The school did not limit itself,
as Vladimir Ilyich would have liked, to politics and economics. It
dealt with philosophy and natural science, the history of art, the
theory of proletarian culture and proletarian "ideological organization," the history of Russian literature, of the Russian state and
Church, problems of revolutionary ethics, and, of course, the "Leftist tactics" on the Duma boycott and other matters that were being
pursued by the bloc built around Bogdanov. Almost insensibly Bogdanov had become a rival to Lenin for the tactical, i.e. the practical
political, leadership of the Bolshevik faction. Even if Lenin had not
been fighting for his very position as head of his group, still his intense concentration on politics, and on theory only insofar as it had
bearing upon immediate problems of practice, would have made
him regard this predominantly cultural school with misgiving. To
understand the peculiar ambivalence of his attitude toward the
goods of culture, we need only ponder this revealing anecdote
from Gorky's *Days with Lenin*:

> One evening Lenin was listening to a sonata by Beetho-
> ven . . . and said: "I know nothing greater than the 'Apas-
> sionata' . . . I always think with pride: what marvelous
> things human beings can do! But I can't listen to music too
> often. It affects your nerves, makes you want to say stupid,
> nice things, and stroke the heads of people who could
> create such beauty while living in this vile hell. And you
> mustn't stroke anyone's head—you might get your hand bit-
> ten off. You have to hit them over the head, without any
> mercy, although our ideal is not to use force against any-
> one. Hm, hm, our duty is infernally hard" . . .

Bogdanov had come to Lenin in 1904 at a time when the latter's political fortunes were at their lowest ebb. As the reader will remember, Lenin had formed his Bolshevik faction only a year earlier (1903), with Plekhanov as its ostensible ideological leader, himself as group organizer, and Krassin as chief lieutenant inside Russia. But by 1904 Vladimir Ilyich had lost Plekhanov to the Mensheviks, had lost control of *Iskra,* and even of the Central Committee, leaving the irreconcilable "Majority" leader of yesterday virtually without a faction. It was at this critical moment that Bogdanov and his friends, most of them just released from Siberia, rallied to Lenin's standard. The newcomers were all men with a penchant for cultural and philosophical speculation, a speculation which in no wise resembled the unquestioning Marxist orthodoxy of Vladimir Ilyich. But it was enough for him that they agreed with him on organization and tactics. Almost the only continuity between the original Bolshevik leadership of 1903 and the new Bolshevik leadership of 1904 was provided by Vladimir Ilyich himself and his tactical-organizational views. This phenomenon would occur again in 1909 (when he broke with Bogdanov) and several times more. Where Lenin and two or three were gathered together, there was bolshevism.

Bogdanov (real name A. A. Malinovsky) was a medical doctor and a writer of considerable reputation on economics, sociology, natural science, and philosophy. He accounted himself a Marxian, but his was an independent and speculative mind which abhorred authoritarian attitudes in the realm of thought and rejected the notion that in the scriptures of Marx and Engels could be found the answers to all problems that might be raised by men who lived after them.

Lenin had known Bogdanov by reputation since 1898, when a copy of the latter's *Short Course in Economic Science* reached him in Siberia. Lenin found the work so good that he himself rejected a proposal from a publisher to write a manual of political economy because "it would be difficult to compete with Bogdanov." (Letters to his mother, February 12 and June 10, 1898.)

When they joined forces in 1904, the two men exchanged presentation copies of their latest works. Lenin's gift was his *One Step Forward, Two Steps Backward,* and Bogdanov's was the first volume of his *Empiriomonism.* (The second volume was published in 1905 and the third and last, written in prison, was published in 1906.) *Empiriomonism,* strongly influenced by the philosophical writings of Ernst Mach, was the work which, in 1909, was to be the chief target of Lenin's philosophical polemic.

Why did he delay for five years before he made his disagreement public? If the work was indeed a service to religion and reaction, as he was later to assert, why did he take its author into leadership in his faction?

One thing is certain: the delay was not because Vladimir Ilyich was slow to read his new associate's book. We have Lenin's own word for it (in a letter to Gorky) that he read it at once, at once disagreed with it, and wrote a long letter of private criticism to its author. When the third and final volume of *Empiriomonism* appeared in 1906, Bogdanov sent him a presentation copy from jail. Lenin immediately wrote a further "declaration of love, a little letter on philosophy which took up three notebooks!" (Lenin to Gorky, February 25, 1908.) But that did not prevent his forming his bloc with the unrepentant and unconvinced philosopher, nor his maintaining that bloc for five years until it broke up, not on philosophical matters but on tactical. This is important to establish beyond a cavil, not merely for the light it throws on Lenin as philosopher, but also for its bearing on the contention of the Leninist epigones that there is a necessary, direct and inescapable correlation between 100 per cent orthodoxy in Marxist philosophy and the very possibility of being a good revolutionist. The whole of Russian philosophical literature under Stalin is based upon this supposed deduction from Lenin's book. And Leon Trotsky has been no less insistent on this matter in the polemic he conducted during the last year of his life against his American followers, James Burnham and Max Shachtman, when they were breaking with him. (See Trotsky: *In Defense of Marxism*, Pioneer Publishers, New York, 1942, pp. 45–48, 52, 54, 79.)

Doubtless the general strength of the moods of "decadence" in 1908 contributed to Lenin's anxiety to reprove his associates publicly for their heterodox philosophy. Yet even then, as he sensed that the Bolshevik tactical bloc might be heading toward a permanent break, he reviewed the whole experiment in a letter to Gorky, and found it right and good. Moreover, he still pleaded for its continuance:

> In the summer and autumn of 1904—he wrote to Gorky in 1908—Bogdanov and I joined each other finally as Bolsheviks, and formed that tacit bloc which tacitly excluded philosophy as neutral ground. The bloc lasted throughout the entire time of the Revolution and gave us the possibility of introducing together into the Revolution those tactics of revolutionary socialism (bolshevism) which, ac-

cording to my deepest conviction, were the only correct ones . . .

A certain amount of conflict among the Bolsheviks on the philosophical question is, I think, unavoidable. But to split on that account would, in my opinion, be stupid. We have formed a bloc for pursuing a given set of tactics in the Party. These tactics we have pursued and are pursuing so far without differences (the only differences of opinion were on the boycott of the Third Duma elections . . .). To hamper the cause of carrying out the tactics of revolutionary Social Democracy in the Party because of arguments as to materialism or Machism would, in my opinion, be an unpardonable folly. We must carry on our scrap with each other about philosophy in such a way as not to affect *Proletarii* at all, or the Bolshevik fraction either . . . You can help . . . [Letter of Feb. 25, 1908.]

"In 1903, when I worked with him on *Iskra*," Lenin wrote to Gorky, "Plekhanov analyzed for me the error in Bogdanov's views." Hence it was after the *caveat* of his teacher that Lenin entered into the "tacit bloc" with Bogdanov.

Nor was Plekhanov slow to taunt his philosophical disciple. Your tactics, he wrote of Lenin in *Iskra*, are a revision of Marxism in politics; Bogdanov's theories are a revision of Marxism in philosophy. Since each theory gets the practice it deserves, Machism is the proper philosophy for bolshevism. You are welcome to your Bogdanov and his Machist philosophy, "and may all possible Machs and Avenariuses be with you!" The embarrassed disciple could only pretend not to understand the taunt:

> Plekhanov drags in Mach and Avenarius by the hair— he told his followers at the Third (All-Bolshevik) Congress of 1905.—It is absolutely incomprehensible to me what these men, for whom I haven't the slightest sympathy, have to do with the social revolution. They write on individual and social organization of experience, or something of the sort, but really they have no ideas on the democratic dictatorship.

It would carry us too far afield to discuss Mach and his school in the present work. But that last sentence of Lenin's is worth holding on to. If not altogether adequate as a characterization of Mach, it is of Bogdanov's "Machism."

"*They write on individual and social organization of experience.*" Those nine words contain a clearer, fairer, more exact account of what Bogdanov had borrowed from Mach's views and assimilated to his own thinking, than Lenin would subsequently give anywhere in all his four hundred pages of philosophical polemics, when the bloc with Bogdanov had been broken. In 1905, disagreeing with Bogdanov's views, he had known how to characterize them briefly, honestly, exactly. In 1909, he distorted those views the better to discredit them. Thus was Lenin's clear intellect ever subject to the torsion of his powerful factional passions.

The year 1908 marked the turning point in his relations with Bogdanov. Until that time, Lenin still hoped for a fresh armed uprising, in which case such matters as the boycott of the Duma would be of secondary significance. But the growing reaction now convinced him that these tactical differences were central instead of marginal. Philosophical differences, too, seemed more important in the midst of the general ideological reaction. Lenin became increasingly restless concerning the tactical bloc "neutral on philosophy."

Bogdanov, Bazarov and Lunacharsky chose that particular moment to join hands with the Mensheviks Yushkevich and Valentinov and other writers, in the publication of a symposium on philosophy. The last straw was the title: *Outlines of the Philosophy of Marxism!* If at least they had not invoked the name of Marx to cover—as he complained to Gorky—"their smuggling of the contraband of neo-Kantianism or Machism." The articles made him "simply mad with indignation. . . . Today I read one Empiriocriticist and scold like a fishwife; tomorrow another and curse like a trooper."

Alarmed for the unity of the faction, Gorky urged him to restrain himself.

> Once a Party man has become convinced that a certain theory is decidedly wrong and harmful—Lenin answered— then he is in duty bound to oppose it . . .
>
> Plekhanov is entirely in the right against them . . . only he doesn't know how, ·or doesn't want to, or is too lazy to say it concretely, completely and simply, without frightening the public with philosophical subtleties. And I shall say this in my own fashion, cost what it may . . .

"*Cost what it may!*" Yet still he hoped, or so he assured Gorky, that they could continue to maintain the tactical bloc while they had it out in philosophy. But in truth the bloc itself was in a bad way, and Lenin was slowly coming to the conclusion that a split was necessary. In December, 1905, he had let "the Siberians and Caucasians" override him on the Duma question, because it seemed

unimportant in the face of imminent armed uprising. In 1907, at
the July Conference of Bolsheviks and Mensheviks to consider elections to the Third Duma, fourteen out of fifteen Bolshevik delegates
(all but Lenin!) had been for boycott and they had named Bogdanov instead of him as spokesman for the faction. All through
1908 this nagging conflict smoldered and flared up again: now as
"boycottism," now as *otzovism* or "recallism," now as "ultimatism."
Not till the middle of 1908 did Lenin win a slender majority on
tactical questions in Moscow, and not until 1909 in Petersburg.

The group which thwarted him on tactical reconversion from the
period of storm to the period of calm were men who had originally
been attracted to him by his call for armed uprising and seizure of
power. Those formerly big issues had become remote and marginal
for Lenin now, while the questions of Duma elections, and practical
trade union work, had become urgent and central. His associates
were poets like Lunacharsky, philosophers and scientists like Bogdanov and Bazarov, historians like Pokrovsky, novelists like Gorky,
romantic revolutionists in politics for whom Lenin's extremism was
attractive, "softs" for whom a "hard line" possessed irresistible
fascination. When they came to Lenin, he appeared to occupy the
extreme red end of the Social Democratic spectrum. Now that from
more somber circumstances he deduced soberer slogans and devices, shifting his place in the tactical spectrum to match the blue
realities of the period, he lost much of his attractiveness and seemed
to them unfaithful to "true bolshevism or Leninism." But Lenin
knew that to repeat the same slogans of armed uprising and seizure
of power now would be to lose contact with the masses and with
reality. Their "true bolshevism" was to him but a caricature. In
this Lenin was wiser than any philosopher, more attuned to social
moods than any novelist, poet, or historian in his faction. The time
had come, he concluded, to bring his old associates to their senses,
or to sweep them aside, lest his group perish from neglect of the
real possibilities and the actual tasks before it. Since the independent and self-confident Bogdanov was the leader of the heteroge-
nous bloc that stood in his way, Bogdanov must be discredited.
Perhaps the faction would listen to him on tactics after he had discredited his opponents on the ground of philosophy. He could get
off his chest the long-suppressed disagreements on philosophical
matters; he could strike a blow, albeit a trifle late, for orthodox
Marxism against this heterodoxy, and contribute to the counter-
offensive against ideological decay and reaction.

While he was turning this over in his mind, new aberrations, not
of the professional philosophers, Bogdanov and Bazarov, but of the

poetic amateurs, Lunacharsky and Gorky, suddenly put into his hand an excellent stick with which to beat the lot of them and arouse the indignation of the rank and file against them all . . .

Lunacharsky and Gorky were prone to talk in the language of metaphor. Return to religion was in the air. Sensitive, as creative writers are apt to be, to all the currents charging the surrounding atmosphere, they now turned their attention to religion, about which the whole intelligentsia had been talking. Not that they proposed to serve religion, as Lenin was to charge against them. Quite the opposite: they sought to fight the recrudescence of religious orthodoxy by borrowing from its arsenal metaphorical weapons to use against it.

In 1908, Lunacharsky published *Religion and Socialism* (the first volume had appeared in 1907). It was a mixture of the history of religion, sociological analysis, and poetic enthusiasm. The second volume culminated in an apotheosis of Marxism as a "natural, earthly, anti-metaphysical, scientific and human religion" which was to put an end to all supernatural, unscientific, fetishistic, authoritarian, hierarchical faiths and substitute the "faith" of man in his socialized self, in his own powers, unity, solidarity. Hitherto God had been a reflection of man's dreams and aspirations projected into an external object of worship. God's omnipotence had been but the reflection of man's potentially unlimited power over nature, once he had socialized his own nature. "Religion is enthusiasm, and without enthusiasm nothing great can be accomplished by man." But Marxism would turn that enthusiasm and faith into their proper channels, from belief in external gods, a belief which humiliates man, into an enthusiasm for, and faith in, man's own creative powers. The future socialized humanity was the only "god" worthy of man's worship.

Gorky, doubtless influenced by Lunacharsky, next wrote a novel, *The Confession*, which reached its climax in such passages as this:

> The people, they are the creators . . . In them dwells God . . . I saw the earth, my mother, in space between the stars . . . And I saw her master, the omnipotent, immortal people . . . and I prayed: *Thou art my God, the creator of all the gods . . .*

Lenin's first impulse was to pronounce anathema against the two of them:

> A Catholic priest who violates young girls—he wrote to Gorky—is much less dangerous to democracy than are priests who do not wear surplices, priests without vulgar

> religion, ideological and democratic priests, who preach
> the creating and construction of little gods . . .

Yet at bottom he was tolerant of the vagaries of artists and had a deep and abiding affection for the two "little-god creators." Moreover, the real opponent was Bogdanov, free, to be sure, from all "god-creating" and all metaphorical talk of "faith" and "worship," but the leading contender in the realm of tactics for the command of his faction.

> I am completely and unconditionally of the opinion—he
> hastened to reassure Gorky—that you possess the most un-
> erring judgment in artistic creation and that, when you
> create such views, both out of your artistic experience and
> out of philosophy, even if this philosophy is an idealistic
> one, you may come to conclusions which may be of enor-
> mous value to the workers' party . . .

This respect for the creative freedom of artists and their "unerring judgment in artistic creation" was one of the nobler aspects of Lenin which he never succeeded in handing down to his disciples.

Significantly, when Lenin's book on philosophy appeared, it did not contain one reference to Maxim Gorky. Lunacharsky, however, had some pretensions as philosopher and sociologist. More important, his metaphorical avowals of "religion" and "faith" were a most useful stick with which to beat Bogdanov. Lunacharsky, therefore, appears on the very first page as if he were going to be the central target in the book:

> Leaning upon all these supposedly most recent doctrines,
> our annihilators of dialectic materialism go so far as to
> speak openly in favor of fideism (in the case of Luna-
> charsky this is most outspoken, but in this he does not
> stand alone by any means!)

Since Lenin defines fideism as "putting faith in place of knowledge," the charge is not even true of Lunacharsky, still less of Bogdanov, who deplored the latter's coquetry with religious terminology. Moreover, if Lunacharsky is indeed "the most outspoken advocate of fideism" and fideism is the objective of Lenin's attack, one would expect that somewhere in the three-hundred-odd pages there would be an analysis and refutation of Lunacharsky's views. But nothing of the sort. He is mentioned a dozen times, but always glancingly and ironically in a series of three names in order to tie up his "outspoken fideism" with Bogdanov and Bazarov.

Bogdanov pointed out in answer (in *Faith and Science,* 1910) that Lunacharsky had already repented of his religious metaphors by the time Lenin's book appeared. Those metaphors of Lunacharsky's, said Bogdanov, could "only hinder the exact scientific analysis of historic religions, which have always been in the first place *authoritarian* . . . and might preserve in the minds of readers remnants of an unconscious respect for notions which ought to be abandoned." It was all right to criticize such terminology *before* Lunacharsky had abandoned it, just as Engels had criticized the similar religious terminology of Feuerbach. But Engels had been careful to expound the real content of Feuerbach's views, and "had not dreamed of confounding those views with actual historical religions, or 'fideism' . . . Lenin uses a diametrically opposite method with Lunacharsky, obscuring and hiding from the reader the true content of the views of his opponent, to give the reader the idea that Lunacharsky speaks of religion in the usual traditional sense . . ."

Lenin's authoritarian attitude toward the founders of scientific socialism, Bogdanov continues, caused him to treat similar aberrations in Dietzgen, and profounder ones in Feuerbach, with gentle respect, for had not "the masters themselves" pronounced Dietzgen a "proletarian philosopher" and had not "they themselves" acknowledged Feuerbach as a precursor and teacher?

> Rudeness and high-handedness toward people whom one holds lower than oneself in position; respectfulness toward those whom one acknowledges as higher than oneself—is a common feature of *authoritarian* psychology in present-day society—concluded Bogdanov (italics in the original).

Lenin might be thus rude with Lunacharsky in public, but privately he confided to Krupskaya concerning the target of this attack:

> He will return to the Party. He is less of an individualist than the other two. He has a highly gifted nature such as is rarely met with. I have a weakness for him. What stupid words—*to have a weakness!* I am really very fond of him, you know, he is a splendid comrade! There is something of French brilliance about him. His levity is the result of his estheticism.

At the end of 1908, Vladimir Ilyich's sister, Anna, found a publisher for *Materialism and Empiriocriticism* by "Vladimir Ilyin," a pen-name already known to us—and to the police.

From what you tell me—he wrote to Anna—everything is arranged. Splendid! I am agreed to the tone of my remarks being softened so far as Bazarov and Bogdanov are concerned. As to Yushkevich and Valentinov, it is not worth altering what I have said . . .

Strange notion, this, that he could keep a comradely tone toward Bolshevik "Machists" and a less comradely one toward Menshevik "Machists."

But on March 19, 1909, as the show-down in the faction nears, he writes:

Please do not tone down the passages against Bogdanov and Lunacharsky. Our relations with them are completely ruptured. It is not worth while to modify the passages . . .

Such statements give us the intimate psychobiography of Lenin's work on philosophy and open a window into the innermost recesses of his temperament and methods of polemics, philosophical as well as political. Indeed, for him philosophy and politics are so closely connected that on April 8, 1909, he writes:

It is *hellishly* important for me that the book should come out at the earliest possible date, not only for literary but also for political reasons.

This "hellish importance" derived from the fact that he had called an enlarged conference of the Editorial Board of *Proletarii* for the end of June. Only an "editorial conference," but he was secretly planning to place political and organizational matters before it. Some time earlier he had already written to Vorovsky that a split would probably occur "at the next conference." He urged Vorovsky to come personally, see to the proper election of delegates from the Russian underground, for whose expenses "we will send money." Now he wrote Vorovsky again: "If the line of the 'Left' prevails, I will leave the faction immediately." Thus the threat to resign, the big book on philosophy, the use of the funds which Victor Taratuta's maneuvers had gotten from the Schmitt estate, and the careful selection of delegates, whose addresses, as always, were in the hands of faction secretary Krupskaya, were so many careful chess moves for the checkmate of the unsuspecting co-editor, Bogdanov, at the forthcoming editorial conference. He even had replacements ready, for he was training two younger men, Zinoviev and Kamenev, to make up the second and third on the new *troika* with him, after Bogdanov had been ousted. If the new co-leaders did not possess the spirit of independence, the unshakable sense of man-to-man equality, the speculative originality, which had made Bogdanov such a troublesome collaborator, so much the better.

At the beginning of May, 1909, the book appeared in Moscow, and from July 4 to 13, the enlarged Editorial Board of *Proletarii* met in Lenin's apartment. Lenin had prepared all the resolutions and motions. On his proposal, the editorial conference set aside the old Bolshevik Center, elected at the London Congress of 1907, and assumed the power to appoint, remove and legislate. It decided that "boycottism, recallism, ultimatism, God-construction and Machism" were all of them "incompatible with membership in the Bolshevik faction." In vain did Bogdanov question the right of a mere editorial conference to remove people appointed by the Bolshevik Center, or to repeal the resolution on "neutrality in philosophy" on which the Bolshevik bloc had been based. In vain did he protest the attempt to split the faction, and the methods of "coup d'état." The moves had been prepared and thought out to the last detail, and Lenin had the votes to carry his motions. There is no way of knowing how much the big book, which nobody had yet had the time to read but which seemed to tie all the "Leftists" up with religion and "God-creation," helped to weigh in the scale. By a small but safe majority, Bogdanov and his associates were declared to have "placed themselves outside the faction."

> Not outside the Party—Lenin explained precisely.—A party can include a wide range of opinions, the extremes of which may even be diametrically opposed to each other . . .

But in 1912, Lenin's faction was to declare itself the Party! And after 1917 it was to make the state a mere instrument of the Party. What then would happen to the "wide range of opinions"?

The dissidents, a sizable minority despite the fact that Lenin had pretty largely in advance determined who should come to the enlarged editorial conference, withdrew at last and proclaimed themselves the only "true Bolsheviks": legally, because they regarded the acts of the conference as a usurpation; ideologically, because in their own minds they were true to the "original tactics of bolshevism" which had so often in recent years commanded a majority against Lenin. In token of the continuity of their bolshevism, they revived for their new journal the name borne by the first Bolshevik paper, founded by Lenin and Bogdanov at the end of 1904: *Vpered* (pronounced *Vperyod*), whence they were called for the next few years the Vperyodist Bolsheviks.

Go your way, friends—Lenin admonished them in the columns of *Proletarii*.—We did our best to teach you Marxism and Social Democratic methods of work. We now declare decisive and irreconcilable war on the Liquidators of the Right [a sub-tendency among the Mensheviks, of which more later], and the Liquidators from the Left, who are corrupting the workers' party by theoretical revisionism and philistine political and tactical methods.

Materialism and Empiriocriticism, then, is first of all a document in an intra-Party struggle. This should not surprise us, for the same can be said of every line Lenin ever wrote for publication. Its primary concerns are to defend orthodox Marxism against every species of modification, revision, criticism or attack, and to convict Bogdanov and his associates of deviations from Marxist orthodoxy. But over and above this, the work has a more ambitious aim: to expound afresh the basic philosophical position of Marx and Engels, and to evaluate from its standpoint the main philosophical currents and scientific discoveries of Lenin's day.

Engels had insisted, and now Lenin insisted after him, that the recognition of a world independent of the percipient subject, and the recognition of man's ability through analysis and action to form an ever more exact notion of the nature of that world, are the prerequisites of modern science. To those who assert that there is no such "objective" world, or that it is forever unknowable, Engels answers that science and industry, man's knowledge-in-action, teach us how the unknown becomes known, how out of ignorance arises knowledge. It is this knowledge-in-action which enables us to test the correctness of our conceptions of a given phenomenon, by producing it out of its elements or determinants, by devising critical tests, by predicting and foreseeing, by revising and refining our hypotheses in terms of crucial experiments and observable errors. Many of the best pages in Lenin's book are quotations from Engels, followed by explanations and illustrations of this view. Passionately he asserts that, though the *known* be little and the *unknown* vast, the area of man's knowing and power to predict and plan and control is capable of indefinite enlargement. To postulate an *unknowable*, however, is to set arbitrary, self-degrading limits upon man's efforts to understand and master his world. In the midst of all the anti-rationalism that surrounded him in the post-1905 reaction, and that surrounds us in our own day, Lenin's plea for a rational, experimental approach to nature and society—however much he may have deviated from it himself in his own dogmatic authoritarianism in the sphere of "Marxist orthodoxy"—represents an important contribution.

> Man's intelligence—he cries—may be only a feeble rush-light in the darkness of night, but I am not going to let that flickering flame be blown out by mystics and meta-physicians . . .

The one chapter of Lenin's book that has meaning beyond the limits of the immediate philosophical-factional controversy is Chapter V, entitled: "The Latest Revolution in Natural Science." Here Lenin handles the "crisis in science" that had just been pro-claimed by Poincaré; the notion that "matter is disappearing," or being swallowed up by energy or dissolved into pure mathematical formulae; or that the material universe was dissolving, merely be-cause science was stumbling from the one-sidedness of inert matter-without-motion into the contrary one-sidedness of motion-without-anything-which-moves. The approach here employed by Lenin, and more skillfully and subtly by Engels before him, is helpful, too, in considering fresh muddles which have arisen since their day: the supposed entrance of "spirit" into every phenomenon by virtue of the alleged inseparability of the thing-observed from the observer; the emergence of "free will" inside the atom via the principle of indeterminacy; along with other bewilderments of certain recent scientists turned amateur philosophers and philosophers turned amateur scientists, without sufficient mastery of the accumulated heritage of philosophic and scientific thought.

The weakness of Lenin's work, as Bogdanov hastened to point out, was its authoritarian character. Its proofs are all proofs by authority—the authority of Marx and Engels. The final touchstone is always a quotation from one of their works. The authority, on closer examination, almost always proves to be Engels. Curiously, though Lenin mentions the name of Marx scores of times, there is only one three-sentence quotation from the philosophical writings of Marx in the entire book. To be sure, Engels' more specialized *Anti-Duehring* and *Feuerbach*, if less seminal, are more systema-tized, more apposite to Lenin's immediate purposes. Still, the neg-lect of Marx by this orthodox Marxist suggests something concern-ing the limitations in his orthodoxy, like the Christianity of a theologian who forever quotes Paul but finds no use for the words of Christ.

When Lenin has succeeded in confronting some quotation from Bogdanov (or from anyone whom he can, by whatever literary stratagem, link up with Bogdanov) with some quotation from Engels, and has shown some divergence between them, his task is finished. Lenin is not only "authoritarian" himself, but he insists that all his opponents must be authoritarian, too:

> Your clamor against argument from authority—he writes —is only a screen to conceal the fact that you substitute for the socialist authorities—Marx, Engels, Lafargue, Mehring, Kautsky—the bourgeois authorities—Mach, Petzold, Avenarius and the immanentists.

In pursuance of this idea that every man must have his authorities, Lenin matches a maze of quotations from Engels with a counter-maze of quotations from the "other camp," lumping together the most diverse names, on the philosophical theory, as Bogdanov wryly observed, that "who is not with us, is against us." By this device Lenin blames Bogdanov for things he has not said, and even for things he specifically rejects. It is sufficient that Mach has said them and that Bogdanov is a "Machist" and therefore "responsible" for all of his "authority's" views. And for all other Machists! And for all the utterances of any who has praised Mach or been praised by him! This "philosophical chain-reaction method," and "quotational shock treatment," as Bogdanov dubbed them, were calculated as much to impress the reader as to overwhelm the opponent. It was the method of all authoritarian organizations, Bogdanov observed shrewdly, to "hold the chief responsible for the activities of his subordinates" and oblige them to "reflect exactly his conceptions." Bogdanov's reply did not do a very good job of defending his own philosophical speculations, but he had probed the weakest spot in Lenin's intellectual armor.

The most notable difference between Engels and Lenin is the angry moral tone of Lenin's attacks, the opprobrious moral epithets that pepper his pages. Engels had spoken of three philosophical "camps": materialism, idealism and agnosticism. Insensibly, Lenin converts "camps" into "parties" and proclaims that "philosophy is a *partisan* struggle." Where Engels finds "philosophical agnosticism" to be a "shame-faced way of accepting materialism by the back door," Lenin enlarges the "shame" until it becomes a monstrous thing, a plot to drag in not materialism but "religion by the back door." Those in the "idealist camp" are at least to be respected as "open agents of reaction and religion," but those in the "agnostic camp" are to be exposed as covert agents, whose agnosticism is "only a despicable cloak of servility to idealism and fideism."

Marx and Engels could be scornful and ironic in theoretical controversy, and devastating and reckless in their private letters to each other. But even in the *Anti-Duehring*, which so largely served Lenin as source and model, all that Engels aims at is to convict Professor Duehring of inconsistency and "higher nonsense." Nowhere do we find the imputations of evil intention that abound in Lenin's pages, or the passionately held belief that defects in a man's epistemological theories are defects in his character, willful immoralities of the spirit leading to inevitable political sin. ("Genuinely scientific works," Engels had admonished Duehring, "avoid such dogmatic-moral expressions as truth and error.")

If Lenin's philosophical targets disavow a view he has imputed to them, it is sinister trickery. If they have modified a view under criticism (his criticism or another's), it is but the better to deceive. If their views seem very close to his, or to his masters'—still worse: they are "surreptitiously and illegally borrowing" from materialism to hide their true intentions and confuse the right-thinking. As a whole, "professors of philosophy are scientific salesmen of theology." Mach and his school are "graduated flunkies of theism." They are all conspirators, plotting against science and the further progress of mankind. "The philosophy of Mach, the scientist, is to science what the kiss of Judas is to Christ."

This method of polemics, and the very epithets employed in it, derive from the intense ethical bias and passionate fanaticism of Russian thought. For reasons suggested in the first chapter, Russian nineteenth-century thought reduced politics to ethics, without so much as a residue of mere practical concern or experimental interest. Art and literature and criticism were no less questions of morality. Even science was a moral creed to live by. "Science," cried the gentle Herzen, "there is no reason why I should hide words in the depth of my soul—Science is Love!" And the problems of epistemology, the most difficult, subtle, and general problems that can engage the thought of mankind, were made into moral issues, too. The reader will find Lenin at enormous pains, by the "chain-reaction and quotational shock-treatment" methods, to reduce every opponent's views to "solipsism." When he has driven his opponent into that corner, his indignation knows no bounds. As we read, we are reminded of the men of the Russian enlightenment, who, like Belinsky and Herzen, regarded solipsism (extreme subjectivism) as a kind of logical-moral defect of character, arrogant, egotistical, vile. Consistent solipsism, they thought, makes the petty ego of its disciple into the measure of truth and error, right and wrong, good and evil, permitting him to betray all ideals, logically leading him

to commit any crime from murder to suicide. When dealing with
such issues, there is more to Lenin's scorn than worked-up indig-
nation and the desire to discredit his factional opponents (more
than his "I shall always act thus whenever a split is involved").
The overtones of anathema and excommunication are part of that
Russian polemical heritage which caused the Slavophiles to brand
Chaadaiev an "apostate," Granovsky a "corrupter of the youth,"
Herzen a "lackey in Western livery." And we can hear no less the
Westernizers retorting with the epithet "Slav gendarmes in the
name of Jesus Christ" or Merezhkowsky accusing Gogol of "betray-
ing Pushkin" by his "all-devouring sickly mysticism."

Belinski, atheist though he was, had proclaimed the need of a
"faith" for "without faith I cannot live." Herzen had rejected "the
heavy cross of disillusioned knowledge." Odoevski had cried that
"to be happy, man must have a luminous axiom, one that is all-
embracing, one that brings deliverance from the torment of doubt."
This spirit, unexpressed, goes far to explain the fury with which
Lenin attacked any slightest "deviation" which might sow in the
solid granite of his own faith the fissuring seed-corn of a doubt:

> You cannot eliminate even one basic assumption, one
> substantial part of this philosophy——it is as if it were a
> solid block of steel——without abandoning objective truth,
> without falling into the arms of bourgeois-reactionary false-
> hood.

Materialism and Empiriocriticism appeared too late to have
much influence upon the conference proceedings which expelled
Bogdanov and his friends. It was little noticed, little sold, little
read. Bogdanov as philosopher was not of large enough caliber to
have attracted much general attention. Moreover, by 1909, the entire controversy, epistemological and ethical, was already on the
wane. Insofar as the book represented a determined counter-thrust
against the religious, mystical, soul-searching, anti-rational moods
of post-1905 Russia, it had been delayed too long because of
Lenin's "tacit bloc" with the "empiriomonist." It turned out to be
a deployment of heavy artillery to a part of the battlefield that had
largely been vacated. It is significant that Lenin failed to follow
it up, as he had his other large works, with a series of special
articles in the press. When Bogdanov answered it in a brief defense
(the eighty-page pamphlet *Vera i nauka*—"Faith and Science"—
Moscow, 1910), Lenin did not even trouble to make a rejoinder.

As Lenin had shrewdly suspected, Lunacharsky did, but Bogdanov did not return to his camp after the tactical and philosophical controversies had blown over. During the war, Bogdanov was an internationalist, which prompted Lenin, despite his previous anathemas, excommunications and thunders concerning the "kiss of Judas," to write Shlyapnikov in October, 1916, suggesting the possibility of a "new bloc with the Machists." (Lenin, Vol. XXXV, p. 185.)

After the Bolshevik seizure of power in 1917, in which he took no part, Bogdanov sought to serve the new society by founding and guiding the Proletcult movement. Driven out of this field by Lenin, he returned to his first love, the medical laboratory. He became founder and Director of the Moscow Institute for Blood Transfusion, a new field in which blood types and their importance had not yet been established. In 1928, because of his uncertainty as to the outcome, Bogdanov performed a blood transfusion on himself, and died in its course.

Bazarov served the new Lenin regime for many years in economic construction and planning, only to be framed up in one of the earliest of the show trials, the "Menshevik Trial" of 1931, whereafter he disappeared, no doubt dying in the purges. Valentinov, who scored third in condemnatory passages in Lenin's book, also served the Soviet Government in the realm of economic planning. Sent abroad with Piatakov in 1928, he is still alive in Paris, well up in his eighties, enfeebled in body, but young and vigorous in spirit. He has contributed a steady stream of essays, memoirs, pamphlets, dealing with Russian philosophical, political and economic thought in—rare virtue in these fields—a beautiful Russian prose. His "Vstrechi s Leninym" ("Meetings with Lenin") is the best closeup of Lenin's spirit that has been done by any one.

Lenin's book against Mach and these "Machists" created no stir when published. But after he came to power, and still more in the hands of his successors, it has acquired considerable influence in the history of contemporary thought. Published in enormous editions, translated into many tongues, it has been studied and cited by zealous disciples all over the world. In Russia it is now a basic text for the "training" of intellectuals and Party theoreticians. As Lenin used Engels, so the Leninists use Lenin: as a sword to slay the lurking dragon of "fideism"; as a "quotational shock treatment and chain reaction" to link up and overwhelm all opposition, dissent, or independent thought; as a thread to guide the faithful through the labyrinth of modern science and philosophy. It has been used as a reagent to test new doctrines in such diverse fields as relativity, atomic theory, psychoanalysis, genetics, cybernetics, and theoretical mathematics. Its exegesis of the philosophical insights of Engels and Marx stands today as a coarsening screen between official Russian Marxist thought and the more flexible, receptive, penetrating thinking of the founders of Marxism. On this exegesis by Lenin has been superimposed an exegesis of the exegesis by Stalin.[2] Thus do commentaries upon commentaries upon texts which have become scriptures continue to grow into a body of official state philosophy. Inevitably, where there is orthodoxy there must be heresy. And where the state enforces the orthodoxy, inevitably there must be the burning of heretical writings and autos-da-fé of the heretics. Not for nothing does purge suggest purification.

Lenin's angry moral tone, dim echo of anathema and excommunication, has become the model for the official polemical style employed in the most subtle fields of abstract thinking and scientific and philosophical discussion. Lacking Lenin's strong intellect and originality, lacking his "weakness" for a Gorky or a Lunacharsky, and possessing infinitely more power and zeal to enforce their anathemas and edicts of excommunication, innumerable disciples hurl their fragments of text and torrents of epithet. If we are to accept the aphorism—a little unjust to philosophy—which holds that "philosophy consists in asking questions, sophistry in answering them, and fanaticism in enforcing the answers," then Lenin's work, though intended as a blow against anti-rationalism and religious obscurantism, has been fated to serve a quasi-religious fanaticism of its own: developing into a state philosophy or a state faith, the faith of a state relentless, irreconcilable and omnipotent in "enforcing the answers."

[2] Stalin: *Dialectical and Historical Materialism.* First published as Chapter IV of Stalin's *Short History of the Communist Party of the Soviet Union,* and then reprinted as a separate work.

CHAPTER XXX

THE SPLIT BECOMES PERMANENT

> When the Central Organ was being discussed, I attacked its
> editors sharply because they forgot at times that *The Social
> Democrat* was not only written for the comrades abroad who
> knew all about the inner party fights . . . but mainly for
> the comrades in Russia. I quoted some unsigned passages
> from *The Social Democrat*, which made rude personal attacks
> on the representative from the Social-Democratic Party of
> Poland-Lithuania on the Editorial Board of *The Social Demo-
> crat*. I demanded to know who had brought such methods
> into our Central Organ . . . But just as I finished the quota-
> tion, I was called to order by the Chairman because of 'the
> uncomradely tone of my attacks.' He had not noticed that it
> was not my words but those of the quotation which I was
> reading. At this point Comrade Lenin rose to declare that
> the words in question were his. The Chairman became con-
> fused and the Party Congress broke into loud laughter.
> —*From Ossip Piatnitski's memories of the Prague Congress
> (1912).*

THE five years preceding World War I are largely a tale of splits
and spies. Lenin's enemies blame all the splits on his lust for
power or his "splitting mania," while his admirers attribute them
to his prophetic foresight. Since he was crowned by the Goddess
Success in 1917, runs their argument, everything he did before must
have been wise and right.

As we shall see, we cannot completely ignore Lenin's role as
"aggressor" in these splits—nor discount the secret intervention of
the police either. Yet the fact that the divisions affected all movements alike, even those with which Lenin had little or no connection, suggests that there must have been some wider social and
political meaning as well.

If the Bolsheviks split into three factions, so did the Mensheviks.
So did the Social Revolutionary Party. The Social Democratic Party
of Poland and Lithuania (Rosa Luxemburg's party) split into two
bitterly hostile parts, as did the Polish Socialist Party (Pilsudski's
party). Clearly, the defeat of 1905 had served to engender a split
atmosphere and bring out differences of political approach in a
previously undifferentiated revolutionary movement.

But if we examine the Polish splits, we arrive at unexpected

518

results. Both factions in the Social Democratic Party, as well as the Left Wing faction of Pilsudski's Polish Socialist Party, all joined Lenin and the Communist International after 1917! Yet, during the bitter years we are examining, they denounce one another with the fury of schismatics, schismatics who must have been very close to each other though each of whom fancied that his minuscule fragment of difference was truth's infallible touchstone. The Leading Committee of the Polish Social Democracy (Luxemburg, Tyszka, Dzierzinski, Warski, Marchlewski), located in Berlin, expels the "Warsaw Opposition" (Radek, Hanecki, Unschlicht, and others), charging them with being "Lenin's splitters," and "agents of the police." The aggressor is not Lenin but Tyszka, who ran his Leading Committee even more dictatorially than did Lenin his Bolshevik faction.

What must be our astonishment then to find Jan Tyszka (Lev Grozowski), under the name of Leo Jogiches, Rosa Luxemburg and Marchlewski among the founders of the Spartacus movement, which became the nucleus of the German Communist Party. Marchlewski in turn becomes a Soviet official and a founder of the Polish Communist Party, while Dzierzinski becomes the head of Lenin's secret political police, the Cheka or GPU! In short, those who voted to expel the "Leninist splitters" and "police spies" were so close to Lenin in spirit that when it came to the test of war and revolution they and he found themselves fighting side by side.

And "the Leninist splitters" whom they expelled also became their co-workers and Lenin's, Radek as chief journalistic spokesman for the Soviet Government and the Comintern, Unschlicht as Assistant Chief of the GPU of which his old opponent Dzierzinski was the Chief. This last fact provides another curious problem for us to consider: why so many Poles became high officials of the Soviet Secret Police. Besides the two top officials, Dzierzinski and Unschlicht, there was the Russified Pole of the Vperyodist Bolsheviks, Menzhinski, acting GPU Chief after Dzierzinski's death. Similarly, three members of the NKVD figure today as rulers of the new Poland: President Beirut, Commissar of Security Radkiewicz, and that silent figure who manipulates things behind the scenes, Henrykowski (real name Saul Amsterdam). We cannot pursue any further here the curious story of Poles in the Soviet Secret Police. What interests us for the moment is that all three Polish factions, the two wings of the Social Democracy, and the Left Wing of the Polish Socialist Party, are found fighting shoulder to shoulder with Lenin after 1917, from which we are forced to conclude that there must have been a good deal that was personal, artificial and atmospheric in their horrendous battles with Lenin and each other in the pre-war years. Actually, the generation of Luxemburg, Tyszka-Jogiches, Dzierzinski, Radek, Warski, Unschlicht, etc., provided the only group of political revolutionaries in Europe comparable to Lenin's group and spiritually close to it.

Leaving on one side the Polish quarrels and those that tore apart the Social Revolutionary Party, let us see if we can extract some political meaning from the splits in which Lenin was more directly concerned.

If we begin with the Bolsheviks, our point of departure is Lenin's expulsion of the Vperyodist Bolsheviks (Duma boycotters, recall-ists, ultimatists, "Machists" and "God-Creators") in 1909: Bogdanov, Lunacharsky, Polyansky, Alexinsky, Manuilsky, Pokrovsky, Men-zhinsky, and others less important to our story. Clearly this is a heterogeneous group, some of whom differed with Lenin mainly on theoretical matters, but all of whom differed with him on the tac-tical matter of the Duma. In the next few years, the Vperyodists split into two groups: a "Proletarian Culture" group (Bogdanov, future founder of the Proletcult; Lunacharsky, future Soviet Com-missar for Education; Polyansky, leading Soviet literary critic)—and an "Orthodox Marxist" group (Alexinsky, Manuilsky, Pokrov-sky and Menzhinsky). Since we have here not only the future Soviet cultural leaders but also a future Comintern leader (Manuil-ski, now "Ukrainian" delegate to the United Nations), and a future GPU leader (Menzhinsky), once more we are confronted with the fact that all these excommunicated heretics—with the exception of Bogdanov, who served the Soviet Government, and Alexinsky, who opposed it—find their way back to Lenin during the World War.

Still it is not as difficult as with the Polish factions to find some meaning in the split between Lenin and the Vperyodists. All of the latter differed with Lenin on a key tactical matter: their attitude toward the Duma. Hence we can reduce their various shadings to a common denominator: all are revolutionary romanticists reluctant to abandon the "pure revolutionary tactics" of 1905 and to utilize the narrow legal opportunities offered by the Stolypin constitution during the years of reaction. They are, therefore, but the one-sided extension of a major aspect of Lenin's more complex and flexible approach to armed uprising. This would explain why they came back to him in the years of direct revolutionary storm.

The question arises: why did Lenin choose to expel such sub-jectively loyal revolutionists, in place of taking his chances on persuading them, or persuading his faction against them, while permitting them to remain within it? The answer to this we find in Lenin's temperament, in the "orthodoxy-heresy" atmosphere of Russian political thought, in the bitterness of the years of reaction, in Lenin's conception of the nature of a faction, and, above all, in his fear that they might capture the group machinery or get in the way of its proper functioning. They were the more dangerous to him because the type of instinctively rebellious Russian workers to whom bolshevism appealed was easily influenced by this one-sided, romantic extension of a major aspect of that in Lenin which appealed to them most.

If we turn to the Mensheviks, we find them in the same year 1909 developing a tendency that is the symmetrically opposite pole to the Vperyodist Bolsheviks: namely, the Menshevik Liquidators. If the Vperyodists made a fetish of illegality and abhorred every effort at legal work in trade union or Duma, their Menshevik antipode was an analogous one-sided extension of the Menshevik zeal to seek opportunities for legal, open, public activity.

The new constitution permitted such activity: Duma elections and campaigns; parliamentary activity inside the Duma; the legal chartering of trade unions; and, after 1910, legal newspapers. To be sure, all this was circumscribed within rather narrow limits and often the new legalism was arbitrarily violated. Yet the opportunities were genuine and their scope slowly expanded.

Many advanced Menshevik workers became so engrossed in these union and electoral activities—particularly the former—that they began to feel that the underground party had outlived its usefulness. Its conspirative methods seemed to them now a handicap; it was honeycombed with spies; its illegal papers with their large phrases and negligible circulations provided pretexts for police raids and withdrawal of union charters. (The Bolsheviks were particular offenders in their carelessness about union legality and their zeal to distribute their illegal press directly through the unions). The efforts of the underground to control from secret places and even from abroad the activities of the legal organizations were so many violations of autonomy and democracy. "Abroad" was a breeding ground of bitter faction controversies that reached Russia muted, dim, divisive and unintelligible. It was time to "crawl out of the cellar hole" into the light of public life. "Liquidationism" was thus as natural and one-sided an extension of an important Menshevik aspiration of the Vperyodist trend was of Leninism.

Lenin was more ruthless than the other Russian leaders in his zeal to excommunicate heresies—in his own camp no less than in the opposing one. He seized upon this antipodal symmetry to proclaim his famous "war on two fronts": against boycottism and against liquidationism. Both movements led "objectively" to the "liquidation" of the kind of movement he thought necessary. He would expel both "the liquidators of the right and the liquidators of the left," and out of the remainder build a revolutionary socialist party which would know how to combine both legal and illegal work—but of course, under the control of the underground. Since Lenin was ready to expel those closest to him, he was in a particularly strong position for his struggle with Martov, who did not believe in expulsions, for Martov was, in Lenin's language, temperamentally a "conciliator." By his fight on two fronts, Lenin was aiming a blow not merely at the two opposed "deviations," but no less at the very core of menshevism, since the Menshevik faction as a whole was striving for a displacement of the main center of gravity from the illegal to a legal party.

On the surface, Martov and Lenin were close to each other. Each was for continuing the underground party, and each was for taking advantage of the legal opportunities afforded by Duma elections and the law of March 4/17, 1906, permitting the forming of legal trade unions. But as Martov conceived the underground, it was to be a mere skeleton apparatus held in reserve in the event of a forced relapse into complete illegality. To Lenin, on the other hand, the legal activities were always a skeletal affair, utilized to broaden the sphere of operations of the underground party.

As we know from his *What's to Be Done*, Lenin distrusted legal trade unions under any circumstances, fearing the independence they might develop and the "bourgeois ideology" they might generate. Hence, his conception of trade union work was largely limited to

> . . . utilizing the trade unions and other organizations, legal and semi-legal, in order to guarantee in them the predominant influence of Social Democracy and to transform them, as far as possible, into points of support of the Social Democratic Party.

He would have the underground build tightly disciplined secret "cells" or "fractions" within them to secure control and "the recognition by the unions of the ideological direction of the Social Democratic Party . . . the leadership of all activities of the unions by the Party."[1]

[1] *Collected Works* of Lenin, Third Russian Edition, Vol. XII, pp. 441, 447-48. For a complete study of Lenin's views on the trade unions, see S. Schwarz: *Lénine et le mouvement syndical*, Ed. Nouveau Prométhée, Paris, 1935.

Martov, on the contrary, regarded the trade unions and the party as two equally justified autonomous forms of the general socialist labor movement.

This distrust of the trade unions and limitation of trade union work largely to organizational and political control was to cost the Leninists dear in 1917. "We did not win the trade unions until after the October Revolution of 1917," Zinoviev was to record in his Party History of 1922. "Up till then the Mensheviks had the majority there." The "dictatorship of the proletariat" had to be set up in 1917 against the will of the majority of the organized proletariat!

An analogous difference of approach is observable in the attitudes of the two men toward the Duma. Martov was inclined to give considerable independent value to parliamentary activity. The Menshevik Deputies were generally men of high leadership caliber; the Bolshevik, with one exception to be noted later, were all simple workmen lacking in self-confidence on the floor of the Duma. The Mensheviks saw in the Duma faction democratically elected spokesmen of broad masses of workers, capable of forming a legal leadership for a broad, legal labor party. The socialist Deputies they thought, should operate as a largely autonomous fraction, guided, to be sure, by the program and major aims of the Party, but empowered to decide matters of policy and technique in their day-to-day activities without continuous dictation and instruction by the émigré underground executive committee. Lenin, however (who, except for the single year 1906-07, always managed to control that underground committee), felt that it should instruct the Social Democratic Deputies on all matters large and small, review and pass on all their speeches, motions, interpellations, projects of "law." Lenin and Zinoviev and Kamenev even wrote entire speeches to be delivered as their own by individual Deputies.

The Mensheviks held that their representatives in parliament should introduce actual legislative proposals in the interest of labor and of democracy generally. They should work, besides, for the independence of the Duma as a whole from the Tsar, for the creation of a cabinet responsible to the Duma, for an opposition bloc of liberals and laborites against reaction and absolutism. The Tauride Palace (where the Duma met) might even serve someday as a symbol and rallying center for the entire nation against the Tsar, much as the Estates General had served in the French Revolution. (It actually served so in March, 1917.)

But to Lenin, the Tauride Palace was only a vast sounding-board from which revolutionists, clothed with Deputies' mandates and parliamentary immunities, might expose this whole game of parliamentarism; expose too the liberals and Constitutional Democrats (Kadets) as "the main enemy of the revolution." The aim of their speeches and proposals inside the Duma was neither to secure parliamentary legislation nor to strengthen the Duma's powers, but to summon the masses to street demonstrations, strikes, and other forms of extra-parliamentary struggle. To parliamentary activities as such, Lenin always assigned an auxiliary, never an independent, value.

No sooner had Lenin expelled the Vperyodist Bolsheviks than a new opposition arose within his ranks: the "Conciliators" or, as they called themselves, the "Party Bolsheviks." They were opposed to his ruthless policy of split and expulsion. They were "conciliatory" not only toward the expelled Bolsheviks, but toward the Mensheviks, too. It was all very well, said they, to form factions and tendencies, argue for one set of tactics rather than another, and seek to get a majority for one's trend. But it was not all right to split the Party into two separate parties or sliver it into fragments. Repeatedly they restrained Lenin, got into the way of his driving energies, forced him into new unity gestures, temporary organizational compromises or retreats.

In January, 1910, shocked by the revelation that Lenin had been the secret guiding hand behind the Tiflis holdup, the "expropriation" of the heirs of the manufacturer Schmitt, and other exploits, they joined with Vperyodists, Mensheviks, Liquidators, and with Trotsky's "non-factional" group, against Lenin. The combination, expressive of the longing for all-in unity among ordinary Russian workers, forced him for a time to the wall. At the "united" plenary session of the Party Central Committee held in January, 1910, Vladimir Ilyich was on the defensive for three rage-filled weeks. He had to agree to burn the remaining five-hundred-ruble banknotes of the Tiflis holdup; he had to turn over the Schmitt money. He had to liquidate his faction paper, *Proletarii*, and agree to a new general Party paper, *Sotsial Demokrat*, with an equal number of Bolshevik and Menshevik editors: Lenin and Zinoviev, Martov and Dan, with a representative of the Polish Social Democracy, Warski, to break any deadlock that this parity editorship might get into. Trotsky's non-factional Vienna *Pravda* was declared an official Party organ: Kamenev was dispatched to assist him in editing it; and the Central Committee was instructed to provide it with funds. Lenin tried to turn the new bloc unity into a narrower "Leninist" political unity "against Liquidators and Boycotters" but in this, too, he was checked. He succeeded in getting the two "heretical" tendencies condemned in a resolution (Plekhanov deserting the Mensheviks for this purpose), but the Plenum voted to invite the Liquidators to participate in the life of the underground party and to name three of their number to the underground Central Committee.

How this "unity" looked to the temporarily cornered Lenin we know from a letter to Gorky of April 11, 1910—the first Lenin had written to him since the quarrels over the Otzovist-Machist-God Creators in 1908:

> In the plenum of the Central Committee ("the long plenum"—three weeks long the torture continued, all nerves went to pieces, a hundred thousand devils!) to the serious and deep-going forces making for unity . . . were added trivial and petty ones. There was a mood of "reconciliation in general" (without clear thoughts as to with whom? for what? how?). There was hate for the Bolshevik Center for its merciless ideological war. There was squabbling and, among the Mensheviks, the desire to make a scandal. And out of all this was born a child suffering from an abscess . . . Either we will lance the abscess, drain it, cure the child and bring it up. Or the child will die. Then we will remain childless for a while (that is: we will rebuild the Bolshevik faction) and then we will give birth to a healthier child . . .
>
> The Plenum wanted to unite *everybody*. Now the Golosites (Martovites) are backing out. This abscess *must* be removed. Without squabble, scandal, torture, filth, and scum, this cannot be accomplished. Here we are sitting now right in the midst of the thickest of the mess. Either the Russian Central Committee will clip the wings of the Golosites by removing them from the important posts (for example, from the Central Organ, etc.) or we will have to restore the faction . . . To sit in the midst of this squabble and scandal, torture and scum is nauseating. But it is unpardonable to yield to one's mood. Emigré life is now a hundred times more oppressive than it was before the revolution. Emigré life and squabbling are inseparable.
>
> But the squabbling will die away . . . The development of the Party on the other hand strides on and on through all the devilish difficulties of the present situation. The cleansing of the Social Democratic Party of its dangerous "deviations," of Liquidationism and Otzovism, strides undeviatingly forward; within the framework of unification it has *advanced significantly farther than before*. With Otzovism we finished, essentially, at the Plenum. With

Liquidationism we didn't; the Mensheviks managed to *hide the snake*, but now it is dragged out into God's light, now we will wipe it out and are wiping it out! . . .

Clearly, the Mensheviks did not yet know their Lenin after all the quarrels they had had with him. They had backed him into a corner at the Plenum. He was morally under a cloud. They had rallied a majority against him and for unity. But they did not use their majority as he would have used it. They did not remove him from the strategical posts. Not only did they misjudge him; they misjudged the Liquidators whom they were trying to protect against him. On Martov's motion and against Lenin's opposition, the Plenum had voted to invite the Liquidators to delegate three of their number to join the underground Central Committee in Russia. But to the Liquidators as to Lenin, the question of an underground party had become a question of principle—from opposite viewpoints. The three invited men flatly refused to have anything to do with his underground committee. ("We will not fall into that trap!"). That was all Lenin needed! "The snake has been dragged out into God's light. . . The Plenum decision has been violated," he cried, and reopened his "merciless war."

When the Bolshevik "Conciliators," who had a majority in Russia, proposed further negotiations with yet other Liquidator-leaders, Lenin ignored them. When Martov and Dan tried to write of their viewpoint in the *Sotsial Demokrat* (which they supposedly edited jointly with Lenin and Zinoviev), he barred its columns to them. (The Polish "arbitrator" Warski, voted with him, giving him a majority of three to two on the Editorial Board, so that the paper no longer represented a united party but only his tendency once more).

At the same time, Lenin sought to make unity with the Plekhanov wing of the Mensheviks, against the Martov majority and against the Liquidators. Plekhanov had been forming a separate grouping since 1909 because he, too, thought Martov too conciliatory toward the Liquidators. "My dear and much respected Comrade," Lenin now wrote to him in San Remo, Italy:

> I fully share your thoughts expressed in Number 11 of *Dnevnik* [*Dnevnik Sotsialdemokrata*—"Diary of a Social Democrat," Plekhanov's own paper], on the need for a close and sincere union between all true Social Democratic elements in the struggle against the Liquidators and Otzovism. I should like very much to talk to you about the new situation arising in the Party. If you think it necessary, too,

and if your health permits, write or wire a few words to me saying when you can arrange a meeting with me in San Remo. I am ready to go to you for that purpose. [Letter of March 29, 1910.]

The rapprochement with Plekhanov was brief and unhappy.

Plekhanov wrote dithyrambs to the underground. He abhorred the Liquidators. He wanted to defeat them, convince them, convert them—anything but expel them. To him they were, after all, advanced socialist workingmen who had "gone astray." Lenin, however, wanted to expel them at once. And not only them! He wanted to expel at the same time, Martov and all the Menshevik majority, who were guilty of "hiding and protecting" the Liquidators. And of course, he wanted to confirm the expulsion of his own private heretics, the Otzovist Bolsheviks. That would have left the Plekhanovites alone in the Party with the Leninists, a situation similar to the one Lenin had tried to bring about after the first split of 1903. Plekhanov had shrunk from it then. He shrank from it now. To cap the climax, Lenin and his supporters lost no time in using their contacts with the Plekhanovites to try to win them away from Plekhanov and his "party-loyal menshevism" over to complete bolshevism—the first example of a method of "uniting" which in later days was to become known under the name of the "united front from below."

All through 1911, a crucial year, Lenin drove steadily ahead toward his own kind of "unity"—unity of those who accepted his political line, which, as always, he was convinced was the only right one; under the leadership of the Central Committee he controlled, which he was convinced was the best possible leadership for the Party. Two events of the year 1911 assured the triumph of his solution of the Party crisis.

When Alexei Rykov, future Premier of the Soviet Union and at that time the outstanding leader of the "Party Bolsheviks" or "Conciliators," left for Russia to line up the Bolshevik faction against Lenin's splitting and expulsion activities, the police intervened. For reasons which will appear in the course of the next chapter, they had detailed reports on where everyone in Lenin's group stood politically, and they knew everybody's whereabouts. When Rykov left for Russia with good prospects of getting a majority for his position in the Bolshevik underground, the police picked him up immediately and prevented him from reaching Lenin's adherents. At the time it seemed a mere accident, one arrest like any other. But it left the "Conciliator" Bolsheviks under such inept, second-string leaders as Lozovsky (real name Solomon Abramovich Dridzo), whom we shall meet later as head of the Communist trade union international. He soon became sick of the squabbling and weary of the effort of opposing the implacably tireless Lenin. He gave up the struggle, concerning himself entirely with activity in the French trade union movement. The police helped to discredit the Conciliators by circulating a report to the effect that Rykov had been picked up with a number of addresses of members of the Russian underground carelessly carried on his person. Writes Krupskaya:

> Later this matter was cleared up . . . In Leipzig, where Piatnitsky was working on the shipping of literature to Russia, there lived a certain Brendinsky, who transported the literature . . . Later it was discovered that this Brendinsky . . . was an *agent provocateur*. He coded the addresses for Rykov. This explains why the police were in possession of all the addresses although nothing was taken from Rykov when he was searched.

The other decisive event of 1911 was an act of desperation on the part of Martov. Only a year ago, he had had a majority against Lenin at the January 1910 Plenum. That majority had voted for re-enlisting the Liquidators, for Party unity, for an equal co-editorship of the Party official organ by Lenin and Zinoviev, Martov and Dan. But they had forborne to remove Lenin from his posts so as "not to provoke a split." Now Lenin ignored the decisions of the Plenum; denied Martov space, even for an individual, signed article in the paper they were supposed to be editing jointly; drove ahead, under more favorable circumstances, toward a split in which he should remain in control of the official apparatus. In desperation, Martov tried to restore the favorable situation of 1910 by exposing once more, in more public fashion, Lenin's complicity in the revolutionary holdups, in the passing of stolen funds, preparations for counterfeiting, extortion from the Schmitt heirs. He published in Paris, in the Russian tongue, his detailed account of all he had been able to learn, insofar as it was already known to the police. The pamphlet, *Saviors or Destroyers*, with which the reader is already familiar, was intended to back Lenin into a corner once more and compel him to moderate his "implacable war." It served only to steel his will and widen the breach. The things Martov exposed seemed to Lenin good and right, if not in themselves, then in their origins (out of the armed bands) and in their sanctifying end, which for him justified all such means. But he was not likely to forgive their exposure, or find it possible to work together with the man who had made it. Kautsky, who in the International Socialist Bureau was working for the reunification of the splintered Russian Party, appraised the pamphlet as a provocation to the widening of the breach.

> We do not see, as you do—he wrote to the Vperyodist Bolshevik Lunacharsky—we do not see in Lenin and his supporters the cause of the split. In the actions of Lenin we see only an answer to the offensive pamphlet of Martov against him, which appears entirely senseless if it doesn't aim to force a split.

Plekhanov made the same appraisal. At the very least, Martov had made a blunder in trying to use the same weapon twice. Its positive effect was bound to be weaker the second time, and its more public use could but embitter further the strained relations in the émigré world and in the underground. Only if he were prepared to seek the expulsion of Lenin and his supporters from the movement, did it have practical sense. But such an expulsion was alien to Martov's thought. Moreover, it would have been only the obverse side of what Lenin was seeking at the moment.

Lenin's answer to this unintended declaration of war was the calling of an "All-Russian Party Conference." He ignored the protests of the Bolshevik Conciliators, and the very existence of the joint Central Committee of which he and Martov were members. As in 1904, he set up a new, rump "Organization Committee" of his own followers, and dispatched invitations to all the units of the Russian underground. As usual, his connections with that underground were superior to those of the other side, since his wife was Party Secretary, and since he had been in possession of the funds necessary to dispatch organizers and agents to the localities.

The Conference was held secretly in Prague, in the People's House of the Czechoslovak Social Democratic Party. But when the delegates arrived from the Russian underground, though they heard only Lenin's version of the splits and schisms, they were deeply upset. Before the Conference began, the first seven to arrive voted over his protest to send invitations to Plekhanov and his group of Party Mensheviks, to Trotsky and his non-factional faction in Vienna, and to others whom Lenin had quietly excluded. The invitations came too late, and were not accepted, which was all right with Lenin. Plekhanov wrote: "The makeup of your conference is so one-sided that it would be better, i.e. more in the interests of Party unity, if I stayed away." Trotsky wrote a long letter (which came too late for the Conference) in which he recognized the non-factional character of some of the delegations from the Russian underground, but urged that the makeup of the Conference was too one-sided, its manner of convocation too arbitrary, and that the way to Party unity lay through an agreement of all tendencies to join in a call for a common convention. Two Plekhanovites showed up, one to protest in Plekhanov's name, the other ripe for winning over by Lenin. The Poles and Latvians and other national border parties stayed away; the Martovites and Liquidators were not invited; the Conciliators were leaderless and in eclipse. Lenin was left alone with some unconditional followers, some waverers, and some uninformed delegates from the Russian underground whose desire for unity was no match for his driving desire for split.

With characteristic boldness, he persuaded the Prague Conference of 1912 to consider itself a "Congress of the Russian Social Democratic Labor Party" and to assume all the rights and functions of a Party congress. The old Central Committee was declared to have broken down and to have ceased its organized existence. The "Congress" elected a new one of Lenin, Zinoviev, Orjonikidze, Goloshekin, Spandaryan, Malinovsky and Schwartzman. The last named was a Plekhanovite who had been won over. The others were 100 per cent Leninists. Neither Rykov, who was in prison, nor any other Conciliator was included. No place was left for Martov or Dan, for Plekhanov or Trotsky or any of their adherents. This was to be a pure, "irreconcilable" Bolshevik Central Committee to speak in the name of the entire Party. The other factions, including even the Conciliator Bolsheviks, would have to submit or be read out. The alternates, too, who were to function in case of arrest of the regular members, were all Lenin's men: Bubnov (later to be Stalin's Commissar for Education); Kalinin (future President of the Supreme Soviet); Stassova (who would take Krupskaya's place as Secretary in 1917 when the affairs of the Bolsheviks became too big to remain in Mrs. Lenin's hands); and A. P. Smirnov.

As in the case of earlier central committees, or leading committees of the Bolshevik faction, Stalin's name does not appear. He had written to Paris a few months earlier, hinting at his desire to be a member and by now Vladimir Ilyich had a high-enough estimate of this daring and secretive agent to favor his candidacy. Moreover, Lenin was soon to assign a new and important task to him, that of presenting a non-Russian voice on the national question in Russia. But, he did not venture to propose Stalin's name to the Prague convention. Instead, he introduced a motion to return to the system of coopting additional members whenever the Central

Committee should see fit—a system which had fallen into disrepute in the more democratic mass party days of 1905–07. Shortly after the Prague Congress adjourned, Lenin had the new committee coopt Djugashvili and Belostotsky as members. Stalin's name never thereafter disappears from the lists of successive Bolshevik leading bodies. But neither then, nor at any subsequent time in his career, was his name to emerge victorious from any general election in which there was a real choice of candidates.

A curious example of the malleability of the past is exhibited in connection with the above. All Party documents published in Russia from 1917 to 1937 confirm the facts as just stated. Even as late as 1937, Volume XV of Lenin's *Collected Works* appeared under the editorship of Adoratsky, Molotov and Savelyev, with exactly the same story. A note on page 653 of the Third Russian Edition reads:

> At the (Prague) conference a C.C. was elected with the following composition: Lenin, Zinoviev, Orjonikidze, Schwartzman, Goloshekin, Spandaryan, Malinovsky. As candidates [alternates] in case of arrest of the members of the C.C. were chosen: Bubnov, Smirnov, Kalinin, Stassova. Shortly after the conference were coopted into the C.C.: Stalin and Belostotsky.

But shortly after Volume XV appeared with the above note, came the great blood purges. Then Stalin himself wrote a history of the Bolshevik Party in which he coolly set down an entirely new version of his and the Party's past.

> The Prague Conference—he wrote—elected a Bolshevik Central Committee of the Party, consisting of Lenin, Stalin, Orjonikidze, Sverdlov, Spandaryan, Goloshekin and others.

Gone was the name of Malinovsky, the *agent provocateur*. Gone the name of Zinoviev, who had appeared second in all Party documents because he was at that time Lenin's closest associate. Wherever, in Stalin's *History*, the words "and others" appear, there the reader may know that Stalin is simply suppressing retroactively the honors and historical services of the men he has since executed. Gone, too, is the information that Stalin was coopted only after the conference adjourned: in fact, retroactively, he is moved up to second place, immediately after Lenin. And gone are the names of the alternates, Bubnov, Smirnov, and Stassova. One (Stassova) has since been demoted to nonentity and two have disappeared in the holocaust of the purges. Therefore, Stalin's *History* reduces the list even as his fury did the survivors.

Before the Prague Conference adjourned, on Lenin's motion it read all the other factions out of the Party. Henceforward, to use the words Lenin employed in answering a query of the International Socialist Bureau, there would only be

> . . . a number of groups abroad which are more or less socialist, but which in any case are completely isolated from the Russian proletariat as well as from socialist work in general, and consequently are completely irresponsible . . . These groups can under no circumstances speak for or pass themselves off as the Russian Social Democratic Labor Party, nor does the Party take any responsibility for these groups. . . . All relations with the Party are to be undertaken only through the agency of the Central Committee elected at Prague . . .

That was Lenin's method of disposing of the Menshevik faction which that same year would be able to elect seven deputies to the Fourth Duma to Lenin's six. That was his method of disposing of Plekhanov, Axelrod, Martov, Trotsky, Chkheidze, Zhordania, or indeed anyone else who was unwilling to accept the rule of the self-proclaimed Central Committee. Thus was consummated a coup d'état, a seizure of power within the Party. As we shall see, it gave Lenin a decided advantage inside Russia, where the labor movement was beginning to bestir itself once more after five years of despair and depression.

Too late, all the other groups raged and stormed and called counter-conferences. Already they were in the ridiculous position of having to assert to the bewildered masses in Russia that "we too are part of the Party." Their chief effort, under the personal leadership of the professional non-factionalist, Leon Trotsky, was a conference of all other groups, called in August of that same year. To it were invited Bolshevik Conciliators, Bolshevik Vperyodists, Martovites, Plekhanovites, Liquidators, Trotskyites. But the "August Bloc," as it came to be known after the month of its assembling, began to fall apart as soon as it came together. Lenin knew what he wanted: he wanted to exclude them and run his own organization according to his own ideas. But they, what did they want? What did they have in common besides the desire not to be excluded from the Party which they had helped to build? Nor did they want Lenin to be excluded either!

Plekhanov refused to attend because he disliked Trotsky, who was the rallying center, because the Liquidators were invited, and because he thought it unseemly to have to demonstrate that he was a part of the party he had founded and whose very program he had written. The Poles refused to attend because they did not know which group to recognize and did not care to unite with a split Russian organization. The Petersburg Liquidators came in reluctantly because they wanted no ties with the old underground. The "Party Bolsheviks" or Conciliators were too close to Lenin tactically to be willing to attend. The Vperyodist Bolsheviks sent two representatives. One of them, Polyakov, who came from the police-ridden Moscow Bolshevik organization, seemed to have attended only with the intention of blowing up the Conference. He bided his time, then raised a rumpus, denounced the whole business for its "anti-bolshevism" and "factional character," and staged a demonstrative walkout. After the revolution it was revealed that he had been acting on the orders of the police to add to the splits and oppose Party unity. He was shot as a spy. The representatives of the Georgian Mensheviks, always a radical group, denounced the Liquidators present, Trotsky joining in the denunciation. The babel of voices and jangle of creeds were a poor counterweight to Lenin's resolute, close-knit organization.

The August Conference set up a provisional committee to unify the Party, but it served only as a battle ground for continuing the quarrels of all against each. There were quarrels between Trotsky and the Party Mensheviks and between both and the "Liquidators." In 1914, Trotsky finally broke away to form a new "non-factional" faction of his own and set up a new "non-factional journal for workers," the legal Petersburg paper *Borba* ("Struggle"). To list the contributors is to mirror the uncertainty and confusion of the moment: Lunacharsky, Radek, Kollontay, Pokrovsky, Polyansky, Trotsky, all of whom were to become Bolsheviks in 1917, along with men like Noah Zhordania, outstanding leader of the Transcaucasian Mensheviks, who was to become President of the non-Bolshevik Georgian Republic. Trotsky's *Borba*, during its brief life from February, 1914, until war broke out in July, attacked Lenin for his factionalism, the Liquidators for their liquidationism, the Martov Mensheviks for "doctrinaire legalism . . . opportunistic overestimation of the liberals . . . clique mentality . . . factional fanaticism." Verily, in the Russian movement the lot of the peacemaker was hard!

Late in 1913, the International Socialist Bureau took a hand to see if it could unify the faction-torn Party. In the Communist International that Lenin was to form later, the authority of such a bureau or executive committee would be so great that no party or faction could resist its orders on unification or anything else. The Communist International would dictate to its "sections" final decisions on tactics, on the rightness and wrongness of each faction, on the very personnel and composition of a given party's leading committee. What would have happened to Lenin and his methods if the Socialist International of that day had been able to exercise upon its Russian section the authority which the International he founded claimed over its affiliates?

Be that as it may, Lenin found it necessary in 1913 and 1914 to resist very circumspectly, albeit stubbornly, for the moral authority of the Socialist International was high among Russian socialists, and the longing of the Russian underground for unity was strong. He was determined that the split should continue, until the other factions accepted his tactics and the authority of the Central Committee he had set up in the Party's name at Prague. But he knew that in the end he would have to yield, unless he could make his opponents appear to have the responsibility for the prolongation of the split.

The International Socialist Bureau, for its part, tried persuasion rather than command. It sent delegates to the Russian foreign colonies scattered through Europe, to investigate, to take testimony, to ask proposals from all sides. Its chairman, Vandervelde, came to Saint Petersburg for three days in June, 1914. Then it called for an all-Russian conference in Brussels on July 17, 1914, and prepared to force unity at its next International Socialist Congress set for August in Vienna. In the last days of July of that fateful year, however, war broke out in Europe; the Congress was never held. Instead, differences on the war appeared in every section of the International. It was torn to pieces by them, Lenin becoming the chief driving force for promoting a split in all its parties and for the foundation of a rival body: the Communist International.

CHAPTER XXXI

THE CASE OF ROMAN MALINOVSKY

"At that time there was not a single local organization into which some provocateur had not crept. Every man regarded his comrade with suspicion, was on his guard against those nearest to him, did not trust his neighbor."—*G. Zinoviev:* History of the Communist Party of Russia.

LENIN had called his congress in the unaccustomed city of Prague to get away from the spies that seemed to be privy to every activity. To Anton Nemec, Czech socialist leader, he made the plea: "Everything must be kept *ultra-conspirative.*" Krupskaya personally examined each delegate, sending Brendinsky, whom she already suspected, on a wild goose chase to Brittany instead of Prague. The police took the hint, paying off their agent with a villa in a Paris suburb, costing forty thousand francs. But they were not too upset, for of the fourteen delegates coming from the Russian underground, two more, Romanov from Tula and Malinovsky from Moscow, were their men. Agent Malinovsky so captivated Lenin that he emerged a member of the new Central Committee and returned to his superiors with the exciting news that Lenin wanted him to run for the Duma.

If we were to list only the more important spies that had so far entered intimately into the life of Vladimir Ilyich, that list would include Gurovich, who financed the first legal Marxist organ, *Nachalo,* with police funds; the surgeon dentist N. N. Mikhailov, who turned in Ulyanov, Martov and the other organizers of the underground League for Struggle at the end of 1895; Dr. Jacob Zhitomirsky, who, as Lenin's confidential agent in Berlin, made the arrangements for Kamo and his case of dynamite, for Krassin's counterfeit banknote paper, and for Litvinov's and other arrests in connection with the disposal of the five-hundred-ruble notes of the Tiflis holdup. So well did he work that Lenin continued to consider him as a "man of confidence," to be used for the most delicate tasks. After the Berlin arrests, Zhitomirsky moved "for safety" to France, whence he visited Geneva in 1909 to urge Vladimir Ilyich to move to Paris, "a large city where there will be less spying." Writes Krupskaya: "The argument was convincing to Ilyich." Thus the shadowed moved in order to be closer to his shadow.

535

In 1911, Zhitomirsky finally fell under suspicion, but it was not his chief who suspected him. Lenin received a warning from Vladimir Burtsev. Now warnings from Burtsev were no small matter, for he was a self-constituted, one-man, counter-espionage agency. As some collect coins or stamps or feminine conquests, he collected spies. He it was who had shortly before exposed the incomparable Azev, director of the Fighting Section of the Social Revolutionary Party. Yet so sure was Lenin of his most trusted agent that he ignored the warning.

A revolutionary bloodhound by vocation, Burtsev, once he had scented a spy, was not to be put off the trail. By 1913 he had gathered so much evidence that he sent Lenin an ultimatum. He would create a public scandal if trust were not withdrawn from this man. "If my charges are false, let him haul me before a revolutionary tribunal. There he will prove his innocence or I my charges."

Alarmed at last, Lenin sent another "man of confidence" to take up the Zhitomirsky matter with Burtsev, and, at the same time, to discuss the whole problem of combatting the spies with which the Bolshevik movement was now obviously infested. The man whom Lenin sent was Roman Malinovsky!

Malinovsky questioned Burtsev with strained interest. Who in the police or the government was giving him his secret tips? what reasons had he for suspecting Dr. Zhitomirsky? how could the Bolsheviks judge the reliability of such grave charges unless they were given the sources? what other Bolsheviks did he suspect? Insistently, Malinovsky pleaded that Burtsev communicate "in strict confidence" his sources in the government. For his part, Burtsev had not the slightest reason to suspect his interlocutor, whom he knew as a prominent trade unionist, as a member of the Central Committee which the Bolsheviks had just set up allegedly as the Central Committee of the entire Party, and as the newly chosen chairman of the Bolshevik fraction in the Fourth Imperial Duma. Yet an old habit of caution and a respect for confidences caused him to withhold the names of the officials.

> I will give you two or three names of agents in your midst—he told the Duma Deputy with a pardonable flourish. —Check them. Check the names of people arrested and their last contacts with men I name. If you are successful, I shall speak further . . .

In 1917, when the Tsar fell and the Provisional Government opened up the police archives, they found proof that Zhitomirsky had been a spy during all the years he enjoyed Lenin's confidence.

This, of course, was no surprise to Burtsev. But what did startle him was the realization that Malinovsky (whom he did not even begin to suspect until the end of 1916) had come to him that day on a double mission, charged simultaneously by Vladimir Ilyich and by the director of the Russian Police, S. P. Beletsky, with the task of finding out which spies Burtsev knew of in the Bolshevik faction, and from what governmental personages he derived his tips concerning these most jealously guarded secrets of the police. How deep must Malinovsky's personal interest have been in learning Burtsev's secret, and knowing what revelations or whose turn was coming next!

Before we go on with our story, we must note a version, less flattering to Burtsev, of his interview with Malinovsky. The account we have just given is Burtsev's own, but from the well-informed Boris Nikolaevsky, biographer of Azev, who had many interviews with Burtsev, I got an account less favorable to the famous counter-espionage specialist. According to Nikolaevsky, Burtsev did not come to suspect Zhitomirsky as a result of his own investigations, but merely received a tip, couched in general terms, that someone very close to Lenin was a police agent. The tip came from Syrkin, a liberal official high in the Moscow Okhrana, who offered to give details to someone whom he could trust. Thereupon, Burtsev wrote to Lenin asking him to come himself or send a man of absolute confidence, to whom he would divulge an important secret. When Lenin sent Roman Malinovsky, Burtsev confided to him that Syrkin of the Moscow Okhrana would give him the name of a police spy close to Lenin. Malinovsky took no chances. Instead of going to Syrkin, he reported the latter's offer to the chief of the Moscow Okhrana. Syrkin was dismissed from his post and exiled to Siberia.

What follows has been reconstructed by me from the police archives as published by the Provisional Government of 1917 and by the subsequent Soviet Government, and from the testimony of Roman Malinovsky's Party and police superiors before the Extraordinary Commission of the Provisional Government which investigated the Ministry of the Interior and its police in 1917.

Among those who testified before the Extraordinary Investigating Commission were former Minister of the Interior Makarov; Assistant Minister Zolotarev; the latter's successor, Assistant Minister Junkovsky; Police Director Beletsky; Assistant Director Vissarionov; Chief of the Moscow Okhrana Martynov; and other lesser officials. Citizens Burtsev, Ulyanov (Lenin) and Radomyslsky (Zinoviev) were summoned to testify before a special subcommission on the Malinovsky case. All the testimony before the main investigating commission was stenogrammed and subsequently published by the Soviet Government in a seven-volume work called *The Fall of the Tsarist Régime*. The testimony of Citizens Ulyanov and Radomyslsky before the subcommission were not so published, but I have been able to reconstruct the text from contemporary accounts in the daily press: *Pravda* (Bolshevik), *Rabochaya Gazeta* (Menshevik), *Den* (Liberal), and *Vestnik Vremennago Pravitelstva* (Official News Bulletin of the Provisional Government). Fortunately, this last contains a fair amount of direct quotation in its issue of June 16, 1917, the accuracy of which is confirmed by the reports in the other dailies, including Lenin's *Pravda*. Other sources are the writings of Burtsev, personal reminiscences of men who knew Malinovsky, and documents summarized from memory by Boris Nikolaevsky, who was director of the Historical Archives of the Russian Revolution in Moscow during the years 1919-21, that is, under the Soviet Government at a time when Lenin was alive and active in the leadership of its affairs. Except where otherwise noted, the source is always the seven-volume publication by the Soviet Government of the stenogram of testimony before the Extraordinary Commission of the Provisional Government.[1]

From these sources we can reconstruct the amazing life and deeds of Roman Malinovsky, as well as the political line pursued by the Police Department in the Bolshevik Faction, the Duma and the Social Democratic Party. For, as is characteristic of Russian officials, the Department had a definite political line.

Roman Vatslavovich Malinovsky was a Russified Polish workingman of peasant stock, born in the Plotsk Province of Russian Poland in the year 1878. When he met Lenin at the Prague Conference of 1912, he was thirty-four, robust, ruddy complexioned, vigorous, excitable, a heavy drinker, a rude and eloquent orator, a gifted leader of men. In the closing years of the preceding century he had been convicted several times of common crimes, the third offense being that of burglary ("robbery with breaking and entry"), for which he had served a prison term from 1899 to 1902. The police noted that he was a heavy spender. Though he earned a living first as tailor and then as metal turner, his wages were never sufficient

---

[1] *Padenie Tsarskogo Rezhima, po materialam Chrezvychainoi Komissii Vremennago Pravitelstva. Stenograficheskie otchety doprosov i pokazanii dannykh v 1917 g. v Chrezvychainoi Sledstvennoi Komissii Vremennago Pravitelstva. Gos. Izdat.* Leningrad, 1924-27.

for his expensive tastes. In his youth he had worked for a while in Germany, then returned to Saint Petersburg. Here he entered the labor movement, probably in 1902, with a perfect background for the role of police informer.

How early he became a regular agent is unclear. For years his chief source of income was his wages as a metal worker, while he used his police connections only to pick up a bit of extra cash. When he thought he had something which would interest them, he would telephone, or send in a written report signed *Portnoi* ("Tailor"), for which he would be paid a sum like twenty-five or fifty rubles. Even after he became a professional agent with a regular salary, he did not become a "professional revolutionist"— his usefulness consisted in his continuing to be a worker at the bench. He himself was to confess to the Bolsheviks, and the police confirm it, that one of his motives was always the ambition to rise to a place of prominence in the revolutionary movement. This ambition felt a double spur: the higher his advancement, the more he meant to the police and the higher the sum they set on the value of his services.

In 1906 he was one of the founders of the Petersburg Metal Workers Union. In 1907 he became its secretary, serving till the end of 1909. Here he steered a careful course between Bolsheviks and Mensheviks. The former were more interested in control and political leadership of the union, the latter in the preservation of its autonomy. Therefore, as an active unionist, he inclined to the Mensheviks. In 1908 he successfully resisted an attempt of the Bolsheviks to capture his union, but, after he went over to them completely, he helped them to win control. Zinoviev, who met him while he was its secretary, testified to the Extraordinary Commission that he thought him to be "rather a Menshevik," and the Mensheviks had the same opinion.

Five times he was arrested for his activities, either by police who had no inkling of his role, or because he was at a meeting which he himself had betrayed, where everybody had to be taken in. His early reappearance on the scene after each arrest was so managed as not to excite suspicion. A typical arrest was that of late November, 1909. He had tipped off a secret caucus of the labor delegates to an impending anti-alcoholic congress and was present when it was raided. Released in January, 1910, he was exiled from Saint Petersburg to avert suspicion from him. This ended his secretaryship of the Petersburg union, but he immediately turned up in Moscow in the spring of 1910, where he was welcomed by the entire labor movement and was able to report to the police on every phase of it. On the rolls of the Moscow Okhrana he appears as of March, 1910, no longer as a "piece worker," but with the regular salary of fifty rubles a month, plus expenses. In addition, of course, to his wages as a metal turner.

The police had come to the conclusion that the chief danger to the régime was the possible unification of all opposition forces against it:

> Malinovsky was given the order to do as much as possible to deepen the split in the Party. [Testimony of Police Director Beletsky, Stenogram Vol. III, p. 281.]
> I admit that the whole purpose of my direction is summed up in this: to give no possibility of the Party's uniting. I worked on the principle of *divide et impera*. [Ibid., p. 286.]

Since this political aim coincided in an essential respect with that of Lenin, Malinovsky was now instructed to take the earliest possible opportunity to come out as a Bolshevik and to attach himself as closely as possible to the Bolshevik leader. Police Director Beletsky testified that, in view of this important mission, he freed his agent at this time from the further necessity of betraying individuals or meetings (though not from reporting on them), as arrests traceable to Malinovsky might endanger his position for the more highly political task. It was the easier for the police to make this exemption since they had by now advanced their men to a number of key posts in the Bolshevik underground, including the headship of the Moscow organization itself, which had just been taken over by agent Kukushkin, aided by the spies Romanov, Poskrebuchin and Marakushev. The agents ascended quickly in the Party hierarchy by the simple expedient of arranging the arrest of incumbents, persons who suspected them, and others who stood in their way.

But Malinovsky seemed to enjoy denunciatory work, and, despite, the exemption, continued it. Indeed, he could not resist one more grand coup before he went to the Bolsheviks. As a leading official of a legal trade union, he was highly esteemed by the "Liquidators" who set their hopes on legal unions and the legalization of other mass activities, and found Lenin's underground a hindrance. Malinovsky helped with the conference which was to plan the fight for legality, then tipped off Police Chief Beletsky to raid the planning committee. Most of the "Liquidators" were bagged and their hopes ended for some time to come. Thus the police aided Lenin against the "Liquidators," while agent Brendinsky was clearing another obstacle from Lenin's path by arranging for the arrest of the Conciliator Bolshevik Rykov. In the retrospective light of the 1917 police testimony, all of Lenin's and Malinovsky's subsequent polemics against the Liquidators as "police agents," "police unionists," and "advocates of a police labor party" make strange reading indeed. Beletsky's testimony on the raid on the Liquidators is confirmed by a note in the official edition of Vol. XVII of Lenin's *Collected Works:*

> Malinovsky clearly did not break with the Liquidators completely. He took part in a conference of their supporters, and played his hand in such fashion that the conference, called by them for the fall of 1911, was raided by the police. At that time a suspicion arose in a narrow circle of Moscow workers and Social Democrats who were in contact with Malinovsky . . . but the rumors concerning him soon died down.

About the same time, Malinovsky learned that Lenin was summoning a Party conference too, at which he was to "remove" the Central Committee regularly elected by the last united party congress, and set up in its place a Bolshevik-dominated central committee. The conference, as we know, was held in Prague in January, 1912. Malinovsky appeared as the representative of the Moscow trade unions and of the Bolshevik underground political organization, of which his fellow-agent Kukushkin was the head. Lenin had of course heard of this well-known trade unionist, newly won from menshevism. As we know, he was so taken with the convert that Malinovsky was elected to the new Central Committee, and was urged to become the Party's standard-bearer in the contest for the Moscow deputyship.

A police spy with a record of convictions for common crimes as a Duma Deputy—the idea was so audacious that the highest authorities had to be consulted. Now Beletsky met with his agent only in private rooms of fashionable restaurants. He claims that he took his agent in person to see the Minister of the Interior, consulted with the Assistant Police Chief, the Assistant Interior Minister, the head of the Moscow Okhrana, the Governor of Moscow, Junkovsky. The testimony of these persons before the Investigating Committee of the Provisional Government is often contradictory. It is probable that Junkovsky, when he claims not to have known, was telling the truth, for it was he who finally caused the dismissal of Malinovsky. In any case, many in high place knew the secret.

Interdepartmental communications on the subject were now so

cautious that they no longer referred to their agent by his old pseudonym of *Portnoi*, but each used such circumlocutions as "the personage of whom I spoke to Your Excellency on such and such occasion."

Both police and Bolsheviks set to work with great energy to secure their candidate's nomination and election. The newly founded daily *Pravda*, the Bolshevik apparatus, and—what proved more important—the whole machinery of the Department of the Interior and its police were mobilized to further Malinovsky's fortunes. The first hurdle was his criminal record. The Ministry saw to it that he got the necessary "certificate of good repute" from local authorities in his native province. Next, all the more popular of his possible rivals were eliminated by the simple expedient of throwing them into jail. This included the most likely candidate of the Moscow workers, Krivov.

As election day approached, Malinovsky reported that a hostile foreman was planning to fire him from his factory. The electoral system provided for workingmen to vote by secret ballot in their factories, where they chose delegates to the next higher nominating body, which in turn chose electors for the Workers' Curiae of the Provincial Electoral College, where actual selection of Deputies was made. (Thus neither voting in the factories nor indirect elections are Soviet inventions, as is so widely believed, but were inherited from tsarism.) But no workingman was eligible to vote or to be chosen as delegate, elector, or Deputy unless he had worked in the given factory for the six months preceding the election. The Police Department came to their candidate's rescue once more by throwing the astonished foreman into jail, releasing him after the elections with the explanation that the arrest had been "an unfortunate mistake." (Neither in Tsarist nor in Soviet Russia has there ever been any recourse against officials for false arrest.) Aided by such campaign methods, the Bolshevik and police joint candidate swept all before him. The Department showed its appreciation of his advancement in the secular world by raising his salary from fifty rubles a month to five hundred. It was the first time that any police spy ever got such princely salary. And this was now supplemented not by a metalworker's wage but by a Duma Deputy's.

> *For the first time* among ours in the Duma—wrote Lenin in a letter full of the underscorings with which he showed his excitement—there is an *outstanding* worker-*leader*. He will read the Declaration [the political declaration of the Social Democratic fraction on the address of the Prime

Minister]. This time it's not another Alexinsky. And the results—perhaps not immediately—will be *great*. . . .

The Fourth Imperial Duma, to which Malinovsky was elected, began its term in late November, 1912. It was to be a long Duma, destined to continue in being until the Revolution of 1917 thrust power into its reluctant hands. Its thirteen Social Democratic Deputies (seven Mensheviks and six Bolsheviks) formed a single Fraction, for the split which Lenin had started abroad at the Prague Conference at the beginning of that year had not yet taken effect inside Russia. The Fraction chose Chkheidze, Georgian Menshevik and leader of the Georgian revolutionary armed forces in 1905, as chairman, and Malinovsky as vice-chairman, and commissioned the latter to read the first political declaration.

Lenin was highly displeased with this unity in the Duma Fraction, for, as long as it endured, here was an authoritative and conspicuously public leading body around which the longing for unity inside Russia might crystallize, as against the Prague (Bolshevik) Central Committee. So strong was "conciliationism," i.e. the mood for unity, that the six Bolsheviks had gotten elected only by pledging themselves to work for a united party. Thus the entire bloc of Deputies lent their names as contributing editors both to the Bolshevik legal daily, *Pravda*, and the Menshevik daily, *Luch*, and four of the six Bolsheviks even signed a call for the fusion of the two papers. Indeed, from reading them, one could not then deduce any very good reason for their remaining separate, for Lenin was having great trouble with his editors. *Pravda* had been founded on the eve of the election campaign to take advantage of the increasing liberality of the government with reference to the press. The better to direct it, Lenin had moved from Paris to Cracow in Austrian (Polish) Galicia, only a day and a night by express from Saint Petersburg.

Despite the closer contact, *Pravda* continued to assume a "Conciliator" attitude in response to the popular mood inside Russia. It went so far as to censor, mutilate, or suppress Lenin's articles where they sought to sharpen the fight against Mensheviks, Liquidators, Bundists and Vperyodists.

> Vladimir Ilyich was so upset when from the outset *Pravda* deliberately struck out from his articles all polemics with the Liquidators . . . Ilyich became nervous, wrote irate letters to *Pravda*, but they did not do much good . . . [writes Krupskaya].

Here are excerpts from some of his "irate letters":

> We received a stupid and impudent letter from the Editorial Board. We will not reply. They must be kicked out . . . We are exceedingly upset by the absence of plans for reorganizing the Board . . . Better yet, complete expulsion of all the veterans . . . They praise the Bund and *Zeit*, which is simply despicable. They don't know how to proceed against *Luch*, and their attitude toward my articles is monstrous . . . [Letter of Jan. 12, 1913.]
>
> We must kick out the present editorial staff . . . Would you call such people editors? They aren't men but pitiful dish rags, who are ruining the cause. . . . [Letter of Jan. 20.]

And to Gorky:

> And how did *you* happen to get mixed up with *Luch???* Is it possible that you are following in the footsteps of the Deputies? But they have simply fallen into a trap!

At the time these angry letters were written, Stalin was in Saint Petersburg and Molotov was secretary of the Editorial Board. The fact that they were on the receiving end of these bursts of anger probably explains why Stalin's recent *History of the Communist Party of the Soviet Union* eliminates all traces of the quarrel.

As early as December 18, 1912, that is to say a few days after the Duma Fraction was organized, the astute Malinovsky was able to report to his superiors the news that he would be able to split the Fraction and would have Lenin's support for this purpose. On that date Assistant Police Director Vissarionov wrote to the Minister of the Interior:

> The situation of the Fraction is now such that it may be possible for the six Bolsheviks to be induced to act in such a way as to split the Fraction into Bolsheviks and Mensheviks. Lenin supports this. See his letter.

The letter referred to, a copy of which Malinovsky supplied to Vissarionov, was one Lenin had written a few days earlier to "Vassiliev" (the name then being used by Stalin). It had been written in invisible ink between the lines of a commercial letter to an official of the Russian Bank for Foreign Trade.

> If all of our six are from the Workers' Curiae—said the secret writing—they cannot silently submit to a lot of Siberians. The six must come out with the sharpest protest if they are being majorityized (*mayoriziruyut,* i.e. being overriden by the seven), they should publish a protest in *Pravda* and announce that they are appealing to the ranks, to the workers' organizations.

This was to be the gist of Lenin's argument and of Malinovsky's strategy for disrupting the united Fraction. Malinovsky of Moscow, Badaev of Saint Petersburg, and the other Bolsheviks from Tula and lesser centers, all six in short, had been chosen by the Workers' Curiae, ran Lenin's argument. Not one of the Menshevik Deputies had come from a Workers' Curia, thus the Georgian Mensheviks, for example, had been elected by the entire Georgian population. Therefore the Bolshevik six must be regarded as representing a majority of the working class and the Menshevik seven a minority. They were not representatives of the industrial working class, but "a lot of Siberians." It was a curious foreshadowing of the argument of 1918 concerning the superior representative character of the Soviets as against the Constituent Assembly.

Finding Malinovsky able and willing ("the other Bolshevik Deputies," writes Krupskaya, "were shy, but it was quite obvious that they were good, reliable proletarians"), Lenin left to him the task of finding pretexts for leading the Bolshevik Duma group toward an open break with the Mensheviks, while he himself turned his attention to *Pravda*. He called Stalin to Cracow to instruct him on the matter, and sent Jacob Sverdlov, his best organizer, to Saint Petersburg to whip the editors into line. Soon he was able to write gratefully to Sverdlov:

> Today we learned about the beginning of reforms on *Pravda*. A thousand greetings, congratulations and good wishes for success . . . You cannot imagine how tired we are of working with a completely hostile editorial staff. [Letter of Feb. 8, 1913.]

Malinovsky dutifully reported the arrival of Sverdlov. He hid in Duma Deputy Petrovsky's home, but was arrested when he left there to "move to a safer place" (Feb. 10, 1913). Thereupon Lenin dispatched Stalin to Saint Petersburg, now fully prepared to carry out the splitting or "irreconcilable" line. On March 13, after confiding his plans for that night to Malinovsky, Stalin went to a concert for the benefit of *Pravda*, where he too was arrested. Both Sverdlov and Stalin were sent to Siberia. This time they stayed, all through the war, until released by the Revolution of February, 1917.

Next Kamenev was sent to take charge. The mood of Lenin's household when Kamenev left is reflected in this passage from Krupskaya's memoirs:

> We all—Inessa Armand, the Zinovievs, Krupskaya and Lenin—went to the station to see them off . . . We spoke very little. Every one was wrapped up in his own thoughts.

> We all asked ourselves how long Kamenev would hold out,
> how soon we should meet again? When would we be able
> to go to Russia? Each of us secretly thought about Russia;
> each of us had a strong desire to go. Night after night I
> would dream of the Nevsky Gate [a suburb of Saint Peters-
> burg]. We avoided speaking on the subject but all of us
> secretly thought about it . . .

Unexpectedly, Kamenev's stay was made legal by an act of the
government: an amnesty for all "literary political" offenders, decreed
to celebrate the three-hundredth anniversary of the founding of
the Romanov dynasty. So, instead of turning Kamenev in, Malinovsky provided him with excellent copy by fiery denunciation of his
Menshevik fellow-Deputies. The new line found a willing supporter
in the new editor-in-chief of *Pravda*, Miron Chernomazov, another
police agent. In October, 1913, Lenin expressed his satisfaction to
Kamenev on *Pravda*'s line:

> Here everybody is satisfied with the newspaper and its
> editor [doubtless, Kamenev is meant, for he was the real
> behind-the-scenes editor]. In all this time I haven't heard
> a single word of criticism.

And Lenin had every reason to be satisfied. The Duma Fraction
had split at last. The mellow mood of conciliationism had vanished.
Pravda was engaged in daily "merciless and irreconcilable war"
with both Menshevik tendencies (now all lumped together as
"Liquidators"), the Bundists, and the Trotskyite "non-factionalists."
Most of the Vperyodists had abandoned their independent standard
and either gone over to Trotsky's league of party-unity advocates
or had returned, repentant, to the Leninist fold.

The police, too, were satisfied. Yet this business of having the
Bolshevik leader of the Duma on their payroll was bringing its
complications. First, there were his speeches. He was undeniably
eloquent and forceful. Sometimes Malinovsky wrote them himself
and sent them to his two chiefs, Lenin and Beletsky, for approval.
At other times Lenin or Zinoviev or Kamenev drafted them, or
even wrote out whole speeches in detail. These, too, were sent to
Police Chief Beletsky for his opinion. In the police files were found
drafts in Malinovsky's hand, with amendments in the handwriting
of both Lenin and Beletsky, as well as drafts by Lenin, Zinoviev
and Kamenev. Realizing how popular their Deputy was, the police
tried to cut out some of the most "subversive" passages. But Malinovsky had difficulty following instructions. In reading the first

declaration of the Fraction, he managed to eliminate an offending passage on "sovereignty of the people" by pretending to get rattled and skipping an entire page of his manuscript. But *Pravda* and *Luch* next day followed his original script. When his speeches were attacks on the Liberals, Constitutional Democrats (Kadets), or Mensheviks, the police were glad to give him full rein. Sometimes he tried to substitute a belligerent "revolutionary" fight with Duma Chairman Rodzyanko for the delivery of the speech itself, thus managing to get himself interrupted and denied the right to continue. Yet, on the whole, the Leninist régime so closely limited the autonomy of a Deputy and of the Duma Fraction that the police had little success in modifying his speeches. Without doubt he enjoyed both roles and there must have been moments when he thought of himself as a Bolshevik doublecrossing the police rather then a police agent spying on the Bolsheviks. So Azev had become confused as to his double role, and Father Gapon, and the Bundist police agent Kaplinsky, who as the "Azev" of the Bund plotted many acts of terror and denounced many terrorists to the police, but conscientiously refused to inform on a single member of the Bund! And so Dmitri Bagrov, who murdered Stolypin under such circumstances that it could never be disentangled whether it was on the order of revolutionaries, on the behest of some other official, or to avenge the pogroms against Jews for which Bagrov, wrongfully, held Stolypin responsible. There was something in the Russian temperament and scene that engendered these men of ambivalent spirit and double role, these Gapons, Azevs, Kaplinskys, Bagrovs, and Malinovskys—figures without parallel in the police and revolutionary movements of other lands.

Another complication was the danger of exposure. Some official high in the Ministry of the Interior or the Police was privy to the arrangement and did not like it. From the outset, this still today unknown personage tried to communicate with the socialist "underworld" without revealing his identity. When Malinovsky was elected, *Luch* received an anonymous warning on his role. A year later the wife of Theodor Dan received a letter telling her that a high police official wanted to see her in confidence, and that she could signify acceptance of the appointment by a code advertisement in a stipulated newspaper. Both warnings were ignored.

When Bukharin, living in Vienna, learned of Malinovsky's election, he wrote to Lenin that he had escaped from exile in 1910 only to be seized again in Moscow, suspiciously, right after a meeting with Malinovsky. He was puzzled by the angry tone of Lenin's answer: there was a dark campaign of slander being waged against this wonderful Bolshevik; if Bukharin joined it, Lenin would brand him publicly as a traitor. He desisted.

Then there were the February and March, 1913, arrests of Elena Rozmirovich (Mrs. Troyanovsky), Sverdlov and Stalin. Acting on a hunch, Troyanovsky wrote from abroad in a "shot-in-the-dark" letter to his wife's relatives in which he said that he knew who had caused her arrest: "a man playing a double role." If she were not freed, he would make an exposure which would "stagger society." As Troyanovsky had calculated, the police opened the letter. Director Beletsky testified in 1917 that when he had shown the letter to Malinovsky the latter had "become hysterical" and demanded her release as a condition for serving the Department further. She was released.

To ward off suspicion, Malinovsky declared at a meeting of the Central Committee that "someone close to the Duma Six was a person who had police connections." The axe fell on agent Miron Chernomazov, already under investigation, in February 1914, he was quietly removed from the editorial board of *Pravda*. He had been its editor-in-chief while Malinovsky was its treasurer. The latter position enabled the Duma Deputy to turn in copies of the paper's balance sheet, and a complete list of the names and addresses of all who contributed money. On the other hand, he held meetings, raised funds for the paper, contributed himself from time to time—amounts which he always added to his Police Department expense accounts. These sums the police more than recouped when they levied fines on the paper, in one case a fine of five hundred rubles for an article written by none other than Duma Deputy Malinovsky.

During all this time he was practically a commuter between Cracow and Petersburg. Aided both by police and Bolshevik underground, it was easy for him to cross the frontier. Lenin summoned him at every important juncture, giving him entry into the most highly confidential meetings, when the only other persons present were Lenin and Krupskaya, Zinoviev, and Kamenev. The Police Department received full transcripts of the decisions taken, all Lenin's most secret acts and plans. Every biographer and historian owes a debt to these complete and competent police reports for the period. Malinovsky went on joint lecture tours with Lenin to all the Russian colonies in emigration. Together they attended a secret congress of the Lettish Social Democrats and another of the Finns. He was entrusted with setting up a secret printing plant inside Russia, which naturally did not remain secret for long. Together with Yakovlev he "helped" start a Bolshevik paper in

Moscow. It, too, ended promptly with the arrest of the editor. Inside Russia, the popular Duma Deputy traveled to all centers. Arrests took place sufficiently later to avert suspicion from him. Thus a Bolshevik "Conciliator" group headed by Miliutin disappeared, as did the regular Bolshevik organization in Tula and other local bodies. The police raised his wage from five hundred to six hundred, and then to seven hundred rubles a month.

On the 8th of May, 1914, Roman Malinovsky handed in his resignation to the Chairman of the Duma, Rodzyanko, "for reasons of health," and the same day left the country. He had notified neither Central Committee nor Duma Fraction nor constituents. The amazement at this inexplicable action was enormous. At each session of the Duma, whenever a Bolshevik arose to speak, the reactionary Deputy Markov would cry out with intentioned malice: *"But where is Malinovsky?"*

The leaderless Fraction—for the others were smallish figures who had let him guide the day-to-day struggle with the Mensheviks—reviewed the events leading up to his disappearance in an effort to find a key to the mystery. Recently he had been quick-tempered, more so even than usual. He had complained of his health, and of wearying with "mere parliamentary means of struggle." On April 22, the new Chairman of the Council of Ministers, the reactionary Goremykin, aroused a storm in the Duma by warning the Socialist spokesman, Chkheidze, against using the Duma for radical attacks on the government. Deputies pounded their desks; Chkheidze and Chkhenkeli had to be dragged out by guards; both Social Democrats and Trudoviks were suspended by Chairman of the Duma, Rodzyanko, for fifteen days. Malinovsky tried to persuade the ousted deputies that it would be "shameful to return to the Duma." But on May 7, he returned with the rest of the Deputies. One by one they attempted to read into the minutes a statement of protest, and one by one they were silenced and declared out of order by Chairman Rodzyanko. When Malinovsky got the floor, he seemed to be beside himself. He refused to be silenced, continuing to shout until the sergeant-at-arms was called to remove him from his seat. Again he urged all Left deputies to resign and "appeal to the people." Next day he went to the astonished Rodzyanko and handed him his resignation.

That same day, Chairman Rodzyanko received a visit from Assistant Minister of the Interior Junkovsky, who informed him, "in strict confidence," that the departed Deputy had been a police agent and had been ordered to resign to avoid a possible scandal. Rodzyanko was told that he might inform the Presidium of the Duma, but that the secret should go no farther, or the good name of the Duma itself would be compromised. The last police entry on Malinovsky was a dismissal bonus of six thousand rubles to start life anew abroad.

Now *Luch* remembered its old anonymous letter. Rumors swirled around the corridors of the Tauride Palace and soon the entire press was speaking of "dark police complications." But when Lenin's friend Bonch-Bruevich, as correspondent of the Kharkov daily *Utro*, sent a dispatch of the same tenor to his paper, he received a sharp telegram from Lenin categorically denying the allegation. For the ever reckless Malinovsky, despite the peril of his situation, had gone straight to Lenin in Cracow!

There he had given several contradictory "political" and "personal" versions of his flight. Then, on closer questioning, he had "confessed" that in his youth he had been sentenced for an attempt at rape, which fact the police now threatened to expose if the most useful of the Bolshevik Deputies did not resign from the Duma. While Lenin was pondering this, the Menshevik and Liquidator press arrived with their reports of rumors that the Bolshevik leader had been a police spy. Martov and Dan raised the question: was it not factionalism itself that enabled unreliable elements to rise so high in the Party? They demanded a non-factional or multi-factional Party tribunal to investigate the case, political and personal, of Roman Malinovsky. For Lenin, and for his faction now representing itself as the Social Democratic Party, the situation was fraught with potential disaster. To accept the proposal of Martov and Dan was to recognize that the "expelled" Mensheviks were still part of the Social Democratic Party. And what a weapon against bolshevism would be provided by the thought that its outstanding spokesman, its leader inside Russia, the driving force of its campaign to split the Duma Fraction, was a police agent! What universal demoralization if this man who knew everybody, had traveled everywhere, had had in his hands all connections, all secret lists of members, sympathizers and contributors of funds to *Pravda*, should turn out to be a spy!

In the name of the Party (i.e. the Bolshevik) Central Committee, an investigating commission was immediately set up. It consisted of Lenin, Zinoviev, and Hanecki, a Polish Social Democrat of the Warsaw Opposition and a close supporter of Lenin's. No Mensheviks were included. This commission heard testimony from Malinovsky, from Bukharin, who reiterated his old charges, from Mrs. Troyanovsky, who told the circumstances of her arrest and release, and testified that her interlocutors had shown knowledge of matters which, in her judgment, only Malinovsky could have told them. Burtsev was asked his opinion. He answered that he thought the Duma Deputy a "dirty fellow but not a police agent."

Bukharin's reminiscences of that difficult moment were published in *Pravda* on January 21, 1925, one year after Lenin's death:

> I distinctly hear Ilyich walking downstairs. He does not sleep. He goes out on the terrace, prepares tea, and up and back he strides on the terrace. He strides and strides, stops and again strides up and down. Thus the night passes. . . .
>
> Morning. I go out. Ilyich is neatly dressed. Under his eyes are yellow circles. His face is that of an ill man. But he laughs gaily, the accustomed gestures, the accustomed sureness:
>
> "Well, what do you say, did you sleep well? Ha, ha, ha! Good. Want tea? Want bread? Let's go for a walk?" Just as if nothing had happened. Just as if there had not been a night of torture, suffering, doubt, cogitation, tense mental effort. No, Ilyich had donned the mail of his steel will. Was there anything that could break it?

That night, sentimentally remembered by Bukharin, Lenin decided to exonerate Malinovsky of the main charge against him, and to pronounce Martov and Dan "malicious slanderers." When Bukharin's reminiscence appeared in 1925, Martov's paper took it to mean that Lenin, during that tortured night, had knowingly decided to defend a police spy and attack his accusers out of cold factional calculation. But the passage we have quoted is capable of another interpretation: that Lenin had succeeded in convincing himself of the truth of the rape story and the falsity of the police agent charge. Which interpretation is correct? Let us examine the available evidence.

> Vladimir Ilyich thought it utterly impossible for Malinovsky to have been an *agent provocateur*—records Krupskaya—These rumors came from Menshevik circles . . . The commission investigated all the rumors but could not obtain any definite proof of the charge . . . Only once did a doubt flash across his mind. I remember one day in Poronino [the summer residence of the Ulyanovs where the trial took place], we were returning from the Zinovievs and talking about these rumors. All of a sudden Ilyich stopped on the little bridge we were crossing and said: "It may be true!"—and his face expressed anxiety. "What are you talking about, it's nonsense," I answered deprecatingly.

Ilyich calmed down and began to abuse the Mensheviks, saying that they were unscrupulous as to the means they employed in the struggle against the Bolsheviks. He had no further doubts on the question.

"These rumors came from Menshevik circles . . ." Here was the key to Lenin's reaction. The Bolshevik press adopted a resolution condemning Malinovsky for "indiscipline . . . desertion of his post . . . disorganizing departure . . . a crime which placed him outside the ranks of the Social Democratic Party." And condemning "the Liquidators" (Martov was now always treated as a Liquidator too) for "hurling dirty and malicious slanders at the former Deputy, like the Rightist press which spreads slanderous rumors in order to bring confusion into the ranks of the workers."

In the Bolshevik theoretical organ, *Prosveshchenie* ("Enlightenment"), Lenin published a long article directed not against Malinovsky but against Martov and Dan, under the title: "The Methods of Struggle of Bourgeois Intellectuals Against the Workers."

In it Dan and Martov are denounced as incurably gossipy old women who live for scandal ("like insects that defend themselves by secreting an evil-smelling fluid"). They are worse than "the other Liquidators." Martov's famous pamphlet against Lenin, *Saviors or Destroyers*, is retroactively denounced as another example of this "impermissible, dirty, slanderous method." To the proposal for an impartial court of investigation, Lenin answered:

> We *do not believe one single* word of Dan and Martov. We *will never* enter into any "investigation" of dark rumors in which the Liquidators and the grouplets which support them may take part . . . If Martov and Dan, plus their concealers, the Bundists, Chkheidze and Co., the "August Bloc People," etc., directly or indirectly invite us to a common "investigation," we answer them: we don't trust Martov and Dan. We do not regard them as honest citizens. We will deal with them only as common criminals—only so, and not otherwise . . . If a man says, make political concessions to me, recognize me as an equal comrade of the Marxist community or I will set up a howl about rumors of the provocateur activity of Malinovsky, that is political blackmail. Against blackmail we are always and unconditionally for the bourgeois legality of the bourgeois court . . . Either you make a public accusation signed with your signature so that the bourgeois court can expose and punish you (there are no other means of fighting blackmail), or you remain as people branded . . . as slanderers by the workers . . .

So far had the atmosphere been embittered since the Unity Congresses of 1906 and 1907! The main steps toward this impasse had been the exposure of Lenin's responsibility for the revolutionary robberies (Martov's *Saviors or Destroyers*, 1911), Lenin's seizure of the Party apparatus at the Prague Conference (January, 1912), the maneuvers of Lenin and Malinovsky to smash the unified Duma Fraction (December, 1912, to October, 1913), and now the rumors that the Bolshevik Duma leader was a police agent. Lenin did not have enough faith in Martov and Dan as fellow Social Democrats to sit on a common committee with them. He refused to recognize either of them "as an equal comrade of the Marxist community." This embitterment, this factional momentum, was one of the incalculable component forces entering into the final split of 1917. Even the fact that Martov became a Menshevik Internationalist and Lenin a Bolshevik Internationalist could not bring them together during the World War, which both opposed.

A sifting of the evidence still leaves doubt in our minds. Did Lenin believe Malinovsky's story of an early conviction for attempted rape, and the resignation of his mandate under threat of exposure? Or did he decide "on balance" that a spy could still be useful?

> One feels ashamed for mankind—wrote Lenin on June 4, 1914—when one sees how a man's personal misfortune is utilized for a struggle against an opposing political tendency.

That was a little over a month before the war began. Lenin's treatment of Malinovsky during the war, when the latter was an obscure prisoner in a German prison camp, demonstrates his conviction of the ex-Deputy's innocence of the spy charge. Lenin sent him reading matter and material for agitation among the other Russian prisoners. Krupskaya sent him food parcels, took care of his laundry and clothes and performed other services that had no political meaning beyond that of personal comradeship. Late in 1916 (two or three months before his exposure) the Bolshevik paper *Sotsial Demokrat* publicly stated that Malinovsky had been "fully rehabilitated" by his subsequent conduct, for his past crime of "desertion of his post."

> I did not believe—testified Citizen Ulyanov before the Extraordinary Investigating Commission of the Provisional Government—in provocateurship here, and for the following reason: If Malinovsky were a provocateur, the Okhrana would not gain from that as much as our Party did from

Pravda and the whole legal apparatus. It is clear that by
bringing a provocateur into the Duma and eliminating for
that purpose all the competitors of bolshevism, etc., the
Okhrana was guided by a gross conception of bolshevism,
I should say rather a crude, homemade (*lubochnii*) caricature. They imagined that the Bolsheviks would arrange
an armed insurrection. In order to keep all the threads of
this coming insurrection in their hands, they thought it
worth while to have recourse to all sorts of things to bring
Malinovsky into the Duma and the Central Committee. But
when the Okhrana succeeded in both these matters, what
happened? It happened that Malinovsky was transformed
into one of the links of the long and solid chain connecting
our illegal base with the two chief legal organs by which
our Party influenced the masses: *Pravda* and the Duma
Fraction. The *agent provocateur* had to serve both these
organs in order to justify his vocation.

Both these organs were under our immediate guidance.
Zinoviev and I wrote daily to *Pravda* and its policy was
entirely determined by the resolutions of the Party. Our
influence over forty to sixty thousand workers was thus
secured . . . [*Vestnik Vremmenago Pravitelstva*—News
Bulletin of the Provisional Government, June 16, 1917,
p. 3.]

As always, to Lenin a gain for the faction was equivalent to a
gain for "our Party" and for "the revolution." Whether he was right
in calculating that the split in the Duma was a gain, or whether the
police were right in thinking it a loss to the revolutionary movement, we must leave to the reader to decide as he considers the
events of the year 1917. At any rate, the police were so convinced
of the desirability of a split that the loss of Malinovsky's services
and the simultaneous alarming news that the International Socialist
Bureau was calling a new unity conference of all Russian factions
caused the police chief to issue a general circular of instructions
to all his subordinates and secret agents. Beletsky was no longer
police head, and Assistant Minister Junkovsky was now the deciding force, yet the political line of the police remained the same.
The circular read:

Information received from political agents points to a
tendency recently exhibited within the ranks of the Russian
Social Democratic Party toward the unification of the different factions . . . In view of the exceptional gravity of this
intention and the undesirability of its taking place, the
Police Department considers it necessary to . . . impress

upon their secret agents the necessity for participating in the various Party conferences, there to insist, firmly and convincingly, upon the utter impossibility of any such fusion, particularly the fusion of the Bolsheviki and the Mensheviki. [Russian text in *Rabochaya Gazeta*, April, 1917; English text in Kerensky: *The Crucifixion of Liberty*, John Day, 1934, p. 246; also in Gankin and Fisher: *The Bolsheviks and the World War*, Stanford University Press, 1940, p. 106.]

The last act in this strange drama of Roman Malinovsky occurred in November, 1918, when Lenin had been in power for a full year. On November 2, reckless adventurer to the end, Malinovsky crossed the Russian border and turned up in Petrograd. For three successive days he visited the Smolny Institute (Bolshevik headquarters), demanding either to be arrested or taken to see Lenin. On the third day, Zinoviev saw him and ordered his arrest. He was taken to Moscow for trial. The Bolshevik Krylenko, who was later to conduct so many prosecutions until he himself disappeared in a purge, was appointed as prosecutor. He knew the defendant well since he too had reason to believe that one of his arrests by the tsarist police was Malinovsky's work. The trial was swift and secret. But the workers' organizations of Moscow sent deputations to attend, for they feared that Lenin might exonerate their ex-Deputy once more.

Accounts of the trial are confused and sometimes deliberately confusing. But from Bolshevik memoirs, and the writings of Burtsev, we are able to reconstruct some scenes of this last act of the drama. A trick of fate put Burtsev in jail in the same cell as ex-Police Chief Beletsky, when the latter was testifying at Malinovsky's trial. Another important source was Malinovsky's old colleague, the Bolshevik Duma Deputy, Badaev. Where Badaev and Burtsev (in *Struggling Russia*, I, No. 9-10) agree, we are likely to be on firm ground.

Malinovsky's bearing at the trial was proud and challenging. He demanded that Lenin be summoned as a witness. According to some accounts, this was refused. But the Bolshevik Olga Anikst, in a memoir in Vol. IV of the series "About Lenin" (*O Lenine*), published by the official Gosizdat (Moscow, 1925, p. 93), tells how she watched Lenin closely during the trial. All through it his head remained bowed, and he took notes. But when the defense counsel in his summary said that if Malinovsky had had friends to guide him properly, he would never have become a spy, Lenin looked up at Malinovsky and emphatically nodded his head. If so, it was his only testimony.

Malinovsky asserted that Lenin must have known of his role after his resignation from the Duma. He had further tried to tell Lenin that his past was "filled with abominations," but Lenin had refused to listen, saying that for Bolsheviks these personal misdeeds of his youth had no meaning. Did not Lenin know that the police had a hold on him? Still Lenin had permitted him to rehabilitate himself in a German prison camp, and the Bolshevik organ, *Sotsial Demokrat,* in December, 1916, declared that he had been "fully rehabilitated."

> The best period of my life was the two and one-half years which I devoted to propaganda among the Russian prisoners in Germany. I did a great deal during that time for the spread of the ideas of Bolshevism. [From Burtsev's article]

And Badaev writes:

> He alleged that he was forced to become an *agent provocateur* because he was already completely in the hands of the police. He represented his career as a long martyrdom, accompanied by suffering and remorse from which he could not escape . . . He tried to prove that he left the Duma of his own free will because of personal unhappiness, and that he obtained permission from the police to quit politics . . . He adopted a pose of sincere repentance while admitting the gravity of his crimes.

A notable procession of witnesses testified in the trial: ex-Police Chief Beletsky; ex-Assistant Chief Vissarionov; ex-Minister of the Interior Makarov; ex-Deputy Minister Junkovsky; former Duma Deputies Badaev and Petrovsky; and many of the Bolshevik men and women whom he had betrayed to the police. Both Junkovsky and Beletsky were asked leading questions tending to elicit "proof" that his activities had benefited the Bolsheviks and "the Revolution" more than the police. Beletsky agreed to this, but Junkovsky answered with dignity that he was "an honest monarchist and that he could not enter into a discussion of that question." (Account of Burtsev.)

How much did Lenin know of Malinovsky's past? How well did he understand what manner of man he was using in the German prison camps, in disregard of the accusations of the Mensheviks, of Bukharin and Rozmirovich, and the scandal of his resignation from the Duma? According to Gorky, Lenin said that he had been able to see through Alexinsky, but not through Malinovsky. At the first meeting with Alexinsky, Lenin said:

> 'I had a feeling of physical repulsion to him. I couldn't conquer it . . . I had to use every method to keep myself in check . . . I simply couldn't stand this degenerate.' Then,

shrugging his shoulders in amazement, he said: 'But I never saw through that scoundrel Malinovsky. That was a very mysterious affair, Malinovsky.' (M. Gorky, *Lenin* Centrizdat, Moscow, 1931, pp. 45-46.)

It was indeed. And so, for all the memoirs and analyses, it remains. Why did Lenin exonerate Malinovsky in 1914, against the evidence and against the world? Why did he rehabilitate him in 1916? Why did Malinovsky return to Russia when Lenin was in power? Did he count on Lenin? Why did Lenin then not lift a finger to save him?

Malinovsky's closing words at the trial, according to Badaev, were a profession of sincere repentance and devotion to the Revolution, a reminder that he had returned voluntarily to Bolshevik Russia.

And according to Burtsev:

When the Revolution triumphed in Germany and Russia and the possibility of participating prominently in political activities was lost to him forever, he decided to go back and die, rather than to flee into the obscurity of an Argentina or a similar place of refuge. Of course, he could have committed suicide, but he preferred to die in the view of everybody, and had no fear of death.

The verdict was "death." Malinovsky was shot that same night, shortly after the trial ended, at 2 o'clock in the morning. Was there a special reason for the speed?

Until the archives of that period are opened, if they still exist, the only certain verdict in the Malinovsky case is the single sentence of Lenin to Gorky: "That was a very mysterious affair, Malinovsky . . ."

Even that sentence, in the course of Stalin's great *operation palimpsest*, vanished from subsequent editions of Gorky's memoirs. And the new writings on the palimpsest by Nikita Sergeevich have not restored it.

CHAPTER XXXII

WAR CLOUDS

"Only war can again open up the question before the people in its entire scope . . . and draw the land into a period of revolutionary events earlier than seems now conceivable."
—*Martov in 1909*

"A war between Austria and Russia would be a very useful thing for the revolution, but it is not likely that Franz Joseph and Nikolasha will give us that pleasure." —*Lenin in 1913*

O N NEW YEAR'S DAY, 1912, Vladimir Ilyich told his sister Anna: "I do not know whether I shall live to see the next rising of the tide." Yet, even as he spoke, the ebb had ceased. Once more Russia's amazing capacity for industrialization was making itself felt: rails laid down; factories springing up; workingmen gaining confidence to make new demands. As in the past, five years had been enough to produce a new generation. The students and workers who had been children in 1907, the peasants fresh from the villages to man the new factories—what did they know of old defeats, old disputes, old hatreds and allegiances? The Mensheviks, resting secure in their predominance among the older, more experienced, organized workers, suddenly learned that a new working class had to be won all over again. It is a lesson that established institutions and ideologies are forever forgetting.

> Now, when a new historical situation offered the masses the possibility of advancing again—wrote the Menshevik party-historian Dan—they appeared on the political arena not only with the same revolutionary mood . . . but with the same revolutionary naïveté.

That spring, in April, some fourteen hundred miles from the nearest railway in the northern wilderness of Siberia, the miners in an English-owned gold mine on the Lena River, protesting concerning the rotten food, were fired on by troops. As the shocking news filtered through to the capitals, intellectuals found their voice again; university halls rang with speeches; the dispersed working class reformed its ranks.

Lenin's luck was with him. He had just finished the job of oust-ing ultra-Leftists, suppressing Conciliator Bolsheviks, seizing the Party label at the Prague Congress. Now he could speak in its name to innumerable workers who had never heard of bolshevism and menshevism, while his surprised opponents were in the ridiculous position of pleading: "we too are of the Party."

> The "Liquidators"—wrote Dan—who till then had believed that their purposeful labor in the years of stagnation would secure for them a position of advantage in the reviving movement, saw to their astonishment that their monopoly position was shattered by these same illegal Bolshevik circles which they had regarded as "living corpses." Now they strove with all their might to accomplish their political consolidation and catch up in all haste with the tasks neglected during the preceding years.

And the underground Mensheviks, weakened by the defection to legal work of these same Liquidators, found that they had no machine to match the single-minded, power-concentrated machine of Lenin.

At that crucial moment, manna fell from heaven into the hands of Vladimir Ilyich. The millionaire Kazan merchant, Tikhomirnov, had recently died, leaving four sons. The oldest continued his business, the second became an actor, the third and fourth joined the little group of Bolshevik intellectuals who were secretly meeting for study and propaganda in the sleepy university town of Kazan. The group's leading figure, Adoratsky, would one day under Stalin become director of the Marx-Engels-Lenin Institute, and would take in the youngest Tikhomirnov as assistant. But our concern is with the third son, Victor (born 1889), who, having received his inheritance, one fine day dropped in on Vladimir Ilyich to offer him one hundred thousand rubles for the purpose of founding a legal Bolshevik daily.

For some time it had been clear that not the rigor of censorship but lack of funds was the chief obstacle to a legal daily paper. The Stolypin Government had entered upon a phase of moderate reforms. Duma elections continued to be held. All opposition parties were permitted to put up candidates (the "higher democracy" of the single ticket had not yet occurred to anyone) and to put out printed matter concerning the electoral issues. The countryside was being rapidly transformed into a system of small farm peasants. Liberty of movement within the country and the right to leave the country were granted more freely than they had ever been before or—after 1917—would ever be again. The number of schools were growing rapidly and the campaign against illiteracy was taking on

serious proportions. The year 1912 saw the enactment of an insurance law against sickness and accident, providing two-thirds to
three-quarters pay, covering virtually all industrial workers. The
workingmen themselves elected their delegates to the insurance
councils.

The year 1913 saw a general amnesty for political offenders in
connection with the three-hundredth anniversary of the founding
of the Romanov dynasty. Martov, Dan, Kamenev returned to Russia
to live there openly and legally. If Lenin did not, it is because he
did not choose to. Trotsky and Stalin were ineligible because they
had escaped from Siberia and had unfilled terms to serve.

In short, the Stolypin constitution, as Lenin assured his romantic
ultra-Leftist followers was a moderate, but "by no means a cardboard or comic opera constitution," and Stolypin was really bent
on reforming and transforming Russia in accordance with his vision
of a modern state. It has become a conventional legend since to
pronounce this time a period of unalloyed reaction, but all signs
pointed to a peaceful, if leaden-footed, progress.

All signs, that is, except the war clouds over the Balkans and
the creeping degeneration at the summit of society: the Court.
There, after Stolypin's assassination, ever more doddering and in-
competent advisers were brought in, under the influence of the
camarilla around the strong-willed, narrow-visioned Tsarina and
her Man of God, Rasputin. But Lenin could not count on war,
though he fearfully hoped he might, nor was he aware of the
progressive paresis in the palace.

> We are fighting better than our fathers fought—he wrote
> frankly in an article on abortion.—Our children will fight
> better still than we, and *they will win.*

This article he published in the new paper he had just founded
with "angel" Tikhomirnov's money. His weekly, *Zvezda,* had been
appearing since December, 1910, and his monthly, *Prosveshchenie,*
since the fall of 1911. Now he set up a daily in Saint Petersburg,
which he called *Pravda* ("Truth"). The name would become world
renowned.

Victor Tikhomirnov became the behind-the-scenes business manager (see Lenin's citation of his reports on finance and circulation in Vol. XVII of the *Collected Works,* pp. 417 ff. and 510 ff).
From Kazan, the "angel" brought with him another local youth,
a year younger than himself, the student Vyacheslav Mikhailovich
Scriabin, to become secretary of the Editorial Board. Young Scriabin
wrote a number of articles experimenting with such unimagina-

tively close pseudonyms as Riabin, then the more poetically proletarian *Prostota* ("Simplicity") and *Molotov* (from *molot*, "hammer"). The aptness of these two names has since received universal
recognition.

The Board of Editors and the mass of Party members and readers
were overwhelmingly in favor of socialist unity. Lenin stood almost
alone in his determination to sharpen the polemical line of the
paper, compel it to fight with the other factions, force a split in the
Duma Fraction and everywhere in Russia. To oblige the paper to
follow his line, Lenin personally wrote controversial articles, which
the editors discreetly censored, blue-penciled or suppressed. Lenin
was infuriated. He wrote threatening letters. He called conferences
of Duma members and Central Committee members in Cracow.
Finally he kept Djugashvili, the Central Committee member then
in charge of *Pravda*, abroad for several months, while he sent
Sverdlov, his best organizer, to Saint Petersburg "for the purpose of
reorganizing the Editorial Board and correcting the line of *Pravda*"
(*Collected Works*, Third Russian Edition, p. 696).

As secretary, it was young Scriabin-Molotov who had to receive
all the furious rebukes. Yet all the editors were responsible. And no
less so the Central Committee member, Djugashvili-Stalin. "During
that period," read the memoirs of Duma Deputy Badaev, "Stalin
ran *Pravda*." Savelyev says the same, as do all the Stalinist Party
histories. When Lenin summoned him to work in Cracow and
Vienna on the national question, and sent Sverdlov to reorganize
the Board, he showed, as always, his ability to "correct" a useful
Party worker without humiliating him or destroying him. Vladimir
Ilyich knew how difficult it was to gather capable people and train
them. So soon as one who had opposed him yielded, his anger
vanished and he had care to save the man's pride and reputation.
If his future "best disciple" had but learned this primary skill of
the art of leadership, the purges of the thirties might have been
avoided.

Once more, because Stalin's relations to Lenin are involved,
literary detective work is necessary to uncover the real outlines of
the controversy with the Editorial Board. Volume II of Krupskaya's
memoirs, already heavily censored, still contains some traces:

> It was necessary to wage a determined struggle against
> the Liquidators. That is why Vladimir Ilyich was so upset
> when *Pravda* at first deliberately struck out from his articles
> all his arguments in opposition to the Liquidators. He wrote
> angry letters . . . [p. 91.]
> Sometimes his articles would be held up . . . This irri-

tated Ilyich and he wrote angry letters to *Pravda* but this
did not improve matters . . . [p. 115.]

Many of these letters have been suppressed, nor are they likely
to appear while the present historiography continues. But enough
were issued before the retroactive revision of the past had begun,
so that we can reconstruct the outlines of Ilyich's unremitting
struggle to force his paper to adopt an irreconcilable split line.

Late November, 1912, Lenin wrote to Stalin urging that the
"Bolshevik Six" in the Duma "come out with a very sharp protest"
against their seven colleagues in the Social Democratic Fraction.
Apparently Stalin did not answer, or the answer has been suppressed. But the real answer came shortly thereafter in the pages of
Pravda itself, in the startling shape of a resolution signed by all
thirteen Deputies, urging the fusion of the Bolshevik *Pravda* with
the Menshevik *Luch*, because "the unity of the Social Democracy
is an urgent need!" And, on December 18, four of the six Bolshevik
Deputies put their names on the masthead of *Luch* as contributing
editors, while *Pravda* displayed the names of all seven Menshevik
Deputies as contributing editors! "As on all other occasions," comments Deputy Badaev cautiously, "our decision was made in agreement with those Party circles with whom we had occasion to discuss
our activities . . ." If we are to believe Stalin's own claims that he
was directing *Pravda* at that time, "those Party circles" meant in
the first instance Central Committee member Djugashvili. It was
at this point that Lenin called a Central Committee conference in
Cracow and insisted that Stalin should make the journey.

No sooner had he left Saint Petersburg than Lenin trained his
heaviest artillery on Editorial Secretary Molotov-Scriabin, and what
was left of the Board. Apparently Molotov must have tried to answer
back, for on January 12, 1913, Lenin wrote the furious letter
already quoted (see page 544) in which he called the answer
"stupid and impudent" and proposed the firing of all the "old-
timers." A week later (on January 20) he wrote:

> . . . we must plant our own editorial staff in *Pravda* and
> kick the present one out . . . Can you call such people
> editors? They are not men but miserable dishrags and they
> are ruining the cause.

The text of these letters can be found in various places, among
them Trotsky's *Stalin*, pp. 146-7. In the third Russian edition

of Lenin's works, Volume XVI (published in 1937 under the editorship of Molotov, Savelyev and Bukharin) one can still find them paraphrased in the notes (pp. 695ff). But in Volume XXIX published the same year by Adoratsky, Molotov and Savelyev, which contains the letters of 1912-13, they are missing without a trace. In the Fourth Russian Edition of Lenin's works it is as if they had never been. The poet's dream "that we might catch ere closed the Book of Fate, and make the Writer on a fairer leaf inscribe our names," has become the principle of present-day historiography.

It was the young secretary of the Editorial Board, Molotov-Scriabin from Kazan, who silently took the abuse and the blame, though Stalin in his *History* takes the credit, for "initiating" and guiding the paper during this period. Between the Central Committee director and the Editorial Board secretary a bond was thus forged that has never since been broken. Molotov then and there attached himself to Stalin, the most important Party functionary he knew, as others might attach themselves to Lenin. As long as Vladimir. Ilyich was alive, Molotov was never highly valued, receiving only second-string posts. In the unanticipated first revolution of 1917, Molotov again happened to be the only one available in Petrograd to edit *Pravda*. Again the line he took infuriated Lenin. An "incurable dumbbell," Vladimir Ilyich pronounced him. Others, who had to work more closely with Molotov, taking note of his dogged stubbornness and intellectual immobility, dubbed him *Zheleznii Zad* ("Iron Backside"). But when Lenin was dead and all his closest comrades had been hurried to their graves, the pseudonym of Stalin's first faithful lieutenant, along with the man's immobile obstinacy, would become known to diplomats throughout the world.

Other editors of *Pravda*, besides Stalin, Sverdlov and Kamenev, who were the successive Central Committee overseers, and Molotov, who acted as secretary, were Olminsky, Baturin, Savelyev, Samoilova, Soltz, Yurev, Gladnev, Raskolnikov, Vasilevsky, Malyshev, Poletaev, Bubnov, Danilov, Eremeev, Skrypnik, Malinovsky and Chernomazov. The last two, as we already know, were police agents. Of Skrypnik, the leading Old Bolshevik of Ukrainian origin, and Bubnov, who became Stalin's Commissar of Education, we shall hear more. The one committed suicide and the other finally disappeared in the course of the great purges, as did many of the others.

Only the tight-mouthed Molotov survives with his closely locked memories.

For the most part, not the real editors but professional "sitting editors" (dummy editors we would call them) were punished, with fines or short prison terms, for offending articles. This was a device made possible by the fact that the government—although, through its spies, it knew better—contented itself with holding responsible the "responsible editor" whose name was given on the masthead, always some loyal, humble and inoffensive person hired especially to "sit" in jail so that the regular editors might continue their work uninterrupted.

It is hard to realize now, since we have become accustomed to think of censorship as total suppression of all opposition literature and extermination of all known and suspected opponents, that the tsarist censorship was in those years little more than a restraining and molesting mechanism. The editors had to keep their real names out of the paper (unless they enjoyed parliamentary immunity— today another vanished institution!). They had to learn a rather humiliating circumspection, an "Aesop" or "slave" language, in which the Central Committee was called "the leading group of Marxists," the Bolsheviks were referred to as "the Pravdists" and the Mensheviks as "the Luchists," and the program of a democratic republic, eight-hour day and land nationalization was advanced under the transparent disguise of "the full and uncurtailed demands of the year 1905." Everything had to be expressed thus in muted and blunted form. But the police knew what was meant and the readers knew also. When, in the eyes of the censor or some zealous official, an expression or an article went too far, an issue might be arbitrarily confiscated, a fine levied, or a "sitting editor" sentenced. In extreme cases, the paper was "suppressed." Yet, even in this, the government respected with surprising literalness and loyalty its own laws and regulations. The paper having been suppressed, it "ceased" to appear. But, the very next day, in the same plant, with the same staff, the same political line, and virtually the same name, a "new" paper was issued. It had to offend afresh before it could in turn be punished. Nine times was *Pravda* thus prohibited. But *Pravda* ("Truth") was succeeded by *Workers' Truth, Northern Truth, Truth of Labor, For Truth, Proletarian Truth, Labor Truth, The Way of Truth*. Always the name *Pravda* reappeared in the title. Always it appeared in the same format. Always the police and the readers knew that it was the self-same paper. Its circulation fluctuated between twenty and forty thousand, running much higher with oversized special numbers. Readers subscribed openly and

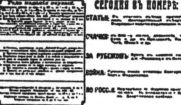

Mastheads of *Pravda, Workers Pravda* and *Northern Pravda*, showing similarity in typography

openly collected money for it. The police, through Malinovsky and
Chernomazov, had a complete list of subscribers and contributors
of funds, but it never occurred to them to make a wholesale raid
throughout the country. Who in those days could think of forty
thousand arrests for reading and supporting an opposition paper?
In this protean form *Pravda* continued to appear, go through the
mails and be sold on the streets, until the eve of the World War.
Then, on July 21, 1914, in a general pre-war shutdown of all labor
papers, the government suppressed "for good" its eighth reincarna-
tion. But it was destined to have nine lives. The ninth it began to
live when the Tsar fell in March, 1917.

> Ilyich became another person—remembers Krupskaya.—
> When the first number of *Pravda* came out, we prepared to
> move to Cracow, in many ways more convenient than
> Paris . . . Whereas the French police assisted the Russian
> police in every possible way, the Polish police was hostile
> to the Russian police as it was to the whole Russian Govern-
> ment. In Cracow we could be sure that our letters would
> not be intercepted and that no one would spy on the new-
> comers.

So many changes have occurred in the map of the world since
the Ulyanovs moved to Cracow, that we must remind ourselves
that the "Polish" police she referred to were really Austrian, Cracow
then being a leading city in Galicia, or Austrian Poland. So great
was the autonomy granted to their Poles by the Danubian monarchy, that it was natural for her to think of the local police and
other administrative officials as "Poles" without qualification.

By moving to Cracow, Lenin was breaking with the long tradition of Russian exile in Switzerland, England, Germany and France.
Many reasons, subtle and explicit, caused the choice. Deepest, and
least conscious, was homesickness, that nostalgia which sooner or
later affects all Russian political émigrés.

> All our people in Paris at that time longed terribly to go
> to Russia . . . We were moving a little nearer . . . Exile
> in Cracow was only semi-exile . . . Ilyich liked Cracow so
> much, it reminded him of Russia . . . Vladimir Ilyich be-
> came quite jolly . . . how joyfully my mother packed her
> things . . . Each of us secretly thought about Russia; each
> had a strong desire to go . . . We avoided speaking about
> this but all of us secretly thought about it . . .

Many such tell-tale phrases can be culled from Krupskaya's
memoirs. To Lenin's mother she wrote from their new Cracow

home that Volodya (Vladimir) was "starved" for Russian novels, had nearly "learned by heart" the works of Nadson and Nekrasov, and had read and re-read "a hundred times," until it was in pieces, *Anna Karenina*, the only novel they had with them. "Greedily" they pored over the book ads in the Russian journals.

> Volodya is a terrible nationalist. He wouldn't go to see the works of Polish painters for anything, but one day he got hold of a catalogue of the Tretyakov Galleries . . . and he frequently becomes absorbed in it . . .

Nostalgia found reinforcement in practical and political considerations. Cracow was only an hour and a half by train from the border, overnight by fast express from Saint Petersburg. Equally important, on both sides of the border lived Poles. On the Russian side Polish revolutionaries plotted secretly, on the Austrian openly, against the Tsar. They were sustained by the passive and active sympathy of their fellow-countrymen, while the Habsburg monarchy looked complacently on because it might sooner or later find itself at war with the Romanovs. An explosive dream, this, of a reunited and autonomous Poland—of course as an Austrian protectorate. But then, all war is a playing with explosives.

When Lenin moved to Cracow in the summer of 1912, it was with the knowledge and consent of the Austrian Ministry of the Interior. Hanecki had taken the matter up with local officials and with certain Social Democratic parliamentary deputies. One of these, Marek from Galicia, had secured assurances from the Austrian Government that Citizen Ulyanov would be welcome. That very autumn was to begin the first of two "little wars" in the Balkans, involving Serbia, Bulgaria, Greece, Montenegro and Turkey. In the background, Russia and Austria-Hungary, two great multi-national empires that had somehow survived into the modern world of nation-states, were maneuvering for position to thrust rival feelers of influence into the Balkan peninsula, each seeking the lion's share of the pieces to be torn out of the third multi-national empire, Turkey, that seemed about to die. If Austria's Polish border officials now became almost as friendly to Russian revolutionaries as they had long been to Polish, the Tsar's Government in turn was secretly encouraging Irredentist Montenegrins and Serbs, to sow disruption in the great Danubian monarchy that ruled over more Slavs than it did Germans, or even Germans and Hungarians put together. And the French republican police were becoming friendly to the secret service of the tsarist autocracy in the same proportion as Habsburg and Romanov agents grew cold toward each other. Nobody had yet invented the terms "Fifth Column" or "ideological" or "psychological warfare," but more than one great power was beginning to play the hazardous game of encouraging its rival's internal and external foes.

Thus it was that Lenin got permission to settle in Cracow, encountered friendly blindness on the part of local officials, and found more than four thousand self-exiled Russian-Polish conspirators, who taught him some tricks of his own chosen trade. The local Polish officials found that their governmental duties, their patriotic feelings, and the sums of money that crossed their palms, all combined delightfully to make them benevolent onlookers while letters, literature and conspirators crossed and recrossed the artificial frontier that Russia, Prussia and Austria had drawn over a century earlier across the living body of their land. It was here that Lenin learned to intermeddle actively in Polish faction disputes, had his awareness of the national question intensified by Polish plots and controversies, and could almost see the war clouds that were rolling up from the Balkans, soon to involve all Europe and the globe in universal war.

> That autumn—writes Krupskaya—the Great Powers intervened in the Balkan affair, and things began to smell of war. The International Socialist Bureau organized protests everywhere . . . but here in Cracow they . . . were more like meetings called to rouse the hatred of the masses towards Russia than protest meetings against war . . . The Polish masses were filled with burning hatred toward tsarism . . . One remembered what his father had experienced during the Polish rebellion . . . another how the tsarist authorities had desecrated the graves of his nearest and dearest, etc. etc.

It was hard for orthodox Marxists (harder for Rosa Luxemburg as a Pole than for Lenin as a Russian) to take account of this long national memory and steadily rising national passion. Was not nationalism a "bourgeois idea"? Was it not supposed to die away as class consciousness and class hatred grew? The *Communist Manifesto* (1847), favorite text of revolutionists (Stalin with his flare for religious terminology would one day call it "The Song of Songs of Marxism"), was a seed-bed of diverse and sometimes contradictory ideas. "The workers have no country," it had said. But it had been said in answer to the charge that "the communists have been accused of wanting to do away with country, with nationality . . . No one can take away from them what they have not got."

And the very next sentence had proclaimed that the proletariat was aiming to "establish itself as the nation."

In the *Manifesto* was embedded the assumption that nationalism had nearly completed its progressive work, and was on the way out. The bourgeoisie was credited with having constructed the modern unified economies, unified national markets, and nation states, eliminating local customs barriers, dialects, laws, petty local rulers, bringing nationalism into being. But the same class was further credited with having undermined the very foundations of the nation-states by establishing a world market, a world interchange of products "spiritual no less than material," and a world literature. The proletariat in its struggle within each nation to "establish itself as the nation" would find necessary "united action, at least among civilized countries." Hence its revolutions would "efface national distinctions and antagonisms even more" than the bourgeoisie had already done, and, by ending exploitation within each nation, would end the exploitation of one nation by another.

Actually, nationalism, democracy and socialism had grown up together as "triplet" sister-ideologies, all engendered simultaneously in the common matrix of modern industrialism. Two of these sisters, however, nationalism and socialism, were potential rivals for a common heritage, since the struggle for national freedom or national existence implies considerable unity of all classes in an oppressed nation, while the socialistic class struggle implies an inner antagonism more powerful than the outer. In a complex society there is a great variety of overlapping loyalties, whence the question becomes: which shall be the overriding loyalty—loyalty to nation or to class?

Economically, and this was the aspect that Marx tended to emphasize, the ideas and institutions of nationalism had arisen as a movement to overcome medieval particularism by creating a nationwide division of labor, a nationwide market, languages viable over wide areas, a uniform system of laws, unified nation-states, self-governing national economic, political and cultural units: in its "pure" form, theoretically, "one people, one language, one state," in which the people, not the sovereign, was the acknowledged repository of a sovereignty henceforward to be called "national." In the first modern states thus created, the sense of nationality soon lost its passionate charge of energy. People born in a great nation take the right to use their own language, to choose their own officials, to follow their own creeds and pursue and determine their own way of life, quite for granted, like the air they breathe, no longer realizing how precious these rights may be to

Catalonians, Lithuanians, or Poles. Nationalism thus loses much of its pathos where successful, or that pathos may perhaps be diverted into new channels of chauvinist, imperialist nationalism. Liberals and progressives, in opposing the latter hateful growth, often develop an abstract "internationalism" that denies the importance of national self-determination to peoples who have not yet attained it. This abstract variety of internationalism expects subject peoples to "outgrow" nationalism without ever having known national freedom or tasted its precious fruits. While in its extreme form triumphant nationalism easily turns into its repressive opposite for peoples awakening a little more tardily to consciousness, in the nationalities still denied their rights, nationalism continues to represent a fundamental democratic demand: the demand for the right of self-determination. All these complexities the *Communist Manifesto* slighted, or telescoped together as, in aphoristic and stirring utterances, one page pronounced nationalism itself on the way out, and the next unconditionally espoused the right of the Poles, for instance, to independent national existence.

The young revolutionaries, Marx and Engels, had written simultaneously as German democrats seeking to create by revolutionary struggle a united German nation, and as long-range social prophets striving to foresee a remoter future in which nationalism itself, having achieved its progressive objects and spent its force, would be absorbed into a higher supra-nationalism or internationalism. But the first order of business for them was the creation of a united Germany in the name of a sovereign German people, by a general revolution calculated to drive out Hohenzollerns, Habsburgs, and scores of pettier rulers, and unite all Germans, including those of Austria, into a single, unified German republic. Moreover, their striving lacked some of the pathos of other national movements since the German people had already achieved cultural unity and cultural self-determination, and only the politico-economic superstructure—or "foundation" was lacking.

In both Prussia and Austria the young socialistic democrats found imbedded large portions of Poland, while the Austrian Hapsburgs, the oldest of medieval houses, ruled over Italians in Lombardy and Venetia in the Italian peninsula, and in what was later (when the peninsula was unified) to be known as the "Italia Irredenta" in portions of Venezia Giulia and the Tyrol; over Hungarians; and, above all, over a variegated assortment of Slavs. Actually, the ruling Germans were in a minority in the Danubian Empire. The total of Germans, Hungarians and Irredentist Italians added together was less than the Slavs, who, after World War I, were destined to constitute Czechoslovakia, Yugoslavia and parts of Poland, and, after World War II, the Galician and Carpathian parts of the Ukraine. By Lenin's day, the Austrian Germans had taken the Magyars of Hungary and the Austrian Poles of Galicia into partnership as ruling layers of the nation. They were in the process of struggle-and-concession that would eventually have given the same rights to the Slavs of Moravia and Bohemia (Czechoslovakia). It was the tensions thus arising between the various nationalities with differing degrees of development and attainment of self-rule that continually threatened to tear the Austrian Social Democracy to pieces and made the national question its central political problem. If one wanted to study the complexities and tensions of the triplet complex, nationalism, democracy, socialism, there was no better laboratory in all the world than the one Vladimir Ilyich had just moved into in the year 1912, as the clouds were gathering for the storms of 1914. In Russia, at least, the Great-Russians had something close to a majority, and, with the exception of Ukrainians, Poles and Finns and Balts, most of the peoples were so backward that they scarcely stirred in their medieval sleep, until the violent earthquakes of 1905 and 1917 shook them from slumber.

Marx and Engels, as Germans and democrats, were quite ready to advocate the right of Italians to unification and independence, of Hungarians to form a separate nation, and of the Poles of Austria, Germany and Russia to break away from all three, to reconstitute an independent Poland. But, as for Czechs, Slovaks, Slovenes, Croatians, Serbs, Montenegrins, Ruthenians, (Ukrainians), indeed, all the other assorted Slavic peoples except the Poles, the two young German revolutionaries repeatedly and dogmatically asserted that they were and would forever be unfit for self-rule and independence. These Slav peoples, Marx and Engels declared, were too variegated to unite, too weak to live as separate splinter nations, culturally too backward to aspire to national self-determination, politically too reactionary to be tolerated by progressive democrats. Their nationalist movements were mere powerless fantasies of utopian intellectuals. If they were given independence they would become inevitable puppets or prey of the steadily expanding Russian state, a state which menaced all democratic movements in western Europe and which therefore must not be permitted to expand.

These conclusions Marx and Engels arrived at partly as a result of their traumatic experiences with Russia and with the Austrian

Slavs in the abortive revolutions of 1848, and partly because they assumed that nationalism had already done most of its progressive historical work.

With the unification of Italy and of Germany, the reconstitution of Poland and the independence of Hungary, they thought that the permanent frontiers of the great "historical" nation-states would be pretty largely fixed. The remaining Slavs were *geschichtslose* ("historyless") peoples destined to be civilized and assimilated by their "more progressive and advanced" neighbors, the Germans, the Hungarians, and the Poles. They failed to recognize that the same processes of industrialization, spread of universal education and literacy, universal military training and general suffrage, would continue to shake up the masses of the more backward nationalities and bring them too as actors onto the political stage. This would give the still weak nationalist intellectual movements the mass support they required, and would arouse the same longing for self-determination in Austria and the Balkans and Russia which, in the past, had produced the national idea and national movements in the West, and which, for a hundred years and more, had maintained the idea of nationality as a subterranean flame among the Poles.

The animus of Marx and Engels toward Russia and the Slav peoples of Austria and the Balkans, as I have already suggested, came from the experiences of the year 1848. They refined and modified, but never fully re-examined, those conclusions during the rest of their lives. In that memorable year 1848, Paris had risen, Berlin had risen, Vienna had risen, Budapest had risen, battered Warsaw had strained once more at the leash, and Italian cities had been up in arms. But Russian troops, and the still Habsburg-loyal, backward Austrian Slavs, had provided the armies to restore Hapsburgs and Hohenzollerns to their capitals and thrones. Marx and Engels then and there became convinced that no revolution could triumph in Western Europe until the power of Russia had been broken or drastically curbed, and that the Slavic peoples of the Danubian monarchy—except for the Poles—would always be instruments of reaction.

Modeling themselves in thought upon the revolutionary wars of the Great French Revolution of 1789, they began, in season and out, to advocate war with Russia.

> Only a war with Russia [Marx wrote in the *Neue Rheinische Zeitung*] is a war for revolutionary Germany, a war in which it can wash away its sins of the past, can become virile, defeat its own autocrats, and, as beseems a people shaking off the chains of a long passive slavery, can purchase the propa-

ganda of civilization with the sacrifice of its own sons, making itself free within while freeing itself externally . . . (July
8, 1848)

Though the situation had soon changed in Germany and in
Europe generally, this was the tangent Marx and Engels continued
to follow for most of the rest of their lives, as they went into life-
long exile after 1848. For many years they continued to urge war
with Russia, urge it on Germany, on Austria, on France, and even
on England! In the middle fifties they supported the Concert of
Powers in the Crimean War, denouncing them only for not making
it a real, all-out effort. Repeatedly they supported Turkey and
Austria-Hungary against all the Danubian and Balkan independence movements, because they thought of Turkey and Austria as
needed barriers to Russian expansion and they held any possible
independent Slavic and Moldavian nations to be inevitable Russian
puppets or prey (Today the Russia calling itself "Marxist" seems determined to show its orthodox zeal by justifying their forebodings.)

Interesting, in view of Marx's conviction that nationalism was a
superstructure of ideas and institutions arising on the economic
foundation of a wide-area market and wide-area division of labor,
is his steady and ardent support of Polish freedom. For here the
considerations of economic unity were completely set aside! In the
case of the Poles, it was recognized that their economic integration
into three other nations (part into the German economy, part the
Russian, part the Austrian) was somehow not decisive or final or
determinant of ideology. Here Marx was giving recognition to
nationalism as a powerful impulsive idea which continued to persist in despite of economic foundations, and which must be given
support though Polish liberation should break up, as it must, considerable portions of the Russian, Austrian and German national
markets and political outlines. In 1833, in 1846-48, in 1863, the
Polish indepedence movement flared up afresh. And, more than a
century after partition, again in 1905. As Krupskaya testified in the
passage quoted above, it was a fierce-burning flame still when they
moved to Cracow in 1912. At present, no reader needs any longer
to be reminded of the pathetic indestructibility of the Polish
national spirit.

This recognition of Polish aspirations in despite of the prevailing
economic foundation suggests that nationalism is first of all not an
economic phenomenon, though certain economic prerequisites must
be there before it arises. Rather is it a moving idea, a phenomenon
of consciousness, a feeling nourished in the matrix of a common

culture and sense of shared historical fate. Perhaps the most fantastic test of this would come in the middle twentieth century in the case of the Jews. All nineteenth-century progressive thought was assimilationist, and all Marxist writers from Marx himself to Kautsky and Lenin, would assert that the Jews were not only not a nationality but that their lack of common territory and common economy and even common language and culture made it impossible for them to become such. Yet, the fearful historical fate thrust upon so many of them in Europe in our time has awakened an unmistakable national consciousness among millions of Jews. After all, was it not the young Hegelian "materialist" Marx who wrote: "The idea, once it takes possession of the masses, becomes itself a material force."

Actually, Marx's deep and abiding interest in the idea which so clearly held possession of the Polish masses, arose primarily from his conviction that Germany itself could not be democratic and internally free as long as it helped to enslave a portion of the Poles:

> As long as we help to oppress the Poles—he wrote in the *Neue Rheinische Zeitung*—and as long as we bind a part of Poland to Germany, so long are we bound to Russia and Russian policy, and will be unable to break fundamentally with patriarchal feudal absolutism here at home . . .
>
> The creation of a democratic Poland is the first condition for the establishment of a democratic Germany . . . And it is not merely a matter of building a Poland that is independent only on paper, but of building a state on a lasting foundation capable of genuine existence. Poland must regain at least the territory that was hers in 1772.

From the reference to the boundaries of 1772 it is once more clear that Marx had no patience with the argument that the Ukrainians of Austrian Galicia should be given to Russia because Russia already ruled over other Ukrainians, nor did he have any inkling that a Ukrainian national movement might one day arise to demand separation from both Austria (or Poland) and Russia, in an independent Ukraine.

Three events went far to change Marx's and Engels's picture of Europe, though only piecemeal and incompletely. The first was the rise of a revolutionary movement (the Narodnaya Volya) in Russia; the second, the unification of Germany from above, without Austria, by Bismarck and the Hohenzollerns; the third the Franco-Prussian War with its sequel of the Paris Commune and the annexation by Germany of Alsace-Lorraine. In 1891, after Marx's death, Engels predicted that the annexation of Alsace-Lorraine would throw republican France into monarchist Russia's arms in a coming war against Germany and Austria. He foresaw the situation as a race between rapidly growing German socialism, which in "a decade or so of peace" would win control of Germany, and that future war. His utterance on this subject was a mixture of prevision of the future with incompletely examined, vestigial remnants of the earlier conceptions we have been tracing. At the rate German socialism was growing, he expected it soon to have a majority. It was not to its interest to resort to force, but if the German ruling class resisted that majority, then universal military training, which already provided one socialist recruit in every five members of the armed forces, would guarantee victory to the Social Democracy. However, if war intervened first "with France and Russia on one side, against Germany, Austria, perhaps Italy on the other," then:

> If Russia should win, and the victory of Russia over Germany should signify the suppression of German socialism, what will then be the duty of the German socialists? . . . In the interests of the European Revolution they are obliged to keep every position they win, not to capitulate, neither to the inner nor to the outer foe. And that they can only do if they fight Russia and all its allies to the utmost, whoever those allies may be. If the French Republic should put itself at the service of his Majesty the Tsar and Autocrat of all the Russias, the German socialists will fight them—with regret, but fight them it would. As against the German kaiserdom, the French Republic can possibly represent the bourgeois revolution. But as against the republic of a Constans, a Rouvier, and even a Clemenceau, especially as against the republic in the service of the Russian Tsar, German socialism represents unconditionally the proletarian revolution.
>
> A war in which Russians and Frenchmen were to break into Germany would be for the latter a life-and-death fight, wherein it could only insure its national existence by the most revolutionary measures. The present régime, if it is not forced, will surely not unleash the revolution. But we have a strong party which can force it to do so, or, in case of need, can replace it: the Social Democratic Party. And we have not forgotten the splendid example which France gave us in 1793 . . .
>
> In short, peace assures the triumph of the German Social Democratic Party in another ten years or so. War will bring with it either victory for the social democracy in two or three years, or complete ruin at least for fifteen or twenty

... No socialist, of any nation whatsoever, can wish for the military victory of either the present German régime or of the French bourgeois republic, least of all of the régime of the Tsar that would be synonymous with the subjection of all Europe. And therefore the Socialists of all lands are for peace. But if war comes just the same, then only one thing is sure: this war in which fifteen or twenty million armed men will kill each other off and lay all Europe waste—this war must either bring the immediate victory of socialism, or so upset the old order of things from top to bottom and leave behind such a mass of ruins that the old capitalist society would be more impossible than ever, and that the socialist revolution might, to be sure, be delayed for ten or fifteen years, but would have to triumph then on a still more rapid and fundamental basis . . .

And now Marx and Engels had died (in 1883 and 1895 respectively). The German Social Democracy had grown still greater so that one in every three army recruits was a socialist voter. In Russia, too, a Social Democratic Party (or two or more skeleton parties) had been founded, and in 1905 there had been a revolutionary movement of wider scope than that of Europe in 1848. Nationalism, far from disappearing, was taking possession of greater masses of men than in the nineteenth century. In the Balkans a little war had begun which gave signs of growing into a big war, the outlines of which Engels had foreseen, albeit imperfectly (he had left out England and America from the lineup). But who was there to interpret, to systematize, to select among the many utterances of Marx and Engels the guide-lines for an attitude toward the new nationalisms arising among the nationalities of Russia, and toward the war itself which was at once different from and the same as the one Engels had foretold?

That war, the parties of the International sensed, must at all costs be prevented. At regular congresses and emergency conferences they were planning, threatening, issuing appeals and pledging themselves to struggle to maintain peace. Rosa Luxemburg, backed by both Lenin and Martov, was building up a "Left Wing" in the International, to define more sharply the attitude toward this question. In Poland, including the Austrian Poland which Lenin had now moved into, Luxemburg and her followers were opposing Polish nationalism in their internationalist zeal. Living now in one multi-national empire and dreaming of revolution in another, Lenin felt that he must come to terms with this problem of nationalism.

He must "consult" once more with the masters. But clearly he must solve, albeit in their spirit, questions they had judged wrongly, or situations that had arisen since their death. With the national excitement in the Balkans and in Austria and the fringe lands of Russia he must somehow reckon, above all with the nationalism of the Polish Socialist Party and the anti-nationalism of the Polish Social Democratic Party. And with the little war clouds that were spreading so rapidly over the sky from the southeastern Balkan storm center.

He set Zinoviev, writes Krupskaya, to "collecting interesting material on foreign affairs for *Pravda*." He selected one of the sons of an oppressed nationality, the Georgian Djugashvili, to write on the national question. He himself wrote much, pondered much, toured all the Russian émigré colonies in Europe to lecture on the national question, and drew up a set of theses on the subject. To Gorky, sensitive as always to rising tides of emotion, he gave an assurance that he and his faction or party were really undertaking to clarify the matter:

> As to nationalism, I am fully in agreement with you that it is necessary to pay more serious attention to it. We have here a wonderful Georgian who is writing a long article for *Prosveshchenie*, for which he has gathered all the Austrian and other material. We are working on it. But that our resolution is "mere copybook maxims, bureaucratic phrases,"—in that you are permitting yourself to scold without justification. No, it is not mere verbiage. In the Caucasus among us Social Democrats, Georgians + Armenians + Tartars + Russians have worked *together* in a *single* Social Democratic organization *more than ten years*. That is not a mere phrase, but a proletarian solution of the national question. The only solution. So it was in Riga, too: Russians + Letts + Lithuanians; *only the separatists* split away: the Bund. The same in Vilna . . . *No, such vileness as in Austria will not appear among us*. We won't permit it. Besides, our brothers, the Great-Russians, are numerically larger. We will not permit the "Austrian spirit" to develop among our workers . . . [Letter to Gorky, written in the second half of February, 1913.]

And, a few days earlier, he had also written to Gorky:

> The Polish Socialist Party is undoubtedly for Austria and will fight for her. A war between Austria and Russia would be a very useful thing for the revolution—in all of Eastern Europe—but it is not likely that Franz Joseph and Nikolasha will give us that pleasure. . . .

CHAPTER XXXIII

THE NATIONAL QUESTION

"Nationality . . . like the processes of life, digestion and breathing . . . has no right to be concerned with itself until that right is denied. That is why the Poles, Italians, Hungarians, and all the oppressed Slav peoples, naturally and rightly stress the principle of nationality; and that is perhaps why we Russians concern ourselves so little with our nationality." — *Bakunin*

"There is a degree of culture where national hatred vanishes, and where one stands to a certain extent above nations and feels the weal and woe of a neighboring people as if it happened to one's own." — *Goethe*

IN STALIN's *History of the Communist Party*, written originally under the cover of anonymity, he puts his own name before Lenin's, but concedes to his teacher a share of the credit for evolving "the national policy of Lenin and Stalin." Says his *History*:

> Only the Bolsheviks had a Marxist program on the national question, as set forth in Comrade Stalin's article, *Marxism and the National Question*, and in Lenin's articles, *The Right of Nations to Self-Determination* and *Critical Notes on the National Question.*

There is no hint here that Stalin's solitary systematic article on this question was written directly under Lenin's guidance, or that it looks impressive only by comparison with Stalin's other works (whether written before or since) and not at all impressive if compared with the sweep, insight and many-sidedness of the theses, resolutions, letters, polemical and programmatic articles that Lenin wrote on the same subject before and during the World War.

As we have already noted, in all the writings of Lenin there is only one reference to the *nationality* of a Bolshevik—namely, the remark to Gorky that a "splendid Georgian was gathering all the Austrian and other material . . . and writing a big article for *Prosveshchenie.*" That he referred to the writer's nationality was not accidental, for at that moment, as we shall see, he especially needed a Transcaucasian to advance some of his views on the subject.

578

Until Lenin moved to Austrian Poland in 1912, his polemics on nationalism had been almost exclusively with the Jewish Bund. Despite Jewish dispersion and lack of a distinct territory, the Bund insisted on considering the Jews as a nationality, and on speaking for all Jews anywhere in Russia. For their scattered peoples, they did not dream of demanding the "right of secession" to form an independent state. Instead of "territorial autonomy" and the "right of secession," they limited self-determination to the more modest demand for "cultural autonomy" or "national-cultural autonomy." By this they meant that the Jewish communities should control their own schools, theaters, press and religious life, free from interference or handicap on the part of the state, should elect their own school and community administrators, and speak for and defend the "national-cultural" interests of people anywhere in Russia who chose to regard themselves as Jews. Still worse, in Lenin's opinion, they wanted the same autonomy to prevail in the Party, for themselves and for other national groups. Lenin was willing to concede nationality to Ukrainians, White Russians, Poles, etc., because they had a distinct territory and language and a strong will to secede from the Russian Empire, and therefore constituted a movement which would weaken tsarism. But Jews, he maintained, were not a nationality but a caste; they spoke not one language but various, lived not in a definite territory but scattered throughout the Empire, and, insofar as they were not "bourgeois-minded" were internationalists. The only "progressive solution" of the Jewish question was emancipation and assimilation. Above all in the Social Democratic Party there was no room for nationalism. The "best and most class-conscious" Jews had set an example by rejecting the Jewish Bund in favor of membership in the local mixed units of the Russian Social Democratic Party. If the Bund were to have its way, it would lead to the recognition of national divisions in the labor movement, and to a federated party in which Jews, Ukrainians, Georgians, Armenians, Great-Russians, White-Russians, Poles, etc., would each be organized separately. Then the Party and the Party Central Committee, instead of being centralized would be a mere federated body. And the new Russia to issue out of the revolution would be a federated, not a centralized, republic.

Obviously, Lenin was not altogether consistent on this. He had never quarreled with the Poles for having a separate organization only loosely federated with the Russian party. Perhaps this might be explained by the fact that Marx and Engels had always envisaged the right of Poland to independence, and the further fact that the Poles cut across three empires, Russian, German and Austrian.

Nor had he quarreled with Latvians and Esthonians, though he had tried sporadically to draw them into closer federal (!) union with the Bolsheviks. Unceasingly he maintained the absolute right of the Ukrainian people to separate from Russia, though he regarded the Ukrainian nationalistic socialist party with hostility and sought to include all Ukrainian workers in the same organizations with the Russians. Above all, Transcaucasia had long been for him a model region in regard to nationalism. Alongside such national socialistic parties as the Armenian Dashnaks and the Georgian Federalists, and quite overshadowing them, was a general, multi-national, social-democratic party, containing Georgians, Armenians, Tartars, Russians and members of other Transcaucasian vest-pocket nationalities, in a single organization. Until 1912, both Georgian Bolsheviks and the far more powerful Georgian Mensheviks had taken this "internationalist," i.e. multi-national, structure for granted.

But in 1912, as we have seen, many things coincided to sharpen Lenin's sensitivity on the national question, drew him into new and extensive polemics, and compelled him to clarify all the hazy aspects of his views. Foremost of these was the Balkan War and the general intensification of national feeling that presaged a coming world war. Then his move to Cracow in Austrian Poland made him aware of the struggle being waged between the Polish Socialist Party (of Pilsudski) and the Polish Social Democratic Party (of Rosa Luxemburg) on the national question. The latter was so ardently internationalist that it zealously combatted all Polish nationalism and the Polish independence movement as "economically and politically retrogressive and out of date." Before long Lenin found it necessary to start a polemic against this, to him, one-sided and abstract internationalism. It might be all right for Polish socialists to fight Polish nationalism as inexpedient, but Russian socialists could do so only at peril to their principles of democracy and self-determination.

Moving to Austria also shocked him into a realization of the difference between the attitude of the Austrian Marxists on the national question and his own. The Austrians were faced with a congeries of more developed nationalities than those of Russia. The Germans of Austria were a leading minority in a majority sea of Hungarians, Poles, Czechs, and other Slavic peoples, some nationally awake and others just beginning to stir. Distinguished Austrian Marxists like Renner and Bauer did not chart their course on the expectation of the immediate disruption of the Danubian state as Lenin did his on the disruption of tsarist Russia. Instead,

they anticipated Austria-Hungary's rapid democratization and fed-
eralization with equal national-cultural and administrative rights
for all the nationalities within it. Hence, as Lenin found to his
dismay, they did not stress, as he did, territorial autonomy and
the right of secession, but national-cultural autonomy and federal-
ism. Since this tended to reinforce the federalist and cultural-
autonomy views of the Bund and other socialistic national parties
in Russia, he began to prepare a trenchant criticism of the Austrian
views. That is why he sent Djugashvili, who knew only the Georgian set-up, to Vienna, "to gather all the Austrian materials."

But his main reason for wanting a Transcaucasian to write such
an article, and not a Great-Russian or a member of some other
nationality, was the fact that the Georgian Social Democracy, the
stronghold and fortress of menshevism, had just begun a slight but
perceptible shift on the national question, and Lenin needed a
Georgian to carry his "national" war into Menshevik-dominated
Transcaucasia.

This shift of views had arisen directly out of the faction struggle.

As the reader will remember, the year 1912 began with Lenin's
seizure of power in the Social Democratic Party by his Prague
Congress.

In August of that year, all the outlawed and excluded had tried
to unite against Lenin in their "August Bloc." In order to present
a common front against Lenin, they had sought to blur their differences on all matters other than Party unity. In order to include
parties like the Jewish Bund, they found it expedient to adopt a
resolution which said that the Bund's "demand for national-
cultural autonomy is not incompatible with the point in the Party
program concerning the right of nations to self-determination."
(In other words, national-cultural autonomy is one of the conceivable forms of national self-determination, and it is up to each people to determine for itself whether it wants national-cultural
autonomy or separation.) When the Georgian Social Democracy
adopted the same resolution at its own Transcausian Conference,
Lenin saw the opportunity to carry the war into the most powerful
stronghold of menshevism. That is the chief reason why he sent
for Stalin early in 1913, initiated him into the basic differences
between the Austrian and Russian Marxist views, and sent him on
from Cracow to Vienna "to gather all the Austrian materials."

Writing the second volume of her *Memories of Lenin* in the early
thirties, under an increasingly rigid Stalinist censorship, Krupskaya

cautiously hints at the relationship between Lenin's many-sided consideration of the national question and Stalin's article. She uses the devices long known to Russian revolutionaries as the "Aesop" or "slave language" which seeks to evade an obtuse or hesitant censorship and yet suggest its point to the perspicacious reader.

> In the middle of February 1913—she writes on page 115-16 (of the English translation)—a conference of the members of the Central Committee was held in Cracow . . . Stalin also came. Ilyich had long discussions with Stalin on the national question. He was glad to meet a man who was seriously interested in this question and who was well informed on it. Prior to his arrival in Cracow [to write his article], Stalin spent two months in Vienna where he studied the national question. There he became closely connected with our people, Bukharin and Troyanovsky.

When she wrote this, Bukharin was already out of favor and within a few years was to be executed. Yet, as Stalin knew no German, it is clear that either Troyanovsky or Bukharin must have helped him "study the national question" in Vienna. From other sources we know that Bukharin was his mentor on Austrian theory, and that Troyanovsky was only mentioned here to cover up.

Three pages later, ostensibly in another connection, Krupskaya launches into a detailed account of how Ilyich helped "inexperienced authors":

> In discussing their work with them, he would get right down to the heart of the subject, to fundamentals, and make suggestions for improvement. But he did all this very discreetly so that these authors hardly noticed that they were being corrected. And Ilyich was very good at helping people in their work. If for example he wanted someone to write an article and was not sure whether he would be able to do it properly, he would start a discussion with him, expound his ideas and get the prospective writer interested. After he had sounded him out on the subject sufficiently, he would say to him: "Would you like to write an article on this subject?" And the author would not even have noticed that his preliminary discussion with Ilyich had helped him and that, in writing his article, he had actually used Ilyich's expressions and turns of phrase.

This was one of the qualities that made Lenin a team-leader and made even his personal leadership assume the guise of a collective leadership. Far from claiming credit for everything others wrote in an effort to build himself up into an all-knowing and infallible *vozhd*, he sought every opportunity to push credit from his person and build up the reputations of those around him.

On page 122, Krupskaya casually returns to the national question long enough to say:

> The other important resolution which was passed [at the "Summer Conference" of 1913] was that on the national question, which expressed the views of Vladimir Ilyich Lenin.

Doubtless she would have liked to put the last eight words in italics if she had dared! In any case, Ilyich could get no "help" from Koba at the "Summer Conference," for the latter was in jail. Therefore, the Bolshevik leader was already looking for another Transcaucasian to carry on in Transcaucasia the war which had been opened by Stalin's article on *Marxism and the National Question*.

That this is so is proved by Lenin's correspondence with other Transcaucasians, particularly with Stepan Grigorevich Shaumyan. There are a number of such letters, from which we select a few typical passages.

> Do not fail to send me as much material as possible on the national question in the Caucasus . . . and the *statistics of nationalities* in the Caucasus, in Persia, Turkey and Russia . . . everything you can get. If a misfortune should befall you [Lenin means the same misfortune as had befallen Stalin, i.e. arrest], so that you cannot write, I hope you will find someone else to hand over the task to. Do not forget either, to *seek out* Caucasian comrades who may be able to write articles on the national question in the Caucasus . . .

The above is from a letter of August 11, 1913, shortly after Stalin had been removed from the scene by arrest and deportation to Siberia. Shaumyan answered, sending both material and a full statement of his views, which deviated from Lenin's in the direction of what Lenin thought a too abstract internationalism and an un-Leninist belief in the superior democracy of a federated state, with regional autonomy and local self-government. In the case of Stalin he had doubtless corrected these common "Transcaucasian errors" by long and tactful personal conversation. But in Shaumyan's case, he had to accomplish the same pedagogical work by mail. He wrote:

Dear Friend,

Your letter of November 15 has given me great joy. You must know that in my situation the opinions of comrades in Russia, especially those who think deeply and occupy themselves with current problems, are most highly appreciated. Your swift answer was therefore particularly pleasant to me. One feels less cut off when one gets such letters. But enough of lyricism. To business. . . .

Follows a gentle but firm correction of those opinions of Shaumyan on the national question which Lenin considers erroneous:

1. An inclination to promote Russian as the general national speech, because it contains the highest culture and the greatest possibilities of unity. ("The Russian tongue," Lenin answered, "would be for a number of unfortunate and backward peoples of progressive significance—no doubt of it. But do you not see that it would be of still greater progressive significance if there were no *compulsion* to use it?")

2. An inclination to prefer local self-government and autonomy, and to give each nationality a choice between the "right of separation" and the "right of federation." ("We are in principle against federation," answered Lenin, "it weakens the economic connection and is inappropriate for a unified state. Do you want to separate? we say. Then go to the devil and cut yourself off altogether if you can break the economic connection or, rather, if the yoke and friction of 'living together' are such that they *spoil* the economic relationship. You don't want to separate? Then, please, don't decide *for me*, don't believe you have the 'right' to federation . . . The right of self-determination is an *exception* from our general premise of centralism. This exception is absolutely necessary in view of Great-Russian arch-reactionary nationalism and the slightest renunciation of this exception is opportunism, it is a simpleminded playing into the hands of Great-Russian arch-reactionary nationalism.")

The letter concludes with the news that Lenin is writing an article on the subject for three issues of *Prosveshchenie*, begs Shaumyan to give his opinion after he has read it, and tactfully suggests that it would be a fine thing if the latter would write a "popular pamphlet on the National Question." Lenin closed "with a tight, tight handclasp."

Several things are notable in this letter. The warm tone—warmer than in any letter Lenin ever wrote to Stalin. The tact and generosity with which Lenin rebutted the views of a man who was "thinking deeply and fundamentally on current problems." The fact that Lenin did not ask any opinion on the supposedly epoch-making article of Djugashvili, but was writing another, actually two more lengthy articles in six issues of *Prosveshchenie*, to clarify the whole question. The fact that he urged Shaumyan to write a popular pamphlet on the subject to follow up on the one he had urged on Stalin. This was in December, 1913. Our next letter brings us to May 19, 1914:

> I hope you will answer me after reading my article on self-determination of nations in *Prosveshchenie* (I am writing it now). You *must* give some self-advertisement (*Selbstanzeige*) or an outline of your own pamphlet against *An* [pseudonym of an Armenian Socialist and cultural autonomist] in *Prosveshchenie*. [Shaumyan had by now written a pamphlet entitled *On National Cultural Autonomy*]. I also propose to you the following plan:
>
> In order to struggle against the stupidity of the cultural-national autonomists, the fraction must introduce into the Duma a draft law on the equality of nations and the definition of the rights of national minorities. I propose that we draw up such a project:
>
> The general situation of equal rights—the division of the country into autonomous and self-governing territorial units according—among other things—to nationality (the local population determines the boundaries, the general parliament confirms them)—the limits of the administration of the autonomous districts and regions, as well as the self-governing local units;—the illegalization of any departure from equality of nations in the decisions of autonomous districts, zemstvos, etc.; general school councils democratically elected etc., freedom and equality of languages—the choice of languages by the municipal institutions, etc. The protection of minorities: the right to a proportional share of the expenditures for school buildings (gratis) for students of "alien" (non-Russian) nationalities, for "alien" teachers, for "alien" departments in museums and libraries, theaters and the like; the right of each citizen to seek redress (before a court) for any departure from the corresponding equality of rights, for any "trampling upon" the rights of national minorities; a census of population every five years in the multi-national districts, a ten-year census in the country as a whole, etc. . . .
>
> The draft might be worked out by the Marxists of *all*, or of very many, of the nations of Russia. Write at once

whether you agree to help. In general, write *oftener,* and
not less often than once a week . . .

These letters are a model of the tact with which Lenin knew how
to suggest ideas and draw others into writing articles and pamphlets embodying them. Moreover, the last letter is striking evidence of how far Lenin had already worked out in his own mind
in 1914 the general outlines of the policy which Stalin himself now
modestly calls "the nationalities policy of Lenin and Stalin." By an
accident of history he confided this detailed plan first not to
Djugashvili but to Shaumyan. Then by another accident of history, Shaumyan was removed from the scene by death in 1918.
If the curious reader picks up Volume XVII of the Third Edition
of Lenin's *Collected Works,* published just before Beria and Stalin
got busy on their wholesale revision of the past, he will find the
following biographical note on S. G. Shaumyan (1878-1918):

> Old Bolshevik Party official . . . Expelled in 1900 from
> Polytechnic Institute for participation in student unrest
> . . . Went to Berlin, studied philosophy and Marxism, be-
> came acquainted with Kautsky, Martov . . . Lenin and
> Plekhanov . . . Took part in the Second Party Congress
> and immediately joined the Bolshevik faction (1903). In
> 1904 returned to Tiflis and stood at the head of the Bolshe-
> vik faction in the Social Democratic organization there. In
> 1906 and 1907 . . . delegate to the Stockholm and London
> Congresses. From this year on he led the entire Party work
> in Baku, editing the legal and illegal Party organs '. . . In
> the February (1917) Revolution, he was chosen by the
> workers as Chairman of the workers' Soviet of Baku.
> Elected to the Central Committee at the Sixth Congress
> (summer of 1917). After the October Revolution he was
> Extraordinary Commissar for the Caucasus and in May,
> 1918, Chairman of the Council of People's Commissars in
> Baku and People's Commissar for Foreign Affairs. On Sep-
> tember 20, 1918, he was one of the 26 People's Commissars
> of Baku shot by the English.

At the head of the Tiflis organization in 1904 . . . from 1907 on
"led the entire Party work" in Baku . . ."! The more we ponder
this biographical note, the clearer it becomes that here is another
Transcaucasian leader whom death so timely removed so that Beria
might "expropriate" his activities and reputation in favor of Joseph
Stalin, even as he had done with Ketskhoveli (died 1903) and
Tsulukidze (died 1905), who had also been Stalin's teachers and
superiors in the early history of Transcaucasia. On the basis of

Lenin's letters to Shaumyan, particularly that of May 19, 1914, it
is not too much to conjecture that, had Shaumyan not been executed in 1918, he and not Stalin might have been the chief executor
of Lenin's nationalities policy in Transcaucasia, perhaps even in all
Russia. Thus, more than once, and, even in greater instances than
these, as we shall see, death was kind to Joseph Stalin and removed
from his path men who might have been obstacles to his climb to
singular greatness and singular power.

If Lenin had written nothing more than his articles on the national question and the right of self-determination, his place in the
history of Russian socialist thought would have been ambiguous.
In them we seem to see Lenin as a complicated strategist and political thinker, and a would-be democrat. On the one hand there is
the Lenin of the mocking formula of "democratic centralism," the
undemocratic splits, contempt for majorities whether of the people,
or the working class, or the unions, or the party, or even of his own
committees and *troikas*. On the other hand, both for tactical reasons and because of unexamined inherited formulae, there is the
Lenin who, in such matters as the national question, appears to
remain a democrat. Both in his polemics with "Great-Russian chau-
vinists" and with those "abstract internationalists" whose zeal for the
unity of the human race found no place for the right of subject
peoples to self-determinatioh, Lenin seemed to speak with conviction in favor of democracy. So embarrassing are these utterances
for latter-day—anti-democratic disciples and practices that when the
Lenin Institute was preparing a twelve-volume edition of his *Selected Works* for wide distribution, it found room for only one of
his articles on the national question. And then it censored Lenin by
omitting two whole sections because they culminated in this categorical affirmation:

> Not a single Social Democrat, unless he is ready to de-
> clare that questions of political freedom and democracy are
> indifferent to him, and in that case it is clear that he has
> ceased to be a Social Democrat . . .

No socialism without democracy! No one is a socialist who is
indifferent to questions of political freedom and political democracy! To lose your attachment to freedom and democracy is to lose
your socialist soul! So Lenin urged in 1905 when his polemic
against Trotsky and Parvus concluded with his "whoever attempts

to achieve socialism by any other route than that of political democracy will inevitably arrive at the most absurd and reactionary
results, both political and economic." So Lenin urged in 1913-14
when he began his polemics on the national question. So he appeared to think until 1917. How he came to abandon democracy and
reveal the anti-democratic essence of his creed and temperament
provides the tragic climax of his life . . .

There is a peculiar ambivalence in the attitude of Lenin toward
nationalism. On the one hand he regarded it with aversion as a product of the bourgeois (bourgeois-democratic) era. Nationalism was
not to be preserved, strengthened, or "purified," but surmounted,
outlived and overcome by internationalism. ("Marxism is incapable
of being united with nationalism, be it ever so 'just,' 'purified,
refined . . . Marxism puts in place of any and every nationalism
its internationalism, the fusion of all nations into a higher unity.")
On the other hand he recognized that it would not be internationalism but nationalistic or imperialistic chauvinism if a victorious
revolution in a dominant nation should deny to peoples incorporated into it by conquest, the right to determine their own fate
themselves, and to separate if they desired. ("The awakening of the
masses from their feudal sleep, their fight against national oppression, for popular sovereignty, for the sovereignty of the nation—
that is progressive. From this it follows that Marxists have the
unconditional obligation to fight for the most determined and consistent democracy in every aspect of the national question. . . . To
demolish every kind of national oppression, every privilege of one
nation over another or of one language over another is the unconditional duty of the proletariat as a democratic force.")
But for Lenin there is a boundary line, hard to determine but
all-important, which must not be overreached. Beyond that, democracy and progress in the national question would turn into their
opposites, into the strengthening of nationalism and the "betrayal"
of proletarian internationalism. ("Struggle *against* every national
oppression—yes indeed. But struggle *for* any national development,
for 'national culture' as such—never!") The slogan of "national-
cultural autonomy" of the Bundists, Ukrainians, Austrian Marxists,
was an attempt to preserve something of national culture and
national values and carry these into the future internationalist
world. That was where the boundary line was overstepped, where
the "negative" task of assuring democratic rights "degenerated"
into the positively dangerous one of trying to preserve national

values. For Lenin there were no such positive national values. ("The proletariat is not only not willing to defend or further the national development of any nation, but on the contrary it warns the masses against such illusions . . . and welcomes any and every assimilation of nationalities—with the exception of those carried out by force or on the basis of privilege.")

In the West, Lenin continued, the national question had already been "settled," the general pattern being *one-nation, one-state*: the national state. But in the East, in Austria and much more in Russia, there still existed the "backward" multi-national state, sign of feudal backwardness, of need for a bourgeois-democratic revolution. The very fact of national oppression was a sign that these were "states whose internal constitution had remained abnormal and underdeveloped." Above all it was Russia, "more Asiatic than Asia, more backward than Austria-Hungary or China," that required a national self-determination program:

> . . . for those non-Russian peoples, which on the whole form the majority of the entire population—57%; which inhabit precisely the borderlands; in which the oppression of these alien races is much worse than in the neighboring states; . . . in which a number of oppressed nationalities in the borderlands have compatriots across the border . . . suffice it to recall Finns, Swedes, Poles, Ukrainians, Rumanians . . . and in which the development of capitalism and the general level of culture is not infrequently higher than in the center of the Great-Russian state.
>
> Can a nation be free if it oppresses other nations? It cannot. The interests of the freedom of the Great-Russian population demand a struggle against such oppression. . . .

But, inside the Empire, the proletariat of all nationalities must be united—regardless of national origin—into a single, centralized, all-Russian party. And all proletarians, regardless of national origin, must be taught to eschew, outgrow and despise all feelings of nationality as "bourgeois or petty bourgeois." If Russia were more advanced, and were facing like the West a socialist-proletarian instead of a bourgeois-democratic revolution, then, thought Lenin, there would be no problem of self-determination:

> It is precisely and solely because Russia and her neighbors are now passing through this epoch of bourgeois-democratic revolution that we require an item in our program on the right of nations to self-determination . . . The question of the *right* of nations to self-determination, i.e. the guarantee by the constitution of the state of an abso-

lutely free and absolutely democratic method of deciding the question of secession, must not be confused with the question of the *expediency* of this or that nation's seceding. The Social Democratic Party must decide the latter question *in each separate case from the point of view of the interests of social development as a whole, and the interests of the proletarian class struggle for socialism.*

What then would happen to the right of self-determination if Lenin should change his mind about Russia's being ripe only for a bourgeois-democratic revolution? And what would happen if the many-nationed, centralized, proletarian party (the duty of whose members is to agitate systematically against their respective nationalisms) should take power simultaneously throughout most of the lands and borderlands of the Russian Empire? What would happen then, not on paper, not in written constitutions, but in practice, to the right of secession? What if all other parties, including all national parties, should be outlawed? What then would be the worth, what the method of implementation, of "the guarantee of an absolutely free and absolutely democratic method of deciding the question of secession?" Would anything then be left, beyond a shadow of that very national-cultural autonomy which Lenin in all his articles (and Stalin in his article on the national question) considered as tantamount to treason to socialism?

By a turn of the screw of fate, the Austrian Marxists would ere long have to grant the "right of secession" which was not in the Austro-Marxist program, while Stalin would one day make "national separatism" a capital charge in the purges, and would adopt the "Austrian" or "Bundist" conception of "national-cultural autonomy" as one of the proudest achievements of the Soviet Union! And then, with a centralized economy, a centralized police control, a single centralized party to determine everything from Moscow, the Soviet "Union" would become a federal state in name only, but in real content the most rigidly centralized state in all history. "National-cultural autonomy" itself would be reduced to little more than the right to propagate in many tongues the same centrally issued directives and slogans and the same centrally organized cult of the Leader. The national autonomy policy, to use Stalin's own phrase, would be "national in form, but socialist in content," by which he means, centralized and total-statist.

Yet, at least until the Second World War, Lenin's ardent fight during the First for the equality and democratic right of self-determination of nationalities would continue to leave some impress upon the "national cultural" life of the Soviet Union.

CHAPTER XXXIV

THE INTERNATIONAL PREPARES

The political impotence of the German Social Democracy,
that is what fills all the peoples of Europe with fear. You
are a great, impressive, wonderful party, but you do not have
any direct influence on the policy of your government.
—*Jean Jaurès at the Amsterdam Congress, 1904*

L ENIN'S INTEREST in the national question came late in his career and
the views we analyzed in the last chapter ripened only slowly.
As a young Social Democrat he had been quite satisfied with the
resolution adopted by the International Socialist Congress of 1896:

> The Congress upholds the full right of self-determina-
> tion of all nations and expresses its sympathy for the workers
> of every country now suffering under the yoke of military,
> national or other despotism . . . and calls upon the workers
> of these countries to join the ranks of the class-conscious
> workers of the entire world in order to fight . . . for the
> aims of international Social Democracy.

Significantly, when the *Iskra* Editorial Board was working in 1902
on a draft program for the Russian movement, Lenin had left to
Martov the task of preparing the section on national self-determination. Lenin's interests lay elsewhere: in organization and the
land question. "It was Martov," Lenin observed ten years later,
"who drafted the national program and got it carried in 1903."
And as late as 1914, the first public address of Vladimir Ilyich after
the war began, once more congratulated Martov—without any reproaches or reservations—for his internationalist stand. Martov's
paper, he said, is today "the best Socialist paper in Europe." As the
war developed, his differences were not with Martov's own stand
and views, but with the latter's willingness to associate with people
who thought differently.

It was in 1907 that Lenin first glimpsed for a moment a thin
crack in the apparently solid structure of the Socialist International.
The occasion was the Stuttgart Congress, a splendid dress parade of
the mighty-seeming forces of the world labor movement. There
were 884 delegates from 25 nations and every continent. The Russian
delegation, this being 1907, was unprecedentedly huge: sixty-three
representatives from all factions and parties: Bolsheviks, Menshe-

viks, Social Revolutionaries, Bundists, Poles, Latvians, Armenians, Finns . . . Lenin, Martov, Plekhanov, Deutsch, Potresov, Trotsky, Khrustalev, Lunacharsky, Knuniyants, Litvinov, Meshkovsky, Evgenia Bosh, and many more whose names need not detain us. And of course, Rosa Luxemburg, looked upon as a leader of the Left Wing of the German party, the outstanding leader of the Polish Social Democracy, and the most active spokesman of the Russian delegation on the questions of war and militarism.

The best International Congress that has ever been held, said Lenin. In a popular calendar for workers he wrote:

> It marked the final consolidation of the Second International and the transformation of International congresses into businesslike meetings . . .

It had made "big strides forward" in the condemnation of "ministerialism" (the entrance of Socialists into coalition cabinets with bourgeois parties).[1]

The Stuttgart Congress was also notable, Lenin continued, for

[1] In the pre-war socialist movement, "ministerialism" was the chief chemical test for distinguishing Left from Right. Whoever opposed the entrance of socialists into bourgeois cabinets was a true revolutionist; whoever favored such action was a personal careerist, or, at best, a class-collaborationist, reformist, gradualist and opportunist. Lenin took this for granted, as did the Mensheviks, although, unlike them, he was "unorthodox" enough to make an exception of a provisional revolutionary government in time of actual revolution. In the war years, he would become the chief denouncer of all socialist Ministers entering wartime emergency coalition governments. Their ministerialism was to him no longer mere misguided opportunism but deliberate and calculated treason. In 1917, the roles of Lenin and the Mensheviks, as we shall see, got somehow reversed. They became advocates of socialists' entering the Provisional Revolutionary Government and he opposed it. In the Communist International he made anti-ministerialism one of the tests of eligibility. But today we have become so used to the spectacle of Communist Ministers entering into coalition governments that Lenin's remark cited above now needs explanation. Of course, "the situation has changed," as has the function of the Communist Ministers, who now enter into coalition governments to get hold of key power posts such as Police, Justice, the Army, in order to eliminate the other parties by purge and set up a Communist police state. They also seek negotiation posts such as Foreign Affairs and Trade so that they may function as agents of the Russian Government within the delegations sent by their own government to negotiate with the Russians. In countries where Russian influence is strongest there are no more zealous collaborationists and ministerialists than the Communist parties. Whether they collaborate or go into opposition, or do both simultaneously, depends primarily on changing Russian interests. Thus Lenin's remark on "the big strides forward of the Stuttgart Congress in condemning ministerialism" sounds today like the echo from another world of primal innocence. Yet, all through the next few chapters we shall have to bear in mind the fact that "ministerialism" was then the chief opportunist sin or treachery, alike to the pre-war Left, to Leninist wartime socialism, and, as long as Lenin lived, to the Communist International.

having adopted admirable resolutions on imperialism, militarism, the colonial question, and the slowly enlarging shadow of impending war.

> And let us note this welcome feature—he added proudly —that *all* the socialists of Russia [Bolsheviks, Mensheviks, Social Revolutionaries, Poles, Finns, Bundists, etc.] unanimously and on *all* questions, voted in a revolutionary spirit.

Never had Vladimir Ilyich been so inclusive in his use of the term "socialist" or so generous in his approbation of the friendly-enemy parties of the common front against tsarism!

Only one smudge did he find on the shining page written by the Congress: the "remarkable and sad feature" that the German Social Democracy, revered leader of the International "which has always hitherto upheld the revolutionary standpoint in Marxism," had wavered on the questions of colonialism and war. And the great August Bebel was among the cautiously equivocal, if not among the waverers or outright opportunists. But Kautsky and Clara Zetkin and others on the German delegation had joined with the Poles and Russians under the lead of Rosa Luxemburg, Lenin and Martov, in stiffening the hesitant Bebel, and repulsing the opportunists.

> On the colonial question—continued Lenin in his Almanac report—an opportunist majority was formed in the Commission, and the following monstrous sentence appeared in the draft resolution reported out by the Commission:
> *"The Congress does not on principle and for all time reject all colonial policy, which, under a socialist régime, may exercize a civilizing influence."*

The German, Eduard David, had led the fight for the adoption of this "monstrous sentence." His argument: "You cannot fight something with nothing. As against capitalist colonial policy, the socialists must propose a positive program of protection of the rights of the natives." But Karl Kautsky, the other German leader whom Lenin admired equally with Bebel, had led the attack on this proposed new departure in colonial policy:

> I contend—he said—that democracy and socialist policy have nothing in common with conquest and foreign rule . . . If we want to exert a civilizing influence upon primitive peoples, the first prerequisite is to gain their confidence by granting them freedom . . . The sentence [proposed by David and the Commission] is at variance with all our socialist and democratic thinking . . .

When it came to a vote, the "monstrous sentence" was defeated. But it was by a bare majority of 127 to 108. And then only because the delegations from colonial lands and from countries having no colonies of their own joined hands with the solid Russian delegation and the Left Wing minorities from Germany, England and France. Lenin was satisfied with the victory, but saddened by the fact that his favorite party, the honored leader of the International, had wavered for a moment before his eyes. It was not until seven years later that he came to realize that the momentary divergence had marked a fork in the road whence would diverge two irreconcilable paths.

More important than the Colonial Question was the related resolution on Militarism and War. All over Europe arms were piling up and arms taxation was becoming an increasingly intolerable burden. Since the turn of the century there had been an unending succession of incidents and alarms: the Fashoda crisis, the Tangier incident, the Algeciras crisis, the Agadir incident. The leaders of the European socialist parties, particularly the German and French, had followed these events with mounting tension. The International Socialist Bureau and Congresses had considered the questions of war and militarism repeatedly, but always their pledges, adjurations, threats and resolves had been shrouded in ambiguity, because they were inclined to distinguish between the duties of socialist parties in defensive wars and in aggressive wars, and because they staked all on preventing war.

But what if both sides plotted war? What if the complicated maneuvers of behind-the-scenes diplomacy should permit all governments to give their participation the appearance of defense against aggression? And what should the socialist parties do if, despite all their efforts to prevent war, it should nevertheless break out? To these questions, up to the Stuttgart Congress of 1907, the International had never given clear and unequivocal answers.

As early as the International Congress held in Brussels in 1890, the general outlines of the coming war of 1914-18 had been foreseen, and the German leader Wilhelm Liebknecht (father of that Karl Liebknecht who will soon figure prominently in our story) had joined with the French leader Eduard Vaillant in a pledge to avert war by joint protests, joint pledges, and the joint cooperation of French and German labor. But a Dutch delegate, Domela Nieuwenhuis, had ventured to ask them: "And what will happen if all our pledges, protests, demonstrations and threats fail to prevent war?" If you are pledged to defend your country when it is attacked, he told the delegates, then all is lost, for the distinction between defensive and offensive wars is really meaningless and diplomats will always know how to convince their own people that the opponent nation was the aggressor. There was only one pledge that would have meaning and be worth while, and that was for the socialist parties of all countries to pledge themselves to refuse to support any war but their own war for socialism. Hence, if war came between their respective nations they must call upon the workers to refuse to render military service and to answer the war by a general strike. His motion was voted down as "impractical" to carry out under the conditions of martial law such as would undoubtedly prevail once war was declared.

In 1893, at the Zurich Congress of the International, he repeated his proposal. Again it was voted down. One of the strongest arguments against it came from Plekhanov, who said that a call for a general strike would be most effective precisely in the freest and most advanced lands with the best organized labor movements, thereby yielding up progressive Western Europe to the mercies of the "Cossacks of Russia," a land which in 1893 had virtually no labor organization or labor press at all. Engels received the news of the vote with satisfaction and wrote a letter to Lafargue in which he praised the Congress for having rejected "high-sounding and empty phrases."

> People must realize—Engels had written in 1890, in an Almanac of the French Party—that if France, in alliance with Russia, should declare war on Germany, she would be fighting against the strongest Social Democracy in Europe; and that we would have no choice but to oppose with all our strength any aggressor who was on the side of Russia. For, if we are defeated, the Social Democratic movement in Europe is smashed for twenty years. But if not, we shall come to power ourselves. The present system in Germany cannot possibly survive a war.

Engels went on to assure the French workers that he thought the French Republic superior to the German monarchy—as a representative of the bourgeois revolution. But not as an ally of tsarist Russia against a Germany that was on the eve of socialist victory. In Germany socialism would soon triumph (within a decade), and then a socialist Germany would of course undo the injustice of the annexation of Alsace-Lorraine, and would liberate Poland. But if France in her impatience should subordinate herself to the Tsar and attack the Rhine while Russia attacked from the East, "then Germany would be fighting for her very existence." If she won, there was nothing to gain. But if she lost, she would be crushed, reduced in size to proportions that would make it impossible for socialism to develop.

At this article, a storm broke out in France. In due course, Engels had replied to his critics:

> If the French socialists do not expressly state that in a defensive war they would be willing to repulse an attack by Kaiser Wilhelm, it is because this is so glaringly obvious, so self-evident, that it is not worth saying. There is not a single socialist in Germany who does not think that in such an event the French socialists would simply be doing their duty in defending their national independence.

And the following year, 1891, he had even written to Bebel:

> If we are convinced that the thing will start next spring, we could hardly be opposed to the credits [of the military budget] on principle, and then we would be in a pretty desperate position. The lick-spittle parties would boast that they had always been right, and that we had had to eat our own words. Also, such an unexpected change of front would cause appalling friction within the Party—and internationally as well.

Rather fantastically, Engels advised that the Party Deputies in the Reichstag should refuse to approve any credits aiming at transforming the existing equipment or at forming new military cadres, since these "would not be ready in time for war in the spring." But they should vote all military credits for those measures

> . . . which will bring our present army nearer to a people's militia, which will simply strengthen our defenses, which will train and arm all men from 17 to 60 who have not yet enlisted . . . We cannot demand that the existing military organization should be completely altered while the danger of war persists. But if there is an attempt to take the great mass of men who are fit for service but have not been trained, and to train them as well as possible and organize them in cadres—for real fighting, not for parading and all that nonsense—then that is an approach to our idea of a people's militia which we can accept. If the danger of war increases, we can tell the government that we would be ready, if they made it possible by decent treatment, to give our support against the foreign enemy—on condition that they (the government) will fight relentlessly and use every means, even revolutionary ones. If Germany is attacked from east and west, then all means of defense are good.

> The existence of the nation is then at stake, and we, too, have a position to maintain, and a future which we have won by hard fighting.

Bebel rejected this suggestion of conditional voting of war credits. He and his colleagues in the Reichstag voted against the war credits, and, by the next year, 1892, Engels spoke no more of such concessions. In 1893, Engels wrote a series in *Vorwaerts* called *Can Europe Disarm?* His answer to this question, verging on what Lenin would, in anyone but Marx or Engels, regard as "utopian pacifism," said:

> Such changes are possible at this moment. They can be made by the existing governments and in the existing political situation . . . I limit myself to such proposals as any existing government can accept without endangering the security of its country. I am endeavoring to show that, from a purely military viewpoint, there is nothing to prevent the gradual abolition of the regular army; and that, if a regular army *is* still maintained, it is maintained not for military but political reasons—in a word, that the army is meant for defense not against a foreign enemy but against a domestic one.

Engels' specific proposals included: the gradual scaling down of the length of military service by international agreement and the ultimate substitution of a system of short-term training of the entire male youth of each country in a locally based militia, easily usable for defense but "useless" for wars of conquest, with every citizen keeping his gun in his home. Since Prussia had begun the arms race, Prussia should take the initiative in calling such an international conference to shorten the term of service in all branches. If France accepted, the war danger would disappear. If she rejected it, she would be worse off, since Russia was not yet in a position to be of real help, while England would doubtless have been won by this appeal to a position of benevolent neutrality toward a Germany that had offered to disarm. In case of war, the final decision would lie with England:

> When she puts her fleet at the disposal of one side, the other will simply be starved out and its imports of grain cut off . . . The blockaded side will have to capitulate as sure as two and two make four.

Again Bebel quietly ignored Engels' proposals as utopian. There the matter had rested after Engels' death (1895), with the armies and navies growing, war incidents multiplying, tension accumulating, and the socialists still uncertain about "defensive" and "aggressive" wars, and with no program on what to do if war came despite their efforts to prevent it. In 1900, without mentioning his name, the Paris International Congress finally rejected Engels' idea of voting war credits under certain conditions. It resolved that:

> The socialist parliamentary deputies in all parliaments pledge themselves unconditionally to vote against every military expenditure and all expenditure for the navy and for colonial military expeditions.

Now it was 1907 and all the socialist parties of the world were at Stuttgart to consider the situation created by back-breaking arms budgets, by the open Franco-Russian alliance, by Kaiser Wilhelm's sword rattling and the repeated crises and alarms. Marx and Engels were dead. Old Wilhelm Liebknecht, who had voted against war credits in the Franco-Prussian War and gone to jail for it, had died in 1900. Marx and Engels had been deceived by Bismarck's forged Ems telegram, and their own general attitude, into believing that the war of 1870 was for Germany a purely defensive war, but Liebknecht had opposed it from the first day. They had not changed their minds until the fall of Napoleon III at Sedan, when they began attacking Bismarck's aggression and defending the new French Republic. Bebel, too, had opposed that war from the first day.

Now, as the grand old man of the German Social Democracy, he prepared the *Resolution on Militarism and War*. Though he was loved and admired more than any other living man in the International, there were in those days no unanimous resolutions or infallible leader cults in this assemblage of men devoted to the cause of freedom and socialism. He was attacked sharply from many points of view. Gustav Hervé of France demanded that the German socialists repudiate "defense of the Fatherland" and that the International repudiate patriotism in every land and pledge itself to "answer" any war by general strike and rebellion. Rosa Luxemburg found his formula "too rigid . . . Hervé is an *enfant*, an *enfant terrible*." But not for that did she exempt Bebel's draft resolution from criticism. Nor reject Hervé's idea of a general strike, if and when a sharpening wartime crisis might make it possible:

> I have asked for the floor—she said—on behalf of the Russian and the Polish Delegations, to remind you that we should think of the Great Russian Revolution in connection with this point (of general strike and war). . . . The Russian Revolution sprang up not merely as a result of the war;

it also served to put an end to the war. Otherwise tsarism
would surely have continued the war . . . After Vollmar's
speech, and partly after Bebel's, we consider it necessary
to sharpen Bebel's resolution, and we have worked out an
amendment which we shall later submit. In our amendment
we go somewhat beyond Comrades Jaurès and Vaillant in
that we contend that, in case of war, the agitation should
be directed not merely toward its termination, but also
toward utilizing the war to hasten the overthrow of class
rule in general.

Bebel answered his critics by contending that a merely inflam-
matory resolution not backed up by the strength to carry it out,
would serve only to give the police pretexts for outlawing parties
and union.

Lenin said nothing, for Rosa Luxemburg was expressing his view
and Martov's and that of the whole group of delegations from
Russia. But here is how he summarized the debate in his Almanac
article from which we have been quoting:

Hervé's scheme to "reply" to any war by a strike and an
uprising, revealed an utter lack of understanding of the
fact that the application of one or other means of struggle
depends not on any decision revolutionaries may have made
previously but on the objective conditions of the particular
crisis, both economic and political, caused by the war. But
even though Hervé did show that he was lightminded,
superficial, easily carried away by resonant phrases, it
would be extreme shortsightedness to reply to him by a
mere dogmatic exposition of the general truths of socialism.
Vollmar (German Right Wing) particularly dropped into
this error, and Bebel and Guesde were not entirely free of
it. With the extraordinary conceit of a man infatuated with
stereotyped parliamentarism, Vollmar attacked Hervé without noticing that his own narrowmindedness and hardened
opportunism *compel* one to recognize the living stream in
Hervéism *in spite* of the theoretical absurdity and folly of
the manner in which Hervé himself presents the question.
It sometimes happens that at a new turning point of a
movement, theoretical absurdities cover up some practical
truth. And this aspect of the question, the appeal that not
only parliamentary methods of struggle should be valued,
the appeal to act in accordance with the new conditions
of the future war and the future crisis, was stressed by the
revolutionary Social Democrats, especially by Rosa Luxemburg in her speech. Together with the Russian Social Democratic delegates—Lenin and Martov both stood together

in agreement on this—Rosa Luxemburg proposed amendments to Bebel's resolution and these amendments emphasized the need for agitation among the youth, the necessity of taking advantage of the crisis created by war for the purpose of hastening the downfall of the bourgeoisie, the necessity of bearing in mind the inevitable change of methods and means of struggle in accordance with the intensification of the class struggle and the changes in the political situation. Thus Bebel's resolution, dogmatically one-sided, lifeless and open to a Vollmarian interpretation, was finally transformed into an altogether different resolution.

The most important amendment offered by Rosa Luxemburg in the name of the delegation proposed to add two final paragraphs to the resolution. They read:

> If a war threatens to break out, it is the duty of the working class and of its parliamentary representatives in the countries involved, supported by the consolidating activity of the International Bureau, to exert every effort to prevent the outbreak of war by means they consider most effective, which naturally vary according to the sharpening of the class struggle and of the general political situation.
>
> Should war break out nonetheless, it is their duty to intervene in favor of its speedy termination and to do all in their power to utilize the economic and political crisis caused by the war to rouse the peoples and thereby to hasten the abolition of capitalist class rule.

After dickering with Luxemburg, Lenin and Martov to tone down the wording of their amendments in the interests of party legality (e.g. the substitution of "agitation among the youth" for "agitation among military recruits")[2] Bebel accepted the above crucial amendment, and three others unanimously by acclamation.

"Should war break out nonetheless," reads the last sentence we have just quoted, *"it is their duty to intervene in favor of its speedy termination."* This Lenin would later play down as "miserable, utopian pacifism." But the rest of the sentence—*"and to do all in their power to utilize the economic and political crisis caused by the war to rouse the peoples and thereby to hasten the abolition of capitalist class rule,"* i.e. attempt to end the war by revolution—

[2] Despite Bebel's precautions, the German Government understood the circumlocution and in April, 1908, passed a law forbidding all persons under twenty years of age to attend political or union meetings. All youth organizations, including the Social Democratic Young, were dissolved, and all youth agitation remained illegal until the revolution of 1918.

this was to be the core of Lenin's and Luxemburg's activities when war did come. And it was to be the cornerstone of the foundation of the Third or Communist International. Thus, in retrospect, the Stuttgart International Socialist Congress of 1907 proves to have been a decisive turning point in the history of the Second International.

So important an event could not go without the usual touch of Stalinist "editing" of history in the course of the nineteen thirties. As late as 1936, a note in Volume XII of Lenin's *Collected Works* still says modestly that "Lenin took an active part in the work of the Stuttgart Congress" (Third Russian Edition, p. 456). But, despite Lenin's own statement to the contrary, Martov's name is omitted from the note, which speaks of "the amendments of Lenin and Rosa Luxemburg to the resolution" (p. 457). And a similar note to the International Publishers' edition of Lenin's *Selected Works*, Volume IV (the notes were prepared by the Marx-Engels-Lenin Institute) further shifts the picture: "The Left Wing of the Congress (Rosa Luxemburg and others), headed by Lenin, moved an amendment . . ." This peculiar use of parentheses and a comma, and this apparently trivial and "innocent" emendation of history, will yet prove of tremendous importance to our story. As for Lenin himself, he never concealed, nor dreamt of concealing, the fact that Martov had joined with him and Rosa Luxemburg in elaborating the amendments, and that Rosa, and not he, had "headed," i.e. been the spokesman for the Left Wing of the Congress and for the Russian and Polish delegations, and the outstanding leader of the fight, both in the commission and on the floor.

On October 17, 1912, tiny Montenegro (population 230,000— "together with the Russians we number 170,000,000!") declared war on Turkey. The Great Powers, still shaken by their glance over the precipice at Agadir (Morocco) in 1911, were in no mood to permit another international crisis. But Montenegro had acted on the basis of a secret alliance with Greece, Bulgaria and Serbia, and in a few days the entire Balkans were ablaze.

Turkey was like a wounded animal, followed by beasts of prey large and small. Like China and Persia, she had begun a desperate effort to modernize and westernize herself as a safeguard against extinction. All three of them had been deeply stirred by Japan's defeat of the "Western" power, Russia, and by the Russian Revolution of 1905, and all three were in the throes of civil war, which, until it should be completed, would leave them helpless. Few spectacles of the first half of our "enlightened twentieth century" were uglier than the attempt of powers large and small—England, France, Germany, Austria-Hungary, Italy, Japan, Tsarist and Stalinist Russia—to partition these countries before they should succeed in their own regeneration.

The Young Turk Revolution had begun in 1908. By the introduction of Western ideas, Western technique, Western nationalism, centralism, parliamentarism and democracy, it sought to save Turkey from disintegration. But the beginning of Turkish civil war was taken as a signal by the Bulgarian prince to end the nominal suzerainty of Turkey and declare its independence and by Crete to revolt and join Greece (1908). Then Austria violated the Treaty of Berlin by annexing the Turkish, Slav-inhabited provinces of Bosnia and Herzegovina, over whose Christians she exercised a "protectorate." Since these provinces were largely inhabited by Serbs, Serbian nationalists were outraged and began to look to Russia for support against Austria, whereupon Austria naturally snuggled closer to Germany. In 1911, Italy too declared war on Turkey long enough to seize Tripoli, Cyrenaica, and some of the islands of the Aegean. And now, in 1912, the allied Balkan powers fell upon Macedonia, Thrace, and the Adriatic provinces (Albania).

The uneasy Great Powers tried to localize the war and bring it to a speedy conclusion. But in 1913 it broke out afresh, then spilled over into a second war between Bulgaria on the one hand and Greece, Rumania, Serbia and Montenegro on the other, over the division of the spoils (Macedonia, Thrace, Albania). Peace was patched up a second time (September 29, 1913), but it left all questions unsettled and all nerves on edge. Bulgaria still coveted all of Macedonia and Thrace and the port of Salonika. Macedonia, divided between Greece, Serbia and Bulgaria, began to develop an independence movement of its own. Serbia and Montenegro were prevented from dividing Albania between them, because the latter was regarded as potential booty both by Italy and Austria, which rivals united to make it into an independent state. To her grievance about Bosnia and Herzegovina, Serbia thus added a fresh grievance concerning the Adriatic. The Russian press increased its talk about "protecting our Slav brothers." Germany increased its support of Austria. The situation was becoming so combustible that the tiniest spark might set off a general conflagration. In less than a year, that spark flew at Sarajevo and the fire spread over Europe, then over all the other continents of the globe.

Lenin seems to have underestimated the significance of the Balkan Wars of 1912 and 1913. His occasional brief articles on the subject denounced Russian chauvinism for seeking to "rob a piece of Turkey"; ridiculed the talk of "Slav brotherhood" as a cover for Russian protectorates and annexations; asserted that Slav peasants and Turk peasants were brothers, and that what was needed was a federation of the Balkan peoples, independent alike of Russian and Austrian "protection." But he thought of the whole conflict as a localized one.

Leon Trotsky, living in Vienna, closer to the boiling Balkan cauldron, hastened to the scene of the "little wars" as correspondent for the *Kievskaya Mysl*, liberal Russian daily. He was glad to escape from the failure of his "August Bloc." And he wanted to see war at first hand. The future War Commissar was shocked by the face of war:

> You in Russia—read his first dispatch—know it and believe in it. My mind does not accept this combination of the things of everyday life, of chicken, cigarettes, barefooted and smut-nosed boys, with the incredibly tragic fact of war. I know that war has been declared, and that it has already begun, but I have not yet learned to believe in it.

In the Balkans he learned something of the politics of Serbia, Bulgaria and Rumania, became convinced of the need of a United Balkan Federation and a United States of Europe, met Balkan socialists whom he was later to bring into the Communist International. Chief of these was Christian Rakovsky, influential in all Balkan socialist parties, a Bulgarian by birth, a Rumanian by virtue of the accidents of map-drawing when frontiers were shuffled, a French physician by education, a master of French, German, Russian, English, Turkish and all the Balkan tongues, and a future leading figure in the Soviet Union, the Communist International and Soviet diplomacy. For a time he would serve as President of the Ukrainian Soviet Republic, which Russia has constantly been supplying with non-Ukrainian leaders from Rakovsky to Krushchev. He would end up by being purged as a Trotskyist.

The news story of "Antid Oto" (Trotsky's pen-name) which attracted most attention was one concerning Bulgarian atrocities on wounded and captured Turkish prisoners. It was a common matter for the Russian press to dwell on Turkish atrocities against Armenians. Indeed, in a letter of Viceroy Vorontsov-Dashkov of Transcaucasia to Tsar Nicholas, dated October 10, 1912, we find:

> It is necessary to take open action in defense of the Armenians in Turkey, especially at the present time, so as to prepare in advance a sympathetic population in those

localities which, as matters stand, might willy-nilly prove
to be in the sphere of our military operations.

But what was unique about "Antid Oto" was his venturing to
write on atrocities committed by "our Slav brothers" against the
Turks. The dispatch attracted national attention, and was met with
the suggestion that the pen-name of "Antid Oto" disguised an
émigré revolutionary who had entered into the pay of Austria-
Hungary. This was an old device: to answer unwelcome criticism
by branding the critic an enemy agent. We shall meet with it
again!

The leaders of the Socialist International, already frightened by
the Agadir incident of 1911, now called a special Emergency International Congress in Basel for November 24, 1912. It met for two
days with no other order of business but the war danger and measures for peace. Every prior demonstration against war in the history of the International was eclipsed by the solemn Emergency
Congress at Basel. But Lenin, who could have gone as representative of his Central Committee, attached more importance to the
problem of completing the split in the Russian party, and especially
in the Duma Fraction. He contented himself with sending a Bolshevik delegation of five, headed by Leo Kamenev. The others
were Shklovsky, Troyanovsky and his wife, Elena Rozmirovich,
and Vladimirsky. The total Russian delegation from all parties and
factions was thirty-six. Lenin's chief interest at the moment was in
the attempt of his people, backed by Plekhanov, to have one of the
thirty-six, Gorbunov, representative of the Petersburg "Initiative
Group" or Liquidators, barred from the meetings of the Russian
delegation at the Basel Congress. Gorbunov was not excluded,
whereupon the Plekhanovists and Leninists walked out of the
Russian delegation meeting, one more success of Lenin's effort to
spread the Prague split throughout every institution of the Party.
But the Congress, intent on the war danger, paid no attention to
the "quarrelsome" Russians and their "private" controversy. When
delegate Shklovsky finally got around to writing Lenin a suggestion
that he should print a pamphlet report on the Basel Congress,
Lenin answered testily:

> Rather late in the day! Evidently something was lacking
> (or was there a surplus of something?) in Basel. Kamenev
> of course was over his ears in work, but what about the
> other four? Surely it was obvious that one ought to have
> written *daily* for *Pravda*. Surely it was not hard to distrib-

ute the work. Not a single letter went to *Pravda* from the place, whereas the Liquidators sent several to *Luch* . . . None of the delegates except Kamenev wrote here about Basel . . . I am *enormously* pleased with the Basel results, for those idiots, the Liquidators, allowed themselves to be caught on the Initiative Group!! Those swine [*svoloch*, "riff-raff," "scum," but with overtones that make it about as harsh an epithet as our "those bastards"] couldn't possibly have been trapped any better. But the inactivity of our delegates, and some inexplicable inability to open their mouths, has outraged me. (After all, four or five *knew how to speak* German.) Who spoke? With whom? How? About what? Not a word from anyone except Kamenev. Yet agitation [on the split] among the Germans is *very* important . . . [Letter of early December, 1912, *Collected Works*, Vol. XXIX, p. 55.]

And that is all! Not a word on the war danger, on possible differences in the International, on the solemn purpose and decisions of the Congress! Yet in retrospect, Lenin would come to realize that the Basel decisions were more important even than those taken at Stuttgart. They would provide him in 1914 with his chief wartime platform and talking point against all those who supported their governments in the war.

The manifesto "On the International Situation" adopted unanimously by the Basel Extraordinary Congress began by quoting once more the pledge of the Stuttgart Congress ("Should war break out nonetheless, it is their duty to intervene in favor of its speedy termination and to do all in their power to utilize the economic and political crisis, caused by the war, to rouse the peoples and thereby to hasten the abolition of capitalist class rule.") Next it noted "with satisfaction the complete unanimity of the socialist parties and trade unions in all countries in the war against war." Upon the Balkan socialists it enjoined opposition to any renewal of hostilities between Serbs, Bulgarians, Rumanians and Greeks, and also the defense of "the rights of the Balkan peoples, Turks and Albanians, who are now in the opposite camp."

It is the duty of the Social Democratic parties of Austria, Hungary, Croatia, Slavonia, Bosnia, and Herzegovina to work for the prevention of an attack of the Danubian monarchy upon Serbia. [Prophetic words!] . . . The Congress expects that the Russian, Finnish, and Polish proletariat . . . will combat every design of tsarism, whether upon Armenia or upon Constantinople, and concentrate all its force upon the revolutionary struggle for liberation from tsarism . . .

But the most important task in the International's activities devolves upon the working class of Germany, France and England . . . to demand that their respective governments withhold all support from both Austria-Hungary and Russia. . . .

Let the governments be mindful of the fact that they cannot let loose a war without danger to themselves. Let them recall that the Franco-German War was followed by the revolutionary uprising of the Commune, that the Russo-Japanese War set in motion the revolutionary forces of the peoples in the Russian Empire . . . It would be sheer madness for the governments to fail to realize that the very thought of the monstrosity of a world war would inevitably call forth the indignation and the revolt of the working class . . .

Thus we have a constant progression: 1900, the Paris International Congress adopts a pledge for all parties "to vote unconditionally against all military expenditures"; 1907, the Stuttgart Congress pledges itself "to utilize the crisis caused by war to hasten the abolition of capitalist rule"; 1912, the Basel Emergency Congress warns that a war "would call forth the revolt of the working class." And there is a similar progression in the definition of the war itself, its Balkan causes, its Anglo-French-German and Russian-Austrian-Serbian components, so that it is no longer talk about war in general but about a specific war, the outlines and salient features of which are precisely foreseen—in short, about a war exactly described in September, 1912, which would even break out as foreseen, with an Austro-Hungarian ultimatum to Serbia in July of 1914.

CHAPTER XXXV

A WORLD ENDS

Our one agreed aim in World War I was to break up German militarism. It was no part of our original intention to break up the Habsburg and Ottoman Empires, to create Czechoslovakia or resurrect Poland, to make a Russian revolution, to treble the size of Serbia and double that of Rumania, to create Iraq and Estonia and Lithuania and a Jewish National Home, or to give the keys of the Brenner and the Adriatic to Italy. Yet, in the outcome, all these—and much else—sprang from the war . . . while the one thing which we promised ourselves, the destruction of German militarism, we failed to achieve. —*H. N. Fieldhouse*

MONTH BY MONTH through the years 1912, 1913 and 1914 international tension mounted. War talk in the air, national feelings rising, the nations spending fantastic sums on "preparations for defense," presidents, kings, ministers, generals, exchanging visits and reviewing each other's armies. Like every acute political observer, Lenin was aware of all this, sensed its meaning; yet he could not quite believe it. To his sister Anna he wrote of his move to Cracow:

> I hope it will be easier for us to see each other, that is, if war does not break out, and I do not believe it will. [Autumn, 1912.]

To his sister Maria:

> There is much talk about war here as you can see by the papers. If war does break out, I shall probably have to go to Vienna or perhaps to the town where we last met [Stockholm], but I do not believe there will be a war. [November, 1912.]

To Gorky in December, 1912:

> There will probably not be a war and we shall stay here for the time being, taking advantage of the Poles' desperate hatred of tsarism.

And yet again, early in 1913, the remark already quoted:

> A war between Austria and Russia would be a very useful thing for the revolution in all of Eastern Europe, but it

is not likely that Franz Joseph and Nikolasha will give us that pleasure . . .

The leaders of the Socialist International, closer to the secrets of their governments because of the powerful parliamentary delegations of socialists in Germany, France and Austria, were more alarmed. They arranged frequent emergency conferences of all sorts, but, as we have seen, Lenin did not even attend the Emergency International Socialist Congress as Basle, called in November, 1912, specifically to meet the war danger.

When the International Socialist Bureau gathered in London in December, 1913, again Lenin did not attend, nor did he send Kamenev, but the less known and less important Litvinov, as the representative of the Bolsheviks. All his energies were absorbed at that time in completing the split in the Duma Fraction and making absolute the split in the Russian Social Democratic Party. The leaders of the International, on the motion of Rosa Luxemburg and Karl Kautsky, were attempting to heal splits in the Russian party as well as in the English movement.[1]

In order that the working class may put forth all its strength in the struggle against capitalism, it is necessary that in every country there should exist only *one* socialist party as there is only *one* proletariat—read Kautsky's motion. Plekhanov, who had till now been supporting Lenin against the Liquidators, joined in the movement for unity, even urging that the time was ripe for uniting the Social Democracy with the Social Revolutionary Party. All Russian factions, including the Social Revolutionaries, agreed, as did both Rosa Luxemburg's faction of the Polish Party and the anti-Luxemburg Warsaw Opposition, and the Left Wing of the Polish Socialist Party, as well. But Lenin would have none of it. Through the Prague Congress he had captured the Party trademark or firm name. With the aid of police agent Malinovsky, he had just split the Duma Fraction and won control of the metal workers' union. *Pravda* was gaining in circulation over the Menshevik *Luch*. The Bolsheviks were beginning to win the upper hand in trade union and social security elections. He had just won a majority in the Lettish Central Committee and had tied up with the Polish Warsaw Opposition against Rosa Luxemburg in the Polish Social Democratic Party. He would press his opponents to the wall. They would accept "unity" on his terms, or he would destroy them. True, the International was the supreme body, the embodiment of internationalism, but what

[1] In England they were trying to unite the Labor Party, the Independent Labor Party, the Fabian Society, and the Socialist Party of Great Britain. Unity was effected on a federated basis.

did its leader know of him and his fight or of Russian conditions? He felt confident that they would remain true to internationalism without his personal presence. He held them at arm's length, sent Litvinov to "their" Bureau meeting with a prepared statement, then sent Inessa Armand, still less important, to the special all-Russian unity conference called by the International at Brussels, for July 16, 1914, a fateful month in a fateful year! Inessa was selected, according to Krupskaya, because Ilyich wanted a "firm" person who could resist a "storm of indignation" from the other Russian factions and from all the leaders of the International, and who could stubbornly repeat his prepared statement in French and German as well as Russian. War was far from his mind now in that fatal summer of 1914. It had yielded first place in his thoughts to the faction war.

The Russian police became alarmed. What if the International, with its great prestige, did force unity, and all the energies that the various factions and parties had been using against each other should suddenly be turned against the government? What if the news of unity should end the bewilderment and sullen rancor of the working class and arouse a new confidence and determination? The Okhrana instructed all its secret agents in the various factions and parties:

> . . . steadfastly and persistently to defend the idea of the complete impossibility of any organizational fusion whatsoever of these tendencies and particularly the union of the Bolsheviks with the Mensheviks.[2]

The police might be worried, but Lenin was not worried. He did not know of their instructions, but even if he had, it would not have stopped him in his determination "steadfastly and persistently to defend the idea of the complete impossibility of any organizational fusion whatsoever . . . and particularly of the union of the Bolsheviks with the Mensheviks." And he was so sure that he was right, on every difference large and small, of organization, of strategy, of tactics, of principle, of personnel, that neither a police instruction nor an instruction from the honored leadership of the entire international working class could swerve him from his path. Surely unity was good, but only the right sort of unity, unity on his terms and under his leadership. Certainly, he was a loyal and zealous internationalist and cherished the International as the embodiment of international solidarity and the means of international action. Of course, he admired the great German Social Democratic Party

[2] *Bolshevik: Dokumenty po istorii bolshevizma s 1903 po 1916 god byvsh. Moskovsk. Okhrannogo Otdeleniya.* Edited by M. A. Tsyavlovsky, Moscow, 1918, pp. 146-48.

above all other parties, and Kautsky above all living Marxists. But in Russia he was right and his methods were right. What did the opposition of all the other Russian factions matter? And the pressure of all the other parties of the International? What did they all know about Russia? Why didn't they let him fight his own fight in his own way? He was winning, and he was not going to let any one stop him. He had his "bull-dog grip" (as Vera Zasulich had phrased it), and he would not let go.

> The Mensheviks only want to scold me before the International. I shall not give them that pleasure. Besides, it would be a waste of time. It is better to serve the cause than to chatter . . .

The Subcommission on Russian Unity of the Socialist International met on July 16-17, 1914. Along with Inessa Armand, Lenin sent Vladimirsky, Popov, and also Hanecki of the anti-Luxemburg faction of the Polish Social Democracy. Altogether there were eleven Russian groups, factions and parties represented. Everybody spoke in favor of unity except his delegation. Everybody was ready to reopen all questions for fresh decision, or regard the past as past and start anew. But his delegation stubbornly refused to vote on anything. Inessa read her statement, and that was that. It accused all of Lenin's opponents of not being socialists, of refusing to accept discipline, of wanting to liquidate the underground organization, of wanting to form a "bourgeois labor party," of desiring blocs with the bourgeoisie, of wanting to wreck the Party program by substituting "cultural autonomy" for "national self-determination." It culminated in a series of ultimatums which may fairly be summed up in the words: "*Let those who want unity with us unconditionally accept the decisions of the Prague Congress and unconditionally submit to the institutions created by it.*"

Inessa was answered with reasoning, pleas, argument, persuasion. A resolution was drawn up to satisfy and dispose of all of Lenin's charges and demands:

> 1. All groups accept the program of the Russian Social Democracy . . .
> 2. All groups recognize as absolutely necessary that the minority within the unified party should always accept the decisions of the majority as binding for party activity.
> 3. The organization of the party must be secret at present; it is compelled to be. The activity of all party members in legal institutions should be under the leadership and control of the leading party institutions.
> 4. All groups renounce any blocs with bourgeois parties.

5. All groups declare that they agree to participate in a general congress which must solve all questions now under dispute concerning the interpretation of the program and the question of national cultural autonomy, and which must determine the details of the general party organization. . . .

The International Bureau refuses to investigate accusations relating to the past history of the various groups . . . as unproductive and even harmful, because they are means by which elements who should be united by their viewpoints on the present and aims for the future, are kept divided . . . No greater crime can be committed against the proletariat of Russia than to interfere with and hinder the rallying of its various groups into a single organism.

Proletarians of Russia, unite!

All the leaders of the International voted for the resolution. Out of the eleven Russian groups present, ten voted for it. Inessa Armand got up for the eleventh group and repeated doggedly: "We abstain. In place of the resolution we offer our statement."

"Lenin desires unity as a man desires unity with a piece of bread: he swallows it," Plekhanov commented.

"Where is Lenin?"—demanded Kautsky and Huysmans—"You are irresponsible underlings who don't understand what you are doing. Where is he? Why didn't he come? In the long run, he must obey the crying need for unity of the Russian masses and the insistent urging of the International."

No answer. Lenin couldn't come. He was too busy. We have our instructions. Here is our statement. We're not voting on anything. Unanimously—with the abstention of one faction—they voted to report the scandalous state of affairs to the forthcoming congress of the Socialist International, to arrange for a unifying congress of the Russian movement to be called over Lenin's head, and to prepare a denunciation of the Bolsheviks before the Russian workers if they continued to stand in the way of unity. All the leaders of the International would sign it. It would be solemnly endorsed by the International Socialist congress to be held in Vienna in August. That would be August 23—not far off. Already it was July 17.

July 17, 1914! But on June 28 a pistol shot had been fired at Sarajevo. *July 17!* Secret mobilization orders were being drafted. Ultimatums were being prepared. Notes were scurrying from chancellory to chancellory and staff to staff. *July 17!* The whole world was ringing with alarms and rumors of war, but Lenin did not seem to hear them. He was not planning to attend the coming

congress of the International either. For him it would be just
another move in the faction war. It was never held. War of another
sort interceded.

Some weight—the reader will have to judge how much—must be
given to a more personal concern that kept Lenin from turning the
full power of his concentrated mind on the mounting international
tension, and kept him away from all the conferences of the two
fateful years, 1913 and 1914, where he might have been joining
with the leaders of other parties in plans to meet the war danger.

Nadezhda, his loyal wife and unquestioning follower, his ever-
dependable secretary, was ill, deeply, seriously, puzzlingly ill. Her
bulging eyes ached so that they could no longer decipher the
secret, invisible writing. Her hands trembled and her knees were
weak as water. Her robust health, so robust that she had never
thought of it, was failing. Her capacity for work dwindled. Weakness, lassitude, dizziness, endless unremitting headaches. One doctor said "nerves" and advised "rest and a change of air." "A proletarian woman doesn't have nerves," she jested. But during the
prescribed mountain walking tour, she fainted. To his sister Maria,
Vladimir wrote:

> We moved here [Poronino, in the Tatra Mountains] the
> other day partly because of Nadya's illness, which greatly
> worries me. We shall spend the summer here . . . I may
> have to take Nadya to Berne to be cured . . . [May 13,
> 1913.]

And in July he wrote from Berne to his mother:

> At last they operated on Nadya on Wednesday in the
> Clinic. The operation evidently went off successfully for
> yesterday (Friday) she already looked fairly well and be-
> gan to drink with pleasure. The operation was apparently
> rather difficult, for about three hours they tortured her
> without an anesthetic, but she bore it heroically. On Thurs-
> day she was very ill—high temperature and delirium—and
> I was thoroughly frightened. Yesterday, however, things
> were obviously better . . . Kocher is a remarkable surgeon
> and people suffering from goiter ought to go to him . . .

And, as a by-product of his experience with "comrade-physicians"
who had treated her earlier and failed to diagnose her goiter
trouble, he wrote to Gorky in November:

> The news that a Bolshevik is treating you by a new
> method, even if he is only a former Bolshevik, verily, verily

upsets me. God save you from doctor-comrades in general, and doctor-Bolsheviks in particular! But really, in 99 cases out of 100, doctor-comrades are asses . . . I assure you that except in trivial cases, one should be treated *only* by men of first-class reputation. To try on yourself the discoveries of a Bolshevik—that's terrifying!!

At the end of April, 1914, he wrote his sister Maria:

In about a fortnight we shall go again to Poronino . . . I hope Nadya's goiter trouble will soon disappear. Mountain air cures this disease . . . Autumn is magnificent in the Tatras . . . If it is fine this autumn, we shall probably stay in the country . . .

The summer and autumn of 1914 were particularly fine. In the midst of those idyllic scenes, those breath-taking vistas, that gentle golden sunshine, those bemusing tranquil hours, who could believe in war? Vladimir clambered over the Tatra range like a mountain goat, stopping to take in the distant view, then to make notes on the national question, or some other question, in his ever-present notebook. That habit of taking a book with him, and stopping on a height to make notes, nearly cost him his life a few weeks later!

A golden summer! "If it is fine this autumn, we shall probably stay in the country."

That golden summer, on June 28, the Archduke Francis Ferdinand, heir to the Hapsburg throne, went riding with his wife in an open carriage through the old Slavic town of Sarajevo, capital of recently annexed Bosnia. Two shots rang out, and the heir apparent and his wife were dead. The murderers, two young Bosnian (Yugoslavian) nationalists, were tried *in camera*—a procedure the world has grown more accustomed to since. The Austrian Government let it be known that the findings "implicated" the Serbian Government and Serbian nationalist agitators. That was ominous—like the chain-reaction trials that Stalin has been using recently in Hungary, Bulgaria, Rumania, Yugoslavia, Czechoslovakia. But who could believe then that a pistol shot in remote, sleepy Sarajevo would involve England, France, Germany, Japan, China, America? that a pistol shot in Sarajevo was sounding the death-knell of the Austro-Hungarian, the German and the Russian Empires, and, indeed, of the entire bourgeois world of the nineteenth century? that a pistol shot in Sarajevo was opening a period of global wars and revolutions that would fill with death and transformation all of the century that had just begun?

Officials, diplomats, labor leaders went on their vacations that
summer more or less as usual. American tourists swarmed over
Europe.

> Peace-loving Russia—wrote General Gurko, who was soon
> to head the Imperial General Staff—was in the midst of the
> summer holiday when the storm clouds hanging over
> Europe for a month finally burst. Petrograd and Moscow
> were practically deserted . . . Dark though the horizon
> was after the assassination of the Austrian heir, few imag-
> ined that the differences between Austria on the one hand
> and Serbia and Russia on the other were so grave that they
> could not be settled by ordinary diplomatic procedure . . .

On July 23, after secret incitement from Kaiser Wilhelm of Germany, Austrian Foreign Minister Berchtold dispatched an ultimatum to Serbia. It demanded an official condemnation of all
anti-Austrian propaganda, the establishment of a friendly government, the suppression of "unfriendly" publications and organizations that incited to contempt toward the Danubian monarchy; the
dismissal of a number of Serbian officials; the arrest of others; the
right of the Austrian police and secret service to enter Serbia to
collaborate with the latter's police in the investigation of the crime.
The demands are curiously like those which in the last few years
Stalin has made upon all his Balkan and other neighbors. Acceptance was demanded within forty-eight hours. Little Serbia's reply
was anxiously conciliatory. It accepted all demands except those
which would have permitted the Austrian police to enter its territory. It offered to submit disputed matters to the Hague Tribunal
or a conference of the Great Powers. Backed by Germany, Austria
rejected the reply. Backed by Russia, and impelled by the knowledge that her very independence was at stake, Serbia refused to go
further in her concessions.

> On July 24th—returning to General Gurko's memoirs—it
> became generally known that a conflict was inevitable. The
> troops had already left for their summer training camps.
> Two days later they were directed to return to their winter
> quarters; orders had been received for preparatory mobili-
> zation . . .

On that same July 24, Philip Scheidemann, one day to become
Prime Minister of the German Weimar Republic, was climbing
Mount Karwendel, over 7,300 feet high in the Austrian Tyrol.
Saddle-maker Ebert, who would become President of the Repub-
lic, was dreaming away the hours on a beach on the Island of

Ruegen. Vladimir Ilyich Ulyanov, future Chairman of the Council of People's Commissars of the Soviet Government, was one hundred miles from Cracow, where the Carpathian Mountains reach their greatest height, in the wild granite peaks of the Tatras.

On July 26, Sir Edward Grey, British Foreign Secretary, suggested a great-power conference of England, France, Germany, and Italy to settle the Austro-Serb conflict. Germany refused on the ground that only Austria and Russia, the most vitally interested, could call such a conference. On July 28, Austria declared war on Serbia. Next day, Russia issued a mobilization order on the Austrian frontier, and Germany a mobilization order on the Russian and French frontiers.

On July 29, the International Socialist Bureau went into emergency session in Brussels. Austria-Hungary had already declared war on Serbia, but none of the other Great Powers had yet declared war. Among those present from Germany were Kautsky, Haase and Rosa Luxemburg; from France, Jaurès, Vaillant, Guesde, Sembat, Longuet; from England, Keir Hardie; from Austria, Victor Adler and his son Friedrich, and the Czech, Nemec; from Holland, Troelstra; from Switzerland, Grimm; from Poland, Valecki; from Belgium, Vandervelde; from Italy, Morgari and Angelica Balabanoff, the Russian girl who had become an Italian socialist leader. There were a number from Russia, Axelrod, Rubanovich (Social Revolutionary) and several lesser figures. Lenin did not come, nor send a man of the caliber of Zinoviev or Kamenev, or even of Litvinov. He contented himself with being "represented" by Inessa Armand and the Lettish Bolshevik, Berzin. He was still thinking in terms of the faction war. He had won control of the apparatus; he had conquered power in the Party, and was not going to yield it, no, not even to the pressure of the entire international movement.

But, at the Emergency Conference, nothing was said about Russia, except Russia as a Great Power. They talked about nothing but war, turning it around and around helplessly in their minds. They voted a manifesto, a huge mass meeting, a universal series of mass meetings, their resolve to maintain the peace, to localize the Austro-Serbian War, to demand its settlement by arbitration, to keep Germany, Russia, France, England out. If only they could hold war off until the great congress of the International already scheduled to be held in Vienna on August 23! They switched the congress to Paris, since Vienna was at war, and moved the date closer, from August 23 to August 9, since the situation was too dangerous for a month's delay.

But on July 31, Germany dispatched an ultimatum to Russia demanding the immediate revocation of Russian mobilization orders. No reply within the brief time limit. On August 1, Germany declared war on Russia. On August 3, Germany declared war on France; on August 4, German troops thrust through Belgium simultaneously with another declaration of war. All powers had been preparing for this moment, but Germany felt that she had the edge in preparations, that time was not on her side, that it was now or never.

Not until August 6 did Austria-Hungary declare war on Russia. Thus, on August 6, Vladimir Ilyich and his wife, Zinoviev and his wife, and various other Bolsheviks in Galicia became Russian enemy aliens on the soil of a country with which Russia was at war. The news surprised Lenin in the Tatra range of the Carpathians, far even from his Cracow home.

War, general universal war, total, all-embracing war, was so new. Nothing like it since the days of Napoleon. Everywhere exaltation and confusion. Everywhere patriotic demonstrations, rumors, alarms, caution about strangers, spies, poisoned water supply. The mighty Russian Army was poised in Russian Poland on the borders of Galicia, ready to drive into Cracow, Przemysl, Poronino, Zakopane, Nowy Targ, one's own fields and doorstep. Peasants hastened to report to the police concerning the stocky, bald-headed Russian who was forever clambering up the heights, "surveying the roads," and making notes in a little notebook. On August 7, one day after Austria declared war, a village policeman visited the lodgings of the strange enemy alien. He paid no attention to the secret addresses of Party members and the Party documents, but pounced upon three notebooks filled with statistical tables and columns of figures—clearly a codebook! Poor Ilyich, would he ever see again his patiently gathered notes on the agrarian question? And the searcher found a pistol, symbol of Lenin's romantic belief in armed uprising, for which the enemy alien had not troubled to take out a permit. Still the village gendarme was a little troubled by the supposed spy's bearing and declarations, and gave him till next morning to report without escort to the police chief at the nearest provincial center, Nowy Targ (Neumarkt).

Would he be arrested? Court-martialed? Interned for the duration? (What duration?) Would he perish, as many did, in the first panicky actions of a universal spy scare? ("During the first days of the war," wrote Krupskaya, "they might easily have put him out of the way.") In this wild corner of the Carpathians, who would know of his fate? Already the Russian army was advancing on Przemysl and Cracow and Novy Targ and Poronino. If he fell into *their* hands, what would happen to him then in time of war?

Lenin used the few remaining hours of freedom to map a campaign for his rescue. He wired to the police director of Cracow, who knew his status and his anti-tsarist political activities, requesting a telegram to the local police to clear him of suspicion of espionage. Hanecki telegraphed to the Social Democratic Deputy Marek, who had arranged with the Austrian Government the permission for Ulyanov to settle in Austria. Both police director and Reformist Social Democrat (both class enemies according to the Leninist schema) responded with telegrams urging his release.

> Zinoviev—writes Krupskaya—despite the pouring rain, cycled ten miles to see the old member of the Narodnaya Volya, the Pole, Dr. Dlussky. Dlussky [whom Lenin also classified as a class enemy] immediately hired a carriage and went to Zakopane, where he did considerable telegraphing and letter writing and then went somewhere to conduct negotiations.

But the notebooks, the columns of figures, the pistol, the mountain climbs in which he had surveyed the horizon and made notes, the enemy alien citizenship and documents, the marching Russian armies, the spirit of alarm, were too much. He was jailed as a spy suspect, and his case handed over to a military tribunal. Leaving his cell after she had brought him food, clothes, and, of course books, Krupskaya heard two patriotic peasant women discussing the "Russian spy" and declaring that if "the authorities released him, the peasants would put out his eyes themselves, cut out his tongue, etc." In many a land many a stranger speaking an alien language was lynched during those first turbulent days.

Lenin wired Victor Adler, an outstanding leader of the Austrian Social Democracy and of the International (another whom he would soon be attacking unceasingly as a class enemy), asking his help. Krupskaya sent a separate plea. Adler went immediately in person to the Minister of the Interior, taking with him another Social Democratic Deputy, Diamant. And yet another, the Right Wing leader of the Austrian Section of the Polish Socialist Party, Daszinski, who had come to Galicia to recruit Poles for Pilsudski's Polish Legion to fight against Russia, sent a message on his own to the Minister of the Interior. Lenin had been attacking both Daszinski and his party for years. But to none of these did it occur for an instant not to help out a fellow-socialist in trouble. Such comradeship was taken for granted in the days of innocence that preceded the great split in the International.

According to the memoirs of Felix Kon, Hanecki, Karpinsky, and other Bolsheviks, all published by the Soviet Government, approximately the following conversation took place in the Ministry of the Interior:

> *Adler:* Ulyanov is no ordinary Russian citizen and no spy. He is a determined opponent of Russian tsarism who has devoted his life to the struggle against the Russian Government. If he were to appear in Russia they would arrest him, possibly execute him. He enjoys a European reputation as a leader of the Russian Social Democratic Party. He is a member with me of the International Bureau of the Socialist International. We both [Adler and Diamant] guarantee personally that he is no spy . . .
>
> *Minister:* Is that really the case? Is he still an opponent of his government?
>
> *Adler:* Ulyanov was an enemy of Russian tsarism when Your Excellency was its friend. He is its enemy now. And he will be its enemy when Your Excellency may again have become its friend.

The Minister was impressed. In his report, dated August 23, he wrote:

> In the opinion of Dr. Adler, Ulyanov may render great services under present conditions.

On the suggestion of the Minister of the Interior, the commandant in Cracow ordered his release. This was the Central Powers' first tentative approach to the idea that Russian revolutionists like Ulyanov might possibly "render great services" to their cause. He was not interned as an enemy alien at all, but given a military pass to travel from Cracow to Vienna. But already he had decided that he could serve his own movement better in some neutral country. With Adler's help once more, military permission being needed to use the railroad or leave the country, he and Krupskaya journeyed unmolested to Switzerland. Zinoviev and his wife, Lilina, saved from internment by the same good offices, joined them two weeks later. On September 5, two days less than a month after his arrest as a spy, Lenin was able to write to Adler from his new home:

> Esteemed Comrade!
> I have arrived safely in Zurich with my whole family. They asked to see my pass only at Innsbruck and Feldskirche: your help therefore was very useful to me. For entry into Switzerland they demanded a passport, but they

admitted me without one when I gave the name of Greu-
lich. My best wishes and utmost gratitude to you.
With Party Greetings,
LENIN (V. I. Ulyanov)

Though these were the last friendly words that Lenin ever
addressed to Victor Adler, they make clear that the feeling of
gratitude was not alien to him. The memoirs published in Lenin's
day and shortly after his death all acknowledge this debt. Karpinsky lists this as one of two celebrated "cases in which our
enemies helped to protect Lenin."

"Just try to imagine," he adds as an afterthought, "what turn the
fate of the Russian Revolution would have taken if Lenin had been
interned and had returned to Russia not on April 3, 1917, but only
in the autumn of 1918, when revolution overthrew the Austro-
Hungarian monarchy!" Try to imagine, indeed! For April 3, 1917,
the day when Lenin arrived at the Finland Station in Petrograd,
was one of those fateful days that altered the whole course of
history. Without April 3 there would have been no November 7!

It remains only to add that by 1943, the Marx-Engels-Lenin
Institute official biography of Lenin had stricken out all gratitude
and all traces of indebtedness to Victor Adler. It merely says:

> On August 8, 1914, he was arrested by the Austrian
> police on a false accusation and taken to the prison at
> Nowy Targ, but was released on August 19, in view of the
> utter absurdity of the charge.

The documents I have used were secured by Hanecki in 1922,
and subsequently, as a representative of the Soviet Government,
and of Lenin personally, to the Polish Government, which opened
the old Austrian police archives to him. It even aided Hanecki to
recover Lenin's and Zinoviev's papers, left in Austrian Poland,
including the three notebooks on the agrarian question, the statistics of which had been the most damning evidence against him.
Hanecki secured from the Polish Government over 60 signed documents of Lenin's, over 50 letters addressed to him, 125 books and
part of the archives of the Bolshevik Duma Fraction and of *Pravda*.
(Ya. Ganetskii: *O Lenine*. Institut Marksa-Engelsa-Lenina, Moscow, 1933, pp. 16-52).

CHAPTER XXXVI

Seven Theses Against War

The experience of the war, like the experience of every crisis
in history, of every great disaster and every sudden turn in
human life, stuns and shatters some, but it enlightens and
hardens others.   —*V. I. Lenin, June 1915*

Trotsky was in Vienna when the storm broke. With unbelieving
eyes he stared at the festive processions of shouting, cheering
workingmen. What had they to cheer about? Where was their
vaunted internationalism? What had war to offer them? What drew
them, rejoicing, to the great square in front of the War Ministry?

> What sort of an idea?—he wrote in his *Autobiography,*
> more than a decade later, still grappling with this mystery.
> —The national idea? But Austria-Hungary was the very
> negation of any national idea. No, the moving force was
> something different. The people, whose lives, day in and
> day out, pass in a monotony of hopelessness . . . the alarm
> of mobilization breaks into their lives like a promise; the
> familiar and long-hated is overthrown, and the new and
> unusual reigns in its place. Changes still more incredible
> are in store for them in the future. For better or for worse?
> For the better, of course—what can seem worse to Pospischil
> (the Viennese-Czech shoemaker's apprentice) than "nor-
> mal" conditions? I strode along the main streets of the
> familiar Vienna and watched a most amazing crowd fill
> the fashionable Ring, a crowd in which hopes had been
> awakened. But wasn't a small part of these hopes already
> being realized? Would it have been possible at any other
> time for porters, laundresses, shoemakers' apprentices and
> youngsters from the suburbs to feel themselves masters of
> the situation in the Ring? War affects everybody, and those
> who are oppressed and deceived by life consequently feel
> that they are on an equal footing with the rich and the
> powerful. It may seem a paradox, but in the moods of
> the Viennese crowd that was demonstrating the glory of the
> Hapsburg arms I detected something familiar to me from
> the October days of 1905 in Saint Petersburg . . . Like
> revolution, war forces life, from top to bottom, away from
> the beaten path. But revolution directs its blows against

620

the established power. War, on the contrary, at first strengthens the state power, which, in the chaos engendered by war seems to be the only firm support . . . Hopes of strong social and national movements, whether in Prague or in Trieste, in Warsaw or in Tiflis, are utterly groundless at the outset of a war. In September, 1914, I wrote to Russia: "The mobilization and declaration of war have veritably swept off the earth all the national and social contradictions in the country. But this is only a political postponement, a sort of political moratorium. The notes have been extended to a new date, but they will have to be paid . . ."

If the internationalism of the masses had been sloughed off like last year's skin, how was it with their leaders? Some, like Hans Deutsch, he found quite obviously pleased and excited, abusive of all Serbs and Russians with little distinction between governments and people, happy that war would rid Austria of the "Serbian nightmare." Others, like Victor Adler, regarded the whole thing as an external cataclysm, not sprung from their activities, beyond their strength to cope with, something to be passively endured until it was over.

Adler intervened for Trotsky, as a few days later he was to do for Lenin. On their way to the chief of the political police, the Russian internationalist drew the attention of the Austrian to the festal mood. "It is those who do not have to go to war who show their joy," Adler sought to reassure himself and his companion. "Besides, all the unbalanced, all the madmen now come out into the streets; it is their day. The murder of Jaurès is only the beginning. War opens the door for all instincts, all forms of madness." Victor Adler was a psychiatrist besides being the outstanding leader of his party. Before the war was over, his own son, Fritz Adler, would commit an act of political desperation which party leaders would attribute to this same "war madness."

Police Chief Geyer hinted to Trotsky that all Russians might be under arrest by morning:

"Good. I will leave with my family for Switzerland tomorrow."

"Hm . . . I should prefer that you do it today."

That was at three. At six-ten that same afternoon, Lev Davidovich and his family were on the train bound for Zurich. Again Adler had helped a comrade who would brand him thereafter as a "class enemy."

The outbreak of war found Joseph Stalin in police exile in the remote Turukhansk Region of Yenisseisk Province on the edge of

the Arctic Circle. There he joined Sverdlov, who had preceded
him. Their arrest, in 1913, had been the result of association with
their fellow Central Committee member, the Duma Deputy and
police agent Malinovsky. Together, Sverdlov and Stalin made plans
for escape, but the latter's request to Duma Deputy Badaev for a
large sum "for food, kerosene and other things before the approach
of the harsh Arctic winter" was turned over by Malinovsky to the
police. Warnings against their plans went to Yenisseisk in August
and December, 1913, and again in early 1914.

> Joseph Djugashvili and I—Sverdlov wrote his sister in
> February of that year—are being transferred a hundred
> versts farther north—eighty versts above the Arctic Circle.
> The surveillance is stronger . . . We have no more than
> eight or nine mail deliveries a year . . . Because he re-
> ceived money, Djugashvili has been deprived of his [gov-
> ernment] allowance for four months. Both he and I need
> money, but you cannot send it in our names . . .
> My arrangements in the new place [the lonely Arctic
> village of Kureika] are considerably worse. For one thing,
> I no longer live alone. There are two of us in the room.
> With me is the Georgian Djugashvili . . . He is a good
> chap, but too much of an individualist in everyday life,
> while I believe at least in a semblance of order. That's
> why I am irritable at times . . . Much worse is the fact
> that there is no seclusion from the landlord's family . . .
> children . . . grownups from the village . . . They come,
> as if for spite, at the very best time for study, in the eve-
> ning . . . We have had to plan our day differently, to give
> up the habit of poring over a book until long after mid-
> night. There is absolutely no kerosene. We use candles.
> Since that provides too little light for my eyes, I do all my
> studying in the daytime now. As a matter of fact, I don't
> study much. We have virtually no books . . .

Thus Jacob Sverdlov, future President of the Executive Committee of the Soviets and future Secretary and leading organizer of
the Party until his death, and Joseph Stalin, who was to succeed
him as Party Secretary, lived in the Arctic wastes through three
dreary war years. Sverdlov wrote a number of letters in addition
to the one quoted. In 1924, when many reminiscences from this
period were being published, a book of Sverdlov's correspondence
was announced. But it was never published! Why, we can deduce
from a few passages from letters which did see the light before
publication was stopped:

The moral atmosphere—he wrote of his worsening relations with his "too individualistic," i.e. inconsiderate, roommate—is not especially favorable . . . A number of clashes, possible only under the conditions of prison and exile, despite their pettiness, have had a pretty strong effect upon my nerves . . . in exile and prison conditions the naked man appears in all his meanness . . .

Sverdlov finally secured transfer to another settlement in the district. Thereafter, Stalin lived pretty much alone. In a letter to his future mother-in-law, Olga Evgenievna Alliluyeva, dated November 25, 1913, he thanked her for gifts (food packages), urging her to save her money for her own large family, and hinted of his loneliness and homesickness:

You need the money yourself. I shall be satisfied if from time to time you send me a picture postcard with scenes of nature and the like. In this accursed region nature is bare to the point of ugliness—in summer, a river, in winter, snow, that's all that nature offers here, and I am stupidly homesick for scenes of nature even if only on paper. My greetings to the boys and girls. I wish you everything, everything good. . . .

This letter, showing the gentler, more sentimental side of his nature, Stalin has excluded from his *Collected Works*. His nearest friend now lived in the "nearby"—125 miles by horse or sleigh— village of Monastyr, the Armenian Central Committee member Suren Spandaryan. He was the leading spirit in a small group of Bolshevik exiles, which included three, his wife (Vera Shveitser), Gaven and Shumyatsky, who have contributed memoirs from which, with the usual "archaeological sifting," we can reconstruct some aspects of Stalin's life in wartime.

Even here, among the Bolshevik prisoner-exiles in the far Arctic northland, there was the same wavering in attitude toward the war and toward the very government that had deported them, that Trotsky had noted among the workingmen of Vienna!

"Defensist tendencies," writes Gaven, "were strong among the exiles. Everybody was disoriented." And the Stalin-supporter Shumyatsky, writing in 1924 when Stalin's star was already rising rapidly, ascribes the leading role in the struggle with the defensist Bolsheviks to Spandaryan:

He saw the matter clearly and distinctly . . . was one of the first to assume an unyielding position of defeatism, and, at the rare gatherings of the comrades, sarcastically chided the social-patriots.

The second place he assigns to Sverdlov, but seeking to find a little opening for an important role for Stalin—a role which becomes enlarged in each subsequent edition of the memoirs—he writes:

> Stalin, being completely isolated in his cave [in later editions the cave becomes a "scientist's laboratory"], without any vacillation assumed a defeatist line . . . by letter supporting Suren against his opponents . . . Only toward the end of 1914 and the beginning of 1915 [actually it was in February, 1915] after Stalin had managed to visit Monastyr and back up Spandaryan, did the latter cease to be subject to attacks . . .

Revealing of Djugashvili's real mood and manner at the time is the following passage from the same work:

> Stalin withdrew inside himself. Preoccupied with hunting and fishing, he lived in almost complete solitude . . . had practically no need for intercourse with people, only once in a while would go to visit his friend Suren Spandaryan at the village of Monastyr, returning several days later to his anchorite's cave. He was sparing in his disjointed remarks whenever he happened to be at gatherings arranged by exiles.

Spandaryan died in the Arctic in 1916, and a flood of memoirs in the later thirties and forties progressively expropriate his role in favor of Joseph Stalin. By 1937, Spandaryan's own wife, writing under the "editorial" direction of Beria, declares:

> Stalin's authority among the Bolsheviks was so great that his very first letter to the exiles put an end to all doubts . . .

Yet even here, another passage suggests the underlying truth that it was a letter from Lenin, containing his "Theses on the War," which strengthened Spandaryan's hand. When Stalin went to Monastyr to visit the Spandaryans in late February, 1915, she writes, she showed him Lenin's letter:

> Lenin's seven theses on the war showed that Comrade Stalin had taken an unerringly correct Leninist position in his appraisal of the complex historical situation. It is difficult to convey the joy, conviction and triumph with which Comrade Stalin read Lenin's theses, which confirmed his ideas and served as a pledge of victory for the revolution in Russia.

Through nearly three years of war, Stalin made no further attempt to escape. ("This time," she writes, "Stalin decided to remain in exile.") And for the entire period, perhaps the most decisive in the history of the Bolshevik Party, besides the letter asking for postcard views of nature (pre-war), there are only three or perhaps four unimportant pieces of writing which come directly or indirectly from Djugashvili's hand. The first is a letter which his biographer Yaroslavsky says was composed jointly by Spandaryan and Stalin to Lenin, "scoffing at national defensists, Plekhanov, Kropotkin, and the French socialist Sembat." In the biographical chronicle accompanying Stalin's *Collected Works*, the author claims this letter exclusively as his own, and, from the wording, this would appear to be so. But it is noteworthy that he did not choose to include the text itself in his *Collected Works*. Since it may be of interest to the reader both as an insight into Stalin's temperament and style of expression, and as a touchstone to compare with Lenin's theses quoted at the end of the present chapter, we give it in full. Dated February 27, 1915, i.e. during his visit with Spandaryan and after he had seen Lenin's theses, it reads:

> My greetings to you, dear Ilyich, warm, warm greetings. Greetings to Zinoviev, greetings to Nadezhda Konstantinovna. How are you? How is your health? I live as before, chew my bread, completing half of my term. It is rather dull, but it can't be helped. But how are things with you? It must be much livelier where you are. I recently read Kropotkin's articles—the old fool must have completely lost his mind. I also read a short article by Plekhanov in *Rech* —an incorrigible old gossip. Ekh-mah! And the Liquidators with their deputy agents of the Free Economic Society? There's no one to beat them, the devil take me! Is it possible that they will get away with it and go unpunished? Make us happy and let us know that in the near future a newspaper will appear that will lash them across their mugs, and do it regularly, and without getting tired. If it should occur to you to write, do so to the address: Turukhansk Territory, Yenisseisk Province, Monastyrskoe Village, for Suren Spandaryan. Your Koba. Timofei [Spandaryan] asks that his sour greetings be conveyed to Guesde, Sembat and Vandervelde on their glorious—ha, ha!—posts as ministers.

The modest tone of the "if it should occur to you to write" hardly suggests the "chief lieutenant" and "close associate" who for many years had supposedly been assisting Lenin in working out all his views. Nor does the letter which Lenin wrote Karpinsky in the autumn of the same year, inquiring:

"I have a big favor to ask you: find out the surname of Koba (Joseph Dj . . .?? we forgot). Very important!!"

Lenin thought it important to keep up correspondence with this lieutenant, but the need to inquire the surname, which has to be used in all letters to police exiles, suggests that there was no constant interchange of communications.

The other documents with which Stalin is connected during the war period up to the Revolution of March, 1917, are, according to the Biographical Chronology, a second letter to Lenin, dated November 10, 1915; an article on the national question, which either went astray or which Lenin did not find good enough to publish; another letter, to Inessa Armand, asking what had happened to the article; and a round-robin greeting, signed by various Bolshevik exiles, to the newspaper *Voprosy Strakhovanya* ("Problems of Insurance"), enclosing the sum of six rubles, eighty-five kopeks, collected among the Turukhansk convicts. Significantly, Joseph Stalin has not considered any of these worthy of inclusion in his *Collected Works*. Thus there is a complete blank space of four years between Volume II, which ends with a manifesto written for May 1, 1913, and Volume III, which begins after the Revolution of March, 1917 had freed Stalin and the other exiles. And, with the greatest zeal and the highest will in the world, his biographers have not been able to make much more than a blank out of his other activities during the same period.

To be sure, one inventive English writer, David M. Cole, professes to have "perused" articles from Turukhansk directed against Leon Trotsky's war position, and speaks of "a series of short letters expressing, in a simple but direct manner, those ideas which Lenin later [!] set out in his book *Against the Current*," [1] which letters from Stalin "kept the small focal centers of bolshevism going in the factories from 1914 to late 1916" (David M. Cole: *Joseph Stalin*, Rich and Cowan, London, 1942, p. 36). But we will be closer to the published record if we accept Yaroslavsky's summary, which limits itself to the following modest claims:

> Thus, even in this remote Siberian village, Comrade Stalin displayed profound attention to, and keen interest in, Party life, read a great deal, kept himself informed of the

[1] The book *Against the Current* was the joint work of Lenin and Zinoviev and published under both their names. But Mr. Cole, with "scruples" more understandable in a historian writing under censorship inside Russia, avoids mentioning the purged Zinoviev as Lenin's closest wartime collaborator.

Party's work in Russia, reacted as far as he was able to every event in Party life, and occupied his leisure with fishing and hunting.

He did not, like Sverdlov, manage to get articles through to Lenin which Lenin would deem worthy of publication in the straitened pages of wartime journals. Nor could he win for himself the spontaneous tributes which the Stalinist Shumyatsky and other memorialists gave to Spandaryan in the memoirs of 1924. ("Clearer than many others in the memory of the Turukhanites is the monumental figure of Suren Spandaryan . . . the intransigent revolutionary Marxist and magnificent orator . . . the most active of the revolutionists and their leader," said the first edition of Shumyatsky's work.) For it takes time and persistence to edit one's memories. But we can safely assume that Yaroslavsky's summary is not too wide of the mark; and, with that favorable if modest verdict, we can leave Stalin out of our further story until 1917. His turn will come later, and will be large indeed.

There is only one more detail to clear up, the question of Stalin's summons to the army. Of this, too, there are several differing versions. His own Biographical Chronology reads:

> December 14, 1916. I. V. Stalin goes by stages to Krasnoyarsk in connection with the calling up of administrative exiles to the army.

To this Yaroslavsky adds his usual romantic touch:

> Comrade Stalin was sent to Krasnoyarsk but he was not taken into the army because the tsarist government knew how dangerous he would be there. From Krasnoyarsk, he was sent to Achinsk to complete his term of exile. This was almost on the eve of the revolution, which broke out while Stalin was in Achinsk.

If Stalin does not explain why he was not inducted, Yaroslavsky's explanation makes it hard to understand why he was ever moved to Krasnoyarsk or Achinsk at all. But Shumyatsky's memoirs, already quoted, state that Stalin was indeed called up, but then rejected for service because of a "stiffness" in his left arm.

The epidemic of war fever which Trotsky had contemplated so incredulously as it set the masses to dancing in the Vienna streets, the war fever which, even among the Bolshevik exiles of Arctic Turukhansk, had "disoriented everybody" and made "defensist tendencies strong" in relation to the very government that held them in exile—that same war fever took possession of the masses in every warring land. I do not speak merely of the unorganized masses, but of the "class-conscious" workers organized into trade unions and socialist parties (and, no less, of the adherents of the "Prince of Peace" organized into the Christian churches).

Not only the Right Wing but the Center and the Left Wing of the socialist parties were affected. Jules Guesde, who had been the leader of the French Left in its fight against reformism and minis-terialism and who had joined with Lenin, Rosa Luxemburg and a handful more to form the Left Wing at the Copenhagen Interna-tional Socialist Congress of 1910, immediately became a Minister without Portfolio in the French War Cabinet. Gustav Hervé, fire-eating leader of the anti-war and anti-imperialist section of the French Socialist Party who had wanted the International to "an-swer" a declaration of war by a general strike, changed the name of his paper from *La Guerre Sociale* to *La Victoire*. Paul Lensch and Parvus (Alexander Helfand) who, like Rosa Luxemburg, had been editors of the Left Wing *Leipziger Volkszeitung,* became ardent war propagandists. Lensch eventually accepted editorship of the *Deutsche Allgemeine Zeitung,* while Parvus founded *Die Glocke* to preach the "socialist meaning" of Germany's war aims. Vladimir Burtsev, whom we have so far known as the chief exposer of the Russian secret police and its agents in the revolutionary movement, published a declaration in the French, English and Russian exile press, calling on all socialists to support the Russian Government in the war. Then, without waiting for permission or promise of amnesty, he set out for Russia to volunteer his services. At the border the police arrested the arch-enemy who had exposed so many of their spies. Only after a year in Siberia, and after inter-vention by the French Ambassador, was he quietly amnestied. Free in Saint Petersburg, he continued to write pro-war articles. The Social Revolutionary leaders Avksentiev, Bunakov (Fundaminsky), Argunov, Savinkov, Lazarev, Moiseenko, Voronov, all of them men who had been in the Tsar's prisons and Siberia and had fled abroad the better to fight the Russian Government, now formed a group called "Beyond the Frontier" with an ardent defensive pro-gram. The veteran leader Breshkovskaya (the *babushka* or "grand-mother" of the Social Revolutionary movement) was with them, as was Rubanovich, their representative on the International Socialist Bureau. "At the present time," wrote this group in *Novosti,* "we consider revolutionary action against tsarism inexpedient, as it would only weaken the military strength of the country." Kropot-kin, the anarchist leader, became an ardent defender of French culture and liberty against Prussian militarism. Plekhanov, the "father" of Russian Social Democracy, author of its program, advocate of proletarian dictatorship, and, after Kautsky, the leading European defender of "orthodox Marxism," became a passionate patriot, defending the Allied cause and actually recruiting volunteers among the Russian émigrés for the French Army.

What must have been most startling to Lenin was the fact that the division did not come on the familiar lines of "opportunism" versus "revolutionary Marxism," or "revisionism" versus "orthodoxy" at all. In the German party, Parvus, Lensch, Cunow, Haenisch, orthodox Marxists all, became ardent war advocates, while the Left revisionist Karl Liebknecht became the outstanding anti-militarist, and the arch-revisionist of the Right, Eduard Bernstein, was one of the first publicly to condemn the abandonment of the old Marxist tactic of refusing to vote war credits (in the *Archiv fuer Sozialwissenschaft*, reprinted as a separate pamphlet, *Die Internationale der Arbeiterklasse und der europaeische Krieg*, in February, 1915). Similarly, Christian socialist, pacifistic and semi-liberal British laborite leaders like Snowden and Macdonald voted against war credits in England while Hyndman, leader of the orthodox Marxist Social Democratic Federation, became a war supporter. The soft-minded humanitarians inclined to pacifism while many a tough-minded "historical materialist" flung himself heart and soul into the war.

Nor was the Bolshevik contingent in Paris exempt from the ravages of war fever. Lenin was far away, in the Carpathian Mountains. *Pravda* had just been suppressed so that there was no guidance from Russia. The Leading Committee of Organizations Abroad, which served in Paris as the connecting center for Bolshevik sections outside Russia, disintegrated. Two of its five members enlisted as volunteers in the French Army. One resigned from the leading committee and the Party. A minority of two, confused and unsure, remained to carry on. At a general meeting of the Bolsheviks in Paris, out of ninety-four present, eleven favored active support for the war and a number of others, how many we do not know, could not make up their minds one way or the other. Antonov-Britman, member of the leading committee of five, volunteered and soon died at the front. N. V. Kuznetzov (Saposhkov) likewise enlisted and fell in battle. Ilya (Japaridze) joined the volunteers, but sobered up later and became anti-war. "A number of others" volunteered, too. A Bolshevik, *Ekk* (Mukhin), drafted a patriotic manifesto in favor of enlistment, which was adopted by a commission of two Bolsheviks, two Mensheviks, and one Social

Revolutionary and was responded to by eighty of these self-exiled opponents of the Russian Government. At the farewell party before they joined the French Army, Plekhanov delivered the valedictory address.[2]

Writes Khonyavko in his memoirs of that time of storm and disorientation:

> Putting it bluntly, the task before everyone—how to be: for or against the war?—was extremely hard for all socialist tendencies. . . . Unexpectedly, in our section too there arose differences on the question. . . . And strangely enough in the bitter two-day meeting of August 2 and 3, 1914 out of ninety-four members of our section eleven were openly on the side of the patriots. We decided to appeal to Comrade Lenin with a letter asking whether our position was right, and he, to our joy, not only approved our position but even praised it as well expressed from the point of view of Marxism . . .

This naive statement, published in *Proletarskaya Revoliutsiya* in 1923, speaks volumes concerning the orphaned condition of the Paris Bolsheviks, with their firm-minded *starik* so far away, their legal Russian paper, *Pravda*, suppressed by the Tsar's Government, and with two of their leading committee volunteering and one dropping out. Lenin and Zinoviev, fleeing from Austria to Switzerland, carried in their pockets or under the domes of their foreheads virtually all that was left of the Bolshevik Central Organization abroad. Once more, there was needed unwavering certitude and iron will for the Sisyphus labor of beginning from the bottom of the slope.

The last days of July, 1914, and the first days of August were full of shocks and surprises. Many convinced pacifists were startled to find their throats open, crying for war. The leaders of the socialist parties were swept off their feet by the advent of what they had so long predicted, prepared for, even exactly described. They were surprised alike by their own actions, and by the reactions of the masses they had been preaching to. On July 25, two days after Austria's ultimatum to Serbia, the mighty German Social Democracy issued an anti-war manifesto condemning the Austrian ultimatum as "precisely calculated to provoke war . . . Not a drop of

[2] Lenin's *Collected Works*, Vol. XVIII, English Edition, p. 413; M. Kharitonov: *Iz vospominanii*, Zapiski Instituta Lenina, II, 119; V. Karpinsky: *Vladimir Ilyich za granitsei v. 1914-1917 g.g. po pismam i vospominanyam* Zapiski Instituta Lenina, II, 72-72; I. P. Khonyakov: *V podpolie i v emigratsii*, Proletarskaya Revolyutsii, No. 4 (16), 1923, p. 168.

blood of a German soldier shall be sacrificed to the power itch of the Austrian rulers . . ."

On July 29-30, the International Socialist Bureau came together at their hastily summoned Emergency Conference in Brussels. Only twenty or so could be assembled in mid-summer on such short notice. Lenin was not there. Missing, too, sorely missing, was the beloved leader of the German movement, the veteran of the anti-war campaign of 1870, August Bebel, whom death had claimed in the Summer of 1913.

Fright, incredulity, improvisation, hope for a miracle, defiance, despair, vied with each other for the possession of the delegates. The war between Austria and Serbia would be localized. The rumors of Russian and German ultimatums were inventions of the jingo press. General war was impossible in the enlightened twentieth century. The masses would not permit it. An International Socialist Congress would unite the peoples, frighten the war makers, stay their hand. "It is remarkable," Kautsky was to write six years later, "that to none of us present did it occur to ask what to do if the war should break out before the Congress convened. What attitude were the socialist parties to take in such a war?"

But this is only a half-truth. With a weary and deadly composure, Victor Adler, whose country was already at war, predicted that the masses would remain passive and the parties likewise:

> Expect no more action from us. We are under martial law. Our papers are suppressed. I am not here to make a speech in a mass meeting, but to tell you the truth, that any action now, when hundreds of thousands are on their way to the frontier and martial law prevails at home, is impossible.

Rosa Luxemburg was too sick at heart to speak. Hugo Haase talked directly at Jean Jaurès as if he must convince that brilliant tribune of the French people that he and his party did not want war and expected the same from the French. Keir Hardie pledged English labor to a general strike before it would permit England to be drawn in, but others signified that they doubted his optimism. Angelica Balabanoff returned to the subject: we have so often pledged ourselves to avert war, now a general strike is the only means left us. Adler and Guesde looked at her with the scornful pity one reserves for a fool. "A general strike," retorted Guesde icily, "would be effective only in countries where socialism is strongest, facilitating the military victory of the backward nations over the progressive ones." What socialist could desire the invasion of his own land, or its defeat by a more backward one? (The only man who might conceivably have cried out: "I" was far off in the Carpathian Mountains, staying away out of confidence that the International would never deliver its soul to the war makers, out of disbelief in the immediacy of war, or out of factional stubbornness.)

The delegates drew up one more stirring, unanimous appeal to the workers of all lands. Beyond a new note of anxiety, there was nothing new in it. Then they hastened to set an earlier date for the coming International Congress, transferring it from war-possessed Vienna to "peaceful" Paris, and changing it from August 25 to August 9. Surely this great International, which was about to celebrate the fiftieth anniversary of its existence, would be the mighty world power able to stop the other world powers from madness. But a whole age was to elapse between August 1 and August 9. The two dates were separated from each other by an abyss. Into the abyss tumbled the fragments of the once great structure of the International, and all the kings' ministers and all the Soviets' commissars would not be able to put it together again in the next half-century.

The two days of feverish, fruitless improvisation ended in a gigantic mass meeting in which the magnificent eloquence of Jean Jaures stirred the multitudes for the last time. Never had he spoken with greater fervor than now, when he pledged himself to continue to his dying breath to wage "war against war." To the heart of Jaurès, a "revisionist" and "ministerialist" for whom Lenin had always had a species of contempt, humanitarianism and pacifism and pity for the victims of poverty and war were ever closer than were class war and revolution. (But, after his death, Lenin's paper would claim his heritage as "pacifism on a revolutionary foundation.") His burning words caught up his hearers jamming the Cirque Royale, overflowed into the streets, where thousands waited who could not get in, took possession of the boulevards and avenues of old Brussels, which rang for hours with the reiterated cries: "*A bas la guerre!*" "*Guerre à la guerre!*" "*Vive l'Internationale Socialiste!*"

Two days later, on his return to Paris, Jean Jaurès was shot dead by an inflamed nationalist assassin. He at least had kept his pledge to his "dying breath." Another two days, and the streets of Brussels, like the streets of Paris, Berlin, Saint Petersburg, London, were ringing with other cries: crowds, often the same crowds, possessed by another fervor, were shouting themselves hoarse for war.

From July 31 to August 4, the German Social Democratic Executive Committee and the mighty Reichstag Fraction of 110 socialist Deputies were in almost continuous session.

Where now were Marx and Engels, who had always known what stand to take on each war in the nineteenth century? (They were never pacifists.) Where were Liebknecht and Bebel, veterans of the opposition to war in 1870?

Habits, formulae, pledges, feelings whirled in a maelstrom. On July 31 they could come to no conclusion except to send Hermann Mueller to Paris to consult with the French socialists . . . But they had just consulted two days before! The French leaders were cautious. Jaures lay dead. Most of the others felt that if France were attacked by Germany, it would have to defend itself. Since Germany would be the aggressor, perhaps the German comrades could vote "no" on war credits, but they would have to vote "yes." Mueller answered that his comrades would surely not vote in the affirmative, but wanted to come to an agreement with the French on voting in the negative or abstaining from voting. The German socialists, he said, felt that Russia was the chief danger, and would invade the Fatherland. Perhaps France could stop the war by pressure on Russia, which was the real aggressor and guilty party. The negotiations stalled; their voices faltered; their thoughts trailed off unexpressed; they did not trust each other chiefly because they no longer trusted themselves. . . .

Perhaps, if Bebel and Jaurès had still been there, they might have understood each other and found a common platform, at least for the first crucial days of the war. Perhaps, perhaps not. Idle to speculate now, but let no one object: what difference could one or two men make? For this was a time of hesitation. For a moment, everything was in suspense, like a tiny spring on the ridge of a watershed which even a twig or a pebble might deflect down one slope or the other. We shall soon see what a difference one or two men could make. . . . The next day or two, and the hesitation was over: the new course had worn itself a deepening channel: another two days later, it was a roaring flood.

On August 3, when Mueller returned to Berlin, the Reichstag Fraction was still in session. But it now knew that the next day the Reichstag would meet and be presented with a bill for war credits. War had been declared on Russia two days earlier, and now (August 3) on France.

Still the maze! *For the war credits*, to show their patriotism and to equip the millions of socialist and trade union members called up to the colors? *Against the war credits*, so as to disclaim responsibility for—but not obstruct—the war? *Against the war credits and the war*, as a preliminary to going underground and carrying on a struggle against their government? As if in a trance, they simultaneously acted on all three premises. By a vote of seventy-eight to fourteen they decided to vote "yes" on the war credits, with a statement disclaiming responsibility for the war. And, incredible as it sounds, they had already secretly sent the Party treasurer, Otto Braun, and the Chairman of the Executive, Friedrich Ebert, to Zurich, to prepare for possible underground existence. (A few days later they came sheepishly back to Berlin.)

The arguments, the statements and counter-statements, the desperate improvisations, the anger and the tears, the searching of souls and the drafting and tearing up of declarations, continued all night. But on August 4, Haase, who was one of these fourteen who had voted "no" inside the Fraction, consented as its chairman to read the declaration of the Social Democratic Reichstag Fraction in the solemn public meeting. Out of a sense of "democratic discipline" the fourteen submitted to the majority will of the seventy-eight. Thus, though one member (Kunert of Halle), unnoticed, walked out while the vote was being taken, so far as the Party, Germany or the world knew, the entire Social Democratic Reichstag Fraction of 110 members had voted solidly to support the war. The French Deputies did the same on the same day, but somehow this was less of a surprise and a shock. For though all the Great Powers had been preparing for war and reaching out for or holding tight to their "spoils," yet the Austrian ultimatum and the Kaiser's support made it clear that Germany and Austria had chosen the time and the way to precipitate the conflict. Moreover, the German party was the party of Marx and Engels, the leading and inspiring, the model party of the Socialist International. With its 110 Reichstag Deputies, its over a million members, its million and a half readers of the socialist press, its almost two and one-half million trade union followers, its specific gravity so great that one soldier out of three who answered the call to arms was a voter for the socialist party—this was the party on which all hopes were laid, toward which all eyes were turned.

When Lenin read the news that the Social Democrats had voted war credits in the Reichstag, he simply refused to believe it. He had not expected the International to be able to prevent war, but he had never doubted that they would reject responsibility for it. They would suffer, and the people would suffer, but in the end they would be justified and, out of the ruins of war, lead the people to revolution and socialism. He had doubted that "Franz Josef and Nikolasha will give us that pleasure," but he had never doubted that the great socialist parties would meet the issue with loyalty to their pledges and principles. The news dispatch, he declared, had been invented by the German Government to deceive its enemies, and to sow confusion in the ranks of the socialists. Even when he saw the report in the *Vorwaerts*, he concluded that that entire issue of the paper was a forgery of the German General Staff. Then he learned that Plekhanov in Paris had turned recruiting agent. "Can Plekhanov be a traitor, too?" he asked again and again, and tried to explain it by the fact that Plekhanov in his youth had served as an army officer. But the blow that was hardest to bear was to learn that Karl Kautsky, the man he had revered most after the founders of Marxism, had counseled abstention from voting, but had followed his advice with sophistries to explain and apologize for, if not justify, the treason of the majority. At this his fury knew no bounds.

First gloom settled over him; then anger seized him; then the steel trap of his mind closed on the new situation. Many a time he had stood alone against all the leaders of his party. Many a time he had split away, and started from scratch to build anew on his own foundation. Now he would stand alone, if need be, against the leaders of the entire International. He had read Martov and Axelrod and all the others leaders out of his party. Now he would read all the pro-war leaders, and all who had truck with them, out of the International. More than once he had declared that he, and those few who stood with him, were the Party. Now he, and those few whom he might recruit, would be the International. Even as he fled from Cracow to Vienna, from Vienna to Zurich to Berne, he was turning this huge, monstrous news over and over in his mind, reducing it to a series of ordered explanations, propositions, slogans, theses. By the time he reached Berne in neutral Switzerland and called together a half-dozen or so of bewildered, frightened, but still faithful friends and comrades, he had it all worked out in his mind, and read off to them *Seven Theses on the War*. The date was September 6 or 7. Present were Lenin and Krupskaya, the Safarovs, Duma Deputy Samoilov, Mokhov, Shklovsky, and possibly Inessa Armand. According to Krupskaya, the meeting was "held in the woods," but this is improbable and is contradicted by Shklovsky, who records that it was in his apartment. Later, when Lenin tried to rally more Bolsheviks, groups and individuals, objections would rain upon his head. But those gathered that day found little to object to.

The European War—said the first thesis—has the sharp and definite character of a bourgeois, imperialist, and dynastic war.

The conduct of the leaders of the German Social Democratic Party of the Second International (1889-1914) [the dates of birth and death were included in the second thesis!] who have voted the war budget and who repeat the bourgeois chauvinist phrases of the Prussian Junkers and of the bourgeoisie, is a direct betrayal of socialism. [Such was the second proposition.]

The conduct of the leaders of the Belgian and French Social Democracy—continued the third—who have betrayed socialism by entering bourgeois cabinets, deserves the same condemnation . . .

The betrayal of socialism by the majority of the leaders of the Second International (1889-1914)—continued the fourth inexorably—means an ideological collapse of that International. The fundamental cause is the actual predominance of petty-bourgeois opportunism . . .

The fifth thesis noted and branded as deceptions the various justifications for their part in the war given by the participating countries.

The task of Social Democracy in Russia—read the sixth—consists in the first place in a merciless and ruthless struggle against the Great-Russian and tsarist-monarchist chauvinism, against the sophistical defense of this chauvinism by Russian Liberals, Constitutional Democrats and the like, and by some of the Narodniks. [No mention of the Mensheviks, for he had learned that the entire Social Democratic delegation to the Duma, Bolsheviks and Mensheviks alike, had voted on August 8 against the war credits!]

From the point of view of the laboring class and the toiling masses of all the peoples of Russia, the lesser evil would be the defeat of the tsarist monarchy and its army, which oppresses Poland, the Ukraine, and a number of other peoples of Russia . . . [This was the most important sentence in the whole document.]

And the seventh thesis:

The slogans of Social Democracy at the present time should be: a thorough propaganda—to be spread also in the Army and the area of military activity—for a socialist revolution and for the necessity of turning weapons not against one's brothers, hired slaves of other lands, but against reaction in the shape of the bourgeois governments and parties of all countries—to carry on such propaganda in all languages it is absolutely necessary to organize illegal cells and groups in the armies of all nations . . . It is imperative to appeal to the revolutionary conscience of the working masses . . . against the leaders of the present International who have betrayed socialism . . . Agitation in favor of German, Polish, Russian and other republics, along with the transformation of all the separate states of Europe into a Republican United States.

These rough-hewn but massive propositions were discussed briefly by those present, and then, with a few changes, launched as best they could be upon an unreceptive and unpropitious world over the signature of "A Group of Social Democrats, Members of the R.S.D.L.P." The principal changes were:

1. The addition of an attack upon "the so-called 'Center,' which has cravenly capitulated before the opportunists" and which should be "resolutely and irrevocably uprooted from the future International."

2. An acknowledgment that not all workers had been immune to the war fever but that "in most cases the workers were hostile to chauvinism and opportunism."

3. The addition of a final group of slogans for Russia:

A struggle against the tsarist monarchy and Great-Russian, pan-Slavist chauvinism, the preaching of a revolution in Russia, the liberation and self-determination of the nationalities oppressed by Russia—on the basis of the immediate slogans: a democratic republic, confiscation of the landowners' lands, the eight-hour day.

The second amendment was apparently forced upon Lenin by someone else present who pointed out that it was not only the leaders who had yielded to the general patriotic fever but also the masses, and even many Bolsheviks. But Lenin would not compromise except to add the evasive words, "in most cases," because already he was envisioning his strategy in terms of rousing "the masses" against "the leaders," imputing to the former, at most, occasional error, to the latter deliberate, systematic treason. The first amendment was doubtless Lenin's own, by way of paying respects to his erstwhile theoretical leader, Karl Kautsky. And the third amendment is a characteristic Leninist formulation of the needs and slogans of a democratic revolution in Russia.

ON TRANSLITERATION AND PRONUNCIATION

IN TRANSLITERATING I have followed generally the system used by the Library of Congress, but have not hesitated to modify it wherever 1) a name has already become familiar to the American reader under a different spelling; 2) a change (as from *ii* and *yi* to plain *y*) might make matters easier for the reader who knows no Russian. The two Russian letters *dzh* I have rendered by the simple English *j* which is its true pronunciation, except in the case of Djugashvili (Dzhugashvili), which has become more familiar in the above forms.

The reader need have no hesitance about pronouncing Russian names with an American or English accent. It is as legitimate to say Trotsky as Trutsky, just as we give so well known a name as Napoleon an Anglo-Saxon pronunciation.

The problem of accenting, which gives so much worry because there are no set rules in Russian, is best met by giving all syllables equal value. A Russian may misunderstand you if you put the accent on the wrong syllable, but will always understand you if you put the accent on no single syllable at all. Thus it is wrong to say Lenín and right to say Lénin, but you will be indistinguishably close to the right pronunciation if you give both syllables equal value.

The vowels which may give the Anglo-Saxon reader most trouble are *e*, normally pronounced *ye* as in Enukidze, pronounced *Yenukidze*, and frequently spelled so in transliteration; the letter *ya*, which is a single letter in Russian; the letter *yu*, to be distinguished from *u* which is pronounced *bo*. The vowels *a*, *i* and *o* (and sometimes *e*) are in general pronounced as in other continental languages.

The troublesome consonants are chiefly the large array of letters that in Russian are single letters and in other languages must be rendered by two or three consonants: *zh*, pronounced like our *z* in azure or like the French *j*; *kh* (Russian *x*) pronounced gutturally with a slight throat-rasping like the German *ch* or the Spanish *j* or *x*; *ts*, a single letter, the transliteration of which is self-explanatory; *sh*, another self-explanatory transliteration of a single letter; and *shch*, a single letter which, given its full value, would sound like the

639

starting of a locomotive, but in actual speech is usually only a prolonged and slightly softened *sh*.

The general reader who is not striving for pedantic perfection can pronounce the names for his own inner ear and for fellow Anglo-Saxons and even Russians by avoiding the accenting of any syllable, by following the transliterations provided, and by using his common sense. Even Krzhizhanovsky looks harder than it is, for Russian is a highly phonetic language.

Index

Abramovich, Rafael, 383, 470-1

Adler, Alfred, 490

Adler, Victor, 213; secures Lenin's release, 617-19; aids Trotsky, 621; at Brussels Conference, 631

Adoratsky, 79, 559

Aesop Language, Slave Language, See Censorship

Agrarian question, military state farms, 22; Decembrists and, 25; Lenin as specialist on, 225; Lenin's *To the Village Poor*, 228-9; Lenin abandons *otrezki* for nationalization, 304-5; Stolypin's agrarian reform, 359-62; its success likely to deprive Social Democrats of their agrarian program, 361; debate at London Congress (Plekhanov's warning on binding peasants to the new state), 364-7; Stalin's proposals carried out in 1917, reversed in thirties, 467-8; state ownership of land and peasants as a foundation for total statism, 364-7, 468

Akhundov, R., 447

Akimov (Vladimir Makhnovets), 221, 235-7

Alakaevka, Lenin's landed estate, 84-5

Albania, 601

Alexander I (1801-25), 22; 24-5; 169

Alexander II (1855-81), 22; 26, 32; 58-9; 169, 184

Alexander III (1881-94), reaction to father's assassination, 58-9; character of reign, 58ff, 67ff; on Lenin's brother, 65; industrialization under, 68; and Jews, 169ff, 184

Alexinsky, G. A., 362, 382; jest on Jewish Menshevism and pogroms, 468-9; on Elizabeth K and Lenin's poem, 469n; 520

Algeciras, 338-9

Alliluev, Sergei, Stalin's father-in-law, 430-1

Allilueva, Nadezhda, Stalin's wife, 431

Amsterdam, Saul (Henrykowski), 519

Anarchists, in Tsarist and Bolshevik Siberia, 135-6; 211-2

"Angels," see Liberals

Anna, see Ulyanova

Antid Oto, pen name of Trotsky, *q.v.*

Anyuta, see Ulyanova, Anna Ilyinishna

Apostolic succession, *see* Stalin, 75, 142-3

Arakcheev and military state farms, 14, 22, 25

Archduke Francis Ferdinand of Austria, 613

Arefeev, Lenin's opponent in lawsuit, 87

Argunov, 628

Armand, Inessa, 610ff

Armed bands, 328; Chap. XXII

Armenia, 447

Asia, and Russia, Asiatic, 15, 17, 18, 161, 269; Lenin and Stalin on, 404

"August Conference," "August Bloc," 532-3

Auntie, see Kalmykova

Austria-Hungary, Lenin moves to, 566; and Poles, 567-8; and national question, 568 and Balkans, 567-8, 601ff

Authoritarianism, root in patriarchalism, 28; authoritarian party necessary to authoritarian state, 259; in Lenin's thought, 508 ff, *see also* Autocracy, Centralism, Democracy, Thought, Totalitarianism

Autocracy, born of Russian expansion, 18; its popular roots, 18-19; develops bondage, 20-1; sets itself against nation, 26-7, 32; and patriarchalism, 28-9; and cruelty, 30-1, *see also* Tsarism, Totalitarianism, Authoritarianism

Autonomy, *see* National Question

Avenarius, 503ff

Avksentev, 316, 628

Axelrod, Pavel Borisovich, and famine, 91; associate of Plekhanov, 93 and *passim*; first meeting with Lenin, 121, 123; answers Economists, 145,

Congress (1903), Chap. XIII,
XV; Third (Bolshevik) Congress
(1905), 306-09, 454-5; Tammerfors Bolshevik Conference (1905),
329-30, 373; Stockholm Congress
(1906) 342-7, 364-8, 376, 434;
London Congress (1907), 343,
358ff, 367, 377, 380, 381-7; Stalin
on, 424; 434, 468-9; Trotsky at,
487ff; Prague Congress (1912),
529-33, 535, August Conference
(1912), 532-3
Congresses of the Transcaucasian Social Democratic Organization:
Fourth, (1906), Bolsheviks and
Mensheviks at, 434; Regional Conference (1912), Bolsheviks and
Mensheviks at, 435
Constitution, Speransky's draft, 25;
after 1905, 32, 321ff, 359-62,
564ff
Constitutional Democratic Party
(Kadets), 183, 265-6, 346, 351-2,
524
Counterfeit money, 394-5
Credit Lyonnais, 338
Czar, see Tsar

Dan, Theodor (Gurvich), 145, 221,
343, 383, 550, 558-9
Dan, Mrs., 547
Danishevsky (Hermann), 384
David, Eduard, colonial proposal, 593
Debts, repudiation of, 328 338-9
Decembrists, 14, 24-6
Defeatism of Khomyakov, 34; in
Russo-Japanese War, 277ff
Degaev, 59
Delyanov, Minister of Education, 68
Democracy, Marxism and Populism
each incomplete without other for
democratic revolution, 107ff; police
overseership of peasants makes for
police state, 107-17; tutelage over
proletariat inimical to, 116, 122,
154-6, 158-66, 220-1, 225, 226-8,
235-9, 240-41, 244-5; Trotsky's
prophecy on Lenin's undemocratic
machine, 253; Zasulich, Plekhanov,
Axelrod and Rosa Luxemburg on,
162n, 255-7; Lenin advocates burocratism as against democratism, 259;
warns Trotsky and Parvus on undemocratic minority dictatorship
and socialism without democracy,
292ff; an undemocratic machine to
make an undemocratic, minority

dictatorship, 293-4; three perspectives of Russian revolution, 289-98;
Lenin's formula for a "democratic
dictatorship," 291-8; his "democratic centralism," 306-9; Axelrod's
broad party and democratic mass
organizations advocated to replace
conspiratorial, dictatorial party,
312ff; press censorship and, 324-
5; danger if peasant is bound to
state (Plekhanov's warning), 366;
Lenin's machine, 461-4; freedom in
party and freedom in faction, 510;
Lenin as democrat in national
question, 587-90
Denikin, A. I., 237n
Deutsch, Leo, 93, 184
Dictatorship of proletariat, 225, 235-9,
324ff
Discipline, 162ff, 240ff, 244-5, 258,
262
Djugashvili, Jacob I., Stalin's oldest
son, 451-2
Documents Concerning the Problem of the Economic Development
of Russia, symposium by K. Tulin
(Lenin), Struve, Plekhanov, Potre-
sov, and others, 120ff
Dolgoruki, Prince, 266
Dostoevsky, on extremism, 32; prophet
of our age, 36; 56
Druzhini, fighting companies, Chap.
XXII
Dubassov, Admiral, 331
Dubrovinsky, I. F., 363, 382n
Duma, conceded, 32; boycott, 345ff;
electoral law anticipates features of
Soviet elections and promotes class
consciousness, 345; Social Democrats and Black Hundreds boycott, 346; Lenin fights boycotters,
346ff; First Duma, 347ff; dissolu-
tion, 353; Stolypin dissolves Second
Duma, 358ff; his "Coup d'Etat" of
June 16, 1907, 359; Third Duma,
362-9; strength of Georgian
Mensheviks in Duma, 429, 434;
boycottism, recallism, ultimatism,
505; Lenin and Malinovsky split
Duma Fraction, 544ff
Durnovo, P. N., Minister of Interior,
322
Dzierzynski (Dzherzhinski), F. E.,
383, 446-7, 519ff.

Eastern Review, Siberian paper for
which Trotsky wrote, 210-11

ment, 155-6; *Where to Begin*, 156; *What's to Be Done*, 156-66; readiness for splits, 157-9, 226-8, Chap. 36; opposes freedom of discussion on matters he regards as settled, 158-9; large task of Russian proletariat, 159; Russian character of his organization plan, 156, 160ff; role of revolutionary intelligentsia, 162ff; hierarchical centralism, 162ff; Rosa Luxemburg's critique of, 162n, 256-7; conception of leadership, 163ff; control of masses, Chap. IX; nominates Trotsky for *Iskra* Board, 168, 217-19; role on *Iskra*, 148-54, 217-20; quarrel with Plekhanov on Program, 223-5; amendments on agrarian question and guardianship over proletariat, 225; acceptance of Plekhanov's program, 225, 234ff; prepares for control of Congress, 226-9; and for split, 226-8; *To the Village Poor*, 228-9; captures Congress majority, Chap. XIV; battle with Martov over definition of member, 240-2; splits *Iskra* caucus, 242-7; wavers between peace and war, 250ff; attitude towards Martov, 250-3; political amoralism, 252, 355-7, and Chap. XXII; warned by Trotsky on his undemocratic party machine, 253; attacked by entire *Iskra* Board, 253ff; and Rosa Luxemburg, Two Steps Backward, 258; espouses "burocratism and centralism" on principle as against democracy, 259; "democratic centralism," 259 and *passim*; tries to force another Congress and loses all committees, 260-2; wins fresh forces and founds Bureau of Committees of the Majority, 263; and *Vpered*, 263-4; defeatism in Russo-Japanese War, 278-9; compared with Stalin's attitude, 278-9; Clausewitz and Cluseret, 287-8; his perspective concerning Russian revolution, 289-98; prophetic warning to Trotsky on undemocratic, minority dictatorship, 292-4; Lenin's and Trotsky's warnings combined, 293-4; position moves between poles of Menshevism and Trotskyism, between his formulae and his revolutionary will, 291-8; *Two Tactics*, 295; "permanent revolution," 296;

"take power and then see," 296; turns Marxian doctrine of economic foundation and political superstructure upsidedown, 297; interview with Gapon, 302-5; revises agrarian program, 304-5, 364-6; modifies centralism during 1905, 306-9; fights his faction on, 306-9; opposes labor party, 312ff; for centralized, directed revolution, traditional Russianism of, 313-4; recognizes importance of Soviet, 315; two perspectives and fight on two fronts, *passim* in Chap. XX, XXI, XXII, XXVIII, XXIX; on unity with Mensheviks in time of storm, 341-2; deserts his faction at Stockholm, 347ff; and London, 358ff; why he yielded at Tammerfors, 348-9; misjudges Tsar and Kadets on Duma, 351-3; Duma as ground for alliance with peasants, 350, 353-4; his party trial, 354-7; estimate of Stolypin, 359-62; prolonged fight on Duma boycott, 346-62 and Chap. XXIX; *troikas*, 363; for nationalization of land at London Congress, 364-6; Plekhanov's warning on danger of restoration if peasant bound to new state, 366-7; significance of combining Lenin's, Trotsky's and Plekhanov's warnings of dangers of undemocratic revolution, 366; reverts to reservations on Soviet, 368-9; compared with Trotsky's view, 369; armed bands, Chap. XXII; Martov's exposure makes split inevitable, 378ff; special estimate of Georgian Menshevism, 436; preparing fight with Stalin on Georgian question, 446-7; on Martov, 471-2; second emigration, 475ff; revives *Proletarii*, 481-2; Lenin as Philosopher (*Materialism and Empiriocriticism*), Chap. XXIX; Lenin and Martov on trade unions, Duma, 521ff; forced into unity, 524-6; proposes bloc with Plekhanov, 526-7; drives for permanent split, 527-34; captures party name and expels all other factions, 530-32; and Malinovsky, Chap. XXXI; controversies with *Pravda* editors, 543-6; moves to Cracow, 566; nostalgia, 566-7; Polish revolutionists, 567ff; national question 577ff; gets Zinoviev, Stalin, Shaumyan working on, 577-87; attitude to Bund and Aus-

OTHER
COOPER SQUARE PRESS
TITLES OF INTEREST

HANNIBAL
G. P. Baker
366 pp., 3 b/w illustrations,
5 maps
0-8154-1005-0
$18.95

MUSSOLINI
Jasper Ridley
464 pp., 24 b/w photos, 3 maps
0-8154-1081-6
$19.95

THE LIFE AND TIMES OF AKHNATON
Pharaoh of Egypt
Arthur Weigall
322 pp., 26 b/w photos,
7 line drawings
0-8154-1092-1
$17.95

GANDHI
A Biography
Geoffrey Ashe
432 pp., 18 b/w photos
0-8154-1107-3
$18.95

T. E. LARWENCE
A Biography
Michael Yardley
303 pp., 71 b/w photos,
5 maps
0-8154-1054-9
$17.95

THE COMPLETE BOLIVIAN DIARIES
OF CHÉ GUEVARA
And Other Captured Documents
Edited by Daniel James
New Introduction by
Henry Butterfield Ryan
376 pp., 47 photos,
3 illustrations, 2 maps
0-8154-1056-5
$18.95

CHÉ GUEVARA
A Biography
Daniel James
New Introduction by
Henry Butterfield Ryan
408 pp., 35 b/w photos
0-8154-1144-8
$18.95

Available at bookstores
or call 1-800-462-6420

150 Fifth Avenue ◆ Suite 817 ◆ New York, New York 10011